CAESAR

CAESAR

A History of the Art of
War among the Romans
down to the end
of the Roman Empire,
with a Detailed Account
of the Campaigns of
Caius Julius Caesar

Theodore Ayrault Dodge

DA CAPO PRESS

Library of Congress Cataloging-in-Publication Data

Dodge, Theodore Ayrault, 1842–1909.
   Caesar: a history of the art of war among the Romans down
to the end of the Roman empire, with a detailed account of the
campaigns of Caius Julius Caesar / Theodore Ayrault Dodge.
      p.   cm.
   Includes index.
   ISBN 0-306-80787-4 (alk. paper)
   1. Rome—History, Military—265–30 B.C. 2. Military art and
science—Rome—History. 3. Caesar, Julius—Military leadership.
I. Title.
DG262.D63 1997
355′.00937—dc21

                                                    97-16027
                                                        CIP

First Da Capo Press edition 1997

This Da Capo Press paperback edition of *Caesar* is an
unabridged republication of the edition published by
Houghton Mifflin Company in 1892.

   5   6   7   8   9   10   02   01

Published by Da Capo Press, Inc.
A Member of the Perseus Books Group

Manufactured in the United States of America

TO
THE AMERICAN SOLDIER

Who, not bred to arms, but nurtured by
independence, has achieved the proudest
rank among the veterans of history

THIS VOLUME IS DEDICATED

"*Faites la guerre offensive comme Alexandre, Annibal, César,
Gustave Adolphe, Turenne, le prince Eugène et Frédéric; lisez, reli-
sez l'histoire de leur quatre-vingt-huit campagnes; modélez-vous sur
eux,* — *c'est le seul moyen de devenir grand capitaine et de surprendre
le sécret de l'art; votre génie, ainsi éclairé, vous fera rejeter des max-
imes opposées à celles de ces grands hommes.*" — NAPOLEON.

"*La tactique, les évolutions, la science de l'officier de génie, de
l'officier d'artillerie peuvent s'apprendre dans les traités;* — *mais la
connaissance de la grande tactique ne s'acquiert que par l'expérience
et par l'étude de l'histoire des campagnes de tous les grands capitaines.*"
— NAPOLEON.

PREFACE.

THE present volume has been delayed nearly a year to enable the author to visit the theatre of Cæsar's campaigns and his many battlefields. To do this is almost a prerequisite to writing intelligently on the subject. Familiarity with the topography gives a quite different understanding of the narrative of the ancient historians. Though Cæsar's Commentaries are among the most exact and picturesque of historical writings, it is by patient study alone that they can be understood otherwise than superficially; without suitable maps they cannot be understood at all. From the days of ingenious but far-fetched Guischard and Turpin de Crissé, topographical descriptions and charts have habitually been copied by one author from another, to the lot of neither of whom it has fallen to personally inspect the terrain; and many errors have been thus propagated. The author hopes that this volume is reasonably free from such.

We owe a great debt to Napoleon III. for patronizing and defraying the expense of the systematic excavations and topographical and military studies which have culminated in his own and Colonel Stoffel's works on Cæsar. To Colonel Stoffel we are peculiarly indebted for one of the most splendid military histories which exists. The present author has made free use of both these works; and though he has personally passed over all the ground covered by Cæsar's campaigns, it would savor of impertinence to seek to better the results of Colonel Stoffel's long and accurate research or of the archæological work of Napoleon. In all cases, however, the author has not been able to agree with these distinguished men; nor is the plan of this volume the one on which the other histories are based. The charts, while lacking the extreme accuracy of detail of the plates of Napoleon and Stoffel, will be found to answer every requirement, at a mere fraction of the cost of those works; and their insertion in the text will aid the average reader as large maps in a separate volume will not.

This history of Cæsar follows the narrative of the Commentaries, and whenever practicable quotes from them, so as to retain the quaintness of their flavor, as far as is consistent with the space allowed. Quotations not ascribed to other sources are uniformly from the Commentaries. As classical names must at times be used, the author has not clung exclusively to the modern equivalents, but has interchangeably used both.

This volume pretends to be only a military history of Cæsar. For clear and brilliant disquisitions on his statecraft or his personal career, or for the history of his era, the reader must go to other sources. But some of the best of the histories of Rome are full of military errors. Even the great Mommsen is by no means free from them. In all the histories which pretend to cover the complicated political and absorbing social conditions of that century, the description of military events is short and superficial. The author seeks to fill the gap.

Many pages will be found too technical to interest the general reader; but they are essential to the tracing out of the history of the art of war. The legend at the head of each chapter will tell the reader what to skip.

The very great array of facts which we possess with regard to the military career of Cæsar makes it hard to compress all that should be said within the limits of even a large volume. But it is believed that no noteworthy fact has been omitted. The history of the art of war during the Empire has been cut down to very meagre limits; but though there were abundant wars, there was much lack of method in war during this period; and it may be said that to omit bodily the fourteen centuries from Cæsar to the invention of gunpowder would not materially alter the general scope proposed for these biographies of the great captains.

Some of the comment indulged in may seem to savor of hypercriticism. But though the author may not meet the views of all in what he says, the reader will at least give him credit for qualifying himself as well as may be by careful study of all the ancient authorities, of the best recognized modern critics, and by personal inspection of the ground. With the sole exception of Colonel Stoffel, the author believes that he is the only writer on this subject who has followed Cæsar entirely around the Mediterranean basin.

The principal sources of our knowledge of Cæsar as a captain are the Commentaries, Cicero's speeches and other writings, Dion Cassius, Plutarch, Suetonius, and Velleius Paterculus; the best commentators are Guischard, Turpin de Crissé, Napoleon I., Lossau, Göler, Rustow, Napoleon III., and above all Colonel Stoffel, of whose lifework one cannot say too much.

TABLE OF CONTENTS.

LIST OF ILLUSTRATIONS.

GENERAL THEATRE

ᵒᶠCÆSAR'S CAMPAIGNS

MILES

0   100.   200   300   400   500

EUXINUS

EPIRUS

MACA

PONTUS

NICOPOLIS

ZELA

CALLATIA

MAZACO

CAPPADOCIA

COMANA

PHARSALUS

MYTILENE

ASIA

EPHESUS

MINOR

TARSUS

HELLAS

ANTIOCH

RHODES

CRETE

CYPRUS

JERUSALEM

ERRANEAN

ALEXANDRIA

PELUSIUM

MEMPHIS

CORCYRA

CÆSAR.

I.

MARIUS AND THE ARMY CHANGES. 110–86 B. C.

CÆSAR's legion was more like the Greek phalanx than like the legion of the
Second Punic War. The latter had intervals between maniples equal to maniple
front, and the maniples stood checkerwise. Each man occupied a space five
feet square. The material of the legion was of the highest order — the burgess-
soldier of the simple republic. But gradually ɩe professional soldier came
into vogue; the citizens avoided military ɩuty; and a less reliable material
filled the ranks. Marius first enlisted men solely for their physical qualifications; and foreign mercenaries were added to th ɩrmy. The general, not the
republic, claimed the soldier's fealty. Arms and equipment remained the same,
but the trustworthiness of the soldier decreased, and the intervals in the line
of battle were lessened. The cohort was no longer a body of citizens marshaled
on a basis of property-standing, but a body of from three hundred to six
hundred of any kind of men, and the legion was marshaled in two or three lines
of cohorts. The army ceased to be a national militia, but was composed of
regulars and auxiliaries. Ballistics and fortification were improved. Sieges
grew to be more expertly managed. The fleets gained in importance. Marius'
great work was the change he wrought in the army; but he was also the means
of rescuing Rome from the invasion of the Teutones and Cimbri, the former
of whom he defeated at Aquæ Sextiæ in Southern Gaul, and the latter at
Vercellæ in Northern Italy. Both victories redound much to his credit.

THE legion with which the Romans vanquished the Grecian phalanx, and which gallantly took the fearful punishment inflicted on it by Hannibal, again and again facing
destruction with unflinching courage, until the Carthaginians,
exhausted by attrition, were forced to abandon Italy, was
a very different body of men from the enthusiastic legion

which Cæsar led victorious to the four quarters of the then known world. Curiously enough, the formation of Cæsar's legion more nearly approached that of the "simple phalanx" of the Greeks than that of the splendid body of burgess-soldiers, whose stanch front to disaster makes the Second Punic War so memorable a page in the annals of Roman courage and intelligence. Cæsar's array in line of battle did not differ as greatly from Hannibal's phalanx in the later battles of this war, as it did from the legion of Marcellus or Nero. At Asculum, Herdonia and Zama, Hannibal's army was set up in two or three lines of legionary phalanxes, so to speak. Adopting the quincunx or checkerwise formation by maniples as the typical idea of the legion of the Second Punic War, Cæsar's army, during all his campaigns, was set up more like Hannibal's phalanx, and at times very nearly approached it.

Let us see how the change came about.

The legion of the Second Punic War was a body composed of citizens rendering service according to the classes of Servius Tullius. This service was as much a privilege as a duty, and was jealously guarded. Only burgesses with a given amount of property were allowed to serve. Those who had less than twelve thousand five hundred asses were excluded from the right. They were *proletarii*, having some slight means, and *capite censi*, having nothing and reckoned merely as so many head of men.

The material of which the legion was made was thus of the very highest order; and originally the armament and place in the legion were determined by the class-rating. But later these were made to depend on length of service, so that the youngest soldiers, from seventeen to twenty-five years of age, were velites or light troops; those from twenty-five to thirty, hastati or heavy troops of the first line; those from thirty to forty, principes or heavy troops of the second line; those from forty to forty-five, triarii or reserves of the third line.

The light troops acted as skirmishers. The legionary soldier occupied a space about five feet square. The lines of hastati and of principes stood in maniples of one hundred and twenty men each, twelve front by ten deep, and between

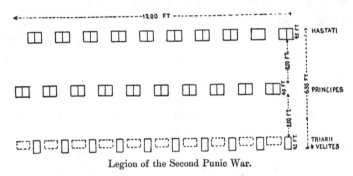

Legion of the Second Punic War.

each two maniples was an interval equal to maniple front. The lines were some two hundred and fifty feet apart, and the maniples of the principes stood behind the intervals of the hastati. The triarii maniples had but sixty men, and stood behind the hastati intervals.

There were ten maniples in each of the three lines, so that there were of line troops twelve hundred hastati, twelve hundred principes and six hundred triarii. To these must be added twelve hundred (or more) velites, making forty-two hundred footmen in the legion, of whom three thousand were heavy.

There were three hundred cavalry in each legion, whose place was on the flanks. The velites often occupied the intervals of the triarii. The details of the formation are fully given in the volume on Hannibal.

This body proved to have extraordinary mobility and capacity to meet unusual conditions, and with the discipline and *esprit de corps* natural to the perfect material of which it was composed made an unequaled body of troops. The wars of the third century B. C. fully proved the qualities of the legion so organized. It was at its very best.

The legion of Cæsar's era was quite a different body. Changes had grown up in the state and army which affected the matter of service and thus the legion; and a number of marked alterations were brought about during the times of the civil wars. The legion descended to Cæsar in a new shape, one that Marcellus and Nero and Scipio would not have recognized.

Caius Marius is a more noteworthy figure in history from his rugged, uncouth personality and his startling political success and failure than from his merit as a captain. Though unquestionably able as a leader, though Rome owed to him the victory at Aquæ Sextiæ, which delivered her from the Cimbri and Teutones, his position in military annals was more distinguished by the new organization of the Roman army than by any other contribution to the art of war.

When internal disquiet began to monopolize the thought and action of the citizens of the Roman republic, the army was not long in feeling its influence for the worse. The civil wars sadly marred the soldierly sentiments of the Romans, but it was Caius Marius who first gave a serious downward impetus to the character of the army. Long before his time many of the old Servian methods had got changed or distinctly modified. The minimum property which entitled a citizen to the privilege of serving had been reduced to four thousand asses. The armament of the legionary had ceased to be determined by census-rating; it had, as above stated, grown to be fixed by length of service. Wealth and luxury had supplanted the ancient habits of simplicity. The burgesses gradually sought to avoid service; the proletariats found in it a means of improving their condition. A certain number of campaigns were no longer essential to secure political preferment. The burgess-cavalry had given up serving in the field, and become a sort of guard of honor. The avoidance of military duty by the rich made it impossible to raise large forces with rapidity by the simple means of calling out the classes; and yet, as after the battle of Arausio, contingencies occurred when large levies must be instantly made. The new barbarian territories of Rome had begun to furnish cavalry, such as the heavy horse of Thrace and the light irregulars from Numidia, as well as light infantry, such as the Ligurians and the Balearic slingers; but the heavy foot had remained Italian.

It was Marius who first gave every free-born citizen, however poor, an equal right to serve. The heavy infantry, hastati, principes, triarii, were all reduced to a level, and it was the officers who decided, from the qualifications of the man, where and with what arms each soldier should be allowed to serve. The armament of all the heavy foot was made the same, and gladiators were employed as masters of arms to teach the recruits the use of their weapons; while Publius Rutilius, Marius's favorite comrade and fellow legate in the African war, compiled a system of tactics for the new legion.

A son of the people, when in 107 B. C. Marius had attained consular rank, he found his advantage in raising his army, not from the self-respecting classes, but from men he could so handle as to subserve his purpose of gaining the supreme control. Later leaders, Sulla, Crassus, Pompey, followed in the steps of Marius. Under such leadership the army soon became another body, no longer representative of Roman courage, honesty and patriotism.

The right to serve in the army ceased to be a privilege, — the sole road to civic honors. The wealthy citizen would no longer consent to serve. Bodily exercises were neglected. The ranks were filled, not by representatives of every class, rich and poor, but by the proletarii; and it was not long before there crept into the ranks numbers of men from peoples tributary to Rome, freedmen, strangers and slaves. Even the criminal classes were greedily recruited, and Marius once made a body-guard of slaves. Some veterans did service in exchange for grants of land, and answered the call for duty as *evocati*, having special privileges.

The legions were not now divided into simple Roman and allied. In the Social War, Roman citizenship was granted broadcast to the Italians, and the legions were composed of Romans, auxiliaries, provincial troops and mercenaries. The test of Marius was simply personal size and strength. Character went for nothing. Cavalry was raised in a manner similar to the infantry, and mostly from foreign elements. If the knights still consented to serve, it was only in posts of peculiar honor. The ancient rules for raising men were utterly disregarded. Any one ready to pay could secure freedom from service; any one physically qualified could bear arms.

The oath of the soldier was no longer an oath to serve the republic; he swore personal fealty to the general. The growing necessity for keeping troops long under arms, which followed the extended conquests of Rome, made generals resort to every means to prevent their forces from disbanding. Gradually the honorable service of the Roman citizen to the fatherland got prostituted to the low grade of soldier of fortune. Mercenaries and standing armies took the place of voluntary service and of armies called out from necessity alone. The conquered provinces were placed under proconsuls, each with a standing army and unlimited power, and were farmed out for revenue with the inevitable result. Rome was following in the footsteps of Greece.

This change from the old method of classified personal service rendered essential corresponding changes in the marshaling of the legion. The ancient distinction of principes, hastati and triarii disappeared, and all troops were either heavy or light. The inherited arms and equipment were not materially altered. The old numerical force of the legion, say four thousand to six thousand heavy infantry and three hundred heavy cavalry as the normal strength, was retained; but the light troops, now all raised from the conquered provinces, were largely increased, both foot and horse, and were no longer an integral part of the legion. The horse grew in importance and effectiveness, for the Roman horseman had imitated the better models of light cavalry which his many wars in every land, from Iberia to the distant Orient, had afforded him. This improvement was traceable in the heavy cavalry in a lesser degree. From about one tenth of the numerical force of the foot, the horse grew to the proportion of one seventh or at times more.

The number of legions in a consular army was no longer four, but ran up to any given number, even to ten, not counting the auxiliaries, horse or foot. Elephants and ballistic machines came into common use. A legion in the field had thirty small catapults and ballistas, each served by ten men. Still, as with Alexander, these machines were not employed in battle, but in the attack and defense of defiles, in crossing rivers, and in the attack and defense of camps and other works.

Up to the time of Marius, the quincuncial form of the legion was retained, and the intervals still remained equal to the maniple front. But when the legions grew to be composed of inexpert recruits, not as in the early days of men trained to war from their youth, the individuality of the legionary could no longer be relied upon. Moreover, the

Romans in their wars with Germanic barbarians and Oriental masses had found that the always present danger of the enemy forcing his way into the intervals grew more serious as the troops deteriorated in quality. This difficulty had formerly been obviated by moving the principes up into or close behind the intervals of the hastati. But Marius introduced another organization, the setting up of the legion in three lines of cohorts. The thirty legionary maniples, each of two centuries, were given up. The word cohort remained, but the body consisted no longer of a maniple each of hastati, principes and triarii, with velites and a turma of horse; it was a body of from four to six maniples of four, five or six hundred legionary soldiers. At first the intervals remained; the five feet space of each soldier, the ten deep file and the distance between lines were not altered; the cohorts had forty,

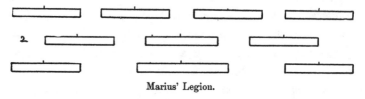

Marius' Legion.

fifty or sixty files. Shortly the intervals between cohorts began to diminish with the individual trustworthiness of the legionary, and the distances beween lines were increased to three hundred feet. These lines were now known as first, second and third; and the first had four, the second and third each three cohorts. The three cohorts in second line stood opposite the diminished intervals of the first, the third line cohorts at the flanks and opposite the centre. The legionary eagle was still carried by the primipilus of the first cohort of the third line, and each cohort had its own special ensign (*signum*). The legionaries of first and second lines, it is thought by some, were the soldiers who were called antesignani; in the third line cohorts were the bravest and strongest soldiers; but they were no longer the triarii.

Upon this formation were grafted, at times not easily determined, yet other changes. The ten cohorts stood in two lines, five in each; or instead of ten there were fifteen cohorts, each of two maniples, and five of these were in each line. The files were now and then split and doubled, making a five deep cohort of double length of front, which in line would close up a full interval. Finally, by a process of steadily decreasing intervals, the cohorts came to all but join each other, and the legion had again become a phalanx. This formation without intervals was not invariable. Cæsar generally set up his cohorts with intervals more or less wide. But a legion whose first line was nearly a solid body was not uncommon. The ancient quincunx had disappeared. This was the inevitable result of the loss of the old Roman patriotism, discipline and stanchness in the legionary soldier, and of his being replaced by a far inferior man who needed to be held well in hand to force him to his work. Finally, the eagle found its way into the front line, but the word antesignani remained, applied to a special body, of which more will be told anon.

The use of the testudo-formation grew into a huge rectangle, much like the modern square against cavalry, for which, indeed, in the Romans' Oriental wars it was frequently used. On open ground, marches were sometimes made in squares, like that of the phalanx of Brasidas — *agmen quadratum.* Marius especially excelled in his dispositions for the march. In the war against Jugurtha, he is said to have moved in a column by legions. Sulla with the cavalry and Manlius with the slingers, bowmen and Ligurians covered the column on right and left. In the van and rear, under command of military tribunes, were some cohorts in light marching order, and scouts in quantities were on the flanks.

In battle order, the Roman legions stood in the centre, the auxiliaries on the flanks, the velites in the spaces between bodies, on the flanks, or in front and rear as needed. Cavalry began to be more of an arm, and was hurled in masses on the enemy or employed to protect the foot. It no longer kept its old stand on both flanks. The method of fighting was not much altered, but grand tactics grew apace, until they reached their highest Roman development under Cæsar.

Other changes of even more importance were made in this period. The office of dictator, that is, the supreme control, was the aim of the ambitious; it was their means of gaining possession of the state. The legates grew to greater importance and acquired more and more the command of legions and armies. They were the general officers. The military tribunes became cohort-commanders, and the centuries were commanded by centurions. The troops were still drilled and exercised in gymnastics, but not so the citizens. Soldiers, to keep them from idleness and turbulence, were put upon the public works, especially the great military roads.

The soldier's pay was doubled by Cæsar at the opening of the Civil War. The footmen received ten asses a day; centurions twenty, cavalrymen thirty, subject to certain deductions, as of old, for rations, arms, equipments and horses.

In this era, discipline and *esprit de corps* were in a transition state from the perfect basis of the Second Punic War to the utter worthlessness of later days. Courage and good behavior were still present, but these were maintained by the severity of the laws. Punishments were cruelly unjust at times, foolishly inadequate at others. They were inflicted no longer in accordance with the code, but to suit the moods or character of the general. The splendid victories of the Romans prove abundantly that much of the old spirit was still there. But it proceeded from a different motive. The ancient love of honor and country had disappeared, and in its place stood an avaricious grasping for booty and a greed of bloodshed and conquest. These men were no longer Roman soldiers. They belonged to the chief who led them, and he used every motive which is peculiarly suited to a low class of military recruits to bind them to his cause and use them for his own purposes. *Ubi bene ibi patria* was the accepted rule; and each general easily persuaded his troops that he represented the chief good. The civil uprisings in Rome had demonstrated how little the Roman soldier of the first century B. C. was like the Roman soldier of the war against Hannibal.

When Cæsar's legions mutinied and demanded their discharge, he addressed them as *quirites*, a title which every Roman soldier in the early days viewed with pride. Just because he was a citizen, he was a soldier. But Cæsar's legionaries were only soldiers. They were not citizens, nor did they care to be. The one word *quirites* shamed or frightened them into obedience.

As punishments in the army were no longer made according to rule, so were unearned rewards distributed. Favoritism grew apace. The simple crown of leaves or grasses gave place to expensive ornaments. The officers, and later the soldiers, were freed from the duty of nightly fortification and other fatigue work. The greater triumph went to the unworthy. Luxury and pomp stepped into the place of simplicity, not only with wealthy citizens, but in the camp.

But because the soldier had degenerated, it does not follow that the ability of the leaders had gone. Rather because of the degeneracy of the rank and file, ability in the captain was enabled to push its way to the front.

The period of the Civil War shows great advance in fortification and ballistics. The form of the camp remained the same, but the walls and defenses were made much more intricate. The wall was higher and thicker; the ditch was wider and usually wet; towers were more numerous and bigger, and covered ways connected them; entanglements in front of the defenses were more common; the camp, especially *castra stativa*, became a fortress.

Even battlefields were fortified. Sulla erected palisades between his lines with ditches on the flanks, against the enemy's chariots at Chæronæa. Marius intrenched himself against the Teutones at the mouth of the Isère. The Romans kept to their own method, but exceeded the Greeks in cleverness at this sort of temporary fortification.

Sieges likewise gained in skillful management. In assaults the telenon of the Greeks was used to swing men up on the enemy's wall. The corona consisted in surrounding a town with two lines of foot and one of horse and gradually decreasing the circumference of the lines until the walls could be reached under cover of penthouses and tortoises. The movable testudo of shields was commonly employed and with good results.

Lines of contra- and circumvallation were made more expertly than of yore. Mounds were used as formerly in Greece, but grew to enormous proportions. Sulla's at Massada was two hundred and eighty-six feet high, and upon these were other constructions and towers of one hundred and fifty-five feet, making four hundred and forty-one feet above the level.

Mines were dexterously used. Sulla's at Athens showed especial ability. Sheds, tortoises, movable towers, rams, all came into play. Catapults and ballistas were in constant use. The big catapult projected beams a horizontal distance of four hundred to eight hundred paces. The small catapult (*scorpio*) shot heavy lances three hundred to five hundred paces. The former was used in sieges, the latter in the field. A burning missile (*falerica*) was also hurled. The big ballista threw stones four hundred to six hundred paces on a curved path like that of a mortar, and was used in sieges. The small one (*onager*) was used in the field. The smallest onager and scorpio could be worked by one man.

In general, the sieges of this day were much like those of the Greeks. They had gained distinctly in skill since the days of Hannibal, but few besiegers reached the clever devices of Alexander; none approached his gallant assaults.

Foreign conquest obliged the Romans to increase the power and effectiveness of their fleet. This was done with their usual push and good sense.

The government owned public forests which were devoted to ship-building, and were well managed. War vessels consisted of biremes, triremes, quinquiremes and up to octoremes; the triremes and quinquiremes were the ones mostly in commission. There were cruisers for light coast duty and spying out the enemy (*naves speculatoriæ*); a smaller class like gunboats; transports and flat bottoms (*pontones*) for river duty. The war vessels mostly had iron rams (*rostra ferramenta*), and their sides were protected by beams and shields of various kinds to save them from the blows of the enemy's. The larger, often the smaller, vessels had decks, and missile-throwers and towers stood upon them. Each vessel was provided with grappling-irons, boarding-bridges, siege implements and machines for casting fire-pots. The use of fireships was well understood.

The fleets were manned by rowers or sailors, and by soldiers or marines. The rowers and sailors were slaves or came from the lower classes; the marines were raised like legionaries. Their oath of fealty was equally to the admiral and not to the state. A quinquireme had four hundred rowers, the others a corresponding number. The marines were armed like the legionaries, but had scythed lances, battle-axes and boarding-swords. The rowers were also armed.

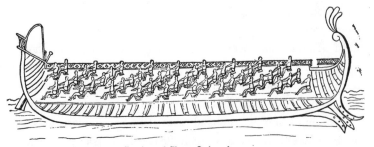

Section of Short Quinquireme.

Each vessel had a chief of rowers who gave the time of the stroke by a hammer-blow on a gong; a sort of boatswain in charge of the sails, anchors, etc.; a steersman (*gubernator*), who was also pilot; a captain (*navarchus*); and a comman-dant of marines (*præfectus navis*). A consul or prætor might be in command of the fleet, or a special officer (*dux præfectusque classis*) might lead it.

Harbors were natural or artificial. A favorite form of the latter was a semicircle from the shore, from which two moles ran out seaward, the entrance between which was closed by a chain. The inner harbor was in several divisions, and well provided with arsenals and wharves. These har-bors were fortified both towards the sea and on the land side.

When a fleet was ready to put to sea the rowers first went aboard, then the marines. An inspection with religious cer-emonies followed and the fleet set sail, the light vessels ahead, then the triremes and other war-galleys, then the transports. On landing, the vessels were drawn up on the beach, and were protected by palisades towards the sea and fieldworks towards the land. This rule, along the rocky coast of Italy, must frequently have been broken; but a fleet always passed the night ashore, when possible.

Naval battles generally took place near land, and vessels were lightened as much as possible by leaving off sails, lowering masts, and clearing decks. Ebb and flood tides were carefully watched and utilized.

The common order of battle was a parallel one in two lines (*acies duplex*), with the lighter ships in the rear line; a

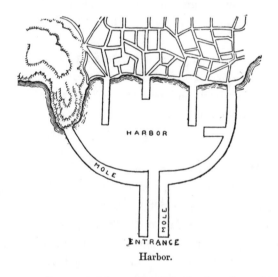

HARBOR

MOLE

MOLE

ENTRANCE

Harbor.

concave order (*acies lunata*), with the heaviest ships on the flanks to outflank the enemy; a convex order, in which the heaviest ships were in the centre; a pincer-like form (*forceps*), against a wedge (*acies cuneata*), or vice versa.

The signal for battle was a red flag at the admiral's masthead, and a trumpet-blast from each ship. Upon this all hands gave the battle-cry and intuned the battle-hymn. The missile-throwers opened the action and then the lines clashed. Each ship endeavored to run down or ram an adversary, cut its oars, board and capture it, or set it afire.

A naval victory was celebrated by songs and music, and by decorating the prows of the vessels with laurel. The admiral was allowed a *triumphus navalis*.

To sum the matter up, the old and perfect militia-system of Rome had disappeared, the soldier had become a professional, and the forces on foot were simple mercenaries. The distinctions in the legions were exclusively military, having nothing to do with civil rank or class. And as everything now depended on the general, so there grew up about him a headquarters-guard (*prœtoriani*) which was the germ of a regular army.

The wonderful campaigns and battles of this era were the work of the leaders. The condition of the army, for good or bad, reflected the spirit and character of the general. It was no longer the Roman citizen who won the victories of Rome, but the genius of great men who aimed at the control of the state.

Much of Marius' success in the Jugurthan war he owed to the skill of Sulla, his then quæstor and later political opponent. Metellus, Marius' chief, deserves the credit for the conquest of Numidia as far as the confines of the desert; Sulla that for the capture of Jugurtha. Marius profited by both. The great army-changes are associated with Marius; but there is little in his military feats which have other than a political significance.

To Marius is, however, due abundant praise for his conduct at Aquæ Sextiæ and Vercellæ. Rome never ran a greater danger than from the invasion of the Teutones and Cimbri; and it was to Marius she owed her rescue. After the defeat of the Romans at Arausio (Orange) in 105 B. C., where the consuls Mallius Maximus and Servilius Cæpio, with eighty thousand Roman soldiers and half as many non-combatants, paid with their lives the penalty of mismanage-

ment,—a blow more seriously threatening than even Cannæ,
— Marius was sent to Gaul to repair the disaster. He had
ample time, for instead of to Italy the barbarians had headed
their column towards Spain. Here, forced back by the
brave Iberians and the difficulties of the Pyrenees, they again
marched towards the north, until they were checked by the
stubborn Belgæ and once more rolled in a vast flood towards
the Roman province.

Route of Cimbri and Teutones.

Marius had established himself at the confluence of the
Rhone and Isère; had reduced the disaffected tribes and confirmed the fealty of others in the Province. At this point he
protected the roads to the only two then available passes, over
the Little St. Bernard and over the Maritime Alps. The
barbarians were in two bodies. One of these essayed the

Eastern Alps and in due time debouched into Italy. The other, the Teutones, aimed to pass down the Rhone and follow the coast to the Maritime Alps. These soon made their appearance before the camp of Marius, which the consul had fortified with extreme care. Though he was an excellent disciplinarian and his men were in good heart, Marius was unwilling to encounter the immense hordes of the Teutones until his men had become accustomed to the sight of their huge stature, their wild demeanor and howling battle-cry. The Romans feared these light-haired bulky barbarians as the Greeks had dreaded the Persians prior to Marathon. Not all the taunts of the enemy could make Marius budge from his secure intrenchments. Finally, tired out, the Teutones assaulted the camp for three days in succession, but were thrust back with heavy loss. They then marched for Italy, filing, say the authorities, six days and nights past the Roman camp, with their armed men and families and baggage-trains, and calling with sneers to the legionaries for messages to their wives and children in Italy.

Now came Marius' chance. Cautiously following up the enemy in the style he had learned in the Jugurthan war, daily camping near by them on inaccessible heights and behind strong works, he finally felt that the temper of his men was equal to an attack on the enemy. Near Aquæ Sextiæ (Aix, Départment des Bouches du Rhône), even before his camp was finished, a fight was begun between the men of both armies who were getting water at the little river Arc, which lay between them. The Romans drove the barbarians — they were Ambrones — across the river and to their wagon-camp. Here took place a severe combat in which the wives of the Ambrones fought beside their husbands and the barbarians lost heavily. But though they had done good work, the day ended by the Romans falling back to their side of the river.

During the succeeding night, Marius placed Marcellus
with three thousand men — some authorities say non-combatants — in ambush in some wooded ravines up the river from
the barbarian camp, with orders, during the battle which he
proposed to force, to debouch on the enemy's rear.   At daybreak the consul drew up the Roman army on some heights

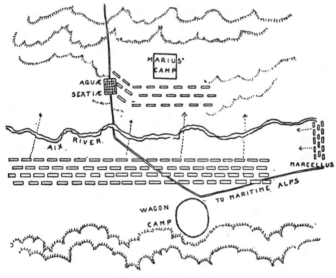

Battle of Aquæ Sextiæ.

lining the river where he had established his camp, and sent
his cavalry out to lure the Teutones to attack.   This was
cleverly accomplished.   The barbarians, under the impression that the Romans would not fight, forded the stream and
rushed tumultuously up the slope.   They were received so
stoutly by the legions that they fell into disorder and were
driven back to the plain.   Unused to the midday heat of the
Mediterranean, the barbarians, after some hours' fighting,
lost their vigor, and at the proper instant the party in ambush emerged and fell, sustained by the cavalry, upon their

rear.   The Teutones were as demoralized as they had formerly been eager.   They fled in disorder and were cut down
in their tracks, with a loss, according to Livy, of ninety
thousand killed and twenty thousand captured.   This was
in 102 B. C.

Meanwhile the Cimbri had crossed the Rhætian Alps, but
did not at once march on Rome.   Marius reached the scene
in time to join his colleague Catulus.   The barbarians, according to their odd but ancient custom, asked of Marius to
appoint a day and place for battle, which to them was but a
huge duel, governed by the same forms.   This Marius did,
and near Vercellæ the hosts met in 101 B. C.   The Cimbri
were beaten and annihilated — no less than one hundred and
forty thousand being killed and sixty thousand captured, as
is claimed by the Latin historians.   The nation disappeared
from history.   Rome was saved from another burning.
Marius was more than a hero.   He was the people's demigod.

Gallic Cuirass.   (?Narbonese.)

II.

SULLA, POMPEY. 90–60 B. C.

SULLA was one of the ablest generals of his era. He learned his trade under Marius. He first used earthworks in battle to protect his lines, and at Orchomenus he used fieldworks to hem in his enemy. Sulla was bold and discreet; he was both lion and fox. Pompey was one of those captains upon whom greatness happens to be thrust. Of good but not high ability, exceptional fortune enabled him to reap the benefit of the hard work of others. He was slow and lacked initiative, but did some of his work well. His early successes in Sicily and Africa earned him the title of Great at twenty-four ; but when he went to Spain and opposed Sertorius, one of the most noteworthy generals of antiquity, he more than met his match. Only the death of Sertorius enabled him to win success. The campaign in which Pompey swept the pirates from the Mediterranean was a simple piece of work excellently done ; his campaign in the East had been already made easy by Lucullus, whose labors redounded to Pompey's credit. On the whole, while Pompey should not be underrated, it must be acknowledged that he earned his great repute on more than usually slender grounds.

SULLA, as a general, stands higher than any of the men immediately preceding Cæsar. He got his training in the Jugurthan war under Marius, and won his first laurels by the able negotiations which mainly contributed to the capture of Jugurtha and the ending of that difficult conflict. He again served under Marius in the campaign against the Cimbri and Teutones. Later on, master and pupil marked an era in the history of Rome by their competition for the supremacy of the state.

Sulla's work in the East in the Mithridatic war was masterly. His siege of Athens, coupled to the earlier siege of Numantia by Scipio Africanus Minor, furnished the pattern

on which Cæsar worked and bettered, though unquestionably
Cæsar had studied the siege operations at Tyre and Rhodes,
and had drawn his inspiration from them. All Sulla's campaigns are of marked interest. There was much in the wars
of the early part of the last century B. C. which was splendid
in skill and accomplishment, and which is specially noteworthy as being the school in which young Cæsar learned his
trade. It is hard to select any one of Sulla's numerous great
deeds which shall stand alone as representative of his soldierly work. The battle of Chæronæa, 86 B. C., on the field
rendered famous by Philip's victory and the youthful daring
of Alexander, is a sample of how to deal with unusual questions in war.

Taxiles and Archelaus, the lieutenants of Mithridates, had

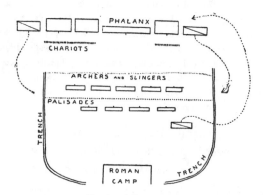

Battle of Chæronæa.

an army of one hundred thousand foot and ten thousand horse
with ninety scythed chariots. Sulla's force, including his
Greek auxiliaries, was less than a third this number, and in
cavalry he was especially wanting, — on these plains a great
source of weakness. His Roman troops were but sixteen thousand five hundred strong. But Sulla despised his enemy,
and was confident of success. He made up for his want of

strength by protecting his flanks with trenches which should save him from the charges of the enemy's horse, and by erecting a row of heavy palisades between his first and second lines, which should arrest the charge of the scythed chariots. Here was an intelligent instance of the use of fieldworks.

The battle was opened in true Oriental fashion by the charge of chariots. Sulla's first line smartly withdrew behind the palisades, which not only checked the onset of the chariots, but these, their horses being terrified by the heavy fire of Sulla's slingers and archers, turned on their own line and produced marked confusion in the Macedonian phalanx and in a corps of Italian auxiliaries serving in the Mithridatic army. To repair the disaster, Archelaus ordered his horse from both flanks to charge the Roman legions. The Orientals rode down on the Romans with great *élan*, and their furious charge, despite the trenches, succeeded in breaking the Roman formation, showing clearly that without the trenches Sulla's line would have been destroyed. But the legionaries did not lose heart. They rapidly formed squares and resisted the horsemen with great determination. Sulla, meanwhile, perceiving that the enemy's phalanx did not readily recover from the disorder into which the chariots had thrown it, and that the moment had arrived when a blow driven home at the right spot was needed, gathered his own small force of cavalry from the right, and heading it in person charged sharply in on the exposed flank of the enemy. As was always the case with Sulla, fortune followed hard upon his boldness. The Asiatic foot offered but little resistance, and its flight unsettled the phalanx. The horse which was assailing the Roman legions found its task too stubborn, and turned to aid in retrieving the disorder of the foot. The legions gained breathing spell, and speedily patching up a new formation advanced sharply on the wavering foot of

Archelaus. This decided the day. The entire Mithridatic army was swept from off the field.

Archelaus managed to retire to his camp, and closed the gates to save what he had got within. Immense slaughter without the walls resulted. When the gates were finally forced by the surging mass, the Romans entered with the enemy and prolonged the massacre. Archelaus saved but a twelfth part of his army. The Roman loss was trivial.

At the battle of Orchomenus, in the succeeding year, Sulla, by clever calculation in cutting ditches and more clever tactics, succeeded in penning up a new army under Archelaus in such a position as to drive him into some swamps and morasses, where he destroyed the entire force. This operation appears to have been a species of siege, by a system of gradually narrowed fieldworks, of an army camped in the open instead of protected by the walls of a fortress, and as such exhibits decided originality of conception and boldness in execution. The accounts of the operation are obscure.

Sulla was equally able as statesman and soldier. He acted, not like Marius, from impulse, but in a well-considered though rapid manner. He was tireless and active, brave and enterprising, and singularly cool in thought and deed. Carbo pronounced Sulla to have the qualities of both the lion and the fox. He won the love of his soldiers, and yet was a stern disciplinarian. He showed as marked skill in his sieges as in tactics.

The most interesting though least creditable part of the military career of Cnæus Pompey will be dealt with at length when we find him measuring swords with Cæsar. In the earlier part of his life, before he had Cæsar to contend with, Pompey showed many characteristics of the great man and soldier. He must not be underrated. But Pompey was perhaps the lightest weight of all the characters who have

enacted a giant's rôle on the stage of life. No man won the
title of Great on such slender merit. No man ever wielded
such vast power with so little to back it up. He compares
favorably with men of a second rank; but as he stood on the
same plane of power with Cæsar, so must we gauge him by
the same large measure. It is due to Pompey to sketch his
early achievements.

Pompey had many of the virtues of the soldier. He was
splendid as an athlete. He was bold in that species of war
which calls not too largely on the intellect or the moral force.
He could charge at the head of his horse with noble gallantry,
when he was unable to plan a good campaign or assume a sudden strategic or tactical risk. He was as simple, modest and
reserved in habit as he was fearless in battle. He had those
qualities which endeared him to the people. Taken up by
Sulla when a mere youth, he climbed into popular favor as
Scipio Africanus Major had done, by belief in and assertion
of his right to commands usually given to those who have
long served the state. But Pompey had less than the ability
of Scipio. He was clean in his private life, and his "honest
countenance" was proverbial. He was upright in his family
relations, but none the less divorced his wife at the nod of
Sulla, while Cæsar, against whom much is charged in his
commerce with women, refused to do so. Pompey was retiring in civil life and lacked the graces of manner much considered at that day, though he had a fair degree of culture.
In council he was slow, and to a habit of silence which came
from a not over quick comprehension, was referred, as it often
is, a judgment he did not possess.

Pompey was but an ordinary man of good abilities. He
had not the first glint of genius. Greatness was thrust upon
him if it ever was upon any man. He was the very reverse
of Cæsar. Circumstances made Pompey; Cæsar made cir-

cumstances. Pompey was cold, passionless and slow at making resolutions. In that era, when every man in power held ultra opinions of some sort, Pompey's very ordinariness sundered him from the ranks of his peers as his assertion and honest belief that he was great raised him above them. Had his conduct risen to a higher plane, other qualities might have been ascribed to him; but he must be judged by the event. In him were blended a singular modesty of bearing and extravagance in demands. He was fortunate in his beginnings; much was done for him; to what he had, more was given; he was never overtaxed, nor did luck run counter to his course. By such easy steps rose Cnæus Pompey, the creation not of brilliant, but of steady good fortune.

Pompey possessed obstinacy to the last degree, — a quality which is often a saving clause. But it was not an intelligent obstinacy. He imagined that he was having his own way when more clever men were outwitting him. From unreadiness to assume a heavy responsibility, when thrust upon him, grew a set habit of caution which well exhibits the average plane of his character. It was not the caution of a Hannibal, who, when called on, could be bold beyond any man; it was rather a want of moral incisiveness. While not lacking good conduct and qualities he was, says Mommsen, "the most starched of artificial great men." Pompey was perhaps the best individual to hold his party together, because he did naught to disrupt it.

Pompey first came into notice in 83 B. C., when he undertook to raise an army for Sulla in Picenum. Here his personal bearing and unquestioned gallantry stood him in good stead. He raised and equipped a superior force, and when three Marian armies faced him, he had the nerve to attack them in detail before they could assemble, and the good fortune to disperse them. He led an attack on the enemy's

camp — an unusual thing at that day — which did credit to
the Roman name. On his joining his chief, Sulla saluted
the young man of twenty-three as Imperator, a title which
few men ever won, and those only at the end of many years
of arduous and brilliant service. In 82 B. C., Pompey was
sent as proprætor to Sicily. The island, on his approach with
six legions and one hundred and twenty galleys, was at once
evacuated by the enemy and afforded him an easy triumph.
From Sicily he shipped to Africa, where, though with larger
forces, he conducted a handsome and successful campaign
against Domitius Ahenobarbus, the Marian. His assault
on the enemy's camp here, too, as well as a speedy and energetic forty days' campaign, revived the Roman name, which
had fallen into disrepute. On his return, "half in irony and
half in recognition," Sulla saluted him as Magnus, and he was
allowed, against all precedent, the greater triumph, never
granted but to those of senatorial rank.

Q. Sertorius, the Marian, had been for some years holding
head against the Sullan faction in Spain. It was essential
that some able soldier should go thither. Pompey as usual
felt that he had a right to demand the place, and it was given
him. He was not fortunate in opposing this extraordinary
general, who, had his work been cast on a winning in lieu of
a losing theatre, might have rivaled any Roman antedating
Cæsar. Sertorius was equally remarkable as a statesman
and a soldier. He had practically set up an independent
kingdom in Iberia. Few men have ever held a difficult
people to its work, or conducted an energetic guerilla warfare so well or on so large a scale. Never coming to battle,
he had wearied the Sullan general Metellus by minor operations, by cutting off his foragers and water-parties, by attacking him on the march, and by remarkable activity in
small-war. Metellus had been unable to cope with him.

It was in the summer of 77 B. C. that Pompey went to
Spain as proconsul.   On his way he made the new road over
the Cottian Alps (Mt. Genèvre) which Cæsar later used, and
settled some troubles in Gaul.   He did not cross the Pyrenees till late in the fall of that year, and wintered in north-

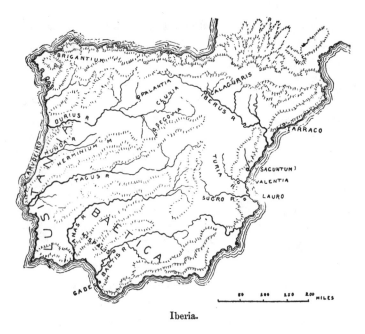

Iberia.

east Spain.   Sertorius was on the upper Ebro; of his lieutenants, Hirtuleius was facing Metellus in Farther Spain,
and Perpenna, sustained by Herennius, held the Ebro against
Pompey's columns.   Pompey, early in the spring, advanced
to and forced the Ebro, defeated Herennius at Valentia, south
of Saguntum, and captured the place.   Sertorius had moved
on Lauro, a town allied to Pompey, on the Sucro (Xucar),
south of Valentia, and was besieging it.   Pompey moved
against him, and sought to shut him in.   So confident was he
of success that he flattered himself that he had got Sertorius

where he must soon surrender. He did not know his opponent. In the struggle which Pompey forced on him, Sertorius utterly outmanœuvred his opponent, penned him up, and
under his very eyes burned Lauro and transported its inhabitants to Lusitania. Pompey was surprised enough at the
turn affairs had taken.

Meanwhile Metellus had defeated Hirtuleius near Hispalis
(Seville). The next year he again defeated him near Segovia
when the Sertorian sought to prevent Metellus from marching
to join Pompey. Foreseeing the arrival of his colleague, and
lest he should be forced to divide his laurels with him, Pompey offered battle to Sertorius on the Sucro, which this general was only too glad to accept before the arrival of Metellus. On the left of the Roman line, Afranius beat back the
enemy and took Sertorius' camp; on the right, however,
Pompey was severely wounded and his troops badly defeated
by Sertorius, who thereupon turned on Afranius and drove
him back in turn. Pompey's army was rescued by the arrival
of Metellus, and Sertorius' quite unreliable forces hereupon
began to disperse. The main difficulty this able man had to
contend with was to keep his irregular levies together and
ready for work. At times he had very large numbers, even
as high as one hundred and fifty thousand men, which he had
with vast labor got together; then, suddenly, on a reverse
or from some unexpected discouragement, the army would
dissolve to a mere handful. So now. On the junction of
Metellus and Pompey, and learning of the defeat of Hirtuleius, Sertorius' army incontinently retired and dispersed to
the mountains. After a period of recuperation they were
again collected and Sertorius faced Pompey south of Saguntum. Meanwhile his galleys interfered with the Roman
victualling fleets along the coast.

After some manœuvring another battle was fought on the

river Turia (Guadalaviar). It was a long and stanch struggle for mastery. Finally Sertorius defeated Pompey and his cavalry, while Metellus broke Perpenna's array. The result was favorable to the Sullans, and Sertorius' army again dispersed. Sertorius betook himself to Clunia, a fortress on the upper Durius (Douro), where he was besieged. But the Spanish army was once more got together, and Sertorius cleverly escaped from Clunia and joined it. The end of the year 75 B. C. saw him again facing the Sullans, with equal chances.

On the whole, however, Metellus and Pompey had done well. Southern and Central Spain had been recovered, and Sertorius had made no gain. This was Metellus' work rather than Pompey's. The colleagues went into winter-quarters, Metellus in Gaul, Pompey between the Durius and Iberus, near modern Valladolid.

In the spring of 74 B. C. Sertorius began a small-war against Pompey. The latter was besieging Pallantia (Pallencia), when Sertorius drove him from it. At Calagurris, though joined by Metellus, he was likewise defeated, and then driven out of the upper Ebro region. Whenever Pompey met Sertorius, he succumbed. The succeeding year was characterized by much the same fortune, though Pompey made some headway in getting allies among the Spanish cities. The war had been going on eight years. It was a serious drain on Italy, and Spain itself by stress of war was lapsing into barbarism. Pompey and Metellus had found their master. The legions were heartily sick of their ill-rewarded labors. Many people in Rome began to fear Sertorius as a second Hannibal, though indeed there was no such danger. It was Sertorius' peculiar abilities, so well suited to the people and mountains of Spain, which enabled him to do such brilliant work. Able as he was, the gigantic conception of a Hannibal was beyond him, — as beyond all others.

Finally, as a piece of good fortune for Pompey, Sertorius was assassinated in 72 B. C. Perpenna, his second in command, was no such opponent, and him Pompey and Metellus speedily put down within the next year. Then regulating the affairs of the two Spanish provinces, they returned to Rome, and together triumphed. This campaign cannot be said to have added to the laurels of Pompey the Great.

In the war against the pirates, Pompey showed considerable skill. Not that the task was one to tax the resources of a great soldier. The Mediterranean pirates were to the

The Mediteranean.

Roman legions and fleets much what a gang of desperadoes is to a well-organized police. But the pirates had long been a scourge to Roman commerce, and their suppression became necessary. In 67 B. C. Pompey was given absolute power in the premises. He began in a business-like way. He divided the entire field into thirteen districts and placed a lieutenant and a sufficient force in each, with instructions to raise and equip men and galleys, search the coasts and hunt down the pirates. Pompey himself undertook the western Mediterranean, and cleared the coast of Sardinia, Sicily and Africa, so as to reëstablish the grain traffic with Rome. Part of his force did the like on the shores of Gaul and Spain. In forty days Pompey had cleared the western half of the Mediterranean, and proceeded to Syria and Cilicia. The resistance offered was slight. There was no general organization. But Pompey was shrewd. He chose to be indulgent to many and moderate to most, rather than to crucify every pirate caught, as it had been the rule to do. This conduct of itself helped break up an already lost cause. The Cilicians alone offered any serious resistance; and these the Roman superior force and well-equipped galleys completely overwhelmed. The land resorts of the pirates were next broken up. Pardon brought many to terms. In three months from the first blow the entire war was finished. Some four hundred vessels, including ninety war-galleys, were taken; thirteen hundred in all were destroyed; ten thousand pirates perished and twenty thousand were captured. Many Roman prisoners were rescued.

The pirates had threatened Rome with starvation. Pompey's victories brought abundance. Every one had feared to go to sea; the Mediterranean was henceforth open to all. No wonder Pompey was heralded as the savior of Rome. Yet he had done only a good piece of work, scarcely a great one.

The consul Lucullus had been ably conducting war in the East against the great Mithridates, who had overrun all Asia Minor (74 B. C.). His colleague, Cotta, having been defeated in the Propontis (Sea of Marmora), Lucullus hastened to his relief and forced the king back with heavy loss. Setting matters to rights at sea, he followed up his advantage with a sharp offensive, crossed the Halys, marched across Pontus, won a fierce battle at Cabira, and fairly drove the great king out of his own kingdom. Capturing many cities by siege, Lucullus advanced into Armenia Minor, while Mithridates took refuge with Tigranes, king of Armenia. In order to forfeit no present advantages, Lucullus, unauthor-

ized by the Senate, crossed the Euphrates into Armenia, and
defeated Tigranes in the great battle of Tigranocerta near the
Tigris. The kings joined forces, but Lucullus beat them
again and marched on Artaxata, the capital of Tigranes. A
mutiny among his legions prevented his reaching his objective, and forced him to retire across the Tigris into Mesopo-
tamia. While Lucullus was taking Nisibis by storm, Mithridates returned to Pontus, and defeated the Roman army
left there, at Zela. Though handicapped by fresh mutinies
and recalled by the Senate, Lucullus still made a handsome
retreat to Asia Minor.

Asia Minor.

While Lucullus had ended unsuccessfully, he had in eight
years of hard campaigning done much to weaken the resources of both Mithridates and Tigranes. In 66 B. C.

Pompey went to Galatia to supplant Lucullus, purposing to advance into Pontus, whither his Cilician legions were to follow him. He had nearly fifty thousand men. Mithridates opposed him with thirty thousand foot, mostly archers, and three thousand horse. He no longer had his ancient ally and son-in-law, Tigranes, to rely upon, and would have gladly made peace; but he would not unconditionally surrender, as Pompey demanded that he should do. Mithridates led Pompey some distance into his territory, harassing him severely with his superior horse. Pompey properly ceased to follow, and marching to the upper Euphrates crossed and entered Mithridates' eastern provinces. The king followed Pompey along the Euphrates and finally arrested his progress at the castle of Dasteira, from which secure position he scoured the lowlands with his cavalry and light troops. Pompey was forced to retire to Armenia Minor until his Cilician legions came up. Then he invested Mithridates in his eyrie and ravaged the land. After six weeks' blockade Mithridates put his sick and wounded to death to save them from falling into the hands of Pompey, and made his escape, marching by a circuit towards Armenia, Tigranes' territory. Pompey followed, but again perceiving Mithridates' intention of luring him away from Pontus, he resorted to a clever stratagem. In front of Mithridates, on the route he was pursuing south of the Lycus, near where Nicopolis was later built, was a narrow valley. Pompey, in lieu of following in Mithridates' rear, by a secret forced march got beyond him and occupied the heights surrounding the valley. Mithridates, unaware of this fact, marched next day as usual, and camped at nightfall in the very spot which placed his army in the trap ably laid for him by Pompey. In the middle of the night Pompey attacked. The army of Mithridates was wrapped in sleep and unable to resist. It was cut to pieces where it stood.

Mithridates fled. Unable to go to Tigranes, he made his way along the east and north shores of the Euxine (Black Sea) to the Chersonesus (Crimea). Tigranes was at the mercy of Pompey. He gave up his recent conquests, and paid six thousand talents into the Roman war chest. Pompey had dictated peace.

In one easy campaign Pompey had thus overcome the two great Oriental kings, — of Pontus and Armenia. The territory of Rome had been indefinitely extended. No wonder that his name was in every mouth.

Pompey for a while pursued Mithridates, which brought about a campaign against the tribes of the Caucasus. The king he could not overtake; the Caucasians he forced into a peace. Mithridates, from his refuge in Panticapæum in the Crimea, harbored extravagant ideas of attacking Rome from the north by enlisting the Scythians and Danubian Celts in his favor as Hannibal had enlisted the Gauls. But this wild plan was ended by his death in 63 B. C. He had waged war against Rome for twenty-six years.

Pompey finished his work by reducing the new provinces, Pontus, Syria, Cilicia, to order, by subduing disorders in Syria, and settling affairs with the Parthians. He then returned to Rome for the reward which was his by right.

Lucullus had made much headway with the conquest of the East, for which his ability and enterprise were well suited. Pompey with his large forces, lack of initiative, and extreme caution, had completed what Lucullus had begun. Had he launched out as boldly as his predecessor he would not have accomplished so much. He had on all hands opportunities for brilliant strokes. He did nothing that was not safe. He kept his superiority of force at all times. His course was the very best to reap what Lucullus had sown, but it would never have conquered the East without such preparation as Lucullus had made. The campaigns of the latter compare favorably with those of Pompey, who was heralded as the representative of all that was most splendid in Roman annals, while Lucullus was forgotten. We shall be better able to gauge Pompey's real abilities when we try him in the same balance with Cæsar.

Ancient Helmet.

III.

CÆSAR'S YOUTH, EDUCATION AND EARLY SERVICES. 100–58 B. C.

CÆSAR was born 100 B. C. of an old Roman family. He owed much to the care given him by his mother. His education was carefully conducted and well bestowed. He was not strong as a lad, but gymnastics and a settled regimen improved his physique, which had a tendency to epilepsy. He was somewhat of a dandy, and a leader of the young society of Rome. He early developed talent as an orator and held many minor offices. His party — the Marian — was out of power, and the young man was wise in keeping out of the whirlpool of politics. Cæsar had less to do with military affairs than most of those who rose to distinction in Rome. His work was in the line of statesmanship. He saw much of the world and at twenty-three made a reputation in his oration against Dolabella. He was well known as an able man, but not as a soldier. At thirty-nine he became prætor and received Spain as province. He was of middle age and had as yet done nothing but accumulate immense debts. In Spain he showed energy and ability, reduced Lusitania, and so managed its finances as to discharge all his debts. When he returned to Rome, Pompey, Cæsar and Crassus became triumvirs; Cæsar was made consul and allotted Gaul. In 58 B. C., at the age of forty-two, he entered upon that part of his career which has made him so great a part of the world's history.

CAIUS JULIUS CÆSAR was born in 100 B. C. (some authorities hold 102 B. C.), of an old patrician family which had come from Alba under the reign of Tullus Hostilius, and which had enjoyed many public trusts. His father had been prætor and had died when Cæsar was about sixteen years old. His mother, Aurelia, was of good stock of plebeian origin, and was a woman of exceptionally fine character. Cæsar was proud of his forbears. In pronouncing the funeral oration of his aunt Julia, who had married Marius, Suëtonius tells us that he thus spoke of his descent: "My aunt Julia, on the maternal side, is of the issue of kings; on the paternal side, she descends from the immortal gods; for her mother was a Marcia, and the family Marcius Rex are the descendants of Ancus Marcius. The Julia family, to which I belong, descends from Venus herself. Thus our house unites to the sacred character of kings, who are the most powerful among men, the venerated holiness of the gods, who keep kings themselves in subjection."

Aurelia devoted her life to her son's education, and by this his natural mental and moral nature enabled him to profit as few youths can. He grew to manhood with many of the best qualities of head and heart stamped upon him. As pedagogue he had a Gaul, M. Antonius Gnipho, who had received all the benefits of an education in Alexandria. His body grew strong, — though originally delicate and having a tendency to epilepsy, — his carriage was erect, his manner open and kindly, and his countenance singularly engaging and expressive, if not handsome. He had black, piercing eyes, pale face, straight aquiline nose, small handsome mouth, with finely curled lips which bore a look of kindliness; large brow showing great intellectual activity and power. In his youth his face was well-rounded. He was moderate in his diet and temperate; his health, harmed by neither excess of labor or of pleasure, was uniformly good, though at Corduba and later at Thapsus he had serious nervous attacks. He exposed himself to all weathers, was an excellent gymnast, and noted as a rider. "From his first youth he was much used to horseback, and had even acquired the facility of riding with dropped reins and his hands joined behind his back " (Plutarch). By judicious exercise he gradually became able to endure great fatigue. His dress was careful, and his person neat and tasteful to the extreme. Like the youth of every age he was over fond of outward adornment. Suetonius speaks of his key-

pattern ornamented toga and loose girdle. Sulla once re-
marked that it would be well to look out for yonder dandy —
and dandies in every age have notably made among the best
of soldiers and men. This habit of personal nicety — not to
say vanity — clung to him through life. "And when," says
Cicero, "I look at his hair, so artistically arranged, and when
I see him scratch his head with one finger," lest perchance
he should disarrange it, "I cannot believe that such a man
could conceive so black a design as to overthrow the Roman
Republic " (Plutarch).

Cæsar was fond of art as of books. He spoke Greek and
Latin with equal ease and fluency, as was common to the cultured classes. He wrote several works which earned him a
reputation for clear and forcible style, but he was not equally
happy as a poet. "For Cæsar and Brutus have also made
verses, and have placed them in the public libraries. They
are poets as feeble as Cicero, but happier in that fewer people know of them," says Tacitus. His life up to manhood
was that of a city youth of good family and breeding, perhaps
according to our notions lax, but within the bounds set by the
age in which he lived; in later years he was a thorough man
of the world. He was fond of female society, and cultivated
it throughout his life. He possessed a marked taste for pictures, jewels, statues; and, as we are told by Dio Cassius,
habitually wore a ring with a very beautiful seal of an armed
Venus. He joined excellent physical endurance to very exceptional mental and nervous strength. "He was liberal to
prodigality, and of a courage above human nature and even
imagination," says Velleius Paterculus. Plutarch calls him
the second orator in Rome. Pliny speaks of his extraordinary memory. Seneca gives him credit for great calmness
in anger, and Plutarch says he was affable, courteous and
gracious to a degree which won him the affection of the

people. "In voice, gesture, a grand and noble personality, he had a certain brilliancy in speaking, without a trace of artifice," testifies Cicero. To the external advantages which distinguished him from all other citizens, Cæsar joined an impetuous and powerful soul, says Velleius. One could scarcely add a single qualification to his equipment for the profession of arms. Such was Caius Julius Cæsar in the estimation of his contemporaries.

At fourteen years of age, Marius procured for him the appointment of priest of Jupiter. At sixteen he was betrothed to Cossutia, the daughter of a wealthy knight, but broke the engagement a year later. At eighteen he married Cornelia, daughter of Cinna. He is said to have been already well known for his personal and intellectual characteristics; but this was doubtless as the promising young scion of a well-known family, rather than from any services actually accomplished.

When Sulla rode into power on the wreck of the Marian party, he would have liked to bring over this brilliant young man to his cause, but he found Cæsar immovable. He ordered him to put away Cornelia, whose father had belonged to the Marian faction, but this Cæsar bluntly refused, though he forfeited his priesthood and his wife's fortune, was declared incapable of inheriting in his own family, and ran danger of his life. This was at a time when such men as Piso and Pompey divorced their wives to suit the politics of the day, and scores a high mark to Cæsar's credit. Finally, after a period of concealment in the Sabine country, through the influence of friends, Cæsar was forgiven by Sulla. But Sulla prophesied truly, says Suetonius, that there was more than one Marius lurking in the personality of Cæsar.

Cæsar deemed it wise, under the circumstances, to keep away from Rome. He could not remain without being thrust actively into the political turmoil, which he could see was but an interlude. Such discretion he manifested all through his political career. He spent some time in Bithynia, where he was guest of King Nicomedes. Here, under the prætor M. Thermus, he served as contubernalis (aide de camp) against

Ægean.

Mithridates, and was (81 B. C.) actively employed both in war and diplomacy. At the siege of Mitylene he received a civic crown for saving the life of a Roman soldier. His reputation for morality of demeanor was rudely compromised by his conduct at the court of Nicomedes; but such facts do not concern the soldier. The morals of each age and clime must stand by themselves. Cæsar in no wise differed from his compeers. He then served at sea under Servilius in the campaign of 78 B. C., against the Cilician pirates. On Sulla's death he returned to Rome.

Here his conduct was marked by great moral courage and independence coupled with common sense and a liberal policy; and in some civil proceedings his powers of oratory, which he studied with great care, raised him high in the estimation of the people. It was an usual means of introducing one's self to the public to pose as advocate in some great political prosecution. Such was Cæsar's part in the prosecution of Dolabella. He was twenty-one years old, and his oration, "which we still read with admiration," says Tacitus, in a moment made him famous. He later attacked Antonius Hybrida, and was engaged in other celebrated causes. These attacks were really aimed at Sulla's party, though still in power, rather than at individuals.

Preferring not to join for the present in the profitless political struggles of Rome, Cæsar set sail for Rhodes, which at that time was a marked centre of learning, intending to devote some time to study. On the way thither he was captured by pirates of Pharmacusa (Fermaco), a small island of the Sporades. The pirates demanded twenty talents ransom, but Cæsar contemptuously volunteered to pay them fifty, a piece of originality which insured him good treatment. While waiting some forty days for the receipt of the ransom-money, Cæsar gained such influence with these men, that he was treated rather as a king than as a prisoner. He disarmed all their suspicions and entertained them by his eloquence and wit. He is said to have told them — which they treated as a jest — that he would return, capture and crucify them all. He was as good as his word. Collecting vessels and men so soon as he was released, he fell unawares upon the pirates, recovered his money, took much booty, and punished them as he had threatened to do. Suetonius states that from motives of pity he had them all strangled first and only nailed their corpses to the cross.

After a short stay in Rhodes, where he studied under Apollonius Molo, the most celebrated of the masters of eloquence, he undertook on his own authority and cost a campaign against Mithridates in Cyzicus, in which he was measurably successful. He now learned from Rome that he had been nominated pontifex, in place of his uncle, L. Aurelius Cotta. He returned, and shortly after was also elected military tribune. He declined service in armies under the command of the Sullan generals, at the time of the campaigns against Sertorius in Spain. He would gladly have gone to the front to learn his duties in the field, but did not care to take a part against one who represented the old Marian party. He as usual cleverly avoided useless complications. Still he was ambitious of power, and set to work to form a party for himself in the state; and by employing fortune, friends, energy and ability, he succeeded in doing this. Being made quæstor, he accompanied the proconsul Antistius Vetus to Spain. Returned to Rome, he was in 68 B. C. made curator of the Appian Way and ædile curulis, and largely increased his popularity by the splendor of the public games he gave.

His next office was that of judex quæstionis, or judge of the criminal court, in 64 B. C., and in the succeeding year he was made pontifex maximus. After still another year he became prætor. During all this time he had been earning the hate of the aristocrats and the favor of the people. He was assigned the charge of the province of Hispania Ulterior, in 61 B. C., but could not leave Rome till some one had become bondsman for his debts, amounting, it is said, to over four thousand talents, or, according to Plutarch, to eight hundred and thirty talents, from one to five million dollars, as the sum. Cæsar's recklessness in money matters was a characteristic which pursued him through life.

Crassus was prevailed on to be his security. He relied for repayment on Cæsar's future successes. He was not deceived. Political preferment in Rome was coupled with opportunities of making money indefinitely great. The control of a province opened endless avenues of gain. And though no one was more careful to observe the forms of law, though no one was more law-abiding in the technical sense, Cæsar was in larger matters as unscrupulous as Napoleon. It was the habit of his day.

Cæsar's province as prætor — Farther Spain, or Bœtica, — possibly included some adjoining territories. He left Rome so soon as his money matters were arranged, without waiting for the instructions of the Senate, whose action was delayed by some political trials. The lowlanders of his province had been long subject to forays by the mountaineers of Lusitania, a section of country only half subject to the Roman power, if at all. Cæsar found two legions, or twenty cohorts, under the colors. These he at once increased by a third legion, or ten additional cohorts, giving him some ten thousand men. The tribes of Mons Herminium (Sierra di Estrella) in Lusitania (Portugal) were constantly troubling the province. Unable to control them by the command of the Roman people, whose authority the hardy uplanders laughed to scorn, Cæsar promptly undertook a campaign against them, and by vigorous measures reduced them to submission. Much of the detail of this campaign is not known. The other tribes of the mountains, lest they should suffer a like harsh fate, migrated beyond the Douro. This enabled Cæsar to possess himself of the strong places of the country in the valley of the Munda (Mondego), basing on which, he set out to pursue the fugitives, whom he soon reached. The barbarians turned upon him, and to unsettle his cohorts by making the legionaries eager for booty, they drove their herds before them. But Cæsar's men always felt the influence of the strong hand, and these cohorts, though new to him, had already learned to obey. An army is the mirror of its captain, reflecting his force and character as well as his intelligence. So now. Not a soldier left the ranks, and the Lusitanians were quickly routed. In this campaign Cæsar scoured the country on both banks of the Durius.

Meanwhile the Mt. Herminianites had again revolted, hoping that Cæsar would be defeated by the migrating tribes, and that they could close the road against his retreat and have him at their mercy. Cæsar had advanced towards the Durius

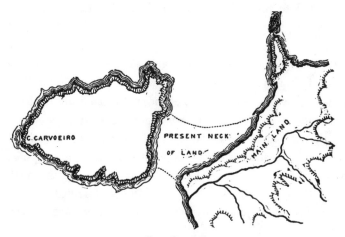

Cape Carvoeiro.

on the eastern slope of one of the minor ranges. Finding that the barbarians had closed this way, and not caring to encounter a guerilla warfare when he could operate to better advantage, he sought an outlet on the slope which descends towards the sea; but this, too, the barbarians closed by occupying the country from the foothills of the mountains to the shore. Cæsar had to fight his way through; but this his legions found no difficulty in doing on the easier terrain near the sea. In attacking the enemy, Cæsar operated by his left and managed to cut them off from the interior so as to drive them towards the sea, where he could more readily handle them. They took refuge on an island, which some critics have identified with the headland of Carvoeiro, now joined to the mainland, some forty-five miles north of Lisbon. The strait could be crossed in places at low tide on foot, but with difficulty. Having cooped up his enemy, Cæsar proposed to destroy him. It was impracticable to cross the strait under the fire of the barbarians. Cæsar built some rafts, and put over a portion of his troops. Part of the rest, over eager, attempted to ford the strait, but, sharply attacked by the barbarians, they were driven back into the rising tide and engulfed. The first attack thus failed, the small part for which the rafts sufficed being unable to effect a landing.

But Cæsar never gave up what was possible of accomplishment. Camping opposite the island, where he could hold the Lusitanians, he dispatched messengers to Gades for ships. On the arrival of these, he was able to put a suitable force over to the island, which done, he had no difficulty in subduing the enemy's force. This matter ended, he sailed to Brigantium (Corunna), whose inhabitants, terrified at the novel sight of such mighty vessels, voluntarily gave up the contest.

This campaign resulted in the submission of all Lusitania, and added much territory to the Roman holding in Spain. Cæsar was saluted Imperator by his soldiers and allowed a triumph by the Senate, which also decreed a holiday in honor of his success. So little is given us by the historians beyond the bare outline of the campaign, that we can say of it only that it was Cæsar's first lesson in war. When he attacked the Gallic question, he showed that he was familiar with war, but not with the management of its greater problems. Gaul was his school in the grand operations of war. It is to be regretted that we do not know how he had learned what unquestionably he knew of the art previous to his first campaign in Gaul. He had manifestly covered an immense territory, but we know naught of his method.

With the civil administration of his province after this war we have no concern. Cæsar accumulated great wealth; as Suetonius says, by the begging of subsidies; as Napoleon III. phrases it, "by contributions of war, a good administration, and even by the gratitude of those whom he governed." The fact remains, but Cæsar did no more than every governor of a Roman province felt it his right to do.

Cæsar unquestionably cared for money, but not from miserly motives. Hannibal was accused of avarice; but every coin he accumulated went to fan the flame of war against his country's oppressors. Cæsar used his gold to create an army, to win to himself the love of his legions. Such an amount of booty was taken in Spain as not only to reward his soldiers with exceptional liberality, but to pay off his own debts. His ambition was satisfied in every way.

That Cæsar was ambitious is no reproach. No man lacking ambition ever rose out of mediocrity, ever accomplished anything in the world's economy. At a small village in crossing the Alps, Cæsar is said to have exclaimed: "I would rather be first here than second in Rome!" Every great man is ambitious. It is the purpose of his ambition and the means he takes to satisfy it which are the test of its being a virtue or a vice. Cæsar's ambition was more personal than Hannibal's. It was akin to that of Alexander and Napoleon. In the temple of Hercules at Gades, standing before the statue of Alexander, Cæsar exclaimed that he had yet done nothing, when long before his age Alexander had conquered the world. Such was not the ambition of Hannibal or Gustavus.

For his victories in Spain, Cæsar was entitled to a triumph, but he denied himself this glory in order to run for the consulship.

The Roman Senate had demonstrated its inability to con-

Cæsar's Provinces.

trol the rival factions which were shaking the foundations of the state. Finally a breach between the Senate and Pompey, who was the strongest man in Rome, was brought about by its refusal to grant an allotment of lands for his Eastern veterans. As a result, Pompey, Cæsar and Crassus formed a secret compact to act together to divide the power and offices of Rome. They and their friends, with the easy methods of the day, could readily control both the Senate and the people.

Cæsar was unanimously elected consul, and with him was chosen Calpurnius Bibulus. The latter was to all purposes, and easily, shelved as a nonentity. Cæsar's first year was passed in law-making. He was able, by Pompey's aid, to procure the passage of a law by which he received for five years control of Illyria and Cisalpine Gaul, with four legions. This was his first great step upward. The governorship would enable him to win renown and to create an army devoted to his own person, a stepping-stone to almost any greatness. Among his other measures he caused Ariovistus, king of the Suevi, one of his later great antagonists, to be declared a friend and ally of Rome.

Before leaving for Gaul he married his daughter Julia to Pompey, as a bond during his absence, and himself — his wife Julia having died some years before — married Calpurnia, daughter of Piso, the ex-consul. Cicero and Cato, Cæsar's rich and powerful opponents, it was agreed should be exiled. The foundation was well laid for permanence.

Cæsar had reached the goal of his political ambition by years of persistent effort and by means of every kind, not always such as were most to his credit. But now began a new life. He was forty-two years old, and politics ceded to arms. We shall hereafter view him in a new and far more worthy rôle, — a rôle which has made one of the great chapters in the history of the art of war.

Gallic Battle-Axe.

IV.

CÆSAR'S NEW PROVINCE. THE HELVETII.
60–58 B. C.

THE Gauls had always been the most dreaded foes of Rome. Whoever put an end to the danger would be the national hero. This fact Cæsar recognized. The Gauls were a fine, hearty people. They had many fortified towns, but the population lived mostly in open villages. There was good agricultural development, much pastoral and some mining industry. The men were warlike and brave, but fickle in temper. Their cavalry was excellent; the foot unreliable, though gallant. The common people were downtrodden by the knights and Druids; the powerful princes and cantons had the weaker population and tribes as clients, exacting service and affording protection. Just before Cæsar's arrival the Helvetii had prepared a descent from their Alpine home to the lowlands. Cæsar saw that this migration would complicate his problem, and refused them the passage they requested across the Roman Province, fortifying the Rhone below Geneva against them. The Helvetii made their way down the north bank of the Rhone. The Gallic tribes, some of whom were under Roman protection, appealed to Cæsar for help. The Helvetii were three hundred and sixty-eight thousand strong, and had begun to ravage the Gallic lands as they marched towards the Saône.

MANY months before Cæsar left for Gaul, reports reached Rome that the Gallic allies on the Arar (Saône) had been defeated by the Germans, and that the Helvetii were in arms. The news created great consternation. All feared a fresh invasion of barbarians such as had been barely averted by Marius. A general levy was ordered. Cæsar had asked as his province only for Cisalpine Gaul and Illyria. Under the pressure of danger the Senate added Transalpine Gaul to his charge.

The Gauls had a memorable record in Roman annals, but the greater part of their warlike feats lie buried in obscurity.

We know that late in the seventh century B. C., an expedition of Celtic Gauls moved through southern Germany to Illyria, while another crossed the Alps and seized on the valley of the Po. It was the descendants of these latter Gauls who burned Rome. In the fourth century, other tribes moved down the Danube to Thrace and ravaged northern Greece. Some of them pursued their way to Byzantium and passed into Asia, where they overran and held a large territory — Gallo-Grecia or Galatia. Rome was constantly fighting the Gauls during the third and fourth centuries, but her knowledge of them was confined to such as lived south of the Alps or in Mediterranean Gaul. She had spilled much blood and spent much treasure to bring the Padane Gauls to terms, but these tribes were no sooner subdued than they again rose when Hannibal crossed the Alps. They were not finally reduced for a generation after the Second Punic war.

The foothold of the Romans in Gaul had been acquired in the usual way, by taking the old Greek colony of Massilia under its protection and subduing the neighboring tribes for its benefit, about the middle of the second century B. C. Next Aquæ Sextiæ was settled as an outpost to Massilia. Between the Rhone and the mountains lay the Vocontii as far as the Isère; from this river to the Rhone lay the Allobroges with Vienna as their capital; from the Rhone to the Saône and Jura mountains the Sequani, with Vesontio; between the Saône and Loire the Ædui, with Bibracte; on both sides of the Allier the Arverni. The Ædui and Arverni had long disputed for the hegemony of Gaul; the Allobroges favored the latter. Rome stepped in and helped the Ædui. In 121 B. C., Domitius Ahenobarbus and Fabius Maximus put down the Allobroges in two great battles. Thus was founded the Roman Province in Gaul. To it was later added Narbo. The irruption of the Teutones and Cimbri about the date of the birth of Cæsar threatened to destroy the structure so carefully reared. The barbarians successively beat five Roman armies. But the victory of Marius at Aquæ Sextiæ forestalled the danger and reëstablished the Roman influence.

The boundaries of the Province had been established from Tolosa and Narbo, south and east of the Cebenna mountains, up to Vienna, thence along the Rhone to the Alps, and thence southerly to the ocean. They were such when Cæsar took it in charge.

There was constant friction among the Gallic tribes in and adjoining the Province, and many of their representatives visited Rome. Among these were Ariovistus the German and Divitiacus the Gaul. From these men, both able and well-informed, Cæsar learned much about the conditions governing the land as well as its geography and topography. It was, except in the remote regions, by no means *terra incognita* which Cæsar was to take in charge. He found a good base for his operations in the Province when Gaul was assigned to him as his share of the triumvirate spoils.

Gaul was in a turbulent state. War had never ceased within its borders. There were ceaseless insurrections; and a Roman army passing through southern Gaul to Spain was sure to have to fight its way. Despite the constant turmoil, the Province was, however, a favorite resort. Its endless wealth of trade with the interior, already begun by the early Greek settlers, was attractive, and its climate was balmy and agreeable. The land still bore traces of Hellenism, but it had gained the practical Roman imprint. Much money was made in trade. Still a residence in the Province had its drawbacks, and was always subject to danger.

"Until the time of Cæsar," says Cicero, "our generals were satisfied with repelling the Gauls, thinking more of putting a period to their aggressions than of carrying war among them. Marius himself did not penetrate to their towns and homes, but confined himself to opposing a barrier to these torrents of peoples which were overflowing Italy. . . . Cæsar alone determined to subject Gaul to our dominion." The Romans looked to conquer other peoples, but only to protect themselves from the Gauls. To resist a Gallic invasion there was always a levy *en masse*, and there was a special treasure in the Capitol to furnish means for only this occasion.

This never-ending terror of the Gauls — equaled only by that of Hannibal, which lasted but eighteen years — explains why the Roman people, after the conquest of these enemies, felt so beholden to Cæsar. The meed due all other conquerors was small compared to his. Other victories had meant aggrandizement; that over the Gauls meant safety. It was a knowledge of all this, of the reputation and power he could thus win, which inspired Cæsar in his task.

Cisalpine Gaul we already know from the campaigns of Hannibal. Transalpine Gaul was bounded by the Rhine, the Alps, the Mediterranean, the Pyrenees and the ocean. It comprised France, the Low Countries, the Rhenish provinces and Switzerland. This huge country had an irregular mountain-backbone running through its centre from north to south, — a watershed on the east of which the streams flowed into the Rhone and the Rhine, and on the west into the Garonne, the Loire and the Seine, or into their affluents. All these rivers flowed in basins well-defined, and furnished excellent means of communication throughout the country. A glance at the course of the rivers shows how excellent the lines of advance or retreat of an army might be. The central mountain chain was readily crossed in many places.

In climate there were the same distinctions in Gaul as to-day. The Province was mild; the north, still covered by dense forests, was colder than to-day. The forest of Arduenna (Ardennes) extended over an area of two hundred miles wide, from the Rhine to the Scheldt and the frontier of the Remi. The country had a wooded character, and deep forests covered territory which to-day is under close cultivation. It is difficult to gauge the population; but to take a reasonable percentage of arms-bearing men, the troops raised on various occasions would argue something over seven million souls. Gaul was divided into numerous tribes, which Tacitus states as sixty-four, but which others place at three or four hundred. This latter number may be accurate, if it be held to comprise the many client-tribes, or small tribes relying upon some powerful neighbor for protection, and bound to send its contingent to its patron's wars. This sort of feudalism existed throughout the country. Powerful individuals had large forces of clients; powerful cantons had numbers of client-cantons. In central Gaul the Arverni and the Ædui strove for the hegemony. Such competition for control created a very loose national tie, and made Gaul all the more ripe for conquest.

To the north of the Sequana (Seine) and Matrona (Marne) and west of the Rhine lived the Belgians, to whom Cæsar accords the palm as the bravest of the barbarians. They remembered with pride that they had defended their borders against the Cimbri and Teutones. Being farthest removed from the Province, and least accessible to merchants, these people had nothing to render them effeminate; while a constant war with the Germans across the Rhine, though they claimed kindred with them, tended to make them bold and hardy. In the southwest of Gaul, back of the Garumna (Garonne) lived the Aquitani. Between these and the Belgians, the land was occupied by various tribes of Celts or Gauls. The Province was in every sense a part of Gaul. Its

peoples had the same origin; they had merely felt the influence of the Greek colony at Massilia, as they now did that
of Rome. The Belgæ comprised several notable tribes. The

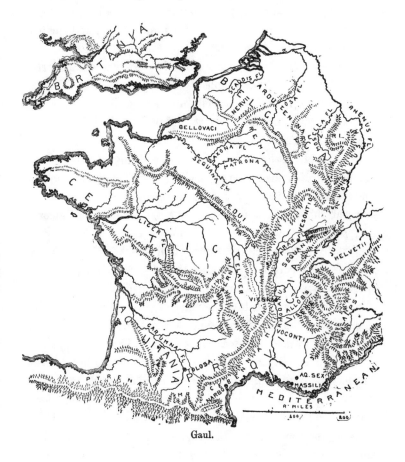

Gaul.

Bellovaci, who abutted on the sea, could put one hundred
thousand men into line. The Nervii placed Cæsar in the
most desperate strait he ever faced. The Treviri and the
Remi were bold and hardy. Central Gaul, or Celtica,
counted the Arverni, the Ædui, the Sequani and the Hel-

vetii as principal nations. The latter stood proudly aloof in their mountain homes; the three former warred much for the supremacy of Gaul. Aquitania, in the era of Cæsar, had less importance to the Romans.

These large cantons were divided into tribes, and further into clans. They had many towns or *oppida* — Cæsar mentions twenty-one — which were mostly well placed and fortified. The bulk of the people lived in open villages. Roads practicable for wheels existed in every section, and there were bridges over many rivers. Navigation on the rivers and sailing vessels at sea were common.

The Gauls were tall in stature, and of light complexion. They dyed their hair; the commoners wore beards, the nobles only a moustache. They were dressed in trowsers and a sleeved shirt, with a mantle among the rich, a skin among the poor. Gold was plentiful among them, and bred the habit of wearing collars, earrings, bracelets and rings. They were fairly expert in agriculture, though some tribes preferred pastoral pursuits, and manufactured linen cloths and felts. Much grain, and cattle and horses, were raised. Their houses were built of wood and wicker-work. Copper was mined and worked. Some tribes wrought in iron and plated it with tin and silver. They ate beef, pork, and other domestic meats, drank milk and brewed ale and mead, in which they frequently over-indulged. Italian wine was highly considered; a jar of it was deemed at times worth a slave. They were pleasant and kindly, but vain and quick-tempered, fickle and restless. Brave in battle, they wilted under defeat. They spoke in precise hyperbole and wrote with Greek letters. The women were strong and beautiful, and often as brave and hardy as the men. The husband had the right of life or death over his wife or child. A free man might not legally be put to the torture; a free woman was not exempt.

In Cæsar's day, as in Hannibal's, the Gauls wielded the long two-edged cutting sword. Some tribes preferred long pikes with wavy blades; all cast darts, and bore both bows and slings. Their metal helmets were ornamented with the horns of animals or with a bird or beast, and were surmounted with a high tuft of feathers. They carried big shields and wore a breast-plate or coat of mail, which they manufactured themselves. The Gallic cavalry was superior to the foot, as it contained the nobles. This arm was their delight. They took pride in their horses and sought noble breeds. Tilting was a frequent sport, and at banquets duels to the death were not unknown.

The Gauls imitated well what they saw of value among others. Their armies were followed by a long array of wagons, and at night they fortified their camps with a circle of them. They challenged to single combat any champion of the enemy before battle, killed their prisoners, and preserved their heads as trophies. Levies *en masse* were common, at which the last arrival forfeited his life. This put every man on the alert. They transmitted news with great rapidity by signals and relays of men, and by peculiar shouts from place to place. The Gauls were superstitious, and part of their religious observances consisted of human sacrifices. The Druids, who originated in Britain, kept them well under control. Their gods approximated to those of all antiquity, there being deities with the attributes of Jupiter, Mars, Apollo and Neptune.

The two classes of distinction were the knights and the Druids. The commonalty was ground between these as between the upper and nether millstone. Each knight or noble had a following of clients, who were devoted to him to the death. The government of each nation lay in a king or an assembly.

Among the Gallic cantons, some one or other was always in the ascendant, and exercised for a time the control of all the land. At the period of Cæsar's receiving Gaul as a province, the Sequani had the upper hand, and had severely oppressed the Ædui, ancient allies of the Romans.

The Helvetii, in modern Switzerland, were then, as history has always shown them to be, a stout-hearted, big-fisted, self-reliant people. They waged a never-ceasing warfare with the Germans, whose tribes constantly invaded their borders or were invaded by them. Orgetorix was a bold, ambitious and wealthy chief of the Helvetii. He had persuaded his people, three years before the beginning of Cæsar's governorship, that their valor would easily conquer for them the more fertile plains of Gaul, and thus enable them to extend their empire beyond the narrow limits of their unproductive hills, all too confined for their numbers, their pride, and their repute in war. Wrought up by the promises of gain and fame which Orgetorix thus held out to them, the Helvetii proceeded to gather together as many beasts of burden and wagons as possible, proposing to move with all their possessions and an abundance of corn, to serve for sowing as well as victual. Orgetorix was appointed to make arrangements with neighboring potentates for passage over their territories. But Orgetorix proved faithless to the trust reposed in him, and instead of serving his fellow-citizens, laid plans for obtaining sovereignty over the Helvetii for himself and his descendants. Being brought to trial, his adherents rose in arms, but Orgetorix died, — it was supposed by suicide, — and this put an end to the matter.

The Helvetian mind, however, excited by the allurements of the fertile plains towards the great sea, still clung to the plan of emigration. In the third year, 60–59 B. C., having made all their preparations, and each one carrying three

months' supply of meal, they fired their twelve towns, four
hundred villages and numberless farms, burned all the corn
which they were unable to carry with them, and in order to
leave no inclination to return, destroyed every vestige of their
homes and habitations. Several neighboring tribes — the
Rauraci, the Tulingi, the Latobriges, and some of the Boii
— cast in their fortunes with the Helvetii.

The Helvetii had to choose between two routes. They
could find an exit from their valleys into Gaul through the
land of the Sequani, across the pass between the Rhone and
the Jura mountains, now the Pas de l'Ecluse, just below

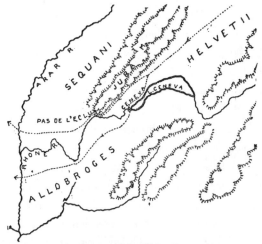

Routes of the Helvetii.

Geneva. This was a rugged road, difficult to march over,
"by which scarcely one wagon at a time could be led," and
which could be easily held and their progress intercepted by
a mere handful of enemies skillfully disposed. Or they could
cross to the south side of the Rhone and pass through the
land of the Allobroges, where the river — the boundary between themselves and this people — was then, it is said, though

it is not now, fordable in many places. The river has somewhat altered its width and course. Genava (Geneva), then
built only on the left bank of the Rhone, was the town of
the Allobroges nearest to the Helvetii, and here was also a
bridge. This latter route was easy. The Helvetii felt confident of their ability to persuade or compel the Allobroges
to allow them to pass, for this people had been recently conquered by the Romans and were bitter accordingly. They
made a rendezvous upon the banks of the Rhone for their
whole people, three hundred and sixty-eight thousand souls,
for the spring equinox of 58 B. C.

All these facts must have come to the ears of Cæsar long
before the time of which we are to write, for the Helvetii had
been openly preparing their expedition for two years, and
one of Cæsar's strong points was his ability to gather news.
Cæsar had not got ready to leave Rome, where political complications and the advocacy of new laws retained him. But
he was carefully watching events. War was what he anticipated. In the division of spoils by the triumvirate, Cæsar
had advisedly chosen Gaul for his consular province. His
purpose was to subdue the country, not only to save Rome
from future incursions, but, equally important to him personally, to create for himself an army, in those troublous times
an essential for the great, the possession of which was to be
his key to abiding success. Cæsar's motives must not be im-
pugned; neither must they be overrated. He was neither a
Gustavus nor a Washington. He worked for Rome; but
Rome was Cæsar. *L'empire, c'est moi!* was his motive if
not his motto.

In March, 58 B. C., the time was rife; events would no
longer wait his leisure. Cæsar hastened from Rome to Geneva, which journey he accomplished, says Plutarch, in eight
days. There was at the time in Transalpine Gaul but a

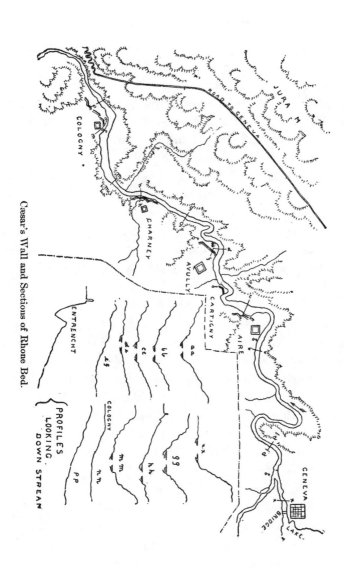

Cæsar's Wall and Sections of Rhone Bed.

single legion, the Tenth. This he at once headed for Geneva, and ordering the Province to raise and equip with utmost
speed as many more men as could be done, he took the only
possible step momentarily to arrest the advance of the barbarians by causing the bridge at that city to be broken down.

So soon as the Helvetii heard of Cæsar's arrival, they sent
an embassy to him composed of their most illustrious men,
requesting the privilege of crossing the Province peacefully,
there being no other available route, and promising good
behavior on the march. But remembering that L. Cassius,
when consul with Marius in 107 B. C., had been defeated and
slain and his army passed under the yoke by the Helvetii, and
far from believing in their pacific intention, Cæsar decided
to decline the request. Moreover, he recognized that it was
impossible for a body of nearly four hundred thousand souls
to pass through the Province without devastating it like a
plague of grasshoppers. And once in Gaul, the Helvetii
would but add one more tribe to conquer, while their territory would almost certainly be speedily filled by the Germans whom the Helvetii now held in check. Still, desiring
to gain time to raise troops and complete his preparations,
Cæsar listened courteously to the ambassadors and declared
his willingness to consider the matter; inviting them to return
two weeks later, on the ides of April, when he would have
his answer ready to give them. It is evident that the Helvetii
believed that Cæsar was sincere. He had conveyed to them
the impression that he would grant their request. The proceeding is a fair sample of Cæsar's political management.
He was a very Talleyrand in statecraft.

Meanwhile, with wonderful expedition and skill, he built
intrenchments at intervals along the left bank of the Rhone
from the lake of Geneva to the Jura range at the Pas de
l'Ecluse. This has been supposed to be continuous fortifica-

tion; but it can scarcely have been such; many critics, however, think that the several redoubts may have been joined by
a simple line of works. A continuous defense was unnecessary. Cæsar had not men enough to man such a line. The
Rhone itself is an enormous ditch with scarp and counterscarp,
which takes the place of intrenchments. Cæsar had the
Tenth legion, say five thousand men, and perhaps an equal
number of new levies, and could have well built in the period
mentioned a wall sixteen feet high and eighteen miles long,
as given in the Commentaries. Colonel Stoffel estimates
that the work assumed to have been actually done could be
performed by three thousand men in three days. Dion Cassius says that Cæsar fortified the most important points, and
much of the course of the Rhone here is so well fortified by
nature that there is no need of art. Cæsar had too much to
do to undertake what was not necessary. The assumption
that *murus fossaque* was a continuous line is untenable.

Only opposite the modern villages of Aire, Cartigny,
Avully, Chaney, Cologny, were fortifications needed, because
at these places the slope of the left bank was gradual. It
was here that Cæsar cut the trenches sixteen feet deep.
With the natural scarp of the river bank the line was complete and continuous. The words cannot be held to mean a
built wall for the entire distance, and the topography clearly
tells the story. The whole line was fortified with well-
manned redoubts at suitable intervals, as at all possible fords
or crossing places, and the fortifications were held with a
strong garrison. Cæsar unquestionably distributed his forces
at the five named points. From there they could easily concentrate on any threatened point in a few hours; and we may
presume that he posted observation parties at the several
places where the Helvetii could best be seen.

It is strange that the Helvetii, who must have clearly perceived what Cæsar was intending to do by thus fortifying the valley against them, should have kept quiet two weeks while waiting for his answer, instead of either attacking his half-finished works, or of moving by the other route. Probably the glib tongue of Cæsar had been employed to such good purpose in his intercourse with them that they gave credit to the words which his acts belied.

When the ambassadors returned on the ides of April to receive their answer, Cæsar, being now well prepared, bluntly informed them that the Roman customs would not allow him to comply with their wishes. He intimated at the same time that he should be compelled to use force if they attempted to pass, and as they could see, was justified in considering himself master of the situation. Some slight efforts were made by the disgusted Helvetii to try the strength of Cæsar's works or to steal a march by night across the fords, but these proved signal failures, and they found that they must turn to the other route, having lost two weeks and been completely outwitted by the Roman.

For this purpose, they endeavored to procure from the Sequani, who occupied substantially the territory covered by the Jura and its foothills, the necessary permission to pass over their land, and, as they could not themselves prevail in this request, they enlisted the services of Dumnorix, the Æduan, who had married the daughter of Orgetorix and who stood in high consideration among the Sequani, to intercede for them. This Dumnorix did, and shortly obtained the desired right. Hostages were given by each party, the Sequani to allow the passage, the Helvetii to refrain from pillaging on the way.

The rumor of this action reaching Cæsar, and hearing, moreover, that the Helvetii were heading for the land of the Santones, on the coast, northwest from the Tolosates, about

modern Toulouse, he determined to prevent this movement
also; for a wandering tribe of warlike barbarians could not
fail to be a danger to the Roman supremacy, and the Tolosates had become Roman clients. What was more, the Helvetii would probably take possession of the best corn-bearing
region of the Province, which he himself might need, and
would keep within no distinct boundaries.

Cæsar estimated correctly that the Helvetii would need
some weeks in completing their preparations for the march;

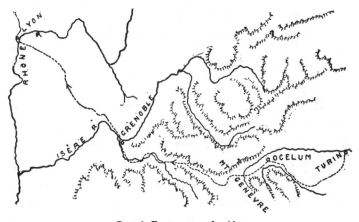

Cæsar's Route across the Alps.

and leaving Titus Labienus, his most trusted legate, in command of his works, he himself hastened to Cisalpine Gaul,
raised two new legions (the Eleventh and Twelfth), called in
three old ones (the Seventh, Eighth and Ninth) which were
wintering at Aquileia, and with these five crossed the Alps
by forced marches into Gaul. His route lay through Ocelum
over Mont Genèvre, and by Grenoble to Lyon, the road
opened by Pompey when he was in command of Spain. He
experienced some difficulty on the road from the opposition
of the mountain tribes, who, despite the reduction of Cisal-

pine Gaul, were still their own masters; but, though they held the commanding points of the passes, he defeated these barbarians in several smart encounters, safely reached the land of the Allobroges with his five legions, and crossed the Rhone near modern Lyon, to the territory of the Segusiani. All this he had accomplished in an incredibly short time. From Ocelum to the land of the Vocontii, about modern Grenoble, he took but seven days, thus making about sixteen miles a day over a rough mountain mule-road. It had taken two months from the refusal of the demand of the Helvetii to raise and place his troops upon the Rhone.

The Helvetii had, indeed, consumed much time in negotiations to secure their passage over the Pas de l'Ecluse, and in their actual march, loaded as they were, still more. But once across this natural obstacle they had made better speed, and, passing through the land of the Sequani, had reached that of the Ædui, which they were ravaging in the most cruel manner in revenge for Cæsar's evident perfidy to them. These people and the Ambarri, their kinsmen, both tribes located north of the Rhone, appealed to Cæsar for help, alleging their ancient friendship for Rome and present distress. The Allobroges also appealed, assuring Cæsar that they had nothing remaining. All were clients of Rome. The Helvetii, to judge by the lay of the land, must have followed the Rhone to modern Culoz and then struck across country to the river Arar, which they reached near modern Trévoux. Their slowness is natural when we consider that some three hundred and sixty-eight thousand men, women and children, followed by a train of ten thousand wagons (for it would take at least so many to carry three months' victual for this number), had to pass through a single defile. Cæsar had relied on this essential slowness to get his troops from Italy. He lost no time in deciding to attack and punish the Helvetii, and told the supplicants that they might rely on his protection. He required from them, however, a number of troops, especially a body of cavalry, of which arm he had none.

It is rather strange that Cæsar, throughout his campaigns in Gaul, relied all but exclusively on native horse; and stran-

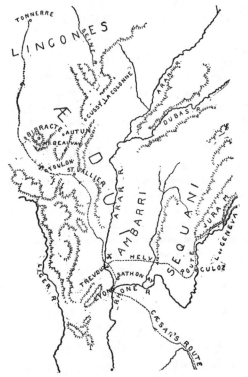

Theatre of Helvetian Campaign.

ger still, that he left the command of this horse to native leaders. His reasons for the last were probably mainly political; but the plan was not always followed by good results, and was constantly attended by danger. The Gallic horse, however, proved for his purposes much better than the Roman. They were an exceptional body of men.

V.

THE BATTLES OF THE ARAR AND BIBRACTE.
JUNE, 58 B. C.

CÆSAR had six legions. He came up with the Helvetii on the Saône above Lyon. Three quarters of the enemy's force had crossed the river. Cæsar by skillful dispositions surprised and destroyed the quarter remaining on the left bank. He then crossed and cautiously followed the rest, who, somewhat abashed, retreated. The Helvetii still had seventy thousand warriors, and were heading down the Loire. At one place Cæsar sought to attack them, but his well-conceived tactical combinations failed to work. Finding that his rations were growing short, Cæsar then ceased from pursuit and moved towards Bibracte, where was much corn. The enemy turned upon him, deeming him to have acted from fear, and offered battle. Cæsar drew up his legions expertly, and awaited their attack. The battle was hotly contested. At one period, having advanced too far, Cæsar was attacked in rear and forced to form two fronts. But Roman discipline finally prevailed; the victory was complete and overwhelming. A bare third of the Helvetians remained. These Cæsar compelled to return to their ancient homes. He had exhibited intelligent decision, coupled to a marked caution, in this first campaign.

AFTER crossing the Rhone, Cæsar had established a camp, not unlikely on the heights of Sathonay, south of where the Helvetii were lying while they effected a passage of the Arar. It was here that Labienus probably joined him, from the Geneva works, which it was now useless to hold. This gave Cæsar six legions, — thirty thousand men; and the Ædui and the Province raised for him some four thousand horse. He was now ready to act with vigor.

Cæsar's reconnoitring parties, of which he had already learned to keep a more than usual number out, soon brought him word that the Helvetii were leisurely crossing the Arar by means of boats and rafts. The Saône flowed then as now so slowly in places that one could scarcely distinguish the direction of its current. At one of these places, north of Trévoux, the Helvetii were ferrying over in boats, for they were not sufficiently clever to bridge the stream. Cæsar at once set out for that vicinity. He dispatched spies to ascertain the enemy's movements, and shortly learned that three quarters of their force — three cantons — had been got over, leaving one canton on the left bank where he himself still was. Here was his opportunity. Breaking up at midnight with the Seventh, Eighth and Ninth legions, he marched between that hour and six A. M. about twelve miles, up the left bank to the place where the enemy was crossing, and sharply pushing in upon the unsuspecting Helvetii, he surprised them, cut a large number to pieces, and dispersed the rest, who fled in terror into the neighboring forests. It was early in June. As a curious fortune would have it, this happened to be the particular canton — the Tigorini, whose home was near modern Zürich — that had defeated and slain Cassius, in which disaster had perished Piso, of the family into which Cæsar had lately married. This defeat crippled the forces of the Helvetii, but left something like two hundred and eighty thousand people still to be dealt with, of whom seventy thousand were warriors; and they had

Camp at Sathonay.

plenty of rations. The locality of the battle is well proven by excavations which have revealed immense numbers of skeletons of men, women and children, some cremated, but all hastily interred, and of broken arms and ornaments.

Cæsar at once bridged the Arar near the battlefield, and crossed. It seems surprising that the Helvetii, under whose very nose this operation took place, should have made no effort to interfere with it, but nothing is said in the Commentaries of an attack. All they did was to observe him closely. Cæsar no doubt had vessels on the river which were transporting rations in his wake, and these aided in the passage. The other three legions soon rejoined him from camp at Sathonay. Astonished to see Cæsar do in one day what they had taken twenty to accomplish, the Helvetii again sent ambassadors to him, to represent that they were desirous of peace and would go and settle wherever Cæsar would allow; but that, if opposed, Cæsar must remember that the Helvetii were brave and numerous and feared no one, as the Romans well knew from experience. Cæsar replied that if they would give him hostages to do as they agreed, he would treat with them; but the ambassadors haughtily answered that they were in the habit of receiving, not giving hostages, and left in high dudgeon.

Still the Helvetii were anxious not to fight. They preferred to carry out their original project, though they must have keenly felt Cæsar's blow in the destruction of a full quarter of their number. They marched away on the succeeding day, intending still to head for the land of the Santones. To do this they could not advance directly west, on account of the intervening mountainous region, which placed two distinct ranges between them and their objective. They headed northwest, so as to strike the lowest part of the watershed between the Saône and Loire, which they could cross and thence move west.

Cæsar was not placed so as readily to bring them to battle, as their column and his own were more or less confined in the narrow space between the Arar and the mountains. A slow, dogged pursuit was his only immediate resource, but he threw out his Gallic cavalry under command of Dumnorix the Æduan, to reconnoitre their movements. A day or two afterwards a body of five hundred Helvetian horse attacked this force, and under unequal conditions inflicted on it a defeat and some considerable loss, though Dumnorix outnumbered them eight to one. Emboldened by this easy success, the Helvetii began to indulge in constant rearguard fighting. Cæsar was cautious. War on so large a scale was still a novelty to him. The teaching of the art in that day did not embrace what we 'now call the grand operations of war. What he knew of them he had assimilated, as no one else had possessed the intelligence to do, from the history of his predecessors, from the splendid deeds of Alexander and Hannibal. But this was theory merely. Cæsar still felt a lack of confidence in his own ability; he knew that his grasp was not yet as large as his problem, and wisely kept without the limits of a general engagement. But he did his best to prevent the Helvetii from plundering and foraging; and thus, at a distance of about five miles, he followed them closely for fifteen days.

Cæsar was being led from the vicinity of the Arar, and the question of supplies was becoming grave. The corn brought up the river to him proved bad, and the crops were not yet ripe. The supply of forage at this season was limited, and was consumed by the immense column of the enemy. The Ædui had agreed to furnish Cæsar with corn, but it was not forthcoming, though he had made a number of demands for it. It seems that the Æduan population, seduced by the representations of Dumnorix, who was, as before stated, serving in Cæsar's army, were neglecting to furnish it, lest Cæsar, having by their help overcome the Helvetii, should in turn deprive them of their liberties. Dumnorix was anxious to see Cæsar thwarted, for the Romans interfered with his own plans of aggrandizement. He had, in fact, played the traitor in the late cavalry conflict with the Helvetii, and had been the cause of the loss of the field by retiring at the first attack. Cæsar suspected that all was not right. He called some of the leading Æduans together, and discovered where the difficulty lay. He was much tempted to make an example of Dumnorix; but, probably from motives of policy, lest the latter's fellow-citizens should feel aggrieved and turn definitely from his alliance, he feigned to forgive him at the intercession of Divitiacus, his brother, who was a great friend of Cæsar's and a faithful ally of the Romans. Cæsar, however, caused Dumnorix to be watched, determined not to allow him to push matters too far.

The Helvetii, at modern St. Vallier, had borne to the west to advance towards the valley of the Liger (Loire), down which they proposed to march, and to cross at Decize. Cæsar's scouts reported that on their march they had encamped at the foot of a hill some seven miles distant (not far from modern Toulon), and he saw at last his opportunity of attacking them to advantage. He reconnoitred the approaches to the hill with care, and sent Labienus after midnight, with two legions and guides, to ascend to the summit by a circuit and get into the Helvetian rear, while he himself, with the other four legions, preceded by cavalry, broke camp long before daylight to approach closer to the enemy's front. The plan, well conceived and ordered, all but succeeded. Labienus actually reached his goal unknown to the Helvetii. The victory of Cæsar, who advanced to within fifteen hundred paces of the enemy, seemed secure. But Considius, an excellent officer and experienced, one of Sulla's old staff, whom Cæsar sent out with the vanguard scouts, in some way lost his head and gave his chief quite erroneous information

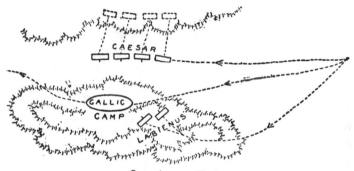

Operation near Toulon.

to the effect that the Helvetii and not the Romans had occupied the summit. He imagined that he had recognized their weapons and standards. This report led Cæsar to believe that Labienus had not reached his post, and he was unwilling to attack without the aid of the ambush. Thus lieutenant and captain failed to work in unison, and the chance of an immediate success was lost. Cæsar withdrew to an adjoining height, where he went into line, to invite an attack by the enemy. Labienus, whose orders on reaching the summit were to wait for Cæsar's attack, refrained from an advance. It was not till the close of the day that Cæsar learned the actual facts. The enemy had meanwhile moved away.

Cæsar was not in the habit of doing his own reconnoitring, even in important cases, if we may judge from a number of such instances as this. He was constant and careful and intelligent in procuring information; but of all the great captains he seems to have relied most upon the eyes of others. In this case, and in others to be narrated, his own observation would have been more fruitful. The Helvetii, having thus escaped from the ambuscade, were much elated that Cæsar had not attacked, — as they deemed from fear; but they had no idea of assaulting Cæsar's strong position.

From passing the Arar, the Helvetii had marched two weeks at the rate of about seven miles a day. It was the end of June. Finding that he was running short of corn, and that the Ædui were still slow in furnishing it, Cæsar decided next day to make a push past the Helvetii for Bibracte (Mt. Beuvray, near Autun).

Bibracte is apt to be located at Autun, but that it was Mt. Beuvray is much more probable. The Gauls were wont to place their towns on hills, like Gergovia or Alesia; or if on a plain, it was surrounded by a stream or marsh, as Avaricum. They would scarcely have located their capital and largest city, Bibracte, at the foot of the mountains where lies Autun. Several ancient roads centre on Mt. Beuvray, and the hilltop is full of the ruins of a town. There is every indication that this was the Bibracte of the Ædui.

From where Cæsar lay the place was about eighteen miles, and here he was sure to find food in plenty. The time for issuing rations, which was usually done every fifteen days, when each man received twenty-five pounds of wheat, was two days hence, and the soldiers were near the end of their supply.

The Helvetii were told of Cæsar's movements by a deserter from the Gallic cavalry, and construed his manœuvre as a retreat. Their assumption that Cæsar was afraid to attack them was strengthened by his thus giving up pursuit, and instead of keeping on towards the Loire valley, they turned back to attack Cæsar and cut him off from retreat. They began to harass the rear of the Romans by more daring though isolated attacks.

Their action accorded well with Cæsar's mood. He deter-

mined to afford them an opportunity for battle. He occupied
the first available eminence which he reached in his march
on Bibracte. The battlefield appears to have been identified
by Colonel Stoffel as near Toulon. Here he drew up his
forces, sending the cavalry forward to arrest the too speedy

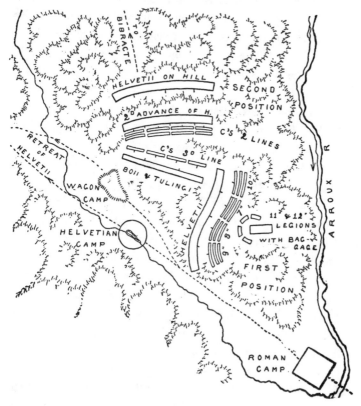

Battle of Bibracte.

approach of the enemy, who had some seventy thousand warriors, while himself had from thirty thousand to thirty-six
thousand legionaries, perhaps twenty thousand auxiliaries
(Appian says Gallic mountaineers), and four thousand horse.

He drew up his four old legions (Seventh, Eighth, Ninth and Tenth), in three lines halfway up the slope, the two legions (Eleventh and Twelfth) recently raised in Cisalpine Gaul and all the auxiliaries on the plateau in the rear, with the baggage parked and intrenched and committed to their care. Here, as on other occasions, Cæsar declined to use his new legions in the fighting lines, but kept them in the background. The baggage referred to is *sarcinæ*, that which the soldiers themselves carried. The legions thus went into action in light order. The location of the train baggage (*impedimenta*) is not given.

These three lines must not be confounded with the old three line formation of the Punic wars, of hastati, principes and triarii. The cohort was now formed in one line, as has been already explained. The two or three lines which Cæsar used were separate and distinct, each legion being drawn up in three lines of cohorts. The Helvetii parked their wagons in an irregular circle on some low ground opposite Cæsar's position, and having repulsed the Roman allied cavalry, drew up in phalangial order, — a formation in which all barbarians are wont to fight pitched battles, — and advanced on the Roman army with closed ranks. They joined their shields together in testudinal fashion, in front, on the flanks and aloft, so as to ward off the first shower of pila, and came on with an impetus which promised hot work.

Cæsar had prepared his men by the usual allocutio, or battle-speech, and in order once for all to encourage his men to feel that he proposed to share their danger, whatever it might be, he dismounted from his own horse and obliged the other mounted officers to do the like. He may have been distrustful of the stanchness of some of his new officers. He did not yet know them. This act with the legionaries meant: "I will stay here and fight with you, for I have given up my means of flight." It was an act the direct reverse of officers dismounting in action, as is sometimes done in these modern days of musketry. The Roman first line, awaiting the Helvetian onset and hurling their javelins from the height on which they stood, succeeded after a while in breaking gaps in the Helvetian phalanx, and immediately charged down upon the barbarians with the sword. A most obstinate combat ensued. Many of the Helvetian shields had been pierced by the Roman pila, whose iron points being turned, the spear could not readily be plucked out, thus making the shields so cumbersome that the barbarians threw them away. The pilum of this era was a little short of two metres, half of which consisted of a long flexible blade with a barbed point, or some equivalent. They could be hurled from sixty to eighty feet; and when cast at a testudo, would often pin two shields together and render them useless. Despite this initial check the barbarians exposed their persons recklessly, as the hardy mountaineers of Helvetia have always done. But robbed of their bucklers, the Romans were enabled to do the greater execution, and after long-sustained effort forced the enemy slowly but surely from the field. In no wise broken or demoralized, the Helvetii retired in good order to an eminence three quarters of a mile away. Here they halted and once again made a stand.

The two new legions and auxiliaries still remained with the wagons. As the old legionaries followed up the retiring foe, they advanced beyond where the Helvetian rearguard, consisting of some fifteen thousand allied Boii and Tulingi, had filed into position which enabled them to protect the Gallic wagon-park. These troops, now on the Roman rear, charged down upon the legions with the utmost fury, perceiving which diversion the Helvetian main line again advanced, giving vent to exultant shouts, and resumed the battle with yet greater vigor. Cæsar states that they fell upon his exposed flank. This does not appear from the topography, and the phrase "exposed flank" may perhaps be the equivalent of the phrase "masked batteries" of 1861. It will be remembered that the right side with the ancients was always weak, as the shield was carried on the left arm, and the right flank of a body of troops was shieldless. It is constantly referred to as *latus apertum*, and the legions were always nervous about this flank. A convenient way of explaining a defeat or suggesting a tactical danger would be to speak of an attack on the exposed flank. Cæsar thus refers to the triarii long after their disappearance from the legions.

Cæsar was thus compelled to form two fronts to receive this double attack. He faced the standards of the third line to the rear to meet the Boii and Tulingi, holding back the new onslaught of the Helvetii with his first two. The danger was grave, but there was still a reserve of two legions, and Cæsar pushed the fighting home. For a long while the combat wavered; the Helvetii would not give up the contest, however unequal, but after a long and obstinate combat the legions drove the enemy back to the hill they had first retired to, and forced the rearguard party of allies to the wagons. The Helvetii had fought like heroes. During the entire action, from noon to eventide, not a man had shown his back. Bitter fighting was now resumed for the possession of the wagon-park and continued till late at night. The enemy threw their weapons from the wagons and intrenched themselves between the wheels, whence they used their long pikes. The women and children took part in the battle. It was only after supreme efforts that the wagon-park was finally captured. The victory was complete. The Helvetii fled after sustaining losses which reduced their number to one hundred and thirty thousand souls. Cæsar did not pursue. His cavalry could not effect much in this hilly country, says Napoleon. But the indisposition to pursue came of the caution of inexperience rather than because Cæsar judged it to be useless.

Cæsar's dispositions for the battle and the vigor of the fighting had been in the highest degree commendable, but he may perhaps be criticised for advancing so far from his reserves as to be liable to be taken in flank and rear. Less than the two legions and the auxiliaries could have guarded the intrenched baggage-park, and the presence of one of them in a supplemental line as at Pharsalus would have rendered victory more speedy and less costly. The loss of the Helvetii was very heavy; but a large part of the entire people escaped from the massacre. These, marching four days and nights without a halt, reached the territory of the Lingones (near Tonnerre), where they hoped to find corn as well as safety. This tribe, however, under Cæsar's declaration sent by couriers that he would treat them in the same manner as the Helvetii if they harbored or traded with these enemies of the Roman people, refused to have any communication with the footsore and famished barbarians. The Helvetii, in the severest distress, at once sent messengers soliciting peace.

Cæsar had remained three days at Bibracte, or near the battlefield, to bury the dead and care for the severely wounded. His loss is not given, but it must have been very large. On the fourth day he followed up the Helvetii, and, having gone into camp near by, he received their embassy, which we can imagine couched in less arrogant language than the last. To the Helvetian petition he assented upon their delivering up hostages, their arms, and a number of slaves who had deserted to them from the Roman camp. Having complied with Cæsar's demands, they were treated with liberality, and furnished with food; but they were obliged to march back to their own country and to rebuild their towns and villages, and until they were able to accomplish this, the Allobroges were instructed to supply them with corn. Cæsar "drove this people back into their country as it were a shepherd driving his flock back into the fold," says Florus. A party of six thousand of the Helvetii (Verbigeni) attempted to escape towards Germany; but they were at Cæsar's order stopped on the way by the tribes through whose territory they tried to pass, brought back and "treated like enemies," which no doubt means that they were sold as slaves or massacred, — one of those cases of unnecessary cruelty which blot the pages of Cæsar's glorious campaigns.

The location of the battle has by some been placed at Cussy la Colonne, but that place does not suit the topography of the Commentaries. Napoleon III. places it nearer Bibracte, but Stoffel's researches are the latest and most reliable.

Lists were found in the Helvetian camp, written in the Greek character, showing that three hundred and sixty-eight thousand in all, men, women and children, Helvetii and allies, had left their homes, to wit: Helvetii, two hundred and sixty-three thousand; Tulingi, thirty-six thousand, Latobrigi, fourteen thousand; Rauraci, twenty-three thousand; Boii, thirty-two thousand. Of these, ninety-two thousand were fighting men. There returned home, according to Cæsar's census, but one hundred and ten thousand; the rest had perished in the migration, the battles or the massacres, or had dispersed. Of the latter it is probable that very many eventually returned to Helvetia. The gallant Boii were allowed to settle among the Ædui, who desired to receive them.

This first campaign of Cæsar's in command of a large army is characterized by great dash and ability coupled to a certain caution apparently bred of self-distrust. He was greatly aided by the want of unity and prompt action among the

Helvetii, who, had they been more alive to their advantages, might have greatly hampered Cæsar's movements. For a first campaign the conduct and results were certainly brilliant.

Cæsar intrenched his camp near Tonnerre, and here he remained until midsummer.

Cæsar, the Citizen.
(Vatican Museum.)

VI.

CAMPAIGN AGAINST ARIOVISTUS. AUGUST AND SEPTEMBER, 58 B. C.

THE Ædui, Sequani and Arverni now invoked Cæsar's aid against the German Ariovistus, who had crossed the Rhine and taken land and hostages from them. Cæsar saw the danger of permitting German invasions. He sent word to Ariovistus that he must restore the hostages and return across the Rhine. The German retorted, haughtily and with truth, that he was doing no more than Cæsar was and with equal right. Cæsar determined to march against him, and moved to Vesontio. Here arose a dissension among the legions, having its origin in a dread of the Germans and of the unknown lands they were about to invade. Cæsar suppressed it by his persuasiveness, and the army marched against Ariovistus. A conference with him led to no results. The German then cleverly marched around Cæsar's flank and cut him from his base — a remarkable manœuvre for a barbarian; but by an equally skillful march Cæsar recovered his communications. Then, learning that Ariovistus was, under advice of his soothsayers, waiting for the new moon before coming to an engagement, he forced battle upon him and signally defeated him. In the two campaigns of this first year, Cæsar had shown much caution, bred probably of inexperience, but he had also shown boldness and skill in abundant measure. The numbers against him had not greatly exceeded his own; and he had not been called on to show the decision of Alexander in Thrace or Hannibal in Iberia.

AFTER the brilliant Helvetian campaign, the Gauls with Cæsar's consent convoked a general assembly of tribes, and the whole of the country sent ambassadors to sue for the victor's good-will. They saw that they now had a Roman consul of a different stamp in their midst. Among the suppliants came embassies from the Ædui, Sequani and Arverni led by the Æduan Divitiacus, who particularly begged Cæsar's assistance against Ariovistus, a king of the Germans (the people dwelling beyond the Rhine), "a savage, passionate and reckless man." This chief, it seemed, having been called in to aid the Sequani and Arverni against their domestic enemies, the Ædui, had as a reward for this help forcibly taken one third of all their land, and was now driving them from another third to accommodate fresh arrivals of his own subjects, of whom one hundred and twenty thousand had already come across the Rhine to settle on the more fertile Gallic lands. Nor was this their only grievance, for Ariovistus had taken all the children of their nobles as hostages, and had treated these tribes with consummate cruelty. Particularly the Ædui had been oppressed and compelled to swear that they would not even complain of their torments, or invite aid from Rome, or ask back their hostages.

The Suevi were the largest of the German nations and the most powerful. They were divided into one hundred cantons, each of which furnished yearly one thousand men for war, and one thousand for tillage, and these alternated, the tillers being bound to maintain the warriors. They were big-framed and hardy in the extreme, strong and savage, and disdained all other peoples. Their land was said to be surrounded by desert wastes, they having devastated the lands of all their neighbors. Two immense forests, the Hercynian and that called Bacenis, began at the Rhine and ran eastward. The former covered the territory between the Danube and the Main, the other was substantially the Thüringerwald of to-day. South of this latter dwelt the Suevi.

Cæsar was of course alive to the danger of allowing tribes of Germans to migrate at will in large bodies across the Rhine, for, emboldened by success, they might soon spread over Gaul, reach the Province, and from thence move to Italy, like the Cimbri and Teutones. The Rhone alone separated the Province from the Sequani, on whose land they were already trenching. Moreover, the Ædui had long been "kinsmen" of Rome and deserved protection. Cæsar had proposed to himself to conquer Gaul. A less conception of his problem is unlikely. As a preliminary, the ejection of the Germans from the land was essential. His method of thought stopped at no halfway measures. He had not come into Gaul merely to protect Roman territory or interests in

The Rhine and the Germans.

the old way. He came for conquest, which as a soldier he saw was the only true way to cut the knot of the Gallic difficulty, and which as a statesman he saw might be a stepping-stone to future greatness. Cæsar was equipped in authority, men and purpose for war, and it was war he desired. The sooner it came, the sooner he would be able to subdue Gaul. One reason was as good as another to serve as a *casus belli*. To examine such questions as these is scarcely within our present purpose. Let us keep as closely as may be to the current of military events.

Cæsar sent messengers to Ariovistus, who was probably on the Rhine somewhere about modern Strasburg, collecting an army among the Tribocci, proposing an interview. Ariovistus returned word that when he desired to see Cæsar, he would come to him; if Cæsar wished to see Ariovistus, he might himself come; that he saw no reason why Cæsar had any business in that part of Gaul which he, Ariovistus, had conquered, as he should not venture into those parts which Cæsar held. This was bold language, but it has the ring of honest bravery in it. Cæsar, who looked at the reply from the stand-point of true Roman arrogance, answered that he was sur-prised that Ariovistus, a man who had been styled "king and friend" by the Roman Senate, should refuse his proposal for a conference; he required this chief to bring no more men from across the Rhine into Gaul, nor seize upon land; at once to cause to be restored the hostages of the Ædui, and to cease from war in Gaul. Should he do so, Cæsar and the Senate and people of Rome would still regard him as a friend; if not, Cæsar, under his instructions to protect the Ædui and other allies of the Roman Republic, would take the case in hand without delay. To this ultimatum, Ariovistus made answer, that he had conquered the Ædui in battle, and had rightfully made them pay tribute in exactly the same fashion as the Romans did by those whom they had subdued; that he should not restore the Æduan hostages; that if the Ædui did not pay tribute, he would compel them to do so, and that their title of "kinsmen" of Rome would avail them naught. He ended his message with a challenge, averring that none had ever entered the lists against him but to be exterminated. Cæsar had certainly met his match in aggressiveness.

It is not quite clear how broad was the authority Cæsar possessed by law. The governors of Roman provinces were usually prohibited from leaving their limits without the express permission of the Senate. But the governor of Gaul had been given, or had assumed, a wider authority, and was expected to protect the allies of the Roman people. As a matter of fact, there was no control whatever over Cæsar, except that exerted by his colleagues in the triumvirate. And this related only to affairs in Rome.

Learning at the same time that the Germans were ravaging the Æduan lands, and that other large bands of Suevi were on the right bank of the Rhine opposite the Treviran district, making preparations to cross the river, Cæsar determined to strike Ariovistus before any reinforcements could come over to his assistance. Accordingly, after rationing his men and accumulating a supply of corn, he set out early in August from the neighborhood of Tonnerre, and by forced marches moved towards the upper Arar, where lay Ariovistus. There

March against Ariovistus.

was subsequently a Roman road which led from Tonnerre to Langres, so that we may fairly assume that there was a previous Gallic path or road, and it was this Cæsar took. Being informed on the way, perhaps near modern Langres, that Ariovistus was on the march to seize Vesontio (Besançon) on the Dubas (Doubs), capital city of the Sequani, a dépôt containing large supplies and an admirable position for strength, of very considerable importance to whomsoever held it, and fearing that Ariovistus might be nearer to the place than he actually was, Cæsar turned from his straight road to the Rhine, which ran by way of Vesoul and Belfort, and forcing his marching day and night, made such speed

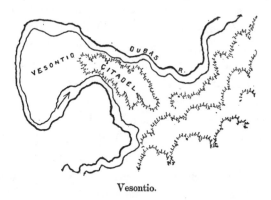

Vesontio.

that he reached Vesontio and threw a garrison into it before Ariovistus could arrive. The Commentaries describe Vesontio so clearly that there can be no mistake in its location. "It was so well fortified by nature that it offered every facility for sustaining war. The Dubas, forming a circle, surrounds it almost entirely, and the space of sixteen hundred feet which is not bathed by the water is occupied by a high mountain, the base of which reaches on each side to the edge of the river." No military narrative exceeds the Commentaries in lucidity; few equal it in its keen descriptions and clear-cut style.

It is evident that Cæsar was active in the pursuit of information, though the Romans as a rule were lax in this particular. Like Alexander and Hannibal — like all great commanders — he had antennæ out in front of the army

which felt its way.   He was at all times abundantly supplied
with knowledge about the countries and peoples he was to
invade and contend with.   This he procured by spies, deserters and reconnoissances, the latter conducted mostly by
native cavalry.   The Roman horse could by no means vie
with the Gallic in doing such work, and Cæsar had a way of
insuring the almost uniform fidelity of the latter.

Ariovistus, learning that Cæsar was moving towards him,
arrested his advance on Vesontio, deeming it wiser to remain
near the reinforcements which he could draw from across the
Rhine.   Moreover, the proximity of the Rhine, near modern
upper Alsace, afforded a *terrain* which was better suited to
the operations of his cavalry.

At Vesontio Cæsar remained some days.   A grave danger
here beset him, — one which well shows how deep was the
decay of the *morale* of the Roman army.   There were in the
army a number of tribunes and præfects, one might call them
volunteer line officers, men who had accompanied Cæsar for
friendship or excitement or profit, having been given their
commissions for political or personal motives, but who were
inexperienced soldiers and lacking in that stanchness which
few men in an army possess unless they have taken up arms
as a business.   Many of these holiday-soldiers, frightened by
the tales they heard of the stature and fierceness of the Germans and of the dangerous route before them, — which tales
were well borne out by the daring courage of the Helvetii,
who themselves feared these Teutons, — besought Cæsar to
allow them to return to Italy, each one alleging some peculiar
personal pretext.   Even those who were willing to remain
strike one as little enough like what we are apt to dub
Romans.   "These could neither compose their countenance
nor even sometimes check their tears; but hidden in their
tents, either bewailed their fate, or deplored with their com-

rades the general danger. Wills were sealed universally throughout the whole camp. By the expressions and cowardice of these men, even those who possessed great experience in the camp, both soldiers and centurions, and those (the decurions) who were in command of the cavalry, were gradually disconcerted. Such of them as wished to be considered less alarmed, said that they did not dread the enemy, but feared the narrowness of the roads and the vastness of the forests which lay between them and Ariovistus, or else that the supplies could not be brought up readily enough. Some even declared to Cæsar that when he gave orders for the camp to be moved and the troops to advance, the soldiers would not be obedient to the command, nor advance in consequence of their fear." This disaffection was spreading to the ranks and threatening the most serious results. Cæsar grasped the grave nature of the matter, and his strong will at once rose to the occasion. He called a council of war to which all the centurions were invited, and with his customary skill and reasonableness, but without weakening his powers as commander to compel, he presented to them the matter of roads, rations, the skill and courage of the enemy and their own, alleging in conclusion that he should march on the enemy immediately, and if the other legions would not follow, he would march himself, with his favorite Tenth legion, alone. But he did not believe, said he, that the rest were afraid to go, having Marius as an example, who, with their ancestors, had defeated these same Germans. His self-reliant persuasiveness — and we know from abundant sources how persuasive Cæsar could be — at once changed the tide of feeling. Dismay gave place to cheerfulness, good heart resumed its sway. The legions expressed their devotion and obedience, the Tenth particularly and instantly, and loudly proclaimed their willingness to follow Cæsar to the end of the world, alleging that they had never thought of usurping the right of the chief to decide on the movements of the army.

This and other similar facts not only show that Roman human nature was pretty much the same as human nature has been all over the world and in all ages, but they show that the most essential quality of an army is discipline. These troops, not yet hardened to service, were acting as militia or unseasoned volunteers will sometimes act. It is probable that Cæsar, himself yet inexperienced in the duties of commanding officer, had not kept his troops sufficiently occupied with drill and camp-duties to prevent their wasting their idle time in foolish gossip. How much the disaffection is overdrawn in the Commentaries, to show Cæsar's eloquence and moral power, cannot be said, but the bald facts must be as stated. Cæsar's management was wise in not having recourse to rigorous measures.

From Vesontio towards the Rhine, if he would go the straight road, Cæsar must cross the northern part of the Jura foothills. That part of the route which lay along the valley of the Dubas was extremely rough, in parts a continuous defile, and much more wooded and difficult then than now. But Divitiacus pointed out to him that by a northerly circuit, of which the Dubas would be the chord, he could move in a comparatively open country and reach the undulating plains of the Rhine valley without danger of ambush. Divitiacus, always intelligent and useful, had been reconnoitring the region in front of the army, and found that the circuit would not exceed fifty miles. Proceeding, towards the end of the third week in August, along this route in the direction of the enemy, in seven days Cæsar reached the vicinity of Ariovistus, who was reported some twenty-four miles off. Unless Cæsar's marches were far below the usual rate, and he would not loiter under the circumstances, he must in seven days have marched at least eighty-five or ninety miles. This would carry him beyond Belfort, usually chosen as the scene of the battle against Ariovistus, to near Cernay. This is Göler's opinion. Rüstow is in error in selecting the upper Saar as the theatre of the approaching campaign.

Not anticipating Cæsar's speedy coming, Ariovistus himself requested a conference, in a way which made Cæsar believe that the German had grown more reasonable, and it was agreed that the two generals should meet on a naked eminence in a large plain between both camps, with an escort only of horse. No large plain exists near Belfort, another reason for placing the scene farther to the east. Cæsar, scarcely trusting his Gallic cavalry under such exceptional circumstances, had "taken away all their horses," and had mounted his trusted Tenth legionaries, so that they might accompany him. They seemed to be ready and expert horsemen. Reaching the place of conference, they were drawn up in line two hundred paces from the mound, the cavalry of Ariovistus taking a similar station on the other side. Each commander was accompanied to the meeting by ten mounted men.

So far from the conference accomplishing any good end, Ariovistus, according to what Cæsar wishes us to infer from the Commentaries, behaved in a most haughty and provoking manner. But even the Commentaries show Ariovistus to have talked in a reasonable way. He claimed only the same right to conquer a province in Gaul that the Romans had exerted, and to collect tribute in the same way; he denied his intention of invading Gaul further, and agreed to a "hands-off" policy, if Cæsar would accept it. But the Commentaries allege that Ariovistus' cavalry showed the bad faith of the transaction by commencing an attack on Cæsar's escort, "hurling stones and weapons at them." Cæsar, forbidding his men to retaliate, lest the blame should be cast upon him, withdrew from the conference. The eagerness of the legions to engage was greatly increased by Ariovistus' treachery. Two days after, Ariovistus again requested a meeting or an embassy, and on Cæsar's sending to him two of his officers, he seized these and cast them into chains, though one was a Gaul and the other bound to him by the sacred ties of hospitality.

At the same time Ariovistus moved to within six miles of

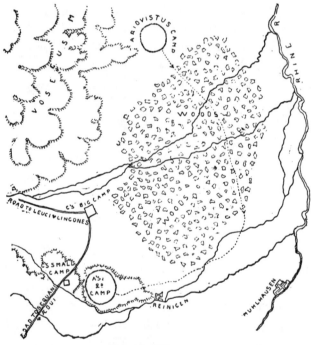

Ariovistus' Manœuvre.

the Romans, and encamped at the foot of the Vosegus (Vosges) mountains; and next day, by a bold and skillful manœuvre, he marched around Cæsar's flank and within his immediate reach, and camped two miles off, west of modern Reinigen, in a position which actually cut the Romans off from their base and the convoys of corn furnished by the Sequani and Ædui. But it fortunately left open the communications with the Leuci and Lingones farther north, on whom in part Cæsar depended, though theirs was a scant province from which to draw his supplies for so large a force.

From the slight description of this manœuvre of Ariovistus in the Commentaries, it would at first blush seem that Cæsar had lost an excellent opportunity of striking his enemy on the flank while thus marching near to and around the Roman camp, and this criticism has been frequently made. During such a manœuvre, any column, especially with baggage, is wont to be more or less out of order, and there can be no better time to attack. The march of Ariovistus was, in this case, protected by the forest, of which a portion still remains at the present time; and Cæsar had not yet learned that power of summary action for which he later grew so noted, and did not attempt to interfere with the march of the enemy. In fact, it is probable that Cæsar did not at the moment know of the manœuvre. Nor was it usual with the ancients to take advantage for attack of a flank march by the enemy.

Cæsar, however, did the next best thing. For five successive days he emerged from his camp and drew up in battle array, inviting action; but Ariovistus, satisfied with his position, the effect of which he perfectly comprehended, kept to his camp, merely throwing out his cavalry, which was six thousand strong, to skirmish with the Roman allied horse. The German horseman at this period was accompanied by a foot soldier, who was practised to run alongside, holding to the horse's mane, and to fight in connection with the cavalry. By these peculiar tactics the Germans puzzled the Gallic squadrons, though it was really nothing new, but an ancient device to be found among many peoples.

Cæsar was unable to provoke Ariovistus to battle. The real reason for this was that the female soothsayers of the Germans had decided by divination that their army could not conquer if it fought before the new moon. This Cæsar did not at the moment know. Fearing to be definitely cut off from his base, which Ariovistus might attempt to accomplish by a further advance, he himself resorted to a similar manœuvre. He was not above taking a lesson from this skillful barbarian. Forming his army in three lines, he marched out as if ready to give battle, and moving by the right, placed his line on the west of the German camp in such a manner as to regain the road along which lay his communications. Halting at a distance of not more than two thirds of a mile from Ariovistus' camp and two miles and a half from his own, Cæsar held the first two lines in readiness to resist the enemy's attack if made, and set the third to intrench a new camp and, as usual, surround it with a rampart. Ariovistus sent some sixteen thousand light troops and all his cavalry to interfere with the Romans in this operation, but this body was driven off. In the new camp, when completed, Cæsar left two legions and some auxiliaries. With the other four legions he marched back and reoccupied the old camp. Though divided, Cæsar was now in better position. He had reëstablished himself upon his own communications, and had placed Ariovistus where he could not undertake the offensive to advantage. In attacking either Roman camp, the troops from the other would.be able to fall upon his flank.

Next day Cæsar marshaled his forces from both camps for battle, taking up a position in advance of the larger one, but as Ariovistus did not accept the gage, the Romans retired to their intrenchments about noon. Then Ariovistus sent part of his forces to attack the lesser camp, and a vigorous combat with some loss ensued, which lasted till night, when Ariovistus retired. From some prisoners captured on this occasion Cæsar finally ascertained why it was Ariovistus was unwilling to fight: "that it was not the will of heaven that the Germans should conquer if they engaged in battle before the new moon," and deemed it wiser to force a general engagement at once, so as to let the moral effect of fighting against fate do its demoralizing work among the German troops.

On the following day, probably September 10, Cæsar secretly drew the two legions from the small camp and joined them to the four of the larger camp. He drew up all his auxiliaries before the lesser camp to impose on the enemy by the number of their array, and to simulate the continued presence of the two legions. This must have been cleverly done to have escaped detection. With all his legionaries, in three lines, Cæsar advanced on Ariovistus' camp. A sufficient force had been left in each of the camps to defend the ramparts. At last Ariovistus saw from Cæsar's pronounced action that it was imperative to fight. He had no intrenched camp, and could probably not resist a determined assault should Cæsar make one. He accordingly drew up his forces by tribes with an interval between each two, — Harudes, Marcomanni, Tribocci, Vangiones, Nemetes, Sedusii, Suevi, — and surrounded the whole rear and flanks with his wagons so "that no hope might be left in flight." The women remained in the wagon-train as witnesses of the battle, and conjured with frantic cries and gestures their husbands, fathers and sons to fight so as not to deliver them to the sword or to slavery, as had been the fate of the women of the Cimbri and Teutones at Aix.

It is probable that Ariovistus much exceeded Cæsar in force, but by how much it is impossible to say. Cæsar's total, after his losses at Bibracte, cannot have been much more than fifty thousand men, allowing a full complement to each legion.

The Romans faced east, Ariovistus west. Cæsar placed his quæstor in command of one of the legions and a legate over each of the others, with instructions to force the fighting. He himself opened the action with the Roman right wing as was his wont, and "because he had observed that part of the enemy (opposite to him) to be the least strong." The Germans were drawn up in a species of phalangial order.

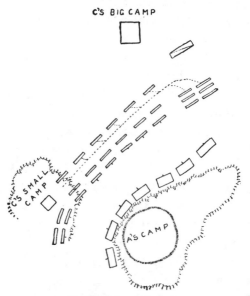

Battle against Ariovistus.

The Roman soldiers attacked the foe with their usual vigorous onslaught, but the Germans met them by a rush given with such impetuosity that the legionaries did not have time to shift ranks so as to cast all their javelins; they were almost immediately constrained to resort to their swords. They were for the moment put on the defensive. But they quickly resumed their ancient habit of offense, and to resist their onset the Germans grouped themselves in bodies of three or four hundred, who made a tortoise, covering themselves with their interlocked shields. The Roman soldiers held to the attack with consummate courage, advancing boldly into the intervals and ranks of the enemy, and tearing away their shields by main force. Some leaped upon the roof of shields so interlocked, forced them apart, and hewed at the Germans from above. The left wing of the barbarians was thus routed, but the enemy still held firmly upon the right, where he was by far stronger. The Roman line was unable to make the least impression, and finally wavered. Perceiving this danger, young P. Crassus, who commanded the cavalry, not being at the moment engaged, but placed where he could see what was going on, took command of the third line which had lain in reserve, ployed it into column, and led it quickly to the support of the Roman left. The shock of these fresh troops broke the enemy's resistance. No doubt the divination of their soothsayers had produced its due effect, and they saw in the Roman success the hand of fate. They turned from the Roman line, ceased resistance, and soon melted into utter rout and flight, nor stopped till they reached the Rhine, a matter of fifty miles distant. Their flight was presumably down the valley of the Ill, up which they had advanced. Some, it is said, swam across the Rhine, near Rheinau. Some others, among them Ariovistus, managed to find boats in which to cross, and thus escaped. The rest were cut down by Cæsar's Gallic cavalry. The two Roman ambassadors who had been cast into chains were recovered.

The Suevi, who had come down to the right bank of the Rhine with intention to cross, hearing of the terrible defeat of Ariovistus, at once decamped. But their enemies, the

Ubii, from lower down the river, hung upon their rear and inflicted severe loss upon them. This victory ended, for the time being, any fear of the Germans.

Cæsar, having thus conducted two successful campaigns in one season, early put his army into winter-quarters in the land of the Sequani, likely enough near Vesontio, under command of Labienus. He himself returned to Cisalpine Gaul to hold the assizes, as well as to be nearer the political turmoils of Rome and to watch for his own interests.

In this initial year of his command of an army, Cæsar showed plainly those qualities of rapid decision and action, courage and intelligent grasp of the situation, which always yielded such vast results. But he was at times more markedly cautious than later in his military life, as if he had not yet learned to trust to his good fortune, nor acquired wide experience in arms. One can notice mistakes and a certain indecision in these campaigns, to which Cæsar was not later so much subject; though the same quality crops up all through his military career. He has been criticised because he did not attack Ariovistus on his dangerous flank march past his camp, but this has already received comment. It has also been observed that the sixteen thousand men sent by Ariovistus against the working-party on the new camp might have been destroyed instead of merely driven back by his protecting lines of legionaries, who much outnumbered them. But Cæsar accomplished his purpose and completed his second camp, which was all he needed to do. Chief criticism of all, Cæsar should apparently have been in command of his left wing opposed to the stronger part of the German line, instead of on the right, where the enemy was weaker. It was the common habit for the commander to open the attack with his right in person; but in this instance it was distinctly unwise, as the bulk of the work had to be done on the left.

If young Crassus had not acted with unusual intelligence and promptness, Cæsar might have forfeited the victory, for his success on the right in no wise demoralized the enemy's other flank. His presence on the right was a tactical lapse.

Though indeed the fact does not detract from Cæsar's merit, it cannot be said that the balance of numbers of the untrained barbarians opposed to his army during this year was so excessive as to make his triumph over them a remarkable thing for Roman legionaries. His army had been trained to war in the best manner then known. He himself was able to command it and manœuvre it by a perfect method. His enemy, while somewhat larger, had no such preponderance as to make the victory of the Romans an extraordinary achievement. One rather admires the Helvetii and Germans, with their comparatively poor discipline, art and equipment, for their noble courage in defense of what they undoubtedly believed to be their rights. In this campaign the odds of the barbarians against Cæsar was in no sense as great as that against Alexander in his Eastern campaigns; while the opposition to Hannibal was many-fold as great. But no general, ancient or modern, ever encountered such overwhelming odds and stood his enemies off so successfully as the great Carthaginian; no general ever attacked with the fury of Alexander.

Gallic Buckler found in Normandy.

VII.

THE BELGÆ. SPRING OF 57 B. C.

THE redoubtable Belgæ had raised a coalition against Cæsar during the winter, and so soon as forage grew he set out with sixty thousand men — legions
and allies — against them. Arriving opportunely among the Remi, he anticipated their defection, and by politic treatment transformed them into allies
who thereafter remained constant. The Belgæ and allies had nearly three
hundred thousand men, but as all were not yet assembled, Cæsar was able to
attack them in detail. He sent a detachment to invade the land of the Bellovaci, one of the most powerful of the coalition, crossed the Aisne, and camped
beyond the then existing bridge in the land of the Remi. He went cautiously
to work, showing none of Alexander's self-confident dash, and sought to induce
the enemy to assault his intrenched camp. This they declined, and made a
clever diversion around Cæsar's left flank, hoping to capture the bridge in his
rear and cut him off. But Cæsar caught them while crossing the fords, and
in a partial engagement routed them with his light troops alone. Easily disheartened, the coalition dissolved, and the Belgian tribes left, each for its own
territory. Cæsar then attacked Noviodunum, but being repulsed, resorted to
a siege with success. Having done this, he could deal with the tribes separately.

DURING the succeeding winter of 58–57 B. C., Cæsar, in
Cisalpine Gaul, received news from Labienus that the Belgæ
were threatening trouble, and had roused their neighbors to
resistance in the fear that Roman success should also overwhelm them, so soon as Gaul south of them was subdued.
They made a coalition and exchanged hostages to insure
mutual action. Thus far, the result of Cæsar's work had
been to save Rome from a possible danger; but it had roused
the Belgæ, perhaps a more redoubtable enemy than the Helvetii or the Germans. This rising was not altogether regretted by Cæsar. He saw in it the opportunity and excuse for

pushing his conquests beyond their present limits. The boundary of conquered Gaul must be the Rhine on the north and east, or there could be no permanent rest. He had his six old legions, the Seventh, Eighth, Ninth, Tenth, Eleventh and Twelfth. Raising two new ones in Italy, the Thirteenth and Fourteenth, he sent them under his nephew and lieutenant, Q. Pedius, into Transalpine Gaul, probably by the Great St. Bernard, to the land of the Sequani. This made eight legions, each probably with not much less than its full complement. If we assume five thousand men to each, he had forty thousand heavy foot. To these we may add Gallic auxiliaries, Cretan archers, slingers and Numidians which, from certain allusions in the Commentaries, we may place at thirteen thousand, or a total of fifty-three thousand foot. Add again five thousand cavalry and some Æduan foot under Divitiacus, and we have an army of over sixty thousand men. The non-combatants (servants and camp-followers) were numerous. His lieutenants were M. Crassus, quæstor, and T. Labienus, C. Fabius, Q. Cicero, L. Roscius, L. Munatius Plancus, C. Trebonius, Q. Titurius Sabinus, and L. Arunculeius Cotta, legates, all good men and tried. We later find some others placed in responsible command. Cæsar had authority from the Senate to appoint ten lieutenants of proprætorian rank. But his legates are not, as a rule, mentioned as such.

When the season had advanced so that there was an abundance of forage, Cæsar joined the army, probably at Vesontio. Learning by scouts and by spies of the Senones and other tribes, neighbors to the Belgæ, whom he sent out as less suspicious than other Gauls, that the Belgæ had raised an army, and that it was encamped in a certain region north of the Axona (Aisne), but apparently not ready to move, Cæsar, after properly providing for rations, broke up and headed towards their boundaries, some fifteen days distant. It was late in May. From Vesontio he marched back over the route he had taken when he moved against Ariovistus, to

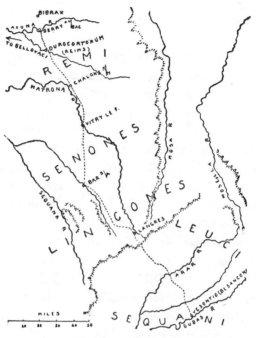

Vesontio to the Axona.

Langres, and thence by Bar-sur-Aube, to Vitry le François, — one hundred and forty-five miles in fifteen days. This route is laid down on the assumption that there was an ancient Gallic road between these points.

This march on the enemy's army as objective was in accordance with Cæsar's energetic mood, as well as in strict conformity with the best rules of warfare. A summary attack on the enemy before his plans are completely developed into action is uniformly the surest means of disconcerting him, and of providing for his discomfiture. It was always Napoleon's plan, and whenever energetically employed is apt to succeed even beyond expectation. Having determined on this course, Cæsar's speed in carrying out his purpose was characteristic of the man, and a first step towards victory.

The result justified Cæsar's anticipations. The nearest tribe of Belgæ, the Remi, at once submitted, awed by the unexpected arrival of Cæsar in their very midst. They had not yet committed themselves to the coalition, but, familiar with its details, their submission put Cæsar into possession of all the facts. They were not unwilling to play in northern Gaul the rôle which was assumed by the Ædui in the centre of the country. It was the safest, and they proved constant to their pledges.

The Belgæ were of German origin. Their distant ancestors had come from beyond the Rhine, and they were equally haughty and warlike. They, alone and unsupported, had thrown back the wave of the Cimbri and Teutones which had come so near to wrecking Rome. The Commentaries open with the statement that the Belgæ were the bravest of the barbarians. They were very numerous. It seemed that the Bellovaci had promised to the common cause one hundred thousand fighting men, of whom sixty thousand picked troops should go into the field; the Suessiones and Nervii, fifty thousand each; and twelve other tribes a total of one hundred and thirty-six thousand more. The actual forces under the colors were as follows: —

Bellovaci, around modern	Beauvais	.	.	.	60,000 men.
Suessiones, " "	Soissons	.	.	.	50,000 "
Nervii, " "	Hainault	.	.	.	50,000 "
Atrebates, " "	St. Quentin	.	.	.	15,000 "
Ambiani, " "	Amiens	.	.	.	10,000 "
Morini, " "	Artois	.	.	.	25,000 "

Menapii, around modern	{ Flanders } { Brabant }		.	.	7,000	men.
Caletes,	"	"	Havre	. . .	10,000	"
Viliocasses,	"	"	lower Seine }	. .	10,000	"
Veromandui,	"	"	Arras }			
Aduatuci,	"	"	Namur	. . .	19,000	"
Four German Tribes		. . . . .			40,000	"
					296,000	"

As the Germans of the left bank of the Rhine had joined the coalition, it was not improbable that additional help would likewise come from across the river. Galba, king of the Suessiones, which tribe Divitiacus had once ruled, was to be commander-in-chief.

This coalition covered the whole of what is now northern France and Belgium. Cæsar plainly saw that he must not allow this gigantic force to assemble, but must speedily attack it in detail if he would not be overwhelmed by it as a whole. He therefore, as a diversion, sent Divitiacus with the contingents of the Ædui, Remi and Senones into the territory of the Bellovaci on a ravaging expedition. This was an excellent thrust, even if Divitiacus should prove unable to accomplish much, for his presence alone was apt to produce present dissension in the ranks of the Belgian cantons. Divitiacus, though allied by friendship to the Bellovaci, did his work in a handsome manner. Cæsar himself, learning that the enemy was near at hand, advanced across the Matrona (Marne) through Durocortorum (Reims), and to the Axona at modern Berry au Bac. Here was a bridge. Cæsar took possession of it, crossed the river and went into camp.

His army was in good spirits and able. His legions were vastly superior to the barbarians ; his Gallic allies probably as good, and Cæsar could of course handle them to better advantage than the enemy his own troops. In his camp there was but one head, one purpose.

The river Axona protected a large part of the territory of his new allies, the Remi, and formed an excellent defensive line. His camp lay north of the Axona, on the hill between the river and a low, marshy brook now called the Miette. There are substantial remains of the camp extant. The hill was eighty feet above the Axona, and the slopes were such as to allow a convenient deployment of the legions. The bridge, if he continued to hold it, made certain that his rations could be securely delivered to him by the contributory tribes in the rear. This bridge he at once fortified on the north side by a bridgehead, with a rampart and palisades twelve feet high and a trench eighteen feet wide; and he placed Q. Titurius Sabinus in command of the south bank with six cohorts, or about three thousand men. Cæsar was, to be sure, astride the

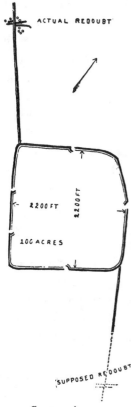

Camp on Axona.

river, but the bulk of his force was on the offensive bank, he had good communications with the Province, and his camp formed an excellent intermediate base for action against the Belgæ.

The enemy was near at hand. They had invaded that part of the territory of the Remi which lay

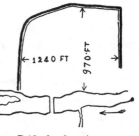

Bridgehead on Axona.

north of the Axona.   They had laid siege to Bibrax (Vieux Laon), some eight miles north of Cæsar's camp.   Their method of siege was to drive the defenders from the ram-

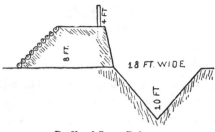

Profile of Camp Defenses.

parts by showers of stones and arrows, and then to advance against the wall a testudo (or tortoise made by the soldiers holding their shields close together over their heads) to cover workmen who should undermine it. At the close of the first day the besieged managed to smuggle some messengers through the lines, never carefully held at night, and sent word to Cæsar that they must be aided or speedily surrender.   Cæsar at once sent them a force of his best Numidian and Cretan archers and Balacrean sling-ers.   This reinforcement probably penetrated the town by the south, where impregnable escarpments made the besieg-ers lax in their watch.   They were active only on the other three sides.

The easily discouraged Belgæ drew off from the siege, and giving up hope of taking the place, devastated the region. They then advanced and took up a position within two miles of the Romans.   Their camp appeared from the fires to have a front some eight miles long.

Cæsar was cautious about engaging this enormous army until he had made essay of their valor and discipline as well as of that of his Æduan horse, and he made daily cavalry reconnoissances by which the Romans could gauge the value of the enemy in action.   They soon ascertained that the allied horse was quite equal to the Belgian; and the Roman soldier was by far his superior.   The legionary's ambition rose accordingly. This caution on Cæsar's part was as much an outcome of his own inexperience as it was the desire of teaching his troops that they were safe in despising numbers. He could not afford to have one bad check now, as its effect might be so far-reaching as to prejudice the results of his whole plan of action in Gaul. But having satisfied himself and his soldiers of their superiority, he concluded to bring on a battle. We admire the method and skill of Cæsar, but we look in vain for that *élan* which characterized even the first campaigns of Alexander — that mettle which made no tale of the enemy. Cæsar's caution was advisable, but it does not appeal to us like the Macedonian's brilliant gallantry.

The ground on the north slope in front of the bridgehead was not only available for ranging the Roman battle-lines, but its left was protected by the Miette and Aisne; the right could lean on the camp. But between the camp and both the Axona and the brook were gaps through which the barbarians with their vast numbers might penetrate, and take the legions in reverse. These gaps Cæsar fortified with a wall and trench four hundred paces long, at right angles to the front of the camp, and built a redoubt at each outer end, where he placed some of his military engines to support his right flank in case the enemy should over-

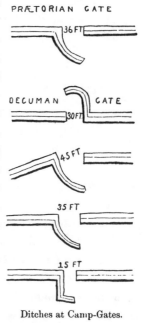

Ditches at Camp-Gates.

lap him. He left the two new legions in camp as a reserve. The other six he drew up in line on the north slope of the hill. The enemy did the same in front of their own camp.

Between the two armies was the marshy bit of land made by the brook.   Neither army appeared willing to cross this strip, lest the disorder into which it might fall during the crossing should enable the other to take it at a disadvantage.

The action was opened by some cavalry exchanges between the two armies, in which the Roman allies again proved their

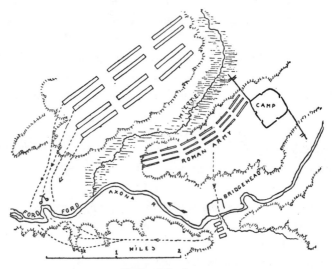

Battle of the Axona.

superiority after a hot contest.   Cæsar, not caring himself to attack, but wishing to lure the Belgians on to begin the engagement, after some hours thus spent in line, led back his forces to camp.   The barbarians, who were really anxious to fight, for their victual was not overabundant, but unwilling to assault Cæsar's intrenchments, now tried another scheme. They marched round the Roman left to the river, where they had discovered a passable and strangely enough to Cæsar unknown ford below the camp; and here they began to make their way across in small parties, purposing to cut off the bridge or the command of Titurius; or failing this, to devastate the region of the Remi on which the Romans relied for much of their corn. It is probable that the country was heavily wooded. Cæsar at all events did not discover the turning manœuvre until informed of it by Titurius. Leaving his legions still in camp, Cæsar himself, with his cavalry and light troops, moved rapidly to the rear, crossed by the bridge and advanced to meet this serious threat. His force consisted of his Gallic cavalry, and of Numidian and Cretan archers and Balacrean slingers, the best of their kind, and of great value and utility. He arrived at the ford not a moment too soon, for the barbarians were already swarming across the river in considerable numbers. The light troops attacked them with vigor. As they were in disorder from the difficulties of the ford, which they were crossing without any preparation or support, Cæsar had them at his mercy, and inflicted enormous losses upon them. The cavalry cut those who had reached the south bank to pieces, and drove back the other warriors who were gallantly seeking to force their way over the river on the bodies of the slain, which all but filled up the ford. The victory was won with small effort. The fact that the legions were not brought on to the field is a fair gauge to the battle of the Axona.

The barbarians, disappointed at not taking Bibrax, nor drawing Cæsar into battle on their own ground, nor being able to cut him off by crossing the river, lost heart and determined to retire. To this they were especially constrained, when on hearing that the Ædui had invaded the land of the Bellovaci, this latter tribe at once decamped to protect its own territory. It was agreed, however, among all the tribes before dispersing, that they should again assemble to resist the Roman army whenever it might invade the country, on the territory of whatever tribe was first attacked.

They accordingly broke camp that night about ten P. M.,

and began their rearward movement.   As the column of each tribe naturally strove to be first in order of march, the army as a whole set out on their retreat in much confusion.   This was increased by the darkness.   Perceiving the disorder, but fearing an ambush, Cæsar, with Fabian caution, remained in camp till daybreak.   Having then satisfied himself that there was no such danger, he sent his cavalry under Pedius and Cotta, and three legions under Labienus, to harass the rear of the retreating enemy.   This was effectually done, and without loss.   The Roman troops cut down many thousands of the barbarians, who had no further idea of resistance, and allowed themselves to be slaughtered like so many brute beasts.   The pursuit was checked at night, and the party returned to camp.   Judging from the account in the Commentaries, the pursuit was not over vigorous.   The remorseless energy with which Alexander followed up his broken and flying enemy was entirely lacking here.

Next day, Cæsar made a forced march of twenty-eight miles down the Axona to a city of the Suessiones which had joined the Belgæ.   It was called Noviodunum (Soissons). He hoped to take the place by storm, as it had but a scanty garrison, the tribe being absent in the general expedition. The wall and ditch were, however, so high and wide that the town could not be captured out of hand.   The Commentaries simply state that Cæsar attempted the assault.   It appears probable that he did so without proper precautions, and being driven back with loss, made no second assault.   Hannibal, it seems, was not the only general who was balked by walls and ditches; and the towns he assaulted were fortified by Roman skill and garrisoned by Roman soldiers.   The Commentaries are our only source of information for the details of this war, and as these were written with a purpose, and are as eminently plausible as they are remarkable as a narrative of

events, it is often difficult to read between the lines so as to
guess at the exact truth. But in this case it is evident that
Cæsar was beaten back by the garrison of Noviodunum.
Finding that the assault was a failure, Cæsar camped near

Axona to Sabis.

by and sent back for the vineæ and other engines of siege.
Vineæ, it will be remembered, were portable, strongly constructed huts, open at both ends, which could be placed
together so as to make galleries to approach the walls of
towns for undermining. They served the same purpose as
parallels in modern war.

The army of the Suessiones meanwhile returned, and a
reinforcement to the garrison was thrown into the place during the following night. The Commentaries lead one to infer
that the entire body of Suessiones filed in. It would seem as
if this should have been prevented by Cæsar. The tribe
could be more easily fought outside than inside the place, and
if he had enough men to besiege it in the presence of the

relieving army, he certainly had enough to prevent their entering the town. It is probable that the barbarians outwitted Cæsar in this matter also. But Cæsar started to make a terrace; and when the siege apparatus arrived, the barbarians, astonished at the enormous preparations made by the Roman engineers, and their speed in the work of the siege, concluded that they had better sue for peace. By intercession of the Remi, whose allies they had always been, their suit was granted, the people were disarmed, and the usual hostages taken. In the town was found a large supply of arms.

Cæsar then marched across the Axona against the Bellovaci, — the most dangerous of the allies, — who retired into their capital town called Bratuspantium (Breteuil, or possibly Beauvais). But when the Roman army came near the place, a deputation of old men was met who sued for peace; and so soon as Cæsar had arrived within sight of its walls, the women and boys made supplication from the ramparts. Divitiacus, who had returned after disbanding his Æduan army, also pleaded for this people, which had been misled by its chiefs, and out of respect to him and to the Æduans, Cæsar took the Bellovaci under his protection, requiring, however, six hundred hostages from them as well as the surrender of their arms. Such hostages were, as a rule, the children of the king, if any, and of important citizens, or else were illustrious men, needful to the state and influential in its councils. The Bellovaci declared that the promoters of the Belgic war had fled to Britain, with which country there was considerable intercourse.

The neighboring people, the Ambiani, on being approached, also brought in their submission, and now Cæsar concluded to turn northeasterly towards the land of the Nervii.

VIII.

BATTLE OF THE SABIS. JULY–SEPTEMBER, 57 B. C.

MANY of the Belgian tribes had sued for peace. Not so the Nervii and
their allies. Cæsar marched against them. At the river Sabis he was surprised
by the barbarians, owing purely to insufficient scouting. While the legions
were preparing to camp, the enemy fell violently upon them. They were
caught unprepared, and came close to being overwhelmed. Cæsar was never,
except at Munda, in so grave a danger. Finally, by superhuman exertions on
his own part, and by cheerful gallantry on the part of his men, the tide of battle turned, and the barbarians were defeated with terrible slaughter. Out of
sixty thousand Nervii, but five hundred remained fit for duty; of six hundred
senators, but three returned from the battle. Cæsar then marched down the
Sabis to a city of the Aduatuci (Namur), which after some trouble he took.
The campaign had been successful and glorious. Cæsar had made serious but
natural mistakes, of which happily the Gauls were not able enough to take
advantage.

THE Nervii were the most warlike of the Belgians, and
they not only absolutely refused to make terms, but reproached
the other Belgians for submission. This people kept themselves entirely aloof from commerce or intercourse with other
nations, and in this manner had preserved their native
strength and hardihood. The Nervii had got the Atrebates
and Veromandui to pool issues with them, and the Aduatuci
were on the way to join the coalition. The women and children had been sent to a spot defended by a marsh, perhaps
Mons, whose hill is now surrounded by low meadows once
marshes. In three days' march Cæsar reached a point near
modern Bavay, not far from the Sabis (Sambre), on which
river, ten miles away, he learned from some prisoners that
the Nervii and the adjoining allied tribes were awaiting the

Roman army, at a place near modern Maubeuge. Cæsar kept up his advance and struck the Sabis on the left or north bank. The Nervii were on the right or south bank. He sent forward his light troops to reconnoitre, and the usual number of centurions to choose a place for camp. The common formation for the march of the Roman army (*i. e.* each legion being followed by its own baggage) had been carefully noted by the neighboring tribes, and its manner reported to the Nervii; some native deserters had also joined them with similar information from the Roman camp; and the Nervian chiefs were advised to promptly attack the leading legion as it approached its new camping ground encumbered with its impedimenta, because, hampered by the baggage-train following it, they would probably be able to destroy it before the other legions could arrive to its support. This would in the opinion of the Gallic advisers quite demoralize the rest of the army and result in Cæsar's complete overthrow. Orders were accordingly issued by the Nervian chiefs to attack as soon as the baggage-train came in view. Such action was all the more promising as the locality was rough and wooded, and suitable for the Nervii to fight in, they having little horse but most excellent infantry.

It was towards the end of July. Cæsar's officers had chosen for camping a place where an uncovered hill sloped gently down to the left bank of the Sabis, at Neuf-Mesnil. On the other side of the river was a like hill (Haumont), the upper slope of which, beginning some two hundred paces away from the river, was heavily wooded. In these woods the Nervii hid their camp. Having no cavalry, they resorted to a clever means to stop the enemy's. They bent down saplings and interlaced their branches with brambles and brushwork, thus making the stiffest kind of hedge. The people of this section still do the same thing to-day to fence in fields. By this

means the Nervii intercepted the advance of the Roman allied
horse which was reconnoitring, and effectually prevented the
discovery of their position. Every warrior was kept out of

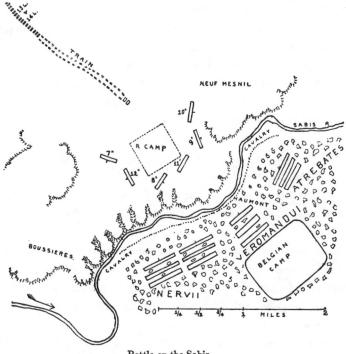

Battle on the Sabis.

sight, excepting only a few videttes near the flats along the
river, which was here but about three feet deep; and these
served to attract the Romans' attention and prevent their
scouting beyond the river. Their skillful dispositions exceeded Cæsar's.

Knowing that he was approaching the enemy, Cæsar, instead of the usual column, adopted an order of march proper
to the occasion. First came the cavalry; then the six old
legions; then the baggage all in one train; last the rear and

baggage guard, consisting of the two new legions. But Cæsar was far from imagining that the whole force of the enemy was close at hand. His scouting was not effective.

On approaching the camping-ground, the cavalry sent a detachment across the river with slingers and archers to drive away the Nervian videttes, while the six leading legions set about fortifying the camp. The Nervian horsemen skirmished well, holding the edge of the wood in such a way that the Romans did not discover the Gallic line of battle.

The Ninth and Tenth legions, meanwhile, began work on the left front of the proposed camp; the Eighth and Eleventh on the front facing the river, the Seventh and Twelfth on the right front. The legionaries, unsuspicious of danger, dispersed to collect palisades and other stuff, with but the slender cordon of horse out as pickets. While all this was passing, and so soon as the wagon-train had come in sight, this being the preconcerted signal, the Nervii and their allies, the Atrebates and Veromandui, rushed impetuously from their ambush, brushed away the Roman skirmish-line of horse like a cobweb, forded the river and fell, as it were an avalanche, upon the Romans, who were entirely unconscious of their presence and unprepared for an assault. It was evident that Cæsar had not yet grown expert in reconnoitring his ground in the presence of the enemy, nor careful in his method of camping. Here was an unwarranted breach of the usual Roman method, which always put out a line of battle to protect a camping party. The surprise was complete. It was all but certain that Cæsar's army would be wiped from existence. In the onslaught the Atrebates were so placed on the enemy's right as to attack the Ninth and Tenth legions; the Veromandui in the centre, the Eighth and Eleventh; the Nervii on their left, the Seventh and Twelfth. The Nervii were opposite the rugged left bank of the Sabis at Boussières.

But for the discipline of the legions, which was in every sense commendable, the Roman army would have been destroyed. Many of the soldiers were at a distance seeking material for the rampart; the rest were busy at work with what they had already brought. Lucky it was that the men had become hardened in their past year's campaigns. Better still, they had gained confidence in their leader. There was not a sign of demoralization. The stanch qualities which later enabled Cæsar with them to complete the overthrow of all his enemies had already taken root. So soon as the enemy was seen to emerge from the woods, every legionary caught the alarm. The trumpet was quickly sounded, and the standards displayed; the officers were happily all at hand, it being one of Cæsar's explicit orders that none such should, under any pretense, leave his legion till the camp was fully fortified; and the Roman soldiers had already learned how to fall quickly into the ranks.

The attack of the barbarians had been so well-timed and sudden that the officers, many of them, had not even time to put on their badges, such as were usual to distinguish the several ranks, or the men to take off the leather covers with which, during the march, they were wont to protect their often beautifully ornamented shields. Nor could they by any means seek each man his own cohort. They fell in under whatever standard was nearest, while Cæsar and his lieutenants rushed to and fro, encouraging the patchwork lines and striving to call order from confusion.

The line was barely formed in this irregular manner, when the enemy reached the ground. They had crossed an open stretch of nearly three quarters of a mile and forded a river, which may have occupied twenty minutes. The surface was considerably cut up by the artificial hedges before referred to, which might be described as a sort of abatis. This cir-

cumstance operated to prevent all manœuvring. The line
thus thrown together was an irregular convex formation,
standing in so confused a manner that the legionaries had no
notion whatsoever of what was going on around them. Each
small body fought where it stood, as it were, for its own sole
safety. There was no possibility of mutually assisting each
other. Aid could not be sent from one to another part of
the line. There was, for the nonce, no head, no purpose.
A worse surprise can scarcely be imagined. Still there was
no manifestation of fear; the legionaries set their teeth and
proposed to fight it out as best they might.

The Ninth and Tenth legions were, as stated, on the left.
These men behaved with all the gallantry for which Cæsar so
loved the Tenth, cast the pilum, fell to with the gladius, and
after a hearty tussle drove back the Atrebates in their front;
for these barbarians had become tired and out of breath with
their sharp rush across the river and their hurried attack.
They were pushed, with great loss, across the ford, followed
up and cut down by thousands. The Atrebates rallied for a
moment, but were again broken and hustled back until the
Ninth and Tenth finally reached the Gallic camp.

The Eleventh and Eighth legions in the centre likewise
behaved with praiseworthy fortitude. After a wavering combat, in which both sides lost heavily, the success of the Ninth
and Tenth on their left so emboldened these two bodies that,
with a shout of triumph, they made a common charge on the
foe and pushed the Veromandui in their front sharply down
to the river, on whose bank they kept up the combat.

But this very success was the cause of the gravest danger.
The advance of the four legions of the left and centre absolutely exposed the front and left of the camp works just
begun, and left naked the flank and rear of the Seventh and
Twelfth legions on the right. While all this was going on, a

heavy force of sixty thousand Nervii, under Boduognatus, the chief in command, had been fording the Sabis and climbing the heights of Boussières. Perceiving the opening, this entire force fell on the two legions, which numbered some ten thousand men, striking them on the right flank (*aperto latere*) with a fierceness which the Romans had never yet

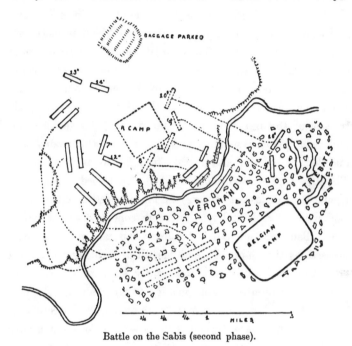

Battle on the Sabis (second phase).

encountered. The cavalry and light troops, who, after being driven in, had just rallied and placed themselves in reserve, were again utterly disorganized by this overwhelming onset; while the host of non-combatants, — drivers, servants and sutlers, — penned up in the camp, seeing a column of the barbarians penetrating into its very midst, made a hasty exit from the half finished rear-gate in the wildest confusion, and made for the woods. So apparently fatal was the disaster and rout, that some auxiliary cavalry, reputed to be the best in Gaul, took to its heels, and conveyed to the tribes along the route by which Cæsar had advanced, and at home, the news that the Romans had been surprised and utterly destroyed.

Cæsar, at the earliest onset of the enemy, had rushed to the left, where the line was first threatened, and encouraged the Ninth and Tenth legions, who under his cheerful words and bearing had gone to work with a will which accomplished wonders.   Thence he galloped to the centre, where his presence exerted a like happy effect.   On his reaching the right, he found matters in the worst possible condition.   On this front had fallen the attack of the Nervii themselves, the bravest of the brave.   The standards of the Twelfth legion had been planted so closely together that the troops were huddled in masses, and unable to fight to any advantage. The files were pressed too close to use the sword.   There had been a terrible loss of officers, the missiles falling on the close ranks with awful fatality.   In some cohorts every centurion was killed or wounded.   If Cæsar had not yet been hard pressed by the Gauls, he had his fill of fighting now.   The efforts of the troops were apparently slackening.   The enemy, in vast numbers, was pushing in front and overlapping the flanks, and more and more were coming.   There was no reserve.   The other legions had not yet worked out their problem.   The matter was at its climax.   Defeat stared Cæsar in the face, — massacre was its result.   Snatching a buckler from a soldier in the rear, with the inspiration of dire necessity, — as he later did at Munda, where, as he said, he fought for his life, — Cæsar rushed on foot to the front to reëstablish order.   Seeing their chief performing the part of the common soldier, the courage of the men near by at once revived, and the good feeling spread.   They opened ranks so as to wield the gladius.   Their battle-cry resumed its normal resonance, and the resistance to the enemy became more resolute. Rushing thence to the Seventh legion, Cæsar reanimated that body in like manner, and brought it sharply up to the support of the Twelfth, and, as some critics read the Commentaries, got the two legions back to back, so as to prevent being surrounded. The benefit of Cæsar's gallantry was immediate. It struck the same key-note as Napoleon's heading the grenadiers at the bridge of Lodi. Such is the effect of a great man's divine fury upon other men. It was the burning genius of the heart within, which could thus in a moment transform disaster into victory, could revive the ardor of courage fast ebbing away. Such, too, was the throbbing heart which turned the tide at Winchester, such the dauntless presence which saved the wreck of Chickamauga. It began to look as if the Seventh and Twelfth could hold their own.

Meanwhile the two legions of the rearguard, having notice of the battle, hastened up, and being seen approaching by the enemy spread a disheartening effect among their ranks. Labienus, who with the Tenth legion had gained possession of the enemy's camp beyond the ford, also perceived from the hill opposite the distress of the Twelfth and Seventh, and speedily sent the Tenth to their succor. This admirable body of men came up at a *pas de charge*, and took the Nervii in the rear with a shock which instantly reëstablished the fighting on the right; and, seeing the change of tide, the camp-followers and cavalry regained their courage, and turning upon the foe drove the flanking column of the barbarians from the camp.

The tide had turned; the battle was won, but so tenacious of their ground were the Nervii that the survivors stood and fought on the bodies of the slain, and even piled them up as breastworks. It was by brute pressure alone that these obstinately gallant barbarians could be forced to cease from fighting. The little remainder Cæsar drove into flight. They had fought with a doggedness exhibited by no foes Cæsar ever encountered. The Roman army was exhausted as it had rarely been, and its losses had been heavy. Camp was at once fortified; the men buried the dead, and took their rest.

The old men from the Nervian retreat shortly sent and sued for peace. They stated that of six hundred senators but three had returned from the battle; that of the sixty thousand men who had been engaged, a bare five hundred could now bear arms. Such had been the splendid valor of the vanquished. Cæsar accepted their plea, arrested further butchery, and commanded the neighboring tribes not to assail them in their utter present weakness.

The Aduatuci had been on the march to the assistance of the Nervii, but frightened at the reports of the battle of the Sabis, they turned back, deserted their other towns, and conveyed all their people and goods into one, peculiarly adapted for defense. This town, whose name is not given, was situated upon a precipitous hill wellnigh inaccessible on every side but one, where a gentle slope not over two hundred feet in width descended to the plain. This slope they had fortified with a very high double wall. These people were descendants of some six thousand of the Cimbri and Teutones, who had been left behind in charge of the baggage, while the bulk of the tribes had marched south and been destroyed by Marius two generations before. This site was doubtless in the angle made by the Sabis and Mosa (Meuse) opposite Namur. Mt. Falhize is suggested as the location, but it does not as well correspond with the text or with the distances marched as the other.

Against this town of the Aduatuci, Cæsar, with seven of the legions — one was detached under Crassus — at once directed his march down the Sabis. Reaching the place, he found its location impregnable, and, seeing that he could not otherwise capture it, he began a siege by the construction of

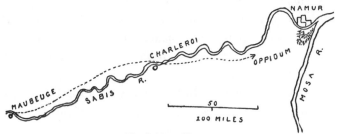

The Sabis to Namur.

a rampart or line of contravallation. This work was twelve feet high and fifteen thousand feet long, with redoubts at intervals. The length of the works is often given as fifteen miles, but this is a manifest error, as the topography plainly shows. After the *quindecim millia* of the text, the word *passuum* must be understood. The barbarians endeavored to interrupt this work by repeated petty attacks, but to no effect. When they saw the construction of a tower and vineæ at a distance, they taunted the Romans for their small stature, which, indeed, then as now, was in marked contrast to the bulky bodies of the Germans, and of the Gauls who were of German lineage, and asked who would bring the tower to their walls. But when this same tower began to move towards them, and actually did approach their walls, they at once sent ambassadors to treat for peace, alleging their belief that the Romans were aided by the gods. They begged that they might retain their arms as a defense against their local enemies. Cæsar demanded unconditional surrender and disarmament, but told them that he would command their neighbors to abstain from attack. The Aduatuci were fain to submit. Their manner of surrendering their arms was to

throw them from the town rampart into the trench, and the
supply was so great that it filled the trench and made a pile
nearly up to the height of the rampart for a considerable distance along its circuit.   Despite their surrender, the chiefs
had acted treacherously, and had yet concealed a third part
of their arms.   After this apparent disarmament the gates
were opened, and the Roman legions marched in and took
possession.

When night came on, the Romans were all ordered from
the town to their camps.   Cæsar feared the violence and

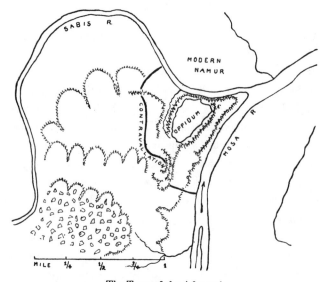

The Town of the Aduatuci.

rapacity of his legionaries, and the ill results which might
flow therefrom.   Still this was a lesser danger than to retire
from a town just captured.   The Aduatuci naturally believed
that the Romans would be less careful now that they had received the surrender of the town, and planned an attack that
very night upon what appeared to be the least strong part of

Cæsar's contravallation wall. They had the arms not surrendered, and they made new bucklers of bark and wickerwork. They delivered the assault shortly after midnight and with considerable vigor. Cæsar, suspecting possible treachery, had provided for just such an occurrence. The usual signal-fire was lighted at the point of attack, and the legionaries at once rushed from all points to the defense of their threatened rampart. The Aduatuci fought like brave men, but, with a loss of some four thousand killed, they were driven back into the town and penned in. Cæsar retaliated for this treachery by marketing the whole spoil of the town. There were fifty-three thousand people sold as slaves. This was early in September.

During this time, Crassus, who had been detached with the Seventh legion against the maritime tribes living on the northwest coast of Belgium, had done his work well, and reported that these peoples had all been brought under the Roman sway. His method of operation is not known.

So great had the fame of Cæsar's conquests become that many of the nations from beyond the Rhine, the Ubii in particular, sent ambassadors to tender their submission to the Romans. But desirous of returning to Italy, and as the cold season was now approaching, Cæsar put his troops into winter-quarters along the river Liger (Loire), among the Carnutes, Andes and Turones, echeloned between Orleans and Angers; and, inviting these ambassadors to return early the next summer, himself set out for the south. Reaching Rome, a thanksgiving (*supplicatio*) of fifteen days was decreed, — a longer period than had ever before been granted a Roman general.

The best praise of this splendid campaign is its own success. The energy, rapidity, clear-sightedness and skill with which Cæsar divided, attacked and overcame the Belgian tribes is a model for study. The fact that he had next to no fighting to do is all the more to the credit of his strategy. But in this his second campaign, he still committed errors.

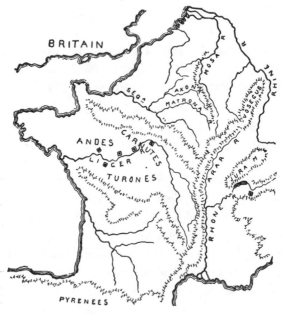

Winter-Quarters, B. C. 57–56.

Many of these are more or less frankly acknowledged in the Commentaries. His miscalculation in his unprepared and therefore unsuccessful assault on Noviodunum was a natural enough mistake, one to which all, even the greatest, commanders are liable. His being surprised, as he was at the river Sabis, by the Nervii was due to a piece of carelessness which came near being, and but for the stanchness of the Roman character would have proved, fatal. He should have placed a garrison at once in the town of the Aduatuci, to forestall the night attack which he suspected might occur, and but for good luck would have proved much more disastrous to him.

He should not have allowed his political desire to visit Rome to prevent his receiving the embassies tendering submission by the German tribes. The surprise at the Sabis is the most grave of these errors. Cæsar appears to have had, contrary to all Roman precedent, no troops out to protect the camping-parties, except a small cavalry detachment, which plainly had been checked by the enemy close to the river and was unable to penetrate the woods. This fact should at once have excited Cæsar's curiosity and have led to greater caution. That he was not absolutely destroyed on this occasion he owed to the excellence of his troops, and by no means to his own skill or care. The Commentaries on this subject show an uphill effort to palliate his error. But it was too glaring to cover. The truth can be easily read between the lines.

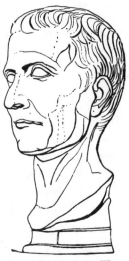

Cæsar, early in Gallic War.
(Campo Santo, Pisa.)

IX.

THE WORK OF CÆSAR'S LIEUTENANTS. 57–56 B.C.

CÆSAR usually spent his winters in Cisalpine Gaul, to be near events in Italy. During this winter, he sent Galba, one of his legates, to open the road from Italy over the Simplon and down the modern Rhone. At Martigny, Galba had a serious battle with the natives, but defeated them. Crassus, another legate, wintered among the Veneti on the coast, and sent ambassadors to gather corn. These officers were seized by the Veneti and held so as to compel the return of their hostages. On learning of this, Cæsar at once made preparations to avenge the act. He must protect his envoys; and to subdue the Veneti would moreover give him easier access to Britain. In order to cover more ground, Cæsar decided to divide his forces. Labienus went to the Rhine region; Crassus to Aquitania, Sabinus to the coast of modern Normandy. Brutus was put in command of the fleet. After a tedious campaign against the Veneti, they were utterly overthrown by Brutus in a naval battle. Meanwhile Sabinus conducted a successful campaign against the Unelli, and Crassus a brilliant one in Aquitania. The year was finished by a partial campaign against the Morini on the Channel, by Cæsar. The work of the year had mostly been done by Cæsar's lieutenants.

ON leaving for Italy for the winter of B. C. 57–56, Cæsar had sent Servius Galba, with the Twelfth legion and some horse, against the tribes south of the lake of Geneva, the Nantuates, Veragri and Seduni, to open one of the most available roads over the Alps between Cis- and Transalpine Gaul, which ran from Milan via the Simplon or the Great St. Bernard to the Rhone valley. The merchants and settlers, in passing through this valley, had generally experienced a good deal of trouble from the native tribes, who subjected them to heavy imposts, if they did not rob them outright. It was essential for military security that this road should be made free to passage. Galba was given permission to winter in the Alps, if he deemed it essential. This Galba did, and having defeated the barbarians in several combats, he received their submission and hostages, and camped in the Rhone valley, where lay the town called Octodorus (Martigny), detailing two cohorts to occupy the land of the Nantuates farther down the river.

The valley is cut in two by the Rhone. The Roman camp lay on one side, the Gallic on the other. The Gauls formed

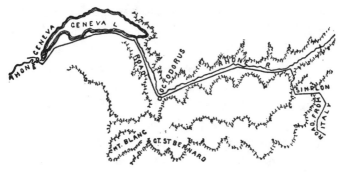

Octodorus Valley.

the plan of cutting off this solitary legion, which by reason of its small number they thought could easily be done. They were indignant at the holding of so many of their children as hostages by the Romans, and they feared annexation to Rome, — the fate of all the tribes of Gaul.

These local clans had accordingly occupied all the surrounding heights and passes, so as to cut Galba off from victual and assistance. This action, taking Galba entirely by surprise, placed him in a most difficult situation. Calling a council of war, it was determined to hold the camp and abide the attack which the barbarians were sure to make. This was the only present resource, though, for some unaccountable reason, the fortifications of the winter-quarters' camp had not yet been completed. Even Roman orders and regulations were not invariably obeyed.

The assault of the Gauls came in due time and was sudden and severe. The defense was obstinate and the legionaries moved from place to place to resist the constantly repeated attacks on the wall. But the number of the defenders was small, and the enemy, whose force was considerable, were able constantly to bring fresh troops to supplant the weary. So vigorously was the fighting pushed that even the Roman wounded could not retire from the trenches. For six long hours the barbarians continued to press on in continual waves, until the Romans had discharged all their darts, and Galba saw that their only hope lay in cutting their way out with the sword. *The sortie was suggested by primipilus P. Sextius Baculus, who had distinguished himself at the Sabis, and C. Volusenus, a military tribune. To carry out the idea, Galba gave orders to collect as many weapons as could be got from those which had fallen into the camp, and then to make a sally from all the gates at once. This desperate venture resulted in unexpected success. Surprised beyond measure at the sudden appearance of the Romans and their vigorous onslaught — for they were momentarily expecting a surrender — the barbarians, disconcerted, turned and fled. This is a fair sample of the inconstancy of the Gaul of that day. Brave to a noteworthy degree, when surprised or once defeated, he could not rally. The bulk of the fighting done by the legions was far from taxing their stanchness.

The legionaries pursued and slaughtered above a third of the enemy, who could not have fallen much short of thirty thousand men. After this victory, having devastated the valley as a punishment for the treachery, and being unwilling to trust to the bad roads and worse population for his supply of corn, Galba passed through the Nantuates, picked up his two cohorts and returned to the Province to winter, pitching his quarters among the Allobroges. His conduct had been brave and sensible.

Cæsar, while in Hither Gaul, believed that he was safe in setting out to Illyricum, as the Belgæ had been subdued, the Germans expelled, the tribes along the most important road over the Alps defeated, and Gaul appeared to be quiet. But peace was not of long duration. Crassus, with one of the legions, had taken up winter-quarters among the Andes, a tribe near the Atlantic on the north shore of the Bay of Biscay. Of the neighboring tribes the Veneti were the strongest. They owned all important harbors on the coast, drove a thriving commerce with Britain and Spain, and possessed great numbers of vessels and considerable wealth. Crassus, running short of victuals during the winter, had sent out some prefects and tribunes among the tribes to negotiate for a supply of corn. T. Terrasidius had gone to the Unelli, M. Trebius to the Curiosolitæ, and Q. Velanius and T. Silius to the Veneti. These tribes, led by the Veneti, having determined among themselves on protecting their territories and made a compact to act together, seized these officers, hoping thereby to be able to compel the return of their own hostages. They sent, in fact, to demand such surrender as the price of the return of Crassus' ambassadors.

Cæsar, being informed of these things by Crassus, but unable to take action during the winter, sent back orders to build a fleet in the Liger, provided rowers, sailors and pilots from the Mediterranean coast of the Province, and commanded everything to be prepared for a marine expedition. So soon as the season of B. C. 56 opened, he hurried to Gaul. The revolted tribes, knowing that they had, by seizing ambassadors, committed the most inexpiable of all offenses, prepared for the worst. They fortified their towns, collected in them all the breadstuffs which they could bring together, and brought their fleet to Venetia, their principal seaport, situated probably in the estuary of the Auray River, which discharges into the Bay of Quiberon. They knew that ignorance of their tides and inlets and harbors would place the Romans

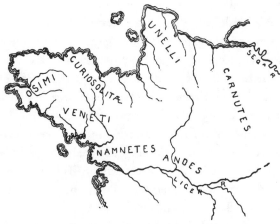

The Venetan Country.

at a great disadvantage. Allies, according to Cæsar, were even sent for to Britain. All the cantons on the coast from the Loire to the Scheldt gave aid, material or moral.

There was not a moment's hesitation in Cæsar's mind as to the necessity of subduing this insurrection. The term insurrection is used, inasmuch as these tribes had once handed in their submission to Crassus, and now again rose in defense of their liberties. But it seems a harsh word to apply to these gallant peoples resisting the encroachments of an invader with no right but that of might to back him. The difficulties Cæsar by no means underrated, but they were as nothing compared to the necessity of punishing the Veneti. If any tribe could, after giving hostages in token of submission, be allowed to transgress, without speedy retribution, the most universally accepted of the laws of nations, observed even among distant barbarians, then all his conquests in Gaul were but a house of cards. This is the motive Cæsar would have us believe he acted on. It is a valid one as far as it goes.

But there was another reason for Cæsar's determination to subdue the Veneti. This people practically owned all the commerce with Britain. They were loath to have Cæsar seize it, as they feared he would do. Strabo tells us that Cæsar had already planned to invade Britain, and to reduce the Veneti was a necessary first step, for they controlled the sea, and while he might push his way between their fleets, they could seriously threaten his rear during his absence.

It must be acknowledged in Cæsar's behalf that the necessity existed of subduing the whole of Gaul, if Rome was to extend her dominion in this direction, if indeed Italy was to be safe; and if Alexander was justified in avenging the attacks of Persia on Greece, so was Cæsar justified in avenging those of the Gauls on Rome. It is hard to criticise the universally claimed right of simple conquest among the ancients; and once we accept so much, nothing remains to blame except unnecessary harshness in the exercise of conquest. Cæsar was justified from his standpoint.

As to the method to be pursued in this campaign, Cæsar decided that it was essential to divide his forces, to occupy the country in a military sense, in order to impose on other tribes who might be tempted to imitate the example of the Veneti. He therefore sent Labienus with part of the cavalry to the Treviri near the Rhine, with orders to sustain the Remi and keep quiet among the Belgæ, and to resist possible inroads of the Germans from across the river; for they had been invited to make another incursion by the Belgæ. Crassus, with twelve legionary cohorts and a stout body of cavalry, he sent to Aquitania, to preserve quiet, and prevent Aquitanian support to the Venetan insurrection. Triturius Sabinus he stationed among the Unelli, and other tribes

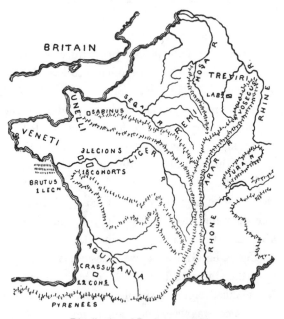

Distribution of Legions, B. C. 56.

along the coast of modern Normandy, for a similar purpose. Decimus Brutus was given command of the fleet. He had brought some galleys from the Mediterranean, and vessels were borrowed from the Pictones, Santones and others.

Cæsar's eight legions at the opening of the campaign were thus distributed: north of the Liger, three legions; in Aquitania one legion and two cohorts; a legion on the fleet; two legions and eight cohorts with Cæsar. Galba had no doubt rejoined from his winter among the Allobroges. Cæsar probably rendezvoused in the vicinity of Nantes, not far from the mouth of the Loire, and thence crossed the Vilaine.

The towns of the Veneti were exceptionally difficult of access. Generally on points of land, they were at high tide inaccessible except by boats; and the retiring tide, while it gave access to land forces, was apt to leave the boats stranded and defenseless. Again, whenever, after great exertions, any town had been cut off from the sea or been put into a desperate strait, the barbarians would simply embark their goods on their own boats, of which they had a vast number, and escape through the creeks and bays, with which the

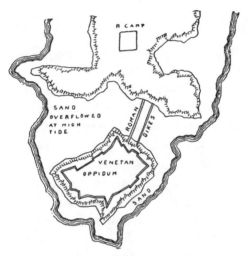

A Venetan Town.

Romans were not familiar. This shifting from place to place they carried on all through the summer of 56 B. C. Their ships were flat-bottomed so as to be the more readily used in inland navigation, but with high bows and stern to resist the waves and the shock of rams. The wood was seasoned oak, the parts of which were held together by heavy iron spikes an inch thick, and their anchors had iron chains. Their bows, made much higher and stronger than those of the Roman galleys, rendered them all the more difficult to attack or to grapple to. Their sails were of soft and thin but tough skins. These boats were in all respects seaworthy, and far better adapted to shoal water warfare than those which the Romans had built on their usual pattern. Only in speed, and this by rowing, did the Roman galley excel that of the Veneti; the latter was impelled by sails alone.

The Roman method of taking the Venetan towns was to build out from the main land two parallel dikes, sometimes as high as the town walls, which when completed excluded tides and gave an excellent approach for engines and men — a place of arms, in fact. It was a vast labor and the operation was rendered nugatory in most cases by the escape of the barbarians as above explained.

The bulk of the season thus passed without success. Cæsar saw that he could accomplish nothing without a fleet, and this was not yet assembled, though it had been ordered many months before and rendezvous given at the mouth of the Liger. The tides, an unknown element to the Romans, the lack of harbors, the inexperience of Roman sailors in these waters, and many other causes had operated to delay the preparations. But there is still something which the Commentaries do not explain. Roman galleys were very speedily constructed. Scipio Africanus, *e. g.*, built and launched twenty quinquiremes and ten quadriremes in forty-five days; Cæsar had been at work nine months, and his fleet was not yet equipped. The delay was not a reasonable one. We know but half the truth.

After taking a number of the Venetan towns, it was plainly brought home to Cæsar that he was making no practical headway. He accordingly determined to risk the event on the result of a naval battle. He camped on the heights of St. Gildas, on the east of the Bay of Quiberon, and waited for his fleet. This was shortly after assembled. So soon as matters were made ready, the Roman fleet moved against the Veneti into the bay. When it hove in sight, about two hundred and twenty of the vessels of the Veneti

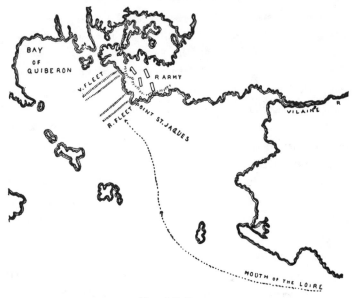

Bay of Quiberon.

sailed out and confidently made ready for battle. The Roman line formed near modern Point St. Jaques, with its right not far from shore.

The Roman ships were lower; even their turrets were not as high as the stern of the barbarian ships, so that the marines could not effectively cast their darts, while fully exposed to those of the enemy. It was a question what tactics could be advantageously employed. The Romans were superior only in courage and discipline, and their vessels in speed, but this was offset by their being unused to and apprehensive of the ocean, to which they ascribed qualities different from their native Mediterranean. But they luckily had on board a great number of grappling hooks (*falces*), not unlike those used in sieges to pull stones from the tops of walls, or, as some construe it, had provided sickles tied to the end of long poles. These Brutus, by a stroke of genius, divined how he could put to use. A falx was slung to the mast; the Romans rowed alongside the enemy and grappled on to the main cable which held up the yard and sail of a Venetan ship; after doing which the oarsmen would pull vigorously away, thus cutting the cable and letting fall the yard and sail. The vessels thus disabled, — for they had no oars, — were then at the mercy of the waves and ready to be boarded by the much superior Roman soldiers. Each one boarded succumbed.

This naval fight, the first of which we have any record on the Atlantic ocean, was witnessed from the hills by Cæsar and the entire Roman army, — a vast encouragement to deeds of valor. It must have been a splendid spectacle. Though the ships of the enemy outnumbered the Romans two or more to one, after many of them had been disabled and boarded, Roman valor prevailed, and the uncaptured ones soon attempted to take refuge in flight. But a dead calm suddenly arose so that they could not move, — Cæsar's fortune always came to his aid at opportune moments. The wind in this bay to-day blows at this season east or northeast till midday, then almost invariably a calm sets in. The attempt at flight was unfortunate. It dispersed the Venetan ships so that when the calm came, the Roman galleys could attack them one by one, without their being able to assist each other. From about ten o'clock till sundown the contest raged, and so effectual were the tactics and discipline of the Romans that very few of the Venetan galleys got to land, — and these under cover of night.

All the valor, youth and strength of the Veneti had been assembled in this one fleet. After its utter destruction there remained to them no means of defense. They had neither men nor vessels. They were fain, therefore, to throw themselves on Cæsar's mercy. But, deeming, as he says in the Commentaries, that he could not forgive their infringement of the sacred rights of ambassadors, Cæsar determined to make an example of this tribe. He put all the senate to death and sold the rest of the people into slavery. It would be hard to decide whether this act was more unpardonable for its mistaken policy or for its ruthless cruelty. Cæsar never considered this latter point. He did not often err in the former; but one or two of his acts of extermination appear to be grave mistakes. While one hardly palliates a similar policy on the part of Alexander, the cruelties of Cæsar appear more monstrous on account of the intervening centuries of growth in civilization and international law. Not only was the military necessity which often constrained Alexander to his acts absent in Cæsar's case, but the latter's destruction of human life far exceeds anything of which Alexander was ever guilty. Almost all critics — including Napoleon — are particularly severe upon Cæsar's unnecessary cruelty to the Veneti. Cæsar had less excuse than precedent for his action. It is strange that Alexander and Hannibal have been so constantly upbraided for what is termed their cruelty, while this quality is rarely imputed to Cæsar.

During the early part of this campaign against the Veneti, Titurius Sabinus had been engaged with the affairs of the Unelli, a canton south of modern Cherbourg, in Normandy, whose king was Viridovix. This chief had collected a large army from all the adjoining tribes, principally the Lexovii and Aulerci-Eburovices, added to which were numbers of robbers and soldiers of fortune from all parts of Gaul.

Sabinus started from the vicinity of Angers on the Loire, marched north, and camped among the Unelli. The remains of a camp some four miles east of modern Avranches, known as Camp du Chastellier, indicate his probable location; and

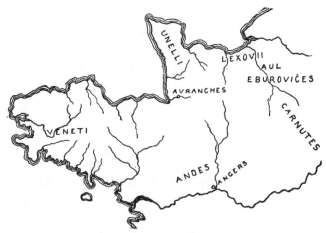

Theatre of Sabinus' Campaign.

though the remains may be those of a later camp, it was not uncommon to pitch new camps on the old locations of predecessors. This camp shows an interesting variation from the usual shape, dictated by the ground.

Sabinus was a cautious officer, with a bent to stratagem. He kept to his camp, which he had established so that his breadstuffs could not be cut off. Viridovix camped over against him some two miles away on the other side of the little river now called the Sée, daily drawing up in battle array, and taunting the Romans for cowardice in not accepting the gage. Even his own men grew dissatisfied and ashamed; but Sabinus had his purpose in thus acting. He wished to bring about a habit of carelessness on the enemy's part by inducing him to underrate his opponents. Having succeeded in so doing, he selected a crafty Gaul, and by promises of valuable gifts, persuaded him to pretend desertion to the enemy, where suitable representations to Viridovix might convince that chief that the Romans were actually cowed by the situation. This spy was directed to state to the chief that the Romans were compelled during the following night to decamp and march towards Cæsar, whose campaign against the Veneti was rumored to be going wrong; and he was to seek to persuade him that the Roman army could be easily attacked and destroyed before its retreat. The spy

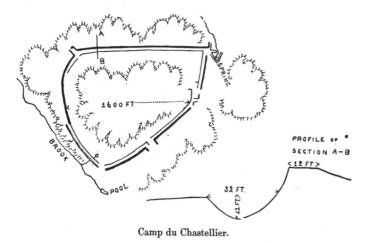

Camp du Chastellier.

proved to be a clever one. Viridovix, in effect, lent a willing ear to his story, and determined on assaulting the Roman camp without loss of time.

This camp was situated on a hill, rocky and steep on the west, less so on the other sides. Towards the north it sloped gradually down a mile or so to the river Sée. In pursuance of their project the Gauls not only armed themselves fully, but carried large quantities of fagots and brushwood to fill up the Roman trench. They were over-eager to reach the

camp before the Roman army should get away; and, loaded
down as the warriors were, in toiling up the ascent, they
arrived in its front wearied and out of breath. Sabinus had

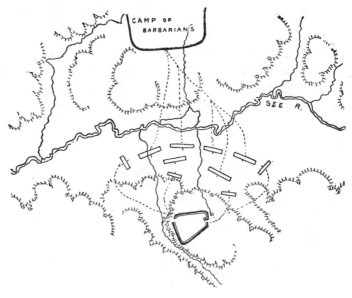

Sabinus' Battle.

been watching for just this chance. The signal was given,
and the Romans, fresh and ready for the combat, rushed out
upon the Unelli from the two corner gates at once. Surprised and overwhelmed, the barbarians offered no resistance
worthy the name; but, turning, sought safety in flight. The
legionaries and horse followed hard at their heels, and
slaughtered the greater part of them. This victory and the
shortly arriving news of Cæsar's triumph over the Veneti —
for Cæsar and Sabinus each heard of the victory of the other
about the same time — so entirely broke up the coalition of
these peoples that tribe now vied with tribe in their anxiety
to bring in their submission and be assured of its acceptance.

This battle is another fair index to the hasty and impetuous, but frail character of the Gauls. Generous, courageous,
patriotic, they were dangerous opponents at the inception of
a campaign. But they became easily discouraged, and were
never long of one mind. Their treaties for mutual support
were wont to be short-lived. They were unable to bear disaster. Polybius and Cæsar gauge the Gauls alike.

P. Crassus, meanwhile, had a large task set him in Aquitania, the territory which is comprised between the Loire

Theatre of Crassus' Campaign.

and the Pyrenees, where the Romans, a few years before,
under Valerius and Manlius, had suffered two galling defeats. Moving south and collecting corn in plenty, summoning to his aid the best men of Tolosa, Carcaso and Narbo, in
the southwest Province, and enlisting auxiliaries, both foot
and horse, among the best material to be had in the cantons
under Roman sway, Crassus crossed the Garumna (Garonne)
and marched into the land of the Sotiates on the left bank.

These barbarians, having brought together a large force
and much cavalry, attempted to attack the Romans on the
march. They opened the action by a diversion with the
horse, meanwhile placing their infantry in ambush. The

horse was speedily routed, and the Roman infantry, somewhat in disorder with the fray, was resuming its march and passing a defile, when it was suddenly assaulted by this force, which debouched from hiding, with exceptional vigor. The combat at once waxed hot. The barbarians were fighting for their soil; the legionaries to show what they could do without their general-in-chief, and under a very young commander, and no doubt also with the clear appreciation which every Roman must have always had of the slender chance to be found in flight. And again Roman discipline prevailed. The Sotiates were defeated with great slaughter.

Crassus then laid siege to their capital, placed variously at modern Lectoure or Sos, the principal of their towns on his line of march. The resistance was so effective that he was obliged to build vineæ and turrets. The Sotiates, many of whom were copper-miners, developed great skill in resisting these means of siege, undermining the Roman ramparts, and themselves building vineæ, but without eventual success. The Romans were so bold and persistent that they were obliged to surrender. During the capitulation the chief, Adcantuannus, with six hundred chosen men bound to him by a special oath, essayed to cut his way out, but was headed off. Despite this fact, he was not denied equal terms, out of regard to his gallantry. Crassus then marched upon the Vocates, also on the left bank of the Garumna, and the Tarusates on the Aturis (Adour).

These peoples were intelligent enough to send for auxiliaries into Hither Spain, where war had been a long time waged with the Romans, and obtained from there not only men, but officers of rank familiar with the Roman method of warfare, many of whom, indeed, had served under Sertorius, the great partisan-chief. These officers, whose training had been of the very best, began to fortify suitable positions, to occupy available defiles, and to harass Crassus to such an extent and in so able a way, that he found that unless he soon came to battle, he would be cut off from his bread and driven to a retreat beset by danger. He therefore called a council, as was usual. These Roman assemblies belie the saying that a council of war never fights, — the Romans held them and remained combative. They now decided to fight.

Next day Crassus drew up in two lines with the auxiliaries in the centre, and offered battle. But the enemy, though

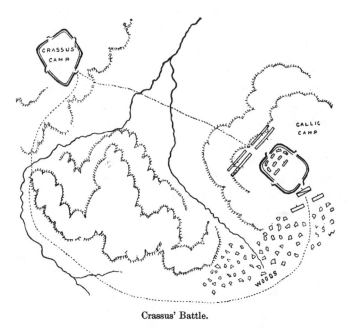

Crassus' Battle.

greatly superior in numbers, preferred their Fabian tactics, intending not to attack the Romans until they could force them into retreat for want of corn, and thus have them at a disadvantage, loaded down, as they would be, with their baggage. Crassus saw that there was nothing left but for himself to attack, though to assault fortifications was much

against the rule. This he did, relying greatly on the eagerness of his troops, who loudly demanded battle, and deemed
the barbarians to be afraid.

The enemy had occupied and intrenched a formidable
camp, in the Roman fashion. The attack was boldly made
on the front and flanks of the enemy's works. By a heavy
fire of missiles the Romans sought to drive the defenders
from the ramparts, so that an assault might be made with
success, if undertaken. The auxiliaries served to supply the
legionaries and light troops with stones and weapons, to bring
turf and material to fill the trench. While the battle was at
its height, Crassus was informed that the Decuman, or rear
gate of the enemy's camp, was not well guarded. Moreover,
as a rule, the rear of every camp was less well intrenched
than the front and flanks. Selecting the horse and such of
the cohorts as had been left to guard his own camp, and
were therefore fresh, Crassus sent this force, with promises
of great reward in case of success, by a long circuit and out
of sight, around to the rear. The barbarians had so little
anticipated this, that the Roman soldiers demolished the fortifications of the rear gate and filed into the enemy's camp,
before the bulk of the foe were aware of their being at hand.
The manœuvre was crowned with success. The Romans fell
upon the enemy's rear with loud shouts and blare of trumpets, encouraged by which the legionaries in front redoubled
the ardor of their fighting. No assault appears to have been
needed. The barbarians were unable to resist this double
onset. Terrified, they turned from the battle, cast themselves from the ramparts, and fled into the plains. Out of
their entire number of fifty thousand men, barely a fourth
escaped the sword of the Roman horse, which pursued them
across the open. This battle, fought in the fall of B. C. 56,
resulted in the submission of substantially all Aquitania.

The whole of Gaul had now been reduced, save only the land of the Morini and Menapii, which extended along the coast southerly from the mouth of the Rhine to modern Boulogne, the land which the Dutch have since so laboriously rescued from the ocean. These peoples had never sent ambassadors to Cæsar, and when he approached their territory, taught by defeat of other Gauls, they retired into the forests

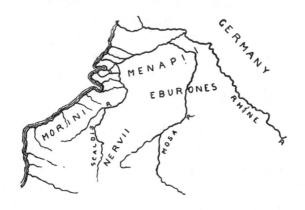

The Morini and Menapii.

and morasses of the coast and bade him defiance. Having no towns, but dwelling in tents or in caverns, this was to them no great hardship. Cæsar in person undertook to drive them from their lairs. Arrived at the edge of the forests bordering on the lowlands of the sea, the vicinity of St. Omer, inland from Calais, to which locality these tribes had removed all their possessions, some slight interchange of hostilities took place, the barbarians attacking the Romans while preparing to camp. Seeing that there was grave danger of ambuscades while advancing through the forests, Cæsar began to cut a wide swath for his line of operations and astonished the enemy beyond measure by the rapidity with which he laid the forest low. For their own poor tools enabled them to work but slowly. The cut timber Cæsar piled on either side of his path as a rampart. He had particularly good engineers (*præfecti fabrum*). Especially L. Cornelius Balbus and the knight Mamurra were noted for cleverness in enginery and sieges. This apparently vast undertaking testifies to the ability of these officers.

The Roman army, say the Commentaries, had already reached the rear of the retreating barbarian forces and had cut out a number of cattle and wagons from their train; but owing to the lateness of the season and the setting in of severe storms, Cæsar was obliged to defer his operations against the Morini and Menapii and to go into winter-quarters. After ravaging the country and burning such dwellings as there were, the troops were camped among the Aulerci and Lexovii on the coast between the Sequana and Liger (Normandy).

Cæsar gives the best complexion to this as to his other campaigns; but the truth is that he never entirely subjugated the northwest of Gaul. The Morini and Menapii were but prevented from spreading mischief. They remained independent.

To Cæsar belongs the credit of the intelligent cutting out of the work of this campaign. But the success of Sabinus and Crassus must remain their own. Their execution of Cæsar's plans came fully up to expectation, and redounds much to their credit. The outcome of Cæsar's fourth campaign, against the Veneti, must be set down in no small measure to the able conduct of Brutus with a quantum of good fortune added. No criticism can belittle the splendid achievements of Cæsar; neither must they be overestimated. With the best troops in the then world, perfect in discipline, commanded by officers trained in all the minutiæ of war, he was contending with peoples all but savage, unapt at regular war, disunited in counsel, and unable to put into the field forces much superior to the Romans in numbers, and in view of all conditions far inferior to them.

The fifth campaign, against the Morini, has been called one of pure ambition, quite unnecessary for the conquest of Gaul. But this does not so readily appear. The Rhine, the ocean and the Pyrenees were the only boundaries which Cæsar could set to his conquest of Gaul, if he was to make it at all; and without entering into the question of Cæsar's right to conquer a square rood of the country, it may be assumed that everything within those boundaries must be counted under the same head.

As usual, Cæsar personally returned to Cisalpine Gaul for the winter months of B. C. 56–55.

Light-Armed Soldier.

X.

THE RHINE. SPRING OF 55 B. C.

SOME German tribes, the Usipetes and Tenchtheri, had crossed the Rhine not far above its mouth, crowded from their homes by the Suevi, the most powerful of the Teutonic nations. Once in Gaul, they had advanced into the Vosegus country. Cæsar's plan necessitated a check to these barbarians, who had over one hundred thousand warriors. From his winter-quarters near Amiens, he marched to the Meuse in May. In the ensuing negotiations, the enemy acted, Cæsar claims, with duplicity. So, confessedly, did he. And when their ambassadors next came to his camp, he detained them, put his legions in order of battle, marched upon the unsuspecting Germans, surprised and put the entire body — four hundred and thirty thousand men, women and children — to the sword. A very few escaped across the Rhine. This is unquestionably the most atrocious act of which any civilized man has ever been guilty. It accomplished its end, but this fact does not palliate its enormity. Cæsar then built his celebrated bridge, and crossed the Rhine, probably near Bonn. The Suevi retired into the forests beyond their domain. After eighteen days he returned and broke down the bridge. The foray had no useful results.

AT the beginning of the next year, B. C. 55, there was an incursion across the Rhine, not far above its mouth, by some German tribes which three years before had been harassed and driven from their lands by the Suevi. They had wandered about in Germany during the three years and finally, as a last resort, had crossed the Rhine and devastated the land of the Menapii with great slaughter. The preceding winter (B. C. 56–55) had been spent there, and no one knew what their next movements might be.

The Suevi have been already mentioned. They had sent over the troops which Cæsar had defeated two years before under Ariovistus. They were a fierce and warlike people.

They subsisted on meat and milk rather than corn, were great hunters, and celebrated for their strength and stature. In the coldest weather they wore nothing but skins which scantily covered their bodies, and constantly bathed in the open rivers. Their cavalry was drilled to dismount and fight on foot, the horses being trained to remain where left, until the riders could again rejoin them. They used no housings upon their horses, and presumably, like the Numidians, no bridle, despised luxury and forbade wine. On the east side of this people the territory was said to be devastated for six hundred miles; on the west they bordered, among other peoples, on the Ubii, whom they had reduced to the payment of tribute. It was some of these Ubian tribes, the Usipetes and Tenchtheri, which had now forced a passage of the Rhine to the number of four hundred and thirty thousand souls, and had advanced some distance inland. It was thought, and truly, that this advance had been made with the consent of some of the Gauls, who hoped by this immigration to be able to increase their power of opposing the Romans. The place of crossing was probably near modern Cleves and Xanten, which were opposite their territory. On the left bank, from Xanten down, is a chain of heights some thirty miles long, at the foot of which the river used to flow. Two gaps pierce these heights, at Xanten and near Cleves. That these passes were used by the Germans in their incursions is shown by their having been fortified by the Romans after the conquest. The Usipetes and Tenchtheri had moved forward nearly to the Mosa (Meuse).

Cæsar joined his legions in Normandy in April, B. C. 55, earlier than usual. He determined to make immediate war upon these Germans, who, justified by the invitation of sundry Gallic tribes, had already made incursions as far as the Eburones and Condrusi, the latter clients of the Treviri.

He mobilized his army in the early spring, from his winter-quarters between the Sequana and Liger. Calling together the tribes of the vicinity at Samarobriva (Amiens), he wisely

Normandy to the Rhine.

refrained from accusing them of complicity with this incursion, but used his powers of persuasion to such effect as to secure from them victual, a goodly number of auxiliary troops, and especially a fine body of five thousand horse. From the winter-quarters of his legions, Cæsar probably rendezvoused, early in May, at Amiens, and thence marched to Cambrai, Charleroi, Tongres and Maestricht, where he crossed the Mosa towards the end of the month. This would have been his most natural route. There was need of prompt measures. The danger was imminent. There must have been over one hundred thousand warriors among these migrating peoples.

Before he reached the Mosa, Cæsar met ambassadors sent by the Germans, who were authorized to treat, provided Cæsar would consent to their keeping the lands they had already conquered. But this Cæsar would by no means permit, informing them that they must go back across the Rhine, where, he suggested, the Ubii, who dwelt near modern Cologne, would now grant them territory willingly; for this tribe had begged his aid against the Suevi, and stood ready to perform his behests. The German ambassadors pretended to assent to these terms, but asked Cæsar to delay his advance for a short space until they could report to their senate and return. This delay Cæsar would not grant, as, according to the Commentaries, he believed that they desired only to gain time until their horse, which had gone on a distant raid among the Ambivariti beyond the Mosa for provision, could return. Crossing the Mosa and continuing his advance to within some twelve miles of the enemy, Cæsar, perhaps near Straelen, again met the ambassadors, who made similar excuses, and prayed for a delay of at least three days, when the tribes would cross the Rhine if the Ubii bound themselves by oath to receive them.

It was early in June. Cæsar had left the vicinity of the Mosa, and had probably advanced beyond modern Venloo. The Usipetes and Tenchtheri were on the levels near Goch on the Niers River. He agreed to advance but four miles, to the nearest place where he could get water for the army. If our topographical assumption is so far correct, this was the Niers. No sooner had his cavalry moved forward to its vicinity than the Germans attacked this body with some eight hundred horse and threw it back in disorder, killing seventy-four of their number. Their tactics were peculiar. They "made an onset on our men and soon threw them into disorder. When our men in their turn made a stand, they according to their practice leaped from their horses to their feet, and, stabbing our horses in the belly and overturning a great many of our men, put the rest to flight, and drove them forward so much alarmed that they did not desist from their retreat till they had come in sight of our army." This looks like a serious case of fright. The attack appears to

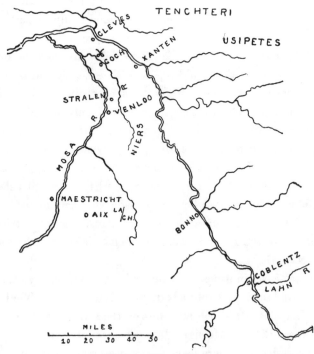

Rhine and Meuse Region.

have been caused by some misunderstanding. It seems curious that five thousand of the Roman allied horse should have been thus driven back by so small a force. The attack must have been vigorously made and weakly met. This German horse was always a fighting arm. Irritated at the defeat, Cæsar determined to avenge it as an act of treachery, for, as he explains, the attack had been made while the ambassadors were still treating, and a truce existed; "after having sued for peace by way of stratagem and treachery, they had made war without provocation." He at once proceeded to do the same act he so heartily condemns, paying no heed to explanations or apologies.

The next day the Germans again sent a large embassy to apologize for the yesterday's misadventure; but Cæsar construed the act to be for the original purpose of obtaining a further truce till their still absent horse could arrive. The ambassadors Cæsar detained, and putting his army in three lines, probably in columns by cohorts, with the cavalry beaten the previous day in the rear, moved forward the intervening eight miles at a double-quick, and reaching their camp in an incredibly short time, took the Germans entirely by surprise, and fell on them with fury. Such was their consternation that, after a short resistance by a few who were not panic-stricken, the Germans threw away their arms and fled in all directions. The cavalry was sent in pursuit and drove the fugitives into the *cul de sac* formed by the confluence of the Mosa and Rhine. Here those who did not perish by the sword threw themselves into the river and were mostly drowned. Few succeeded in getting across. All, including women and children, were indiscriminately butchered, to the number of four hundred and thirty thousand souls. The whole nation was exterminated, save only the absent cavalry, and but a few Romans were wounded.

This whole campaign lacks clearness in the Commentaries. Florus confuses it still more by placing the defeat of the Usipetes and Tenchtheri in the confluence of the Moselle and Rhine, and Dion Cassius by stating that Cæsar reached them among the Treviri. This latter has been the theory of many, who, in compiling their data, stray unwarranted from the Commentaries. The country in the Moselle-Rhine angle is much cut up, has no traces of ancient roads, and could scarcely have supported these tribes. To conduct his march on the theory that he reached the enemy there, Cæsar would have been led through the Forest of Ardennes, a fact which he does not mention, as he most likely would have done. It looks more probable that the situation was as described, and that, on learning of Cæsar's approach, the Usipetes and Tenchtheri withdrew their foragers and retired towards their base among the Menapii. To cross the Rhine near the Moselle would have led them to their enemies, the Ubii; and to make them head that way is an improbable assumption.

This awful act in the Gallic drama has uniformly received the severest condemnation of thinking men. None of the extensive acts of retaliation of Alexander, not all the deeds of Punic cruelty charged upon Hannibal by his bitterest enemies during his fifteen years in Italy put together, can equal the sum of destruction of human life here wantonly exhibited. Unlike some of the holocausts of Alexander, — which were required for his own and his army's safety at the distance from his base at which he found himself, — this slaughter appears to have been absolutely uncalled for. If the barbarians broke the laws of international intercourse, Cæsar had done the like. So indignant were his political enemies in Rome, that Cato openly proposed that Cæsar's head should be sent to the surviving Usipetes and Tenchtheri in expiation of his attack while their ambassadors were in his camp. Perhaps no more inexcusable act was ever perpetrated. Even the plausible tone of the Commentaries quite fails to convey an extenuation.

The unnecessarily harsh measures of Cæsar would not be thus insisted on were it not that of all the great soldiers of antiquity, the one least deserving the accusation, Hannibal, has come down to us bearing the reproach of cruelty. That the charge is unjust has been abundantly proven. It may be that none of these captains can be properly taxed with inhumanity; that the trait belongs to the age and not to the men. But if cruelty is to be imputed to any of them, it is certain that, of the three great captains of antiquity, Cæsar was by far the most reprehensible, Hannibal the least.

Having accomplished this "brilliant success," as Napoleon III. phrases it, Cæsar determined, as a means of imposing on the Germans, to cross the Rhine, so that those tribes which were still unconvinced of his power might feel that they were not safe from Cæsar's reach even in their own territory. He deemed it wise to show the Germans that no obstacle, natural or national, could arrest the Roman arms, and to make them see that, however distant, they could be reached and punished if they indulged in any more incursions into Gaul.

The occasion was good. The party of cavalry which had been on a raid at the time of the destruction of the Usipetes and Tenchtheri had retired across the Rhine and joined the Sugambri, which was one of the most powerful tribes between where the modern Ruhr and Sieg join the Rhine. Cæsar sent and demanded their surrender by the Sugambri, as belonging to those who had treacherously attacked the Romans. This demand was refused, and at the same time the Ubii sent again to beg for aid against the Suevi, who were grievously oppressing them. They offered all their ships for transportation across the river, but this means Cæsar neither deemed safe, nor, says he, was it consistent with the dignity of the Roman republic to depend on others.

This invasion of German soil was dictated solely by ambition. It was beyond Cæsar's province. Without an unprecedented construction of the rule of the Roman Senate, he had indeed no authority to go beyond Gaul. Under the then well-understood laws of nations, he had no right to attack a tribe which had committed no covert or overt act of hostility against himself or Rome, other than the right of conquest. This it is not desired to deny to him.   So much is said of his rights and motives only to brush away the often made assertion that Cæsar was actuated by no motive save the patriotic one of defending the Roman republic.

The refusal of the ships and the project of building a

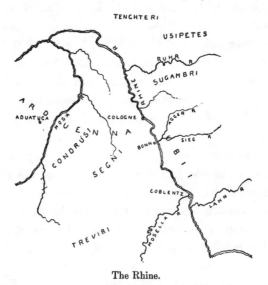

The Rhine.

bridge was probably the result of a desire to have a perfectly secure means of returning to Gaul in case of any reverse. This was wise.   But it is a question whether the invasion itself was wise.   In Gaul, Cæsar had of course maintained the offensive, as he must, if he was to subdue the whole country.   But it is scarcely doubtful that the best military policy beyond the borders of Gaul was a strict defensive, especially at so distinct a natural barrier as the Rhine.   He had made an example of all who had crossed it into Gaul, and this was sufficient.

The location of the bridge has been much disputed.   It

cannot be absolutely proven. The confluence of the Rhine and Moselle below modern Coblentz has many advocates. Those who place the slaughter of the Usipetes and Tenchtheri at this place naturally favor it as the crossing point. Some authorities put the passage as far down the river as Cologne.

There is reason for selecting Bonn as the crossing point. The fact given in the Commentaries, that Cæsar passed from the land of the Treviri to that of the Ubii, would suit many localities. But he was at no great distance from the Sugambri, and the confluence of the Moselle and Rhine is far above the territory of this people. The next year but one, having crossed "a little above" the present bridge, Cæsar started from the Rhine and marched to Aduatuca (Tongres) through the forest of Arduenna, from east to west, near by the Segni and Condrusi. From Cologne he would have marched north of these peoples; from Coblentz, south. The bed of the Rhine about Bonn is well suited for piles; south of Bonn it is more rocky, and the mountainous banks would make the location less desirable for a bridge. Fifty years later, as we are told by Florus, Drusus crossed at this place to attack the Sugambri; and Drusus would likely have profited by Cæsar's experience. The probabilities run strongly in favor of Bonn.

To rapidly build a bridge at this point over the Rhine, without previous preparation or a bridge train, is to-day no contemptible engineering feat. The river is over a quarter of a mile wide. Cæsar accomplished the task in ten days from the time when he began to cut the timber. It was mid-June. The bridge was supported on piles driven into the bed of the river and held firmly in place by cross pieces and braces. His own description is clear: "He devised this plan of a bridge. He joined together at the distance of two feet, two piles, each a foot and a half thick, sharpened a little at the lower end, and proportioned in length to the depth of the river. After he had, by means of engines, sunk these into the river, and fixed them at the bottom and then driven them in with rammers, not quite perpendicularly, like a stake, but bending forward and sloping, so as to incline in the direction of the current of the river; he also placed two (other piles) opposite to these, at the distance of forty feet lower down, fastened together in the same manner, but directed against the force and current of the river. Both these, moreover, were kept firmly apart by beams two feet thick

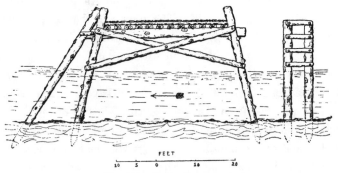

FEET

The Rhine Bridge (cross section).

(the space which the binding of the piles occupied), laid in at their extremities between two braces on each side; and in consequence of these being in different directions and fastened on sides the one opposite to the other, so great was the strength of the work, and such the arrangement of the materials, that in proportion as the greater body of water dashed against the bridge, so much the closer were its parts held fastened together. These beams were bound together by timber laid over them in the direction of the length of the, bridge, and were (then) covered over with laths and hurdles; and, in addition to this, piles were driven into the water obliquely, at the lower side of the bridge, and these

serving as buttresses, and being connected with every portion
of the work, sustained the force of the stream; and there were
others also above the bridge at a moderate distance, that if

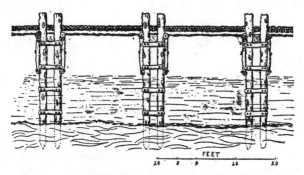

The Rhine Bridge (elevation).

trunks of trees or vessels were floated down the river by the
barbarians for the purpose of destroying the work, the violence of such things might be diminished by these defenses,

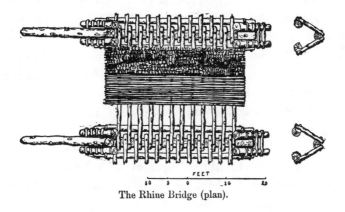

The Rhine Bridge (plan).

and might not injure the bridge." Plans best describe
the structure.

Engineering feats are measured largely by the amount of
available material and labor. As Cæsar had all the men he

could use and more, as the material was close at hand, and as the form of bridge was one well-known to the Romans, the construction is noted chiefly for its great size and the remarkable speed with which it was accomplished. And it has already been stated that Cæsar had exceptionally good engineers. He did not have to contend with opposition to his passage.

Having completed the structure and posting a strong guard at either end in a suitable bridgehead, Cæsar led his army across and moved up the Sieg and Agger. Several nations at once offered submission; the Sugambri retired from their territory with all their wealth, "and concealed themselves in deserts and woods." Cæsar devastated their country, and marched into the land of the Ubii. This fact also points to the vicinity of Bonn as the crossing-place. Had it been at Coblentz, he would have been in Ubian territory on reaching the right bank.

Among the Ubii, Cæsar learned that the Suevi had also sent away all their possessions and wives and children; had collected all their fighting men at a spot about the centre of their land, a number of days' march to the east, and were awaiting the arrival of the Romans. But having, as the Commentaries state, accomplished all he intended, and having spent eighteen days beyond the Rhine, Cæsar returned to Gaul and broke down the bridge.

He had really accomplished nothing. He had not recovered the cavalry demanded of the Sugambri; he had done no more than promise help to the Ubii; he had failed to attack the Suevi. The question arises whether he would not have stood better in the eyes of the Germans if he had not crossed at all, except, indeed, for their wonder at the bridge. In a military sense, he would, perhaps, have acted more wisely if he had remained in Gaul. This land had been sufficiently defended by twice driving the Germans back across the Rhine with so savage a punishment; his invasion of the German territory had brought absolutely no result. In fact, it may be said, that his failure to accomplish anything on the east shore of the Rhine must have tended to lower his standing among the Germans. But his reputation in Rome and his self-esteem had been greatly raised by the performance, to which his letters, as well as the Commentaries, lent great lustre. And his friends in Rome had something to offset against the avalanche of reproach with which his enemies sought to overwhelm him for his slaughter of the Usipetes and Tenchtheri. The passage of the Rhine was as splendid a subject to enlarge on as it was, in a certain sense, a brilliant achievement.

Gallic Horseman.
(From a Sarcophagus.)

XI.

BRITAIN. FALL OF 55 B. C.

CÆSAR had the traveler's instinct. To invade Britain was even less a part of his Gallic problem than to cross the Rhine. But he determined to see that island, and a pretext — that they had given help to resisting Gallic tribes — was readily conjured up. He sought information from merchants and leading Gauls and sent a subordinate over to Britain to prospect; but he learned little. He shipped two legions and some cavalry in transports and crossed in August. He reached the Dover cliffs and actually landed at Deal, though with difficulty, owing to the warlike opposition of the Britons. After a few days, a storm damaged the fleet; the Britons attacked Cæsar, but were defeated; a peace was patched up; hostages were promised, who were never delivered; and having accomplished nothing whatever except as a discoverer, Cæsar returned to Gaul. He had run great risk of being cut off, and had illy provided against probable contingencies. There is little commendable in a military sense in the first invasion of Britain. It had no connection with the Gallic theatre of war.

THOUGH the season was well advanced — it was late in the summer — Cæsar determined to move over to Britain, "because," as he says, "he discovered that in almost all the wars with the Gauls succors had been furnished to our enemy from that country; and even if the time of year should be insufficient for carrying on the war, yet he thought it would be of great service to him if he only entered the island and saw into the character of the people, and got knowledge of their localities, harbors and landing-places, all which were, for the most part, unknown to the Gauls." This explanation has the look of an afterthought. The fact of British aid to the Gauls seems doubtful, and rests almost entirely on this statement and another that the Suessiones, under Divitiacus, had extended their control to Britain.

It is probable that Cæsar had a good deal of the traveler's instinct in addition to his ambition, and desired to know something about the island and its people, its harbors, resources and accessibility. Plutarch and Dion Cassius agree that the expedition against Britain was of no use to Rome. Suetonius says Cæsar was in search for pearls, a rather weak motive. Any reason, good or bad, which could plausibly be used, sufficed for a *casus belli* when Cæsar wished to invade a country. And so it was with Britain. Returning to the coast in July, and calling to him all the merchants he could find, he interrogated them, and ascertained that these people knew only that part of the British coast which was immediately opposite to Gaul, and little indeed of that, inasmuch as they had never been able to go inland, and had traded only in one or two places.

Cæsar's description of Britain is vague, but good considering the difficulties of obtaining information. He thought the climate of Britain more temperate than that of Gaul. The same products of the soil were known, but ripened more slowly. The population was considerable, and the east and south coasts had been peopled by the Belgæ, who had crossed the Channel for spoil and ended by settling in Britain. Cantium (Kent) had thus been settled. Each tribe had its king. Cæsar mentions the Trinobantes, in modern Essex and Middlesex, whose oppidum was no doubt London; the Cenimagni in Suffolk; the Segontiaci in Hampshire and Berkshire; the Bibroci in Sussex and Surrey; the Ancalites and the Cassii farther north. The Britons were, on the whole, less advanced in civilization than the Gauls. Their habitations were huts of wood and rough thatch. They buried their corn in underground vaults. Their towns were mere places of refuge in forests, defended by a ditch and rampart. They had the same bodily structure as the Gauls, but the Britons were taller and bolder, with long blond, rather than red hair. They wore skins and lived on flesh and milk, with little vegetable food. They painted their bodies blue with woad. Polyandry was common. They sold tin to the Phœnicians at a very early age, but relied on foreign nations for bronze. They had no ships. Their religion was Druidical. They fought with long swords and small bucklers, and skirmished, rather than fought in masses, as the Gauls did. Their chariots were numerous and able.

As Cæsar could ascertain little about Britain, he sent Caius Volusenus with a ship of war to make a rapid examination of the coast, to ascertain what harbors there might be for a large fleet, and something about the peoples, their system of war and customs. He ordered the fleet to assemble in one of the harbors of the Morini,— later Portus Itius,

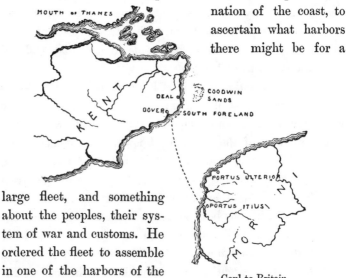

Gaul to Britain.

not improbably Boulogne, though it cannot be taken as settled,— whither he himself, by steady marches from the Rhine, repaired with all his forces, and commanded to be brought many ships from all directions, including those with which he had fought the Veneti. While this was going on, several tribes from Britain, who had, no doubt, heard through merchants of Cæsar's victories, and of his preparations to invade their land, sent in their offers of submission. These ambassadors he received with courtesy, and sent back with them Commius, a Gallic chief, whom Cæsar had made king of the Atrebates, and in whom he reposed great confidence. This man, Cæsar says, stood high in the sight of many leading Britons. Commius was to visit as many of the British tribes as he could; make them familiar with Cæsar's exploits; tell them what manner of people the Romans were; satisfy them that the new-comers would be friends and not foes; and say that Cæsar in person would shortly arrive.

Volusenus brought back his report in five days. He had not even landed. He had seen and could tell but little. This brief time, and apparent lack of push, had enabled him to catch but a glimpse of the coast.

The Morini had luckily given in their submission and surrendered numerous hostages, excusing their late resistance on the score of want of knowledge of the Romans. This had been done without a further campaign, which Cæsar had anticipated; there was now no enemy left to prejudice his rear. He had, during August, provided eighty transports, which sufficed for the two legions, the Seventh and Tenth, presumably under Galba and Labienus, which he proposed to take with him, to be escorted by a suitable number of war galleys. The two legions must have been less than ten thousand strong. The horse, four hundred and fifty effective, was marched to and embarked on eighteen transports from another harbor some eight miles up the coast, Portus Ulterior (Ambleteuse), where, in addition to some tardiness, they had been held by contrary winds. The quæstor, the legates and præfects were divided up among the men of war, in such a manner that each had a certain number under his charge. The rest of the army Cæsar left with Titurius Sabinus and

Arunculeius Cotta to hold head against those coast-tribes of the Menapii and Morini which had not yet so frankly submitted as to make him feel confident he could trust them unwatched. A garrison under Sulpicius Rufus was also left in camp in the harbor of departure.

Cæsar set sail with the first favorable wind, towards the end of August, B. C. 55, and in a few hours (one to ten A. M.) arrived on the British shore opposite the chalk cliffs of Dover. In Cæsar's day the sea came so close to the cliffs that a dart thrown from the top would reach the tide-covered beach: but by about 950 A. D., the old port had been quite blocked up by alluvium. As this spot did not appear to be a good place for landing, after cautioning his officers to act promptly in their orders, he sailed — at about three P. M. — some seven miles farther up the coast, doubling, according to Dion Cassius, a lofty promontory, no doubt South Foreland, and stopped at Deal.

The Britons, who had assembled in great numbers on the shore to oppose his landing, guessed his intention and followed up his movement, sending cavalry and chariots on ahead. Their opposition to the landing of the Romans was very spirited. This they conducted by advancing into the water and casting their javelins at the Roman legionaries as they attempted to land. The men thus found it difficult to get out of the boats, because these drew too much water to get close to shore, and they themselves were heavy-armed and laden with camp-gear. Cæsar, to escape from this dilemma, sent some ships of war to a cove close by, where, with sling-stones, arrows and engines he could attack the Britons in flank. This diversion surprised them and obliged them to retire somewhat up the beach. Perceiving that the soldiers were still slow to land, the standard-bearer of the Tenth legion leaped into the waves with the legionary eagle, and

called on the men to follow him if they would not see their
sacred emblem captured by the enemy under their very eyes.
The soldiers of the Tenth at once swarmed to the shore,
which example so encouraged the whole body of the Romans
that they speedily leaped into the water to drive away the
enemy.

"The battle was maintained vigorously on both sides.
Our men, however, as they could neither keep their ranks,
nor get firm footing, nor follow their standards, and as one
from one ship and another from another assembled around
whatever standard they met, were thrown into great confusion. But the enemy, who were acquainted with all the
shallows, when from the shore they saw any coming from a
ship one by one, spurred on their horses and attacked them
while embarrassed; many surrounded a few, others threw
their weapons upon our collected forces on their exposed
flank. When Cæsar observed this, he ordered the boats of
the ships of war and the spy-sloops to be filled with soldiers
and sent them up to the succor of those whom he had observed in distress. Our men, as soon as they made good
their footing on dry ground, and all their comrades had
joined them, made an attack upon the enemy, and put them
to flight, but could not pursue them very far, because the
horse had not been able to maintain their course at sea and
reach the island. This alone was wanting to Cæsar's accustomed success."

It is little items like these which enable one to draw a comparison between the ancient and modern soldier. To read
of a disembarkation of troops to-day, under heavy fire, conducted in such a haphazard way, where each man appeared
to consult his own ideas of prudence or courage instead of
acting under the orders of his officers, would savor of absurdity. Discipline of old was good, but even under Cæsar it

did not seem to reach the grade of the best discipline of to-day; that is, what they called discipline was a different thing from ours.

The particular tribe of Britons which had been thus beaten concluded to sue for peace, and there came back with the British ambassadors Commius, whom Cæsar had sent into Britain with the messengers that had been dispatched to him into Gaul. This man the Britons had seized and thrown into chains, a fact which seems to deny the influence the Commentaries claim that Commius had in Britain. The Britons now returned Commius with pretended excuses for their conduct, saying that the multitude had overwhelmed them. The apparent complete submission of these coast-tribes constrained Cæsar to forgive this breach of the law of nations. He felt that he was not strong enough to do less. He took some hostages and required more. These were promised, but not presently delivered. Thus in four days after the legions had landed, a peace was patched up with the peoples who inhabited the shore line on which he had landed, to wit, Kent.

The cavalry, which had sailed in eighteen transports from another port, reached the coast, but met with a serious storm near by. They were unable to land, though they tried to do so, and returned to Gaul. At the same time a very high tide destroyed and damaged a large number of the vessels in which the legions had crossed the Channel. This was the season of full moon and high tides, at the end of August, 55 B. C. The Romans had not drawn their ships far enough up on the shore. The war-galleys had been beached; the transports were riding at anchor. The heavy seas filled the galleys and dashed the transports one against the other. Those that were not crushed lost their anchors, tackling and sails. The inability to repair this loss, and the fact that the Romans had not corn enough to winter in Britain, not only caused a certain feeling of insecurity among the soldiery, but afforded the Britons an opportunity to reconsider their action in submitting to Cæsar. Therefore, instead of bringing in their promised hostages, they conferred together, and agreed to attack Cæsar's camp, in the belief that if they could destroy this army, none other would ever cross to Britain. Cæsar's camp was small. The legionaries had come without much baggage. Cæsar, we hear, had but three servants with him, though this does not give one much of an idea of the general impedimenta. The barbarians saw he had no cavalry and had lost many ships. The opportunity looked favorable to expel him.

Suspecting, though not informed of their designs, Cæsar made provision against every probable contingency, and saw personally to it that the discipline of the camp was stringently enforced. Peace was not ruptured, and the barbarians went to and fro in the Roman quarters. The ships were duly repaired — for there were numberless shipwrights in the expedition — by using the seasoned timber and the brass of the worst damaged ones to repair the rest. Such materials as had been lost in the wreckage were sent for to the continent. Only twelve remained unfit for further use.

Not long after, the Seventh legion, having gone out as usual to forage at the only place left near by where the wheat had not been cut, was attacked by the enemy from an ambush while the men were scattered filling their sacks. This legion, surrounded by a host of cavalry and chariots, was on the point of succumbing, for the novelty of the dashing chariots and the strange shouts given by the Britons had greatly demoralized the men. They had huddled together in a mass, and the barbarians were casting weapons on them from all sides. Even the Gallic wars had not yet made them proof to panic.

"Their mode of fighting with their chariots is this: firstly, they drive about in all directions and throw their weapons, and generally break the ranks of the enemy with the very dread of their horses and the noise of their wheels; and when they have worked themselves in between the troops of horse, leap from their chariots and engage on foot. The charioteers in the mean time withdraw some little distance from the battle, and so place themselves with the chariots that, if their masters are overpowered by the number of the enemy, they may have a ready retreat to their own troops. Thus they display in battle the speed of horse, together with the firmness of infantry; and by daily practice and exercise attain to such expertness that they are accustomed, even on a declining and steep place, to check their horses at full speed, and manage and turn them in an instant, and run along the pole and stand on the yoke, and thence betake themselves, with the greatest celerity, to their chariots again."

Cæsar, perceiving that something was wrong from the great clouds of dust which could be seen from the camp, had speeded to the assistance of the legion attacked, with those cohorts of the Tenth which happened to be on duty. Disengaging it by a vigorous assault on the Britons, who promptly retreated, he deemed it wise to retire at once to the shelter of the camp. The Seventh legion had lost heavily. For several days no further action was taken on account of the rainy weather; Cæsar was kept close to the limits of his works preparing for a further attack; while the Britons collected troops from all the neighboring tribes, urging that now was their opportunity to redeem their cause. Cæsar had no cavalry save about thirty horsemen brought over by Commius, but he determined nevertheless to engage the enemy so soon as his troops were again in proper condition. He thought he could accomplish something with even thirty

horsemen. After the lapse of a few days, the Britons made
a demonstration on the camp. Cæsar drew up his legions
in its front with the purpose of accepting battle. But the
Britons, though they made a smart assault, were unable long
to withstand the well-drilled ranks of the legions, and being
routed and pursued, lost many men; whereupon the Romans
devastated the vicinity and returned to camp.

The Britons now again sued for peace, which Cæsar deemed
it wise to grant after doubling the number of hostages they
were to furnish. And, no doubt fearing that he could not
enforce their present delivery, he ordered these to be brought
over to the continent by a given time. Then, the autumnal
equinox being near at hand, which Cæsar desired not to
encounter at sea, he embarked and safely reached the shores
of Gaul. He had been less than three weeks in Britain.

Two ships were, however, carried farther down the coast.
The three hundred soldiers in these, after safely landing,
were on the march to rejoin the main army, when they were
surrounded and attacked by some warriors belonging to the
Morini, who were shortly reinforced up to six thousand men.
The legionaries defended themselves manfully, drawn up in a
circle for nearly four hours, until Cæsar's cavalry, which he
had sent out in quest of them, happened at the eleventh hour
to come to the rescue. The Morini were penned in by the
cavalry and large numbers were killed.

For this act of the Morini speedy vengeance was taken.
Labienus, with the Seventh and Tenth legions, just back
from Britain, marched into their land, and, as the morasses
were almost dry at this season, was able to reach and capture
all the tribes which had taken part in the attack. These
were no doubt summarily dealt with.

The legions under Sabinus and Cotta, which had been sent
out among the Menapii, had been unable to hunt up the

natives in their forest retreats. Having, therefore, mowed down all the crops and burned the habitations, they returned to camp.

The limited effect of Cæsar's invasion of Britain is well shown by the fact that out of all the tribes who handed in their submission, only two sent over the hostages demanded. The peace and its security had been a mere farce.

Cæsar now took up winter-quarters among the Belgæ, and, returning himself to Rome, was decreed a thanksgiving of twenty days. This decree was, however, violently opposed by his enemies under leadership of Cato, who depreciated or laughed at his performances as much as his friends extolled and overrated them.

It cannot be claimed that the campaigns of this year had been brilliant. The crossing of both the Rhine and the Channel had been without result. In the former case this has already been pointed out. The campaign into Britain is subject to equal criticism. Cæsar's preparations for crossing were lamentably wanting. He had too few ships; he sailed without his cavalry, absolutely essential among tribes which had chariots and horses in plenty. The expedition may be said to have been undertaken in a happy-go-lucky way.

The invasion of Britain was no part of Cæsar's military scheme so far as concerned the mere protection of Rome by the conquest of Gaul. But Cæsar was looking to his own interests quite as much as to those of Rome. To him his own success was Rome's. Each conquered land enhanced his reputation and might add to his riches; fame and wealth furthered his political aspirations. This ambition was proper enough. It is what has inspired some of the greatest of men and soldiers. But it was the ambition of a Napoleon, not of a Gustavus. It led to over-rapid operations, not carefully planned, the results, or rather the lack of failure of which are

largely due to good fortune. The most necessary elements of
the work of a great captain are: a distinct conception of his
plan; scrupulous preparation for what he undertakes; and
courage tempered with caution in its execution. He should
not undertake operations without full consideration of what
every step may mean. These elements scarcely appeared in
either the German or British campaign of this year. Cæsar's
right to go to Britain he based upon an unproven, perhaps
quite improbable assertion, that the Britons had aided the
Gauls during his campaign against them. He made no pretense of examining the ground. Volusenus, sailing alone
along the coast, could at best bring him but little information — quite insufficient to warrant him in risking his
two legions. His preparations and conduct were deficient in
that he left no force whose special duty it was to protect his
return should he be driven back; that he carried along no
victuals or baggage; that he left his cavalry to come behind
in a haphazard way; that he had no vessels in reserve; that
he apparently knew nothing about the ebb and flow of the
tide on the shores of Britain, or had not thought of it;
that he inflicted harm on the enemy rather than gained an
advantage himself ; and that he showed an unnecessary
cruelty against the Britons as he had against the Gauls
and Germans. Some of the best critics go so far as to say
that both campaigns of this year were awkward and deficient
in conception and execution, and were as far from useful as
from glorious. Had Alexander planned his steps after this
fashion, he would never have penetrated beyond the edge of
the Persian empire; had Hannibal contrived his work in
Italy as carelessly, he would not have held his own for one
campaign. Indeed, it may be said that Cæsar's good star
was at the bottom of his coming out whole.

And yet, if viewed in the light of reconnoissances in force, to ascertain, in unknown lands, what he might be able to do with a stronger expedition thereafter, perhaps both these campaigns may be absolved from such criticism. On no other ground, however, are they even tenable. But is the commander-in-chief, whose death would mean the destruction of his army, warranted in leading such a reconnoissance in person?

Gallic Swords.

XII.

CASSIVELLAUNUS. SPRING AND SUMMER, 54 B. C.

Not satisfied with his first trip to Britain, Cæsar prepared to cross again. This time he took better precautions, though there is little to justify either invasion from a military point of view. In all he had eight hundred craft, carrying eight legions and four thousand horse. The balance of his force he left on the Gallic coast under Labienus, to protect his base. He set sail in July, landed safely, and marched inland to attack the Britons. Once more a storm damaged the fleet. Cæsar returned, hauled up the fleet on the beach, intrenched it, and again set out. After several engagements with the Britons, he forced a passage of the Thames near Kingston. Cassivellaunus, who commanded the Britons, opposed him ably, but Cæsar marched as far as St. Albans, for many tribes deserted the national standard, and Cassivellaunus was unable to do much to check him. When Cæsar was at a distance, the tribes in the rear attacked the fleet camp and compelled his retreat. Cæsar recognized that there was nothing for him to gain by subduing the island. He had seen what manner of land and people there were in Britain. He retired, having accomplished much as a traveler, nothing as a soldier, and returned to Gaul in two embarkations without accident.

Cæsar had not yet satisfied his curiosity with regard to Britain. When leaving for Italy to attend to political affairs after the campaign of the preceding year, he commanded his lieutenants to construct as many new vessels as possible during the winter, and to have the old ones well repaired, purposing to cross the Channel a second time. He planned the new ships himself, making them somewhat broader, so as better to accommodate the cavalry and other burden, and with lower sides, so as to be more easily loaded and unloaded. They could also be more readily drawn up on the beach. These, as described by Cæsar, were for a similar purpose substantially imitated by Napoleon, in 1804, showing

the conditions to have remained practically the same for the
intervening centuries. They were fitted to row or to sail.
The equipments were brought from Spain. No doubt Cæsar
recognized the failure and faults in his first invasion of Britain. No man was more ready to profit by his own or his
opponent's errors than he. This is really one of Cæsar's
strong points, though in writing the Commentaries he is unapt
to acknowledge as much. He determined that he would do
the work over again in a more business-like manner, so that
it might not only add to the dominion of Rome, but to his
own reputation in such a fashion as to silence those wordy
and troublesome adversaries who had laughed at his first
expedition.

During Cæsar's winter absence from his Gallic legions, he
was called on to settle what promised to prove a warlike
question in Illyricum. The Pirustæ had been laying waste
the boundaries of that province. To meet the emergency
Cæsar at once began to raise troops. But seeing his promptness and having heard of his Gallic exploits, the Pirustæ sent
ambassadors to make their peace, praying humbly for pardon,
and offering to make compensation for all damage committed.
These terms were accepted, for Cæsar did not wish to turn
from the Gallic problem, and hostages were given for their
performance.

On returning to his Gallic army in June, Cæsar found that
about six hundred transports and twenty-eight ships of war
had been constructed or repaired and made ready to launch.
Strabo says he had established a naval arsenal at the mouth
of the Sequana. Ordering the fleet, when ready, to rendezvous and await his arrival at Portus Itius, which was the
nearest harbor, as he supposed, to Britain, he himself took
four legions without baggage and eight hundred horse, and
marched against the Treviri, who were threatening trouble,

and it was said had again invited the Germans across the Rhine. There is no clue to which legions he took. The Treviri, we remember, were very numerous and strong in cavalry, and occupied territory bordering on the great river. Two chiefs, Indutiomarus and Cingetorix, his son-in-law, were contending among the Treviri for the upper hand in the government. Indutiomarus placed in the Ardennes forest all the people incapable of bearing arms, raised an army and prepared to fight. But when many chiefs deserted him to make submission to Cæsar, he concluded to do the like. Cæsar gave the power to Cingetorix, who had been singularly attached to him. This made of Indutiomarus an implacable enemy. Both having brought in their submission and delivered up two hundred hostages, including Indutiomarus' relatives, Cæsar, being anxious to go to Britain, settled the matter for the time being, though leaving the two chieftains unreconciled, and returned to Portus Itius. His trip had consumed the month of June.

Here he found that all the ships, save forty, which had not been able to reach this port from the Matrona, where they were built, stood ready for sailing. He had six hundred transports and twenty-eight galleys, plus a number of private barks, eight hundred in all. In order to leave less chance of trouble in the rear during his coming absence, he proposed to carry with him nearly all the Gallic horse, numbering four thousand men. They would be in the nature of hostages for the good behavior of the tribes to which they belonged. With them he also insisted upon taking Dumnorix, the chief of the Ædui, a man "fond of change, fond of power, possessing great resolution and great influence among the Gauls," with whom he had heretofore had difficulty, for Dumnorix was aiming at the chieftaincy of the Ædui, and the autocracy of Gaul. This man used every artifice to persuade Cæsar to leave him behind, and finally, unable to accomplish his purpose, he broke out into open revolt and rode away with the whole cavalry force of the Ædui. Though Cæsar had been detained twenty-five days waiting for a favorable wind, and one had just begun to blow, he saw that he could not for a moment temporize with so grave a matter. He sent the bulk of his horse in pursuit. The fugitives were caught up with, and the mutiny came to a speedy termination by the killing of Dumnorix; for the commanders of the pursuing troops had been ordered to bring him back, dead or alive.

Cæsar made much more careful preparations for his present descent on Britain, and for the protection of his rear. There were assembled at Boulogne eight legions and four thousand cavalry. His legate, Labienus, was placed in command of the detachment left in Gaul, which consisted of three legions and two thousand horse, — seventeen thousand men, at normal strength, — a force amply large to provide temporarily for the safety of the land. Labienus was also to take steps to insure Cæsar a steady supply of corn. His orders were general, to act for the best interests of Cæsar under any circumstances which might arise. Labienus was, to all appearances, a faithful, and was unquestionably a clever lieutenant. One can but wonder how he could prove so treacherous as he later did, or sink so low in ability. Cæsar took with him the other five legions and two thousand horse, — some twenty-seven thousand men, if we assume the legions to be full. There is no means of telling how strong the legions at this time were. Later they were greatly depleted, and it is probable that at this date they fell below the numbers given.

Cæsar embarked and set sail, with over eight hundred craft, one day at sunset, thought to have been the twentieth of July. The fleet sailed with a southwest wind till midnight, when the wind fell; but, by dint of hard rowing and continuous, the British coast was made in the morning, and next midday, after having been carried somewhat too far

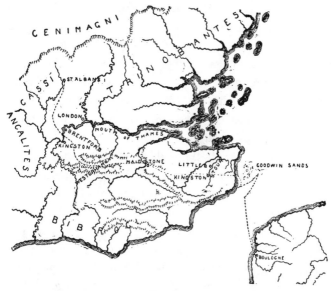

Britain.

north, probably to Goodwin Sands, from whence the vessels were rowed back, made good the landing at several points, at a place which the preceding year Cæsar had discovered to be a suitable spot.

The Britons had been frightened by the appearance of this enormous fleet, — the like of which they had never imagined, — and in lieu of opposing the landing, had, as Cæsar learned from some prisoners, concealed themselves some distance back of the coast on the high land.

The operation of this year stands out in marked contrast to that of the last. Cæsar had brought victuals, baggage, a sufficient fleet, his cavalry, and enough troops to enable him to accomplish some result. For quite a season he could subsist on what he had, and he had perfected arrangements for future supplies. Cæsar probably chose his camp in a safer place, taught by the experience of the last year.

Leaving Q. Atrius in charge of the ships, with a strong guard of ten cohorts — two from each legion — and three hundred horse, Cæsar marched by night towards the place, some twelve miles distant, where prisoners had told him the enemy lay encamped. Here he was met by an advanced party of warriors, who, with chariots and horsemen, essayed to dispute his passage of a small river, very probably the Little Stour, near Kingston or Littlebourne. The Gallic cavalry, however, easily threw this force back, and following it up, Cæsar found the main army strongly intrenched in a fort well protected by felled trees, "which the Britons had before prepared on account of a civil war." The locality cannot be identified, nor indeed are most of the places settled beyond dispute. But some of them may be considered as practically determined. The Britons, not content with having harassed the marching column very materially, offered in a desultory way quite a stubborn defense of their fort; but the Seventh legionaries, having thrown up a temporary terrace and forming a testudo, overwhelmed the barbarians with missiles, captured the fort, and drove the Britons out of the woods. The loss of the Romans was small. Cæsar forbade their pursuing to any distance, lest they should fall into an ambuscade. He desired, moreover, to intrench his camp more carefully than usual.

On the morrow, when Cæsar was about to pursue the Britons, and had already given marching orders to several detachments of foot and horse, three of which had proceeded some distance, had caught up with the barbarian rear, and were pushing them to a fight in retreat, he received by mounted messengers word from Atrius that a storm had destroyed and damaged a number of the ships. These had been left at anchor, and had been violently dashed against each other by the heavy sea. The experience of the last year had not been heeded, and the same danger had been incurred. Recalling the cohorts already in pursuit, Cæsar marched back to the fleet. Here he found that forty of the vessels had been seriously broken, but that the damage to the rest could be repaired with time and labor. He detailed skilled workmen from the legions for this purpose. He also deêmed it wise to send to Labienus in Gaul to have additional ships built. And he now took the precaution, though at great labor, to haul the ships up on the beach out of the reach of the waves, and strongly fortified the position. This work consumed ten days and nights of unremitting toil, for eight hundred ships would take up much space and were not easily handled. If each was eighty feet long by twenty wide, and they were put six feet apart and in four lines ten feet apart, they would occupy a mile of beach three hundred and fifty feet wide. To add the space required for the crews and room to receive the legions as well would make a camp covering much ground. This was, however, no unusual feat for the Romans. The time occupied was mainly used in putting the fortifications beyond fear of capture. August had come, and Cæsar had made small headway.

The same cohorts were left to protect the new camp, and Cæsar marched back to the place where he had last met the enemy. Here he found the Britons assembled under command of Cassivellaunus, a noble chieftain whose territories were separated from the maritime states by the Tamesis (Thames) about eighty miles up from the sea, above London. The several tribes, who were constantly at war, had laid aside their own feuds in order to meet the common enemy, and though Cassivellaunus was universally disliked, he had been recognized as the best commander.

The British foot was useless against the legions. Cassivellaunus recognized this fact, and appears to have discharged it. But the cavalry and chariots proved useful. They hovered about Cæsar's column on the march, made frequent attacks, and gave unceasing trouble to the Romans, who, at first, daunted by the fierce looks of these barbarians, their woad-stained skins, and their courageous demeanor, ended by finding discipline more than a match for their wild tactics. After camping, a constant skirmish was kept up with the outposts. The Britons at one time appeared suddenly from the woods and drove in a Roman guard with serious loss. But Cæsar sent forward two cohorts as reinforcement, and the action after some time resulted in greater loss, by far, to the Britons, who were driven back to the forest. The method of fighting of the Britons was novel to the Romans. The charioteers did not act in large bodies, nor indeed the cavalry, but in small squads, relying upon their individual prowess. They would often purposely retreat and then turn furiously upon the pursuers, and as often as necessary they relieved the fighting men with fresh ones. The drill and heavy masses of the Roman legions were by no means suited to this method of warfare. The Roman allied horse was subjected to the same difficulty, for the Britons, seeing that they could not meet the squadrons on equal terms, merely skirmished in loose order and cut out an occasional horseman whenever chance offered.

Cæsar does not give us details of just what means he adopted to meet these novel tactics. One is led to believe that Cæsar's legionaries in this their fifth year of campaigning were not as apt at coping with the unusual as Alexander's phalangites, who could and did skirmish as well as they fought in line or column, against any and all comers. Still, Cæsar's legionary was an adaptable fellow, able to turn his hand to almost anything. He had already had considerable experience in dealing with new methods of warfare, and to rank him as he was at this period after the Macedonians, who had been trained by Philip, is no disgrace. Later, he came well up to their standard. Probably without altering anything of the regular formation or manœuvring of the legion, Cæsar was able to meet the Britons at their own tactics.

Next day the enemy assembled "with less spirit than the day before," on the hills surrounding the camp, and challenged the Romans to battle by advancing cavalry skirmishers, who galloped tauntingly around the Roman horse without venturing to make a serious attack. This challenge being refused, when towards noon Cæsar sent out the legate Trebonius with three legions and all the cavalry on a foraging expedition, the Britons, who lay in ambush, suddenly and from all sides, fell upon them. The barbarians fought with uncommon vigor and daring. They pressed on so sharply that the legionaries were compelled to close in round their standards. But, as always, Roman discipline under able leadership prevailed; the Britons were driven back and broken, and in the pursuit, a vast number of them were killed. The cavalry, finding itself sustained by the foot, kept so close to their heels that they were unable to display their peculiar tactics. Reinforcements which came up to their aid were likewise dispersed. The punishment was severe, and thereafter no attack in force was made on the Roman columns.

After these preliminary combats, Cæsar advanced on Cassivellaunus via Maidstone and Westerham. He saw that the enemy proposed to draw the war out to a great length and believed that he had better force the fighting. In order to reach Cassivellaunus, he must cross the Thames. Several places were fordable, and at each of these localities the enemy had erected defenses. Cæsar chose a spot between Kingston and Brentford. Here he found that Cassivellaunus had driven sharp stakes into the farther bank and into the river bed near by, with the points below the surface of the water, and expected to be able to overwhelm the Romans when they should get into disorder in forcing the ford. These stakes were probably driven both above and below. Cæsar had got wind of this device from prisoners, and was able to avoid the snare. Sending his cavalry to points up or down the river so as to cross and take the Britons in flank, and following up its manœuvre with the legions, who, though the water was up to their necks, dashed into the ford with courage, the combined onset was so sharp and vigorous that Cassivellaunus' men sought safety in flight. Polyænus says Cæsar had an elephant, the sight of which greatly disturbed the Britons. This is not elsewhere mentioned, and is doubtful.

It was the middle of August. Many of the auxiliaries of Cassivellaunus now deserted him, and he was reduced to defend himself with his own forces, amounting to four thousand men in chariots, perhaps seven or eight hundred chariots, with their auxiliary fighters. He showed himself an adept in a small system of warfare. Knowing all the paths of the country, he was able adequately to hide his people, cattle and goods, and to fall upon the Roman foragers wherever they went, from one ambush after another. So clever were his devices, that he succeeded in almost entirely preventing foraging at a distance from the main body of the legions; and so effectively did he interfere with their obtaining corn, that one is tempted to make the same criticism upon Cæsar's passing over to the north side of the Thames which was applied as a whole to his first invasion of Britain.

At this time, the Trinobantes, who lived in modern Essex and Middlesex, came in and surrendered, they being one of the most powerful tribes and inimical to Cassivellaunus. No doubt Cæsar had exerted all his diplomacy to bring about this result. The Trinobantes were secured from plundering by the Roman soldiers, and on giving forty hostages, and furnishing corn for the troops, Cæsar reinstated their chief, Mandubratius, who had been to Gaul to see Cæsar, and was still with him. The old king, his father, Cassivellaunus had killed. Other tribes, the Cenimagni, Segontiaci, Ancalites, Bibroci and Cassi, soon followed this example. These tribes covered substantially the entire southeast section of Britain. Learning from the new allies to what place Cassivellaunus had retired, that he had fortified his capital, — at modern St. Albans, probably,— though it could have been little more than a camp, and had collected in it a large force and much cattle, Cæsar took up his march thither. After reconnoitring the camp, — it had a rampart and ditch, "admirably fortified by nature and by art," and lay in a thickly wooded district, — he determined upon attacking it from two directions. The storming columns made short work. The Britons did not long resist the assault, but hurriedly retreated by the gate on one of the sides which had not been attacked, leaving behind corn and cattle, and losing many people in the flight and pursuit. This was not a very flattering victory, nor a decisive, but it furnished a pretext to declare the advance a success, and enabled Cæsar to withdraw from a campaign which promised no eventual gain.

While Cæsar was thus engaged, Cassivellaunus sent messengers to the tribes in Kent whose kings were Cingetorix, Carvilius, Taximagulus, and Segonax, and persuaded them to make a sudden attack on the Roman fleet and camp. This they did with a large force, but the Romans, expertly sallying out upon them, routed them, killed a vast number, and captured Lugotorix, a celebrated leader. This was, indeed, fortunate. A disaster at the rear would have meant destruction of all Cæsar's forces.

After this defeat Cassivellaunus, thoroughly alarmed by his want of success, by the wasting of the country, and by the desertion of many tribes, concluded to treat for peace. He employed Commius to make advances for him. Cæsar, as the summer was far spent, — it was now the end of August, and he felt that he must return to Gaul, where some tribes had revolted and others were threatening to follow suit, — after taking great numbers of hostages and prescribing a tribute to be paid the Roman people, and forbidding Cassivellaunus, moreover, to attack the Trinobantes or Mandubratius, concluded peace. By no means all of the vessels which had been sent back to Gaul for supplies had returned to Britain. Many had gone astray. Cæsar had fewer ships by far than he had brought over. He was compelled to convey his army back to Gaul in two trips, for his numbers were swelled by an array of hostages and prisoners. There were many disasters to vessels returning empty from the first crossing, but the transfer was managed without loss of a ship containing soldiers, and Cæsar reached Gaul after an absence of two months. Having housed his ships, he called a great congress of the Gallic tribes at Samarobriva (Amiens) in the land of the Ambiani.

The operations of this year in Britain were practically as resultless as those of the previous one, though the care and skill with which the invasion was conducted were in this case commendable. Cæsar had accomplished nothing substantial. As Tacitus remarks, he had made rather a survey than a reduction of Britain. He had not added a new province to Rome, nor indeed paved the way for so doing. He had not left a force to hold what he had conquered. He had brought back hostages, to be sure, but their possession was unable to assure him any control over the island. We are constrained to look upon the expeditions to Britain in the light of invasions made without proper warranty, consideration or effect. They had no influence upon the military problem in Gaul. However valuable as giving historians their earliest bird's-eye view of Britain, from a military point of view they were unnecessary and ineffective.

Wounded Gaul.
(From a Sarcophagus.)

XIII.

AMBIORIX. WINTER, 54–53 B. C.

THE crops had been poor. Cæsar spread his legions in winter-quarters over a large area, so as more readily to subsist. The camps were three hundred miles apart between extremes. Of this fact the Gauls took advantage. Ambiorix attacked Sabinus at Aduatuca. Instead of fighting it out, Sabinus relied upon Ambiorix's promise of free exit, and sought to march to Cicero's camp, the nearest to his own. But he did this carelessly, was attacked, and entirely cut up. Ambiorix then marched to Cicero's camp and tried the same artifice of promising free exit. Cicero acted the soldier's part and held to his camp. Cæsar heard of these events. He had but seven thousand men whom on the spur of the moment he could concentrate. With these he set out to rescue Cicero. So soon as he reached the vicinity, Ambiorix quitted the siege of Cicero's camp and advanced to meet him. It was nine to one. Cæsar, with admirable ruse, led on Ambiorix, who despised his meagre numbers, to attack him in careless order; and falling suddenly on him, defeated his army and dispersed it. He thus released Cicero from his bad case. Few of Cicero's men had escaped wounds or death. Labienus meanwhile had been attacked by the Treviri, but had won a brilliant victory.

OWING to an exceptionally dry season the corn-crop had not been good in Gaul during the year 54 B. C.; so that Cæsar, as he says, was obliged to disperse his legions to provide them food in winter-quarters during the succeeding winter. Fabius, with one legion, was sent to the Morini, and established himself at modern St. Pol; Q. Cicero, brother of the orator, went with one to the Nervii, between the Scaldis and Sabis, and camped probably at Charleroi; Roscius, with one, was placed among the Esuvii, in southern Normandy, near Séez; Labienus, with one, was among the Remi, near the Treviri, very likely at Lavacherie; Crassus, Plancus and Trebonius, with three legions, occupied Bel-

gium, between the Scaldis and Isara, — Trebonius at Amiens, Crassus among the Bellovaci at Montdidier, twenty-
five miles from Amiens, Plancus near the confluence of the

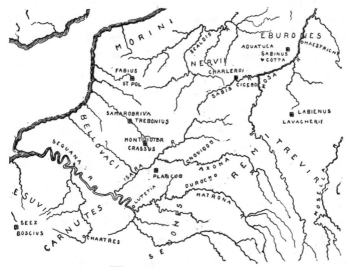

Winter-Quarters, B. C. 54–53.

Oise and Aisne; and the new legion last raised on the Po,
and five cohorts, under Sabinus and Cotta, were placed near
the Meuse, among the Eburones, the country governed by
Ambiorix and Cativolcus, at Aduatuca (Tongres). The bulk
of the legions were thus in the northwest section of Gaul.
The exact locations are, of course, not certain. The only
ones which are determined are Samarobriva and Aduatuca.
The others are set down according as topographical features
or the subsequent establishment of Roman oppida, or camps,
suggest the probable earlier locations, and are approximately
correct.

These forces made up a grand total of eight legions and
five cohorts. This was the same number Cæsar had had for
a year. No new ones were raised till later, — though some

authorities claim that there was, at this time, one extra one, or nine legions and a half.

Cæsar determined to remain with the army until the camps were all fortified. One legion (Plancus') was later hastily sent to the Carnutes in the neighborhood of modern Chartres, where Tasgetius, who was one of Cæsar's firm allies, — for Cæsar had replaced him on the throne of his forefathers from which he had been driven, — had been murdered by his subjects. Plancus' orders were to hunt up the murderers, and send them to Cæsar for trial.

It proved in the event that these several camps were unable to support each other in case of need. They were, as the crow flies, over three hundred miles distant between extremes; or if the camp of Roscius be left out, the other camps could not be contained in a circle of a diameter less than one hundred and sixty miles. Why Cæsar chose to so divide his forces can be explained only on the score of extreme stress of victual. Even this scarcely suffices. Corn he had or must procure, despite the bad harvests, and he could in some fashion have brought the supplies into magazines. His method was clearly a miscalculation, natural enough, but not Cæsarian.

Having, not far from the end of October, received word from his quæstor that the camps were all intrenched, — it appears that he did not personally inspect the camps, — Cæsar prepared to leave for Cisalpine Gaul.

Gaul was only outwardly quiet. The Roman legions were really camping on a volcano. The Gallic tribes had been fearfully maltreated, and the mistaken policy was now bearing fruit. The people were poor, their chiefs had lost all power and influence, large districts had been devastated, and starvation promised to be the lot of thousands. The Romans were always careless in providing for conquered peoples. Cæsar had been particularly so in Gaul. He imagined that this very fact would prevent insurrection; but it produced the reverse effect. Fury and despair outweighed calculation or common sense.

It does not appear that a general rendezvous had been given the legions, in case it became essential for them to concentrate. To do this was, in fact, not the method of Cæsar, who had not yet taught himself some of the most necessary lessons of the military art, which even among barbarians require to be observed. In the African campaign, we shall see a still more glaring instance of this, the outcome of a certain habit of carelessness on Cæsar's part. Cæsar's theory was that each isolated body, as was possible in a well intrenched and victualed Roman camp, should defend itself, and take the most available means of procuring succor from neighboring legions. When he was absent, he did not, in fact, leave any one in command. Each legate was independent. With his enormous grasp of the requisites of any military situation, this is somewhat curious.

Two weeks after all the legions had been settled, a sudden insurrection arose among the Eburones (a tribe south of the confluence of the Meuse and the Rhine), under leadership of Ambiorix and Cativolcus. These chiefs had apparently been friendly. They had at least brought in provisions to Sabinus and Cotta. Though these chiefs struck the first blow, Indutiomarus of the Treviri is thought to have been the prime mover of the rising.

The insurgents began by making an assault on the Roman soldiers who were gathering forage and wood for the camp under Sabinus at Aduatuca. That this was Tongres is not doubtful. No other place satisfies all the requirements of distances and topography made by the Commentaries. These parties rallied, held together and reached camp, whose defenses had just been completed. The Spanish cavalry made a successful sortie, which, coupled to the stanch front of the legionaries, broke up the attack. Then, after their usual treacherous manner, the barbarians asked for a conference. This was unwisely granted. C. Arpineius, a Roman knight, and Q. Junius, a Spaniard, who personally knew Ambiorix, being sent on the parley, the Gallic chief informed the messengers, with every show of truth, that he had been compelled by his people to make the attack on the camp; that he himself was Cæsar's constant friend; that this day had been selected throughout Gaul for an attack on the isolated legions; that a large force of Germans was within two days' march; that for their own safety, Sabinus and Cotta had best retire; and he promised under oath that he would give them a safe-conduct.

Upon these statements being reported, a council of war was held, at which the most opposite opinions were stormily expressed. Cotta, backed by many of the tribunes and centurions, was for holding on. They had rations; he believed that Cæsar would come to their relief, and that untold forces of the Germans could be encountered in their fortified winter-quarters; why, then, should they, on the advice of the enemy, cast aside these advantages? But finally, late at night, Sabinus succeeded in imposing his opinion on the others. This was to the effect that though the information did come from an enemy, they would do well to regard it and not wait till the Germans arrived; that Cæsar had probably started for Italy; that they had the choice of quick retreat or a prolonged siege; that they could easily join the nearest Roman winter-quarters, which were but sixty miles away; that the statement of Ambiorix bore the stamp of probability, though he was an enemy. It was determined to retreat towards Cicero at early dawn.

The soldiers spent the night without sleep, making preparations for the march.   At daybreak the column started on its way, not in close order and with due precautions, but strung out and hampered by an immense amount of baggage, as if relying solely on Ambiorix's promise of safe-conduct, and not in the least on their own resources.   This utterly

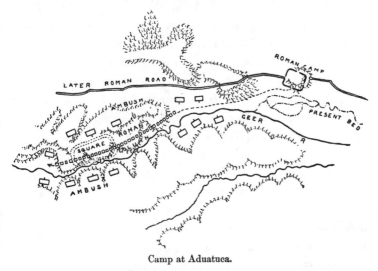

Camp at Aduatuca.

un-Roman conduct shows how much more the safety of an army depends upon the commander than upon the men.

The enemy, from the stir of the camp, quickly perceived that the Romans had decided on retreat.   They accordingly placed an ambuscade in the woods about two miles from the camp, on the road the Romans must pursue on the march towards Cicero's camp.   This was in the defile of Lowaige, on the heights north and south of the village, where the Geer flows between two hills.   The Gauls occupied both exits and the adjoining eminences.

The Roman army started on its ill-fated march.   No sooner had it descended into the valley where the Gallic troops lay hid, than the barbarians emerged from cover and attacked the head and rear of the Roman column. Sabinus, who had been for retreat, quite lost his head; Cotta, who had yielded to his views only after long persuasion, was active and full of vigor. The discipline of the soldiers was lax, and each one, instead of rallying on the standards, sought rather to save some of his goods from the baggage-train. The column was much extended. It was hard to convey orders. The march had been begun without the precautions essential to such an operation. The men were not kept closed up; no method of defense was apparent; every one worked on an independent basis. The train soon had to be abandoned. Danger crowded the legionaries together, and the army was drawn up in a square (*orbis*) for defense.

The Gauls behaved wisely. They did not seek plunder, but first victory. They began a system of tiring out the Roman legions. Out of the square, from time to time, certain cohorts would charge on the enemy and uniformly defeat him; then retire again to their place in the line. The barbarians soon ceased to offer resistance to these charges. Whenever one was made, they would retire; but so soon as the Roman cohorts turned back, being lighter armed, they would rush forward and beset their flanks, and the flanks of the cohorts exposed by their advance. Though, in the square, the Roman lost his initiative, the impetus which made him strong, yet from early morning till near nightfall the legionaries held their ground without disgrace, but at a serious loss in men and officers. Sabinus, still weakly relying on Ambiorix's word, sent Cnæus Pompeius, during a lull in the fighting, to ask a conference with him. To this being granted and protection again promised under oath, he himself and a number of tribunes went; but during the conference they were surrounded and slain; whereupon the Gauls again attacked the circle, and, owing to the demoralization of the men, speedily forced their way into it. Cotta was slain; a few of the cohorts cut their way out of the mêlée and managed to get back to the camp, where the survivors all committed suicide during the night. A handful of fugitives found their way to the camp of Labienus, nearly seventy miles distant.

Ambiorix, elated at his victory, made forced marches with his cavalry, — the infantry following as rapidly as possible, — to the westerly clans of the Aduatuci and the Nervii, to rouse them to embrace this opportunity of revenge and freedom. These tribes, elated by his exaggerated promises, willingly joined him, and all the neighboring and dependent tribes were sent for. Having assembled a large force with the utmost dispatch, they attacked some foraging parties, and then the camp of Cicero at Charleroi, who had heard not a word of the disaster to Sabinus and Cotta, and who was expecting nothing so little as an insurrection. The legionaries rushed to arms and manned the vallum, and the Gauls were foiled in their hope of seizing the place out of hand. Cicero at once dispatched messengers to Cæsar, but of these — despite great promises of reward — none made their way through the enemy's lines. The roads and passes had been all beset by the Gauls. Ambiorix had taken his precautions well.

The Romans had got together a great deal of timber for winter-quarter fortifications. During the night after the attack they worked hard at the defenses of the camp, shortly building one hundred and twenty towers (the towers were built as they still build scaffolds in Italy, by lashing together upright and cross poles), weaving hurdles and preparing burned stakes and mural spikes for use from the battlements. Not even the wounded could cease from labor. The enemy attacked next day, and thanks to the preparations were

beaten back. Desultory attempts to take the camp continued
for some days. Cicero, though sick, would give himself no
rest until obliged to do so by his men. The legionaries defended the camp well, though with difficulty. A winter camp
was more extended than the daily camp and gave a much

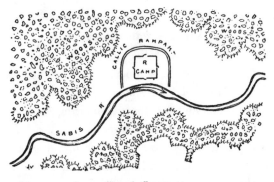

Cicero's Camp.

longer rampart to defend. Unable to make sensible progress, the Gallic chiefs signified their desire to confer with
Cicero. On this being granted, Ambiorix plausibly stated
the same things with which he had persuaded Sabinus, re-
fraining however, from promises, and told of the destruction
of that legion. He claimed that the cause of war was the
burden laid on the Gauls by the Romans in wintering regu-
larly in the country and consuming the corn which was
needed to keep their own people in life. To all this Cicero
made the soldier's answer that the Romans never treated with
foes in arms, but that if the enemy would lay down their
arms and state their case as supplicants, no doubt Cæsar
would do them ample justice. Ambiorix retired baffled.

The Nervii then set about to besiege the Roman camp, and
built around it a rampart eleven feet high and a ditch thirteen feet deep. They had learned these methods from Roman

prisoners and former wars. Though they had few tools to
work with, but were "forced to cut the turf with their swords
and to empty out the earth with their hands and cloaks," so
vast was their number that in three hours they had made
a rampart fifteen thousand feet long. The text here says
passuum, but it is probably meant for *pedum*. The former
would make the length of the rampart ten miles; it was in
effect less than three, for they had to surround only the
camp of a legion. Next day they built towers, mantelets
and galleries, and made mural hooks. They had attained
some skill in the minutiæ of sieges.

Cicero was now entirely shut in. On the seventh day there
was a high wind, and the barbarians, by means of hot clay
balls and heated javelins, set on fire the camp-huts which
were thatched after the Gallic fashion, and under cover of
the confusion of the flames made a vehement assault. The
legionaries stood manfully to their work, despite the fact
that their baggage was being consumed, and utterly worsted
the enemy.

The Commentaries give prominence to some acts of personal
gallantry. "In that legion there were two very brave men,
centurions, who were now approaching the first ranks, T.
Pulfio and L. Varenus. These used to have continual disputes between them which of them should be preferred, and
every year used to contend for promotion with the utmost
animosity. When the fight was going on most vigorously
before the fortifications, Pulfio, one of them, says: 'Why do
you hesitate Varenus? or what better opportunity of signal-
izing your valor do you seek? This very day shall decide
our disputes.' When he had uttered these words, he pro-
ceeds beyond the fortifications, and rushes on that part of the
enemy which appeared the thickest. Nor does Varenus remain within the rampart, but respecting the high opinion of

all, follows close after. Then, when an inconsiderable space intervened, Pulfio throws his javelin at the enemy, and pierces one of the multitude who was running up, and while the latter was wounded and slain, the enemy cover him with their shields and all throw their weapons at the other and afford him no opportunity of retreating. The shield of Pulfio is pierced and a javelin is fastened in his belt. This circumstance turns aside his scabbard and obstructs his right hand when attempting to draw his sword; the enemy crowd around him when thus embarrassed. His rival runs up to him and succors him in this emergency. Immediately, the whole host turn from Pulfio to him, supposing the other to be pierced through by the javelin. Varenus rushes on briskly with his sword and carries on the combat hand to hand, and having slain one man, for a short time drove back the rest; while he urges on too eagerly, slipping into a hollow, he fell. To him, in his turn, when surrounded, Pulfio brings relief; and both having slain a great number, retreat into the fortifications amidst the highest applause. Fortune so dealt with both in this rivalry and conflict, that the one competitor was a succor and a safeguard to the other, nor could it be determined which of the two appeared worthy of being preferred to the other." This story lends local color to the rivalries of the Roman soldier's life.

The number of defenders of the Roman camp was daily becoming smaller, and these were weakened by exertion. Of the messengers dispatched to Cæsar, none reached him. Some were captured and tortured in sight of the camp. Finally, a Nervian who had deserted to the Romans undertook to carry a message and succeeded in reaching the chief.

Cæsar was at Samarobriva. He had not left for Italy so soon as he expected. He at once headed Trebonius' legion for the scene of danger, and ordered Crassus, who was at

Montdidier, to march to headquarters with his legion to replace Trebonius. Fabius, with his legion, was directed to march from St. Pol toward the Nervian frontiers, and join Cæsar among the Atrebates.

Cæsar received notice of Cicero's peril about four P. M. So rapid was his message and so alert was Crassus that this officer reached Cæsar at ten A. M. next day, a march of fully

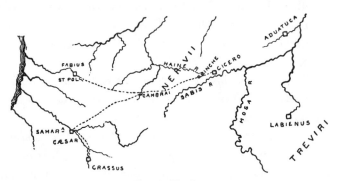

Cæsar's March.

twenty-five miles. The camp at Samarobriva was protected by the rearguard of Trebonius' legion until Crassus' arrival, when it set out to rejoin the column. Crassus was left behind at the main camp to protect the baggage, treasure, prisoners, archives and the vast amount of corn there collected.

At the same moment Cæsar had sent word to Labienus to march to meet him in the vicinity of Cicero's camp; but Labienus replied, explaining the state of revolt of the Eburones and the imminent danger from the Treviri. He knew the confidence Cæsar reposed in his judgment and relied on his properly gauging the reason of his failure to obey orders. He was right.

Cæsar instantly followed Trebonius' legion. He had, in addition to that body, but four hundred horse available at headquarters, or a total of only two small legions, perhaps seven thousand to eight thousand men. One of the most singular facts in the military history of Cæsar is the manner in which he was repeatedly caught in dilemmas with but a handful of troops at his disposal. We shall see him at Alexandria, Zela and Hadrumetum in a desperate strait from lack of foresight. It required luck superior to Alexander's, as well as his own splendid resources, to save him from destruction in these false positions. Cæsar's fortune will ever remain proverbial, and indeed, had not the fickle goddess laid aside her wonted character to favor him, Cæsar would have ended his career before he had made himself an enduring name. No great captain was ever rescued from the results of his own neglect so often as was Cæsar.

Cæsar now had but a handful, but he felt that dispatch was of more moment than larger forces. On the first day he covered twenty miles in the direction of modern Cambrai, and was joined on the road by Fabius, not far from that place. Pushing on, he reached the borders of the Nervii, and learned from prisoners what the conditions were. He managed to send word to Cicero that he was coming, by a Gallic horseman, who shot an arrow, or threw a javelin with the message tied to the thong into his camp, and urged him to hold out to the last. The message was in Greek. Polyænus says it was brief: "Courage! Expect succor!"

In five days Cæsar marched from Samarobriva to near the winter-quarters of Cicero, not far from one hundred and ten miles, twenty-two miles a day, over winter roads, a good but not wonderful performance. He camped in the vicinity of Binche. So soon as the Nervii discovered Cæsar's approach, they raised the blockade and marched towards him, some sixty thousand strong. Cicero sent Cæsar word that the enemy had turned against him. He had no men left to send as a reinforcement to his chief. Cæsar had but about seven thousand men, and saw the necessity for caution. His having but one man to nine of the enemy was due to his miscalculated system of winter-quarters. He broke camp at Binche, advanced, and soon ran across the enemy. He first caught sight of them across the valley of the Haine. He camped on Mount St. Aldegonde in a very contracted space, to make the Nervii underestimate even the paltry force he had with him. He then sent forward his horse to skirmish

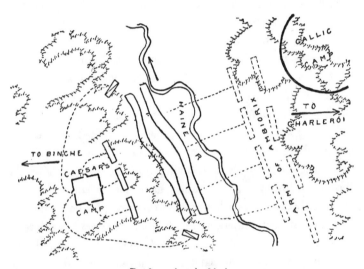

Battle against Ambiorix.

with the enemy, and by simulating retreat, draw them on to attack the camp. He and his legion lay west of the Haine; the barbarians were on its east bank; Cæsar manœuvred so as to get them to cross the stream to the attack. He also began fortifying and gave orders to the soldiers to act with apparent confusion, as if in fear, so as still more to lure the Nervii on.

The ruse succeeded, and the barbarians advanced, took up

a disadvantageous and careless position, and sent out a proclamation that they would receive and spare any deserters from the Roman legions. They believed that they had bagged their game. They then began the fight as if nothing were so sure as victory, advancing to the gates and ramparts in enthusiastic disorder. Cæsar still simulated fear, to render them yet more careless, and held his men sharply in hand, intending to take them unawares. At the proper moment he gave the signal. The legionaries rushed from all the gates at once; and the cavalry sallied out with unexpected dash. So entirely surprised were the barbarians by the vigor and courage of their opponents that they fled in dismay. They were pursued with great loss, but the pursuit was not kept up to any distance, owing to the wooded and cut-up nature of the country. In pursuit, Cæsar was never equal to the great Macedonian. No one but Napoleon was.

Having thus opened the way, Cæsar marched to Cicero's camp, where he found the garrison in sad case, but still full of courage. "The legion having been drawn out he finds that even every tenth soldier had not escaped without wounds." This was a heavy loss, which might be estimated at seven per cent. killed, and eighty-three per cent. wounded; or, out of a legion of five thousand men, three hundred and fifty killed and four thousand one hundred wounded. Cæsar highly commended the legions and officers for their valor, and distributed rewards among the bravest. Both praise and gifts had been gallantly won.

News of this victory was speedily conveyed to the Treviri. This determined Indutiomarus, who had been on the point of attacking Labienus, to withdraw from his front, — at least for the time being. The news had traveled sixty miles between the ninth hour and midnight. Cæsar had reached Cicero's camp at three P. M.; before midnight some of the

Remi raised a shout of joy which announced the victory to Labienus. This is not so wonderful a performance as it sounds. A single courier might have done it; three or four, relieving each other, very handily. Fifty miles have been run in less than seven hours, in these so-called degenerate days.

No sooner was the campaign thus happily decided than Fabius was sent back to his winter-quarters. Cæsar determined to remain in Gaul. Profiting by his bitter experience, he concentrated his forces; established his own headquarters at Samarobriva, with three legions, Crassus', Cicero's, Trebonius', in three several camps. Of these there are some relics still: a camp at the citadel of Amiens; the Camp de l'Etoile; and one near modern Tirancourt. Labienus, Plancus and Roscius remained *in situ.*

The defeat of Sabinus and Cotta had bred a feeling of uncertainty all through the land; nocturnal meetings were held,

New Camps.

and insurrections were threatened and expected on every hand. An attack on Roscius had all but occurred. Among the Senones, on the Upper Sequana, there was a political

upheaval, and a refusal to comply with Cæsar's demands,
which he does not appear to have felt in a position to enforce. This badly affected the tribes. The Remi and Ædui
alone remained quite true. By calling together the principal
citizens and alternately using threats and courtesies, most
troubles were for the moment averted, though a constant
turmoil went on.

Indutiomarus, chief of the Treviri, was, it appears, the
head and front of this entire movement. He tried to get

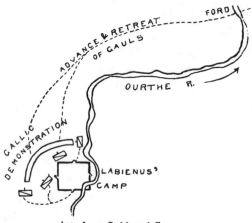

Attack on Labienus' Camp.

the Germans across the Rhine, but they had conceived a
hearty dread of Cæsar. Still Indutiomarus ceased not his
work, and finally his efforts induced some isolated tribes of
the Senones and Carnutes to join him; and the Aduatuci and
Nervii seemed ready to help. But his army was largely
composed of outlaws and criminals. He called an armed
assembly of chiefs, and under its inspiration advanced and
camped again before Labienus. This officer kept to his
ramparts, simulating fear, — a trick whose repetition never
seemed to make it stale, — but watching keenly for a good

chance for attack. Growing more careless day by day, Indutiomarus finally laid himself open.

Labienus had a good body of native horse which he had quietly assembled and introduced into the camp. Indutiomarus made, as usual, a threatening advance to the Roman ramparts, and towards evening withdrew in more than usually careless order, no doubt laughing at the cowardice of the legionaries. This was Labienus' opportunity. Throwing open the two main gates of the camp, the cavalry issued, followed by the cohorts. Taken by surprise the enemy fled. Indutiomarus himself was slain, and much loss was inflicted on the barbarians. This victory and the death of the chief plotter allayed the turmoil greatly; but though the Nervii and Eburones dispersed to their homes, it was far from quieting Cæsar's apprehensions of further trouble.

These operations show the immense rôle the Roman fortified camp played in the days of short-carry weapons. Gunpowder first nullified the importance of the camp. A modern field battery would with a few rounds demolish a Roman vallum. To-day, anything like a camp would be subject to irresistible concentric fire. Well chosen natural positions had to be sought as a defense against artillery.

Cicero's defense at Charleroi leads Napoleon to contrast ancient war with modern very skillfully: "Si l'on disait aujourd'hui à un général: 'Vous aurez, comme Cicéron, sous vos ordres, 5,000 hommes, 16 pièces de canon, 5,000 outils de pionniers, 5,000 sacs à terre; vous serez a portée d'une forêt, dans un terrain ordinaire; dans quinze jours vous serez attaqué par une armée de 60,000 hommes ayant 120 pièces de canon; vous ne serez secouru que quatre-vingts ou quatre-vingt-seize heures après avoir été attaqué.' Quels sont les ouvrages, quels sont les tracés, quels sont les profils que l'art lui préscrit? L'art de l'ingénieur a-t-il des secrets qui puissent satisfaire à ce problème?"

The quartering of the legions in such widely separated localities was certainly a grave error, severely punished in the event. But the rapid, able and decisive measures adopted by Cæsar to retrieve the disaster are quite beyond praise. The superb courage with which he set out with a mere handful of men to relieve his beleaguered lieutenant, and the skill he showed in dealing with the barbarians when he met them, cannot but excite the highest admiration. It is this sort of conduct on Cæsar's part which makes one forget the carelessness which lay at the root of so many of his brilliant strokes. Criticism seems to be almost out of order.

Sabinus had given proofs of ability. How he contrived to allow himself, against the advice of Cotta and his other fellow officers, to enter into negotiations with the crafty Ambiorix is an enigma. And having left his camp to make a junction with Cicero, why he should have marched in loose order and without proper precautions is still more of a puzzle. His only real chance was to stick to his camp and defend it as Cicero did, and as he had Cæsar's orders as well as all precedent to do. There can be no excuse for the shiftlessness of his order of march. This disaster is one more instance of the folly of divided command, for Sabinus and Cotta were equal. Cæsar should have given absolute command to one or the other legate. That the system of rotation and division of authority did not wreck the Roman army, is referable solely to the wonderful character of the people of Rome. No other army has ever had such a system and survived it.

The conduct of Cicero stands out in marked contrast to that of Sabinus.

The incisive conduct of Cæsar in remedying the disaster did not fail of effect among the Gallic tribes, and produced its full influence, political and military. The Nervii, Menapii and Aduatuci, who had been in arms, returned home; the maritime cantons followed suit; the Treviri, and their clients, the Eburones, retired from before Labienus. In Rome Cæsar's reputation stood higher than ever.

Cæsar, from a Coin.

XIV.

THE TREVIRI AND EBURONES. SPRING, 53 B. C.

During the winter another uprising was planned, headed by the Treviri. Cæsar determined to take the rebels unawares. He set out, despite the winter season, and successively surprised and punished the Nervii, Senones and Carnutes. He then reduced the Menapii on the lower Meuse, while Labienus a second time defeated the Treviri. Cæsar again crossed the Rhine, to impose on the Germans, having done which he begun his pursuit of Ambiorix, who was now isolated. He sent his cavalry ahead to surprise and capture this chief, if possible, but without success. The Eburones were now hunted down without mercy. Cæsar divided his force into three columns, which advanced on three several lines throughout northern Gaul. His baggage he left at Aduatuca. During his absence, some German tribes, who had crossed on a foray, attacked the camp at that place and came close to capturing it. Though Cæsar thoroughly suppressed the rising of this year, he was unable to catch Ambiorix. He went into winter-quarters near Sens.

It had become necessary to raise and have on hand a greater number of men, as well as to fill large gaps occasioned by the last campaigns. Cæsar deemed it essential to show the Gauls that the resources of Rome were ample; that to destroy one legion meant to have two others spring ready equipped from the earth. By negotiation with Pompey, whom business retained in Rome, he was able to obtain a legion which the latter had raised in Gaul when he was proconsul in Spain. The men had been furloughed to their homes, but they were recalled to the eagles and the legion took its place in line. Two additional legions were enlisted in Gaul by Cæsar's lieutenants, Silanus, Reginus and Sextius. The three new legions were the First, the Fourteenth (it took the number of the one destroyed at Aduatuca), and the Fifteenth. Thus thirty cohorts replaced the fifteen lost by Sabinus. Cæsar now commanded ten legions.

After Indutiomarus' death, the Treviri elected new chiefs from his family. They were unable to induce the near-by Germans to join their cause, but persuaded some of the Suevi to do so. Ambiorix joined them. Rumors of war were far spread. The Senones were still antagonistic, and the Carnutes abetted them. The Nervii, despite their fearful punishment, the Aduatuci and Menapii were under arms.

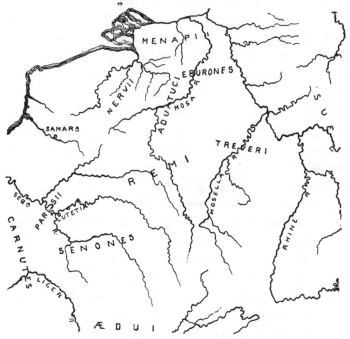

Campaign against Nervii and other Tribes.

Anticipating trouble with the tribes which had placed themselves under the leadership of the Nervii, and knowing that they were constantly striving to induce the Germans to undertake another invasion, Cæsar determined to strike them unawares. Suddenly and before the season for campaigning opened, perhaps in March, he concentrated the four legions nearest headquarters at Samarobriva (under Fabius, Crassus, Cicero, Trebonius), marched upon the Nervii, rushed like a hurricane over their territory, captured great booty, devastated the land and carried off victual. By taking them off their guard, he had them at his mercy. Having cowed them, he compelled them to give him hostages for good behavior, and returned to his winter-quarters.

Here he called an assembly of the Gauls. All sent representatives except the Senones, the Carnutes and the Treviri. Cæsar transferred the congress to Lutetia (modern Paris), so as to do both his political and military scheme justice at the same time. From here, he made a demonstration against the Senones and Carnutes, whose territory adjoined the Parisii. These tribes, under Acco, retired into their oppida; but they were unable to resist Cæsar's prompt measures. They respectively begged the Ædui and Remi to intercede for them; and on giving the hitherto refused hostages, Cæsar overlooked their defection. He had no time to split hairs. He was content to check a growing disposition to revolt. The hostages given were confided to the Ædui for security. Cæsar then closed the congress. His rapid and well-considered action had tranquillized central Gaul, and he could devote himself to the war with Ambiorix, chief of the Eburones. It was of the highest importance, Cæsar thought, in a military as well as a political sense, that the disgrace of Aduatuca should be wiped out.

As a part of his scheme, Cæsar had imposed a fresh levy of horse on the Gallic tribes. The Senonian cavalry under Cavarinus he ordered to accompany him. He was distrustful of its fidelity, as it contained many of the chief men of the tribe, unless he had it under his eye.

The Menapii, north of and next to the Eburones, were the only tribe which had never sent ambassadors to Cæsar. They were allies of Ambiorix, and Cæsar desired first to detach this people from his alliance. So long as they were unsubdued, Ambiorix retained an inaccessible place of refuge in their woods and morasses. Next to the fear that Ambiorix would persuade the Germans to a fresh war, was the safety this chief possessed in this alliance. The two things to be accomplished were the reduction of the Treviri and the detaching from Ambiorix of the Menapii. The last task he

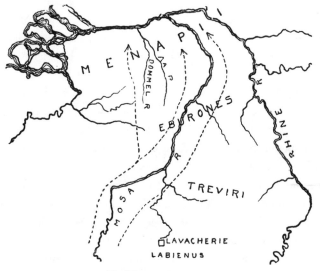

The Menapii Campaign.

undertook himself, the first he left to the management of Labienus, who knew the problem well, as he had wintered on the borders of the Treviri, and had already tried issues with them.

Sending all his baggage and two legions to Labienus, Cæsar moved with five legions, in light marching order and in three columns, against the Menapii, who at once took refuge in their natural fastnesses. They had assembled no forces. Cæsar divided his five legions into three columns, under Fabius, Crassus and himself. By the aid of the Senonian cavalry, and by bridging the marshes and streams, he advanced on three lines into their land. These lines were probably down both banks of the Meuse and down the Aa or Dommel, affluents of the Meuse, running from south to north through the Menapian territory. Cæsar began by relentlessly devastating their country, capturing their cattle, and taking prisoners all the prominent men he could reach. Shortly the Menapii sued for peace. Though independent from their isolation, they were not wont to act in unison, and were quite unable to resist organized invasion. Cæsar granted their petition on their undertaking by no means to harbor Ambiorix; and leaving some of the cavalry, under Commius the Atrebatian, among them, he marched towards Labienus and the Treviri. His route was probably up the Rhine, for we next find him at Bonn.

Labienus had wintered in his old camp at modern La-vacherie. The Treviri had harbored certain designs against him, and even since the victory over Indutiomarus made sundry demonstrations against his camp; but hearing that he had received two fresh legions from Cæsar, they deter-mined to await the Germans, whom they had now some reason to expect. They established themselves on the right bank of the Ourthe. Labienus did not await the barbarians. Taking twenty-five of his thirty cohorts and his cavalry, five remain-ing to guard the baggage, he anticipated their advance by marching against them, and camping on the other side of the Ourthe, a mile distant from their station.

The enemy were evidently anxious to wait for German suc-cor. Labienus desired to bring them to speedy battle. He stated in public, in such a manner that the rumor might be

carried to them, that, not desiring to measure swords with
both Treviri and Germans, he proposed to retreat the next
day, and made certain preparations which looked like hurried
and confused withdrawal, actually leaving his intrenchments.
This fact the enemy's scouts soon saw, and some deserters
carried to them the statement of Labienus. Fearing that
they might lose the booty of the Roman camp, and encouraged
by the apparent flight, the barbarians crossed the river and
attacked the Roman rear so soon as it had filed out of camp,
with the expectation of an easy victory. They had placed
themselves in a danger-
ous position, with the
river at their back, and,
the river banks being
precipitous, had lost all
semblance of order in
the crossing. Labienus
had explained the whole
purpose to his lieuten-
ants and centurions, and
had placed his baggage
under its guard on a
secure eminence. Ex-
horting his legions to

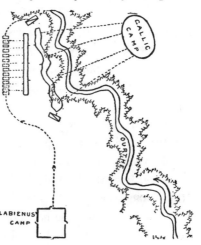

The Treviri Campaign.

fight as they should, Labienus, whose troops were well in
hand and whose simulated retreat was but a well-drilled
manœuvre, speedily gave the order to face the eagles to the
enemy, and deploy into line. The command was executed
with clockwork precision. The horse was thrown in on the
enemy's flanks. The battle-shout was clear and crisp. The
Treviri, taken utterly at a disadvantage, showed little fight.
Falling upon them with the utmost fury, the legions and
cavalry cut most of them to pieces. The rest fled to the

forests.   Labienus had ably used his knowledge of the impetuosity and lack of cool calculation in the Gauls.   This sharp lesson forestalled the threatened irruption of the Germans, who returned home.   The state was turned over to Cingetorix, who had always been an ally of Rome, in the place of Indutiomarus.

It will be noticed that whenever the Roman troops fought with steady discipline, the Gauls, whatever their numbers, were inevitably beaten.   There were no open-field pitched battles in the Gallic war, in the sense we understand the words.   At the river Sabis, Cæsar had to fight, because he had allowed himself to be surprised.   The Gauls were always ready to fight; they clung strenuously to their struggle against the Roman conquest, and deserve credit for heroic efforts.   But in line of battle they could never face the legions.

Ambiorix was now isolated.   The Menapii on one hand and the Treviri on the other were subdued, and the Germans could no longer be counted on.

Cæsar, from the land of the Menapii, had marched up the Rhine, and hearing of Labienus' victory, remained at Bonn, near the place where he had crossed two years before.   He determined again to cross the river, principally, as he states, to impose upon the Germans by a show of force, because they had assisted the Treviri, but also in order to prevent their receiving Ambiorix.   He built again a similar bridge at a place a little above where he had built the first one.   This bridge was completed yet more quickly; still "by great exertion of the soldiers."   Leaving a large and suitable guard at the west bridgehead, he crossed with the legions and cavalry and advanced into the German territory.   The Ubii at once approached and easily proved to him that they had been faithful to their alliance, and that it was the Suevi who had sent auxiliaries to Ambiorix. The Suevi had gone so far as to make drafts on their clients and assemble a large army ready for invasion. Cæsar employed the Ubii as scouts to discover the movements of the Suevi, and through them ascertained that, on learning of Cæsar's approach, they had retreated to the Bacenis forest (Hartz mountains) on the boundary of their territory. Cæsar did not deem it wise to march against them, on account of the impossibility of rationing his men in a land whose inhabitants had paid no heed to agriculture, and which would therefore be little better than a desert after the Suevi had driven off their flocks and herds. The barbarians had calculated shrewdly. But in order to leave them convinced that he would return and thereby prevent their undertaking immediate operations, after recrossing his army to the west bank, he broke down two hundred feet of the farther end of the bridge and "at the extremity of the bridge raised towers of four stories," and "strengthening the place with considerable fortifications" on the left bank, left therein a strong guard of twelve cohorts under Volcatius Tullus. He himself with the bulk of his ten legions, so soon as corn began to ripen, set out across the Forest of Arduenna against Ambiorix, determined to punish him for his treachery to Sabinus.

Cæsar marched from the bridge via Zulpich and Eupen. He sent forward all the cavalry force, under L. Minucius Basilus, to endeavor to surprise Ambiorix, promising to follow rapidly with the legions. He instructed Basilus to march secretly and refrain from lighting camp-fires. This officer performed his duty with excellent discretion and skill, directing his course by information got from prisoners taken on the way to a place where Ambiorix was said to be hiding with a small body of cavalry. So speedily did he march that he reached the retreat of Ambiorix before any rumor of his

being on the road had come to the ears of this chief; surprised
and almost succeeded in capturing him. But "Fortune
accomplishes much," says Cæsar, "not only in other matters,

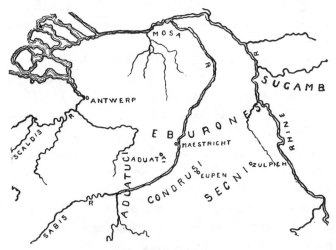

Pursuit of Ambiorix.

but also in the chances of war." And Ambiorix, by a rare
stroke of luck, made good his escape. His escort proved
loyal, made a smart fight, and under cover of it he mounted
a horse and fled.

It seems that this chieftain had begun to see the folly of
continuing the struggle against Cæsar, for he sent notice to
his allies that each one must now provide for his own security, — an act of desertion which roused up fury against
him. Cativolcus, king of the Eburones, committed suicide.
Many of the tribes which had risen in arms fled with their
possessions from the anger of Cæsar into the forests and
morasses. The Segni and Condrusi threw themselves on his
mercy and were forgiven, having proven that they had not
abetted Ambiorix. But they were cautioned to secure and surrender to Cæsar all Eburones who took refuge among them.

Cæsar's task was now vastly easier. He could deal with the barbarians in detail, and needed much fewer men under his own command. Having reached the ancient ford on the Mosa (at Visé), he divided his army into three parts. His baggage he sent to the camp at Aduatuca, among the Eburones, where Sabinus' legion had been destroyed, and where many of the fortifications still stood, which would relieve the soldiers from much of the work incident to preparing a fresh camp. He left the Fourteenth legion and two hundred cavalry to guard it, under command of Cicero. Labienus with

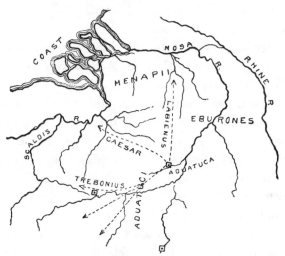

The Three Columns.

three legions he sent toward the ocean, near the boundary between the Eburones and Menapii, on a reconnoissance to ascertain the standing of this part of Gaul, and to take measures accordingly. Trebonius he sent southwest with three to lay waste the region contiguous to the Aduatuci; he himself, with three legions, marched towards the Scaldis (Scheldt), intending to pursue Ambiorix to the confines of the Forest of Arduenna, between modern Brussels and Antwerp, whither he had retired with a few mounted companions.

By some authorities the river Sabis is read instead of the Scheldt, because the latter does not flow into the Mosa, as is stated by the Commentaries. The phrase is, "the river Scaldis which flows into the Mosa." But Cæsar could readily be in error geographically, and the Scheldt does empty into the sea not far from the mouth of the Meuse; the Scheldt was more likely to be the objective of one of the columns than the Sabis. A column which marched only so far as the Sabis could accomplish nothing, and this, moreover, was Trebonius' direction.

A rendezvous was given to both Labienus and Trebonius if possible to again rejoin Cæsar at Aduatuca on the seventh day, when, from their several reports, Cæsar would be able to determine the situation and decide upon future operations. On this day rations were due to the troops remaining in garrison. The amount of work thus cut out for the short space of a se'nnight reminds one forcibly of some of Alexander's campaigns against mountain barbarians. The three columns were really more like three forced reconnoissances. Little could be accomplished in so short a time.

The tribes which had scattered from their allegiance to Ambiorix had so effectually done this, that there was neither town nor camp nor army to attack. They had retreated in small parties to the woods, and the only warfare they could wage was to attack isolated soldiers who were foraging or straggling for booty. "There was, as we have observed, no regular army, nor a town, nor a garrison which could defend itself by arms; but the people were scattered in all directions. Where either a hidden valley, or a woody spot, or a difficult morass furnished any hope of protection or of security to any one, there he had fixed himself. These places were known

to those that dwell in the neighborhood, and the matter
demanded great attention, not so much in protecting the
main body of the army (for no peril could occur to them
all together from those alarmed and scattered troops), as in
preserving individual soldiers, which in some measure tended
to the safety of the army. For both the desire of booty was
leading many too far, and the woods with their unknown and
hidden routes would not allow them to go in large bodies.
If he desired the business to be completed and the race of
those infamous people to be cut off, more bodies of men must
be sent in several directions, and the soldiers must be
detached on all sides; if he were disposed to keep the companies at their standards, as the established discipline and
practice of the Roman army required, the situation itself was
a safeguard to the barbarians, nor was there wanting to
individuals the daring to lay secret ambuscades and beset
scattered soldiers. But amidst difficulties of this nature, as
far as precautions could be taken by vigilance, such precautions were taken; so that some opportunities of injuring the
enemy were neglected, though the minds of all were burning
to take revenge, rather than that injury should be effected
with any loss to our soldiers."

Cæsar found that his time would not admit of his dealing
single-handed with the question as it stood; and he desired
to spare his legionaries. He invited the neighboring tribes,
by promise of abundant booty, to come and aid in exter-
minating these tribes, which were chiefly Eburones. This
he had made up his mind to do, as a punishment for their
destruction of the legion of Sabinus and Cotta, under circumstances which, according to his view, were treacherous in
the extreme. Cæsar could not forgive the tribes the bad
faith of their leader. He visited them with punishment the
more terrible as it ended only with their extinction.

Rumor of this invitation reached the Germans across the Rhine, who deemed that it also applied to them, and gave them a rare chance of plunder. A certain tribe, the Sugambri, abutting on the Rhine, crossed a force of two thousand horsemen in boats thirty miles below Cæsar's bridge, and began collecting and driving off cattle, "of which the barbarians are extremely covetous." Learning at the same time that the camp at Aduatuca had been left without much of a garrison, and drawing small distinction between friend and foe, their greed of gain tempted them to try their fortunes there. They concealed their booty and marched on Aduatuca, crossing the Mosa at Maestricht.

Cæsar and his lieutenants were unable to return to the camp at Aduatuca by the seventh day, — by no means a remarkable circumstance, — and the garrison, which had been left with but seven days' rations, began to clamor to go foraging. Cicero had so far kept them closely within the ramparts. To collect victuals soon became a matter of necessity, and Cicero determined to send out some parties for food, not imagining that there could be any grave danger, as all the tribes had been scattered and there must be nine legions at no great distance. He erred in sending out too large a force, — five cohorts, and these probably the best, — leaving the camp by no means safely garrisoned. As ill-luck would have it, not long after these foraging parties had left camp, the two thousand German horse put in an appearance and found the camp insufficiently defended. Though his position had indeed been a trying one, the condition of affairs showed lack of care on the part of Cicero. A soldier must assume that the improbable will happen.

The Germans had so suddenly approached by the Decuman gate, that a number of sutlers had been surprised with their booths outside, and the cohort there on guard was unable to

do aught but retire in confusion and close the entrance behind
them. Inside the camp everything was in disorder, and the
forces all but lost their power to act. It was even surmised
that Cæsar must have been defeated, and that this was the
van of the victorious army of Gauls. But for the presence
of mind of Sextius Baculus, who was invalided by wounds,
but who nevertheless seized weapons and encouraged the men

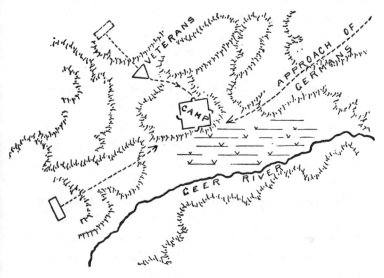

Cicero at Aduatuca.

to defend the ramparts, the enemy could readily have forced
an entrance. Thus state the Commentaries; but it seems as
if five cohorts inside a camp were more than a match for two
thousand horsemen outside. Where Cicero was is not stated;
yet he had earned reputation last year by stanchly defending
his camp. Aduatuca seemed to be a pitfall to Cæsar.

But while the German horsemen were debating how to
make good their capture, the foragers returned. These, in
their turn, were unable to effect an entrance; for the whole

camp was surrounded by the barbarians. Different counsels prevailed among them; the veterans urging one course, the new soldiers and camp-followers another. The foragers had apparently been sent out under several officers. No one seems to have had sole authority. The veterans, under command of C. Trebonius, a knight, took the only reasonable view of the case and resolved to cut their way through. Forming a compact column, a wedge or triangle (*cuneus*), by a bold push they reached the camp in good order and in safety, with the horse and camp-attendants. Another party, less well-led, had endeavored to make a stand on an adjoining knoll; but on perceiving the success of the veterans, attempted to do the same thing. Of this party, however, a number were cut out and slain; for not only were the Germans on the lookout for such a manœuvre, but the party presumably acted inexpertly, and passed over unfavorable ground. The entire matter shows demoralization and lack of management.

The camp having been regarrisoned, the Germans saw their chance of success gone, and withdrew, carrying their plunder beyond the Rhine. The forces in the camp were in a sorry state, and scarcely believed that Cæsar was safe when his cavalry vanguard, under Volusenus, actually arrived. Cæsar had returned with his work half done, because he had promised Cicero to do so, and had agreed to meet Labienus and Trebonius.

Having reëstablished affairs in the camp, he again set forth in pursuit of Ambiorix, this time accompanied by auxiliaries from all the neighboring tribes, who scouted the country traversed by the army, and burned and ravaged to such an extent that those insurgents who escaped the sword would surely perish by hunger. But despite the greatest rewards offered for the capture of Ambiorix, this wily chief eluded every snare, though frequently nearly taken. With but four companions, it is said, he moved from one fort or hiding-place to another and escaped the closest pursuit.

Cæsar next marched back to Durocortorum (Reims), the chief town of the Remi, the tribe which of all others, except the Ædui, was most faithful to and most highly esteemed by Rome. Here he held a council of the Gallic tribes, to decide upon the conspiracy of the Senones and Carnutes. Acco, the chief of the conspirators, was found guilty, together with a number of others. Acco was punished "according to the

Winter-Quarters, B. C. 53–52.

custom of our ancestors" (*more majorum*), by being stood in a collar and beaten to death. Some of the conspirators fled, and to these all allies were forbidden to furnish fire and water.

Cæsar now went into winter-quarters. Two legions were camped on the frontiers of the Treviri, two among the Lingones; the remaining six at Agendicum (Sens) in the land of the Senones. The legions were thus within better supporting distance of each other, in lieu of isolated, as they had been the year before. Corn having been provided in abundance and stored in safety, Cæsar himself set out for Italy, feeling that his army was safe from insurrections for some months.

The operations of this year are characterized by the able and rapid dispositions and manœuvres of Cæsar against the equally subtle work of Ambiorix in northeast Gaul. The campaign was accompanied by thorough devastation of the country, but in this instance the devastation was not only not an unusual act, but it may perhaps be claimed to be the only means of subduing the tribes actually in revolt. Such measures have to be judged, even at that day, by the attendant circumstances. What on one occasion was a simple act of war, on another occasion might be an act of simple barbarity.

The one point of criticism in this year's operations is the carelessness of Cicero at Aduatuca, which Cæsar felt called on gravely to rebuke. As good fortune would have it, no great evil came of it, but it might well have resulted in another Sabinus affair.

Gallic Helmet.

XV.

VERCINGETORIX. WINTER 53–52 B. C.

GAUL had apparently been reduced; Cæsar could look back on a good six years' work. But Gaul was really ripe for a fresh revolt, for the Roman yoke was bitter. No one was habitually left by Cæsar in supreme command while he was absent; the Gauls had free play. They rose under Vercingetorix, a man of remarkable ability and breadth, and before Cæsar could rejoin his legions they had cut off his access to them. The outlook was desperate; so soon as Cæsar reached the Province, he saw his dilemma. The Province was threatened; but by activity he was able sufficiently to protect it. By a bold and difficult winter march across the Cebenna mountains with a few cohorts, Cæsar attracted the attention of Vercingetorix, who, surprised at his audacity, advanced to meet him. Upon this, Cæsar with a mere escort of horse pushed through the gap the enemy had opened, and by riding night and day kept well ahead of danger, rejoined his legions, and concentrated them at Agendicum in February. He had a critical war on his hands. Vercingetorix finding that Cæsar had eluded him, retraced his steps to the Liger. Cæsar advanced from Agendicum south, taking Vellaunodunum and Genabum.

WHEN Cæsar reached Cisalpine Gaul, he heard of the intestine turmoils in Rome, of the murder of Clodius, and the report that all the youth had been ordered to take the military oath, or in other words to report for duty with the eagles. He therefore felt warranted in ordering a general draft in Cisalpine Gaul and the Province. His six years' campaign had borne good fruit. To all appearance Gaul had been subdued and her neighbors in Germany and Britain taught not to interfere with her internal economies. Rumors of these grave troubles in Roman politics had also reached Gaul, and though this country had been fully tranquillized, the quiet was but skin deep. No sooner had Cæsar's back been turned than the chiefs of the leading tribes began conspiring to rid their country of the burden of the Roman people. This was a favorable season, as Cæsar, they thought, would be obliged to remain in Italy to protect his own interests in the home government; a necessity they deemed of far greater consequence to him than the allegiance of Gaul.

The conspirators met in secret and retired places; they discussed their grievances; they made especial complaint of the cruel death of Acco, and other leading Gauls; they foresaw the possibility of a similar fate befalling themselves; they denounced the devastation of their land; they bewailed the yoke put upon their country, and they bound themselves with a solemn oath to die, if need be, in freeing her. It was planned to attack, or at least blockade, the Roman camps before Cæsar could return, and to try to cut him off from return by waylaying him on the road. This seemed all the more easy to accomplish because these chieftains knew that not one of the legions could move its camp without Cæsar's personal orders, — it was not Cæsar's custom to leave any special officer in full command, — and with the roads beset, Cæsar could not himself reach the legions without an escorting army.

That there should be no one left in supreme command during Cæsar's absence strikes us as a singularly weak method. Lack of positive rules of rank and command had more than once brought about disastrous results; but this custom, as well as the constant rotation in command among Roman officers, appears to have wrought less injury than might be expected. It worked, barely worked, in the Roman army; in no other army could such a system have worked at all.

The Carnutes, who had been most seriously struck by the

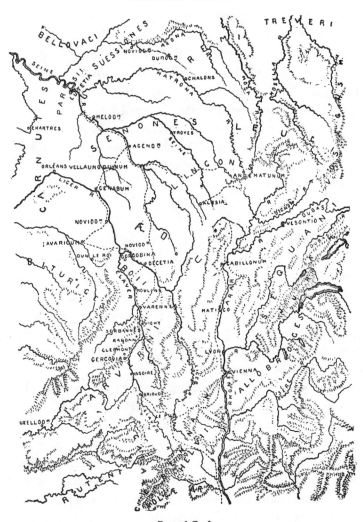

Central Gaul.

death of Acco, were first under arms and agreed to begin the
war, providing the other tribes would sustain them. An
oath so to do was taken by all, and was pledged on their
military standards in the most solemn manner. Accord-

ingly, on the day set for the insurrection, under command of Cotuatus and Conetodunus, two desperate men, the Carnutes rendezvoused at Genabum (perhaps Orleans, but more likely Gien, to the east of Orleans) and massacred all the Romans, mostly traders, in the place. Among them was C. Fusius Cita, Cæsar's commissary of this department.

The intelligence of this act traveled like lightning. It is said to have reached the Arverni (Auvergne), in other words, to have gone from Genabum to Gergovia, one hundred and sixty miles through the valleys of the Loire and Allier, from sunrise to the end of the first watch, nine A. M. The news was passed along by men stationed in towers on convenient hills, who gave out shouts of peculiar kinds, or as it is phrased "sonorous monosyllables." The habit of thus conveying intelligence continued in Gaul through the Middle Ages. Some remains of these towers still exist. If the wind was contrary, fire was employed in lieu of the voice. Similar means have been used in many lands and ages. It is a natural thing to do. Signaling is very old; but alphabetical signaling is of quite recent origin.

Vercingetorix, a young, intelligent and powerful chief, born in Gergovia, — son of Celtillus the Arvernian who had been put to death for aspiring to the sovereignty of all Gaul, — excited the passions of his subjects and caused them to rise against their Roman tyrants. The older chiefs did not deem the movement opportune, for the Arverni had long been faithful allies of Rome. They caused Vercingetorix to be expelled from Gergovia, their chief fortress. But Vercingetorix was not to be so readily turned from his purpose. He called to his standard all the poor and desperate, and many of the young and ambitious; and in a short period of time grew so strong that he drove out all the other chiefs and established himself in Gergovia. Saluted as king, he won the ear of all the neighboring tribes along the Liger to the sea, and even beyond that river, — Senones, Parisii, Pictones, Cadurci, Turones, Aulerci, Lemnovices, — and was chosen chief leader of the uprising. The Ædui declined to take part, and kept some of the tribes east of the Liger from joining in the insurrection.

Vercingetorix' army grew apace, though his discipline was so severe and cruel that he is said often to have forced recruits into his ranks from fear of death or mayhem. In one fashion or another, at all events, he assembled an army of vast numbers, which was especially excellent in cavalry. The infantry was not so good, but the horse was increased in numbers by mixing light troops with the squadrons.

Vercingetorix was undoubtedly a man of exceptional ability. His time, as it turned out, was inopportune, but this error can scarcely be attributed to want of judgment. At that moment, neither he nor any person could foresee how much more dangerous for the Romans and promising of success to his countrymen an uprising would be, if put off a few years, until Cæsar was so deeply engaged in the Civil War that he could not personally come to Gaul. Fortunate indeed for Cæsar, that so strong an adversary as Vercingetorix should not have delayed his action until after the final rupture with Pompey.

Vercingetorix opened his campaign by sending a force under the Cadurcan Lucterius into the land of the Ruteni in southern Gaul, while he himself marched on the Bituriges south of the Liger, who had not joined his cause. The latter sent for aid to the Ædui, the ever faithful allies of Rome, who dispatched a force to their assistance. On arriving at the Liger, which is the boundary of the Ædui, this force heard, or the anti-Romans in it pretended to hear, that the Bituriges had treacherously planned to attack them; and, acting on this ground, returned home. The Bituriges then joined Vercingetorix.

Cæsar heard of these things while in Italy. Pompey and he had again placed affairs in Rome on a basis satisfactory to both, and Cæsar was enabled to leave. But so soon as he reached Cisalpine Gaul, perhaps at the Rhone, he perceived his dilemma. He was quite at a loss how to join his army. The Gallic chieftains had been shrewd in their plans. He could not send for the legions. He could get no messengers through to any one of his camps, nor indeed direct their movements. Isolated as they were, they might each be cut to pieces in detail if they attempted to move, and before they could concentrate. They had no special head on whom he could rely to do the wisest thing under the circumstances. Nor could he go to the legions, for he dare not trust himself to any one, the disaffection had become so general.

Meanwhile Lucterius had gained over the Ruteni and the Nitiobriges and Gabali, adjoining tribes, and was preparing to make a descent on Narbo, in the Province near the coast. But Cæsar was fertile in expedients. His restless nature recognized no impossibilities. Like all great soldiers he rose to the occasion, and gained in strength as the dangers thickened. He set out for Narbo, and reaching the place, — as he readily could, for the Province was in no wise associated with the uprising, — he took the reins in hand.

Cæsar's appearance restored confidence; he garrisoned Narbo, and by encouraging the populations near by, raised a sufficient body of recruits to enable him to protect the border towns along the Tarnis river, adjoining the Ruteni, and those among the Volcæ Arecomici and Tolosates. He thus made it impossible for Lucterius to invade the Province, for the front presented to him was too bold to promise lasting results.

Having secured the left flank of the Province front, Cæsar moved northward towards the Helvii, where he had meanwhile ordered to assemble a number of recruits from Italy and some forces from the Province. He feared that Vercingetorix would move against his legions, and he planned to attract his attention away from them and towards himself.

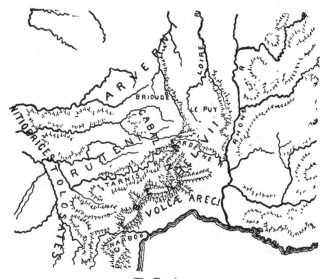

The Province.

Something must be done to draw the Gallic leader near the Province, where he could be neutralized. Cæsar saw that he must undertake some daring operation to arrest the notice of Vercingetorix, if he would gain a chance to reach his army; and though the snow was six feet deep, he marched his troops with incredible labor and sufferings across the Cebenna mountains, — substantially up the Ardèche and down the Loire valleys by modern Aps, Aubenas, and St. Cirgues, — debouched into the territory of the Arverni towards Le Puy, and advanced to Brioude. He then sent his cavalry forward to cut a wide swath through the land to inspire dread and terror.

Dumfounded at seeing their land made the scene of war

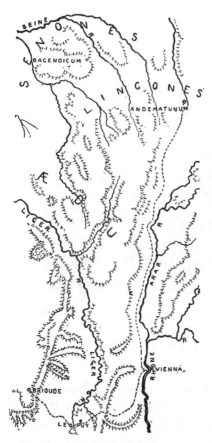

in lieu of the Province, as well as at the sight of a fully equipped army emerging from mountains which not even an individual had ever before attempted to cross in winter, the Arverni cried aloud to Vercingetorix for aid. The latter left the Bituriges question to settle itself, and with his best troops moved by forced marches towards the Roman army. Cæsar's diversion had lured Vercingetorix away from where he was most useful to his cause. Leaving the younger Brutus in command, with orders to use his cavalry in vigorous scouting and to keep restlessly on the move, Cæsar

Cæsar's March to his Legions.

himself hurried to Vienna on the Rhone; there, finding some cavalry which had been newly recruited, and had at his orders assembled in this town, he placed himself at their head, set out and marched day and night through the land of the Ædui to that of the Lingones, where two of his legions were wintering at Andæmatunum (Langres). He had thrust aside a danger which menaced his entire scheme of conquest

Agendicum to Avaricum.

by a markedly fine diversion; he had, without a moment's hesitation, run a serious personal risk, — which, however, was unavoidable, and therefore advisable, — and had completely baffled the enemy. He was now safe. He had traveled so rapidly that he had kept ahead of the danger of discovery. From Andæmatunum Cæsar sent orders to the two legions among the Treviri to move towards him, so as again to gather his forces into one body. The other six had wintered at Agendicum, among the Senones. At this place he summarily rendezvoused all the legions. These exceedingly rapid and well conceived movements puzzled the Gauls as to his intentions, and forestalled any of the tribes engaged in the plot in an attack which they might otherwise have made on the legions during their concentration. Cæsar reached Agendicum about the end of February. One cannot admire his conduct of this affair too highly.

Hearing that Cæsar was thus concentrating, Vercingetorix moved back to the land of the Bituriges, and thence to Gergobina Bojorum (St. Parize le Chatel) at the confluence of the Liger and Elaver, which he determined to attack. This was the capital of the Boii, who had remained faithful to Rome. They had been settled there by Cæsar after their defeat in the Helvetian campaign. It was a difficult task for Cæsar to undertake a winter campaign, as the transportation of supplies was almost impossible; one can scarcely imagine how bad the few roads there were could be; but everything must be risked, lest the allied tribes should lose confidence in Rome, and, still more important, lose confidence in Cæsar, which they would be sure to do if he allowed one of their chief towns to be taken. He concluded to rely largely on the good will of the Ædui to keep him supplied with corn.

Having got his forces well in hand, he left two legions and the baggage at Agendicum, and moved towards the Boii, hoping to keep them in allegiance by extending to them his protection. He sent forward messengers to encourage them to stout resistance and assure them of his speedy arrival. Coming on the second day after starting to Vellaunodunum (Triguères), he made arrangements to capture it, as he not only needed it for a storehouse, but could not leave it in the enemy's hands in his rear. In two days Cæsar had drawn up his lines of contravallation, and the town, seeing plainly that resistance would be useless, capitulated, and gave up its arms and six hundred hostages. Leaving Trebonius to complete the surrender, Cæsar marched without delay on Genabum of the Carnutes. This, as above said, was probably modern Gien, though generally assumed to be Orleans. In pushing for Gergobina, which he aimed quickly to reach, it would be much out of Cæsar's way and over a bad tract of country to march to Orleans, and as it was not essential to do so, he would not be likely at this moment to vary from his straight course. Moreover, Gien is a better location for an oppidum, being on a hill, while Orleans is on a slope. This town, Genabum, the Carnutes had not yet garrisoned, as they expected Cæsar would be delayed a long time at Vellaunodunum, whereas he reached Genabum, much to the surprise of the inhabitants, in two days after Vellaunodunum had capitulated, when they had barely received news of the fact. He could scarcely have reached Orleans, hampered by his considerable trains, which is fifty miles as the crow flies, in this short time — another argument in favor of Gien. The population at midnight endeavored to escape across the Liger, near by, over which there was a bridge, but Cæsar had already detailed two legions to observe the town; and the inhabitants, being much delayed at the bridge on account of its narrowness, were prevented from escaping and driven back into the place. Cæsar entered the town and gave it up to pillage, as punishment for the recent murder of Romans within its walls. Thence he marched south on Noviodunum (Sancerre) and Avaricum of the Bituriges (Bourges).

Gallic Horseman.
(From a terra-cotta Statuette.)

XVI.

AVARICUM. LATE WINTER AND EARLY SPRING, 52 B. C.

VERCINGETORIX sought to interfere with Cæsar's siege of Noviodunum, but to no effect. He conceived the idea that it was unwise to risk battle with the Romans; that more could be accomplished by a system of small-war. This was a remarkable plan of campaign for a barbarian. It is what gave Fabius his fame in the second Punic War. The Gauls burned their crops and towns to prevent Cæsar from victualling his army. Avaricum alone in that section was spared. This town (Bourges) had but one approach. Here Cæsar began siege works and built a mound. Vercingetorix tried to raise the siege by harassing the Roman army. He suffered much from the jealousies and dissensions of the allied tribes, but his ability and character sufficed to hold them together. The Gauls ably managed the siege. The wall, built up of logs, stones and earth, was strong and tough. Sallies were made with considerable success, still there was but one end possible; the place was taken and forty thousand souls perished. Cæsar found on hand much corn. Labienus was sent from here against the Parisii. Vercingetorix, foreseeing Cæsar's plans, sought to defend the line of the Elaver, but Cæsar cleverly stole a passage, and marched on Gergovia.

VERCINGETORIX, on hearing of the havoc Cæsar was playing with his allied towns, gave up the siege of Gergobina and moved forward to meet the Romans. Cæsar had just completed the siege of Noviodunum. The inhabitants were in the act of delivering up hostages, horses and arms to the centurions, when the arrival of Vercingetorix' cavalry vanguard was seen in the distance. Encouraged by this apparent relief, a certain party of citizens again resorted to arms, shut the gates, manned the walls and refused to surrender. They were with difficulty suppressed, though the centurions receiving the surrender behaved with consummate skill. At the same time Cæsar, by a smart attack of his cavalry, drove back the van of the Gauls with considerable loss. In the combat his native cavalry came near to being beaten, but a body of four hundred Germans newly recruited proved equal to their reputation, and by their vigorous and unusual tactics turned the tide.

Vercingetorix retired, and Cæsar marched to Avaricum, the best fortified town of the Bituriges. He proposed to besiege it, in the belief that its capture would reduce all the region to obedience. The name Avaricum comes from the River Avara (Euse); Bourges is a relic of Bituriges.

Vercingetorix, who was by long odds the strongest opponent Cæsar ever had in Gaul, was taught by the failures at Vellaunodunum, Genabum and Noviodunum, that he could not deal with Cæsar in open warfare. He convoked an assembly of the tribes, and informed the chiefs that, in order to win success, he must undertake a system of small-war, so as, if possible, to cut the Romans off from rations and forage for their beasts, the want of which latter would render Cæsar's cavalry more or less harmless. By self-sacrifice alone could they save Gaul from Roman oppression. They must burn and destroy their own farms and villages; everything not beyond capture from its defenses or position must be made unavailable to the enemy. This course would oblige the Romans to send to a distance to gather supplies, and Vercingetorix could then fall upon their detachments and beat them in detail. So long as the legions could keep together, there was no Gallic courage or discipline which could cope with them.

This plan, however severely it fell on his own people, was full of wisdom in regard to the enemy. With a sufficiency of victual in his own rear, Vercingetorix proposed to starve out the Roman armies. As much credit is due to this barba-

rian chief for his masterly conception of the proper means of
opposing Cæsar's legions as was due to Fabius for the same
method of meeting the victorious phalanxes of Hannibal.
The plan was the more easy for the barbarians to carry out,
as they scoured the country to a much greater extent than
the soldiers of Cæsar; were more familiar with its resources
and topography, and had the population on their side.

Acting on the scheme thus devised for them by Vercingetorix, the Bituriges began to destroy all the towns and provisions which could possibly fall into the Roman possession.
It was a hard lot, but they preferred this loss to the prospect
of death themselves, and the sale of their wives and daugh-
ters into slavery — a certain fate, as they believed, if Cæsar
should now succeed in conquering the land.   Twenty towns
were burned in one day. Almost alone and after long debate,
Avaricum was spared on account of its exceptional situation
for defense, and a proper garrison was thrown into the town.
And, at a distance of fifteen miles, Vercingetorix camped
with his army in a spot defended by woods and marshes,
probably near Dun-le-roy, at the confluence of the Taisseau
and Auron, some eighteen miles southeast of Avaricum. The
marshes have now dried up and the streams have been narrowed.   He did not dare to interfere with the siege of Avaricum, but closely watched the operations of the Romans,
faithfully scouted the neighborhood, attacked their foraging
parties whenever he could safely do so, and kept well posted
in all their movements.   He "received intelligence every
hour in the day:"

Avaricum, in the middle of an extended level stretch of
country, was surrounded on north and east and west by
marshy rivers, the modern Yèvres, Yèvrette and Auron,
affluents of the Liger, and the marsh they produced.   It had
but one narrow approach on the southwest.   This is now

much wider than it used to be. The rivers of Bourges have
gradually been canalled, a work which has broadened the
strip of land, while constant accretions have raised the level
of its slopes. The entire marsh has by the industry of generations been reclaimed, and rich fields and gardens now
occupy its site. The plateau descends to these low-lying
fields in a gentle grade. The general height of the plateau
above the meadows is still what Cæsar gives it, but its edges
are less abrupt.

Avaricum had forty thousand souls. Cæsar camped between the Auron and Yèvrette, on an eminence half a mile

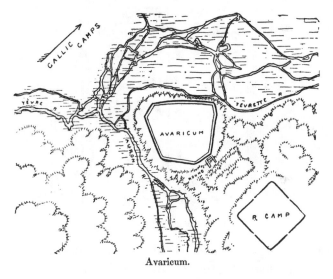

Avaricum.

from the gates. The site of his camp is now, appropriately
enough, occupied by a government gun-foundry and shop,
and by other military establishments. Between the camp
and town was a depression in the ground protecting the latter like a huge ditch. This has now been filled up to accommodate modern structures, though it can still be traced, if
carefully sought. Cæsar began the erection of a terrace,

vineæ and two towers. Owing to the marshes, a line of
contravallation was neither feasible nor necessary. He must
attack along the narrow approach, which was not over four
hundred feet wide. The top of the wall of Avaricum was
eighty feet higher than the floor of the ravine.

Vercingetorix carried out his small-war programme well.

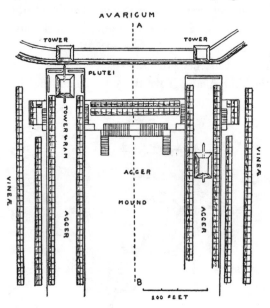

Terrace at Avaricum (plan).

The Romans could not go far to forage without being
attacked. Rations began to fail; the Ædui, growing lax in
their fealty, were by no means prompt in furnishing corn;
the Boii were poor; foraging was an altogether uncertain
resource, now that the country was devastated. Still, the
soldiers bore their deprivations well. Cæsar not infrequently
consulted the wishes of his army, as a matter of policy as
well as precedent. Now, in his anxiety for the welfare of his
legions, he went so far as to offer to raise the siege if the

men felt that their hardships were too great; the answer
came promptly, an emphatic "No." They would avenge the
manes of their comrades at any cost. Thus rings with no
uncertain sound the voice of all soldiers who recognize the
great captain in their chief.

While the siege was progressing, and it was pressed with
all vigor, Vercingetorix, from his camp to the south,
approached near to Avaricum and camped on its northwest.
He hoped for some chance to deal the Romans a blow. With
his horse and the attendant light foot he soon after made his

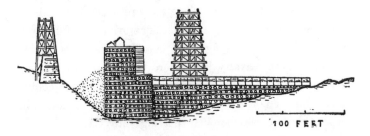

Terrace at Avaricum (section on line A-B).

way to a place which the Roman foragers were wont to pass
in going out on this daily duty, hoping to catch a large
party of them in an ambush. Cæsar fortunately learned of
this attempt.

We do not hear much of the details of Cæsar's scouting
and spy system, but he was generally so well informed of
what went on in the enemy's camp that we can but draw the
conclusion that he had organized an effective "secret service" system.

Cæsar set out at midnight with the bulk of his force to
checkmate the scheme of the barbarian leader by attacking
his camp in his absence, where no person, he heard, was left
in absolute command. On reaching the place he "ordered

the baggage to be piled and the arms to be got ready," in other words, prepared for battle. Vercingetorix had placed his camp on a height surrounded by the Avaricum morass, where it was but fifty feet wide; had broken down the bridges leading to it, and occupied the few fords in force. On reconnoitring it, Cæsar found the position so strong, that he sensibly declined an unequal combat from which nothing could be gained. The soldiers, not recognizing the dangers of the ground, demanded battle, but Cæsar showed them that it would be too costly in life, and as he had already accomplished his aim in forestalling the ambush of Vercingetorix, it was not worth the doing. The army returned to the siege.

On the return to camp of Vercingetorix, the failure to bring the Romans to a fight on unequal terms, his having gone off with the cavalry just before Cæsar appeared before the camp, and the general delay in affairs, raised a clamor against him among his fickle-minded Gallic allies, who accused him of treacherously playing into Cæsar's hands. But this accusation and feeling Vercingetorix, by representing his case and prospects with great cleverness, managed to turn aside, and, indeed, change into so favorable a sentiment. that the Gauls determined to send ten thousand men to Avaricum, lest the Bituriges alone should reap all the glory of defeating Cæsar. Still, the difference between the hearty coöperation of Cæsar's legionaries, and the suspicious and jealous dissensions in the camp of Vercingetorix was marked, and made the chances run all the more in favor of the Romans. That Vercingetorix was able to hold these conflicting elements together redounds much to his credit.

The Gauls ably managed the defense of Avaricum. They opposed the Roman method of sieges with great ingenuity. The mural hooks and rams used by the Romans to pull and batter down the walls they would catch with a noose, and drag into the town. They undermined the Roman mound, at which work they were expert, as there were many iron and copper miners in the country; they raised towers as high as the Romans on the threatened side of their wall, and covered the woodwork with skins; they set the vineæ on fire by nocturnal sallies; they made sorties every day, and impeded the work greatly by throwing sharp stakes, stones and hot pitch upon the besiegers. A civilized garrison could scarcely have done the defense greater justice.

The Gallic wall, of heavy logs and stones, was peculiarly difficult to attack with battering-ram or fire. The logs were laid across the line of the wall, two feet apart, and held in place by heavy cross logs mortised together. These were packed with earth, and the ends of the logs at the outer side of the wall were held in place with the stones which made its facing. The stone protected the walls from fire; the ends of the logs would only char, and the logs and earth, from their greater elasticity, resisted the rams far better than stone alone could do. The

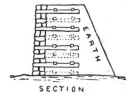

SECTION

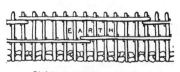

PLAN OF ONE LAYER

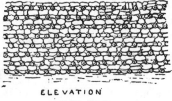

ELEVATION
Gallic Wall.

wall had to be broken down piecemeal; it would not tumble together.

Still, the legions persevered, despite wet and cold, and in twenty-five days had raised a mound three hundred and thirty feet broad and eighty feet high. These figures are disputed by some critics, though given by the Commentaries. They are not exceptional, and the topography bears them out. When the mound had all but reached the enemy's walls, it began to sink. It had been undermined, and was, moreover, fired from the mine. This occurred at midnight, when Cæsar happened to be making a tour of inspection, and at the same moment a vigorous sally from two gates on each side of the tower was made by the besieged. The Avaricans threw torches, pitch, dry wood and other inflammables on the towers and terrace. Two legions were generally on guard at night, and these were taken unawares. The fight lasted all night. The pent-houses were destroyed, and the Romans for a while had to march to and fro from the towers without cover. The besieged now saw a good chance of victory.

Cæsar here mentions an occurrence which enables us to compare ancient with modern gallantry under fire: "There happened in my own view a circumstance which, having appeared to be worthy of record, we thought it ought not to be omitted. A certain Gaul before the gate of the town, who was casting into the fire opposite the turret balls of tallow and fire which were passed along to him, was pierced with a dart on the right side and fell dead. One of those next him stepped over him as he lay, and discharged the same office; when the second man was slain in the same manner by a wound from a cross-bow, a third succeeded him, and a fourth succeeded the third; nor was this post left vacant by the besieged, until, the fire of the mound having been extinguished and the enemy repulsed in every direction, an end was put to the fighting." It seems that three men or more were shot down at their post, and that the post was at once filled by fresh men. This is mentioned as an exceptional piece of courage. In our day we have seen many such. Entire color-guards have not infrequently been shot down in battle; but there has never been a lack of men eager to take their places.

The sortie was, after a fierce struggle, beaten back. The Gallic soldiers in the city now formed a project of leaving the town by retiring across the marshes in its rear by night, and making for the camp of Vercingetorix; but the clamor of the women, who were to be left behind to the tender mercies of the besiegers, gave notice to the Romans of this evasion, and, for fear of being cut off, the garrison desisted.

Next day, a heavy rain coming on, the ramparts of the town were carelessly guarded. Cæsar, perceiving this, quietly made his preparations, sharply advanced the towers and ordered the walls to be scaled, offering great rewards to those who first mounted them. The Romans broke from cover with exceptional energy, and assaulted in good form. The enemy, surprised and disconcerted, was driven in; but with admirable constancy drew up in the market-place in wedges (or close order), determined to resist to the end. And here no doubt they would have stubbornly fought; but when they saw the Romans moving along the walls so as to surround all who should be left in the city, the columns dissolved, and each man sought his individual safety in flight. Most fled to the northern extremity of the oppidum. Thus broken up, the Gauls lost head; and having thrown away their arms, the Romans had them at their mercy, and cut them down remorselessly, sparing neither age nor sex. What the infantry could not reach fell at the hands of the cavalry. Out of forty thousand men, women and children, barely eight hundred escaped across the marshes to Vercingetorix' camp. The Gallic chief received and distributed them among the several divisions of his army, lest in one body their sad tale should breed a mutiny.

Once again, Vercingetorix had a hard task in reconciling

his fellow-citizens to this disaster; and nothing shows the native ability of this remarkable man better than the way in which, under the stress of misfortune, he kept his ascendancy over this fickle, unreasonable people. "As ill success weakens the authority of other generals, so on the contrary his dignity increased daily, though a loss had been sustained." Vercingetorix now advised the Gauls to imitate the Roman method and to fortify their camps. This counsel they followed and thenceforward continued to do. He also by skillful appeals to the neighboring tribes succeeded in winning all over to his cause, and very shortly replaced the troops lost at Avaricum with a still larger force. Especially a fine body of cavalry came to him under Teutomatus, prince of the Nitiobriges. But though he would have been backed up by public sentiment in an offensive policy, this barbarian chief refrained from an attack on Cæsar's lines. He wisely kept to small-war.

Cæsar found in Avaricum also a large supply of corn and provender, and gave his army a much needed, well-earned rest. The spring and the time for more active operations were at hand, when the Ædui sent urgent messages to Cæsar praying him to come to their assistance, as there had arisen a serious division in the state, two parties respectively under Cotus and Convictolitavis, both of high lineage and much power, claiming the government, which was governed by an annual chief magistrate. Cæsar was loath to leave operations against Vercingetorix, whom he now hoped either to drive from the forest retreats to which he had retired, or else to close in and trap. But Cæsar could neither allow danger to lurk in his rear, nor temporize with the fealty of the Ædui. He therefore turned backward. It was through their land that his line of operations ran from his base, in the Province. If the Ædui were to waver in their allegiance, it would

become a question of subsistence and not strategy. It was
they kept his granary full of corn. They were indeed an
intermediate base. Arrived
among this people, — at
Decetia (Decize) on the
Liger, — Cæsar sent for the
senate of the Ædui to meet
him, and not only decided
the matter in dispute by
making Cotus, who had but
a minority at his back, re-
sign, and by placing the
government in the hands of
Convictolitavis, whom the
priests favored; but he induced the Ædui to promise
ten thousand infantry and
all their horse for him to
use in garrisons along his
line of operations, to protect the trains of corn which
they should forward him.

Having shelved this
danger, Cæsar sent Labie-
nus with four legions, two
from the army and the two
left at Agendicum, against
the Senones and Parisii
(or Lutetii), who had been

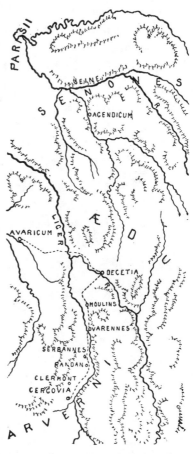

Avaricum to Gergovia.

roused by Vercingetorix; while he, with the six remaining,
marched on Gergovia in the land of the Arverni, proposing to besiege it. The Arverni, though they had long been
faithful allies of Rome, were now the centre of the rebellion.

The cavalry was divided between Labienus and Cæsar.
What Vercingetorix had been doing during Cæsar's absence
is not told us.   It looks as if he had retired into the hills
and woods of the Bituriges, and had been watching his opponent.   On learning Cæsar's direction, he guessed his objective and betook himself to the farther (left) bank of the
Elaver (Allier), and occupied it before Cæsar reached the

right bank.   This move-
ment shows that Vercin-
getorix, too, had either
the true instincts of the
soldier, or else possessed
an equally good corps of
scouts and spies.   His
manœuvre   placed   him
athwart Cæsar's path.   He
was intent on barring the
Romans from approach to
Gergovia, and he took
care to break down all
the bridges over the river.
The Elaver is still a good-
sized stream; it was then
a mighty bulwark of his
territory, and he must
keep it intact at all haz-

The Elaver.

ards.   This river was not
then fordable except in the low-water season in autumn,
and it was essential to Cæsar to cross without delay —
unless he was to acknowledge that Vercingetorix could
force him to change his plans.   He moved up the river,
struck it near modern Moulins — from Decetia was an old
Gaulish road which led to Moulins and was later made a

Roman road — and sought a chance to cross. From day to day Vercingetorix moved exactly as far as the Romans moved, and camped opposite to them at night.

Cæsar saw that he must resort to some stratagem to cross. Having camped one night at one of the broken bridges, most likely near Varennes, Cæsar next morning sent forward only two thirds of the army and all the baggage, ordering it to march in six corps, and in such order as to appear to be the entire force of six legions. With two legions he remained behind in hiding in the woods well back of the river. Vercingetorix followed the moving column on the other side up the river. So soon as the enemy was out of the way, Cæsar emerged from his hiding-place, and speedily rebuilt the bridge on the old piles which had been left standing, crossed to the left bank and intrenched a bridgehead; having done which he sent on and recalled the body which had marched ahead. This rejoined by stealing a march on Vercingetorix during the coming night. Vercingetorix, when he saw that he had been outwitted and knew that the whole Roman army had crossed, moved by forced marches on Gergovia, so as not to be brought to battle against his will.

This passage was skillfully accomplished. Cæsar here earned as much credit for a clever stratagem as Vercingetorix showed that he had been careless in scouting the river-banks. But we cannot too much praise the native ability of this barbarian chief, who without military education or example was able to do so much to oppose one of the greatest soldiers the world has ever seen. We cannot compare Cæsar's operation at the Elaver to the passage of the Hydaspes by Alexander, or that of the Rhone by Hannibal. It was far from as distinguished an operation. But nevertheless it was skillful and well-conceived; and was so well executed as to deceive a very keen-eyed opponent.

XVII.

THE SIEGE OF GERGOVIA. SPRING, 52 B. C.

THE height of Gergovia stands twelve hundred feet above the plain, and has at the summit a plateau over a mile long. It could be attacked most easily from the south. Vercingetorix had drawn up his forces on this slope. So soon as the Romans arrived, cavalry skirmishes became common, but the Gallic infantry remained behind the defenses. Cæsar camped southeast of the town and later seized a hill on its south, intrenched a second camp, and joined the two camps by works. This cut the Gergovians off from the river, and made their water supply uncertain. The Ædui, Cæsar's chief allies, had been giving him anxiety; rebellion now broke out in their army, which was on its way to join him. Cæsar left Fabius in command at Gergovia, made a speedy march to the rear, brought the rebels to terms, and returned. In twenty-four hours, his column of four legions had marched fifty miles. After due consideration, Cæsar determined to assault Gergovia. He laid his plans skillfully. Sending a force to make a demonstration against the west front, which the Gauls felt was not very strong, he drew all the Gallic troops to that quarter. He then suddenly threw forward his legions, which gallantly advanced and reached the very walls of the town. But they had not been furnished with scaling-ladders; few only mounted the top of the walls; the Gauls returned from the western front; Cæsar was driven back with heavy loss. He essays to gloss over this defeat in the Commentaries, but the facts are plain. The Ædui now broke out into open revolt, and Cæsar had to give over the siege. He had been roundly defeated.

IN five days' march, the first one being short on account of the fatigue of the column which moved up the river and back, and the last one short because he reached Gergovia early in the day, Cæsar arrived at the capital of the Arverni. The enemy opposed him only by a slight cavalry skirmish, and then retired to the upper slope of the very high hill on which the town was built, where, outside the wall of the oppidum, they camped.

Gergovia and Vicinity.

The heights of Gergovia, four miles south of modern Clermont-Ferrand, stand boldly up twelve hundred feet above the plain. It has been rechristened its ancient name. At the top is a quadrangular plateau a mile long by over a third of a mile wide. On the north and east the slope was probably wooded; access to the plateau by a body of troops might have been difficult. The south slope is a succession of terraces rather wide and not over steep. These apparently were not wooded. On the west lie the heights of Risolles, whose top is only one hundred feet lower than Gergovia and is connected with it by a neck of land. Two other hills, Monts Rognon and Puy Giroux, flank the Risolles, and are northwest and southwest of Gergovia respectively. On the south, like a huge buttress, is the Roche Blanche, a long and narrow hill, with rocky face on the south and east, and easy slopes elsewhere, about five hundred feet below the plateau of Gergovia. The Auzon flows south of Gergovia, and falls into the Allier. On the northwest runs a small brook. On the east was a large shallow lake, now drained. On the south and southeast, Gergovia was thought to be most accessible to attack.

Cæsar established his main camp on high and healthful ground south of the lake, perhaps one hundred feet above the plain. The Auzon ran behind his camp. It was certainly a task of some danger to attempt to take Gergovia by storm until Vercingetorix' army was disposed of, and Cæsar must get together victual in abundance before he could blockade or besiege it.

Descriptions and pictures of Gergovia are somewhat misleading. One is apt to conceive of a rocky eminence with top palisaded by nature and practically inaccessible. The north slope is wont to be described as impossible to capture. It is not so. The slope is not steep, though it is long. The

cultivation of many generations — it is now covered with rich
fields and vineyards — may have softened the slopes, but it
cannot have materially altered them.   It is probable that in
Cæsar's day the slope was concealed by woods, and that he
did not reconnoitre it thoroughly.   But the position could
have been surprised on the north far more easily than assaulted on the south.   So far from being, as it is generally

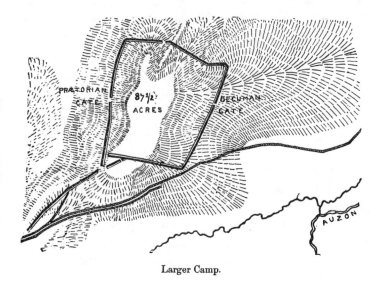

Larger Camp.

said to be, inexpugnable, the men who captured Lookout
Mountain, or who charged with Pickett up Cemetery Ridge,
would have laughed at the idea.   But ancient warfare was
different.

The terraces of the southern slopes were no doubt more
open, and it was on these terraces that Vercingetorix drew
up his army, which was protected by a wall of heavy stones,
six feet high, running along its front.   Here Vercingetorix
posted his allies, in order by tribes, in the most skillful manner, and daily exercised his troops — especially his cavalry

mixed with light armed foot — in skirmishes with the
Romans, so as to ascertain and improve their courage and
discipline. These combats took place on the plains between
Cæsar's camp and the slopes of Gergovia; the barbarians
debouching from the outlets of
the south and east front of the
oppidum.

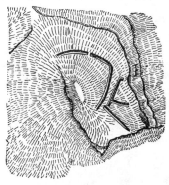

Cæsar soon discovered that
a hill south of the town, and
opposite the eminence on which
was built Gergovia (Roche
Blanche), was essential to the
enemy. By its posesssion the
Gauls were able to protect
themselves in getting at their
water, corn and forage, and

Small Camp at Gergovia.

here Vercingetorix had a small advanced post. He should
have held it in heavier force. The hill in places was no
doubt steeper in Cæsar's day than it now is. Slides have
since altered its slopes, but towards the plateau it could not
have been steep. Cæsar determined to capture this hill.
By a carefully planned night attack he drove off the meagre
garrison, and placing two le-
gions in their stead, speedily
intrenched a small camp upon
it, and connected this hill with
the main camp by a double
trench, twelve feet wide, and a

Profile of Double Trench.

parapet, such that access from one to the other was secure.
The two camps have been excavated. Their outlines are
still distinct. This act of Cæsar's cut the Gergovians off
from their main supply of water, for the Auzon, to which
they had been going by the glen road from the plateau, was

not easily accessible from another place. They now had to rely on springs on the plateau, which still exist and are fed from the higher mountains to the west, and on the brook at the northwest of the town. On this side Cæsar had made no demonstration.

Meanwhile the young Æduan nobles had been tampered with by the emissaries of Vercingetorix, who had contrived, by misrepresentations and gold, to abuse their minds about Cæsar's intentions respecting their nation. Convictolitavis, even, whom Cæsar had made chief of this tribe, partook of this feeling, and ordered the ten thousand men who, it had been agreed, should guard Cæsar's line of supplies, and who were just setting out with a large convoy, to march ostensibly to join Cæsar, but really to make a junction with Vercingetorix. The leader of this body was Litavicus. On the way, he and his men first exhibited their treachery, perhaps near modern Serbannes, by massacring the Romans who accompanied the train. The plot was revealed to Cæsar by Eporedorix, the Æduan noble, who was part of his *entourage*.

The matter was pressing. Cæsar was between two fires. The danger was to the rations on which he relied. He delayed not a moment. Leaving Fabius in command at Gergovia, he hastened with four legions in light order, accompanied by all his cavalry, to the Æduan army, which was at Randan on the way to join Vercingetorix. Surrounding it, he speedily brought it to terms. He convinced the soldiers of the faithlessness of their leaders, all of whom had fled to Gergovia so soon as their real intentions had been discovered. Eporedorix and Viridomarus, both serving with Cæsar, added their words to his; and their explanation and the conspirators' flight restored quiet in the Æduan army.

Cæsar was, however, unable to reach the disaffected Æduan citizens at home. These, stirred up by sedition, fell to massacring the Romans in their midst, and incited many others to take up arms. The whole nation was in turmoil. Many, indeed, when they heard that Cæsar had done no harm to the Æduan army for its treachery, — as he had not because he was obliged to temporize, — were desirous of returning to their allegiance; others were boldly for insurrection. In Bibracte, Convictolitavis murdered the Roman residents and plundered every Roman's property. All this made it essential that Cæsar should return to quell this tumult, which threatened his very base. Vercingetorix had by his machinations attacked him in his weakest spot.

Many of the Æduans had acted with duplicity and faithlessness; when they were put in the wrong, they professed contrition and humbly craved forgiveness. Part had been really misguided. It was hard to distinguish the honest from the perfidious. A Fabian policy had to be resorted to. Cæsar's military and political resources were taxed to the utmost. Though he had regained control of the Æduan army, the Æduan state was still capable of vast mischief.

During Cæsar's absence to suppress the mutiny of the leaders of the Æduan army, Vercingetorix attacked the Roman camp; and owing to its large extent, the two legions left behind had much ado to defend the ramparts. Vercingetorix forced the fighting, and constantly sent on relays of fresh troops. Though the defenses were strong, it was only with the aid of the engines and at great loss in men that the enemy could be held at bay. Fabius sent messengers to Cæsar, who speeded his return, leaving the revolt in the Æduan territory — however dangerous — for the future.

Cæsar's men made their long forced march with great alacrity. From the Gergovian camp to Randan, where Cæsar met the Æduan army, is twenty-five miles. He heard of the plot "almost at midnight." He left the camp presumably at sunrise, say at four A. M., reached Randan at noon, spent six or seven hours in negotiations and consequent action, then gave "three hours of the night to his soldiers for repose," say seven to ten P. M. (the night watches began at six P. M.), and returned from Randan to the camp in six hours more, making twenty-four hours in all, during which his column covered fifty miles. Nor did they reach the camp any too soon to avert serious disaster. The two legions were well-nigh exhausted.

Some days after, a favorable opportunity occurred for attacking the enemy. Cæsar gives us to understand that he had already determined to give up his attempt on Gergovia, owing partly to its difficulties, and especially to the Æduan imbroglio; but that he desired to make some demonstration, so as to retire with credit, and not allow Vercingetorix to accuse the legions of cowardice. He was not really besieging Gergovia. He was only observing it. Except that he was annoying the enemy, he had in no sense even blockaded him. Vercingetorix could have retired at any time.

This part of the Commentaries is plainly disingenuous. It may be true that Cæsar felt that he would have to return to the Æduan territory before long, but the fact remains plain that he attacked the Gergovian stronghold in the full expectation that he could capture it out of hand, and that he was repulsed with a heavy loss. We have nothing but the Commentaries, with an occasional reference in other authors, added to the topography, on which to base our narrative; but, reading the Commentaries between the lines, and in the light of our other knowledge (as in the case of Hannibal, we must sometimes read Livy), and keeping the topography clearly in view, the fact of an assault in good faith and a bloody repulse is manifest.

Cæsar had a keen eye. In the days when field-glasses

were unknown, the eye, if naturally good, was trained, like those of our Indians, to a surprising degree of accuracy. He noticed from the Roche Blanche, where he had located his lesser camp, that the defenses of the main plateau of the town, so far strongly beset, were quite disgarnished of troops. Deserters, "a great number of whom flocked to him daily," informed him that the top of one of the adjoining heights, the Risolles, marked 1 on the chart, was level, and communicated with the oppidum by a wooded and narrow neck (2); and that Vercingetorix had conceived some danger from that quarter. The north of the Gergovian height, it will be remembered, was not attempted by Cæsar in any sense; but he had seized the Roche Blanche, and might seize the Risolles, and thus win a nearer, and to the Gauls more dangerous, access to the plateau. The gate (3) of the oppidum, and the road to it from the westerly height (1), has been dug out so as to show the lay of the land in Cæsar's day. It varied but little from what it now is, except from a certain amount of natural débris, and gradual smoothing of the surface by generations of plowing since. Should Cæsar get possession of the Risolles height (1), he could do more towards cutting the enemy off from water and forage, — a fact which they cared not to face. What Cæsar might do next was the unknown quantity of the Gallic problem. Vercingetorix had foreseen the danger, and had sent all his force to fortify this flanking height. Some authors pick out Mont Rognon or Puy Giroux as the object of Vercingetorix' solicitude; but for Cæsar to take either of these would by no means compromise the Gergovians, both being beyond the range, and neither being connected with the plateau. Besides, the facts related show that the Gergovians were at work near at hand, at a place from which they could in a few minutes return to the oppidum.

Acting on this information, Cæsar saw that here was an excellent opening for a general assault. He sent some turmæ of cavalry at night round towards the height in question, to make a noisy demonstration on the west and south of it (6), and, to add to their number, he helmeted many of his muleteers, and sent them at daylight on the same errand, instructing them by ranging about in the skirts of the woods to attract the attention of the Gauls, and lead them to believe that an attack was coming from that quarter. He also sent a legion in support, with orders to take post below Puy Giroux, and to pretend to be hiding in the hollows and woods as if preparing a surprise. This demonstration, seen from the oppidum, resulted, as Cæsar anticipated, in the enemy withdrawing nearly all his force from the south front of the oppidum, and marching it over to the position (1) they thus deemed to be threatened. It was evident to them that Vercingetorix had been right in apprehending trouble from this quarter. They set to work to fortify its west front (a to b), and presumably the neck of land, for this was not precipitous enough to be its own defense. Cæsar's capital feint had succeeded as it deserved to succeed. This Gergovia affair is one of the earliest where the terrain is so well explored as to give us a thorough insight into the manœuvre. Barring the

Gergovia, from Roche Blanche.

use of artillery, the whole operation closely resembles a modern assault, in its method of preparation and execution.

Thus much accomplished, Cæsar, under cover of his feint, transferred the bulk of his force secretly and in small detachments from the greater to the lesser camp. The men marched behind the wall, as Polyænus says, crouching down so as not to be seen, and the ensigns, plumes and shields, which would have betrayed them, were covered so as not to attract attention to the manœuvre. Then he gave out his instructions to his legates. The place, he said, could not be taken by assault, but only by surprise; the men were to be kept well in hand and not allowed to go beyond orders, either from zeal or hope of plunder, lest they should be taken in flank when in confused order ; of which, to judge from Cæsar's description, there was some danger, which would not otherwise appear. The Ædui were sent from the greater camp by another circuit on the right to attack in another place. This was probably on the southeast angle of the oppidum (4).

The town wall was twelve hundred paces distant from the

foot of the mountain, as the crow flies. Irregularities in the ground made the access circuitous, and added to this distance at least a half. The road up the mountain now runs by the glen where lies Merdogne, and must always have done so. Midway up the ascent there was the stone wall six feet high, already mentioned. No defenses or camps were below; but above the stone wall were the barbarians' camps very closely packed together.

The signal of attack was given. With a rush the legionaries debouched from the gates of the lesser camp, advanced the short mile up the hill (9 and 10), and, swarming over the wall, at once became possessors of the camp. The surprise was complete. So much was this the fact that the king of the Nitiobriges, Teutomatus, barely escaped half-clothed from his tent, where he was resting during the noon-tide.

At this point, and having made this gain, for some strange reason Cæsar paused, and halted the Tenth legion, which he was with. This is one of the most inexplicable circumstances of his career. He states in his Commentaries that this much was all he intended to do. "Cæsar, having accomplished the object which he had in view, ordered the signal to be sounded for retreat." But this is clearly an excuse framed after the event. It is probable that, from his position when the troops were swarming over the stone wall (it may have been the knoll marked 5 on the chart), he was better able to recognize the questionable nature of the task than from below, and decided to call off his men. It is not impossible that he purposed to hold this position and erect vineæ and mounds; though, indeed, from what subsequently happened, it seems as if he might have been successful in a summary assault on the town, had he then and there pressed on. Writing afterwards, he says that "success depended on a surprise," and he had succeeded in surprising the enemy. Sounding the recall, he endeavored to arrest the onset of the other legions; but though the centurions and tribunes did their utmost, the legionaries, with the flush of past victories and the hope of plunder, either would not or did not hear. There were accidents in the ground between Cæsar and them to intercept the trumpet-blasts, but the legions at Thapsus broke away from Cæsar, and perhaps they did so here. They pressed on till they reached the wall of the town, where they were stopped for want of means of escalading the rampart, which had not been provided — a curious lapse, if a surprise and assault was intended. So little defended were the walls, that the women were seen hanging over them and imploring for mercy, expecting no less than immediate capture or death, as at Avaricum. Some of the men did reach the top of the wall. L. Fabius, centurion of the Eighth legion, lifted by his soldiers, scaled it, and others followed. Had the legionaries been furnished with ladders, it seems as if one vigorous effort would have met with success. Even as it was, the fact that some managed to scale the wall shows that in the absence of the garrison the thing was feasible.

By this time the Gauls had heard of the Roman assault, and, preceded by the cavalry, came rushing back to the defense of the city. In a few moments the ground back of the wall was beset by defenders, and the women, who had been imploring mercy, now — as was their wont, with disheveled hair and holding up their infants — bade their husbands defend them. The speedy return of the Gergovians proves that they could not have been so far away as Mont Rognon or Puy Giroux. The contest was now quite unequal, so much so that Cæsar was constrained to send back to the camp for the cohorts left there on guard under T. Sextius, ordering them to take up a position at the foot of the hill, so as to threaten Vercingetorix' right (8), and to protect the retreat if it should have to be made, by attacking the Gauls in flank. He himself, with the Tenth legion, now advanced somewhat to the support of the other legions which had gone beyond the position where he had halted the Tenth, and awaited the issue, holding his men well in hand. The other legionaries were still fighting bravely, but against odds of position and numbers, the Gauls having been able to make a sortie on their flank. T. Sextius and the others who had climbed it were thrown from the wall; the centurion, M. Petronius, also of the Eighth, attempting to burst the gates, was killed in trying to save his men.

At this instant the Ædui emerged on the Roman right, and though they had their right shoulders bared, — as the Gallic allies of Cæsar were in the habit of doing to distinguish them from the other barbarians, — the legionaries assumed that these were fresh troops of the enemy who had bared their shoulders as a stratagem, and at once began to retire somewhat confusedly. They had lost in killed, seven hundred men and forty-six centurions, but had illustrated Roman valor in every phase. The great loss in officers shows that these by no means lacked devotion.

The Tenth legion, by changes of position to suit the several cases, abundantly protected the retreat by threatening Vercingetorix' flank; the cohorts from the camp did their share, taking position on high ground to impose on Vercingetorix by endangering his advance. So soon as they reached the plain, the legions all turned and faced the enemy. Vercingetorix, who had hoped to have them at his mercy and who had followed in pursuit, impressed by this bold front, decided not to risk an attack, but led back his forces into the town.

On the return to camp, Cæsar took occasion to "censure the rashness" of the legionaries for not heeding the orders of their officers, while commending their valor; and showed them how nearly they had come to suffering a fatal defeat. As at Avaricum, said he, he had desired not to risk the lives of his men in a futile assault; and he bade them remember that he, their general, was the best judge of what it was wise to do, and that he required in his soldiers forbearance and self-command not less than valor and magnanimity. At the same time he encouraged them not to lose heart from one piece of bad luck, "nor attribute to the valor of the enemy what disadvantage of position had caused."

Cæsar had, as he says, not obtained such success over the enemy as would enable him under its cover to retire from the siege with honor. He felt that he must do more. On the next day he led out his army into the plain and offered battle to Vercingetorix, which this chief declined, and hostilities were confined to a cavalry skirmish, in which the Romans proved the victors. The succeeding day Cæsar did the like, having made all preparations to raise the siege. But as Vercingetorix would not accept his gage and descend into the level, Cæsar began to withdraw in open daylight, in full view of the enemy. Vercingetorix did not pursue.

One cannot refrain from contrasting this assault on Gergovia with some of Alexander's, — as, *e. g.*, the Rock of Chorienes, or Aornus, or the city of the Malli. The energy of Hannibal, one of whose weak points was his conduct of sieges, in more than one instance — as at Saguntum — stands out in marked relief from the lack of vigor here exhibited by Cæsar. And we have to judge Hannibal from the accounts of his enemies; Cæsar, by his own statements.

Nor is this the only similar case. We shall see how he paused at Thapsus, until his men took matters into their own hands. At Munda he stopped at the brook which separated him from Cnæus Pompey. With all Cæsar's consummate strategic courage, and a personal bearing above reproach, he was wont to lack the tremendous vitality in tactical initiative which we admire so heartily in other captains.

There are in other authors hints that this Gergovia affair is not accurately given by Cæsar, but that a really serious defeat is explained away in a manner which would do justice to the report of a modern general. It is related by Servirus Maurus Honoratus that so marked was the defeat that Cæsar was taken prisoner in the confusion, and only escaped by a lucky accident. Plutarch, indeed, says the Arverni had a sword captured from Cæsar's person, either here or at the battle preceding the siege of Alesia. However apochryphal these statements may be, Cæsar was clearly compelled to give up the siege for want of success in his assault. The Æduan question had, however, become so pressing that he was no doubt wise, for that reason alone, in retiring from Gergovia. That it was the only place he had failed to take in the Gallic war abundantly condones the failure.

Cæsar moved east, and on the third day after the assault he reached the Elaver, and repairing the bridge over the river, perhaps at Vichy, he retired to the right bank on the way to the territory of his former "kinsmen."

Cæsar now deliberately took up the question of the Ædui, the treachery of many of whose prominent men was apparent, despite the manner in which he had honored and protected them. The Æduan army, under Viridomarus and Eporedorix, probably disgusted at the late defeat, was leaving for home, and "Litivacus had set out with all the cavalry to raise the Ædui," but Cæsar made no effort to retain them. He merely represented to them how he had found the Ædui at the mercy of their neighbors and had placed them in the highest position of any tribe in Gaul, and left them to draw the inference.

Cæsar had collected a large amount of baggage, corn, horses and all his hostages in Noviodunum (Nevers), a town of the Ædui on the Liger.   When the Æduan army came to this place, they found that the chief men of the state had

Gergovia to Agendicum.

sent to Vercingetorix to negotiate a peace, and that the Roman alliance had been thrown over. This act still more confirms the idea of a serious defeat at Gergovia. Not willing to neglect so favorable an opportunity for regaining their independence, Eporedorix and Viridomarus seized and massacred the garrison of Noviodunum and all its traders, divided the spoil, sent the hostages to Bibracte, drove off the reserve horses which Cæsar had got from Italy and Spain for remounts, and burned the town, together with all the corn they could not carry away.   They then placed troops at the fords of the Liger to prevent the Romans from crossing.   They hoped to force Cæsar by lack of provisions to retire to the Narbonese.   They would then have Labienus, who was at Lutetia, at their mercy.

Learning of these things on the march from the Elaver towards the Liger, Cæsar saw that he was in a very dangerous position. His enemies were in high spirits at his late defeat; he was surrounded by troops in revolt — the victorious Arverni were on his rear, the Ædui in his front holding the Liger, the Bituriges on his left. But he also saw that it would be a shameful as well as a perilous thing to allow himself to be driven back to the Province, for this would isolate Labienus. He proposed, come what might, to go to the bottom of the matter, join Labienus, and punish the traitors at their own threshold.

Here we have Cæsar at his best. No one ever rose to the occasion more splendidly than this captain. The graver the danger, the bolder the front this great man presented to it. At times Cæsar appeared to lack a certain spirit of enterprise, in which Alexander and Napoleon excelled. But once put impending disaster before him, and no general ever proved himself more energetic, more able.

Cæsar made speed to reach the Liger, and sought a ford. At modern Bourbon-Lancy there has always been one; it was on his direct road; and though this ford was not what he could have desired, it was the only one he could secure. He drove off the enemy and crossed, the legionaries being up to their armpits in water, but having the current broken for them by stationing cavalry obliquely in the water above them. On the other side he found corn — for the harvest was at hand — and cattle, and refreshed his troops. He then marched rapidly to the land of the Senones to join Labienus. It was still early in the year.

XVIII.

LABIENUS' CAMPAIGN. SPRING, 52 B. C.

LABIENUS had been conducting a campaign against the Parisii. He reached Lutetia, but shortly heard of Cæsar's failure before Gergovia. He was opposed by Camulogenus, an able man, and saw that he could not safely retire, as he ought to do, towards Cæsar, without first imposing on the enemy. This he did in a bold and well-planned battle, and promptly retreated to Agendicum. The Æduan rebellion practically cut Cæsar off from his lieutenant; and Vercingetorix was all the more active since Cæsar's defeat at Gergovia. But by a bold march northward, Cæsar made a junction with Labienus, and thus reunited his eleven legions in one body. His manifest policy was now to push for the Province, from which he was cut off, reëstablish his base securely, and again advance on the Gallic allies. He set out by the most promising route. Vercingetorix believed the moment to have come for a *coup de grace*. He gave up his policy of small-war, and intercepted Cæsar on the way. But in the ensuing battle the Romans won, and Vercingetorix retired to Alesia, the last and main stronghold of the Gauls. This victory reopened Cæsar's communications with the Province, and he followed the Gauls to Alesia.

DURING Cæsar's Gergovia campaign Labienus had marched on Lutetia of the Parisii with four legions, having left a suitable force of new recruits from Italy with his baggage and victuals at Agendicum. He marched down the left bank of the Icauna (Yonne) and the Sequana. A large army from the neighboring states assembled to oppose him as soon as his arrival was known. The town of Lutetia occupied the island in the Seine where now stands Notre Dame de Paris. The chief command had been given to an aged but excellent soldier named Camulogenus. This officer, perceiving that Labienus was marching along the left bank, camped and drew up his army near a neighboring marsh. This was unquestionably where the Esonne flows into the Seine. It could not have been Le Marais, a part of Paris, as has been claimed. His position prevented the Romans from advan-

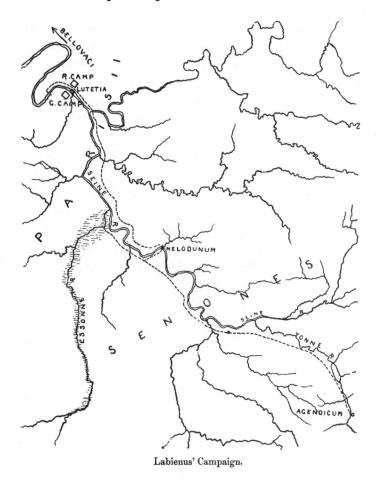

Labienus' Campaign.

cing. Labienus tried to make a road across the marsh by using hurdles and branches, a sort of corduroy-road, but failed in the attempt.

He then resorted to stratagem, and sought to steal a march

on Camulogenus by a flank manœuvre. He marched back at night by the way he came, along the left bank, on which he had so far been, to Melodunum (Melun), which was likewise on an island in the Seine. Here, by seizing boats, he crossed the left branch of the river to the island, captured the town and, having repaired the bridge which led to the right bank, moved down on the other side towards Lutetia. He reached the latter oppidum before Camulogenus, who did not at once see through Labienus' manœuvre. But his delay was not long. He soon followed the Roman army. On his arrival he ordered Lutetia to be set on fire and its bridges to be destroyed. The two armies camped on either bank of the Sequana opposite the city.

Labienus now heard of Cæsar's ill success at Gergovia, and the Gauls added to the story that his chief had been forced back to the Province by hunger. The near-by Bellovaci, hearing of the revolt of the Ædui, assembled forces for war. Labienus was thus placed with this inimical tribe on one side, only separated from him by the Isara, and with the Sequana and the Parisii, on the other side. He was cut off from his dépôts at Agendicum, which was on the farther bank of the Sequana, and from the road to it leading up the left bank, the way he had advanced. He very properly thought it of no use to attempt to reduce the Parisii under these adverse conditions, but deemed that he had best retire towards his base and seek to preserve his army intact for Cæsar. Single-handed, he could not suppress the insurrection.

In order to escape from his awkward situation, Labienus must recross to the left bank of the Sequana. To accomplish this in face of the army which was still on the other side and would oppose his passage, required ruse. To retrace his steps was to invite Camulogenus to oppose his crossing at

Melodunum, and his boats would be hard to get so far up
the river. A slow process would not accomplish his end.
Labienus was a good soldier and a bold. He saw that it was
safer to impose on the enemy by daring than to encourage
him by a retreat, which would convey the idea of weakness.
He called his lieutenants together and impressed their task

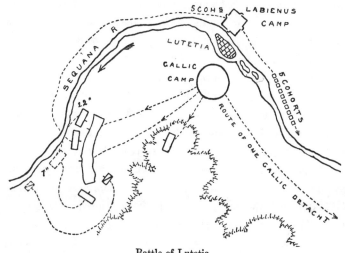

Battle of Lutetia.

upon them. He placed the boats which he had brought from
Melodunum under trusted Roman knights and ordered them
quietly to fall down the river about four miles at an early
hour of the night. He left a force of five steady cohorts in
camp; the other five cohorts of the same legion he ordered up
the river and sent some boats with them, instructing them
to proceed in a noisy manner, to lead the enemy to suppose
that he was marching that way. His other three legions he
led downstream to the boats and crossed them unperceived
under cover of a storm. This was probably near modern
Point du Joir. The Gallic posts were sheltering themselves
from the weather, and were easily dispersed.

Not knowing what Labienus was doing, but learning of these three parties, the enemy drew the inference that Labienus was trying to steal away in detachments, hoping that some might be saved by the sacrifice of the rest, and determined to capture all three. They broke up into three divisions, sending part up and part down the river, and leaving a part in camp. Camulogenus led the party which went down the river. By daylight the Romans were across, drew up in line and fell smartly upon the Gauls, who encountered them with equal boldness. The Seventh legion on the right at once routed the force opposed to it, but the Twelfth legion on the left, though it inflicted heavy loss on the barbarians, who were under the eye of their chief, was unable to break their ranks until the Seventh legion wheeled to the right and took them in flank and rear, and the cavalry rode them down. Even then the Gauls stood their ground until they were cut to pieces. The party in the camp, at the sound of battle, marched towards its chief, and took position on a hill (perhaps Vaugiraud). But they could not hold it. The cavalry cut down all who did not reach the woods. Camulogenus was killed. The detached forces of the enemy were next dispersed; and Labienus, having drawn in his own detachments, marched to Agendicum, where the baggage had been left. From here he moved towards Cæsar.

This campaign proves Labienus to have been an able officer. His manœuvring was excellent in every respect. It is a grievous pity that the latter part of his military career was clouded with ingratitude to his former chief. Under Cæsar's control, Labienus did far better work than he later did when opposed to Cæsar.

The revolt of the Ædui, the outbreak of which was an immediate consequence of the Gergovia defeat, gave a dangerous aspect to the war, for this people was all the more influential as having been long under Roman control. In order to terrify the neighboring tribes into joining the war, they murdered the hostages Cæsar had committed to their keeping, and threatened to do the like by those of such nations as did not join them. They were all the more determined now that they had broken loose. A council of all Gaul was summoned to Bibracte. All but the Remi, Lingones and Treviri came. Here the Ædui claimed the chief command; but it was given by universal choice to Vercingetorix, to whom, in consequence, the Æduan chiefs gave half-hearted support.

Vercingetorix exacted hostages from the allies, and ordered a general levy of cavalry, to the number of fifteen thousand, which he used as body-guard. Of infantry he already had an abundance. All Gaul had risen, save only the Remi and their clients, the Suessiones, Leuci and Lingones. It was the only occasion when the entire country was in arms. Vercingetorix proposed to continue his cunctatory policy of harassing the Romans and keeping them from obtaining corn; and advised the allies again to set fire to the crops and houses and thus to hamper Cæsar, as they had done before. An Æduan and Segusian army of ten thousand foot and eight hundred horse under Eporedorix, he sent against the Allobroges; some of the Arvernian tribes and the Gabali he sent into the land of the Helvii, in the Province, to devastate it; the Ruteni and Cadurci he sent against the Volcæ Arecomici, hoping to tamper with some of the tribes in the Province. He tried to gain over the Allobroges by flattery and promises.

The only force in the Province to oppose this host consisted of twenty-two cohorts put in the field by the legate Lucius Cæsar. The Helvii were defeated by the enemy and driven within walls, with loss of many of their leading men;

but the Allobroges held their boundary, the line of the Rhone, by a multitude of posts.

Knowing how large the enemy's force of cavalry had grown to be, Cæsar was obliged to send to Germany, to those tribes he had rendered tributary, to increase his own squadrons, as the peculiar warfare waged by the barbarians made this arm one on which at all times great reliance could be placed, and which sometimes was indispensable. In this effort he succeeded, and raised beyond the Rhine, in the states he had so far subdued, a most excellent though small body of cavalry, perhaps one thousand men, which he mixed with light troops. To add to its efficiency, as their horses were of poor quality, he dismounted the tribunes, knights and evocati, and gave their horses to the Germans. This was a radical measure, but Cæsar never stopped halfway; nor was this the time to do so.

After crossing the Liger on his way from Gergovia, Cæsar apparently directed his march due north to join Labienus, who, when he had defeated Camulogenus, had made his way towards his chief. Not far south of Agendicum, the captain and lieutenant met. The enemy's plan to divide the Romans had failed.

Cæsar now had eleven legions, the First, Sixth, Seventh, Eighth, Ninth, Tenth, Eleventh, Twelfth, Thirteenth, Fourteenth and Fifteenth. The First was the one lent by Pompey. In 58 B. C. Cæsar had six legions, the Seventh, Eighth, Ninth, Tenth, Eleventh, Twelfth. In 57 B. C. two new ones were raised, the Thirteenth and Fourteenth. In the winter of 55–54 B. C. he got five cohorts more. He lost at Aduatuca fifteen cohorts, a legion and a half, but in 53 B. C. he raised three more legions, *i. e.*, the new First, Fourteenth and the Fifteenth. Later the First and Fifteenth were lent to Pompey, and the Fifteenth became the

Third. The legions were usually four to five thousand men strong. When reduced, they were so soon as possible recruited up to standard. When Cæsar raised new levies, they were not generally made into new legions, but were distributed among the old ones. These legions, during the Gallic War, were thus about fifty thousand strong. Cæsar had also some twenty thousand Gallic, Cretan or Numidian light troops, and five thousand cavalry, of which one thousand were Germans; a total of seventy-five thousand men. This is an estimate, but it is not far from accurate. Later, in the Civil War, the legions were more depleted, the average being not much over three thousand men.

Having made his junction with Labienus, Cæsar deemed it essential to direct his march as speedily as possible on his base. He could not move south, straight towards the Province, because the Ædui lay between him and it, and they were in insurrection. He moved through the land of the Lingones to the east, and then heading south, purposed to make his way through the territory of the Sequani towards the Province. He had a good storehouse and intermediate base, should he require it, at Vesontio. He followed the same route he had pursued when going to meet Ariovistus, and when moving from Vienna to Agendicum. He intended to march up the valley of the Vingeanne and cross the Arar, on his way to Vesontio. This is what the Commentaries mean by saying that he marched "through the confines of the Lingones into the country of the Sequani, in order that he might the more easily render aid to the Province."

Cæsar's purpose in regaining the Province was not only to be able to protect this almost Roman territory; but, foreseeing that the uprising would probably be general, he preferred to base himself afresh on what was unquestionably a safe place of retreat, and the only place from which he

could be certain to obtain victual, — in other words, to make
a fresh start for the conquest of Gaul.

Meanwhile, Vercingetorix, after driving Cæsar from Gergovia, had concentrated his forces, some eighty thousand

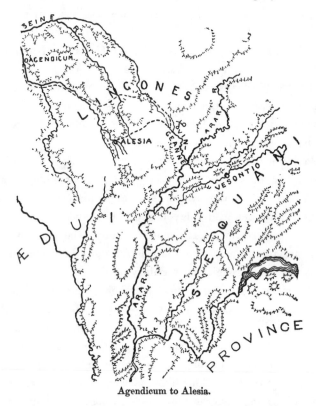

Agendicum to Alesia.

men, near Bibracte, and had moved up and encamped on the
road he divined the Romans would pursue. He placed his
army so as to bar Cæsar's passage through the land of the
Sequani. He camped at a fork in the roads in three divisions, each covering one of the paths Cæsar might choose
towards the Arar and Vesontio. Cæsar marched to within
ten miles of his enemy, ignorant of his presence.

Vercingetorix' position on the modern heights of Sacquenay was very strong. The heights bulged out in three
promontories, so to speak, on each one of which lay a third
of Vercingetorix' army. The right flank of his army thus
rested on the Vingeanne. The Badin brook was in its front.

That this is the field of battle seems to be proven by the
tumuli of the region, which contain skeletons identified from
their ornaments as Gallic, and by the horseshoes, still occasionally dug up by the peasants. Moreover, it suits the
distance from Alesia given by the Commentaries.

Calling a council of war, Vercingetorix declared to the
chiefs that now was the moment forever to put down Roman
tyranny, as even at that moment the enemy was flying to
the Province. If he reached it, he would return with even
larger forces; if destroyed without delay, which he could be
if attacked on the march, no Roman would ever return. He
especially encouraged his mounted troops, and the men of
this body bound themselves by solemn oath to deprive of all
his rights any soldier who did not ride twice through and
through the Roman army.

While Vercingetorix was camping on the heights of
Sacquenay, Cæsar kept on his march up the Vingeanne,
camping near Longeau. Next day, Vercingetorix moved his
foot up to the Badin and sent out his cavalry to attack Cæsar
as he should debouch on the plain north of the brook. The
Gallic cavalry was divided into three bodies. Of these one
was to attack each flank of the Roman army and one the
head of column. As Cæsar reached the plain, he saw
Vercingetorix' central division of cavalry opposite his own
head of column. Shortly the other two columns appeared on
its right and left. He was taken by surprise.

Cæsar had not anticipated this attack, but he was marching with care and with his troops well in hand. He met

the attack by ordering out three bodies of his own cavalry.
He called a halt, collected his baggage, and drew up the
army in battle order, probably in three lines of legions, — a

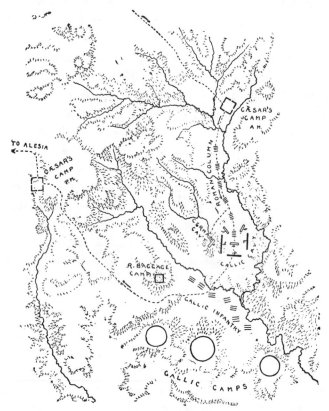

Battle of the Vingeanne.

sort of square, for "the baggage was received within the
ranks of the legions." Whenever the horse seemed hard
pressed, Cæsar supported it by an advance of infantry, and
by making a sharp demonstration in that quarter, and thus
kept up the courage of the fighting line. The affair was
only a cavalry fight; Cæsar's cavalry was supported by his

foot, which was near at hand. Vercingetorix' foot was not put in at all. After considerable skirmishing, the German cavalry on Cæsar's right got possession of the hill of Montsaugeon, drove the Gallic horse from it, and pursuing it to the infantry at the Badin, produced such demoralization as to weaken the other columns of the enemy's cavalry, which, thus taken in reverse, precipitately retired from the field. This retreat enabled Cæsar's horse to kill many and capture more prisoners; among them Eporedorix and two other noted Æduan chiefs, Cotus commanding the cavalry, and Cavarillus commanding the foot.

This check was a serious blow to the prestige of Vercingetorix, and determined him to retire to Alesia (Mont Auxois) with his infantry and the baggage from his camp. Cæsar followed up his advantage, parked his baggage on a hill near by, and by pursuing the retreating Gauls, inflicted a loss of three thousand men on the enemy's rearguard. Vercingetorix was wise enough not to return to his camps on the hills of Sacquenay. Had he done so, Cæsar could have cut him off from Alesia. But he risked his baggage to secure Alesia, which latter he did by moving at once by his left to the town. His baggage hurried thither by a parallel road farther to the south. Cæsar, as it happened, made no effort to capture it.

Vercingetorix had been unwise in the last degree to give up his system of small-war. We do not know how much he was impelled to do this by the insistence of those who did not appreciate his Fabian policy. So long as he pursued this method, he might be more than a match for Cæsar's army. A fighting machine can accomplish little unless it can fight, and meanwhile it must subsist. But Vercingetorix should have known that he could not meet the well-drilled legionaries in the open, especially when commanded by Cæsar in person, and that Cæsar's German horse, manœuvred under his direction, would be more than a match for his own.

Cæsar, in this movement, showed distinctly his great qualities. Having drawn in the forces of Labienus, his one object was to reach the Province, from which he was now cut off, drive from its borders the hosts of hostiles which were threatening it, and thence make a fresh start. He proposed that no obstacle should obstruct him in his march. Vercingetorix could not have attacked him at a less opportune moment. Nor when met by Vercingetorix, had Cæsar any idea of fighting on the defensive. He at once undertook a sharp offensive. He sustained his cavalry handsomely, and by his able manœuvres carried off a victory vastly more important in its moral effect than in its dimensions. For the affair itself was only a cavalry combat, and scarcely rose to the dignity of an engagement.

When Vercingetorix retired towards Alesia, the road to the Province was thereby opened to Cæsar. There was no more need for him to fray a path through the enemy's lines to his base. He could now rely on the fact that Vercingetorix would recall his outlying forces which were threatening the Province, or that the cohorts there would be able to defend themselves. He decided not to continue his march to his base, but to march directly upon the enemy's army. There was no fear for his communications. He might at once pass over into a sharp offensive.

Gallic Sword.

XIX.

THE SIEGE OF ALESIA. SUMMER AND FALL OF 52 B. C.

THE siege of Alesia was foreseen by both parties to be the final act in the struggle. Vercingetorix retired into the city with his army, eighty thousand strong; Cæsar sat down before it with sixty thousand men, and began to draw his lines of contravallation. Meanwhile cavalry skirmishes were frequent. Vercingetorix had provisions for thirty days; he sent away his cavalry, and by them word to the allies that before that period was past he must be rescued or surrender. Cæsar set to work on his defenses. These were strongest at the western approaches, where there was a large plain. Aware that an army of relief would speedily come, lines of circumvallation were added. The works were singularly complete, and skillfully adapted to the ground. After about six weeks, an immense army of relief did, in fact, come up, numbering nearly a quarter of a million of men. This shortly attacked, and Vercingetorix from within lent his aid. But the attack was partial and did not succeed. A second attack had no better result. The Romans held their own. The failure of these two attacks did much to depress the Gauls.

ON the day but one (*altero die*) after the battle of the Vingeanne, Cæsar reached Alesia, and determined upon its siege. This siege is one of the most notable of antiquity, and shows Cæsar's genius in high relief. The stronghold lay on an isolated hill (Mt. Auxois), or rather an elevated oval plateau, one and a quarter miles long east and west, by a half mile wide at the centre north and south, five hundred feet above the surrounding valleys, in the confluence of two of the small tributaries of the upper Sequana, the Lutosa (Ose) and Osera (Oserain) which bounded it on north and south. In front of the town to the west was a plain over three miles in length north and south — now called the

Alesia.

Plaine des Laumes — bisected by the Oserain and a little brook. Around the town on the three other sides, north, east and south, at the distance of a mile or so measured from the edges of the plateau, was a line of hills of about equal height as Mt. Auxois, separated each from the other by smoothly sloping valleys. There were springs on the plateau and many wells. The streams at the foot of the hill of Alesia were accessible by paths. The grade up the hill was easy, but at the top was a wall of rock interrupted at intervals, but on the whole steep and impracticable to assault.

It has been the habit of most authors to overrate the difficulties of the position at Alesia. It is a sort of pocket edition of Gergovia. While the slopes are unquestionably easier to-day than they were in Cæsar's time, made so by the continuous labors of sixty generations of farmers, yet the ground itself can have changed comparatively little. This is abundantly demonstrated by the excavations of Cæsar's lines; and though the position of Alesia, considered in the light of ancient warfare, was very strong, it was by no means inexpugnable. The place could readily be taken along the neck of land leading from the heights on the southeast, which was a sort of a natural siege-mound. Cæsar's real difficulty lay in his knowledge of the fact that all Gaul would join hands in sending an army of relief before he could take the place by regular approaches.

The Roman army approached from the east, south of Mt. Bussy. The Gauls were encamped on the east of the town under the walls, with a trench and stone wall six feet high (z) as defense. This was their weak spot, and here they expected the struggle. They had prolonged their wall down hill to the streams on either hand; and because this wall could be readily taken in reverse, they had made a double crotchet at either end. On reconnoitring the place, Cæsar deemed it inexpedient to attempt to carry it by storm, from the number of its defenders and especially in view of his recent failure at Gergovia; but that it might be starved out by a complete investment he believed. He no doubt appreciated the advantages of moving along the neck on the southeast; but having decided on a siege and not an assault, he threw his decision in favor of an approach from the west at the plain. He manifestly desired to shut in Vercingetorix, and he made his chief works where the position was weakest.

He had eleven legions, a scant fifty thousand men, five thousand Gallic and German horse, and perhaps ten thousand Gallic and other auxiliary foot. Vercingetorix is said to have had eighty thousand men. This has been doubted by many critics on account of the small size of the plateau and consequent lack of space to hold so large a body. But according to all the accounts, Cæsar was undertaking with sixty to seventy thousand men to besiege eighty thousand. In all eras, a force less than twice that of the besieged has been considered too small to predicate success. But the question of number adds to or detracts little from the ability, boldness and far-reaching results of this noted siege. It is probable that Cæsar had made up his mind that here was his last chance. Another failure would mean such encouragement of the Gauls as to prejudice his entire campaign. This must not be another Gergovia failure.

Cæsar's first step was to seize all the hills on the north, east and south, place thereon suitable detachments, and determine where the lines of contravallation should run. The cavalry was established near the watercourses; the infantry on the hilltops. He then began along the slope of the hills, from point to point, the erection of intrenchments which were eleven miles in length. The camps were protected by twenty-three square and high earthwork redoubts near the

Alesia, from the South.

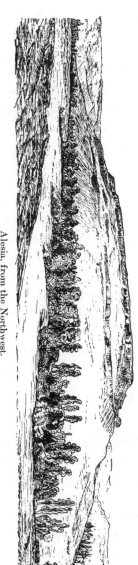

Alesia, from the Northwest.

foot of the slopes, and these were well guarded to prevent sallies, being held by day by small posts, at night by forces which bivouacked in them. The redoubts were as usual the first defenses constructed, and were later joined by lines of earthworks.

There appear to have been four infantry camps, two (A and B) on the hilltop south of Alesia, one on the hill northeast (C), one on the hill northwest (D). The topography dictated the shape of these camps; the intrenchments commanded the ground in their front. The naturally weak side was made the stronger by art; the camp A, for instance, had three lines on the south front. It may have been Cæsar's headquarters. The camp B was larger. The debouches of the camps were all towards Alesia. The ditches of D were excavated and found full of relics, coins and weapons, bones and helmets, collars and rings. Four cavalry camps, three in the big plain (H, I, K), one north of Alesia (G), have been found. Their ditches were less deep than those of the infantry camps. Of the twenty-three castella, five have been exhumed, 10, 11, 15, 18, 22. These are, no doubt, the stoutest ones that were made. The others were presumably mere block-houses, which have disappeared. The probable positions of the other eighteen are indicated by the topography.

The work on the lines had hardly been begun, when a cavalry action was brought about by Vercingetorix, who advanced into the open plain to the west. The fighting was obstinate. The Roman horse was at first unsuccessful. But the Roman infantry was ordered into line in front of the camps to forestall a sally from the town by its imposing front. Reanimated by the presence of the legions, which they had learned in the late battle could be relied on to sustain them heartily, the German horse took courage,

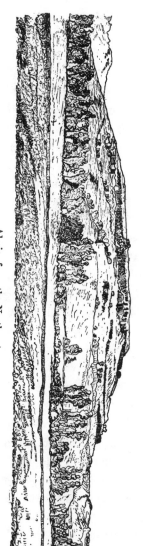

Alesia, from the Northeast.

Alesia, from the Southeast.

redoubled the vigor of its charges, put the enemy's horse to flight, and pursued them to the gates of the intrenchments. Cæsar advanced the infantry at the proper moment, and this demonstration increased the rout.   The Gauls endeavored to retire into the town, but Vercingetorix ordered the gates to be shut, so that the camp outside the city proper should not be left undefended.   Many Gauls sought to climb the ditch and wall but failed.   After inflicting a heavy loss on the enemy the Roman allied horse withdrew.   It will be noted with curiosity how many of the engagements of the Gallic war were mere combats of cavalry.   This arm did Cæsar good service; and yet it was never used like the "Companions " or the Numidian horse.

Vercingetorix now saw that a siege was inevitable.   Still he was not bold enough to cut his way out before it was too late.   He feared again to encounter the legionaries in the open; but he had strong hopes that this siege might result like the one of Gergovia, and determined to abide by the result.   The position was, if anything, stronger.   He sent away his fifteen thousand cavalry one night in the second watch, before the lines of contravallation were completed, not only because he was unable to provide forage for them, but particularly because he desired these men to visit and arouse all the tribes to his aid.   The squadrons escaped up the valleys of the two rivers.   Vercingetorix sent word by them that he and his sixty-five thousand foot had beef and corn for thirty days, which, by good management, might be made to last a trifle longer, and that they must have succor before the expiration of that time, or else Alesia and the whole cause would fall together.   He then withdrew all the forces to the plateau, and took into his own hands the distribution of rations.   He divided the cattle, but kept the corn for regular issue.   It remains a question as to whether sixty-five thousand men could actually crowd into the small limits of the place. The old city walls have in places been found. By close camping it might be done; and the barbarians were used to herding together in a very small space. Vercingetorix was now inclosed in a town whose well constructed walls rested on the edge of a cliff of stone which may have stood forty to sixty feet above the slope of the ground as it rises from the valley. This is the character, more or less marked, of all of the surrounding plateaux. Part of the slope and of the edge of the plateau was wooded or covered with bushes. Except from the neck of land on the east, nothing but hunger was apt to drive him out. He had a water-supply on the plateau. But his mouths were many. His main reliance was on the arrival of an army of relief.

Cæsar went at the business of the siege in the most workmanlike manner despite its exceptional difficulties. The earth in some places was rocky and unsuited to intrenchments, and the land was, no doubt, rougher than it is to-day. As Vercingetorix could escape only by the plain or up one of the north ravines, Cæsar devoted most of his attention to fortifying at these points. On the other sides the ground was in itself a defense, and less was needed. While the men were at work they had constantly to be protected by outlying guards of light troops against the sallies of the garrison, which were many and fierce.

Cæsar's preparations were on a remarkable scale of magnitude. He dug a trench on the west side of the town twenty feet deep and wide, with perpendicular sides, to protect the building of his other works (f). This trench was four hundred feet in front of the main line of contravallation, at the foot of the slope at the west end of the oppidum, and stretched from one stream to the other. It both prevented sudden sallies and left the regular lines beyond the throw of

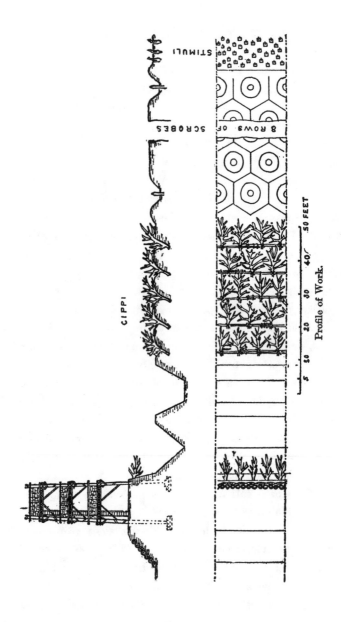

STIMULI

8 ROWS OF SCROBES

CIPPI

5 10 20 30 40 50 FEET

Profile of Work.

javelins. The earth from the trench was piled up behind it.
In front of the main line of works came two other trenches;
first one trench (g) on low ground, fifteen feet wide and
deep, which he located so as to be readily filled with water
from the Osera. It now shows only eight or nine feet deep.
Then back of it another equally big, dry trench on the same
level. These ditches continued half a mile south of the
Osera up the slope of the hill on the south. Thence the
ditch was single. Back of these a rampart (*agger*) and wall
(*vallum*) twelve feet high. The top of this wall had a parapet of hurdles (*lorica*) and battlements (*pinna*) and the top
of the rampart was provided with stakes "like stags' horns,"
projecting outward and downward so as to hinder scalers,

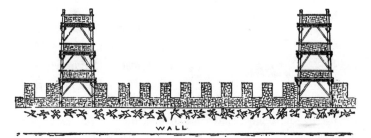

Face of Work.

and was armed with towers eighty feet apart. When the
length of the line is considered, — the front thus protected
was over a mile and a half long, — this was indeed a fine
piece of work. Cæsar's legionaries handled the pick and
spade as effectively as the pilum and gladius.

Performing all this work and foraging for corn at the
same time made the duties severe on the men; and so long a
line really needed more force than Cæsar had at command.
There were but three men per metre front; or if the men
were all continuously on duty in three reliefs, there was but

one man per metre front, and no reserves to draw on. The enemy made many assaults or demonstrations during the progress of the work, which added to the annoyance. For this reason Cæsar deemed the defenses not yet strong enough. He wanted to make them such that a small body of men could defend them, so that he could detach at need the bulk of his command to other points. The undertaking was one which demanded every possible aid from art, and he did not cease one instant from perfecting his lines. He devised several kinds of obstacles against sallies and drew up still another threefold line of entanglements. Five rows of slanting trenches, five feet deep, were dug, and sharpened branches like abatis sunk in the bottom. The men called these *cippi*. These five rows of cippi were close together, so that the abatis could be interlaced. Eight rows of conical pits (*scrobes*) three feet deep and three feet apart were placed checkerwise, each

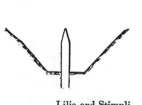

Lilia and Stimuli.

with a fire-hardened sharp stake as thick as one's thigh at the bottom, and the surface covered with osiers and twigs. These wolf-pits with stakes were nicknamed "lilies." Many of these *trous de loup* have been found. In front of these were sunk stakes close together, armed with iron hooks called *stimuli* (spurs), somewhat resembling huge fishing tackle. The fact that the Romans gave these devices new names looks as if they had not been previously used.

Outside this vast line of contravallation and two hundred yards back, Cæsar drew another similar line of circumvallation (x) to provide defense against the Gauls who would certainly soon arrive to raise the siege. These latter works covered an area of fourteen miles in circumference. The defenses stopped at the perpendicular sides of the hills, and began again on the plateaux, as shown in the map. The line varied at places according to topography. Some authorities have attempted to cast a doubt on the accuracy of the extent of these lines; but the Commentaries give the figures as eleven and fourteen miles, and they have been completely verified by modern excavations. These have proved very fruitful. Cæsar's intrenchments have been traced through their entire length, and many parts of the defenses plainly shown. There is no reason, if the work of an ancient historian has come down to us intact, why, within the limits of his intelligence, his statements should not be as worthy of credit as those of an author of to-day. Cæsar's works at Alesia are clearly as described in the Commentaries. They are no more wonderful than those of Vicksburg or of Petersburg. Unlimited numbers of men at work always accomplish wonders. To man these works facing both ways, Cæsar had in three reliefs but two men per five metres front.

Cæsar's defenses, immense as were their dimensions, were completed in about forty days. Despite their hardships, the legionaries worked with the best of good will. Cæsar said in later days that he could have overturned the heavens with such men. At Rome his friends were wont to say that scarcely a mortal man could imagine, none but a god execute such a work; his enemies, for once, were silenced.

It is probable that camp D had two legions. The size of the others leads one to place one legion in A, two in B, three in C, in all eight. The other three were in castella. The eleven-mile circuit was the line of the camps and redoubts.

Having completed this extraordinary task, each man was ordered to lay in provisions for thirty days, so as to reduce the danger due to foraging, and to provide against their being themselves blockaded by the army of relief.

Acting on the message of Vercingetorix sent out by his retiring cavalry, the Gauls immediately convened an assembly, probably at Bibracte, and decreed, from all the states, a levy, not a general but a specified levy, lest too large an army should be hard to ration, — two hundred and forty thousand foot, and eight thousand horse in all. The paper strength was two hundred and eighty-three thousand. Even those Gauls whom Cæsar had best treated now caught the national infection, revolted and put their best efforts at the service of the cause. The Bellovaci alone declined to send their contingent, but sent two thousand men as an act of friendship. They proposed to be subject to no control. The chief command of this enormous army was given to Commius the Atrebatian, the man Cæsar had sent to Britain, Vercasivelaunus the Arvernian, cousin to Vercingetorix, Viridomarus and Eporedorix the Æduan. How the latter escaped from imprisonment, for he was captured in the last battle, is not explained. A war council of members from each tribe was added to these chiefs. Full of confidence, as well it might be, for to barbarians strength resides solely in numbers, this huge army rendezvoused on Æduan soil, and marched to Alesia, imagining that the Romans could not, for a moment, withstand such a multitude, especially when sallies should also be made from within.

Not aware of the speedy arrival of this army, the besieged were already at a loss what to do. Six weeks had elapsed since Vercingetorix sent out his message, and he then had barely corn for thirty days. Starvation was at hand. It was proposed by Cirtognatus, an Arvernian, to eat the useless soldiers and inhabitants; but this yielded to a project to send them away. The whole population (Mandubii) was accordingly marched out; but the Romans declined to receive them even as slaves, and drove them back into the city.

Commius and the great army finally reached the Roman
lines, and, camping on the heights southwest of the town,
within a mile of Cæsar's lines, led out their cavalry the very
next day to the large plain, where it was supported by their
infantry on the hills at their back. It covered the entire
plain. Every movement could be distinctly seen from
Alesia. Vercingetorix responded by marshaling his own
army outside the city walls and making ready to sustain any
assault by the relieving force. He had prepared great numbers of hurdles to fill up the trenches and cover the entanglements.

Vercingetorix' troops advanced. They had actually begun to fill up the first ditch, and the affair promised to
develop into a general engagement of infantry. Posting his
forces on the walls facing both to the city and towards the
army of relief, Cæsar opened the action by sending in his
German and Gallic allied cavalry. The enemy had light
troops mixed with their cavalry, to lend it steadiness. In a
short while the battle waxed hot, the Gauls feeling confident
of victory from mere force of numbers, and urging on their
men by yells and shouts. The people of Alesia encouraged
their friends by equal clamor. The action lasted from noon
till sundown. Vercingetorix did not push on, nor did the
army of relief put in its foot. The action does not appear to
have gone beyond a combat of cavalry aided by slingers and
bowmen. Finally, after the cavalry of Cæsar had been all
but defeated, the Germans, rallying in column for a final
effort, drove in the Gauls despite their numbers, and broke
them up. Once fairly routed, they could not recover themselves; Cæsar's squadrons pursued them to camp, killing
many of the archers who were supporting them, and who
could not so speedily get away. The forces from Alesia
retired dejected. There had been no organized attack upon

the intrenchments. The prominent rôle played by the cavalry in all Cæsar's wars shows that most of his battles were confined to a skirmishing contact. For pitched battle the legions alone were available. Cæsar had no cavalry proper.

The next day but one the army of relief again attacked, having, in the mean time, made a much greater number of hurdles, and provided themselves with scaling-ladders and wall-hooks. They selected midnight for the hour and delivered the assault suddenly at the westerly plain. Their shouts aroused Vercingetorix and the forces in the town, who at once sallied forth to lend assistance to their friends outside. The Gauls, as best they might in the darkness, filled up the pits and trenches with fascines and hurdles, covering their operation with a fire of sling-stones and arrows. The Romans were fully alive to the necessities of the occasion. Each man knew his place. They sent for troops from those redoubts which were least exposed, to resist the onset where it was hottest. The legates Trebonius and Antonius brought up reinforcements. The Romans replied to the Gallic fire with arrows, sling-stones, hand-hurled stones of about a pound weight, of which they had gathered a large supply, and pointed stakes kept on the walls in reserve. The military engines also came into play. In the dark, shields were almost useless. While the enemy's line was at a distance, the assault proved more harmful in loss to the Romans than when the barbarians neared the walls, for then many of them fell into the pits and trenches; this bred confusion and dismay; their aim grew wild, and their weapons inflicted little damage; the Romans, on the other hand, threw down their heavy siege pila from the intrenchments with deadly effect. Before long the vigor of the Gauls slackened. Finally, at daylight they conceived a fear of a demonstration on their uncovered right flank from the Roman lines on the hills south of the town, which, coupled to fatigue and loss of men, induced them to retire. Vercingetorix, from the town side, suffered equally from the entanglements. His men used up most of their time in filling the twenty-foot ditch, and did not get beyond it; and as daylight came on, seeing that the assault by the army of relief had failed, he also blew the signal to retire.

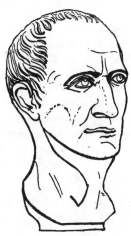

Cæsar, late in Gallic War.
(British Museum.)

XX.

THE BATTLE OF ALESIA. FALL OF 52 B. C.

THE Gallic army of relief made a third and last assault on Cæsar's lines, after careful preparation. They skillfully probed the weakest spot in the Roman line, which was at the northwest camp, and made a violent attack on it with a chosen body of sixty thousand men. At the same moment the cavalry made a demonstration at the western plain. The legions were put to it as never before to hold their own. Perceiving the attack by the army of relief, Vercingetorix moved against the lines from within. Cæsar had an army equal to his own on either side of him, each delivering a desperate assault at the same moment, and with huge reserves in support. He' himself was omnipresent and kept his men heartily to their work. The value of the defenses was now apparent. The Gauls could nowhere penetrate the line, though attacks were made at several places, and came dangerously close to success. Finally, by a well-timed sortie with the sword and a simultaneous cavalry charge on their flank, the Gauls were driven back, and discouraged at their threefold defeat, the army of relief retired; Vercingetorix surrendered. The siege of Alesia practically sealed the doom of Gaul.

THE Gauls had now been defeated in two assaults. These, indeed, had been partial ones, but want of success had begun to discourage the men. The leaders distinctly foresaw failure unless they could wrest a victory from the Romans in the next encounter. The Gallic character before the Christian era is universally described as illy adapted to bear the strain of continued disaster. Commius proposed to make one more strong effort to break through Cæsar's lines, and the Gauls went to work systematically to discover the weakest part of the Roman walls. By inquiries of the country people they learned what were the troops and kinds of defenses at each point.

On the northwest of the town was a hill which the

engineers had not included in the circumvallation, on account
of its area. They had been obliged to run the wall at its
foot on comparatively low ground. Here was the camp D of
two legions, under the legates Anstitius and Caninius. It
was located on the steep slope of the hillside. Back of this
point the Gallic chiefs decided to assemble sixty thousand
men chosen from the tribes most noted for valor, and to
attack on a given day at noon, — Vercasivelaunus being
given the command of the assaulting party. This force was
moved at night by a circuit of a dozen miles to near the spot
selected and was concealed under cover of the hill on its
north slope.

As noon approached, his men being well rested, fed and
eager for the fray, Vercasivelaunus drew them up in order
and marched rapidly against the Roman camp. There
appear to have been some works on Mt. Rea; probably only
an outpost. This body, at all events, was hustled out and
the Gauls moved down the slope on camp D. At the same
time, as agreed, the cavalry made a sharp demonstration
upon the Roman defenses fronting the plain, sustained by an
advance of the foot. Vercingetorix, in the town, was not
slow to perceive what his countrymen were about, — he was
constantly and anxiously on the outlook for their assault, —
and sallied forth with all his implements, movable pent-
houses, ladders, mural hooks and other tools, of which he had
prepared a large supply for such an occasion. His attack
was delivered opposite Vercasivelaunus, somewhat to the
left. Thus, while at the plain the cavalry demonstration
caused Cæsar no little anxiety, two infantry armies, each
nearly equal to the entire Roman force, were again attacking
his lines front and rear on the side where perhaps he was
weakest. The Roman forces were widely distributed, and it
was hard to say what other part of the line might be

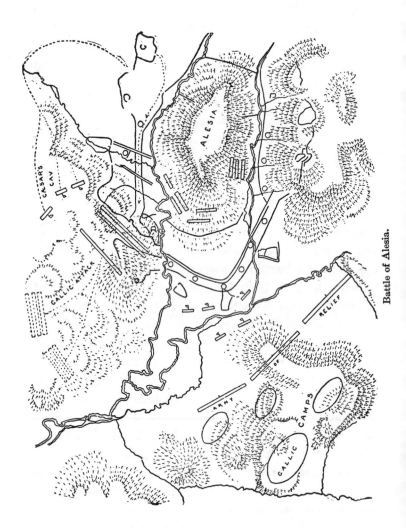

Battle of Alesia.

attempted. In fact, Cæsar could scarcely expect that with some three hundred thousand men the Gauls within and without would put into action less than half their force.

The attack was sudden and severe. The Gauls, with every kind of expedient, pressed in on whatever part of the wall appeared most weak. They were evidently in earnest, and they fought as if they expected and meant to win. Their gallantry was consummate. Cæsar had prepared several outlooks from which he could get a commanding view of the whole field. In one of these he stationed himself, probably near the south end of the twenty-foot trench, and dispatched troops from place to place, wherever they seemed to be most needed. Each party was nerved up to do its best. The Gauls evidently felt this to be their last chance of freeing themselves from the hated Roman yoke; the Romans understood that this battle, if gained, would be the term of their labors. Moreover, they recognized their certain fate if they did not win.

The brunt of the struggle came at the northwest camp, where, owing to the high ground above the Roman defenses, missiles could be more effectively hurled by the barbarians, and testudos put to use. Here, too, were the most renowned warriors, while at the main lines the Gauls were, however numerous, of no marked fighting quality. The abundant force at the northwest camp enabled the enemy to relieve the weary with fresh men at frequent intervals, and to heap mounds up against the Roman wall, which put them on a par with the legionaries. After some hours of combat the Roman soldiers at this point had used up all their missiles.

Observing their distress, Cæsar ordered Labienus with six cohorts from the northeast camp (C) to go to their relief, and if compelled to do so, to make a sally with the sword, while he himself repaired to the plain to encourage the troops.

The Gauls under Vercingetorix, within, in despair of effecting a lodgment in the Roman lines at the point where they had been fighting, made a fresh attempt on a more precipitous but less guarded place, probably the foot of the south camp; and having brought engines and tools, which they used under cover of a storm of missiles, they succeeded in driving the defenders from the walls, in filling the ditches and tearing down the wattling cover of the palisades with mural hooks. To meet this new and threatening danger, Cæsar dispatched Brutus with six cohorts to the point assailed, and as this did not appear to suffice, followed him up by Fabius with seven more. Even this did not turn the tide; he was at last personally obliged to hurry to this point in order to rehabilitate the battle, a matter which he succeeded in accomplishing after some time and with considerable effort.

As Labienus had been unable to hold the enemy in check at the northwest camp (D), Cæsar sent a portion of his cavalry by a circuit outside the walls, to debouch from the north ravine, file up along the slope of the hills, and attack the enemy in the rear. He himself, so soon as the assault of Vercingetorix had been beaten off, taking four cohorts and some horse, rushed to the support of Labienus. The latter, meanwhile, had drawn a large number of cohorts from the redoubts which could best spare them. The bulk of the barbarians, happily for Cæsar, remained inactive in reserve. His arrival — which all the legionaries could see, for he wore the imperator's robe, the purple *paludamentum*, over his armor — yielded the utmost encouragement to his men. They could always do wonders under the eye of Cæsar. In their ardor they ceased the use of missiles and betook themselves to the sword.

At this moment the German cavalry, which Cæsar had sent out, charged sharply in on the left rear of the Gauls, and raising a great shout the legionaries rushed upon them. Nothing could withstand their onset. Broken by its vigor, the enemy turned and fled, but only to be cut down by the cavalry. A number of the chiefs, among them Sedulius, prince of the Lemovices, were slain; others, principal among whom was Vercasivelaunus, were captured; and seventy-four standards were taken. The men under Vercingetorix, seeing their auxiliaries thus defeated, and Cæsar ready to turn on them, withdrew from their attack and retired into Alesia, in the utmost dejection. The troops which had not been engaged caught the alarm and made haste to retreat; retreat soon became rout. The flight of the Gauls from the battlefield was by no means arrested at their camp; the whole body of warriors began to seek safety wherever each could find it; had the cavalry been fresh, they could have been annihilated. As it was, a large number were cut down and the rest dispersed into the woods. Only after long wandering did they find their way to their respective states.

The stake having been nobly played and lost, Vercingetorix surrendered himself to his countrymen to be dealt with as they saw fit; and these at once sent ambassadors to Cæsar. There was no alternative. Cæsar disarmed the Gallic soldiers and ordered them to surrender their leaders. "Vercingetorix, who was the chief spring of the war, putting his best armor on, and adorning his horse, rode out of the gates, and made a turn about Cæsar as he was sitting, then quitting his horse, threw off his armor and remained quietly sitting at Cæsar's feet until he was led away." (Plutarch.) This gallant chieftain was kept for exhibition in Cæsar's triumph, and immediate death thereafter, a thing which, whatever the precedent, is scarcely creditable to the Roman, for though an enemy, Vercingetorix was assuredly a hero. The Æduan and Arvernian prisoners were reserved to use in once more gaining over their respective tribes. Of all the other prisoners, Cæsar gave one apiece to the soldiers as plunder. These were sold to the traders, of whom there were always plenty not far from a Roman camp. After a battle, they always appeared, ready to profit by the abundance of bargains.

The siege of Alesia exhibits the greatest art in Cæsar and equal courage and endurance on the part of his troops. The inaction of the bulk of the barbarians in the last battle had been his salvation, as well as led to the loss of Gallic independence. Though there were, thereafter, isolated cases of insurrection, the country never again rose *en masse*. In a year Gaul was practically a Roman province. Her spirit of resistance had been finally crushed.

After this brilliant success, Cæsar marched back to the land of the Ædui, and found no difficulty in recovering that state; and the Arverni made haste to bring in their submission and hostages. To both these tribes Cæsar restored some twenty thousand prisoners. After his great victory he could well afford to make use of generosity in his treatment of the Gauls. He was then enabled to put his army into winterquarters. Labienus, with the Seventh and Fifteenth legions and some cavalry, was placed among the Sequani with Rutilius as his lieutenant; Fabius with the Eighth, and Basilius with the Ninth, among the Remi to protect them against the Bellovaci; the legion of Antistius, the Eleventh, among the Ambivereti; that of Sextius, the Thirteenth, among the Bituriges; that of Caninius, the First, among the Ruteni; Cicero, with the Sixth at Matisco (Macon), and Sulpicius, with the Fourteenth, at Cabillonum (Chalons), charged with procuring corn along the Arar in the land of the Ædui. Cæsar himself fixed his headquarters at Bibracte. The location of Antonius, with the Tenth and Twelfth, is not given. It was likely enough at headquarters. A supplicatio of twenty days was granted Cæsar in Rome.

During none of the campaigns in Gaul did the tribes put so large a force into the field as on this occasion. Forty of the eighty-five tribes, in the course of a month, contributed

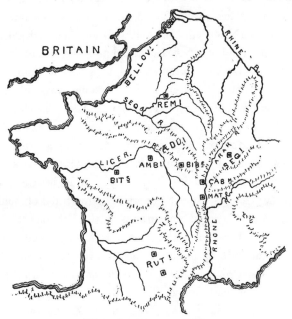

Winter-Quarters, B. C. 52–51.

a quarter of a million men which, added to the eighty thousand under Vercingetorix, made a grand total of three hundred and thirty thousand, almost five times as many as the Roman legions, light troops and allied cavalry together. The danger had been grave for Cæsar. But his own genius, the stanchness of the Roman legionaries and especially the divided counsels of the barbarians, had saved him. The sixty thousand men who assaulted at the northwest camp at Alesia had been picked; the bulk of the barbarians on the

west plain were of poor stuff.   But had even this force
attacked from the western face, while Cæsar was with difficulty driving back the front and rear assaults on the northern
camp, and meeting Vercingetorix from within on the south,
however good his lines, he must, it seems, have been overwhelmed.   His own account of how hard pushed he was by
the partial attack proves how near he came to a fatal outcome.   Cæsar's courage, the ambition and brilliant gallantry
of his men, the loyalty of the allied and the splendid qualities of the German horse, added to good fortune, which
smiled on him with even more constancy than it did on
Alexander, yielded him the victory.   And this victory led
to results which were far reaching.

This seventh year is the most interesting as well as the
most important of the entire war.   It exhibits Cæsar's power
in engineering, in tactics, in strategy, in logistics.   Let us
recapitulate events, so as to group the superb list of achievements.   Cæsar's rapid appearance in the Province on hearing of the Gallic insurrection; his raising troops and crossing
the Cebennæ into the land of the Arverni, to forestall their
invading the Province and deceive the enemy as to his intentions; his personal forced march thence through a network
of dangers to the land of the Lingones, where he concentrated
his legions on the rear of Vercingetorix, made a splendid and
successful strategical opening, particularly as Vercingetorix
flattered himself that he had cut Cæsar off from his army,
and had that army at his mercy.   Following this concentration of his legions in the face of opposition came his march
from Agendicum to Vellaunodunum, Genabum, Noviodunum
and Avaricum, and his rapid successive capture of these
towns.   Thence he marched up the Elaver, cleverly stole a
passage of that river under the very eyes of Vercingetorix,
and besieged Gergovia.   Called away from the siege by the

Æduan imbroglio, as he represents, or beaten back from his assault of it, as is the truth, which he could well afford to acknowledge, Cæsar moved back over the Elaver through the land of the revolted Ædui and Senones, forcing the Liger and making his way to Agendicum, where he joined Labienus. Having recruited his forces, he retired through the land of the Lingones on his way to the Province, beat in fair fight Vercingetorix, who stood across his path, and reopened his communications. Thence following the enemy to Alesia, Cæsar finished the year by his wonderful siege and capture of this stronghold. These operations, alike splendid in conception and execution, make a string of military jewels hard to match.

Vercingetorix had proved a worthy antagonist. His plan to avoid open conflict with Cæsar and to fight him by a Fabian policy is an extraordinary conception for a barbarian. Vercingetorix exhibited a true natural genius for arms. His mistake lay in not clinging to his original plan. So soon as he wavered in it, he lost. This was not his fault, but that of the political combination against him among his own people. Despite the capacity of Vercingetorix and the fact that the Gauls had more than five times Cæsar's force, the genius of this great captain, added to Roman discipline and training, overcame the courage, but lack of unity, of the Gallic allies. Art versus mere strength — as always — could have but one ending.

XXI.

THE BELLOVACI. JANUARY TO APRIL, 51 B. C.

THE Gauls had learned that they were not equal to the Romans in whatever combination; but they saw that a number of isolated insurrections gave Cæsar vastly more trouble than a single combined one. Several uprisings were therefore initiated; but Cæsar did not delay an instant. He made a series of winter campaigns, and by taking them unawares, successively reduced the Bituriges and Carnutes. He then marched against the Bellovaci, who, with their allies, had rendezvoused in what is now the Forest of Compiègne. Cæsar found them strongly intrenched. He camped on an adjacent hill, making a ditch and his wall in two stories. After some skirmishing between the rival outposts and cavalry, the barbarians prepared to retire, fearing another Alesia. Cæsar made ready to follow, but the Gauls detained him by a clever stratagem, and escaped. Seeking shortly to entrap him in an ambuscade, the barbarians were themselves surprised and defeated. Cæsar then distributed his legions so as best to cope with the several insurrections, whose extent he could not yet gauge.

THE rest which the Roman legions had fairly earned in the splendid campaign just ended was not destined to last long. The Gauls had been beaten, to be sure, but not all of them were subdued. Then as now they added to native gallantry the habit of not yielding until they had tried a number of ways to accomplish a desired end. They had tried the experiment of rising in one body and had been distinctly worsted; they had learned that they were, in whatever numbers, no match for Roman discipline, courage and intellect. But they had also learned that the most grievous blows they had inflicted on Cæsar were those they had given by waging a judicious small-war in many localities at the same time. This system they determined once more to try. They were intelligent enough to understand that while Cæsar could, no

doubt, defeat them wherever he might be, he was unable to
be everywhere at once.   If the Gauls had all been willing to
come within the scope of this plan, and if they had had
another leader like Vercingetorix to carry through such a
policy to the end, Cæsar's conquest of Gaul might never
have been completed.   But fortune did not favor the Gauls
in their brave struggle for liberty.   It was destined, happily
for them and for us, that they, too, should bear the Roman
yoke.

Cæsar was shortly informed of the consultations of the

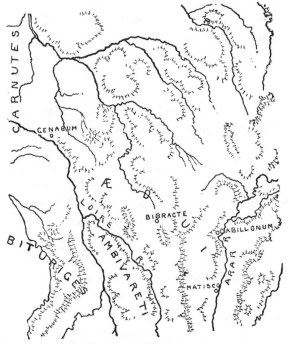

Campaign against Bituriges.

Gauls to this end, and determined to crush the uprising in
the bud.   While the leaders of the several tribes were still
arguing and preparing, he went to work.   Leaving Mark

Antony in charge of headquarters at Bibracte, on the day before the kalends of January, he set out with a body of horse for the Thirteenth legion, which was wintering among the Bituriges on their boundary nearest the Ædui. Lest a single legion should not be sufficient to keep the enemy in control, he added to the Thirteenth the Eleventh legion, which was stationed among the Ambivareti near by. Leaving two cohorts of each to guard the baggage and winter-quarters, he moved by forced marches upon the Bituriges and surprised them completely. He made many prisoners, but forbade plundering or burning, promising his men two hundred sestertii each, and every centurion two thousand sestertii in lieu thereof. He not only desired not to disaffect the population too seriously, but also to preserve the corn and forage for his own use. The burning stacks and farms would moreover serve to give warning of their danger to adjoining tribes, and it was Cæsar's plan to attack and compel each tribe separately to bring in its submission.

The chiefs of the Bituriges endeavored to escape, for their preparations were barely begun, but so hot was Cæsar's pursuit of them wherever they fled, that, by heading them off, and capturing them one by one, he speedily broke up their combinations. Those of the population who desired to retain their allegiance to Rome he protected by taking from their midst the conspirators who were leading them astray. This policy of vigor flavored with generosity forestalled a general uprising. The campaign had lasted but forty days. In its rapidity and success, it approaches some of Alexander's short operations against mountain tribes. The two legions went back to winter-quarters.

Eighteen days after Cæsar had returned to Bibracte at the end of February, the Bituriges invoked his aid against the Carnutes who had begun war upon them. In order not to disappoint this tribe in its newly sworn allegiance, Cæsar called in Cicero's Sixth legion from Cabillonum and Sulpicius' Fourteenth legion from Matisco, on the Arar, and marched to Genabum. From this place as a centre he conducted a partisan warfare against the Carnutes with his allied horse. This tribe made no pretense at resistance but dispersed into the country, where at this season they had much ado to get provisions, and finally fled to other tribes. The soldiers gathered much booty. Cæsar had scarcely used his infantry. He preferred for the sake of his men not to undertake further active operations at this inclement season, and left the two legions in Genabum, where he could quarter them to advantage.

Cæsar and Hannibal both disliked winter campaigns. Unlike Alexander, for whose exuberant physical and moral hardihood no season was too severe, they kept their troops in winter-quarters unless operations became imperative. But on this occasion Cæsar sent out his cavalry detachments through the length and breadth of the land, and these, backed up by the presence of the legions, broke down all present opposition. He was fain to be content with so much at this season.

This task finished, he placed Trebonius in command of the two legions at Genabum, and left for the land of the Remi, who had appealed to him against the Bellovaci and neighboring tribes; for these were preparing war upon them and the Suessiones, their clients, under the leadership of Correus the Bellovacian and the so long faithful Caninius the Atrebatian. The Remi were allies of Rome and had been stanch friends, who must be helped at any cost. Their early usefulness in the Belgian campaign will be remembered. Cæsar hastened to Durocortorum with the Eleventh legion and one drawn from Labienus at Vesontio. The Commentaries say that the

legion was drawn from Trebonius, but as this legate was
later ordered to bring up both his from Genabum, it is
probable that Labienus was meant.   Cæsar ordered Fabius

Campaign of Bellovaci.

to march to the land of the Suessiones with the two which,
under his command, had been wintering among the Remi.
By these details he endeavored to give duty alternately to
the legions.   He, individually, ceased not from work.

Arrived in the territory of the Bellovaci, Cæsar camped
and sent his cavalry out to reconnoitre.   He ascertained that
all the able-bodied men of this and adjacent tribes (the
Ambiani, Aulerci, Caletes, Veliocasses and Atrebates) had
left their dwellings, were on a war footing, and camped on
a hill surrounded by a morass — modern Mt. St. Marc in
the Forest of Compiègne — with their baggage hidden in the
depths of the forest farther away; that Correus was in gen-

eral command, Commius being away to gather auxiliaries
from the Germans on the Mosa; that they proposed to fight
if Cæsar had but three legions, but to remain in camp and
harass him with small-war and cut off his forage, which was
in any event hard to get, if he had more than three. "Cæsar was convinced of the truth of this account by the concur-
ring testimony of several prisoners."

This prudent resolution, so far as it applied to fighting
only a small force, Cæsar determined to encourage. Though

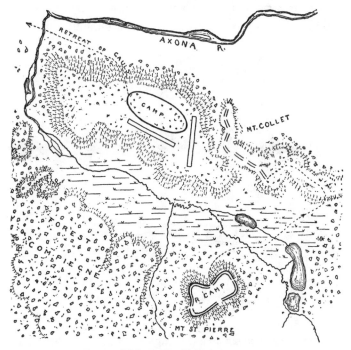

Fight against Bellovaci.

he had four legions with him, — three veteran, the Seventh,
Eighth and Ninth, and the Eleventh " composed of chosen
young men of great hopes, who had served eight campaigns,
but who, compared to the others, had not yet acquired any

great reputation for experience or valor," — he endeavored
to make the enemy believe he had only three. He therefore
marched the Seventh, Eighth and Ninth by themselves in the
van, and left the Eleventh to follow the train at a convenient
distance. "By this disposition he formed his army almost
into a square, and brought them within sight of the enemy
sooner than was anticipated." He had given his officers full
instructions as to his plans. There are frequent rather puzzling statements in the Commentaries. This was largely a
wooded country, and how Cæsar could move his column in
anything like a square seems to us, who are familiar with the

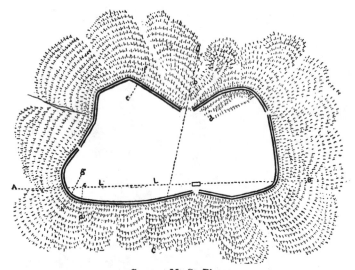

Camp at Mt. St. Pierre.

limitations of modern armies, highly singular. But infan'-
try or cavalry, with no baggage except pack-mules, can, and
on our Western plains does, get over ground which would be
considered utterly impracticable for an army if hampered by
artillery and trains. We may accept Cæsar's statement as a
broad description of his order of march, and not assume his

square to have been an exact equivalent of our modern square.

On perceiving Cæsar's approach, the enemy drew up in front of their camp, but declined to leave their advantageous position on the heights. Cæsar saw that their number was

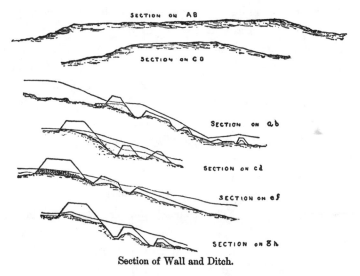

SECTION ON A B

SECTION ON C D

SECTION ON a b

SECTION ON c d

SECTION ON e f

SECTION ON g h

Section of Wall and Ditch.

much too great to attack without proper preparation, and went into camp on the other side of a deep valley, — on Mt. St. Pierre. His camp he fortified with a twelve-foot rampart, with roofed breastworks on it and down the slope two trenches fifteen feet wide, with, as he says, perpendicular sides and square bottom, though the excavations do not show them such. It was easy, when he later wrote about it, to forget the kind of trench he may have dug. He built several turrets three stories high, intercommunicating with galleries, all protected by hurdles. Two rows of men, one above the other, could fight on the ramparts. Those on the galleries could throw their darts farther, while the lower rank on the vallum would be protected by the plat-

form against falling darts.   The gates were flanked by
heavy turrets.   This camp would be secure when a part of
the garrison had gone foraging; would make a safe magazine for stores; and Cæsar hoped the enemy would suppose
from all this preparation that he felt concerned for his
safety and be induced to attack him in his intrenchments.
This camp of Cæsar's at Mt. St. Pierre has been exploited,
and its contours and area and many of its details have been
brought to light.   These are interesting to show how the
accentuation of the ground was put to use to facilitate the
erection of defenses.   Cæsar was fond of doing things in a
novel way.   Any new idea which occurred to him he was apt
to carry out, to test its adaptability and usefulness.

There was constant skirmishing at a ford across the marsh,
now a piece of low meadow land, which lay between the rival
camps; either party crossing and engaging the other with
alternate success.   The Roman foragers were constantly
attacked by the barbarians.   Some successes thus obtained,
and particularly the arrival of five hundred German horse,
under Commius, greatly encouraged the barbarians.

Cæsar deemed it wise to send back for more troops, as the
Gauls were many and in a peculiarly strong situation, and
as he deemed an investment the only safe means of attacking
the barbarian stronghold.   He ordered Trebonius to draw
in the Thirteenth legion, which under Sextius was in the
territory of the Bituriges, and with it and his own two, the
Sixth and Fourteenth at Genabum, to join him by forced
marches.

Meanwhile the barbarians were all the more encouraged
by an ambuscade into which they led the Reman, Lingonian,
and other allied horse, and during which a number were
killed, including their chief.   Cæsar had drafted a considerable tale of mounted men from all the tribes which he had

subdued. This was an easy and effectual way of insuring their good behavior, for it took from among them their leading citizens, — in other words, those able to serve mounted, — and kept them under Cæsar's own eye. It had its corresponding danger in keeping with the army a sometimes uncertain element; but under Cæsar's immediate control the danger was minimized.

A few days after the above defeat, some of the German foot auxiliaries crossed the marsh, and in a hand-to-hand combat drove the enemy into and a few even beyond their camp. This defeat and the arrival of Trebonius frightened and disheartened the enemy as much as they had been before encouraged. Fearing another Alesia siege they prepared to leave, and sent forward by night their baggage and old people. As daylight overtook them during this operation, not daring openly to continue the retreat, they drew up part of their army in front of their camp to protect it and conceal the movement in retreat.

Cæsar saw what the barbarians were doing. He bridged the morass in his front (there are still traces of this road), and making his way to a hill — Mt. Collet — overlooking the enemy, he drew up in line of battle. He did not wish to assault, nor was it worth while to follow the flying column, as owing to the river Axona on one side and the marsh on the other, he could not reach it except by exposing his flank. The enemy declined to leave their position. Cæsar camped and fortified in that place and then remained in line of battle, the horses bridled ready for attack or pursuit, in case the enemy should divide in order to get away. The hill on which he lay had abrupt sides, and was separated from the Bellovacian position by a narrow valley in places but two hundred yards apart. The engines, it appears, could fire across it. This fire, which they were unable to return, galled

the barbarians sensibly.   Observing Cæsar's intention, the
Bellovaci resorted to the following clever stratagem.   Piling
bundles of straw, of which they used much to sit and lie
upon, with hurdles and other inflammables in their front, at

Theatre of Bellovacian Campaign.

nightfall they set all this on fire.   Under cover of the smoke
they precipitately retired.

Cæsar guessed as much, but advanced   cautiously, naturally fearing some ambuscade.   The horse could not easily
advance through the line of fire.   Thus the enemy was able
to retreat in safety ten miles, where they took up another
strong position on a hill fortified by nature.   This is thought
to have been Mont Ganelon, north of the confluence of the
Aisne and Oise.   It is only six miles from Mt. St. Marc as
the crow flies, but a circuit may have been necessary to cross
the rivers.   It is not stated that Cæsar followed them up.
He probably kept to his camp and reconnoitred the vicinity

to await a favorable chance of action. From their new camp the barbarians again engaged in their small-war by a number of lesser ambushes, doing much harm to the Roman foragers.

Learning soon after that Correus, the chief of the Bellovaci, had placed six thousand of his best foot and one thousand horse in an ambush where the Roman foragers were

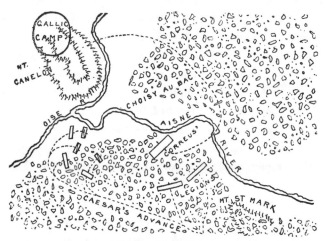

Combat with Bellovaci.

apt to go because there was considerable provision, Cæsar himself accompanied these, and made his party somewhat larger than usual. His cavalry he mixed with light infantry and sustained by some cohorts of legionaries. The ground for the ambush was a plain about a mile in extent, — not far from Choisy au Bac, — surrounded by woods and the river Aisne. The enemy's force was led by Correus. At the proper moment Correus emerged from the woods and attacked the column of foragers, expecting entire victory. The ambush proved a failure, as the Romans were in force and fully prepared for it; the cavalry was quickly sustained by the bowmen, and after a severe combat of the van, in which the cavalry and light troops fought with commendable bravery, the legions arrived and hemmed in the barbarians. Correus tried to retire, but he was himself in the trap he had laid for the Romans, with the river closing him in. The Romans killed all but a very few, Correus among them, despite the latter's desperate resistance.

Cæsar then marched sharply upon the camp of the main body, but the other chiefs, believing resistance useless, sued for peace. Commius the Atrebatian, who was the chief instigator of the revolt, fled to the Germans. Cæsar gave the Bellovaci to understand that they themselves were the cause of all their own troubles, but pursued a liberal policy in dealing with them. He had become convinced that his system of extermination was politically unsound.

Cæsar now saw that these nations were quite subjugated, but that many were endeavoring to get rid of the Roman dominion by emigration. To this he desired to put a stop. He distributed his army, the better to control the tribes. The legate, C. Caninius, had been previously sent south to the land of the Ruteni, with his two legions, the First and Tenth; but he found himself too weak to control the turbulent population on his route, and had stopped on the way, among the Pictones. To Caninius' assistance, Cæsar now sent C. Fabius with twenty-five cohorts. He ordered the Fifteenth legion to Cisalpine Gaul to protect that province from inroads of mountain tribes, and smaller detachments to one or other place where they were needed. He retained for his own disposition Mark Antony, now quæstor, and the Twelfth legion, together with Labienus and some of the other legions, and marched to the country of Ambiorix.

This chief had fled, but Cæsar thoroughly devastated the Eburonian territory by fire, sword and rapine. This was the second time he had thus visited the land. It was an act which was entirely uncalled for, and as inexcusable as it was inhuman and unworthy of Cæsar. The Commentaries give as a reason that Cæsar desired to leave no territory for Ambiorix to return to which could afford him support, and to make the few remaining people hate this chief for the evils he had brought on them. But this is no valid excuse even for ancient days. Ambiorix was an enemy and had inflicted a heavy penalty on Sabinus and Cotta. Revenge against Ambiorix' person should not have been thus late carried forward upon his people. He had previously punished the Eburones with sufficient severity. Cæsar shines most when he is magnanimous, least when he is cruel.

From the Eburonean land Cæsar sent Labienus with two legions to overawe the Treviri, who were much like the Germans, and never abode long in their allegiance.

It is rare that the Commentaries mention the legions by name or number. They cannot, therefore, always be followed with certainty. Subsequent mention often enables a legion to be identified, but not in every instance. Occasionally the Commentaries are manifestly in error. Whenever possible, the legions have been specified by number, but generally they have to be dealt with in gross. The rotation in command of the officers of the Roman army conflicts with the individuality of the legion. Only the Tenth, Cæsar's favorite, and the one he was wont to have on the wing where he commanded, is specially prominent. This legion Cæsar continually refers to.

XXII.

UXELLODUNUM. SPRING OF 51 B. C.

CANINIUS and Fabius, with four legions and a half, had pursued an army of freebooters heading for the Province under Drappes and Lucterius, as far south as Uxellodunum, which these outlaws had seized. This oppidum was almost as difficult of access as Gergovia or Alesia. The barbarians having sent out a party to bring provisions to the place, the Romans managed to capture the entire convoy. Caninius and Fabius had the place invested when Cæsar arrived. The enemy had enough corn, but relied for water on a stream flowing on the west of the place. Cæsar cut off this supply by a system of outposts, and the Gauls were then confined to a spring on the hillside. Cæsar set to work to cut this off also. He built a mound and tower from which he could direct missiles upon the water-carriers, and gradually undermined the spring, so as to tap and divert its flow. Uxellodunum then surrendered. Cæsar spent the rest of the year in traversing Gaul from end to end to confirm the people in their allegiance, and to rectify the many abuses naturally arising from the war.

C. CANINIUS, meanwhile, hearing that Duracius, a friendly ally, was besieged in Limonum (Poitiers), a town of the Pictones, by Dumnacus, chief of the Andes, marched from his winter-quarters among the Ruteni with his two legions, the First and Tenth, to his assistance. Finding himself unable to cope with the barbarians, who were in large force, he camped near by in a strong position. The barbarians attacked his camp but without success; they were driven back with loss. When it was reported, soon thereafter, that Caninius was to be reinforced by C. Fabius, whom Cæsar had sent to his aid with twenty-five cohorts, the besiegers not only raised the siege and decamped, but retired beyond the Liger. Fabius, coming from the north, — he had been among the Remi, — caught them on the march, harassed their rear with great loss at the bridge where now stands Saumur, and gained much booty. The next day, the horse in pursuit, having gone too far beyond the infantry for the

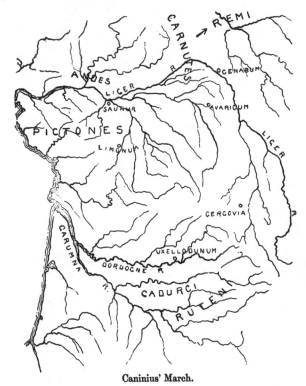

Caninius' March.

purpose of bringing the fugitive army to a halt, engaged in a combat with the rear of the enemy, who turned upon them and, sustaining their cavalry with foot, pressed them hard. The legions arrived when the Roman allied horse was all but exhausted, reëstablished matters, and put the enemy to rout with a loss of not far from twelve thousand men. Their entire baggage-train was captured.

The Andes having been disposed of and the land quieted by the destruction of all its warriors and warlike material,

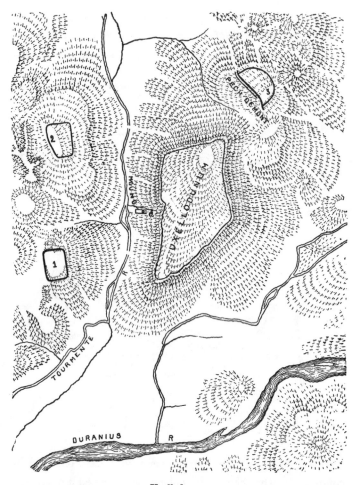

Uxellodunum.

Caninius was called on to follow towards the Province a body
of some five thousand men, consisting of robbers, runaway
slaves and other desperate characters, who under Drappes and
Lucterius were moving thither.   Fabius, with his twenty-
five cohorts, marched to the land of the Carnutes, who had
been engaged in the recent uprising, but with all the Armor-

ican tribes between them and the ocean now brought in their submission. Dumnacus was obliged to flee to remotest Gaul.

Caninius followed Drappes and Lucterius, who, knowing that they could accomplish nothing in the Province against his legions, had stopped in the land of the Cadurci, and seized Uxellodunum (Puy d'Issolu), a stronghold on very inaccessible rocks and hardly needing defenses. It had been formerly a vassal town of Drappes. The location of Uxellodunum has been put on the Oltis (Lot), but late excavations have proved it to be modern Puy d'Issolu. Caninius followed the enemy, camped on three adjacent hills, and began to draw lines of contravallation to besiege the place.

The plateau of Uxellodunum covers some two hundred acres and is six hundred feet above the plain. It is north of the Duranius (Dordogne), between which and it lies a flat plain. On its west is a range of hills separated from it by a narrow valley, and on its northeast is a smaller plateau (Pech Demont) joined to it by a ravine. On these heights Caninius established his camps, which were on a level with the oppidum. On the west and south of the Uxellodunum plateau were perpendicular rocks one hundred and forty feet high. On the east was an easier slope. Of the three camps, 1 and 2 were not intrenched, as from the lay of the land it was not necessary, and there were few men in Uxellodunum; 3 was intrenched because it was accessible from the oppidum. The position of camps 1 and 2 is fixed upon from the topography. No remains have been found of their walls.

The barbarians, fearing another Alesia and determined not to be starved into surrender, sent out all but two thousand of their force to gather corn, of which they established a dépôt some ten miles away. Meanwhile the garrison simulated numbers by sundry attacks on Caninius' camps, and

Uxelloduum, from the South.

Uxelloduum, from the North.

interrupted his work. Lucterius and Drappes proposed to gradually convey the provision to the oppidum in small trains. But when Lucterius sought to carry some corn by night into the town on beasts of burden by a steep and wooded path, probably on the north side, passing camp 3 on the west, Caninius, notified by his outposts who had heard the sound of the moving convoy, fell upon and captured the whole train. Lucterius was cut off and could not rejoin Drappes, who, back in the supply-camp, knew nothing of the disaster but assumed his colleague to have reached the oppidum. Caninius then left one legion to guard his own camps and with the other and his cavalry he advanced on the enemy's supply-camp itself. This was on low ground, enabling Caninius to seize the hills around it and corral the whole party. Having well disposed his men, he fell on and destroyed the entire foraging force with the loss of but a few men wounded. Drappes was taken prisoner. Caninius then completed the lines around the town, and Fabius shortly joined him on completion of his work north of the Liger, thus giving him enough men to finish and man the lines. Fabius took one side of the town, Caninius the other.

Cæsar had, meanwhile, left Mark Antony and fifteen cohorts in the territory of the Bellovaci to keep them in subjection, while he himself was making a tour of Gaul. He visited each region in turn, and by politic generosity and some necessary severity he won over each tribe. Among the Carnutes, he caused Guturvatus, said to have been the instigator of the late rebellion, to be brought to him and on the clamor of the soldiers executed *more majorum, i. e.,* beaten to death and decapitated. He did this, it is said, to save executing vengeance on the whole people.

Learning by letters from Caninius the situation at Uxellodunum, Cæsar put Q. Calenus in charge of the two legions which he had kept with himself, ordered him to follow by regular marches and, taking only the cavalry, moved rapidly to the aid of Caninius. This he did because it had now become essential speedily to stamp out all opposition; the natives well knew that his term in Gaul lasted but one summer more, and he feared they might argue that if they could hold out so much longer they would eventually get rid of the Romans. He therefore determined to make an example of this body of freebooters.

Cæsar was wont to leave as little to his lieutenants and to do as much personally as he could.   While abundantly busy with the political questions of Gaul and Italy, he yet deemed it wise never to allow a military operation to drag for want of his own supervision.   To this personal activity is traceable the remarkable success of his Gallic campaigns, which from beginning to end breathe of Cæsar's genius, cool head, clear judgment, presence of mind, boldness and never-tiring energy.

On his arrival he found that the inhabitants of Uxellodunum had abundance of corn, and that, in order to accomplish his end, he must cut them off from water.   This he could not easily do, for a stream (the Tourmente) flowed at the foot of the crags on the west side of the town, and through a narrow ravine, so that its waters could not be diverted.   But, by disposing slingers, archers and engines in certain places in the ravine, Cæsar rendered the operation of getting water so hazardous, that he finally confined the enemy to procuring it in one place.

This was between the town and the stream, where, near the walls, gushed out an ample spring (a). Cæsar saw that he must also cut this off. He advanced vineæ and a mound towards the place with great labor and constant skirmishing, in which a number of Romans were wounded. He also undertook to tap the sources of the spring by a subterranean passage which was run some distance in the rock towards it.

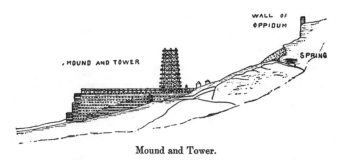

Mound and Tower.

This passage has been discovered, and some traces also of the mound and works.

Finally, the outside works were advanced so near the spring that the Romans from the mound, which was sixty feet high and surmounted by a ten-story turret, could cast their darts with marked effect upon any of the garrison who came for water; thus they succeeded in all but preventing its use. The tower was too far below the walls of the oppidum to attack the latter. Thus deprived of the spring, many people and all the cattle in the town died of thirst.

But the besieged, with the fury of despair, determined to make a supreme effort for their salvation. They accumulated an enormous amount of inflammable material, — tallow, pitch and tar, — and filling barrels, rolled them down upon the Roman works, at the same time making a desperate sortie in force against them. The patiently constructed works speedily caught fire. To beat back this sortie and at the same time to enable his men to handle the fire to advantage, Cæsar ordered a feigned general attack from all sides at once, which being stoutly given, the barbarians withdrew quickly into their town, for they did not know which quarter was most in danger, and they feared that the Romans might

enter the town.   This enabled the legions to extinguish the
flames and to gain a material amount of ground as well.

Some days after, the Roman mine reached the sources of
the spring and diverted its flow.   The barbarians, considering this to be an act of the gods and not of men, for they
had deemed the spring unreachable, were compelled both by
fear and by thirst to surrender.   In pursuance of his determination above explained, Cæsar cut off the hands of all
those who had here borne arms.   Both leaders had been previously captured and imprisoned.   Drappes starved himself
to death in prison to save himself from a worse fate.

Meanwhile Labienus, among the Treviri, had got the

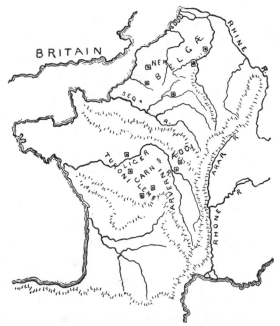

Winter-Quarters, B. C. 51-50.

insurgent chiefs into his hands, and Cæsar, seeing that his
return thither would not be necessary, marched throughout

Aquitania, where he received the submission of all the tribes which Crassus had already partly brought under control. This occupied the summer. When the time arrived for going into winter-quarters, four legions (under Mark Antony, C. Trebonius, P. Vatinius and Q. Tullius) were left among the Belgæ; two among the Ædui; two among the Turoni near the Carnutes to hold the seaside tribes in check; two among the Lemnovices near the Arverni. Cæsar then personally went to the Province, where he attended to the duties of the state, returned to the legions among the Belgæ, and wintered at Nemetocenna (Arras). There were no rebels left except a few bands of rovers, who could accomplish nothing unaided. But Cæsar had to rest content with a merely nominal submission, in the north of Gaul. There was always a relic of war in that quarter. Commius, after some cavalry exchanges with Volusenus, turned freebooter. According to Frontinus, he retired to Britain. Only he and Ambiorix, of all the Gallic chieftains, survived.

Cæsar now devoted his time to demonstrating to the Gallic tribes the advantages of the Roman alliance, as he had shown them the dangers of revolt. "Cæsar, whilst in winter-quarters in the country of the Belgæ, made it his only business to keep the states in amity with him, and to give none either hopes of or pretext for revolt. For nothing was further from his wishes than to be under the necessity of engaging in another war at his departure; lest, when he was drawing his army out of the country, any war should be left unfinished, which the Gauls would cheerfully undertake when there was no immediate danger. Therefore, by treating the states with respect, making rich presents to the leading men, imposing no new burdens, and making the terms of their subjection lighter, he easily kept Gaul (already exhausted by so many unsuccessful battles) in obedience."

Thus Cæsar spent the winter, and when the spring opened, he proceeded towards Italy, visiting all the towns by the way, and confirming them in their allegiance, as far as Cisalpine Gaul. He was received with the greatest honor and acclamations. He then returned to Nemetocenna, ordered his legions to the territory of the Treviri, and held there a grand review of his troops. Having settled the affairs of Gaul on a solid basis, Cæsar journeyed to Ravenna to be near the events in Italy when his consulate should expire. He left Labienus in command, regarding whom, though warned that he was solicited by his enemies, he harbored no suspicion.

The Gallic campaigns are peculiarly interesting to the military student as showing how Cæsar schooled himself and his legions. He began with but the ordinary military training, on a small basis of experience; he ended as a great general, with an experience which enabled him to rise to the most astounding height. His legions commenced green and untried; they ended as veterans equal to conquering the world. Each became so wedded to the other that mutual confidence and affection made the army commanded by Cæsar irresistible.

It was impossible that during this period of schooling Cæsar should not make mistakes, — grave ones. But all his mistakes bore fruit, and raised the qualities of both general and legions. One can see, step by step, how Cæsar's successes and failures alike produced their effect; how his inborn ability came to the surface; how he impressed his own individuality on whatever he did; and how his intelligence led him to apply whatever he learned to his future conduct.

No praise is too high for the conduct or moral qualities of the army. From Cæsar down, through every grade, all military virtues were pronounced. In organization and dis-

cipline, ability to do almost any work, endurance of danger
and trial, toughness and courage, it was a model for the rest
of Rome, — but a model unhappily not imitated.   And not
only his legionaries, but his auxiliary troops, were imbued
with the same spirit, — all breathed not only devotion to
Cæsar, but reflected in a measure his own great qualities.

All this, however, was of a nature different from the high
qualities of the legions of the Punic wars.   These were wonderful in their devotion, discipline and effectiveness because
the material in them was incomparable.   Cæsar's legions
were equally wonderful, but it was because Cæsar had fash-
ioned and always commanded them.   The discipline of the
earlier legion depended largely on the men; that of Cæsar's
entirely on himself.   As in the case of Napoleon, the discipline of Cæsar's legions was often terribly lax; but in that
quality which may be called battle-discipline they were
unsurpassed.

Cæsar had in Gaul some opponents worthy even of him.
Vercingetorix, Ariovistus, Casivelaunus were, each in his
way, great leaders.   That they were overcome by Cæsar was
but natural.   Disciplined troops well led cannot but win
against barbarians.   The end could not be otherwise.   And
while the Gallic War does not show Cæsar — as the Second
Punic War did Hannibal — opposed to the strongest military machine in existence, it did show him opposed to generals and troops quite equal to most of those encountered by
Alexander.   The Gauls must not be underrated.   Some of
their operations and some of their fighting were of the highest order.   They contended nobly for their independence.
Defeat did not discourage them.   Once put down, they again
rose in rebellion so soon as the strong hand was removed.
They were in no sense weak opponents, and while in all
things Cæsar's army was superior to theirs, yet in their

motives and hearty coöperation they certainly were more commendable than Cæsar in his mere love of conquest.

Gaul was conquered. Even though the master's grasp of the reins was soon relaxed, to reach for other and greater things, the subjected province rose not. There were small wars and rumors of wars, but these were so isolated and unimportant that the local governors could do them justice. In the remote corners of the new territory, the Pyrenees, the Scheldt, and the coast, some tribes were still *de facto* free. But time itself reduced these. Cæsar's work had been thorough, and it was the work of civilization. Whatever fault can be found with his method, or indeed his abstract rights, that Gaul should be conquered was a historical necessity, and it is well that it fell to the lot of a man as broad, as thorough, as enlightened as Cæsar.

Gallic Horseman.
(From a terra-cotta Statuette.)

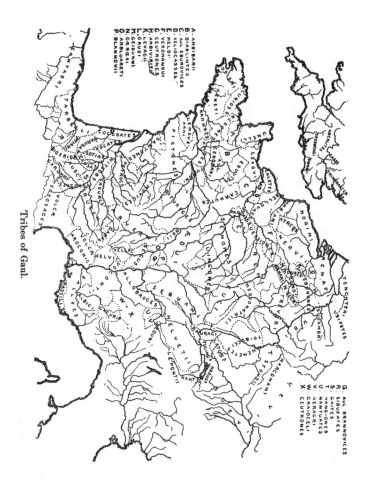

Tribes of Gaul.

XXIII.

CÆSAR'S METHOD.

THE Gauls had been the terror of Rome for centuries. Whoever conquered them would be the national hero. Cæsar understood this. His mission was to protect the Province; he purposed to subdue Gaul. He worked for his own ends as much as for Rome, but he understood his problem thoroughly. He considered the strategic field of Gaul with a clear eye, and committed no errors in his general plan. It was natural that he should make early mistakes of detail, for Cæsar had not been brought up as a soldier; and we find a hesitancy in his first campaigns which later he threw off. His line of advance from the Province through central Gaul was in strict accord with the topographical values, and he studied the tribal instincts keenly. He educated himself as he went along, profiting by all his mistakes. His campaigns across the Rhine and to Britain were useless; they did not aid the general scheme. Cæsar was energetic in obtaining information, ingenious in contending with new obstacles, intelligent in selecting his objective, careful of his base. He demanded severe exertions from his men, but rewarded them handsomely. He was much aided by fortune, but under trial was doubly energetic. In view of the fact that Cæsar entered the Gallic campaign without experience in war, it was a marvelous success.

IT has already been pointed out that Cæsar, on being appointed governor of Gaul, had been vested with no right to do more than protect the exposed boundaries of the then Province. All prefects had confined themselves to this rôle. The laws of nations in Cæsar's day had already received some recognition; but right was no valid argument against might, and few rights were accorded to barbarian tribes by Rome in the last century before the Christian era, least of all to the redoubted Gauls, who had so often brought Rome to the verge of ruin. Rome at that day was lawless. Every great man wrought for himself. Cæsar had been brought up

in a school which prompted him to bend all things to his ambition. He represented a great party; only by his personal
success could his party succeed. War meant to him an
army; an army was to him but a means of winning power.
When he went to Gaul, Pompey was distinctly the leader
of the triumvirate. With a man of Cæsar's make-up, this
could not last. Like his colleague, Cæsar soon recognized
that he must aim at the sole control of Rome if he would
win any standing. Without war and conquest, he could
gain neither the experience, fame nor influence requisite to
this end. This was no unworthy ambition. Cæsar could
not be great with a lesser end in view, and the importance of
his object was equaled by the splendor of his means. To
deliver the republic forever from the Gauls was to make their
conqueror the foremost of the Romans, as the Gauls had been
the most dreaded of the foes of Rome. To subdue Gaul
was a stepping-stone to certain and unapproached renown.

Cæsar was fortunate. At the very inception of his charge
of Gaul, the outbreak of the Helvetii opportunely occurred,
and led, in its progress, to the current of events which ended
in the conquest of the entire country. One thing after
another, with Cæsar's uniform good fortune, was sure to
happen, to give him at least a pretense of right in extending
his conquests. The Helvetian question solved, the Ædui
called in his aid against the Germans under Ariovistus. In
this, too, Cæsar could assert that he was but protecting the
allies of the Province. The Romans always helped their
allies when by so doing they could help themselves. Cæsar
worked on the like theory. Gaul publicly thanked the
consul for freeing her from the Helvetii and the Germans;
but Gaul did not then anticipate her own subjugation.

Cæsar's next step requires more of his own plausible
explanation. It is hard to justify his action in carrying the

war among the Belgæ, but he solves the enigma by reciting the danger to which the Province would be subjected by any combination of tribes, even if not offensively meant. The same course of argument carried Cæsar beyond the Rhine, and into Britain, and was the motive of all his other conquests. However unjustifiable this may have been, — and yet we see the same process of conquest going on in the nineteenth century, — Cæsar's purpose was clear and definite, and he played his cards well. His course was consistent throughout; and he had the happy faculty in his public utterances of arguing the law to his side, of placing there the appearance of right. Whatever he undertook resulted in his favor, and, greatest accomplishment of all, he disciplined and hardened an army devoted to himself, by means of which he was able to make himself master of Rome.

All this is by no means to Cæsar's discredit. He did but what other leading men had been doing in Rome for generations. The old-fashioned Roman patriotism had long since vanished. There was scarce another road to honor and power than the selfish one, scarce another means of safety for those who held high rank. Cæsar cannot fairly be blamed for self-seeking; neither should he be held up as a model patriot. Judged by his own Commentaries, he never rose to the plane of a Washington, a Gustavus, a Hannibal. *Ubi bene, ibi patria* was a serviceable motto for him, so long as the good ran in his own favor. Rome needed a Cæsar to shape the destiny to which she was manifestly drifting. It is well that such a man was at hand, and that he did his work with thoroughness; but though Cæsar was as useful to the ancient world as Napoleon to modern Europe, it cannot be said that either worked on the instincts of elevated patriotism.

Whatever criticism may be passed upon Cæsar in a political aspect, as a great captain he is almost beyond cavil. Barring such errors of vigilance and judgment as are of peculiar interest in showing certain characteristics as well as how Cæsar educated himself to arms, his military conduct through this memorable series of campaigns is a fruitful study. His errors were more often in policy than in war. At times he could be generous, even magnanimous, to subjugated peoples. At times he was cruel beyond what any civilized conqueror has ever been, unnecessarily, unwisely cruel. The world had advanced since the days of Alexander, and while what is now known as the law of nations was not then a code, certain of its tenets had been established. But Cæsar absolutely disregarded any such when they interfered with his own projects.

Statecraft counts for much in a great captain's work. Cæsar's policy in Gaul was on the whole so harsh as scarcely to rate as policy at all. This is the civil aspect of the matter. From another point of view it was as masterly as the problem was difficult. Cæsar had to conciliate some tribes while attacking other neighboring and friendly tribes. He had to supply himself while destroying victual for the enemy. He had to elevate part of the people in order to suppress another part. He had to play one half of the population against the other half. He had a population of eight million Gauls to oppose his dozen legions. In no other way could he do his work. So far as this his military policy goes, his conduct was irreproachable.

Cæsar's strategy was farsighted and sound. The Province, when Gaul fell to his lot, as one of the triumvirs, was a sort of salient thrust forward into the midst of the country. West and north of its boundary, the Rhone, lived allied peoples; from the mountains on the east danger threatened from a number of restless tribes. The advantages of this

salient position were by no means lost on Cæsar, nor the
power of concentrated action which it gave him. His first
campaign, against the Helvetii, was intended to protect and

Physical Features of Gaul.

resulted in protecting the right flank of the salient, an absolute essential to safety in advancing into north or northwest
Gaul. From this point duly secured, northerly, the Rhine
and the Jura and Vosegus mountains protected to a certain
degree the right of an advancing army, provided the tribes on
the left bank of the great river were not unfriendly; and it
will be noticed that one of Cæsar's early efforts was directed
to making as many of these tribes as possible his firm friends
by generous treatment and effective protection against their
enemies. When he could not quickly accomplish his end by

negotiation, he resorted to drastic measures. In carrying out his scheme of conquest, Cæsar advanced his salient along the Arar and the Mosa as far as the Sabis, and could then debouch from the watershed to the west of these rivers down the valleys of the Sequana and its tributaries, the Matrona and Axona, with perfect safety. And Cæsar not only secured the friendship of the abutting tribes, but always kept several strongly fortified camps among them as an additional protection.

The flow of the Axona across his line of operations furnished Cæsar an advanced base from which he could move against the Belgæ. This line from his first base in the Province to the secondary one on the Axona lay along the Arar and the Mosa. From Belgian territory, when once in his hands, Cæsar could safely move even so far as Britain, provided he properly protected his rear and was careful that his victuals were accumulated or certain to be delivered by friendly tribes. Having subdued the Belgæ, he could turn without danger to the southwest corner of Gaul, against Aquitania. Cæsar thus exemplified in the fullest degree the advantage in grand strategy of central lines of operation. Neither Alexander nor Hannibal exhibited a clearer grasp of his strategical problem than Cæsar. It is noticeable that the hardest part of Cæsar's work was to establish this central salient by alliance or conquest of the tribes which abutted on it; his gravest danger when the Ædui, who guarded his line of operations, joined their revolting brethren. But this salient definitely gained, Cæsar was able to reduce the operations of the war to the basis of single isolated campaigns. These, indeed, were difficult, but dangerous only when they threatened with intestine broils the military structure he had erected.

The several campaigns, from the cautious handling of the

Helvetian question to the splendid management of the siege of Alesia, have each received comment in its proper place.

Cæsar, as a Roman general, carried out the Roman idea of a conquest of the world by virtue of a constant offensive. In studying Cæsar, one studies the Roman military status at its best, so far as generalship goes; so far as concerns the soldier, all that was best in the burgess-militia of Rome had long ago disappeared. Cæsar's legionary was a professional soldier in every sense. Cæsar began the war by a defensive operation against the Helvetii; after that he always assumed the offensive, though in the Commentaries he frequently goes out of his way to convince his readers that he was the aggrieved party. If he ever resorted to the defensive it was but for a moment, shortly to resume the offensive and push it vigorously.

Like all generals who are careful of their men, Cæsar preferred to campaign only in the season of good weather, and to lie in quarters in winter. But that he could conduct a winter campaign was more than once demonstrated. While in quarters he appears to have been fairly careful of good discipline and studious to keep his men busy. The panic at Vesontio was a good object-lesson, by which he profited. His teachableness was one of Cæsar's admirable qualities.

Cæsar was energetic in procuring information on which to form his plans. This was often both hard to get and unreliable when got, but he sought it intelligently. He constantly kept afoot some of his Gallic officers or horsemen; used spies from allied tribes or gained friends within the enemy's lines. Deserters were put to use and were handsomely rewarded. If information could not be otherwise procured, Cæsar made reconnoissances in force. As such we may well treat Cæsar's first expeditions against Germany and

Britain. On no other ground can these be justified as military operations; and a reconnoissance in force should never risk the existence of army or commander, — as the first crossing to Britain did.

Cæsar as a rule was numerically weaker than the enemy, but he was not so vastly overmatched as was Alexander, nor can the opposition to him be in any sense compared to what Hannibal encountered during his entire military life. Cæsar was far stronger than his enemies in everything but numbers, especially in self-confidence and power of work. His legionaries would bear anything and could do anything. They were very Yankees for ingenuity. Cæsar did not willingly mix the allies with his legions; he employed the native foot mostly as bowmen and slingers; his cavalry was uniformly native. He worked his army habitually well concentrated. If he divided his forces it was but for a short time, soon again to concentrate. This is an almost uniform test of military capacity. But Cæsar sought to attack the enemy before the latter had concentrated, and generally made good use of such a chance. Nimbleness of movement stood in the stead of numbers. He understood how, as Napoleon phrases it, "se multiplier par la vitesse."

Cæsar's objective was always well chosen. It was either the most important strategic point, or more usually the army of the enemy. Thus in the campaign against the Belgæ, he threw himself upon the Remi, who had not yet decided whether to join the confederacy, and by preventing their so doing at once made secure a secondary base. He chose the shortest road to march by. In 52 the enemy concentrated his forces between the Cebennæ mountains and the upper Liger. Cæsar's army lay between the Sequana and Matrona. He joined it, got his forces well in hand, and marched from Agendicum by way of Genabum straight on the enemy. In the division of his forces he was usually careful so to march as to be able again to make a junction of the bulk of his forces. In the campaign against the Veneti, while the army was divided into several parts, two of these, comprising six legions under himself and Titurius, were placed where they could easily be concentrated.

Cæsar was careful of his base. This cannot be said to apply to the first British expedition, but in the second he left half of all his cavalry and three legions on the coast of Gaul as an intermediate base. In 52, in the general insurrection, the Province was his first base, with twenty-two cohorts under L. Cæsar the legate. The second base was the land of the friendly Remi, and the line from the first to the second base lay along the Arar, through the land of the likewise friendly Sequani and Lingones, and was strengthened by Vesontio midway. In order to secure another line along the Liger, Cæsar left Labienus with two (later reinforced to four) legions at Agendicum, well intrenched. Even these dispositions barely saved him. His leaving the fleet protected by an intrenched camp on the coast of Britain was a simpler instance of his care for his base, taught by unfortunate experience.

Cæsar always sought to induce his enemy to divide his forces. In the war with the Belgæ he sent the Ædui to attack the Bellovacian territory, thus easily detaching this powerful tribe from the confederacy. His diversions were well conceived and well timed. When he drew Vercingetorix down to meet him by crossing the Cebennæ, and when, after so doing, he personally hurried to his legions, Cæsar showed that he was a master of the art of blinding the enemy as to his real intentions. This was a device in the style of Hannibal.

Cæsar was careful of his soldiers. But he called on them

for the severest exertions at any time or under any circumstances. His logistics was good. He showed in Gaul more foresight in the matter of rations and magazines than in later campaigns. Protection of Gallic tribes was paid for by victual. He got rations from those neighboring tribes whose alliance he had accepted. A beaten people was always mulcted in a given amount of corn. He was rarely in a strait for bread. Still he campaigned only when there was forage, if this was possible. A train of pack-animals accompanied his column, loaded with a supply in addition to what the men themselves carried.

Cæsar speaks in his Commentaries of a threefold advantage of the Roman, or what Napoleon called the methodical system of conducting war, over that of any other nation, namely: the holding of decisive points, the intrenching of camps, and the breaking up of the enemy's communications. The capture of decisive points opened the campaign, and placed the troops where they were advantageously located for winning a victory; the Roman intrenched camp was a movable fortress which from its effect on the *morale* of the troops made victory more certain as well as neutralized defeat; by the breaking up of his communications the enemy was compelled to shift his ground, to fight under adverse circumstances, or surrender.

Decisive points were to be reached if possible through friendly or at least neutral territory. If they must be reached through the enemy's, then every step must be protected to secure his own communications. On Cæsar's march from Agendicum to the Bituriges, he could not leave Vellaunodunum in his rear, but must capture it to keep open his communications with Labienus. Cæsar describes a decisive point as one having many advantages, the most important being that of opening and holding an entrance into the enemy's country. In the march above instanced, such a point was Genabum where there was a bridge over the Liger. This bridge Cæsar must have in order to approach Vercingetorix. In his campaign against the Belgæ, so soon as he had crossed the Axona he was on the enemy's territory, and therefore his camp on the Axona was located at a decisive point. In moving on the Helvetii, after crossing the Rhone, Cæsar intrenched in the angle of that river and the Arar, where he was among the friendly Ædui, and from here he could readily attack the enemy. This was a decisive point.

Whether Cæsar laid much stress on secrecy in relation to his plans among his own men does not appear. In secrecy, even to his lieutenants, Hannibal was unapproached. Alexander, too, kept his own counsel, but rather as master than for military reasons. Hephæstion knew his every purpose. Cæsar deemed great speed in executing his projects the equivalent of secrecy.

A captain must be largely gauged by the strength of his opponents. Cæsar's in Gaul by no means lacked ability. Ariovistus was a man of exceptional strength, and Vercingetorix came near to being a genius. Both recognized the value of decisive points as well as Cæsar, — though war to them was not a science, and what Cæsar relied on against such men was not so much secrecy as the rapidity of his marches and the discipline of his legions.

The decisive point secured, a battle was sought or an attack on a town was made, or some operation was undertaken to bring the enemy to such action that he might be overwhelmed. Cæsar preferred a battle in the open field because a victory so won was apt to result in many towns falling into his hands or in making their capture easier. But if the enemy constantly avoided it, he was compelled to forego a battle and to resort to a siege or a blockade.

While it is true that Cæsar sought battle, the fact that there were few pitched battles proper in the Gallic campaign shows how much stronger the legions were than any troops opposed to them. Defeat was often inflicted by Cæsar's native cavalry alone.

When Cæsar camped in the presence of the enemy in expectation of battle, he sought to lure him away from his camp so that should he win a victory, he might make the most of it by pursuit, without the enemy taking refuge within it and compelling an assault. With secret forced marches he approached the foe, camped a short march from him, and next day endeavored to take him unawares. Thus he approached Ariovistus, thus the Usipetes and Tenchtheri. Sometimes Cæsar would move nearer to the enemy the evening before he intended to bring on a battle, if there was some obstacle behind which he could easily camp unobserved, or he would do the same thing in case he needed more information before engaging. Occasionally he camped at a distance of two short marches.

In determining the locality of a camp, Cæsar paid strict heed to his own communications and sought to prejudice the enemy's. At the outset he paid the more heed to his own. Later he showed more dash, more reliance on the enemy's inertia. When Ariovistus moved around his flank, Cæsar at once took up a defensive and moved only a small body on Ariovistus' flank. In Britain Cassivellaunus moved on Cæsar's communications. Vercingetorix cut Cæsar's line at Gergovia by rousing the Ædui in his rear. There is sometimes a lack of strategic dash in Cæsar's movements in the Gallic campaign. We do not see him moving on the enemy's communications by the great turning movements he afterwards employed. He simply secured his own communications and fought. In besieging towns he disturbed the enemy's communications after a fashion, but not by turning movements. This was caution bred of self-distrust which wore away before the Civil War.

When Cæsar conquered in open fight, he pursued vigorously, as a rule with his cavalry, but not infrequently with the legions, — unless he had been very much exhausted. It was only the cavalry, however, which actually reached the enemy. No one ever pursued so remorselessly as Alexander, until Napoleon dawned upon the world and showed it how to utilize victories to the fullest. Cæsar followed up the political chances keenly, and appearing after a victory in the very midst of his enemies had no difficulty in subjecting them and in forcing them to furnish victuals and transportation. He insisted on dictating what their government should be. After a victory, when danger was over, he divided his forces, the better to work on the moral nature of the people by a sudden display of his legions in many places at once.

The results of the summer's campaign having been gathered, Cæsar went into such winter-quarters as best fostered what had been accomplished. He avoided loading the Province with the care of the legions. His winter-quarters accustomed the newly subjected tribes to the army, to the Roman yoke and to furnishing regular supplies. After the victory over Ariovistus, winter-quarters were taken up in the east part of the land of the Sequani about Vesontio, where were rich supplies, with the Province near by; and at the same time Cæsar was threatening the Belgæ and keeping the Sequani well in hand. In 57 he took up winter-quarters on the lower Liger, when Crassus had already accustomed the Belgæ to their masters. The Sequani needed rest from furnishing provisions, the Remi had been on Cæsar's side, the Belgæ were exhausted, and the Ædui and neighbors were friendly. Besides, Cæsar wished to see what effect his eastern victories had had in the west, and whether it would still require force to subdue the western tribes. In 56 and 55 winter-quarters were taken with reference to the British expedition. In 54, after this expedition, he had winter-quarters near the coast, but spread over a large area because of the late bad harvest. In consequence of the terrible experience gained by distributing the legions too widely, in 53 and 52 they were kept close together; six were in Agendicum.

When Cæsar had bad luck, his energy markedly grew. He particularly watched for and guarded against any loss of *morale* among his men. In such circumstances he could use his fluent tongue to the greatest advantage. He would convince his men that they were not beaten, turn to another field and by redoubled energy wrest victory out of failure. This he did after Gergovia. Cæsar throughout his campaigns shows best after a backset. We shall meet notable instances of this in the Civil War.

It has been said that ancient differs so entirely from modern war that one can learn little from the great deeds of the captains antedating the Christian era. But what can be said of Cæsar would be high praise for the best of the generals of modern times. When we read the old campaigns, not superficially but for their inmost meaning, they convey to us the same broad lessons which the most able captains since the Middle Ages have given us. An artist learns his technique in a modern studio; he gathers his inspiration from the old masters. So with war. In no better way can the characteristic quality essential to the soldier be developed than by the study of the work of the ancient captains; by searching earnestly for the reasons which led them to what they did. Every great general has confessed his debt to the soldiers of antiquity.

XXIV.

CÆSAR'S ARMY.

CÆSAR'S legionary was no longer a citizen-soldier, as in the Punic wars; he was a professional, or a mercenary. He served for a livelihood, not as a duty. The legion was no longer set up in three lines according to property rating; it was marshaled in two or three lines of cohorts, the cohort being a body of four to six hundred men, ranked according to military qualities, and ten cohorts went to the legion. The men retained substantially the old equipment; they occupied in line a space of but three feet front instead of five. The intervals between cohorts had sensibly decreased. The camp and camp-followers, musicians, standards and petty details of all kinds remained much as before. Light troops and cavalry were recruited from conquered tribes. Each legion had six tribunes who commanded it in turn under a legate. The general staff of the army had quartermasters, aides, engineers, lictors, scouts and a body-guard. The legionary's pay was about that of a day-laborer, but largesses and booty were bountiful. For defense, the legion or army formed square or circle. It readily ployed into column or deployed into line. The orders of march were accurately laid down and well observed. The average march was about fifteen miles. The train was less long than ours, there being neither artillery nor ammunition. For battle the army was drawn up on the slope of a hill; it still attacked, as had always been its habit. The legion of the Punic war was good because the men were good; Cæsar's was effective because he was able.

THE tactical formation of the early Roman army was described in the volume on Hannibal. Considerable changes in this tactical formation had taken place since the Punic wars; some were introduced by Marius, or by Cæsar as a consequence of his campaigns. The Roman soldier as to arms, equipment and minor tactics, was to all intents and purposes the same as he had been in the time of Hannibal. He still wore helmet, cuirass, and greave on right leg; he still bore spear, shield and sword. But in character, quality and discipline, he was no longer the splendid citizen-soldier of that day. He was a professional if a Roman; a mercenary if a foreigner; and as such he was exactly what his commander made him. A similar change had obtained in the officers. The six tribunes of a legion were no longer appointed for their military qualifications or long service, but claimed their rank on the score of political or social standing, or of friendship for the chief.

The original smaller tactical unit of the Romans had been the century. It next became the maniple of two centuries. Later the three maniples of the hastati, principes and triarii, with some cavalry and velites, were merged into one body called a cohort. But the name alone remained. Under Cæsar the cohort was no longer the ancient one, but a body the evolution of which has already been traced. It was divided only for the smaller details. It was practically the tactical unit of the legion, and all manœuvres were by cohorts. The three-class formation of each cohort had entirely disappeared.

It seems odd, with all that has been written about Roman tactics and organization from Polybius to Vegetius and Onosander, that the exact structure of Cæsar's legion, cohort, maniple and century cannot be given. The addition of a few words in some paragraphs would elucidate the difficulties we encounter in construing these authors. But, as the omission of the name of some single well-known spot by Polybius has given rise to endless discussion as to Hannibal's route across the Alps, so a certain lapse in explanation in all the Latin authors who treat of tactics has produced many different views as to the details of organization of Cæsar's legion. Particularly Rüstow, Göler and Stoffel have discussed the matter *au fond*. But they disagree on many points.

The maniples of the cohort, according to Rüstow, stood beside each other; according to Göler still in rear of each

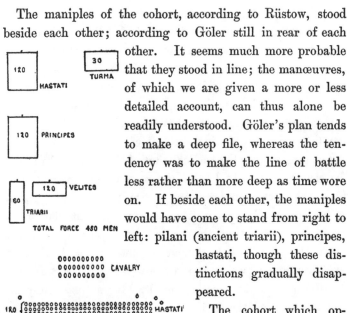

other. It seems much more probable that they stood in line; the manœuvres, of which we are given a more or less detailed account, can thus alone be readily understood. Göler's plan tends to make a deep file, whereas the tendency was to make the line of battle less rather than more deep as time wore on. If beside each other, the maniples would have come to stand from right to left: pilani (ancient triarii), principes, hastati, though these distinctions gradually disappeared.

The cohort which opposed Hannibal was formed of three maniples or companies, each maniple in two centuries or platoons, and the maniples standing in rear of each other with intervals between hastati, prin-

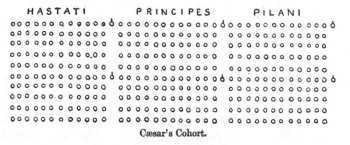

Cæsar's Cohort.

cipes, triarii, and with cavalry and light troops conveniently disposed. The cohort with which Cæsar conquered the world was a body of three maniples, each in two centuries (*ordines*) and the maniples standing side by side without intervals. The first ordo comprised the front five ranks of the maniple, the second ordo the rear five ranks. Or if the cohort was set up in eight ranks, there were four in each century.

The normal numerical force of Cæsar's legions cannot be determined with the accuracy of the legions of the Punic wars. At times they had five or even six thousand men; at Pharsalus they had been reduced by service to an average of but twenty-seven hundred and fifty. Rüstow construes the various authorities to give the legion an average field strength of thirty-six hundred men; Göler puts it at forty-eight hundred. This latter is perhaps nearer the normal force, not often reached in time of war.

Ten cohorts composed the legion. If the cohorts had three hundred and sixty men, ten deep, there would be thirty-six men in each rank. If eight deep, which was not unlikely the usual case, and at Pharsalus probably so, there would be forty-five men in each rank. If these thirty-six men in close order for the march or parade or column of assault took up three feet each in breadth and six feet in depth and there was six feet between maniples, the size of a cohort would be one hundred and twenty feet front by sixty feet depth. If there were forty-five men in rank and eight in file, the size of a cohort would be, in close order, with say seven and a half feet between maniples, one hundred and fifty feet front by fifty feet depth.

But three feet front was not sufficient to enable the legionary to hurl his pilum or use his gladius to advantage. There was therefore an open order of battle. This was either taken by each odd-numbered man stepping three feet forward to gain arm-room, or more likely each rank deployed by a face to right or left from the centre and took distance as needed. This doubled the front of a cohort. On this latter supposition there must have been, in close order, intervals between cohorts equal to their front so as to provide for deployment; in open order — after deployment — there would be no intervals at all.

Taking the eight-deep formation, with close-order intervals equal to cohort front added, the cohort would occupy, in open or in close order, three hundred feet front by fifty depth. Taking the ten-deep formation, equally with intervals, it would occupy two hundred and forty feet front by sixty feet depth.

Rüstow makes calculations on the average strength of a legion in active service being thirty-six hundred men. At

Ilerda, Cæsar tells us that a certain ridge, well identified to-day, was wide enough for three cohorts in line. The ridge, says Rüstow, measures three hundred and sixty feet in width — which gives one hundred and twenty feet front to a cohort — as they stood without intervals. But the actual width of the ridge varies as it descends to the plain. This vitiates the calculation, though the deduction is not far from correct. We may fairly assume the average front of Cæsar's cohort without intervals as one hundred and twenty to one hundred and fifty feet, and the cohort as commonly numbering not over three hundred and sixty men during his campaigns.

Maniple of 120 Men.

Each maniple had two centurions, a senior and a junior, and to each centurion there was a sub-centurion. These, like our company officers, all served on foot. The senior centurion of the cohort was its commander. While, like the non-commissioned officers of modern armies, the centurions could not rise in rank beyond their own grade, and while their duties were assimilated to these, they more nearly approached, in the extent of their command, our company officers than our sergeants. Their relative rank in the legion was well determined.

The music and standards of the cohorts and legions were much like those of the Punic wars.

Maniple of 200 Men.

Each maniple had an ensign; each cohort an eagle. The baggage consisted of pack-train (*impedimenta*) and the soldier's own load (*sarcinæ*), which Cicero says was sixty pounds in addition to his armor and weapons, — a possible maximum. Sutlers (*mercatores*) were the only persons accompanying the army who used carts. The tents were of skins, ten feet square. Each tent could accommodate ten men, of whom two would probably be on duty. Each centurion had a tent; the camp-followers must be sheltered; the higher officers had servants and more tents than the lesser. With tools for intrenching, tent-poles and pegs and the usual baggage carried, Rüstow estimates five hundred and twenty sumpter-mules for a field legion of thirty-six hundred men, — or one animal for every seven men. This was all there was to the pack-train, and is not far astray. Marius invented a forked stick or pole (*muli Mariani*) for convenience in carrying the sarcinæ. The bundles of rations, clothing, etc., were tied to this, and it was borne on the shoulder. The ration for fifteen days, grain

Muli Mariani.

unground, weighed probably twenty-five pounds. The rest
of the kit, armor, etc., much more than doubled this load.
Cicero's estimate may be considered high.

The allied legions of old times had all disappeared. A

Legion in One Line.

legion no longer meant one Roman and one allied legion, or
ten thousand men. It meant simply a body of ten cohorts.
In place of the allied legions there was a larger force than

theretofore of light troops armed like
legionaries, but less heavily, and considerably more bowmen and slingers. The
light troops had a leather jerkin but
no armor, and carried the round shield
(*parma*) instead of the cylindrical *scutum*.
The bowmen and slingers wore no armor
at all.

The six tribunes were divided into sets
of two. Each set com-
manded the legion for
two months, the two tri-
bunes alternating daily,
after the odd Roman

Light-Armed Man.

fashion, which only among them could
work without destroying all idea of discipline. The four tribunes off duty acted
much as quartermasters, commissaries or
aides de camp do in modern times. All
of them served mounted. To be sure that
each legion should not suffer from the
divided command, a legate was put in supreme supervisory control. Later Cæsar

Legionary ready for
Battle.

put him in actual command, and under him the two tribunes on duty probably acted as chief of staff and adjutant general of a modern brigade.

The general staff of Cæsar's army comprised:—

Legates, assigned by the Senate to the consul, and deriving their authority from him. They were the general officers. Cæsar had one for each of his legions. This was the first time their duty had been made definite.

Quæstors, who superintended the business of a province or of an army. The quæstor was a sort of quartermaster-general.

Contubernales and comites prætorii, who were volunteer aides, or if numerous a sort of gentleman body-guard.

The Cohors prætoria, consisting of lictors, secretaries, marshals, spies, servants and orderlies.

Speculatores (scouts), who acted as vanguard and flankers on the march, — each legion had ten, — and who were generally sent out to reconnoitre. We must conclude that these had placed under them such details as the immediate circumstances called for.

The Body-guard, sometimes a small cavalry detachment, but principally evocati, — veterans past duty years who remained voluntarily in service. Though footmen, they had horses and servants, were highly honored, served near the general, and were put into places of trust.

Fabri, or engineers, under a *præfectus fabrorum*, of whom mention has already been made. They were used to repair weapons, construct bridges, siege-mounds and towers, and generally do the engineering work of the army. Cæsar had some very able engineers.

Antesignani, thought by some historians to have been a select body of a few men from each cohort, for service in delicate cases requiring skill and experience. They carried no baggage, and from them were often selected the centurions. But it is not improbable that the antesignani were actually what their name designates; that in each maniple they formed the first two ranks, to protect the ensign, which was carried in the second rank; and that they were thus a quarter or a fifth of the entire body. Some events, as at Ilerda, lead up to this belief.

The pay of Cæsar's legionaries was two hundred and twenty-five denarii (forty dollars) a year. This was about the pay of a day-laborer. His rations and clothing were deducted from his pay, but booty and largesses greatly increased it. His ration is variously stated to have been from one to three pecks of wheat, or other grain, a month; which was probably supplemented by beef, and such vegetables and fruit as the foragers could find.

The offensive formation of the legion was in two, three or four lines (*acies duplex, triplex* or *quadruplex*). In two

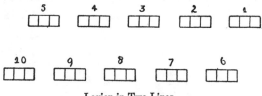

Legion in Two Lines.

lines there were five cohorts in each, standing checkerwise. In three lines, which was usual, four cohorts were in the first and three in each of the others, also checkerwise. Intervals between cohorts in battle order are, by many commentators, said to have been equal to the cohort front; but though this was true of the era of the Punic wars, there is much room to doubt such intervals in Cæsar's time. No doubt there was an interval, especially when the men stood in close order, that is, three feet apart; but the quincuncial formation, whose intervals must be equal to the front of the bodies and so remain in battle, had tended to disappear by gradual decrease of the intervals. What these actually were at this time we do not know. They may have been prescribed in the Drill Regulations, and used on parade; but it is probable that in action they were often reduced to a minimum. The best explanation of which the involved statements of the old authorities are capable seems to be the one already given, that in close (three-

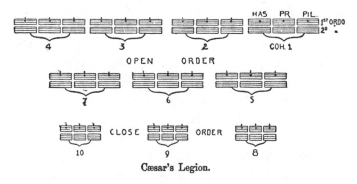

Legion in Three Lines.

foot) order there were intervals between cohorts equal to cohort front; and in open or battle (six-foot) order, these intervals were quite filled up. As the third line was apt to be held in reserve and in close order, a legion in battle order would have the first two lines deployed, — *i. e.*, without intervals between cohorts and the third line ployed into close order with intervals equal to cohort front.

Cæsar's Legion.

The lines were some one hundred and fifty feet apart, though this distance is also disputed. This would give, in

an eight-rank formation, about four hundred and fifty feet
depth and ten hundred and fifty feet front for a legion in
three lines.   The weight of such a legion was, therefore,
very great, and still its mobility was well preserved.   The
phalanx of Alexander had twenty-eight men per metre of
front line.   The legion of the Second Punic War and Cæsar's era had eleven men.   The modern army has not far
from seven.

An army of seven legions in three lines — twenty - five
thousand men field strength — would take up somewhat less
than a mile and a half of front.

The defensive formation of the legion was in one line
(*acies simplex*), or in a square (*acies quadrata*), or a circle
(*orbis*).   The one line was usual for the defense of breast-

Seven Legions in Three Lines.

works or of the camp, — depth being unnecessary, as reserves were kept for the protection of the gates and for
sorties.   The five front ranks were on the rampart without
intervals, the five rear ones at the foot of the rampart.
Sometimes only two ranks were on the rampart and the
three other ranks of the ordo back of it in reserve, while the
rear ordo of five ranks was similarly disposed at the left of
the front ordo.   The space allowed for the usual defensive
line was six feet per man; or with only ordo depth and
assuming that the centurions were not in line, two hundred
and sixteen feet for the maniple, four hundred and thirty-
two feet for the cohort, and forty-three hundred and twenty
feet, four fifths of a mile, for the legion.   A single line disposition was sometimes practiced to resist attacks in the

field, but the cohort retained its front of about one hundred and twenty feet, and the intervals being closed, the legion had but twelve hundred feet front. How much of a circle the orbis was, we do not know. It was formed for defense in the field against overwhelming and surrounding forces. To resist such an attack, the cohorts drew up in what was the equivalent of our hollow square. Smaller bodies might form circular groups, using their shields and hurling their spears and occasionally falling to with the sword. Were not the hollow square also described we should be tempted to believe that the orbis was the same formation.

A legion in three lines could readily form square by leaving the first, second and third cohorts facing to the front; by facing the fifth and sixth to the right; the fourth and seventh to the left, and by facing the eighth, ninth and tenth to the rear. The term *orbis* may have come from the natural habit of flattening out the corners of such a square for easier defense. It is difficult to imagine the manœuvre by which a legion ployed into anything approaching an actual circle and again deployed into line. It may have been an irregular half-square, half-circle, according to the accentuation of the ground or to the conditions demanding a defensive formation.

On rare occasions there was a quadruple line. The fourth was intended to protect a flank and might consist of some cohorts specially detailed and marshaled at an angle to the general line. Such was Cæsar's disposition at Pharsalus.

The auxiliary troops were drilled to conform to the same methods. They had not the cohort formation, but they were utilized so as to sustain the legionary tactics, much as the velites of old had been. The bowmen and slingers were mere skirmishers having no definite tactical position.

In the cavalry, the *turma* of thirty-two enlisted men was

the tactical unit.   It rode in four ranks of eight front.   It

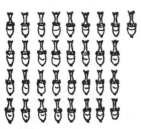

Turma.

has been thought that the ranks were open so that the men stood checkerwise.   There were three decurions to each turma, the senior being its chief.   The turma must have been a body about forty feet square, reckoning crudely five feet front and ten feet depth per mounted man.   Twelve turmæ were an *ala* (wing) or regiment, which may have been formed in two (or three) lines, each say four hundred and forty (or two hundred and eighty)

Ala in Two Lines.

feet long, counting intervals equal to turma-front between turmæ, which were more essential in the cavalry than the infantry.   The cavalry was commanded by a *præfectus equi-*

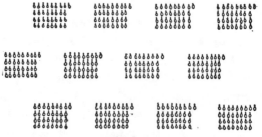

Ala in Three Lines.

tum.   In larger bodies, in which the cavalry often acted, we must guess at the formation.   It no doubt, at this era, conformed much to the habits of the peoples furnishing the troops, modified by Roman experience and the necessities of the army. Cæsar had no Roman cavalry, properly speaking. It was all recruited among the Gauls or Germans.

The order of march (*agmen*) was quickly formed by facing the legion to the right or left, according as it was to move. The cohorts thus followed each other in order. If to the right, the maniples of each cohort would be pilani, principes, hastati; if to the left, the reverse. The depth of the file, on facing to the right or left, would be column front, *i. e.*, eight or ten men; and as the men could comfortably march in a breadth of three feet each, this front could be reduced to twenty-four or thirty feet by simply dressing on the front rank man; or by making each second ordo fall in behind its first, this could be again reduced to fifteen or twelve feet front.

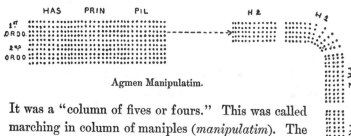

Agmen Manipulatim.

It was a "column of fives or fours." This was called marching in column of maniples (*manipulatim*). The legion in column of maniples could then file in any direction.

Or the legion could march in column of centuries (*centuriatim* or *ordinatim*) by the maniple on the right or left marching straight forward, followed in order by each succeeding maniple. In this order each cohort would march with its centuries in regular sequence: first ordo of pilani, second ditto; first ordo of principes, second ditto; first ordo of hastati, second ditto. In other words, the centuries (*ordines*) would successively follow each other. This column would have a front of twelve men if the cohort had only field strength; but

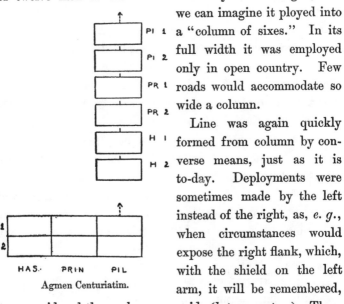

Agmen Centuriatim.

we can imagine it ployed into a "column of sixes." In its full width it was employed only in open country. Few roads would accommodate so wide a column.

Line was again quickly formed from column by converse means, just as it is to-day. Deployments were sometimes made by the left instead of the right, as, *e. g.*, when circumstances would expose the right flank, which, with the shield on the left arm, it will be remembered, was considered the weak or open side (*latus apertum*). Thus, in debouching from a defile, to deploy at its mouth, the column might issue left in front, and deploy to the right of the leading century or cohort. The open side would not be thus exposed.

The men could readily march each in a space of four feet from front to rear. A cohort of field strength (three hundred and sixty men) would thus take up, in length of column, if marching *centuriatim*, full front, one hundred and twenty feet; half front, two hundred and forty feet. If *manipulatim*, and the men kept their distance of three feet, as they could for short distances, it would be one hundred and eight feet long; if the column was extended so as to allow each man four feet, it would be one hundred and fifty-two feet long in full front, three hundred and four feet in

half front. It scarcely seems probable that the column could
be allowed to drag its length out so much beyond the space
required by the line of battle. But marches then were governed by the condition of the roads as they are to-day, and
it was, no doubt, difficult to keep the column closed up.

The legion could march in line (*acies instructa*); in
column (*agmen pilatum*); in square (*agmen quadratum*).

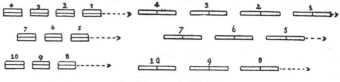

By Lines to the Right.

The march in line was only employed on the battlefield and
had the same advantages and disadvantages, saving the
absence of artillery, as it has to-day. If the legion in three

lines wished to take ground to
the right, and still remain in
line of battle, it could do so by
facing the whole body to the
right and marching the three
columns so made as far as desired. By a halt and front the
line of battle was again formed
in three lines. This enabled a
legion to change its position obliquely without great difficulty.

If the line was on difficult
ground it could advance by column of wings (*cornu*). The right
wing would have cohorts 1, 5,
8; the centre would have co-
horts 2, 6, 9; the left wing would have cohorts 4, 3, 7, 10.

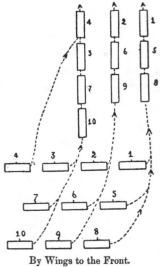

By Wings to the Front.

Each of these would march by the flank and file to the front, like our forward by the right of companies. On halting, each cohort would file to its proper place in line and dress forward on its right.

In marching in column the cohorts followed each other according to number (No. 1 to No. 10 from right to left). Thus marching *centuriatim* gave the legion, with an interval of twenty feet between cohorts, some fourteen hundred feet of length; if doubled up, twenty-six hundred feet.

The baggage-train of a legion Rüstow has estimated at five hundred and twenty pack-animals. In a breadth of forty feet eight animals could go abreast, which gave sixty-five ranks of them; or allowing ten feet for each, six hundred and fifty feet for the pack-train, or thirteen hundred feet if doubled on a road twenty feet wide. Thus the marching length of a legion of thirty-six hundred men, with its train, was not far from two thousand feet, or doubled, four thousand feet, say three quarters of a mile. If the legion was marching *manipulatim* in "column of fives," the cohorts would take up over three thousand feet, and with baggage added would stretch out somewhat more; on a bad road, a full mile.

In presence of the enemy, or in line of battle, the troops were drilled to ploy into column or deploy back into line, to march by the right or left flank, to the front or rear, much as modern armies do. The drill-ground or battlefield manœuvres of a legion were almost identical in principle and performance with our own, the variation relating mainly to the greater depth of the Roman lines, the difference in arms and the absence of artillery. The manœuvres of one of our civil war brigades, in a line of battalion-columns doubled on the centre, would not be much unlike those of a legion.

The legion in presence of the enemy also marched, when the ground permitted, in a sort of square formed by a van and rear with baggage between, and heavy flanking columns on each side of the train. The square was quickly formed for the march from the legion in line. Cohorts 1, 2 and 3 kept straight on. Cohorts 5 and 6 formed column left in front so as to face outwardly when coming to a front. Cohorts 4 and 7 formed column right in front. Cohorts 8, 9 and 10 formed line to the rear, and then broke by the right of cohorts or maniples to the rear and marched behind the baggage. These last were then in such order as readily to form line to the rear and complete the square. The baggage was thus inclosed in the centre; its length might somewhat modify the formation of the marching square. We hear of the Roman army marching over what we know must have been very difficult ground in this formation. It is not to be presumed that accurate order was preserved when the ground was wooded or much cut up.

March Forward in Square.

Cæsar is as perfectly exact in his use of terms to describe these manœuvres as if writing a book of tactics. And the Roman "drill-regulations" had been established for generations and modified only as requirements from age to age dictated. Still there are many minor points which cannot be positively elucidated.

The cavalry wings of four hundred men marched by turmæ

forty feet wide, taking up, without baggage, nearly five
hundred feet length of column. The train probably added
half as much. The ranks of the turmæ column were also
doubled in narrow ways, just how is not known. They must
often have been obliged to reduce front and thus lengthen
the column. A body of four thousand horse, such as Cæsar
had in Gaul, with baggage, would take up, in simple column,
nearly a mile and a half; doubled up, three miles.

All this was naturally subject to precisely the same difficulties which are encountered by every army in the field.
And the more wooded and broken the territory the less
accurately could the "tactics" be conformed to. In Gaul,
no doubt, there was constant and great deviation from the
regulations.

The day's march (*iter*) was reckoned from camp to camp.
A day of rest was customary after every three or four
marches. Each night, or whenever a stop was made, the
camp was fortified. This intrenching practically took the
place of our outpost system, besides being something else.
The legions usually fought with their camp in their rear.
If they came across the enemy on the march, they stopped,
half the men fortified a camp, while the others protected
them, placed the baggage in it and then fought, — provided,
indeed, they could so long fend off the enemy. The ordinary
day's march was from fifteen to eighteen miles, theoretically
supposed to be done in five summer hours, nearly seven of
ours, generally from early morning to noon, there being thus
enough time left for camping.

The step (*gradus*) was two and one half Roman feet long;
the route step one hundred to the minute; the quick step one
hundred and twenty. This is about our own standard. The
pace (*passus*) was two steps, from right heel to right heel.
The Roman foot was nine tenths of ours.

The average Roman march was no greater than that of modern days. Some exceptional marches were remarkable. Cæsar left Gergovia at daybreak to move on Litavicus, marched twenty - five Roman miles, struck him and brought him to reason the same day, marched back twenty-five miles, and the next day reached Gergovia before daybreak, the legions having rested three hours during the twenty - four, and six more having been consumed in watching the enemy under arms. The only superior to this march which can be quickly recalled is that of the Spartans to Marathon, one hundred and fifty miles in three days. Crassus marched to join Cæsar, who was moving to the assistance of Cicero, and made from midnight to

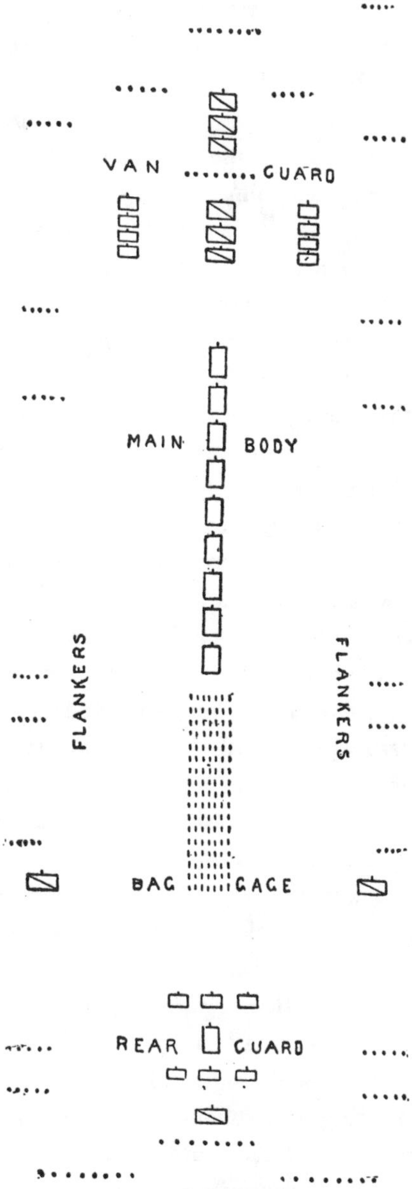

VAN .... GUARD

MAIN BODY

FLANKERS   FLANKERS

BAG ....GAGE

REAR GUARD

Army on the March.

nine A. M. twenty-five Roman miles. In the Zeta raid, Cæsar's legions marched thirty-six miles from before daybreak to nightfall, capturing a town and fighting four hours in retreat on the way. We do not know just what periods of rest were allowed during the day's march. We rest usually ten minutes every hour. On occasion marches were made without baggage. It goes without saying that the Roman marches were subject to the same interruptions, difficulties and delays as our own. Muddy roads and freshets in rivers were as common in Gaul as in Mexico or Virginia.

A vanguard (*primum agmen*) was usual, and consisted of the bulk of the cavalry and light troops, scouts, staff-officers and camp men supported by some cohorts without baggage. The main body followed. A guard brought up the rear. The duty of the van was to attack and hold the enemy, if met, so as to enable the main body to form; to reconnoitre the front and advance flanks; to select and stake out a camp. The cavalry Cæsar sometimes kept with the main body when he did not deem it reliable, or when one of the flanks had to be protected from danger of attack. Light troops alone were used as vanguard when the cavalry was on other duty.

The rearguard (*agmen extremum*) in marches towards the enemy had no duties except to keep order at the tail of the column and pick up stragglers.

The main body marched in simple column or in battle order by the flank, according as the enemy was far or near, or the land was friendly or inimical. An army of five legions, with baggage, eighteen to twenty thousand men, all told, took, in a forty-foot wide order, from two to two and a half miles of length, with ranks doubled twice as much. In practice, the column was much more strung out than this when the roads were not good.

Out of presence of the enemy, the train of each legion

accompanied it for greater convenience; in his presence, the train was kept together in one body. When moving on the enemy, the bulk — say three quarters — of the main army was in front, then the train, then the remainder as baggage and rearguard.

In battle order the legions were not intended to march any distance. This order was used only in the immediate vicinity of the enemy. When Cæsar moved against the Usipetes and Tenchtheri, each legion is supposed to have marched ployed into three columns at deploying distance. There were thus fifteen parallel columns for the five legions. The whole could at once deploy forward into line. The legionaries had their helmets on, their shields uncovered and their weapons ready; the baggage had been left in the camp.

We remember that on the march the legionary had his helmet hanging on his chest, his shield in a case, and his plumes, and other insignia of rank or corps, wrapped up. If suddenly attacked the men must lay down their baggage, prepare and put on their badges and get ready their weapons. At the river Sabis the Romans had to fight without this preparation.

The marches in retreat were conducted on reverse principles, with similar precautions. The baggage went with the vanguard, followed by the bulk of the army; then came a strong rearguard. The marches in squares were made through an enemy's territory, or in times of insurrection, or when the enemy was on every side. Sometimes the square was composed of the whole army; sometimes each legion marched in square. On every front of such a square, cavalry, bowmen and slingers were thrown out as skirmishers. The baggage was in the centre of the one large square, or that of the legion in the centre of each legionary square.

Flank marches were made in battle order, with baggage

on the side opposite the enemy, or between the lines if there were more than one. Such marches were not usually made for any great distance. In the open field the legions so marching were protected by flankers. In a valley a stream might serve to protect the column. Cæsar marched up the Elaver in battle order by the flank for several days.

The order of march was changed daily, to equalize the labor of the legionaries. Cæsar's legions crossed rivers with ease, wading fords up to the waist, breast and even neck. They carried no ammunition; their armor and weapons could not be spoiled. Bridges took as a rule too long to build; Cæsar preferred fords when available. If the river was deep and the current rapid, a line of cavalry was stationed above and below, the first in an oblique line to break the current, the last to catch men who were carried down. Fords were now and then passed in line of battle, as at the Thames.

Bridges were as quickly built as to-day. The absence of pontoon-trains was no apparent hindrance. They were built of boats picked up along the river, as often as on piles; whichever was at the moment handier. But once did Cæsar in the Gallic War cross a river directly in the face of the enemy. This was the Thames. Bridgeheads usually protected both ends of a bridge.

Cæsar kept to the uniform ancient habit of drawing up his legions for battle on the gentle slope of a hill, so that they might have the advantage of the descent for casting their pila as well as for the rush upon the enemy. The utmost reliance was put upon the initiative so as to make the first shock a telling one when possible. The legions were wont to await the advance of the enemy to within two hundred and fifty paces (if, indeed, he would advance), then at the common step to move upon him, and when within half this space to take the run (*cursus*). The distance was not great enough to wind the men, even in their heavy armor. The first two ranks held their spears aloft in readiness and hurled them at ten to twenty paces from the enemy. If the volley produced sufficient gaps, falling to with the sword the legionaries would penetrate into these and have the enemy at their mercy. In case the enemy was brave and determined, the legions often remained longer at javelin-casting distance and used their spears only, the rear ranks advancing through the front ranks to hurl their pila in their turn. The ten ranks could thus deliver five heavy volleys of javelins, having exhausted which, the first line of cohorts drew the sword or allowed the second line to advance in its turn. It sometimes occurred that the enemy was so rapid as to leave no time to hurl the pila, and the legionaries set to at once with the gladius. But this was rare. The light troops kept the fighting line supplied with javelins, collected from those hurled at it. Or again the two first lines, after casting their pila, would at once close in with the sword. When exhausted they would allow the next two ranks to come forward, hurl their pila and use the sword; and thus the ranks worked successively, — hours being often consumed in this array of duels between the individuals of each fighting line.

The old legionary always pushed his enemy with his bossed shield. He was so well armed and so expert that he could sometimes fight all day without receiving a wound. He was physically strong and could gradually force the enemy back in places by sheer pressure and thus make gaps into which he could penetrate with deadly effect. During battle, few legionaries were either killed or wounded, — but when one line broke, the other could cut it to pieces.

In case the enemy awaited the Roman advance, this was

conducted in similar manner. The first ranks were sustained by the backward ones in such a manner that there was a never-ceasing motion in each cohort as those who still held their pila in their turn advanced to hurl them; yet there was no loss of formation, as the space occupied by each man gave ample room to advance and retire within the body of the cohort. The second and third lines remained at a suitable distance in the rear, — two hundred feet or more, — ready to support the front line by advancing into or through its intervals. The second line was ordered forward when the first line ceased to gain a perceptible advantage over the enemy. All the lines gradually came into action, — the third at the critical moment.

The legion in Cæsar's time excelled because he was at its head. It was not without its disadvantages. The soldiery was brave and well disciplined, but the Roman army was not independent of terrain. The work of the skirmishers, slingers and bowmen, of the auxiliaries, and of the veteran antesignani did not always chime in with that of the legions. The two kinds of infantry would sometimes clash, owing to their different formation. The cavalry was often inefficient, and had to be strengthened by bodies of light infantry placed in the intervals of the turmæ. This infantry, when the shock with the enemy's horse came, could inflict serious damage on it. It helped to steady the movements of the turmæ, while protected at the same time from being run down by the enemy's cavalry. This mixing cavalry and foot is one of the most ancient of devices. In a modified form it has survived to our day. The Roman cavalry was serviceable, but at its very best it was not cavalry, such as were Alexander's Companions or the squadrons of Seidlitz.

The real battle was fought out by the legions. In fact, the legions could be independent of any other troops. Cavalry could attack cavalry; it could cut up broken infantry; but unbroken cohorts could not be successfully attacked by cavalry except in flank. By a front attack, steady infantry could drive cavalry in every instance. During battle, cavalry was useful only against the enemy's squadrons. The cavalry and skirmishers were chiefly of use in outpost and reconnoitring duties and in pursuit. In actual battle, the cavalry was not much employed. Since Alexander's day, it will be seen, cavalry had degenerated.

The cohorts were all-sufficient. When cavalry and light troops were not on hand, the legions found no difficulty in doing all the work themselves. Still they relied on the cavalry and light troops, if present, to protect their flanks while fighting. In case there was grave danger of a flank attack, especially on the right, a fourth line was more than once made by Cæsar, the duty of which it was to stand near and defend the threatened quarter.

Habitually the line of cohorts in each legion was threefold as before detailed. This arrangement in an army of six legions in line would give twenty-four cohorts in the first line and eighteen cohorts in each of the others. The third was considered as a reserve not to go into action till ordered by the general. It was on occasion used to sustain the flanks of the legions, or threaten the enemy's. Its utility was shown at Bibracte and in the battle against Ariovistus. A curious feature of Cæsar's formation, due probably to Marius, was that the oldest and best cohorts were placed in the front line, and the younger ones in the rear. This was the direct reverse of the principle which in the old legion had ranked the three class-lines as hastati, principes, triarii.

The cavalry was placed as occasion required. As a rule it was on the flanks. It might be posted in the rear, as was the case at Bibracte, because it was not deemed reliable, and in the battle against Ariovistus because the barbarians were protected in flank and rear by their wagons set up as defense, and cavalry against these was useless.

The light troops were only available as a curtain or as skirmishers. In battle they were harmful rather than of use. They do not appear to have been employed to open the action as uniformly as in earlier days, but rather in collateral duties. But they collected darts and kept the legionaries supplied with them.

The line had a centre (*acies media*), and right and left wing (*cornu dextrum, sinistrum*). The cavalry wings sometimes first advanced; then legion after legion under the legates in command. This was, as it were, an order of battle with the centre withdrawn. The oldest and most experienced legions were posted on the right and left. If there were no prevailing reasons to the contrary, Cæsar preferred to attack with his right in advance, where, like Alexander, he was wont to take his stand. This resulted in a species of oblique order of battle. It was more the result of Cæsar's predilection for personally leading off in action than a definite tactical oblique order, like that of Epaminondas, or as most perfectly exemplified by Frederick at Leuthen. On the signal being blown, the right cohorts at once advanced, those on their left successively following. It was not a tactical advance in echelon with heavily reinforced right flank, but a gradual rushing to battle of the cohorts from right to left. In a measure it had similar results. The best legions would naturally be stationed on the attacking wing.

The line of cohorts impinged upon the enemy only along part of its front when there were intervals between the cohorts; and the enemy might and sometimes did penetrate into these intervals, and take the cohorts on the sensitive

right flank. But the second line was always on the watch
for just this thing, and was ready to correct the evil by a
vigorous onset. Cæsar's probable formation, by which the
cohorts deployed into a battle order without intervals, elimi-
nated this danger. During the fighting contact there was
not only a succession of smaller shocks by the several ranks
of each cohort, but the first, second and third lines could
deliver their heavier blows in succession, following each
other as the tired lines got rest from the advance of those in
rear. A hard-fought field was one of incessant motion.

The different acts of a battle might be stated as these.
Before the action opened — unless it was precipitated — the
general rode the lines and made a short address (*cohortatio*)
to each of his legions, to rouse their martial ardor. He
then went to the attacking flank and gave the trumpet signal,
which was repeated down the line. The legions of the
attacking flank advanced with their battle-cry and the
legions on their right or left successively came on in a species of rough echelon. The legions of the first line were
followed after a certain lapse of time, perhaps minutes, perhaps hours, by the second and third lines, the cavalry riding
forward at the same time to protect the flank or attack the
enemy's cavalry, or — when this was beaten — the flank of
the infantry line. When the first line was exhausted, the
lines in rear replaced them in places or along the whole
front as ordered, and special bodies of troops were brought
up to support decimated legions much as in our own days;
moving forward through intervals when these existed, or
allowing the broken lines in front to fall irregularly through
intervals specially opened for the purpose. Victory being
won, the cavalry pursued. Defeat ensuing, the legions
withdrew to the fortified camp and re-formed there, the
general holding back the enemy with his reserves or the

legions least exhausted, and the cavalry. The battles of
remote antiquity were very different; the battles of Alexander, Hannibal and Cæsar bear more resemblance, in a
general way, to our own.

Defensive battles were not fought unless the terrain was
especially suitable. The flanks were then leaned on natural
obstacles, and the front was protected by wolf-pits or other
entanglements. If possible, the army backed on the camp,
protected their flanks, and gave the enemy only one approach,
in front and up a slope. The camp of Cæsar on the Axona,
where he invited an attack, was a good sample of this. If
the barbarians had crossed the morass in his front, they
must have broken ranks in so doing, and Cæsar could have
charged down on their phalanx with decisive effect, for his
flanks were protected by ramparts. At Alesia, the fighting
was defensive, coupled with sallies. But in the open field,
the Roman strength lay in attack, or in inviting attack and
in meeting it halfway.

Gallic Buckler.

XXV.

CAMPS, SIEGES AND BALLISTICS.

IN camp the men had tents, which were carried in the column by pack-mules. In winter-quarters the camps were larger and more carefully intrenched, but similar to the daily camps. These latter could be intrenched in a few hours. Little change in fortification and siege work took place from Alexander's era to Cæsar's. The walls of the Italian cities were by no means like those of Babylon and Nineveh; but they were high and well built, and much skill was put to defend and take them. The same sheds and screens for approaching walls were used; mounds and towers were built, and the lines of contra- and circumvallation were thrown up as of yore. The walls were undermined or battered down by rams. Sorties were made by the garrison to destroy the besieger's works. The ballistic machines of the Romans do not strike us as being as good as those of Alexander, whose field artillery was excellent and easily transported. Still there were small engines used on the walls of camps and sometimes in line of battle. Cæsar's sieges were expert; that of Alesia is one of the finest of antiquity.

WE do not know exactly how Cæsar's camps were laid out. Polybius gives us the plan of the Roman camps in the Second Punic War; Hyginus gives us that of the time of the Empire. As Rüstow says, what is common to both was no doubt a constituent of Cæsar's camp. Cæsar's was presumably much the same as either, the changes relating merely to the differences in organization of troops. Cæsar had no definite number of auxiliaries, as was usual in the War against Hannibal, and the camp was calculated accordingly. Its general arrangement was what it had been for centuries. It was pitched on high ground, fronting down a slope, favorably near wood and water, and away from probable opportunity for ambush. A desirable place was the slope towards a stream, particularly if the enemy lay beyond. But the Romans camped where they must, if the best site was not at hand, and the shape of the camp was modified by the ground.

A camping party always went ahead to select and stake out camp, and the legionaries pitched and intrenched it in the course of a few hours, while the cavalry served as outposts. Each legion and cohort as it arrived was marched into its appointed place, the detail for guard was selected, the baggage was laid down, the weapons, except the sword, put aside. The camp was then fortified, and the tents afterwards put up. If the weather was stormy the tents were put up first. Then the troops took supper,

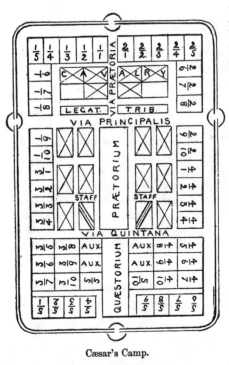

Cæsar's Camp.

the officers assembled for orders, and much the same routine was gone through which has been described in a previous volume. The fortifications took the place of outpost-duty, which the Romans did not practice in our sense. In the immediate presence of the enemy the work would be done by the third line, the two first being sent out to protect the fatigue party; or by the second line if only two, the first standing in line in front, ready to meet an attack. When the legions marched out to battle, the camp was left in entire order under a guard, usually composed of the younger troops, who were fully able to hold it. The camps were rectangular unless modified by the ground.

The same thing applies to the little camps or redoubts (*castella*) which were built in siege operations or for outpost defenses of a general camp. Of these castella the smallest were one hundred and twenty feet square, for a garrison of a cohort. The corners of all camps were rounded off to prevent the enemy getting a footing on them in the assault. The gates, wide enough for a maniple front (forty feet), were protected by half-moons, and materials were on hand for closing them quickly in case of threatened attack. Gates like our modern ones seem to have been unknown, except in permanent fortifications.

The ditch (*fossa*) was nine to twelve feet wide at the top, with a depth of seven to nine feet. It was often deeper and

Camp Wall (section).

wider, the ratio being preserved. The scarp and counter-scarp had, one or both, a slope or not, according to the nature of the soil. The height of the wall (*agger*) was not deemed so important, for the shield of the ancient soldier protected him abundantly. The percentage of darts which took actual effect was, as in the case of bullets, very small. From the wall the soldier could, however, cast his own missiles with better effect upon the enemy below, whom the ditch stopped at a good spear-hurling distance. This, indeed, was the main object of the wall. The height of the wall was supposed to be about two thirds of the surface-width of the ditch. Its thickness was about equal to the height, or a bit greater. The slopes were covered with sods, or interlaced with branches, fascines or hurdles. There was a banquette of suitable width, and palisades (*vallum*) were planted at the top. The word vallum is often used for the entire palisaded wall. Embrasures in the palisades were common and towers were generally built. The inside slope of the wall was cut in steps for easy access, or faced with logs in steps.

It took, as a rule, four or five hours to complete the intrenching of a camp. It could, under favorable conditions, be done in three. The Roman used his spade to good effect. If the troops reached camp by noon, they would have finished their work by sundown of a short day.

The division of the camp was, in nomenclature, much like that of the War against Hannibal. The cohorts camped in their regular order. Each cohort took up a space one hundred and twenty feet wide, with a depth of one hundred and eighty feet, cut into six parts, thirty feet wide, one for each century. The century tents were pitched back to back and front to front, in streets. A cavalry turma took up one hundred and twenty feet by thirty. A regiment of twelve turmæ took up as much space as two cohorts.

The accompanying sketch, added to what has already been given in a previous volume, suffices to show the details of Cæsar's camp.

A cavalry picket was usual, which sent out scouts and spies. The gates were specially guarded, the wall was duly lined with sentinels, averaging one every thirty feet. The

Cohort Tents (Hyginus).

reliefs, every three hours, were called by the trumpet, and there was blown a sort of tattoo and reveille. The same rounds were made by an officer of the day as of yore.

The winter-quarters were the same as the summer-quarters, but more permanently and comfortably arranged. Huts took the place of tents. It may again be mentioned here that the Roman day was divided into two parts, the day from six A. M. to six P. M., and the night from six P. M. to six A. M. The hours were: the first, from six to seven A. M., the second, seven to eight A. M., and so on. Thus noon was the sixth hour, and four P. M. the tenth hour of the day, or midnight the sixth hour of the night. The day and night were also divided into four watches of three hours each. Thus six to nine A. M. was the first watch of the day; midnight to three A. M. was the third watch of the night.

Occasionally summer hours are spoken of, being the time from sunrise to sunset, divided into twelve hours. This would at times lengthen the hour materially from what it would be if the day had been reckoned as from six A. M. to six P. M.

The art of attacking and defending strong places underwent comparatively little change for more than a thousand years. As far back as there are any records, written or sculptured, the processes of a siege are shown to be substantially the same. The following verses from Ezekiel iv. 1, 2, 3, speak of a siege about 600 B. C.: "Thou also, son of man, take thee a tile, and lay it before thee, and portray upon it a city, even Jerusalem." This was the plan of the works to be undertaken. "And lay siege against it, and build forts against it, and cast up a mount (mound) against it; set camps also against it, and plant battering rams against it round about." These are the usual steps of the siege. "Moreover take thou unto thee an iron pan, and set it for a wall of iron between thee and the city,"—this refers to iron mantelets used in preparing the approaches, — "and set thy face against it, and it shall be besieged, and thou shalt lay siege against it."

At certain periods, as during the wonderful activity of Alexander's military career, or during the siege of Rhodes by Demetrius Poliorcetes, or the defense of Syracuse by Archimedes, or Sylla's siege of Athens, a marked advance was made, but this again was wont to be lost, and the methods and machines remained almost identical. In fact, from dim antiquity they were so.

The walls of towns were generally of stone, and very high and thick. Those of the Gauls were, as we have seen, sometimes of earth, logs and stone. They were guarded by towers at regular intervals, and were apt to be fronted by a

ditch, wet or dry. Immense skill and patience were devoted
to the defenses of cities and their interior citadels. To
capture a town, one must resort to blockade, or siege, or
assault. To attack the walls there was no artillery capable
of making breaches. The catapults and ballistas could throw
heavy stones and huge arrows to a remarkable distance, but
had not penetration enough to break down walls. To operate a breach, it was essential to approach near to the wall,
and either undermine it, or break it down by battering-rams
or mural hooks. This approach could not be made except
under artificial cover, and hence arose the more or less
effective series of tortoises, galleries and mantelets, terraces
and towers, added to mining and countermining, which were
good or poor according as the skill and energy of the besiegers varied. All this remained unchanged so far as principle
was concerned, until the invention of gunpowder reduced the
ancient walls to uselessness in the same summary fashion as
it unseated the knight in armor.

In sieges either towers were erected to override the wall,
or else simple battering was resorted to at its foot. In the
former case, so soon as the place had been approached, the
army was camped, generally in several suitable locations,
having heed to health, sustenance and siege operations.
Each camp was fortified by a stockade and ditch, and often
much more elaborately. Communications were established
between these camps, and a line of investment — or contravallation — was drawn around the city. If there was danger of an enemy's army coming to the relief of the place,
another line — of circumvallation — was drawn outside the
besieger's camps, facing outward to forestall an attempt to
raise the siege. Cæsar generally uses the term circumvallation for what was earlier and more properly known as
contravallation, — *i. e.*, the works erected against a town.

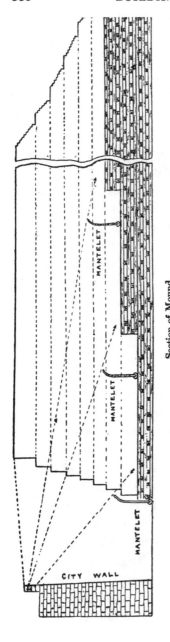

Section of Mound.

A terrace or mound (*agger*) was then begun, which should slope up to the bottom of the city wall. In case the city was on a level a terrace was not essential. It might be raised to a point part way up the wall, but this was not usual. Its surface was smooth enough to allow the moving of towers along it. The labor was performed by the soldiers and such part of the surrounding population as could be set at it. It was built of any material at hand. As terraces were often set on fire, it is to be presumed that much wood was used in their construction, — logs, hurdles, etc. That it was generally a sort of cob-house work, on the edges at least, filled with loose material in the middle, is to be inferred from the rapidity with which it was set on fire and burned, a fact which argues a strong draft. The terrace was probably built a story at a time. A line of mantelets (*plutei*) was placed as near the wall as possible, but still out of range. Behind these, galleries made

of a succession of small pent-houses (*vineæ*), placed end to
end, protected the men going to and fro, who brought material through the galleries and began work behind the man-

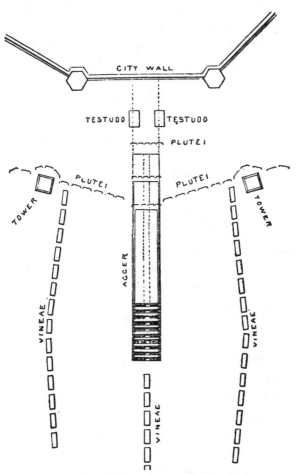

Plan of Approaches to a Town.

telets. Movable towers with artillery and bowmen kept up
a constant fire upon the walls to clear from them the missile-
throwers of the enemy who interfered with the work, and

suitable details were posted to check sorties. When as much was finished as one set of mantelets were calculated to protect, these were advanced and another section built. Upon this first section or story a second was constructed, and a third and more, as desirable. The end near the wall was made especially strong so as to bear the weight of heavy towers.

The size of some of these terraces excites the same wonder as temporary structures that the Pyramids do as monuments for all time. They are explained by the fact that so many thousands of hands worked at them. The terrace was made as wide as convenient, to contain all the necessary engines — if these were to be used on it — and to allow a storming column to advance along it, say fifty feet. When completed the terrace was crowned by towers which were higher than the city walls, and which were connected by curtains or walls. Such a terrace appears at first blush to be a work more gigantic than called for; but it was made necessary by the fact that so long as the garrison could hold the platform of the wall, they could prevent the approach of the battering-ram or the filling of the ditch, by throwing missiles, inflammables, hot tar and heavy stones from above; or they could interfere by grappling tackle with the free swing of the ram essential to an effective blow, or deaden its effect by cable-aprons hung at its point of impact. But so soon as the besiegers had reached the height of the wall, so as to be able by their greater numbers to drive the garrison from the platform, they could secure free play for the ram, fill up the ditch, and make ready to storm the walls by bridges from the towers, or through a breach after one had been operated.

When the ram was got fairly at work, the capture of the place was deemed secure, and no capitulation was received on any save harsh terms. Sometimes, on a breach being made, a new wall or demi-lune was found to have been constructed within, which obliged the besiegers to begin their work all over again.

The pent-house galleries (*vineæ, musculi*) took the place

Musculus, light.

of our trenches and parallels. But these latter were not unknown. The galleries were set up obliquely to the wall as trenches are to - day, but less so. Accidents in the ground were utilized for cover, but so soon as the approaches arrived in the open, they were run with regularity on a most intelligent system. Parallels were not so deep as ours because the missiles were not so destructive. Portable curtains and defenses were common for surprises.

Mantelets (*plutei*) were made of skins, cable-mats, mattresses, etc., suspended on masts, and not infrequently iron plates or heavy lumber. They were not unlike

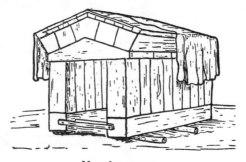

Musculus, strong.

huge snow-plows mounted on wheels.

The vineæ were constructed of a roof of plank and wicker-work covered with rawhide, ropes and wet cloth to resist missiles and fire, and were usually sixteen feet long and seven feet wide, resting on posts eight feet high. The sides were also protected by wicker-work. These vineæ were carried forward by the men. If heavier, they were rolled on wheels. They were then pushed forward obliquely, a number were joined together, and under their cover the

terrace foundations were laid close to the ditch. Wet ditches were tapped and drained. The *musculus* was a low triangular hut on rollers for the protection of the men; when working near the walls it was heavier. The testudo

Vinea.

was much like the musculus, but larger.

The building of the terrace was opposed by every contrivance imaginable. Sorties were made at night to destroy the work of the day. Mines were driven underneath the terrace

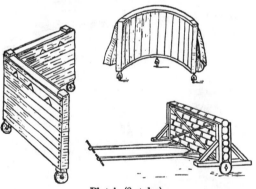

Plutei (3 styles).

and filled with inflammables which, set on fire, would crumble the earth and drop in its foundation. These were opposed by counter-mines. Mines were run under the walls by the besiegers with a similar object; and they were often run as a means of throwing a force into a town under its walls, which force, once in, would open the gates to the besiegers. Such mines often showed ability to a high degree in design and execution.

The towers with which the terraces were surmounted were often many stories in height. They were usually structures of wood, but sometimes of earth, stone or brick, so high as to dominate the walls of the town.

The heavy machines of the city were within the walls on the level. Only soldiers and light engines occupied the walls and towers. Where a wall was escaladed and the assaulting party had reached the platform, it still had to descend into the inclosure, a work of yet greater danger. On the platform the party had to encounter the cross-fire from the towers, and must get ropes and ladders to descend on the inner side. The operation was difficult. Hence the greater practicability of breaches.

The walls were not usually of solid masonry; one front and one back wall were built of stone, perhaps twenty feet apart; the space between was filled in with the earth taken from the ditch, or with rubble or other available material. Huge earthen ramparts were not uncommon, as at Gaza.

The immensity of the towers which surmounted the terraces is perhaps the most astonishing feature of sieges. Vitruvius (who was one of Cæsar's engineers in the African war) speaks of two ordinary sizes. The smaller had sixty cubits of height (a cubit is one and a half feet) by seventeen cubits square, and decreased one fifth in going up. The larger was one hundred and twenty cubits high by twenty-seven cubits square. Each had ten stories. Demetrius at Rhodes made one much larger than even this.

These towers were usually prepared in advance with fitted beams, were brought as close to the walls as could be under cover of mantelets, and there set up. They generally carried

a ram in the lower story, and were furnished with drawbridges to drop on the enemy's wall. The ram could operate
under cover of the armed men above, who kept the platform
clear by their missiles. These towers were furnished with

Tower.

huge wheels on which they were moved forward. The
approach of such a tower to the walls was generally followed
by the capture of the town, unless it could be destroyed by
fire.

Fire and heavy missiles were the means of combating the
approach of these towers. The object of sorties was to fire
the towers. The falling drawbridges were kept off by long
sharpened beams fastened on the walls of the city.

Rams were either mounted on wheels or suspended by ropes

or chains. A huge beam (or one made of several lashed together) was furnished with a heavy cast-iron end, frequently in the form of a ram's head, fixed to it by iron bands. The beam was reinforced in the centre, the better to withstand the shock. The head was at times furnished with a mural hook as well as a ram. The ram was hung or mounted in a

Ram and Tongs.

shed, well protected from fire, and was manipulated by soldiers. The size and weight of these rams excite our surprise. Demetrius used a ram one hundred and twenty feet long against Rhodes. Appian speaks of one, at the siege of Carthage, which required six thousand men to mount it. Perhaps this means their labor used in speedily building its emplacement and covering.

To resist the ram, the walls were covered with soft material hung upon them from above, such as bags of feathers and wool, or mattresses, or plaited cordage. Heavy suspended beams were dropped upon it to disable it. Big grappling devices to seize not only rams but other machines, and even to pick up men, were common. Callias, at Rhodes, enjoyed a great reputation for such fishing tackle, until Demetrius constructed such heavy rams and engines that Callias' tackling would no longer work.

The telenon was a rude crane by which was raised a cage

containing sol-diers who could thus reach and at-tack the platform, or make observa-tions of what was being done inside the walls.

The artillery of the ancients was far from despica-ble. Cæsar calls all the missile-throwers *tor-menta*, because they derived their propulsive power from *twisted* ropes, sinews or

Telenon.

hair (*torquere*). The catapults and ballistas of the Greeks had no doubt survived and been little altered. These have been described in previous volumes. The ballistas were able to throw stones weighing five hundred to six hundred pounds. Smaller ballistas (*scorpiones*) threw one-hundred pound stones, and were known as *centenaria*. A bundle of arrows placed on the horizontal upper beam at the proper angle and struck by the ballista head could be thrown a great distance. Dead pestilential bodies or other such matter were thrown into the enemy's lines. The average ballista could hurl up to twelve hundred feet.

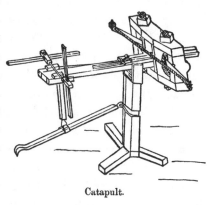

Catapult.

The catapults were on the principle of huge bows, and threw sharpened beams, darts, leaden bullets, fire-pots and fire-darts with great effect. These machines were really,

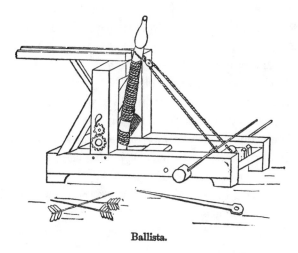

Ballista.

except for size and convenience, almost as powerful as the early artillery. Their aim was good.

The walls of cities and towns were plentifully provided with missile-throwers. Besiegers had to await the bringing up of a siege-train or the construction of fresh machines, which was a long process. There is nothing to show that Cæsar had anything like as effective artillery, or artillery as easily transported, as Alexander. But Cæsar had missile-throwers with his army, for they are mentioned as being mounted on the walls of his camp.

After a breach was opened, heavy columns assaulted it and were met with the resistance of like bodies. A breach by no means always brought about the capture of a city. A half-moon, or reëntering angle, which the besieged could build in rear of the place where a breach was being made, was all the more difficult to take because the besieged during its attack lay on the besieger's flanks and rear. At Rhodes such a half-moon was faced with a ditch.

Ancient sieges were much more obstinately contested than modern ones, and for good reason. The besieged had to face the alternative of victory, or of slavery or death.

The ordinary course of a siege might be stated as: —

1. A reconnoissance of the place.

2. The establishment of camps in suitable positions.

3. The collection of material for the siege.

4. The manufacture of *vineæ, plutei, musculi,* etc.

5. The building of redoubts and joining them with lines of contra- and perhaps circumvallation.

6. The preparation of covered ways to the town, mines and subterranean passages.

7. The building of a terrace, by legionaries within reach of darts, by natives beyond range.

8. The erection of towers on the terrace, or pushing them forward along it.

9. The operation of breaches.

10. Storming the breaches.

This chapter is largely a recapitulation of what has been told in former volumes; but it has been deemed essential to the proper appreciation of Cæsar's numerous sieges.

Scorpion.

XXVI.

THE OPENING OF THE CIVIL WAR. DECEMBER, 50, TO MAY, 49 B. C.

THE triumvirate had been broken up by the death of Crassus in the Parthian campaign. The friendship of Cæsar and Pompey had ended in competition for the sole control. Cæsar represented the democratic, Pompey the aristocratic party. War was forced on Cæsar. Though he entered into it in self-protection, it was he who took the initiative, when the tribunes of the people fled to him for safety. He marched into Italy with one legion; Pompey had many, — but they were on paper. Great numbers of recruits joined Cæsar's standard, while Pompey, from lack of preparation and energy, found his forces dwindle. Cæsar's legions were veterans; Pompey had but fresh levies. Gradually Cæsar forced his way down the Adriatic coast to Brundisium, where Pompey with his adherents had taken refuge. On the way, the gates of most of the towns were opened to Cæsar; some, especially Corfinium, had to be besieged. Many of Pompey's cohorts voluntarily went over to Cæsar; others were captured, and then joined his cause. The people were with Cæsar; the Senate, the aristocrats and the rich with Pompey. The latter, overwhelmed by Cæsar's rapidity and his own lethargy, resolved to transfer the war to Greece instead of fighting in Italy.

WHEN the triumvirs assumed power, Pompey was looked upon as the ruling spirit, Cæsar and Crassus much in the light of Pompey's adjutants. To Pompey were opened the treasures and the power of the entire state; to Cæsar only those he was given by law. Pompey's term was unlimited; Cæsar's was a long but fixed term. Pompey remained at the capital; Cæsar was sent to a distant province. But the important work undertaken by Pompey soon developed his weakness. So far from ruling Rome, its rival factions reduced the capital to a state of anarchy which Pompey had not the ability to check. "The rabble of every sort never found a merrier arena." The leaders of the several bands which played fast and loose in the city followed their own sweet will. Never was capital so ungoverned. It is no part of the purpose of this volume to describe political imbroglios; suffice it that Pompey gradually lost his grasp and his standing. He was at times reduced to the condition of a mere puppet. Cæsar was gaining laurels in the north, while Pompey's military reputation was in a way to be forgotten. Having lost control of the rabble, Pompey was unable to control the popular assembly; his strength and ability were unequal to the exceptional conditions, and his failure to perform his share in the scheme of joint government necessarily ended by estranging himself and Cæsar. This state of things worked against Cæsar, who was distant from Rome and with difficulty able to control what friends he had. Power might slip away from him.

The triumvirs held a meeting at Luca in the spring of 56 B. C. There were two hundred senators present and numbers of other men of mark. Here a further division of provinces was agreed upon, but it was evident that Pompey had ceded a substantial part of the controlling voice to Cæsar.

The aristocrats, meanwhile, were combining against the triumvirate. Yet every one seemed to be his own master. Cæsar raised legions without authority; Crassus equally so conducted the Parthian war. The forms of law were observed, but money or violence carried the votes in every election. There was abundant manifestation of the unlicensed spirit of all in the constant armed conflicts in the streets. These finally culminated in the murder of Clodius by Milo, an episode which roused the energy of Pompey to the point of seizing the dictatorship, and to a certain degree bringing the law again into operation.

Crassus had been a make-weight between Cæsar and Pompey, but steadily leaned to Cæsar's side. In the late division of provinces he was afforded a chance to gain military power and still greater wealth in a Parthian war, which had come about by Pompey's bad faith in failing to respect the line of the Euphrates. Crassus reached Syria instinct with the purpose of another Alexander, resolved to penetrate to India. He had two routes. He could invade Parthia through mountainous and allied Armenia, or through the

Crassus' Routes.

Mesopotamian desert. He chose the latter route, on the mistaken testimony of a native friendly prince. He had seven full legions, four thousand cavalry and an equal number of archers and slingers, — nearly fifty thousand men. The great Macedonian had made this march nearly three centuries before.

Careless scouting led Crassus into an ambush of the enemy not far from Carrhæ. Surenas, the Parthian vizier who commanded the enemy, had recognized the fact that Eastern foot could accomplish nothing against Roman legions; he had utilized his infantry to keep a large body of Armenian horse from joining Crassus, and with a keen tactical appreciation of the conditions had chosen to do his fighting solely with cavalry. Crassus advanced into the desert; soon his marching column of foot was met by a body of mail-clad horsemen, partly heavy lancers, partly lighter

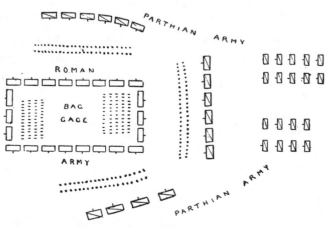

Battle of Carrhæ.

archers. The legionary was more than a match for his man when he could get at him, but here the foe could fight or decline to fight as he chose; could cut the Roman communications by his superior activity; could move with twice the Roman's speed. The armies were on a limitless rolling plain, the very arena for a huge body of horse, a very pitfall for foot in those days of short-carry weapons. There was on the sandy soil scarce a chance to intrench a camp; water was at distant intervals; the Roman was out of his bearing, the Oriental in his element. For the first time the legions met a native tactical array with which they could npt cope. Close combat weapons were useless. The mounted archer was master of the situation, and the Parthian had made the bow a national weapon.

The battle of Carrhæ is interesting as a defeat of the best of infantry by inferior horse, and yet not by cavalry tactics so called. The Parthians drew up in an extended order affording the greatest scope for their fire. The Romans drew up in their usual dense square. Here we have the deployed line of superior fire — generally assumed to be a modern idea — against a dense mass limited in its ability to hurl missiles. There was but one outcome. The Parthian mounted archers were accompanied by camel-loads of spare arrows. The legions had absolutely no means of attack or defense. Their own archers were of small avail. They were speedily defeated when sent out.

Gradually the thin Oriental line swept by and outflanked the Roman square. Fearing to be surrounded and thus have his progress checked, Crassus sent his son Publius, one of Cæsar's young veterans, to attack the enemy with a select body of six thousand mixed troops. This diversion for a moment arrested the Orientals, who summarily retired, pursued by the brave young soldier. But his gallantry had sealed his fate. Luring him to a distance, the Parthians made about face on his column, and, surrounding it, cut the entire force to pieces. They then turned again on the re-treating Roman square.

Darkness alone saved the wreck of the Roman army. The Orientals, fearing a night surprise, rode off to camp at a distance, intending to return to their prey next day. But the Romans, by leaving behind some four thousand wounded to be massacred, continued the march and reached Carrhæ. Thence, after a brief rest, the mere remnant of the force, some five thousand men, made their way to Sinnaca, a for-tress on the foothills of Armenia, only to be followed by the Parthians, and again cut up. The entire army was lost, and Crassus killed. This was in June, B. C. 53.

The end of the triumvirate thus came. Cæsar and Pompey between them controlled the state, but they had already begun to be politically estranged; socially, the death of Julia, in 54 B. C., severed the last tie. When Pompey had secured for himself the undivided consulship, he was fully prepared to fling his gauntlet at the feet of the man who, he foresaw, would soon outstrip him unless overridden before he acquired more headway. The death of Crassus was a grievous blow to Cæsar, who could uniformly rely on his colleague's fidelity. It was in this same year that the insurrection of Vercingetorix occurred; had Pompey taken the vigorous step of having Cæsar recalled from Gaul, it would have put a term to Cæsar's career. But Pompey was never ready to seize an opportunity; lack of incisiveness was fatally characteristic of the man.

Cæsar was strictly and from the beginning a democrat, and was now the leader of the party. Pompey had been playing with democracy and shortly reverted to his old Sullan traditions. He easily effected a reconciliation with the Catonians, and became the head of the aristocratic party. Thus Cæsar and he were formally arrayed against each other. Cæsar desired no rupture. He had, at Luca, been promised the consulship in B. C. 48, and this he was anxious to obtain peacefully, as a base from which to exert his influence. Through the legal trickery of Pompey and the Catonians this was denied him, and it was sought to disable him by an order to break up his legions. Cæsar offered to disarm whenever Pompey was made to do the like. It was during the debate on this matter that Cæsar was completing the pacification of Gaul, holding his grand review on the Scheldt, and making his triumphal march through the province of Cisalpine Gaul. Finally, through the management of Curio, Cæsar's henchman in Rome, the Senate voted that both Pompey and Cæsar, as proconsuls of Spain and Gaul, should lay down their offices. Cæsar was willing to do so; Pompey declined. On the assumption that Cæsar was disobeying orders, Pompey asked to be instructed by the Senate to march against him. This was refused. But the old consul and the newly elected ones gave Pompey the authority the Senate had denied. On this slender pretense Pompey put himself at the head of the only two legions at hand, — they were the two sent by Cæsar to be used in the Parthian war, but wrongfully detained by Pompey, and were far from reliable against their old commander, — and began levies of fresh troops.

Of the prominent Pompeians, Cicero remained in Campania to recruit; Minucius Thermus was sent to Umbria; Lentulus Spinther and Attius Varus to Picenum; Scribonius Libo to Etruria; Domitius Ahenobarbus, whom the Senate had designated as Cæsar's successor in Gaul, went to Corfinium.

This proceeding was substantially a declaration of war. Cæsar, if forced to it, was ready to strike the first blow.

Cæsar had passed the winter at Ravenna, some two hundred and forty miles from Rome. Here Curio joined him. The news he brought decided Cæsar's action. He ordered his nearest legion to Ravenna, — the Thirteenth from Tergeste (Trieste), — a body which he speedily recruited up to nearly or quite normal strength, five thousand foot and three hundred horse. His other eight legions were far away: four among the Belgæ, under Trebonius; four among the Ædui, under Fabius; all in winter-quarters. He had already ordered Fabius to send him the Eighth and Twelfth, and Trebonius to give over one of his own to Fabius, and with the rest to approach the Arar. Fabius, with the three legions thus under his command, was sent to Narbo, lest Pompey's seven legions in the Spanish peninsula should invade Gaul. The strength of Cæsar's legions in Gaul varied from three thousand to thirty-five hundred men each.

Cæsar, in due course, sent an ultimatum to Rome, couched in a reasonable spirit. Under Pompey's dictation the Senate replied by ordering Cæsar to lay down his arms unconditionally, or be deemed a traitor. The tribunes of the people, Mark Antony and Q. Cassius, vetoed the resolution, but were forced by Pompey's adherents to flee for their lives. They started north to join Cæsar, who was the recognized centre point of the democratic party.

Cæsar's mind was soon made up. War was his only resource. He harangued the Thirteenth legion, to explain why he struck the first blow in a civil war. His cause was equaled by his eloquence, and he found a generous response. With these cohorts he advanced towards the border of his province, December 16, 50 B. C. The Thirteenth legion crossed the Rubicon on the night of December 16-17. The Civil War had begun.

In Gaul, Cæsar had not been noted for foolhardy operations. Bold as Alexander when boldness was demanded, as when he started with seven thousand men to rescue Cicero from sixty thousand Nervii, yet Cæsar exhibited as a rule the virtue of caution rather than the error of untimely boldness. We shall, from the outbreak of the Civil War, however, find him in a new rôle, constantly committing acts of precipitancy which are never altogether admirable, and sometimes much to be condemned. For the present proceeding, even, he has been severely blamed by many critics and historians. It can scarcely be classed as prudent generalship, it is said, however bold, for Cæsar to set out with five thousand men against Pompey, an excellent tactician and a man of large experience, who would probably array considerable forces

against him. But in this instance it the rather appears that
Cæsar was both bold and prudent. The temerity was in
Cæsar's own style. He knew the condition of his enemy's
forces: that Pompey had not got his levies made in season;
that the two Apulian legions were too far off to be immediately available, even if they were reliable; that the towns
on his route were illy garrisoned; that there was a strong
sentiment in his own favor if suitably met. Moreover, he
could not afford to wait; he believed that a surprise of the
enemy before he increased his numbers was his safest course,
and that rapid work would secure him control of the northern
provinces of Italy. His course, fortunately, was the right
as it was the bold one.

Cæsar had no difficulty in assuring himself of the personal
fidelity of the rest of his legions, of which he ordered some
in from Gaul so soon as he learned that the tribunes of the
people had fled to him from Rome for protection. This
latter fact gave him the required appearance of right. It
was in a mood distinctly conciliatory, but determined to give
his enemies no unfair advantage, that Cæsar set out towards
Ariminum. The handful of troops he had with him reflected
the feeling of the rest in declaring that they would know how
to protect their insulted chief and the tribunes of the people.

Cæsar's pause at the Rubicon has pointed many morals.
With his quick habit of judgment and action, it was unquestionably of short duration.

From Ravenna were two roads to Rome. One ran from
Bononia across the Apennines to Arretium; one down the
coast to Fanum, thence southwest. Cæsar chose the coast
road. His plan was not to move on Rome. He proposed to
seize the Adriatic coast, with its many and rich towns, and
thus not only rob Pompey of much of his territory, but create
a base for himself in Italy.

At Ariminum, taken by surprise December 17, Cæsar met the tribunes, and also messengers from Pompey. The latter were Roscius the prætor, and young L. Cæsar, whose father was one of Cæsar's legates. They offered in indefinite terms an accommodation. Pompey, no doubt, had been alarmed lest Cæsar should take him unawares. Cæsar replied by a message agreeing to lay down arms and retire to his province if Pompey would do the like at the same moment and retire to Spain; and requested an interview either in Pompey's camp or his own. To this message, which Roscius and Cæsar conveyed to their chief, Pompey, and the Senate, replied by the same messengers that whenever Cæsar had disbanded his army and gone to Gaul, he, Pompey, would do the like and go to Spain. It is not improbable that Pompey was desirous of coming to an accommodation; but he did not adopt the proper tone or terms to secure such a result. Cæsar was reasonable, but he demanded a crisp understanding. One of our authorities for the tone of these messages is the Commentaries. They are presumably accurate as to facts, but they were penned by one of the negotiating parties. Either rival was right in opposing the sole exercise of authority by the other; but we must judge mainly from the facts and from the other authorities, and not from the statements of Cæsar, which was least to blame for the war that for years decimated the republic.

The material power of the two chiefs when they should be properly concentrated was very different. Cæsar at this time had nine legions; two had been spirited away from him to Pompey, and were now arrayed against him. He had no fleet, and but himself to rely on. Pompey, on the contrary, had the formal power of the Roman state in his own or his friends' hands, and could retain it, if it was not forfeited by some signal error; he practically controlled the entire Italian

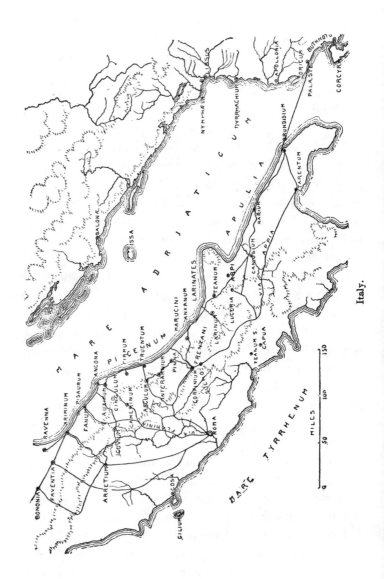

Italy.

peninsula except the regions abutting on Cæsar's province; he had his Spanish and African legions, and all the forces of Italy, Greece, Egypt and the East. Cæsar controlled Gaul — Cisalpine, Narbonese and Transalpine, the latter only just subdued — and Illyricum; Pompey practically controlled the rest of Rome's enormous territory, and especially in the provinces was Pompey's influence still strong. Pompey had the chief officers of the republic, the Senate, the aristocracy, the rich burgesses on his side; Cæsar had but his few adherents, the tribunes of the people and the many headed.

But Cæsar possessed what Pompey lacked. His authority was undivided within his camp and his party. His lieutenants were truly such. His legions were his, body and soul, and were veterans used to victory. He could do with them what no other captain could do. Their imperator was the embodiment of success not only in their eyes, but in the eyes of all soldiers in the service of Rome. Wherever Cæsar went, armies would gather from the multitude. Moreover, Cæsar was untrammeled and able to act as best to him seemed, while Pompey was really little more than the tool of his party. And above all, deeming the power to be all in their own hands, Pompey's party had taken no immediate measures to defend themselves against Cæsar. What they had was scattered at arm's length; what Cæsar had he could put to instant use. The material weight was on Pompey's side, the moral weight and the power of initiative on Cæsar's. Pompey's reputation was for deeds long gone by; Cæsar's was fresh in the minds of all.

Of Cæsar's lieutenants every man, save Labienus, who aspired to higher office, had remained faithful. Cæsar's plan of keeping his lieutenants in subordinate positions worked well with him, who purposed to do everything himself; but it robbed him sometimes of efficient marshals, who, on occasion, would have served him better.

Pompey's military forces were enormous, but they were scattered. He had seven legions in Spain, and numberless cohorts in every part of the empire, — Sicily, Africa, Syria, Asia, Macedonia. In addition to the two legions at Luceria, there were three legions of the levy of 55 B. C., and men already sworn in of the general levy of 52 B. C. in Italy. There was a total of ten legions in the peninsula, not counting the seven in Spain, — not far from one hundred thousand men; but they were not yet under the eagles. It was really no idle boast that "Pompey had but to stamp with his foot to cover the ground with armed men." But time is of the essence in war. Pompey's army was yet a skeleton. As we have seen, he had recognized the fact and had at once sent out eminent nobles to bring in the levies to rendezvous in the various provinces.

The force of Cæsar's legions is very hard to gauge. Judging by what they were afterwards at Pharsalus, when they had been reduced by campaigning, Cæsar's cohorts may at this time have been three hundred to three hundred and fifty men strong. This would have made the average of each legion three thousand to thirty-five hundred men, so that Cæsar had under his control a minimum of some thirty-two thousand heavy infantry. No better ever bore arms. Added to this force was a body of auxiliaries and some cavalry. All told, Cæsar's army exceeded forty thousand men. Closer calculations are often made, but the data are all founded on estimates. Cæsar's manifest advantage lay in the fact that his legions were veteran and at hand; Pompey's weakness was that the legions he might have had ready for the field, though strong on the morning reports, had yet to be assembled.

From Ariminum Cæsar sent Mark Antony with five cohorts to Arretium. This was for the purpose of anticipating an advance against his line of communications with Gaul by way of that place, and across the Apennines to either Faventia or Bononia. Libo, at Arretium, had taken no measures of defense; Antony seized the place the 20th. Cæsar himself remained at Ariminum with two cohorts, to raise levies, while he made Pisaurum, Fanum and Ancona secure, with a cohort each, on the succeeding two days. If he could get possession of Iguvium, on the Flaminian Way, he would thus gain a base line from Arretium to Ancona, securely protecting Gaul.

Learning that the prætor Thermus, with five cohorts, was fortifying Iguvium, whose inhabitants were well disposed towards Cæsar, he sent Curio, on the 23d, to that town, with the three cohorts drawn from Ariminum and Pisaurum. On his approach, December 25, Thermus drew out his forces and marched away; but his troops dispersed to their homes, unwilling probably to oppose Cæsar. Curio entered the town and later occupied Iguvium. This put an end to any danger to Cæsar's rear.

Pompey being nowhere within reach, Cæsar then withdrew Antony from Arretium, for by advancing down the coast he would minimize any danger of operations against his communications. Antony drew in Curio at Iguvium and moved to Ancona, where he joined his chief, and Cæsar gave the men a day's rest on January 4.

Brief repose was all Cæsar could give his troops. In two days he marched on Attius Varus at Auximum, southwest of Ancona, where this legate was recruiting for Pompey. His chief, Lentulus Spinther, was at Asculum. The senate of Auximum refused support to Attius. The latter retired from the place. Cæsar's van pursued and struck Attius' soldiers. These either dispersed or were for the most part glad to join Cæsar, who was welcomed by the inhabitants with loud acclaim. Lucius Pupius, the chief centurion of Attius Varus, on being brought to Cæsar as a prisoner, was at once released. Cæsar had no quarrel with the individuals of his enemy's army. He knew the value of generous treatment. About the same time Hirrus evacuated Camerinum with three thousand men.

At Auximum Cæsar was dealt a heavy blow by learning the desertion of Labienus, his hitherto apparently most devoted and able lieutenant. Cæsar made no attempt to stop him, but sent his properties and money after him. What was the immediate cause of this sad mishap is not known, but Labienus, after joining the cause of Pompey, exhibited the greatest hatred towards the chief he had for ten years so ably and cordially served.

Though thousands of recruits were willing to leave their homes and cast in their fortunes with Pompey, thus testifying to a strong sentiment for his party, this manifest leaning towards Cæsar on the part of the population produced great consternation in Rome, where news of his Umbrian successes arrived the 20th and 21st. It was rumored that "the monster" was marching on the city. The consuls, Lentulus and Marcellus, followed by most of the magistrates, within two days fled from the protection of its walls. It is curious how infectious the dread of the conqueror of the Gauls could be. It was as if these dreaded barbarians themselves had once more marched on Rome. The enemies of Cæsar did not feel secure at any point north of Capua. Here they arrested their flight, and reëstablished the Roman government. But in their haste they forgot to make the usual sacrifices to the gods, and, worse still, omitted to carry away the public treasure.

Having abandoned Rome, Pompey held a conference with his chief supporters at Teanum Sidicinum on the 27th. The various chances of the campaign were canvassed, Labienus being present, and Pompey decided to take the two legions in Apulia and advance on Picenum, where, by hurrying up the collection of the levies, he might gather a force sufficient to arrest Cæsar's farther progress. It was in this province, thirty-five years before, that Pompey had first acquired his reputation by raising troops for Sulla.

Pompey accordingly repaired to Luceria to carry out his plan of campaign. But with his usual listless method he sat down, gave out his work to others to do, and practically accomplished nothing until it was too late.

Cæsar moved down Picenum, received with hearty good will and material support by most of the towns, and recruiting with success in each locality. Even Cingulum, a town Labienus had founded, — in fact owned, — offered to join him and sent him soldiers. How great the number of his recruits may have been it is impossible to say. The Twelfth legion now joined him, and with these two, the Twelfth and Thirteenth, Cæsar marched, via Firmum and Truentum, to Asculum, the chief town of Picenum. Lentulus Spinther here had ten cohorts, — five thousand men; but he, too, fled at Cæsar's approach, and his soldiers largely deserted to the new chief. Cæsar entered the town January 11. Military glory is contagious. All soldiers were anxious to serve under a chief who had accomplished such wonders in Gaul, and in the company of men who had served in so many glorious campaigns.

Vibullius Rufus, an old soldier and a good, had been sent by Pompey into Picenum to check the growing sentiment for Cæsar. Meeting Lentulus Spinther on his retreat, Vibullius took his few remaining cohorts and dismissed him. To these he added those of Hirrus. He then collected as many as possible of the new levies which had been made for Pompey; these with some other retreating Pompeian garrisons made up thirteen cohorts, with which he fell back January 11 on Domitius Ahenobarbus, Pompey's lieutenant at Corfinium, — a recruiting rendezvous, — and reported Cæsar's advance.

Domitius had about twenty cohorts, collected in neighboring states where recruiting seemed better than elsewhere. With those of Vibullius he made up thirty-three cohorts. Had these lieutenants possessed the true soldier's instinct, they would have marched north on Cæsar, to seek, by a bold offense, to hold head against him. They might not have succeeded, but it was the thing to do.

Cæsar had two legions. He added to their numbers by seeking out the deserters from Lentulus and bringing them under the colors. Having delayed but one day beyond the time needed for the muster of these men to provide corn, he at once marched south to Corfinium, by way of Interamnum and Pinna. In Corfinium were assembled many notables and refugees.

Meanwhile the Senate at Capua was laying the blame of all these losses on Pompey; the new levies did not come in; volunteers were few; and the cause of the aristocrats looked worse and worse. Instead of Pompey's collecting endless cohorts to oppose Cæsar, it was Cæsar whose forces were growing in number and enthusiasm, while Pompey had but two legions rather weak in their allegiance, and a few newly recruited cohorts, not yet consolidated into legions.

Cæsar found the outposts of Domitius, five cohorts strong, breaking down the bridge over the Aternus, three miles north of Corfinium. By an unexpected and impetuous attack his van was able to drive off the party and save the structure. Cæsar passed over and sat down before Corfinium

on the 18th of January. His position was on the east of
Corfinium, cutting Domitius off from communication with
Pompey. Domitius, who had thirty cohorts, prepared for
vigorous defense. He had previously sent hurriedly for aid
to Pompey, who was still in Apulia. He told Pompey that
Cæsar could between them easily be surrounded in the
narrow valley in which lay Corfinium, but that without help
he himself was apt to be shut up and to lose his army. He
promised his men largesses out of his own estate, in the
event of success, — to each soldier four acres, with corresponding increase to veterans and centurions. Corfinium
was situated on a plain surrounded by high and abrupt
mountains, — the bed of an ancient lake. It was a place of
much importance and strength. It was protected by a
wall compassing over one hundred acres, and could only be
attacked from the sou*h. The plain can alone be entered
from the north through the two ravines of the Aternus.
Domitius had been wise in selecting Corfinium for his base.
Cæsar, who was awaiting farther reinforcements from Gaul,
pitched two camps before it, on the road to Sulmo.

Cæsar shortly received notice that Sulmo, ten miles
southeast from Corfinium, was ready to declare for him, but
was held in check by a garrison of seven cohorts under
Lucretius and Attius. Sending Antony thither with five
cohorts of the Thirteenth legion, the gates were opened to
him and the cohorts enlisted under Cæsar's standards.
Cæsar cared naught for the leaders. Lucretius escaped;
Attius, taken prisoner, was sent away in safety. Antony
returned the same day to Cæsar's camp, having made a
successful campaign in a few hours.

At Corfinium Cæsar determined to gather corn, fortify
and wait for some of his other troops. In addition to the
Eighth legion there shortly arrived twenty-two newly levied

cohorts, with three hundred Gallic horse from Noricum. He formed a camp in his investment line for these troops, such that it would hold the Via Valeria, and placed Curio in command. He went on with his contravallation, joining the two camps with a line of works crowned by towers. The

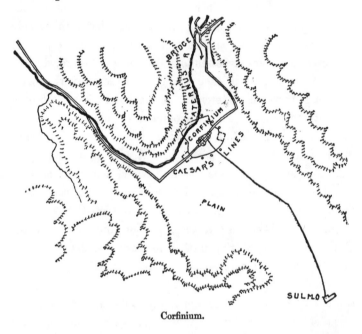

Corfinium.

entire line was nearly five miles long. His three old legions, the Eighth, Twelfth and Thirteenth, and some thirty cohorts of new levies made up an army approaching twenty thousand men. Of the new cohorts he formed three new legions.

By the time that the works in front of Corfinium were completed, Pompey, after some exchanges of correspondence, had finally replied that he could send no help to Domitius, but that the latter must save his force as best he might and join him. Domitius now changed his conduct; he misled the soldiers by false declarations while personally contemplating flight; and the men, discovering the treachery, mutinied, seized his person, January 23, and sent word to Cæsar that they would surrender him. While believing in their intention, Cæsar left nothing to chance. He paraded his entire force on his works, exhorted the officers to extra caution, and ordered that no man should sleep that night. Every one was on the alert. During the night Lentulus was surrendered, and on being pardoned by Cæsar returned to Corfinium, where he reported Cæsar's generosity. Next morning, January 24, Domitius, Vibullius, Varus and Rubrius were given up, with many other magnates. Cæsar forgave them all for their ingratitude, each one being indebted to him for past favors, protected them from the taunts of the soldiers, and restored to Domitius six millions of sestertii which he had brought with him to pay the soldiers, and which had been taken from him. Cæsar's clemency at Corfinium was as much a surprise to Rome as his advance had been a terror. He was no longer "the monster." The popular tide began to set in his favor.

Having sworn in the legionaries of Domitius under his own eagles, Cæsar, after only a week's delay before Corfinium, marched into Apulia, along the coast through the land of the Marrucini, Frentani and Larinates. He guessed that Pompey would seek to leave Italy for Greece. He knew his man as well as the conditions. The port of Brundisium was the most available one for this purpose, in fact all but the only one, and Cæsar hoped that he could succeed in anticipating Pompey at this place, and thus confine him to Italy and all the sooner bring him to battle.

This was, indeed, since early in January, Pompey's intention. He saw that almost all the available men in the peninsula were joining the enemy's standard. In all he had lost by defection nearly sixty cohorts. He had got together a

number of men in the vicinity of Rome, and these had been
marched down to Campania. He was certain about no other
levies. As matters had eventuated, Pompey could scarcely
expect to hold himself in Italy. With a potential army at
his command, large enough to crush out Cæsar before he
fairly reached Picenum, he had allowed all his chances to
slip away. His ancient habit of procrastination had grown
on him; and it was Cæsar's just estimate of this fact which
had made his temerity in advancing into Italy safe. Pompey, who now had only the two Luceria legions, the recent
recruits from Campania, together with the few remaining
faithful cohorts in Picenum, was no longer a match for his
rapid-thrusting opponent. He deemed it advisable not to
come to a general encounter with Cæsar in Italy, but to draw
him over to Greece, where he could assemble many more
troops, and where Cæsar would not be so near a friendly
population to support him. Every step taken by either of
the two men is characteristic. Cæsar was positive in what he
did. He knew his own intentions well; he was ready and
anxious to fight. Pompey was hesitating and uncertain in
his purpose; he appeared shy of crossing swords.

Instead of taking the matter personally in hand, he had
been lying in and near Luceria, the "key of Apulia," often
so valuable to Hannibal. His headquarters were at Lari-
num. Some cohorts had previously moved from Luceria to
Canusium; all were now marched to Brundisium, and his
levies were instructed to repair thither to join him. He
himself reached the place January 28. Not a few, however,
of his new cohorts deserted and went over to Cæsar. Thither
he also ordered all available galleys and transports from
every near-by port.

Pompey's calculations had from the outset been essentially
wrong. He had taken no seasonable means to defend Italy,

and he was now leaving it to Cæsar as a prize. He was giving up what he ought to have been prepared to hold at all hazards for its mere moral effect. When he had once abandoned Italy, Cæsar would have full control of Rome, and would not again afford him a chance to return. Driven from Rome, how long could Pompey maintain his influence over the provinces? His leaving was to all intents and purposes a flight. Unprepared when the struggle came, — though himself had brought it about, — he had now taken such action as to throw a first great advantage over to Cæsar's side. His conduct showed a lack of calculation and decision as marked as his apparent dread of Cæsar. It is but fair to his colleagues to say that most of them objected strenuously to Pompey's policy.

Cæsar, at Opening of Civil War.
(Berlin Museum.)

XXVII.

BRUNDISIUM AND MASSILIA. FEBRUARY TO APRIL, 49 B. C.

LACKING force to meet Cæsar in Italy, Pompey retired to Epirus. Cæsar had no fleet and could not at once follow. He sought to pen Pompey in Brundisium, and there bring him to a decisive conflict, surrounded the place, and built moles to close the harbor mouth. But Pompey managed his escape with great cleverness, and took with him to Epirus the Senate, consuls and many notables. He had rejected all Cæsar's overtures of peace. There were seven Pompeian legions in Spain, under good lieutenants. Cæsar feared that these might invade Gaul and thus strike him at his weakest point. Relying on Pompey's inertia, he determined to go first to Spain and neutralize these legions before he followed Pompey to Greece. He placed affairs in Rome on a basis to uphold his own interests, and set out for Massilia. This city he found in the hands of the Pompeians. He laid siege to it, and, placing Trebonius in command, left for Spain.

HAVING concluded that he could not hold Italy, and having made Brundisium his headquarters, Pompey there collected his troops. He had armed a large number of slaves and had made a corps of three hundred horse from the Campanian herders, — the cow-boys of Italy, — a good material for irregular cavalry. A considerable fraction of his levies failed to reach him, the cohorts breaking up on the way. Some further bodies deserted to Cæsar while on the march to Pompey; but there assembled at Brundisium a motley crowd of politicians and soldiers intermixed, numbering some twenty-five thousand men. Pompey sent Metellus Scipio to Syria to recruit. He dispatched the consuls to Dyrrachium in Epirus with a van of thirty cohorts in January, 49 B. C., promising soon to follow with the balance of the army. But the effect of his mistaken policy was still apparent; desertions continued. His two prætors, Manlius and Rutilus, went over to Cæsar with nine cohorts.

Cæsar, in all his communications to Pompey, and repeatedly, had asked for a personal interview, with the feeling that matters could be amicably adjusted. He again made overtures here through Magius, Pompey's chief engineer, whom he had captured. He was wise enough to see that if Pompey escaped to Greece there was a long, tedious and very uncertain war thrust upon him, and was not so blinded by political passion as not to allow this fact to weigh for all it was worth in his calculations. But his efforts were vain; Pompey sedulously avoided a meeting, personal or tactical.

Cæsar, having been delayed but seven days before Corfinium, marched on Brundisium via Anxanum and Teanum, Arpi, Canusium and Barium. He reached the place February 9, after a march of seventeen days at the rate of nearly seventeen miles a day. He had now six legions, the Eighth, Twelfth and Thirteenth veteran, the rest made up of what he had raised and what had voluntarily joined his ranks, in all, at least twenty-five thousand legionaries. Domitius' cohorts he had sent to Sicily.

Brundisium was one of the best of the old-world harbors. The town was well defended from the land side by a towered wall. It was a rich city and the principal port on the Adriatic.

Cæsar ascertained that the consuls had gone to Dyrrachium with thirty cohorts, while Pompey remained at Brundisium with twenty. These fifty cohorts numbered some thirty thousand men. Pompey had not had enough vessels to transport all the troops, and non-combatants as well, at one trip. Cæsar grasped immediately at the advantage of cutting Pompey off from joining them. This he could do

only by depriving Pompey of the use of the harbor of Brundisium, which commanded the Adriatic, and in which Pompey was awaiting the return of his fleet.

Cæsar went to work. He blockaded the town from the
land side by a circle of works, placing his legions in three
camps joined by contravallation walls, and proceeded to build
out into the harbor, from opposite sides and near its mouth,

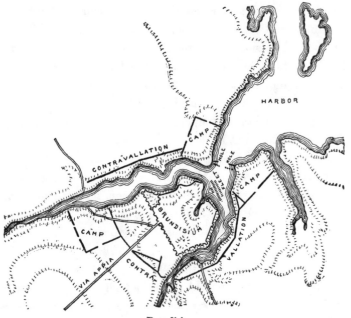

Brundisium.

where he had located two camps and where it was narrowest
and shallow, two moles some twenty feet wide, extending
towards each other. These moles were constructed of rough
stone, wood or other material near at hand. After building
out from each shore a distance of some two hundred and fifty
feet, the depth of the water made the work too difficult for
speedy completion, and in order to join these moles, yet over

five hundred feet apart, Cæsar devised a number of floating rafts, thirty feet square, which he joined together, anchored at each corner, covered with earth and protected with a parapet of wicker-work. On every fourth one he built a tower of two stories, to get an effective cross-fire. To offset this proceeding, Pompey on his side fitted out a number of merchantmen with three-story towers, and sent them out to interrupt and break through Cæsar's works. Skirmishing between these rival naval forces was of daily occurrence, with heavy interchanges of fire from bowmen and slingers.

For the third time Cæsar now sought a personal interview, through Scribonius Libo, to whom he sent a messenger. But Pompey evaded it on the pretext that without the advice and consent of the consuls he could take no action, and they were in Dyrrachium. This subterfuge determined Cæsar to push the war with vigor.

When Cæsar's works were about half finished, — on the ninth day of the blockade, February 17, — the fleet that had conveyed the forces of the consuls to Dyrrachium returned and made its way into the harbor. Pompey determined at once to leave Brundisium with the balance of his force. He strengthened the city walls and barricaded the streets, lest Cæsar should enter the town from the land side while he was embarking. The citizens were distinctly in favor of Cæsar, and gave him notice of Pompey's designs. But owing to the defenses erected by Pompey, consisting of entanglements of various kinds and excellent intrenchments, and to a rear-guard of chosen men that he left on the walls while he was embarking, which he did at night, Cæsar was entirely deceived as to Pompey's actual movements, and was prepared to do nothing to harass his retreat. This, though the citizens, irritated at the high-handedness of Pompey's soldiers, sought to give Cæsar notice of what Pompey was doing. The manner in which Pompey managed the retreat was markedly good. He got embarked before Cæsar reached the walls with his scaling ladders, and as the notice of the entanglements within had made the latter overcautious, Pompey sailed out of the port before Cæsar could get to it. The only mishap which befell Pompey was that two of his ships laden with soldiers became entangled in the harbor chain and at the mole, and were captured.

Pompey thus escaped, despite Cæsar's efforts to bring him to battle in Italy; and as he had taken possession of all the ships on the coast, and Cæsar could procure none from nearer than Gaul and Spain, the latter was, as he says, compelled to give over all present idea of following his enemy. Had he shut Pompey up in Brundisium, he might have ended the war there, instead of having to spend more than four additional years in pursuing Pompey's partisans all around the Mediterranean basin. It is certain that Cæsar began to appreciate the difference between fighting barbarians and Romans. Still he had good cause to be satisfied with what he had accomplished. He had been waging war against Pompey the Great, — the idol of the Roman people. Yet in sixty days from crossing the Rubicon, he had put himself in possession of all Italy. He must have been keenly alive to his own superiority in all that breeds military success. His decision, energy and speed stand out in strange contrast to the weakness, the vacillation of Pompey.

Cæsar had unquestionably gained by getting possession of Italy. But his responsibilities and risks had increased in equal measure. A very considerable part of his entire force must now go to garrison the peninsula, which would reduce his military power correspondingly. As he had no fleet, Italy was largely at Pompey's mercy, who could cut it off from its grain supplies in Sicily, Sardinia and Egypt. The revenues of the East would no longer flow into Roman coffers; they would all be stopped midway by Pompey; and yet Italy had grave need of these contributions, for everything had been organized on a spendthrift scale. Moreover, Cæsar was not at first looked on, even by the people whose champion he was, with a feeling of security. Many of his adherents in power were dissolute, irresponsible men, deeply in debt and reckless. People had seriously feared a return of the Marius-Sulla horrors. But it was not long before Cæsar succeeded in reassuring people on this head. Italy became tranquil. Though Cæsar was practically monarch, every one saw that the change of masters was for the better.

Cæsar now changed his plans to accord with Pompey's escape to Greece. He commanded the coast towns to procure ships from whatever source, and send them to Brundisium. He ordered the construction of two new fleets, one on the Adriatic, one in Etruria, which Dolabella and Hortensius should respectively command. Valerius the legate he sent to Sardinia with one legion; Curio the proprætor he ordered to Sicily — which was of the highest importance as a granary — with three legions made up of cohorts captured at Corfinium and one of new levies, and instructed him, after securing the island, to proceed to Africa, where the government was in dispute by rival Pompeian factions and could perhaps be brought over to his side. On their arrival, these lieutenants found both Sardinia and Sicily hastily abandoned by their respective governors, M. Cotta and M. Cato (who, like the rest, seemed to have taken fright at Cæsar's approach), and the population fallen from Pompey's and favorably disposed towards Cæsar's cause. The Cavalitans in Sardinia drove out Cotta; Cato, who was energetically equipping vessels and recruiting for Pompey, feeling that he was unable to hold the island for his chief, took ship for Epirus to join him.   Here was a large and easily gotten advantage.

The province of Africa had fallen by lot to Tubero; but when he reached his province the new governor found Attius Varus in control.   This officer, it will be remembered, had lost his army at Auximum, had fled to Africa, which seemed to be a limitless refuge for all the aristocrats, and finding no governor on hand had assumed the reins, and raised two legions.   Having formerly been prætor in Africa, he had been able to do this without much opposition.   As the days of law and order seemed past, Varus did not propose to give up his power, resisted the attempt of Tubero to land at Utica, and drove him from the coast.

Pompey had been misled by his calculation on the influence of the aristocratic party in Italy.   It had proved unequal to facing the democrats headed by Cæsar.   This was one of the facts which had determined him to leave Italy and to make Greece his battle-ground.   He had abandoned the best part of the national prize to Cæsar, and it was now Cæsar's part to hold it.

There were seven legions of Pompey's in Spain.   These were, say the Commentaries, a constant and serious threat to Gaul; or they might indeed be brought to Italy.   Cæsar deemed these legions more immediately dangerous than Pompey.   While, therefore, Pompey was flying from Cæsar to Hellas, Cæsar saw that he might be compelled to turn from Pompey to Iberia.

It is probable that Pompey had formulated a broad strategic plan.   We are not told what it was, but an occasional statement in the Commentaries and elsewhere helps us to guess. Not anticipating Cæsar's sudden irruption into Italy, Pompey had expected to quietly finish his preparations and then carry the war against Cæsar into Gaul, from Spain and

Italy at the same moment. With time in his favor he could have thus marched into Gaul with from fifteen to twenty legions, and have utilized Massilia, whose favor he had won, as his base. When this plan was frustrated by Cæsar's active campaign, Pompey himself might have done well to go to Spain, where his legions and lieutenants were both efficient, and to make that country his theatre of war, leaving Greece under a legate. But Pompey was tied down to his political associates, and his Oriental resources were the greater. He could not look at the matter coolly as a mere military problem. His vacillation persuaded him to ship to Greece and abandon Italy to the democratic party, headed by Cæsar.

There is no question that Pompey, with half the mental activity of Cæsar, could have held himself in the Italian peninsula instead of decamping from it. But the keystone of war is preparation, and Pompey had not made any. His temperament and actions were always of a *laissez aller* nature. If he had begun his levies, Italian and Eastern, in season; if he had brought half his Spanish legions to Italy, Cæsar's task could have been made all but impossible on the lines he had chosen. As it was, Pompey's personal presence in Picenum might have turned the scale. For Pompey, at his best, could exercise an influence few men could equal. If he could not hold Rome, he might have held some point on the coast, every rood of which he controlled with his fleet; and having summoned forces from all the provinces he would have vastly outnumbered Cæsar. It stands to reason that to sit still while your opponent is actively pursuing his advantages can result but in disaster. We shall see that Cæsar, in his contests with Roman troops and third-rate generals, was wont to exhibit great caution. Would he not have been less apt to make rapid progress had he known, so soon as he

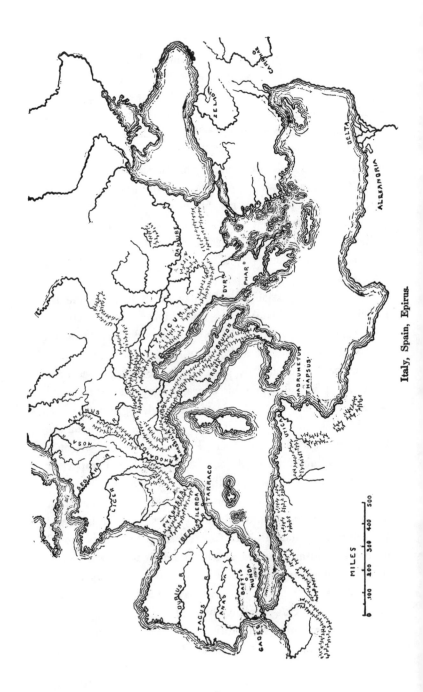

Italy, Spain, Epirus.

reached Ancona, that Pompey the Great stood personally at
the head of even the fresh levies which lay athwart his path?
For Cæsar had not then as fully gauged his opponent as he
later did. Pompey's first great error lay in entering on without preparing for war; this he followed up by a greater one
in deserting Italy without a struggle.

As to Cæsar, it is by no means clear that he acted wisely
in undertaking a campaign to Spain, instead of at once
following up Pompey. Every month he gave Pompey
enabled the latter to collect more men and material and made
him a more dangerous opponent. Though Spain was rich
and a valuable acquisition, though Cæsar must prevent the
Spanish forces from operating on his rear, it would seem that
to leave Italy, not to follow Pompey but to go to Spain
directly away from Pompey, threatened to lose him a part
of the moral strength which he had acquired by his own
boldness in pushing into Italy and by Pompey's hebetude in
crossing to Greece. Cæsar had to march overland to Spain;
why not march through Illyricum to Greece, and following up
Pompey push him to the wall? It may be said that Cæsar
counted on Pompey's character, which he well knew, and
concluded that Pompey would not attempt to return to Italy.
But was this not reckoning without his host? How could
Cæsar believe that Pompey would behave with such unmili-
tary laxness? Was he not underrating his opponent? His
reasons given in the Commentaries are, taken alone, quite
insufficient to account for his movement to Spain instead of
on Pompey, in Greece. And Cæsar's dangerous campaign
and narrow escape from disaster in Epirus, after Pompey had
raised his Eastern army, show that he was giving his opponent a manifest advantage by not attacking him before he
collected his forces.

We may assume that Cæsar argued that if he left for

Greece, his absence might give rise to partisan movements in Italy, which the presence of the seven Pompeian legions, easily transferred from Spain to Rome, might turn to his disfavor; that Pompey might draw him away from his natural base, which was Italy backed by Gaul; that he hoped that by eliminating the Spanish question he would be more able to attack Pompey to advantage.   In other words, he felt that Italy was not his so long as Pompey had seven legions in Spain, and he was unwilling to move on Pompey, with Italy for a base, unless this base was secure beyond a peradventure.   This was well enough.   But could he not have neutralized the seven Pompeian legions *quoad* Gaul by a lesser force of his veterans at the Pyrenees, and still be strategically stronger by moving on Pompey through Illyricum before the latter had concentrated all his forces, or raised more?   The time to strike Pompey was when he most feared to be struck.   And was not Pompey in Greece, with his limitless resources, a far graver threat than the seven legions in Spain?   How could Cæsar safely reckon on Pompey's not returning to Italy so soon as himself had left?   It will always remain a question whether Cæsar could not have moved on Pompey, through Illyricum, — most of his legions were easily available for such a march, — and have defeated him, or driven him into flight with a hearty dread of his enemy, before any serious danger would happen from the activity of the Spanish legions.   And Cæsar's Gallic lieutenants were better men than Pompey's Spanish legates, and might be fairly relied on to hold the Pyrenean country against them.

All these arguments are based on assumptions.   Little is told us by the Commentaries about Cæsar's reasons for his actions.   "I am setting forth to fight an army without a leader," said he, "so as by and by to fight a leader without

an army." Aphorisms do not explain. All we are told is
that Cæsar determined to go to Spain.

After quartering his legions for rest in the chief municipal
towns, Cæsar went to Rome, had the tribunes call together
on the 3d of March what remained of the Senate and
stated his grievances. He claimed that Pompey should be
made to obey the law as he himself was willing to do, and
demanded that ambassadors should be sent to Pompey to
effect a reconciliation between them. But no one was
found who cared to act as envoy, for Pompey had declared
that those who remained in Rome were as much his enemies
as those who were in Cæsar's camp.

Cæsar was able to accomplish little. His secret enemies
were still numerous in Rome. Before he left the city, he
appropriated from the treasury the fund deposited there to
defend the city against the Gauls, alleging that, as he had
conquered them, there was no further use for it. The tribune Metellus attempted to prevent him from so doing, but
Cæsar drew his sword upon him, exclaiming: "Young man,
it is as easy to do this as to say it!" The money was soon
expended, and Cæsar, not long after, was obliged to borrow
money from his officers to pay his legions. It must have
been a strange spectacle to Roman citizens to see the treasury thus despoiled; but they were powerless. Cæsar was
sole master.

Cæsar had his legions strung out from Gaul to Sicily.
He was not well concentrated and had to make many changes
to accord with his new plans. His fresh troops he stationed
in Apulia and along the Adriatic Sea, garrisoned the coast
towns having good harbors, ordered the Eighth, Twelfth
and Thirteenth legions back towards Gaul, whence he had
already drawn Trebonius with his three legions, and concentrated these and Fabius' three in the Narbonese. Then he

placed his Roman interests in the hands of Marcus Lepidus, gave the military command in Italy to Mark Antony, and put Illyricum under Caius Antonius and Cisalpine Gaul under Licinius Crassus. He released Aristobulus, king of the Jews, who was captive in Rome, hoping he would on his return home oppose the recruiting of Pompey's lieutenant, Scipio, in Syria. After completing these preparations he left Rome March 9, and went to the province of Transalpine Gaul, thence over the Corniche towards Massilia, the vicinity of which he reached in about twelve days.

Meanwhile Vibullius Rufus, whom Cæsar set at liberty at Corfinium, had gone to Spain to act for Pompey. Domitius, who, we remember, was Cæsar's successor as governor of Gaul, on the appointment of the Senate, had got friends at Igilium and Cosa to fit out seven rowing galleys for him, and had sailed for Massilia. As Cæsar marched along the coast he heard that Massilia had collected all the corn from the vicinity and fortified the town, and that Pompey's adherents had roused the citizens in his favor. They had also procured the aid of the Albici, near-by mountain tribes of the Western Alps, between the modern Durance and Verdon rivers. So soon as he reached the place Cæsar invited some of the principal citizens of Massilia to come to him, and endeavored to talk them over to his cause. But for once his eloquence proved vain. The magistrates claimed that they had received equal favors from Pompey as from Cæsar, and could in good faith give allegiance to neither, nor admit the forces of either to their town or harbor. Domitius, during the parley, arrived with his fleet, was admitted to the harbor, and made governor of the place. Cæsar, without ships, had no means of stopping him.

Domitius at once set to fitting out a fleet. He seized on all the merchantmen which were in the harbor or in the vicinity, and confiscated their cargoes, mostly corn, which was laid up for a siege. Cæsar, incensed that a town in the Province should thus turn against him, as well as all but compromised by its treachery — for Massilia, with the aid of the Albici, might cut at Aquæ Sextiæ the road from Italy to Spain — began to provide means for besieging the place. He could not leave it in his rear without at least a blockade, for it was one of the most important towns on the Mediterranean, and its example might prove disastrous. He built and equipped twelve vessels in the short space of thirty days, at Arelas near by, placed these under Decimus Brutus, the skillful victor of the Veneti, and left Trebonius with the three legions he was marching towards Narbo to invest the place. He himself began the construction of a line of contravallation.

Fabius' three legions had, we remember, been wintering in Narbo. Cæsar sent word to Antony to hurry up the Eighth, Twelfth and Thirteenth, already on the march, and diverted them from Gaul towards Spain. Meanwhile he dispatched Fabius into Spain, with the three legions at Narbo, to occupy the passes in the Pyrenees, in advance of his own coming. Fabius marched with speed enough to dislodge a small party of Pompey's adherents (part of the forces under L. Afranius) from the passes in the Pyrenees, and descended into Spain. It had been the purpose of Afranius and Petreius to occupy the Pyrenees, but Fabius anticipated them.

Vibullius Rufus had recently arrived with instructions to assume supervisory charge on behalf of Pompey of all Hispania. But the several generals remained in command of their respective armies. The lieutenants who had been there before, L. Afranius, M. Petreius and M. Varro, with seven legions, divided the peninsula between them, each practically

independent. Afranius, who had served under Pompey
against Sertorius and Mithridates, had three legions in
Hither Spain, *i. e.*, Catalonia and the territory south and
west; Petreius had two near the river Anas; and Varro had
two between the Anas and the west coast. On getting news
of the happenings in Italy and at Massilia, Petreius marched
towards Afranius, and joined forces near Ilerda (Lerida), on
the Sicoris (Segre), early in April, while Varro was left to

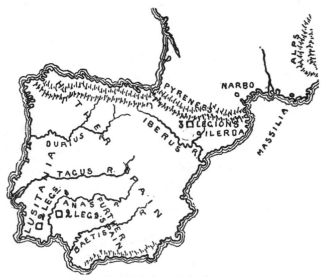

Pompey's Spanish Legions.

hold the western part of the peninsula. The five legions of
Afranius and Petreius were increased by a large force of
auxiliaries and horse recruited by these legates. In all Spain
there were the seven legions mentioned, six being old Italian
legions and one Spanish; eighty cohorts of auxiliaries, those
from Hither Spain with shields, those from Farther Spain
with round leather targets; and five thousand Spanish horse.

It is difficult to estimate these forces. At normal

strength they would number eighty-seven thousand men. But if they were of good average field strength alone, say four hundred men to a cohort, they would count but sixty-five thousand, with cavalry some seventy thousand men. Cæsar counted Fabius with three legions on the ground, the three to arrive by and by from Italy, five thousand Gallic foot-auxiliaries, three thousand horse of old German and Gallic troops, and the same number of new foot and horse recruited of the best material, of whom those of most repute were from the Aquitani and neighboring mountaineers. The total of these forces is equally hard to estimate. Probably the Cæsarian cohorts fell below those of Pompey's lieutenants, which had not been ground down by the attrition of war. If his cohort numbered three hundred and sixty men, as we formerly called them, the total under the eagles would have been thirty-seven thousand six hundred. It was no doubt under forty thousand men; but the army was veteran and included many of the best of the Gallic chiefs. Stoffel estimates that Fabius had twenty-five thousand men, or with the three legions yet to arrive thirty-six thousand men. These are, as estimates, close enough.

Cæsar had used up all his moneys, including the large sum which he took from the Roman treasury, to pay his legions. He now adopted a novel course of conduct to raise more. He borrowed various sums from his tribunes and centurions and distributed the money among the private soldiers. He thus secured the good will of the latter by his gifts and the adherence of the former on account of the loan. This certainly original proceeding was perhaps justifiable in view of the fact that Roman legionaries were now for the first time in this war to meet Romans in hostile array, and a double hold on the fidelity of his men was a further bond to fortune.

XXVIII.

ILERDA. APRIL TO JUNE, 49 B. C.

AFRANIUS and Petreius held Ilerda. Cæsar sent Fabius ahead with his army, leaving the fleet at Massilia. When he himself came up he at once advanced on the Pompeians, who declined battle. Cæsar camped near by and shortly essayed to capture a hill which lay between the Pompeian camp and the city. In this he was checked by his veterans becoming demoralized, but in a fight under the walls of Ilerda got the better of the enemy. For a long while the contention of each army was confined to foraging and seeking to disturb its rival in foraging. But shortly a serious storm and flood cut Cæsar off from his base, by destroying his bridges over the Sicoris; the enemy kept theirs which was a solid one of stone. In Cæsar's camp there was great distress, and a convoy coming to him from Gaul was almost captured by the Pompeians. Cæsar contrived a bridge of boats by which he saved the convoy and again victualed his army. The Pompeians began to lose energy.

FROM the Iberus to the vicinity of Ilerda the country is mountainous and in Cæsar's day was in part heavily wooded. North of Ilerda the country was level, and it is well commanded by the city, which stands on a bold, prominent rock on the bank of the Sicoris. While Ilerda was an excellent place for tactical defensive purposes, it was not a strategic point from which central Spain could be controlled or even protected. The river Ebro was the true line of defense, but the Pompeian lieutenants not only did not hold this, but did not even have secure communications with the river and the interior beyond. Having by delay forfeited the Pyrenees, they were short-sighted in relying solely on Ilerda to protect Spain. They took up the position "on account of the advantages of the situation."

On reaching Ilerda, about April 20, which he had done

"by hasty marches" from the Pyrenees, Fabius found
Afranius strongly camped, some eight hundred paces south

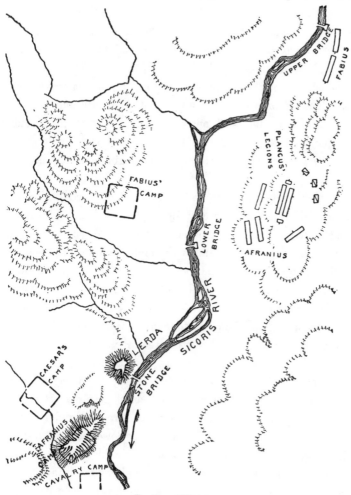

Ilerda and Vicinity.

of the town, on an isolated hill on the right bank of the
river Sicoris. The cavalry lay between this camp and
the river, in the plain. The situation of the town made it

inexpugnable. Between camp and town lay another piece
of slightly elevated ground, the south part of it nearer the
camp than the town. In this location Afranius and Petreius had determined to keep on the defensive till Pompey
could arrive, for their chief was reported to be on his way
through Mauretania to join them. How the rumor originated
it is hard to say. There was no foundation whatsoever for
it. The Pompeians had accumulated goodly supplies of
food in Ilerda, but still not enough to last through a long
campaign. They imagined, however, that they could here
hold the road into the interior of Spain against Cæsar's
forces.

Fabius went into camp and intrenched on the right bank
of the Sicoris, about three miles upstream from Afranius,
on the slope of a hill, between two brooks discharging into
the river. Here he "sounded the inclinations of the neighboring states by letters and messengers." He was joined not
far from the middle of May by the three legions from Italy.
He had made two bridges over the Sicoris, one near the left
flank of his camp, the other four miles upstream. Afranius
had control of the stone bridge at the town.

Each army used to send across their own bridges on foraging expeditions, because the corn supply on the right bank
was exhausted, and constant skirmishing resulted. On the
21st of May, when Fabius had sent his foragers, under cover
of his cavalry and two legions, across the lower of the bridges,
the weight of the train and troops, and the high water, broke
it down before the horse could cross, and cut the infantry off
from that in camp. The party none the less kept on its way,
anticipating no danger. Seeing the débris of the bridge
floating down the stream, Afranius guessed the reason and,
marching four legions and all his cavalry from Ilerda over
his own bridge, attacked the two legions thus left without

support. L. Plancus, the legate who was in command of
the Cæsarian party, "took post on a rising ground and drew
up his army with two fronts," — perhaps meaning a square,
perhaps that each legion backed on the other with a cohort
drawn up across the flanks, — so as to resist the enemy's
cavalry. This was a formation later used by Cæsar at
Ruspina, and may have been more or less in use. Here
Plancus bravely held head against a furious attack by Afranius. His defense succeeded. Before the enemy had
inflicted any serious injury on him, Fabius was seen to be
approaching with a reinforcement of two legions. He had
made the circuit over the upper bridge by a forced march in
light order. This put an end to the combat, as Afranius
deemed it wise to withdraw. The broken bridge was speedily
repaired.

Two days after this encounter, Cæsar arrived with a body-
guard of nine hundred horse. After thoroughly reconnoitring the topography of the region, he at once began active
operations. He felt that he had no time to waste. Every
week was adding to the potential strength of Pompey in
Greece. One of the most noticeable features of all Cæsar's
campaigns is the restless, unceasing activity of the man.
He never sits down to await events. He puts his hand to
working out the problem so soon as he encounters it. His
speed in planning is as remarkable as the rapidity of his
execution. He never waits for the enemy to initiate operations. This prerogative he reserves to himself. He now
left six cohorts — one from each legion — to guard the camp,
bridges and baggage, and "with all his forces drawn up in
three lines" in battle order, and then faced to the right into
column of march, he moved to Ilerda, marshaled his legions
opposite the Pompeian camp, and offered Afranius battle on
equal terms. But Afranius, though he drew out his forces

with a show of resolution, finally declined it. He was well enough off as he was, and wished to wait for Pompey's arrival. Cæsar, after remaining in line all day, though barely half a mile from the enemy's camp and at the foot of the hill on which it lay, determined to remain where he was, instead of giving the enemy the moral gain of seeing him retire; kept out his two first lines for protection, and with his third line unobserved began to fortify the front line of a camp with a trench some two thousand feet from the foot of the hill. No rampart was at first added, lest Afranius should attack during the inception of the work, which he would be able to see from the greater prominence of the rampart. He could not see the ditch, hidden in rear of the two first lines. An additional reason for omitting the rampart may have been that the legionaries were not provided with palisades; there were none to be obtained close at hand, and it would have been dangerous to send to a distance for them.

This camping in the open plain in the close vicinity of the enemy was a bold thing to do, if it was not a wise one. It reminds one of old Friedrich camping in the very teeth of the Austrians before the battle of Hochkirch. Cæsar does not sufficiently explain what he purposed to accomplish by this proceeding, quite un-Roman and without precedent. The troops lay on their arms all night behind the ditch. Having thus made a beginning, for a day or two Cæsar continued to intrench the other fronts of the camp, keeping at all times a large force behind the front ditch for protection, and paid no heed to Afranius and Petreius, who each day drew up as for battle not far off but on their slope. When the ditch was finished, on the third day, Cæsar added a rampart to the camp; and after the whole thing was completed, on the same day drew in the baggage and cohorts from the first camp up the river. The location of the camp was in every sense unfavorable; but it enabled Cæsar to cut the Pompeians off from foraging on the right bank of the river.

Afranius and Petreius were, as stated, encamped upon a hill. Between them and Ilerda was a plain some five hundred yards broad, with the slight eminence in the middle, already mentioned, which had abrupt sides about fifty feet high on the south. It occurred to Cæsar that he would try to take this eminence, which Afranius had neglected to fortify, because its possession would cut the Pompeian camp off from the town where were the supplies, and from safe access to the bridge by the use of which alone they could contrive to forage on the left bank. This was of itself an admirable diversion, but it was not expertly managed. The hill was nearer the enemy than to Cæsar, so that the latter must employ ruse to seize it, as the Pompeians were always on the watch. Instead of sending a party thither by night, which would seem to have been his better plan, Cæsar drew up three legions of his army as if again to offer battle, extending them from opposite the Pompeian camp to opposite Ilerda. The Ninth and Fourteenth legions were respectively in the centre and on the left. The duty of the latter was at the proper moment to advance and take the hill. It is probable that only the first two ranks, or the antesignani, of the Fourteenth were thrown upon the hill. At all events the attack was not perfectly planned, nor delivered with sufficient vim or speed. Afranius was on the watch. He had no intention of accepting an offer of battle by Cæsar, but divining his purpose from some of his movements, he proved too quick for his opponent. He could not permit himself to be thus cut off. He threw forward those of his cohorts which happened to be on guard on the north of his camp to anticipate the movement. These cohorts, having "a nearer way" to the hill, as Cæsar alleges, though this is not borne out by the topography, reached it first and drove back Cæsar's men.

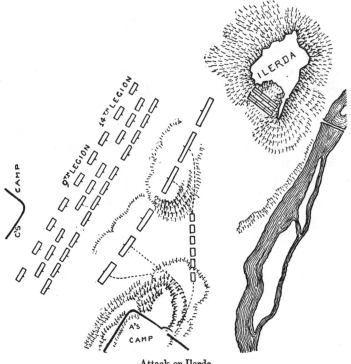

Attack on Ilerda.

Even a reinforcement did not suffice to carry the hill. "They were obliged to turn their backs, and retreat to the standard of the legions."

The method of fighting of Afranius' men, and they were war-hardened veterans, was peculiar. They had learned it in combats with the Lusitanians and other barbarians of Spain. Instead of fighting in close order in the usual legionary manner, they scattered in small parties, and taking advantage of the accidents of the ground advanced or retired, fighting in loose order. "If hard pressed they thought it no disgrace to retire and give up the post." It seems to have been a sort of loose order in groups, which advanced by short rushes from one cover to another much like the system which has obtained in recent days against the decimation of the arms of precision. Unused to this method and fearing that the rushes of some of these small groups from hiding would jeopardize their exposed (right) flank, Cæsar's legionaries were at first considerably unsettled, and when its "advanced guard," *i. e.*, antesignani, fell back from the eminence, the Fourteenth legion also gave way, and retreating to the next hill in its rear, not only weakened the entire line, but imparted a feeling of insecurity to all the legionaries.

The effect of this loss of confidence Cæsar saw that he must immediately overcome. He seized on and headed the Ninth legion, which was in line on the right of the Fourteenth, and while covering the retirement of his beaten men, by a bold onslaught drove the enemy back in confusion. Part retreated over the hill in dispute, as far as the walls of Ilerda, where they stopped and drew up; part appear to have retired to their camp.

Ilerda was built on a rock which stands up boldly five hundred feet above the plain, with a plateau of some one hundred and fifty acres on the top. Every side of this rock is practically inaccessible to assault except that on the south. Here, in a sort of ravine, is a slope, up which ran the road to the town, some six hundred yards long from the plain. Near the plain the mouth of the ravine is some three hundred and fifty yards wide; at the town, about a third that width.

It was between the two walls of the ravine that the enemy turned, and backing against the fortifications of the town awaited Cæsar's Ninth legion. Emboldened by their success, and advancing too far in their eagerness to efface

their comrades' defeat, this legion got engaged on an up-slope
where it had difficulty in disengaging itself. Its situation
was critical. It had advanced well up the rocky hillside, and
there met the enemy's line, which it could not destroy; when
it essayed to retire the enemy fell upon it from the higher
ground. The approach to the town on which they stood was
flanked with craggy sides. There was but one way down, —

Ilerda, from the Northeast.

the way they had come. The enemy's men not only stood
where they could use their weapons to excellent effect, but no
aid could be put in on the flanks of the Ninth, nor the
cavalry be of the slightest service. Meanwhile the enemy
was fighting with his back to the town, and felt confidence
accordingly. There was room along the approach for but a
front of three cohorts, and though Cæsar had had no idea of
coming to close quarters on such bad ground, he was constrained to send in, from time to time, out of the troops he
could not use, fresh forces to relieve the weary. And this the
enemy likewise did. "Cohorts were frequently sent to their
aid by a circuit from the camp through the town," which
seems to argue that there was access to the plateau from the
river side, at least for friends.

The contest raged on this narrow slope for five hours.
Neither line gave way, and Cæsar could not well extricate

his men without danger of demoralization. He had apparently sent in as many successive cohorts as could fight on the narrow front, and kept on putting in fresh ones. This it was which enabled the three cohorts front to continue to fight five hours without loss of heart. Finally Cæsar's legionaries exhausted their javelins. At the sight of this the enemy renewed their efforts, resolved to hold their own. Cæsar was threatened with disaster; but under the inspiration of his personal appeals the men persuaded themselves to make one last effort, drew their swords, and charging up the hill on the enemy's cohorts, drove them in disorder to the very walls of Ilerda. Under cover of this charge they withdrew down to a point where the cavalry was able to file in on the flanks, "which though stationed on sloping or low ground, yet bravely struggled to the top of the hill and riding between the two armies made our retreat more easy and secure." Cavalry here was enacting one of its chief rôles to great advantage. This, added to the smart attack of the foot, prevented the enemy from following.

The combat was drawn. Retiring to camp, Cæsar found that he had lost in all one centurion and seventy men killed and six hundred wounded. The enemy's loss in killed alone, as the Commentaries claim, was two hundred, with five centurions. The wounded are not given. Considering that the combat had been hotly contested for five hours, this was not so serious a loss. It shows how safe the Roman legionary was with his excellent armor and broad and skillfully handled shield, so long as he did not break his ranks.

It is to be observed in a general way that while the losses of a thoroughly defeated enemy were often in olden times awful beyond anything we know to-day, the losses of the victors were usually by no means heavy; and the casualties of ordinary campaign work, — outpost and picket fighting,

— such as we are familiar with and which are frequently far more numerous than those of pitched battles, were small compared to those of modern days. The percentage of loss by wounds in one of Cæsar's campaigns was as a rule low.

Each party claimed the victory in the fight at Ilerda; Cæsar's men because, though they had at first fallen back, they had forced the enemy to his gates and held him there, and had moreover driven him uphill with the sword, — an unusual feat; Afranius' men because they had kept and were able to fortify the eminence in dispute. This they did with strong works and put a garrison in them.

Cæsar's operation so far had for result that his cavalry — which was far superior to Afranius' — could hold the surrounding territory, and by watching the bridges could prevent Afranius from foraging at large on the farther side of the Sicoris. He foresaw that want of bread would sooner or later drive Afranius from his position. Still Cæsar must have keenly felt the fact that he had in his first combat with Roman troops quite failed to accomplish what he set out to do. His luck had for the moment turned on him, and this in a contest with an officer of minor rank and ability. No doubt here, too, his persuasive words were employed to advantage in satisfying his soldiers that they had really won the fight. But to construe the Commentaries as we often have to do in the Gallic War, this affair at Ilerda looks more like a defeat for Cæsar than a drawn battle. Nor can it be said that the attempt to seize the hill in question was brilliantly conceived or executed. Rather is Afranius' defense to be commended.

Two days after the battle a serious disaster happened. A severe storm arose. The melting snows poured down from the mountains in a vast flood, and the waters of the river overflowed their banks — "it was agreed that there had never been seen higher floods in those countries" — and swept away both of Cæsar's bridges, which were of but temporary construction. The camp was flooded by the brook which ran through it. Cæsar found himself cut off from his communications with Gaul, and shut in between the two rivers Cinga and Sicoris, over the latter of which Afranius still had a bridge, and Cæsar now had none. No fords were within thirty miles. Afranius had previously gathered all the corn of the immediate vicinity, so that foraging was difficult, and the light troops attached to the army of Afranius kept up a harassing small-war. His Lusitanians and targeteers of Hither Spain could easily swim the river, "because it is the custom of all those people not to join the army without bladders," and Cæsar was no longer able to interfere with the foraging of Afranius on the left bank.

Worse than all, Cæsar's convoys could not reach him. A large force of foragers had been prevented from returning to camp. The friendly states could not get to him with corn, and the new crops were not yet ripe. All the cattle had been removed to a great distance. There were no boats to be had, for Afranius had secured these long ago. Cæsar's rations grew short. Afranius, on the contrary, was well supplied, and his own bridge was still intact, which enabled him to cross the Sicoris, not only to forage, but to receive supplies from the interior of Spain. The tables were turned. The height of water, the rough banks and the enemy's opposition prevented Cæsar from repairing the bridges, — "it was no easy matter at one and the same time to execute a work in a very rapid flood and to avoid the darts," — and any attempt to cross small parties was headed off by the cohorts of the enemy, which lined the banks.

A still more fatal matter was that a large convoy from Gaul — including slaves and freedmen, some six thousand souls all told — was near at hand, and Afranius knew the fact, and had set out with three legions and all his cavalry to attack it. In this convoy "there was no order or regular discipline, as every one followed his own humor, and all traveled without apprehension," knowing nothing of the disaster to Cæsar's bridges. Reaching the convoy, Afranius summarily fell upon it, and but for the courage of the Gallic horse — which now as always behaved with consummate gallantry — might have corralled the whole body, in which "there were several young noblemen, sons of senators and of equestrian rank; there were ambassadors from several states; there were lieutenants of Cæsar's." But to the aid of the skill and daring of the Gallic horse came the faultiness of Afranius' dispositions, which lacked both vigor and ability. These men held Afranius' forces at a distance by skirmishing about his legions in their own peculiar manner, and thus enabled the convoy to retreat to the uplands. The loss was two hundred bowmen, some horse and non-combatants, and a little baggage.

All these disasters made provisions scarce and high. Corn reached fifty denarii a bushel. "The want of corn had diminished the strength of the soldiers." Cattle were got, but by great efforts only. Cæsar was obliged to forage at a considerable distance. This series of misadventures tended to encourage the enemy, and, reported at Rome, as they were very circumstantially by Afranius, began to lead people to believe that Cæsar's fortunes were at an end. Had Pompey actually come to Spain at this moment, — as he should have done, — Cæsar might well have been in bad case. But Pompey did not deem it essential to come. He was waiting for Cæsar in Greece.

Cæsar's resources in corn were small; but in intelligence and audacity they had as yet scarcely been taxed. He determined to cross the Sicoris, whatever the difficulty or danger, reëstablish his communications with Gaul, and rescue his convoy. He built a lot of boats whose keels and ribs were of light timber, covered with wickerwork and hides, — a

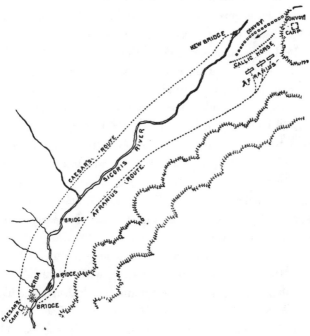

Rescue of Convoy.

trick he had learned in Britain. These he now transported on wagons in one night, twenty-two miles from camp, up the river to a place already selected, near the modern village of San Llorens. Here he sent a body of men across, who seized upon and fortified unperceived a hill on the opposite shore; and to this place he soon transported a legion. Then, by beginning a bridge at both ends under cover of this force, he finished it in two days and safely brought his convoy and foragers across to camp (June 11). At the same time he put over a large body of horse, and sending it out at an opportune moment, he surrounded the enemy dispersed as foragers, and captured a great store of men and provisions; and when some Spanish light-armed cohorts came to the rescue, a part of the horse protected the plunder, while another advanced against the enemy, cut off one cohort, put it to the sword, drove off the rest in disorder, and returned to camp, across the bridge, with much booty. The question of provisions was thus settled, and the superiority of Afranius and Petreius at once vanished into thin air.

During this time, there was a naval engagement at Massilia between the forces of Domitius and Brutus, near an island (modern Rattonneaux), opposite the town, where Cæsar's fleet was stationed. The enemy was largely superior in the number of his vessels. He had seventeen war-galleys, eleven decked and many smaller ones, well manned by archers and the auxiliary Albici, and was the attacking party. Brutus bravely sallied out to meet the enemy. The Romans, though their rowers were new, had aboard antesignani and centurions, all veterans of stanch courage, who for its honor had requested this service. For a while the skillful manœuvring of the Massilians threatened disaster. "The Massilians themselves, confiding in the quickness of their ships and the skill of their pilots, eluded ours, and evaded the shock, and as long as they were permitted by clear space, lengthening their line they endeavored to surround us, or to attack single ships with several of theirs, or to run across our ships and carry away our oars, if possible; but when necessity obliged them to come nearer, they had recourse, from the skill and art of the pilots, to the valor of the mountaineers. But our men, not having such expert seamen, or skillful pilots, for they had been hastily drafted from the merchant ships, and were not yet acquainted even with the names of the rigging, were, moreover, impeded by the heaviness and slowness of our vessels, which having been built in a hurry and of green timber, were not so easily manœuvred. Therefore, when Cæsar's men had an opportunity of a close engagement, they cheerfully opposed two of the enemy's ships with one of theirs. And throwing in the grappling irons, and holding both ships fast, they fought on both sides of the deck, and boarded the enemy's; and having killed numbers of the Albici and shepherds, they sank some of their ships, took others with the men on board, and drove the rest into the harbor. That day the Massilians lost nine ships, including those that were taken."

The news of this victory tended much to encourage the forces at Ilerda. Cæsar purposely exaggerated the success, and as a result a number of towns and native tribes tendered fealty and corn, — Osca, Calagurris, Tarraco, the Jacetani at the mouth of the Iberus, the Illurgari south of them, and the Ausitani on the sea near the eastern end of the Pyrenees. Even a cohort of Illurgari, in the enemy's camp, deserted to Cæsar in a body.

Signum.

XXIX.

GOOD MANŒUVRING. JUNE, 49 B. C.

CÆSAR's desire was to capture the Pompeian army instead of destroying it in battle. His new bridge was many miles up river. The stream was too full to build one farther down. In order to have a means of crossing near Ilerda, he cut a number of canals in a low island in the middle of the river to divert the stream into many channels, thus lower the water and make an artificial ford. The plan succeeded well. The Pompeians determined to retire to the Ebro. They crossed the Sicoris on their bridge; Cæsar followed by way of his ford. The enemy sought to escape to the mountain-passes; Cæsar anticipated them and thus cut off their retreat. They then tried to return to Ilerda; Cæsar followed, harassed and finally surrounded them. The legions demanded battle; Cæsar, anxious to spare Roman lives, refused. Finally, cut off from water, the entire Pompeian army surrendered, on agreement that they should be discharged. Cæsar had thus neutralized Pompey's whole force in Spain without a general engagement. It is one of his finest feats of manœuvring. The Ilerda campaign had lasted but six weeks.

THUS Fortune took a turn. Soon the vigor of Cæsar's Gallic horse intimidated Afranius' foragers. "The enemy, daunted by the courage of our horse, did not scour the country as freely or as boldly as before; but sometimes advancing a small distance from the camp, that they might have a ready retreat, they foraged within narrower bounds; at other times, they took a longer circuit to avoid our outposts and parties of horse; or having sustained some loss, or descried our horse at a distance, they fled in the midst of their expedition, leaving their baggage behind them; at length they resolved to leave off foraging for several days and, contrary to the practice of all nations, to go out at night." The neighboring tribes, too, and many distant ones, so soon as Cæsar's success was demonstrated, began to send in their allegiance and desert Afranius; and furnished the army with plenty of corn and cattle. More than this, the rumors of Pompey approaching through Mauretania died away, which still more encouraged the adherents of Cæsar.

In order to provide a nearer means of crossing the Sicoris than the bridge lately built, and one less liable to interruption than those which the floods had carried away, Cæsar, with his restless ingenuity, devised an artificial ford. Why he did not rebuild the bridges which had been destroyed by the high water, or construct others, it is hard to say. A new flood was improbable. Unless the water was too high and rapid, or unless the enemy was more than usually active in opposing the construction of bridges, the labor involved in building several bridges would have been small compared to that he undertook. Wood was not near by, but it could be floated down from the mountains.

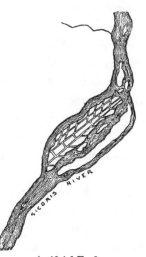

Artificial Ford.

There have been numberless constructions of the passage in the Commentaries which narrates this engineering feat; and many clever designs have been made to show how Cæsar produced this celebrated ford. What he really did — and there can be no doubt that it was what is now to be explained — is as remarkable by its simplicity as by its ingenuity.

The Sicoris, a mile or more above Ilerda, has a wide bed, in which, in Cæsar's day as now, it flowed in three channels, leaving broad, sandy islands between them. The island nearest the right bank is half a mile long. Here, out of dart-throwing distance from the enemy, by sinking a number of drains thirty feet wide, he managed to draw off part of the current of the Sicoris into the beds of these drains, and by thus giving the volume of water more channel room, lowered the depth of the river so as to make it fordable in places. The plan succeeded well. The horse needed no longer to make the long détour by the San Llorens bridge.

This energetic and clever piece of engineering discouraged Afranius and Petreius, as much as the fact that Cæsar's horse had proved so much the stronger, and had annoyed them so sorely. Here, as in the Gallic campaigns, these gallant fellows were one of his mainstays. The Roman or native cavalry of Afranius and Petreius could by no means cope with them.

With Cæsar in possession of the right bank of the Sicoris, and able to scour the country on the left bank, the Pompeians threatened to be in evil case. They must take decided action, and that at once. After long consultation, the legates resolved to retire across the Iberus into Celtiberia, where Pompey was well liked by many and feared by others, and where his influence consequently predominated. This was partly because he had been the Roman general who had got the credit of putting down Sertorius. This sentiment led the Pompeians to believe that they could there prolong the war till winter, whose snows in the Pyrenees would weaken Cæsar's communications with Gaul; and Cæsar, being unknown in that region, could not readily make adherents or victual his army. They therefore collected all the vessels they could in the Iberus at Octogesa (modern Mequinensa), at its confluence with the Sicoris, and ordered a bridge of boats to be there built.

The nearest and easiest road to Octogesa was along the right bank of the Sicoris; but an easy road meant easy pursuit by Cæsar's cavalry, and this the Pompeians dreaded.

They decided on the more rugged road on the farther bank, which had the advantage of yielding many places of ready defense; but the country had the very objectionable feature of being all but waterless. Only rain-water is there used to-day, and the inhabitants store this up in reservoirs.

The Pompeians accordingly transported two legions over the Sicoris,— they still retained the stone bridge,— and about June 21 fortified a camp and bridgehead with a rampart twelve feet high on the left bank. All their preparations had been some time completed; but Afranius and Petreius, with the slowness bred of lax purpose, had delayed their retirement too long. What they had done, moreover, had betrayed their intentions. Cæsar, by severe toil day and night, had so far completed his ford as to be able — though with some danger — to get his mounted troops across, but "the foot had only their shoulders and the upper part of their breast above the water." The enemy recognized the mistake they had made in their delay, and saw that they must speedily move away or forfeit their chance of doing so unmolested. Afranius and Petreius were growing morally weaker. Though their success had been fair in their several encounters with the Cæsarians, they did not care to face Cæsar in a pitched battle in the open. This looks as if, though Cæsar had not won a success in the late engagement, he had impressed himself strongly on his enemies. At all events, the Pompeians had concluded to abandon his front and retreat to a safer country. Leaving two auxiliary cohorts in garrison at Ilerda to cover the withdrawal, they moved their whole army on the night of June 23 to the new camp across the river. "The legionaries had been ordered" to carry " sufficient corn to last twenty-two days."

The country from Ilerda to the Iberus, on the left bank of the Sicoris, was at first rolling and fertile, then strongly

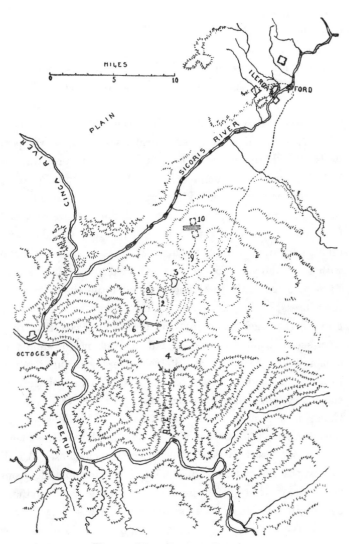

Theatre of Operations near Ilerda.

accentuated, and within five miles or so of the Iberus became much cut up by rocky and mountainous country, difficult to traverse. The march of Afranius and Petreius, if speedy and well conducted, might be free from pursuit. If they could get beyond the level and into the mountains, they were safe.

Cæsar saw with regret that his prey was escaping. His only chance now lay in harassing the enemy's rear with a view of bringing them to terms. He sent his cavalry across the Sicoris to do this, and the nimble Gauls performed the duty efficiently. "When Afranius and Petreius had broken up their camp about the third watch, they suddenly appeared on their rear, and, spreading round them in great numbers, began to retard and impede their march." Cæsar had given up the idea of forcing battle on the Pompeians. He saw that it would be better, if it was possible, to conquer Afranius and Petreius without destroying the Roman legions opposed to him. His hope was to bring these legions, or at least many of the men, over to his cause. What would have been vacillation in many of his movements may really be ascribed to a sound military motive. He wished to win by manœuvring rather than by fighting. Let us see how he did it.

On the left bank of the Sicoris, Afranius and Petreius had choice of two routes: one close to the river and through rather flat country, one by a circuit inland over the cut up country. This latter they chose for the same reason as they chose the left rather than the right bank. But it is evident that they had not carefully reconnoitred their ground, for even the latter route was not so cut up as to prevent the cavalry from keeping on their heels.

From the eminences on the right bank of the Sicoris Cæsar's army could watch the operations of the horse, and

see how greatly they interfered with the movements of
Afranius and Petreius.   The squadrons swept around the
enemy's flanks and rear, thus demoralizing the legionaries,
but retired when smartly attacked.   The Cæsarians were in
the forks of the two rivers, Cinga and Sicoris, with their one
bridge twenty-two miles upstream.   A circuit would be too
long to enable them to take part in the action; and the stone
bridge being, as we must assume, well held, they could not join
their comrades except by the ford, which was up to their necks.
But with the eye of veterans they at once perceived that the
enemy was about to escape them; and they understood that
this meant a long pursuit and a tedious campaign in an
unknown territory.   "They applied to their tribunes and
centurions, and entreated them to inform Cæsar that he need
not spare their labor or consider their danger; that they were
ready and able and would venture to ford the river where the
horse had crossed."   Cæsar took advantage of this enthusiasm, and determined to try the experiment.   It is neither
stated in the Commentaries that Afranius and Petreius had
broken down the stone bridge, nor that they had left a
garrison to hold it; but one or the other must be the fact, or
Cæsar would certainly have used it at the present moment to
cross.   If broken down, he could not do so; unless held by
many cohorts, it would seem as if Cæsar might have brushed
away the force at the bridgehead, and have thus frayed himself a passage across the river.   The habit of the day, to be
sure, was to avoid assaulting breastworks even when held by
a handful of men, and anything but an immediate assault
would have consumed too much time.   But it appears
curious, when so much was at stake, and the odds were so
greatly in his favor, that Cæsar should have hesitated to
assault and capture the bridge.   Roman legions during the
Punic Wars, and at other times, stormed breastworks held

by large bodies of regular troops; Cæsar's legionaries had before now stormed town walls, and did so later; the defenses of the stone bridge could not have been other than the usual ditch and rampart. However it may have been, Cæsar preferred the risk of the ford to attacking the bridge, if still standing. The only explanation lies in the probability, either that the ford was easier than assumed by the Commentaries, or that the Pompeian generals had left behind, out of their Spanish cohorts, a goodly body to hold the bridge defenses. In Ilerda, the two cohorts were probably enough as a garrison.

Leaving the weaker soldiers and one legion to guard the camp, taking no baggage and stationing horse obliquely across, above to break the current and below to catch those who might be swept away, the legions were marched down to the ford and across the river. Though a number were carried off their feet, they were all caught by the horsemen, and not a man was lost.

Cæsar ployed his legionaries into three columns, — the usual three-line order of battle forward by wings, — and advanced. The good will of the men was such that they speedily gained the rear of the enemy, whose advance had been much retarded by the cavalry. "So great was the ardor of the soldiers that, notwithstanding the addition of a circuit of six miles and a considerable delay in fording the river, before the ninth hour of the day — three P. M. — they came up with those who had set out at the third watch," — midnight. The cavalry had so cleverly harassed the march of Afranius that his column had been unable to advance any considerable stretch, — not more than six miles.

The appearance of Cæsar's legions in his rear constrained Afranius to pause in his retreat and to draw up his army on a rising ground, probably 1 on the chart. The Commentaries give certain hints as to time and distances which have helped to locate the operations of the coming days with fair accuracy. Cæsar also called a halt and gave his men time to rest and refresh themselves, for they had marched more than twenty miles. He was loath to attack in earnest; but whenever Afranius resumed his retreat, Cæsar advanced again upon him. In this manner both armies, in a sort of skirmishing fight, drifted six miles farther to the southwest. Both finally camped, Afranius on some hills which enabled him to avoid Cæsar's cavalry (2), and Cæsar on an adjoining height (3).

The original purpose of Afranius had been to continue his route nearly west over the hills to Octogesa; but Cæsar's proximity led him to fear the effects of further interference by his cavalry. Some five miles to the south was a range too rough for the operations of horse; and through it ran a defile. If, by a sudden march, he could reach the mouth of the defile, he would be safe from pursuit, and could perhaps cross the Iberus farther down than Octogesa, or follow up its bank to that place. At all events the defile, at less than half the distance of Octogesa, was a temporary refuge, and the Pompeian clutched at a straw. It was a vacillating thing to do, and a useless; for Cæsar, by marching straight on Octogesa, could head him off from that place; but any port in a storm.

The position of Afranius and Petreius was highly delicate; they had been marching and fending off Cæsar's cavalry some sixteen hours. Their men were broken up with fatigue and the leaders were equally unsettled. Out of sheer dread of the cavalry it was determined not to push for Octogesa by the straight road, but to make a dash for the Iberus river by way of the defile; and with a view to this manœuvre they reconnoitred the ground. Cæsar, always active, did the like.

Having come to this conclusion, it was the height of folly for the Pompeians not to push for the defile, at all hazards, before Cæsar could seriously attack; but, "fatigued by the skirmishes all day and by the labor of their march, they deferred it till the following day." They should have sacrificed part of their army and all their baggage to save the rest. Some generals never know when affairs need a desperate remedy.

After dark it occurred to Afranius that he might steal a march on Cæsar. The Gallic cavalry, which continued scouting all night, discovered from some prisoners whom they took at midnight that the enemy was making an effort to retire under cover of the darkness. When this fact was reported to him, Cæsar ordered the signal for packing baggage — a certain note on the horns accompanied by a shout — to be given in his own camp. Hearing this signal, and assuming that Cæsar was about to break camp, — lest his march should be disturbed by Cæsar's legionaries as well as his cavalry, — Afranius decided not to move. A night attack with his large train would be apt to be disastrous. Next day (June 26), both generals again reconnoitred the country, and Afranius and Petreius held a council of war. Some advised to move by night, hoping to escape the more easily in the darkness. Others argued that as Cæsar's horse was patrolling all night, it would be sure to discover them, and that the soldiers in the dark would not fight by any means as well as under the eye of their commanders. Daylight, said they, raised a strong sense of shame and duty in the soldiers which they lost in the darkness. After weighing the pros and cons, it was decided to move at daylight on the succeeding morning, and to risk whatever losses they must. This they prepared to do; but it was too late.

Cæsar had divined the change of plan and decided to make

an effort to cut the enemy off from the defile. He set out considerably earlier, "the moment the sky began to grow white," by a long circuit around the enemy's right flank, — to the east of them, — for the mountains. He could not take the main road, for Afranius and Petreius lay across it. He resorted to a clever ruse. He ordered his legions to leave camp by the west gate in the direction opposite to the defile. The movement was perceived by the Pompeians, but it was their opinion that Cæsar was retiring. So soon as he could move his legions under cover, Cæsar bore to the east and south. The road ahead of him was rough and cut up. "His soldiers were obliged to cross extensive and difficult valleys. In several places craggy cliffs interrupted their march, insomuch that their arms had to be handed to one another, and the soldiers were forced to perform a great part of their march unarmed, and were lifted up the rocks by each other. But not a man murmured at the fatigue, because they imagined that there would be a period to all their toils if they could cut off the enemy from the Ebro and intercept their convoys."

The idea that Cæsar was retiring emboldened Afranius and Petreius to take their time. "Afranius' soldiers ran in high spirits from their camp to look at us, and in contumelious language upbraided us, 'that we were forced, for want of necessary subsistence, to run away, and return to Ilerda.' For our route was different from what we proposed, and we appeared to be going a contrary way." But by and by it was perceived that Cæsar's head of column had filed to the right, and that his van had passed the line of their camp. This at once showed the enemy their error, and urged them on to dispatch. If Cæsar should cut them off from the defile, their game was lost. Afranius detailed a guard for the camp, and set out at a rapid pace with the bulk of his

forces, without baggage, for the defile. The enemy's movements were somewhat hasty and irregular, and Cæsar's
horse managed seriously to impede their march. "The
affair was necessarily reduced to this point, with respect to
Afranius' men, that if they first gained the mountains, which
they desired, they would themselves avoid all danger, but
could not save the baggage of their whole army, nor the
cohorts which they had left behind in the camps, to which,
being intercepted by Cæsar's army, by no means could
assistance be given."

As above stated, Afranius and Petreius had decided,
because the road was more rugged and they thought would
better preserve them from the stinging pursuit of the Gallic
horse, to head directly south for the defile of modern Riva-
roja. Cæsar had divined their purpose and had pushed for
the same point.

Though the circuit he was compelled to make lay through
a very broken country, where there were no roads, such was
the eagerness of his men and the enforced slowness of
Afranius' party, that Cæsar first reached the point where
he could hold the mouth of the defile. Here he drew up his
army athwart Afranius' path, "in a plain behind large rocks "
(5). Afranius was strategically beaten. The men rested,
elated with their success and more than ever confident of the
ability of their chief. The horse continued to sweep around
Afranius' flanks and rear. It was one of those cases where
the problem was plain and every man could see success or
failure.

Afranius, seeing the miscarriage of his plan, again changed
his mind, and determined to push for the road he had originally chosen, due west over the mountains. He sent out four
cohorts of Spanish foot to take possession of one of the
eminences (6), which seemed from its position to afford a

probable opportunity of holding Cæsar in check until he could pass in its rear with the main column. But Cæsar's horse was on the alert, and smartly attacked these cohorts; "nor were they able to withstand the charge of the cavalry even for a moment, but were all surrounded and cut to pieces in the sight of the two armies."

The occasion was now so plainly excellent for an attack in force on the enemy, purposeless and held in place by the horse, that Cæsar's legates, centurions and tribunes crowded round him begging him to engage battle, for the men were most eager for it, especially as all could see that the enemy was demoralized and pressing in irregular groups around their standards as if uncertain what to do. Or if not at the moment, battle should be prepared for, as the enemy must soon come down from the hill for lack of water. Cæsar plainly saw that a battle at this moment meant fearful slaughter of the enemy, and was not only anxious to spare Roman blood, but to keep these legions intact if possible, for his own use. He had the utmost faith in his ability to bring Afranius and Petreius to a surrender without decimation of either his own legions or the Pompeian. This decision excited great opposition and discontent among the soldiers, many of whom openly declared to each other that if Cæsar would not fight when he was so advantageously placed, perhaps they themselves would not fight when Cæsar called on them. But Cæsar was not the man to change. He paid not the least heed to this exhibition of temper, which he knew really proceeded from soldierly motives. He had other more important things to consider. He allowed the enemy to retire to their camp ; and having placed strong outposts on all the avenues to the mountains so as to cut off every road to the Iberus, he fortified his camps close to Afranius and Petreius, the better to observe their movements (7).

There were but two places to which these officers could now retire, Ilerda or Tarraco (Tarragona) on the coast. The latter was too far to attempt to reach it.

Not satisfied with merely observing them, Cæsar now made an effort to cut the Pompeians off from water, and sent out his horse to attack the watering parties, which had to go some distance from camp to find reservoirs which were full. This new and serious danger obliged Afranius and Petreius to put out a line of posts to protect the march of the watering parties, and later determined them to throw up a rampart (8) from their camp to the water, a work of some magnitude and one necessitating the absence of both the generals from camp. "Petreius and Afranius divided the task between themselves and went in person to some distance from their camp for the purpose of seeing it accomplished." "The soldiers, having obtained by their absence a free opportunity of conversing with each other," which they eagerly embraced, — for among the soldiers of both armies there were naturally many old friends, — it was soon ascertained by the Cæsarians that there was grave disaffection in the enemy's camp. Many of the tribunes and centurions came over to see Cæsar, and the intercourse between the camps quickly became universal. The Pompeian soldiers openly expressed their regrets that they were not in Cæsar's army. The fraternizing even went so far that the legionaries deputed some centurions of the first rank to visit Cæsar and state that they were ready to surrender their generals and join Cæsar if the latter would spare the lives of Afranius and Petreius. They keenly felt that Cæsar had spared them the day before, when they were so open to attack. "Every place was filled with mirth and congratulations; in the one army, because they thought they had escaped so impending danger; in the other, because they thought they had completed so important a matter without blows; and Cæsar, in every man's judgment, reaped the advantage of his former lenity, and his conduct was applauded by all."

The Pompeian generals soon heard this news. Afranius was disposed not to resist the inclinations of the soldiers, but was ready to accept the situation. Petreius, who had been at a greater distance, on learning of what was going on, either distrustful of Cæsar, or from greater native combativeness, decided on action, armed his domestics and a few personal followers, and with the Spanish prætorian cohort and a few foreign horse flew to the camp, seized and put to death a number of Cæsar's men who were still in his lines, and forced the rest to hide or flee. The latter "wrapped their left arms in their cloaks, drew their swords and defended themselves against the Spaniards and the horse." He then by threats, entreaties and tears brought the legions back to a sense of their duty, and having administered an oath to Afranius and all the officers, — he himself joining in it, — under no circumstances to desert the cause of Pompey, he obliged them to surrender all Cæsarians who could be found, many of whom were still within the camp. These he put publicly to death in the prætorium. Many, however, were kept concealed by the men and allowed to depart at night over the ramparts. Cæsar was too wise to indulge in such slaughter. After searching out all the enemy's soldiers in his own camp, he allowed them to depart unharmed, with a friendly word to each. A number of officers concluded to remain with him. These he "treated with great respect. The centurions he promoted to higher ranks" (a very unusual step), "and conferred on the Roman knights the honor of tribunes." Matters reverted to a war footing; but Cæsar had certainly gained ground with his enemy's legions.

Afranius and Petreius had made a series of blunders.

Their management was extremely weak. Each error bred a new one. Cæsar's energy and skill stand out in contrast. His constant watchfulness made both foraging and watering difficult to the enemy. The Pompeian legionaries had some corn, having started with a larger than usual supply; but the Spaniards and auxiliaries had none, being unused to carrying burdens, and many daily deserted to Cæsar. Afranius and Petreius finally decided to make an effort to retire to Ilerda, — where they had left much victual, — and by the nearest road, which led north to the river and thence along the left bank. Their old camp there seemed the only harbor of refuge. To do this, they set out at daybreak, took their march along the high ground, to avoid as much as possible Cæsar's cavalry, which harassed their rear as sharply as it could. "Not a moment passed in which their rear was not engaged with our horse." Their own cavalry proved to be useless, owing to the demoralization bred of the late combats. They could not be got to face the Gallic squadrons, and to prevent their breaking up had finally to be put in the middle of the legions.

On the march the Pompeian foot would turn at every piece of rising ground from which they could cast their darts, and engage Cæsar's cavalry to advantage, the cohorts which first reached it turning and defending those which followed; but at every descent, where the pursuing horse was on higher ground, they were obliged to make a violent attack to drive it back a distance and enable them to retire at a run to the plain and beyond to the next high ground, where they could again place themselves on a fighting equality with it. These rearguard combats became so dangerous and unsettling to the enemy that they were finally driven to halt and camp on an eminence, having retired but four miles. Cæsar also camped (9) and sent out to forage. But the Pompeians had

only gone into camp as a ruse and had fortified nothing but
the front line.   Cæsar fell into the trap and allowed his
foragers to disperse.   The same day at noon, when they saw
Cæsar's horse was at a distance, the Pompeians endeavored to
escape; but Cæsar, on perceiving their withdrawal, leaving
a few cohorts to guard the camp and pack the baggage,
followed them sharply up with his legions in light marching
order, instructed the foragers to come in at four o'clock, and
the horse to follow as soon as may be.   On the return of the
troopers they made their way to the front, and again began
to harass the march of Afranius and Petreius.   Cæsar kept
on their heels, incessantly edging in on their left and forcing
them farther from the Sicoris, whose banks he patrolled with
his cavalry.   By skillful manœuvring he finally forced them
to camp at a distance from water, and in a highly disadvantageous place (10).   He had completed a good day's work.

   Cæsar did not attack them.   He ordered his men to lie on
their arms instead of camping, and waited for the still better
chance he could see approaching.   But he took measures to
confine the Pompeians to this place, as well as to protect his
own legions from sudden assault, by a wall and trench which
he extended about them on all sides.   In the course of a day
or two, having no fodder, Afranius and Petreius were obliged
to kill all their baggage cattle.   They perhaps contemplated
making a sudden push for freedom.   On the third day, July
1, at two P. M., they drew out their army in battle front to
interrupt the completion of Cæsar's works.   Cæsar did the
like, but awaited their attack.   Neither army seemed willing
to take the initiative.   Cæsar did not care to do so;   the
Pompeians dreaded the conflict.   They had lost *morale* since
the fight at Ilerda.   The camps, say the Commentaries, were
not distant from each other above two thousand feet, — a space
that gave small room for so many men to manœuvre or to

follow up a victory, for each army had five legions. Afranius' five legions were in two lines, and the auxiliary cohorts in a third line, in reserve. Cæsar had three lines in the following formation: "four cohorts out of each of the five legions formed the first line; three more from each legion followed them as reserves, and three others were behind those; the slingers and archers were stationed in the centre of the line, and the cavalry closed the flanks." The battle was not engaged; both parties at sunset retired to camp. The next day, while Cæsar was continuing the construction of his works, the Pompeians made a move as if to fray themselves a path and cross the Sicoris by a ford near by, — if perchance they might reach Ilerda. Cæsar headed them off with his cavalry, which he ordered to occupy all the fords and patrol the river banks on the other side.

Beset on all sides, having no fodder, water, wood or corn, seeing no chance of exit, and lacking resolution to cut their way out, Afranius and Petreius asked for a private conference on July 2. This Cæsar refused, but granted the Pompeians a public conference to be held in the presence of both armies. The latter took place. Afranius spoke humbly and asked for easy terms; Cæsar spoke in his usual persuasive manner, complimenting Afranius and Petreius and their legions for avoiding battle to save Roman life, though reproaching them for massacring his soldiers in their camp; paying a tribute to the high qualities of the troops and promising his good offices to all, but yet with a clear hint that the terms stated were his ultimatum. He knew full well when to be diplomatically generous. As a result of the meeting it was agreed that the legions of the enemy should be discharged from service and sent back to their homes, and that Afranius and Petreius should evacuate Spain and Gaul.

Cæsar might have obliged the legions to join his cause, and

he was anxious to have them do so. But he was too politic to use force. He accepted only voluntary enlistments. How many of these there were we do not know. He disbanded the legions and furnished corn to all. The Spanish troops were discharged at once, and the Romans were to be discharged at the river Varus on the confines of Italy. Whatever each man had lost, which was found in the possession of Cæsar's troops, was returned to him, the soldier having captured it being compensated at a just valuation. The Pompeian soldiers marched to the Varus in charge of four of Cæsar's legions, under Calenus, two in the van, two as rearguard, and there they were disbanded. The four escorting legions were subsequently ordered to join the Italian army against Pompey. Thus ended a series of blunders on the part of Afranius and Petreius, — by which Pompey not only lost Spain, but his oldest and best legions, — and a series of brilliant manœuvres on the part of Cæsar.

Cæsar retained the other two legions, giving command of them to Cassius, for the purpose of completing the conquest of Farther Spain.

The rapidity of these brilliant campaigns has scarce a parallel. Cæsar crossed the Rubicon December 17, B. C. 50, by the Julian calendar. In two months he victoriously traversed the length of the Italian peninsula, and Pompey, declining a battle, sailed from Brundisium for Epirus. Cæsar then moved his army to Massilia and Spain. On the 23d of May he reached Ilerda. After a manœuvring campaign of six weeks, Afranius and Petreius surrendered, July 2. In a period so short as scarcely to afford more time than was needed to make the marches through the countries named, he had reduced Italy and neutralized Pompey's forces in Spain.

Italy had succumbed so soon as Cæsar trod her soil. No

one had dared fight for her possession against the conqueror of Gaul. While Cæsar had turned to Spain, Pompey had lifted no hand against him. Cæsar had not counted on his good fortune in vain; but it was as fitting that fortune should attend so able and vigorous a conduct as that it should forsake the weakness and lack of enterprise of Pompey. In this instance, Cæsar had made good use of the smiles of Fortune; he had labored when she was willing to lend her aid ; he had avoided her displeasure on the rare occasions when her back was turned.

On the other hand, Pompey's inactivity lay at the root of the forfeiture by his lieutenants in Spain of their seven fine legions and the entire peninsula; and of this weakness and loss of moral courage Cæsar made the utmost use. Pompey's weakness was reflected upon his lieutenants. His lack of initiative was such that one can scarcely hold them to blame for not putting to good use Cæsar's really grave danger after the flood in Ilerda. Like master, like man.

Cæsar's complete accomplishment of his object by manœuvring instead of fighting is one of the best examples of its kind in antiquity. It stands alone as a sample of successful avoidance of battle.

The creation of a ford at the Sicoris has always been considered a noteworthy engineering feat. It certainly was bold and ingenious.

The Italian and Ilerda campaigns have few parallels except in other campaigns by Cæsar himself.

XXX.

MASSILIA, GADES, AFRICA. APRIL TO SEPTEMBER, 49 B. C.

THE siege of Massilia, begun by Cæsar, had been pushed by Trebonius while his chief was in Spain. The city resisted well, and the garrison made gallant sorties, but its fleet, despite reinforcements, was twice beaten by Cæsar's, and the siege works gradually compelled an inevitable surrender. After the Ilerda campaign Cæsar had subdued the rest of Spain as far as Gades, and had then returned to Massilia, where he received its surrender and spared it a sack; but heavy penalties were imposed. Pompey's original plan had been to advance on Cæsar in Gaul from both Italy and Spain; but Cæsar by his speed and ability had anticipated him, driven him out of Italy and captured Spain. Pompey was still engrossed in raising additional forces in Greece. Cæsar's luck for once failed him. He sent Curio to reduce Sicily and Africa. In Sicily Curio succeeded in restoring to Rome its usual and necessary grain traffic; in Africa he was defeated by the Pompeians and his army destroyed. This enabled the aristocrats to make their holding in Africa secure. Cæsar's means of reaching Greece were limited; Pompey controlled the sea. Pompey's land forces were likewise more than double Cæsar's. But the moral force was all on the side of Cæsar and his legions. He now prepared to attack his enemy in Greece.

WHILE Cæsar was settling matters in northern Spain, Trebonius, with his three legions, had been active in collecting material and building ships for besieging Massilia.

Massilia was founded 600 years B. C., by Phocean refugees, and had grown, owing to its unusual position and advantages, to great prosperity. It had spread Greek civilization in southern Gaul, and taught the barbarians agriculture, learning and art. It had numerous colonies, and an enormous commerce. The port of Massilia was naturally excellent; the town was built to the north of it on a point of land crowned by three hills. Two ravines, each of which ran down to the sea, separated the point from the mainland; the south of the harbor was covered with factories, arsenals and works; the eastern wall was at the edge of the ravines. It was solid, and boasted many towers. Several gates pierced it; the principal one, near the middle, opened on the Via Aurelia, the main road from Gaul to Spain. The town was

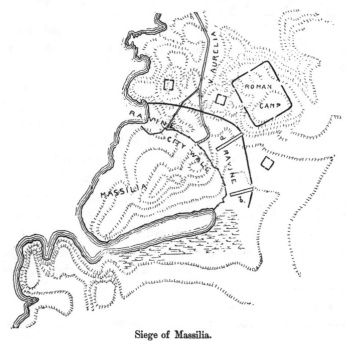

Siege of Massilia.

fortified by nature as well as by art, and was difficult of approach. The habits of the people were honest and simple, and their houses plain; but their public buildings and temples were noteworthy. Trebonius established his camp opposite the centre of the eastern wall, on modern St. Charles hill, which was somewhat higher than any of the city hills and looked down on the ravines which served as a ditch, — about one third of a mile from the city wall. As the Massilians commanded the sea, Trebonius could only invest the place by land. The point he chose for his main attack (a) was just south of the junction of the two ravines near the main gate. Deeming one insufficient, Trebonius opened a second point of attack (b), which was nearer the harbor, four hundred yards from the first one.

To reach the wall across the ravine at the main point of attack Trebonius had been forced to build a mound, which in one place was eighty feet high, and sixty feet wide everywhere. There was such abundance of war engines of great strength in the town that the ordinary material for making vineæ was useless. Some of these engines shot iron-tipped poles twelve feet long, which penetrated even four rows of hurdles and went into the ground some depth. The roofs of the vineæ had to be constructed of twelve-inch lumber, and in their front was a testudo sixty feet long, very stoutly made and covered against fire to protect the men who leveled the ground in front of the approaches. Under such cover alone could the men work with safety. The frequent sallies from the town were uniformly beaten back, but owing to these and the vastness of the works, progress was slow at both points.

Cæsar had remained at Massilia, superintending the opening of the siege up to about the 6th of May, when he found it necessary to go to Spain.

Late in the same month there took place the naval battle mentioned in the last chapter; and about a month after this event, L. Nasidius reached Tauroentum, near Massilia, with a fleet of sixteen brass-prowed galleys sent by Pompey. He had passed the straits of Sicily without the knowledge of Curio, Cæsar's legate there, had put into Messana and carried off a ship, and had made his way to the vicinity of Massilia. Here he got word to Domitius in the town,

advising him to risk another sea-fight against Brutus, in
which he, Nasidius, would join, and do his share. The
Massiliots had a large supply of seamen and pilots, — the
very best of their kind. They had covered some fishing

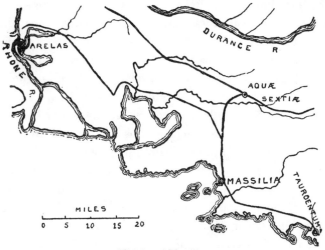

Vicinity of Massilia.

smacks with decks and arranged them to carry archers and
engines; had again repaired their war-galleys and built an
equal number of other ships. They at once acted on
Nasidius' suggestion, and sailed out to join him at one of the
forts named Taurois. "With a fleet thus appointed, encouraged by the entreaties and tears of all the old men, matrons,
and virgins to succor the state in this hour of distress, they
went on board with no less spirit and confidence than they
had fought before." The Massiliots were to have the right
of the line, Nasidius the left. It was the 30th of June.

Brutus, with courage always uppermost, was not loath to
meet them. He had the ships built by Cæsar at Arelas
(Arles) and six taken from the Massiliots. "Accordingly,
having encouraged his men to despise a vanquished people,

whom they had conquered when yet unbroken, he advanced against them full of confidence and spirit." Collected on the city walls, all the population of Massilia watched the boats which contained the flower of their youth and manhood; from Trebonius' high pitched camp, the Romans were equally intent. The combat was not lacking in spirit. The Massiliots fought with great courage. Brutus' line was the more open, which allowed better manœuvring on the part of the Massiliots. The ships came to close quarters and, grappling to each other, boarded and fought with desperation. Brutus' ship was all but run down in the mêlée, and escaped only by a hair's breadth. But Roman valor again prevailed. The ships of Nasidius, proved to be of little use despite his boasting, soon gave up the fight and fled; of the Massilian ships five were sunk and four captured, one sailed away with Nasidius, and but one got back to the town. Those which escaped made for Hither Spain. This happy victory shut the port and reduced Massilia to a condition of siege.

Taught by the frequent sallies from the main gate that their wooden siege works were insufficient, the Roman legionaries built, on the right side of their terrace, near the gate, a thirty-foot square tower of brick or slate, with walls five feet thick, instead of one of wood. Soon this grew in height to six stories. It had an overhanging roof, and this was gradually raised by screws so as to build the walls of the tower underneath it higher and higher. The outside was protected by heavy rope mats, hanging loose upon the walls. These Trebonius found best resisted the missiles. From this tower the Cæsarians built a musculus to the enemy's wall. This consisted of a roof sixty feet long but not very wide, and built of much heavier timbers than usual. It was covered with tiles laid in mortar, to save it from fire thrown down by the besieged; the tiles were covered with hides, to

protect them against water which the besieged poured down
in spouts to dissolve the mortar; and the whole was topped
by mattresses, to protect it against heavy stones and the iron-
tipped missiles. This musculus, when completed, was run on
rollers from the brick tower up to the city wall close to the
tower selected for breaching, and under cover of the musculus
the wall began to be undermined. The musculus resisted the

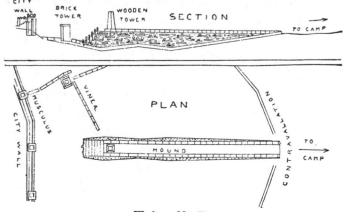

Works at Massilia.

heaviest stones; fire barrels rolled off it, and were then
pushed away by poles from within. From this tower the
soldiers kept up a fire of darts to protect the musculus. It
was intended to guard the flank of the terrace from sudden
sallies from the main gate. As matters eventuated, the
terrace never was completed.

It was not long before the wall of the city, undermined at
more than thirty places, began to topple, despite the fact that
the citizens had flooded the Roman mines by placing reservoirs of water where the mines would tap them; had counter-
mined and had resorted to every known method to arrest the
approaching crisis. Fearing then the capture and sack of
the city, the inhabitants crowded to the gates, and begged

the soldiers for a truce till the arrival of Cæsar, who, in fact, had ordered Trebonius not to suffer the storming of the city, lest the infuriated soldiers should, as they had threatened to do, put to the sword all the men, which out of policy he desired to avoid. It is evident from many such items, — and the Commentaries are full of them, — that Cæsar had not the best of control over his legionaries; and if he himself could not hold them in hand, his lieutenants could scarcely expect to do so. They were not the old burgess soldiers, who obeyed orders because they had, in their intelligent patriotism, the true instinct of discipline; they were professionals, of a far from high grade, who were held down only by the strong hand, and often with difficulty, who broke from restraint whenever a chance occurred. The truce begged by the Massiliots was granted, though the soldiers were hard to restrain from plunder and revenge.

The Massiliots proved treacherous. One day at noon, towards the end of July, when there was a high wind, — the mistral from the northwest, — and the legionaries were off their guard, the inhabitants sallied forth with incendiary utensils, and in an instant set all the works of the Romans on fire. A short hour consumed the labor of months. Next day again the towns-people made a sally, but the Romans were prepared for it, gave them due chastisement, and drove them back within the walls.

The soldiers then set to work, with renewed vigor, to make good the loss occasioned by the sally. The new agger was constructed with brick walls floored with timbers, which were shored up at intervals so as to sustain great weight. It was much less liable to be set on fire. In a few days the Cæsarians had replaced what had been destroyed, much to the amazement of the citizens, who saw their engines made ineffective by the solidity of the Roman works, their soldiers driven off the walls by the Romans from their equally high towers, and no safety in any course but surrender.

Time-serving Varro, in Farther Spain (Andalusia), had been wavering in his allegiance to Pompey until he heard rumors of Cæsar's troubles before Ilerda and at Massilia, when he began to act with more vigor for his chief. Whereas he had theretofore deemed it prudent to praise Cæsar, he now loudly denounced him. He was active in raising money,

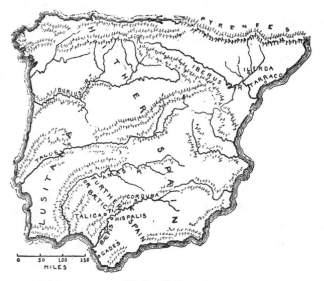

Farther Spain.

corn and troops, — some of the corn for Ilerda, some for Massilia, — and in preparing for war. He added thirty auxiliary cohorts to his force of two legions. As the whole province was somewhat pronounced for Cæsar, Varro proposed to carry on the war from Gades (Cadiz), which lay near the coast on an island, and, being a prosperous city with a fine harbor, was most suitable as a base. Here he had built ten ships, and here, too, he accumulated large materials and stores. He constructed a number of vessels in Hispalis, on the Bætis. He despoiled the temple of Hercules, carried the riches into the city of Gades, and sent six cohorts there to guard them under C. Gallonius. He laid heavy taxes on the states, and by representing that Cæsar was being defeated at Ilerda, got from the Roman citizens of the province eighteen millions of sestercii, twenty thousand pounds of silver and one hundred and twenty thousand bushels of wheat to be used in the war. He persecuted Cæsar's friends and confiscated much private property. He made himself many enemies and generally blustered about, instead of taking real steps to meet Cæsar, who was rapidly approaching, though with only two legions.

Cæsar, although, after the surrender of Afranius and Petreius, he felt called to Italy by the pressure of the war and public affairs, yet did not feel as if he ought to leave Spain without finishing its subjection. From Ilerda, therefore, about July 9, he sent Q. Cassius, the tribune of the people, with two legions against Varro, — the four others had gone to Italy under Calenus as a guard for the captured Pompeian legions,— and, rather than leave the Iberian question unsettled, preceded them himself. He relied on his knowledge of Pompey's character, believing that he would lie quiet till Spain was finally disposed of. Cæsar was lucky in his opponent. At the head of an escort of six hundred horse he marched to Bætica, and notified all the states to send embassies to meet him at Corduba early in August.

The response was unequivocal. Every town and state sent representatives to Corduba, and many towns turned out Varro's cohorts or shut their gates on them. Gades, when the citizens had heard of all that had happened, ejected Gallonius, Varro's lieutenant, and declared for Cæsar. When this news reached Varro's camp, even one of his Spanish legions mutinied in Cæsar's favor and marched to Hispalis. Varro withdrew to Italica, but this, too, declared against him, and he was reduced to surrender with his other legion. He gave up all the military stores, money collected and other booty. Cæsar thanked the towns and inhabitants for their fealty, conferred honors on the principal citizens, remitted the taxes Varro had raised, and returned property he had taken. Then about August 20 he visited Gades, where he restored the moneys taken from the temple of Hercules, and left Cassius in command with Varro's two legions, promising him two more of new levies. Thence he sailed with his two old legions, on the ships Varro had constructed, to Tarraco, where he arrived the end of the month, and was received with acclamations. Here, also, he conferred honors on those who had sustained his cause. From Tarraco he marched by land to Massilia, where he received word that, in accordance with his own proposition, he had been created dictator, under a new law, at the nomination of M. Lepidus. From henceforth he was legally acting for the Roman state.

Massilia had surrendered to Trebonius September 6, after a five months' siege, but Domitius managed to escape by sea, and, though pursued, could not be taken. The Massiliots, greatly against the wishes of the enraged soldiery, who desired to sack the town, were spared on account of their ancient reputation; but they were disarmed, their treasure and fleet taken, and a garrison of two legions left in the place. The rest of the troops proceeded to Italy. Cæsar himself set out for Rome.

Thus was finally thwarted Pompey's first general plan of advancing on Cæsar in his old province of Gaul, from Spain and Italy at once. Originally Pompey had intended to anticipate Cæsar in the offensive. When Cæsar's remarkable activity resulted in his losing Italy, Pompey had conceived the idea of operating offensively from Macedonia as a diversion to aid his lieutenants in Spain, never doubting that Cæsar would consume a year or more in his operations there. But Pompey was never rapid in preparation or action; in comparison with his present opponent he was procrastination itself. Before he had fairly begun the organization of his new levies in Macedonia, Cæsar had finished the Spanish campaign and had robbed him of an entire province and seven fine legions. Pompey had been permanently reduced to a defensive strategic rôle. He took the offensive tactically at Dyrrachium, but he never recovered his strategic initiative.

A misfortune now befell Cæsar's arms. His legate Curio, after regaining Sicily, had been sent from there into Africa early in July, to reclaim that land from Pompey's cause. Curio, a young but able officer, vigorous and enterprising, was unwise enough to underrate the army of Attius Varus, the Pompeian legate in Africa, and took with him but two out of his four legions and five hundred horse. The legions he selected were the ones which had belonged to Pompey, but had come over to Cæsar at Corfinium, and were not quite trustworthy. Curio crossed, landed and marched to Utica, where Varus lay. At the inception of his campaign he acted with good judgment, and in a pitched battle with Varus, near Utica, inflicted upon the latter a bitter defeat with loss of six hundred killed and one thousand wounded. The population was largely favorable to Cæsar, but shortly after the defeat of Varus, king Juba, who was friendly to Pompey and a personal enemy of Curio's, came to Varus' assistance with an overwhelming force.

Curio retired to the Cornelian camp (Scipio's old and excellent position of the Second Punic War), and should have remained there on the defensive until he had sent for his other legions; for he had supplies, water and timber at hand, and everything could come to him by sea. But being informed that the reinforcing army was only a small one, under command of Sabura, and not Juba's entire force, and elated with his recent successes, Curio was tempted out to risk another battle without sufficient reconnoitring. Otherwise intelligent, he was here lacking in discretion. He acted on partial information without testing its accuracy,

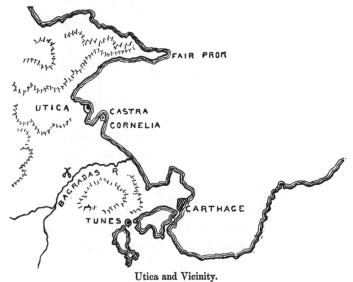

Utica and Vicinity.

and Rebilus, whom Cæsar had given him as "chief of staff," or adviser, did not hold him back. Sabura did, in fact, command Juba's vanguard, but Juba was not far behind with his whole army.

So soon as Curio put in an appearance, Sabura feigned retreat, but only to lure the Roman into disadvantageous ground where the king's force lay in wait to surround him. And this, indeed, took place. Curio followed up Sabura's retreat to a distance of over twenty miles from his camp, in full confidence of another easy victory. He reached the place in careless order, with tired troops and anticipating no danger, and fell heedlessly into Juba's ambuscade. The king debouched from cover on all hands and took him unawares. His entire army was destroyed. He himself refused to fly, and died in the midst of his men (July 24). The forces left in the Cornelian camp attempted to escape by sea, but, owing to fear and careless loading of the vessels, few got away. King Juba put most of them to the sword.

This disaster, traceable to Curio's errors of judgment and over-eagerness to fight, was a serious blow to Cæsar, and enabled the Pompeian party to gain enough ground in Africa to overawe the entire population of the continent. But Curio had previously taken possession of Sicily, and this had relieved the threatened scarcity of corn in Italy. Pompey's plan of starving out the peninsula was frustrated.

Mark Antony had been in command of the army of Italy, as proprætor. The ports of Sipus, Brundisium and Tarentum had been held by three legions to forestall a descent by Pompey's fleet. M. Crassus was in charge of Cisalpine Gaul. Two small fleets lay in the Tyrrhenian and Adriatic waters. Caius Antonius was in northern Illyricum, on the island of Curicta, with two legions. Dolabella, with forty galleys, was in the straits.

To Pompey's admirals the situation at Curicta afforded a good chance of action. Octavius and Scribonius Libo, with a much larger fleet, attacked Dolabella, defeated him, and cooped up Antonius on the island. Despite some reinforcements sent from Italy and the aid of the Tyrrhenian fleet, the superior numbers and skill of Pompey's vessels prevented any rescue. Antonius' legions had to be abandoned to their fate. The cohorts were finally captured, taken to Macedonia and incorporated with the Pompeian army. Octavius continued his efforts to reduce Illyricum. Issa joined his cause; but Cæsar's adherents held Lissus, and at Salonæ severely defeated Octavius, who retired to Dyrrachium.

Cæsar found no difficulty in causing himself to be elected consul the next year, B. C. 48. His associate was Publius Servilius. This gave him a power equal to that of dictator and one which sounded more satisfactorily in Roman ears. He resigned the dictatorship, and after eleven days spent in passing some essential laws, celebrating the Feriæ Latinæ and holding all the elections, began preparations to move on Pompey. Inasmuch as Pompey controlled the sea, Cæsar was compelled to look forward to crossing the Adriatic by ruse. Pompey, he knew, would not suppose that he was about to expose his army to the dangers of a winter passage, or to the difficulties of subsisting it in Epirus during this season. His opponent would believe him too busy with affairs of state, and especially the consulship, to leave Italy so soon. For these very reasons, Cæsar determined to steal a passage of the Adriatic in midwinter.

Cæsar had ordered to Brundisium all his cavalry, several thousand in number, and the twelve legions — nine old, three new — which he now had under the eagles. Of these, four had marched to the Varus under Calenus, escorting Pompey's disbanded legions; two had gone to Bætica under Cassius; three had besieged Massilia under Trebonius. Calenus' legions had become available in mid-August; those of Cassius towards the end of August; those of Trebonius a month later. All had successively been headed for Brundisium, but they had shown signs of discontent and had been marching slowly.

At Placentia occurred the mutiny of the Ninth legion, which Cæsar suppressed by sharp action added to his own personal influence. He ordered the legions decimated; but after a while commuted the punishment to beheading twelve of the ringleaders.

What Cæsar's army numbered, it is impossible to say. Two of the new legions no doubt had somewhere near the normal complement, which has been stated at some forty-eight hundred men. The ten old ones, however, had been much depleted, and while no mention is made of recruiting them up to normal standard, probably something of the kind had been done. If they averaged thirty-three hundred men, — as is not improbable, — Cæsar's forces, with light troops and cavalry, must still have been under fifty thousand men, all told.

Cæsar reached Brundisium the 17th of November. His means of transportation were very limited,— twelve galleys and about one hundred transports. Barely fifteen thousand men and five hundred horse out of his twelve legions and ten thousand cavalry could, according to the Commentaries, be embarked on what bottoms he had at command. Why this was so is not very clear. Nearly a year had elapsed since he ordered vessels to be built in the Italian, Sicilian and Gallic ports and collected at Brundisium; and Cæsar was wont to look well to the logistics of the future. Some of the ships had been destroyed in Illyricum, but this accounted for but a part of the proposed fleet. Hortensius and Dolabella had carried out their orders, and had built and brought together a goodly number of vessels; but the disaster at Curicta, and the necessity of protecting Sicily and Sardinia, had reduced the quota to this limit.

The size of the seven legions selected by Cæsar to be carried over to Epirus — the six old ones of Calenus and Cassius and one new one — must have been much smaller than the above given estimate. The authorities, as well as the Commentaries themselves, are contradictory on this point.

"Even these troops embarked very short of their number, because many had fallen in the wars in Gaul, and the long march from Spain had lessened their number very much, and a severe autumn in Apulia and the district about Brundisium, after the very wholesome countries of Spain and Gaul, had impaired the health of the whole army." The seven legions probably numbered twenty thousand men; and six hundred horse went along.

Pompey had spent a year in inactivity, so far as meeting Cæsar was concerned. But he had been industrious in gathering a fleet, "from Asia and the Cyclades, from Corcyra, Athens, Pontus, Bithynia, Syria, Cilicia, Phœnicia and Egypt, and had given directions that a great number should be built in every other place. He had exacted a large sum of money from Asia, Syria and all the kings, dynasts, tertarchs and free states of Achaia; and had obliged the corporations of these provinces, of which he himself had the government, to count down to him a large sum." He had reached Epirus from Italy with five partial legions; he now had nine full ones of Roman citizens from Italy or resident in the provinces; a veteran one from Cilicia (called Gemella, because consolidated out of two others); one from Crete and Macedonia, of veterans settled in that province after their discharge; two from Asia. "Besides, he had distributed among his legions a considerable number, by way of recruits, from Thessaly, Bœotia, Achaia and Epirus; with his legions he also intermixed the soldiers taken from Caius Antonius, at Curicta." He expected two more legions from Syria, making eleven in all. He had a large number of Greek and other auxiliary bowmen and slingers,—probably not less than six thousand, many of distinguished valor,—two thousand volunteers and seven thousand horse, all chosen men. These latter comprised Celts from the Alexandria garrison,

Thracians, Cappadocians, Galatians, Armenians, Numidians and mounted archers from Commagene. Some authorities figure Pompey's force as high as ninety thousand men; in fact, it was not more than fifty thousand strong. He had laid in a vast amount of corn from his various tributary provinces, and by holding Dyrrachium, Apollonia and other seaports, imagined that he could prevent Cæsar from crossing the Adriatic. His fleet was "stationed along the seacoast."

Whatever the actual force of each, Pompey certainly outnumbered Cæsar in land troops, while at sea he was far superior. The number of the vessels he had collected was five hundred, of which one hundred were Roman and the rest furnished by clients. Unwilling to trust M. Cato, he had placed this fleet under the orders of Marcus Bibulus, who with one hundred and ten large ships lay near Corcyra. Under him the younger Pompey commanded the Egyptian contingent; Dec. Lælius and C. Triarius the Asiatic; C. Cassius the Syrian; C. Marcellus and C. Coponius the Rhodian; Scribonius Libo and M. Octavius the Liburnian and Achaian. It would seem that this enormous fleet, used with any kind of energy, must have seriously interfered with Cæsar's campaigns in 49 B. C.; have all but starved out Italy, and in many ways have manœuvred to advantage. But barring the small operation on the Illyrian coast, it had practically accomplished nothing. Under Cato, it would have shown a better record.

At the outset Pompey had lacked nothing with which to carry on the war. All that Cæsar wanted Pompey had possessed. But the energy, never splendid to be sure, still such that in former days it had enabled him to triumph over all enemies,— such, says Plutarch, as to have made him conqueror of three continents,— was now on the wane. From youth up, Pompey had been used to a life of self-indulgence. At periods he had been capable of successful exertion, and aided largely by what others had done before him, and unexampled good fortune, had accomplished much; he had no inconsiderable native ability, and had in a measure earned the reputation he possessed. But for the past year he had seemed incapable of exertion. His moral force appeared to have shrunk into nothing before the superior energy and character of his wonderful opponent, and as he had refused to meet Cæsar in the cabinet, so now he seemed unwilling to face him in the field. In the case of each man the moral qualities stood in inverse ratio to the material.

Not that Pompey had been absolutely inactive. He had kept busy in drilling and disciplining his troops and in making his forces compact and pliable. Despite his fifty-eight years he had daily taken personal share in the work of organization, and had given his own countenance and example to his troops in their drill and manœuvring at the camp at Berœa, on the Haliacmon. But this was not war. It was not even preparation for war. While Pompey had been reviewing his legions, Cæsar had obtained complete control of Italy and had riven Spain from his dominions. Cæsar was working with a perfect army, instinct with a perfect purpose. Pompey was creating a perfect outward military body, but was doing nothing to breathe that soul into it, without which an army is but a well-drilled mob. Cæsar had a definite object and was working towards it by direct means. Pompey was taking his time, in the belief that when Cæsar finally confronted him, he would be able to demolish him by mere weight of mass. He imagined that in this civil war a simple defensive would enable him to win. This was a thoroughly false conception of the problem. He had as yet not dared to encounter Cæsar. He put off the fatal day. This of itself weakened him, as well as his troops and his adherents, more and more.

Cæsar on the contrary looked at the matter squarely. He no doubt felt, and he certainly so held out to the world, that he only drew the sword to right the wrongs of the Roman people. And in his course he made no pause, he asked no rest, but carried through his intelligently conceived plan with consummate skill and untiring energy. He had now secured his rear by the subjection of Spain; his base was Italy, with Gaul and Spain, and all their resources behind it, and he was ready to undertake an active offensive against the army under Pompey's personal command. He felt that he was superior to his opponent in all that makes war successful, except numbers, and Cæsar was not one of those who believed that the gods were on the side of the heaviest battalions. His faith in his own star was almost blind, and he was willing and anxious to risk his own smaller army in a contest with his bulky but inactive opponent.

Since the opening of the civil war, Pompey had made no offensive movement; Cæsar, on the contrary, had operated offensively against Spain, Sardinia, Sicily and Africa. In Spain he had been fully successful; Sardinia had been recovered; in Sicily Curio had succeeded to the extent of effecting a relief in the threatened famine in Italy; in Africa he had failed. Pompey had been checked in all his plans, save only in the success of his ally, Juba, in Africa, and the capture of Antonius' legions in Illyricum. So deliberate had he been in his preparations, that, despite the Spanish interlude, Cæsar was still able to take the offensive against him in Greece. These facts are a fair measure of the men.

XXXI.

EPIRUS. NOVEMBER, 49, TO FEBRUARY, 48 B. C.

CÆSAR had transports enough for but seven small legions and six hundred horse. He set sail, reached Epirus in safety, and landed at an uninhabited roadstead. He ran grave risk in thus moving against Pompey with so small a force. He would have done better to march with his entire army by way of Illyricum, his own province. On reaching Epirus, Cæsar renewed his offers of peace to Pompey, but was again refused. He then made a bold demonstration on Dyrrachium, but Pompey returned to this valuable port in season to save it. There was some manœuvring between the rival armies, but nothing definitive. Cæsar had brought over but half his army; the other half was still in Brundisium, watched by Pompey's fleet. Only after many weeks could Mark Antony venture to sea. When finally he reached the Epirotic coast he found himself on the north of Pompey's army, as Cæsar was on its south; but by clever marching on their side and want of energy on Pompey's the Cæsarians joined hands. Cæsar then made some detachments of troops to various provinces of Greece to secure corn and allies. By a bold manœuvre shortly after, he cut Pompey off from Dyrrachium, and though he could not capture the town, he established himself south and east of the city, between it and Pompey.

"WHEN Cæsar came to Brundisium he made a speech to the soldiers: 'That since they were now almost arrived at the termination of their toils and dangers, they should patiently submit to leave their slaves and baggage in Italy, and to embark without luggage, that a greater number of men might be put on board; that they might expect everything from victory and his liberality.' They cried out with one voice, 'he might give what orders he pleased, that they would cheerfully fulfill them.'" Cæsar's small force was largely veteran, tried in the campaigns of Gaul and Spain, hardened by work and accustomed to victory. They believed absolutely in their chief and blindly followed and obeyed him. Cæsar

could rely on them as on himself.   There had been some
symptoms of dissatisfaction in the legions, specially exemplified by the mutiny of the Ninth at Placentia, on its way to
Brundisium.   But Cæsar had put this down by his superior
moral weight.   So far as field work was concerned, the
legions left nothing to be desired.   Those which had lately
mutinied were anxious to rehabilitate themselves.

On the 28th of November, 49 B. C., Cæsar, after waiting
many days for a north wind, set sail with his seven legions
and six hundred horse, but without baggage, on some one
hundred transports convoyed by twelve galleys, only four of
which had decks.   After a lucky passage towards the southeast the army landed next day on the Epirotic coast north of
Corcyra, at a place known as Palæste (Paljassa), in an uninhabited roadway.   He had run considerable risk, but had
succeeded in avoiding an encounter with any part of Pompey's fleet.

Cæsar had no doubt carefully studied his chances of
encountering storms and enemy, and had deliberately taken
them.   But his thus risking his entire cause, by shipping half
his army to encounter Pompey's threefold forces on the
latter's territory, savors more of foolhardiness than the well-
pondered courage of the great captain.   It again suggests
itself, that to march his entire army through Illyria, and thus
base on his ancient province, was preferable to shipping half
of it by sea, with a base to create, the chance of capture of
his first convoy, and the serious question as to whether the
second would ever reach him.   Illyria had, to be sure, no
great resources; but Cæsar's line of communications would
have been free from danger.

Still Cæsar's venture succeeded, so far as the first convoy
went.   Such of Pompey's ships as were near at hand — one
hundred and ten at Corcyra, thirty-six at Oricum — had not

known of the sailing. They had kept to the eastern coast of the Adriatic and had not sought to discover Cæsar's movements. They imagined that he was wintering at Brundisium. There was not even a squad of men at any point along the coast, except in the harbors and towns. This argues as much carelessness on the part of Bibulus as Pompey had exhibited listlessness. But it was well in keeping with all which had so far been done, or failed to be done, by all the Pompeian generals. Pompey was confident that Cæsar would not seek to open the campaign before spring. When, therefore, his army had been collected, drilled and organized so as to be fit for service, he leisurely broke up his camp of instruction at Berœa and began to move his legions by the Via Egnatia to the Adriatic, where he proposed to put them in winter-quarters, in Dyrrachium, Apollonia and other coast towns, while Cæsar was still at Brundisium. He relied so absolutely on the strength of his numbers that, even if he expected it, which is doubtful, he seemed to care little whether or not Cæsar advanced against him. He imagined that a single overwhelming victory — which he never doubted he should win — would recover for him all the power, all the influence which for months he had been losing. As Cæsar alleges, his arrival was unexpected; no preparation had been made to receive him.

No sooner had he landed than Cæsar sent back his ships under Calenus for the rest of his legions. But though for greater security they sailed by night, his fortune no longer attended them; the vessels were delayed by adverse winds, and some thirty, which were driven back, were caught and barbarously burned by Bibulus, — who was watching at Corcyra, — with all the crews on board. The Pompeian admiral hoped "by the severity of the punishment to deter the rest." He also hoped thus to atone for his lack of care in permit-

ting Cæsar's fleet to pass him with half the army. Now
that Cæsar had effected a landing, it occurred to Bibulus that
he had better close the ports of Illyricum and Epirus and
watch the coast,— which he did, from Salonæ to Oricum.   It
had not been lack of courage on his part, but the fact that
no one expected Cæsar at this season; for now, "having
disposed his guard with great care, he lay on board himself
in the depth of winter, declining no fatigue or duty, and not
waiting for reinforcements, in hopes that he might come
within Cæsar's reach."

Pompey had posted his fleet on the coast of Epirus as a
curtain behind which to organize and assemble his army.
The latter had been strung out from the Haliacmon to Thessalonica, with two legions still in Syria, recently raised by
Metellus Scipio.   To his headquarters not only came his
levies, but his friends and his defeated generals,— Domitius
from Massilia, Cato from Sicily, numberless refugees from
Rome, men of means and standing.   A senate of two hundred members began its sessions at Thessalonica.   All this
by no means strengthened Pompey's army.   Unlike Alexander, he could not control a court and camp in one body.
Nor did his presence near Pella, the ancient capital of Macedon, infuse into his conduct aught of the glowing energy of
Philip or his splendid son.

Having reached Epirus, where he must absolutely and at
once either make terms with Pompey or fight him, Cæsar
again sent proposals to his opponent to treat for peace and
a disbandment of all forces, agreeing to leave the questions
between them to the decision of the Senate and people.   He
certainly showed every appearance of honestly desiring an
accommodation; and as, indeed, the chances were by no
means in his favor, he may have been sincere.   The bearer
of these proposals was Pompey's legate, Vibullius Rufus,

whom Cæsar had captured, for the second time, in Spain, and had freely forgiven. Vibullius found Pompey in distant Macedonia and gave him the proposals, which, however, met

Epirus and Macedonia.

with the same fate as previous ones. Pompey had but just received the first news of Cæsar's landing. Already on the march, so soon as he heard of Cæsar's advance, he hurried to the coast towards Apollonia. He had until now been so slow that Cæsar, despite the Spanish campaign and the siege of Massilia, could still take the offensive. Startled out of his security, not only by Cæsar's landing but by his activity, Pompey now conceived the fear that Cæsar might get possession of the whole seaboard, and was spurred on to unusual exertions.

Cæsar had, the same day he landed, November 29, marched over the difficult mountain paths from Palæste, on Oricum, which, after some show of resistance by Pompey's lieutenant, L. Torquatus, the citizens surrendered to him; following which the garrison did the like with the citadel. The fleet there stationed escaped to Corcyra. Thence, notwithstanding the fatigues of the previous night's march, Cæsar pushed on to Apollonia, a rich town on a branch of the Via Egnatia, leaving his new legion under Acilius and Marcus in Oricum. He reached Apollonia next day. Straberius, the governor, tried to hold the place for Pompey, watching the citadel and striving to control the citizens. But Apollonia likewise gave Cæsar admittance, refusing to do otherwise than as the Roman people and Senate had done in electing Cæsar consul. Straberius fled. Cæsar headed, December 2, for Dyrrachium. Many distant and more neighboring states and towns, among them Bullis, Amantia and substantially all Epirus, followed suit.

Pompey, meanwhile, thoroughly frightened at the unexpected turn given to matters by Cæsar's arrival, forged ahead by stout marching, day and night, for Apollonia and Dyrrachium. His speed tired, as his evident nervousness demoralized, his men. They were not campaign - seasoned, like the Gallic veterans; they had received but the superficial training of the drill-ground. It is said that the fear of Cæsar was such in Pompey's army that many Epirotic soldiers threw down their arms and deserted so soon as they learned of his arrival. So strong was this sentiment that Labienus, Cæsar's old lieutenant and now Pompey's right-hand man, was obliged, when they reached Dyrrachium, December 3, to subject the men to a new oath not to desert Pompey whatever might happen.

Though Pompey hastened his march with the utmost endeavor, he barely reached Dyrrachium in time to save it from capture. His head of column just anticipated Cæsar, who was already on the road towards this to him essential city. Pompey went into an intrenched camp south of Dyrrachium, and, learning that his opponent had secured possession of the town, Cæsar, no doubt disappointed, but scarcely expecting uninterrupted success, and in any event too weak to attack his adversary, moved backward and camped in the territory of Apollonia, on the south side of the river Apsus. Pompey, so soon as his army had recovered its tone, thinking to defend the line of this river and thus hold the Dyrrachium territory intact, shortly came and camped opposite Cæsar and began to call in all his troops to this place. He made his cohorts comfortable, intending, if necessary, to winter here. Each army thus lay somewhat back from the river, facing the other across the Apsus. Cæsar was waiting for his other legions. He protected by his position his new allies in the country south of where he lay. He was midway between the two harbors of Dyrrachium and Oricum, where alone Pompey's fleet, his chief danger, could find suitable anchorage.

Pompey had won the rank of a great soldier without the herculean labors usually incident thereto; and at this period, age or luxury had robbed him of whatever moral energy he had once boasted. He had never possessed the mental activity of Napoleon, but like the latter at Waterloo he had lost his old-time bodily activity. Nothing demonstrates the weakness of his present condition more than the fact that he remained in this position in front of Cæsar two whole months, vastly Cæsar's superior in numbers, and without taking any step to attack him. A bold offensive at this moment might well have been fatal to Cæsar. He had but half Pompey's forces. The rest were still at Brundisium, and might indefinitely be kept there by weather and Pompey's fleet; for the latter was well equipped and by good management ought to control the Adriatic. Now was the time, if ever, for Pompey to crush his adversary. A lucky circumstance might any day enable Calenus to bring over Cæsar's other legions. Nor were opportunities wanting. Holding as he did the entire coast, Pompey by a simple forward movement of his right, with reasonable precautions, could scarcely have failed to force Cæsar into the interior of Epirus, thus dividing his forces beyond a chance of junction, and putting his enemy, if it could be done at all, at his mercy. Moreover, Cæsar was placed where victualing his army was already a serious task and might be made all but impossible. For he had no fleet.

Calenus, in the port of Brundisium, having been joined by the Massilia legions, had already put the cohorts and cavalry on board the vessels which had returned from Epirus and had actually set sail, when he received notice from Cæsar to exercise the greatest caution, as Bibulus commanded the entire coast and was awake to everything that went on. Thus admonished, Calenus recalled the fleet and disembarked, rather than run the risk of capture. It was as well that he did. Bibulus had left Corcyra and come to Oricum, keenly on the watch for him, and seizing one ship which, on starting, had strayed from the rest and been driven out to sea, put the entire crew to death.

In this position in the roadway at Oricum, while Bibulus

kept Cæsar from the sea, so likewise Cæsar's lieutenants kept Bibulus from the land, and cut him off from wood and water, reducing him to great straits. All his supplies and even water had to be brought from Corcyra. On one occasion his men were reduced to the dew which they could collect on wool-hides laid upon the decks. Though Bibulus' men bore their deprivations with fortitude, these hardships were the occasion of a stratagem, taking the form of a request by Bibulus for a truce and conference with Cæsar. Cæsar had gone with a legion to Buthrotum, opposite Corcyra, to forage and gain allies. But he personally returned on hearing from Acilius and Marcus that Bibulus had asked for a truce. The conference was granted, as Cæsar had always been anxious to come to terms with Pompey, but the truce was refused. Cæsar saw through the ruse,— that the Pompeian admiral only sought to revictual and water his vessels. Bibulus did not come to the conference, but sent Libo in his stead. This officer, however, offered to bear Cæsar's message to Pompey, and renewed the request for a truce meanwhile. This Cæsar naturally declined, as he saw that he was harassing the fleet more than the fleet was annoying him, and could not afford to give it the opportunity it was seeking.

About this time Bibulus died from the exposures of a command he would not desert, and the several fleets were permitted by Pompey to remain under their respective commanders without any one head. This was fortunate for Cæsar, as Pompey's naval management thus lacked unity of action, which was worse than even a half-competent leader.

Cæsar's latest messages to Pompey evoked, it is said, no other reply than that "even life or Rome were not worth holding by the grace of Cæsar." Still he persevered in efforts to bring about a conference. The Apsus — which is a narrow river — alone lay between the camps. There was a general understanding among the soldiers that no darts should be hurled across, or arrows shot, whenever either party approached the banks, and they freely conversed at frequent intervals, assembling in groups on the river shore. This suspension of hostilities was similar to what occurred on the Peninsula, at Petersburg, and other places during our civil war. It is not an unusual species of truce, which has always obtained between armies in immediate contact, especially if speaking the same language. To this meeting-place Cæsar, who was still sincerely anxious for a personal interview, and who no doubt felt his superiority over Pompey in council as well as in war, sent P. Vatinius to solicit, by a publicly proclaimed request, "the right — granted even to fugitives from justice and to robbers — for Roman citizens to send deputies to Roman citizens to treat for peace." Thus a conference was arranged between Vatinius and Aulus Varro; but when this was being held, and Labienus, who was present, was conversing with Vatinius, it was interrupted by a shower of darts from the Pompeian side, by which many, including three centurions, were wounded. Labienus is said to have exclaimed, "There can be no thought of peace unless we carry back with us Cæsar's head!" — apparently seeing in the temper of some of the troops the impossibility of a settlement. Thus again were Cæsar's pacific intentions defeated and the heated feelings of Pompey's chief adherents demonstrated. These are the statements of the Commentaries. There is no special reason for doubting them, and they are lent color by other authorities. Cæsar was always careful to keep the appearance of right and reason on his side, and even if he did not desire the peace he asked, he would have been likely, knowing that Pompey would decline all his advances, to continue to make them.

Libo, after Bibulus' death, sailed over from Oricum to Brundisium about the middle of January, and blockaded that port, which was the only exit to sea for Cæsar's forces still in Italy. He occupied the small island at its mouth. Arriving suddenly, he caught and fired some of Cæsar's transports and carried off one laden with corn. Landing, he drove in a party of Antony's men; whereupon he boastingly wrote that Pompey might haul up for repairs the rest of his fleet, for he could with his own force, unaided, keep Cæsar's reinforcements from joining him.

Antony was at the time in the town. To oppose Libo, he patrolled the shores and prevented his watering. And in order to come to a combat with him, which he could not well do at sea, he covered with pent-houses a number of the long boats belonging to war-galleys, armed them with veterans, and hid them along the harbor shores. Then sending two three-banked galleys out to the mouth of the port to manœuvre, he induced Libo to put five four-banked galleys out to intercept them. Antony's galleys retired within the harbor, as if flying, and induced Libo's to follow. So soon as they came within the harbor, the long boats advanced, inclosed the galleys of the enemy, attacked them, captured one and drove the others away. Libo, seeing that he was unable to accomplish anything by lying off the place, and starved for water, which Antony prevented his getting by stationing cavalry posts along the coast, finally gave over the blockade.

Cæsar was becoming anxious about his other legions. He had waited nearly three months for them, winter was coming to an end, and he felt that he must run some risk in order to get them. He was, in fact, almost without news of their condition and that of Italy; for he had few ships he could use as couriers. He wrote to his lieutenants at Brundisium that the troops must be sent at all hazards by the first fair wind, even if some vessels were lost. "I need soldiers, not vessels," he wrote. Indeed, he attempted himself to go across on a small twelve-oared boat. It was on this occasion that he is said to have exclaimed to the boatman, who feared to put to sea owing to high running water, "What dreadest thou? Thou carriest Cæsar and his fortunes !" But he was unable, for all that, to cross. The voyage was too dangerous, beset by the perils of the sea and the enemy alike.

Antony, Calenus, and especially the rank and file, were all as fretful to join their chief as Cæsar was to have them do so. The old soldiers could hardly be held in hand, so anxious were they to be beside their general. On the blowing of the first south wind, — February 15, — they weighed anchor and set sail at nightfall. They were carried past Apollonia and Dyrrachium, were seen by the enemy, and, being caught in a lull of wind, were chased by his fleet, under Q. Coponius, who emerged from the latter place. Just as these war-vessels had all but reached Cæsar's transports, the south wind again sprang up and enabled them to make Nymphæum, above Lissus. This port, with the sailing vessels of that day, could be entered by a south but not a southwest wind, and after Antony's transports had made the roadway, Cæsar's luck came in, the wind veered to southwest and not only prevented the enemy from entering, but drove a part of their fleet upon the rocks and lost them sixteen out of twenty ships and many men. Cæsar liberated those who were captured. Only one of Cæsar's vessels was taken by the enemy, and though the crew of two hundred and twenty recruits, unsuspicious of the enemy's treachery, surrendered on promise of being spared, they were every one put to death. One other ship went ashore, but the veteran legionaries aboard of her declined terms and happily made their way to shore and joined the army.

On landing, the near-by town of Lissus, which Cæsar had fortified while Illyria was one of his provinces, received Antony and his men and gave them all assistance. Otacilius, Pompey's lieutenant, took to flight. From here Antony notified Cæsar of his safe arrival by native couriers. He had brought the three veteran Massilia legions and one new one, the Twenty-seventh, about eight hundred horse, and some convalescents belonging to the legions already in Epirus, — something under twenty thousand men. The ships were sent back to Italy for the rest of Cæsar's army, save thirty transports, kept on the chance of their being needed.

Cæsar and Pompey received the news of Antony's landing about the same time, — perhaps February 18. The ships had been sighted from both Apollonia and Dyrrachium, but had then been lost to view. The immediate duty of each leader was clear. Cæsar instantly but openly broke camp February 19, and set out to join Antony, who was at least four days' march away; Pompey had secretly marched the night before, via Dyrrachium, on Tirana, to cut him off from moving towards Cæsar and if possible fall on him from ambush. Pompey had the easier task. He could hold the line of the Apsus against Cæsar, as well as move directly upon the newcomers. Cæsar was obliged to go some distance up the Apsus to find a ford and perhaps to force a crossing.

Pompey was not rapid in his march, but nevertheless reached the vicinity of Antony one day the sooner, — February 21, — and camped in ambush near the road to which Antony was limited in marching toward Cæsar, hoping to catch him unawares. He camped without fires and kept his men close in hiding. News of this proceeding luckily reached Antony through friendly Greeks. He remained in camp, where he was entirely safe, and sent word of his whereabouts to Cæsar. This chief, meanwhile, had passed the Apsus, twenty miles above his camp, reached Scampa, and on the 22d was reconnoitring to ascertain his lieutenant's location. Here he was found by Antony's messengers. On

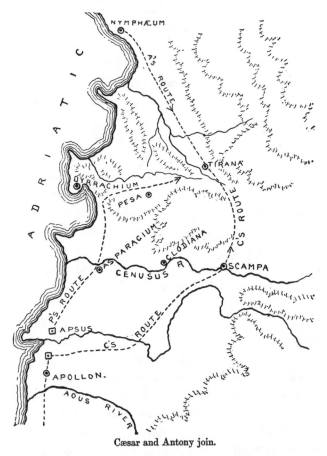

Cæsar and Antony join.

the 23d he crossed the mountains and marched on Tirana. Pompey had no idea of being caught between the two armies, and decamped, lest he should be forced into immediate battle. That Pompey should have allowed this junction to be made is as much a reproach to him as a credit to Cæsar. But it was of a part with his phlegmatic character. The ability or rather the nerve of the two men is well shown in this, as in other minor operations. Pompey's every step was marked by hesitating, not to say timorous, conduct; Cæsar's every step by good fortune, to be sure, but good fortune well utilized. All the luck in the world could not have helped Pompey accomplish his ends when he would not put his hand to the work to be done, under even the most favorable conditions.

Up to this moment, Pompey had been acting on a misconception of what was the proper plan of campaign. He had deemed it wise to seek to confine Cæsar to a given territory by his largely superior cavalry, and thus starve him out, — a very questionable possibility; whereas when he had outnumbered him three to one, his manifest duty was to attack him. If Pompey had hitherto avoided battle, now that Cæsar had been reinforced, he had a double reason for so doing. Though it is clear that Pompey showed distinct lack of enterprise during this period of his great superiority, his plan of starving out Cæsar may have been a good one after the latter's junction with Antony.

During this time, Scipio, Pompey's lieutenant in Syria, had, on Cæsar's crossing to Epirus, been ordered by Pompey to return to Macedonia and join him there. He apparently did not feel strong enough to cope with Cæsar single-handed, however much he might outnumber him.

Cæsar held his army well in hand. He had joined Antony and had drawn in most of his garrisons. He had a total of thirty-five thousand men, and circumstances, if not forces, were in his favor. He was entirely ready to come to a decisive struggle with Pompey. Thessaly and Ætolia had sent ambassadors to him, agreeing to support his cause if he would send them troops. Though he could ill afford to make details from his meagre force, Cæsar answered these appeals by dispatching a young legion, the Twenty-seventh, and two hundred horse to Thessaly, under L. Cassius Longinus,' and five cohorts from Oricum and some cavalry into Ætolia, under C. Calvisius Sabinus. Each of these lieutenants had instructions, in addition to protecting and gaining the friendly coöperation of the several provinces, to adopt measures to provide Cæsar with corn. Into Macedonia by the Egnatian highway he sent the Eleventh and Twelfth legions and five hundred horse, under Domitius Calvinus, to head off the corps of Scipio, which would soon approach from Thessalonica.

When these detachments were all made, Cæsar had but seven legions, — the Sixth, Seventh, Eighth, Ninth, Tenth, Thirteenth and Fourteenth, — say twenty-two thousand men, but his situation was vastly improved. He undertook to try conclusions with Pompey and determined to hold him on the seacoast near Dyrrachium, and thus cut him off from Greece. It was Cæsar, though far weaker, who began to force the fighting. He saw through Pompey's intentions, and, like a bold player, met his adversary, though with but half his strength, on his own ground.

Calvisius was well received in Ætolia, "dislodged the enemy from Calydon and Naupactus, and made himself master of the whole country." Cassius found two factions in Thessaly, — Hegasaretus in power and favoring Pompey, Petreius favoring Cæsar. This made his work more difficult.

While Domitius was marching on Macedonia from the west, Scipio was moving on the same province from the east. When the latter came within twenty miles of Domitius' army, instead of manœuvring against it he suddenly filed off southerly towards Longinus in Thessaly, hoping to catch this general napping, and to interfere with his reduction of the country. In order to do this the better, he started in light marching order, having left his baggage with eight cohorts, under M. Favonius, south of the Haliacmon, ordering him to strongly fortify himself there. He sent Cotus' cavalry ahead, to fall on Longinus' camp.

Longinus, whose force was fresh and weak, at once retired towards the foothills, intending to cross to Ambracia, and was vigorously followed up by Scipio's cavalry. Domitius, however, was expert enough to make an immediate demonstration against Favonius. The rumor of this danger obliged Scipio to return to his lieutenant and baggage-camp, which he only reached in season to head off Domitius, whose van was already in sight. "The dust raised by Domitius' army and Scipio's advance-guard were observed at the same instant." Domitius was still north of the river. Scipio shortly crossed by a ford above him and camped.

There was a plain six miles wide between the camps. Scipio drew up in front of his camp. Domitius advanced towards him and invited battle. After some skirmishing and an advance and show of battle, Scipio, though he had crossed the Haliacmon to close with his enemy, concluded it to be best to decline the engagement with Domitius' legions, which were very eager for the fray, and to retire across the river to his first camp. In two cavalry combats which supervened in their mutual reconnoitring, Scipio was worsted. Each officer endeavored to lure the other into some stratagem, but neither succeeded. Domitius apparently had the best of the interchanges. Both remained *in situ.*

Cæsar, wishing to concentrate, left but three cohorts at Oricum, under Acilius, to protect the shipping which was in the bay, and drew in the rest of his garrisons to the main army. Acilius blocked up the harbor by sinking a merchantman in the mouth and anchoring a war-vessel near by. But he was not fortunate. Pompey's son, Cnæus, whom we shall later meet in Spain, and who commanded the Egyptian contingent, anxious to distinguish himself, sailed for the place, captured the man-of-war, raised the sunken 'ship, and made his way into the harbor. Here he burned the main part of Cæsar's fleet, and leaving Decimus Lælius to blockade the port and hinder the entering of corn, he sailed to Nymphæum and up the river to Lissus, where he also burned the thirty transports Antony had kept there. These losses were highly disadvantageous to Cæsar, for they took all the vessels he had on the east of the Adriatic. ' In landing at Lissus, young Pompey had, however, less fortune, being foiled in his effort to capture the place. But it would appear that Cnæus possessed the spirit of enterprise, which at this time seemed to have deserted his father.

After the failure of his ambuscade at Tirana, Pompey had retired on Dyrrachium. In pursuance of his plan of avoiding armed conflict, he then determined to defend the line of the Genusus, just south of Dyrrachium, and moved to Asparagium, a town whose location is variously stated, but which, to accord with the operations detailed in the Commentaries, must have lain some ten miles up from the mouth of that river and on the south bank. After joining Antony, Cæsar had returned to Scampa, had conducted a raid up the Genusus, for the sake of capturing the capital of the Parthenians (a place which cannot be identified at this day) with its Pompeian garrison, and had then followed Pompey to Asparagium. In three days' march he reached a position opposite Pompey and camped. Next day he moved out of camp, drew up in order and offered battle. Pompey declined to accept Cæsar's challenge, emerging, to be sure, from camp, but remaining on his heights, where he could not be attacked without much danger.

Cæsar, never at a loss for a plan, and determined to leave

Pompey no rest, conceived and executed one of those bold
operations which show the head and hand of the master. He
determined to cut Pompey off from Dyrrachium. By a long
and secret circuit over a rugged road, he set out, March 3,
to move about Pompey's flank straight on his base of supplies. His route lay over a difficult wooded country, probably with but the barest roads, up the Genusus to Clodiana
(modern Pelium), and across the mountains which separated
the Genusus from the modern Arzen, whose mouth is north
of Dyrrachium, thence down the latter river. From river

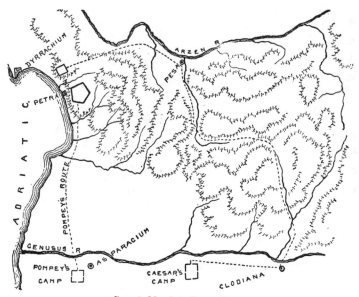

Cæsar's March to Dyrrachium.

to river he must ascend and descend the affluents of either,
by a circuit of some forty-five miles, which distance, with
the route so badly cut up, could not be made at a greater rate
than two miles an hour, if that. At the same time, speed
was imperative. Success depended on Cæsar's keeping
Pompey in ignorance of his intentions during a whole day,

and on his making the march in not much over twenty-four
hours; for Pompey's road to Dyrrachium was straight and
easy and less than twenty-five miles long.

Pompey had no idea that Cæsar was heading for his communications; he thought he was moving camp for lack of
corn. When, by his cavalry scouts reporting Cæsar's direction, he awoke to the fact, though he was on a shorter line,
which he at once took, it was too late. Cæsar, by vigorous
efforts and by stopping but for a short rest at night, reached

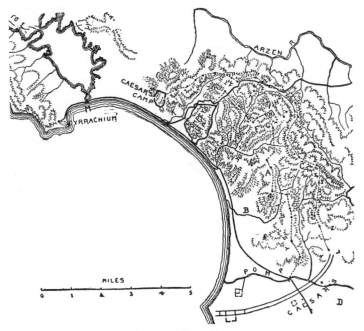

Theatre of Dyrrachium.

the Arzen, followed it down to where it turns northwesterly
along the coast, and thence pushing rapidly towards the seashore, seized the adjoining heights, "when the van of Pompey's army was visible at a distance," and shut Pompey off
from approach to Dyrrachium, where the latter had stored

all his war material and much provision. Cæsar camped north of the Arzen, on slightly rolling ground. He had conducted an operation of remarkable boldness and brilliancy.

Cut off from Dyrrachium, though his garrison still held the place, Pompey, much aggrieved, camped and intrenched on rising ground at Petra, south of the Arzen, where was a harbor for small ships, by the use of which he could still victual at Dyrrachium.

The bay of Dyrrachium describes a bow whose chord runs northwest and southeast. As you approach the coast from the sea you have a perfect *coup d'œil* of the entire theatre; but the details you must study on the ground. Back of this bow, in an irregular semicircle, runs the watershed of the streams which feed the Arzen or descend to the sea. This bow is threefold. The outer curve is of lofty hills, which make a rugged frame for the scene of the coming operations; the next inner one consists of irregular chalk-hills, rough and difficult; the inmost curve is one of rolling upland, well covered by verdure and occasional bunches of trees. The entire country is more or less accentuated. The population of Epirus to-day is smaller than in Cæsar's time. This terrain was probably much then as now. The bolder hills of this watershed, from three hundred to twelve hundred feet in height, advance to the sea about the centre of the bow, and form a defile of over one third of a mile in length between the water and the cliffs, which latter are in places almost erect, but are wooded at the summits. At the south of the bow the hills slope down into the plain of modern Cavaia. The ground contained within the bow of the watershed is cut up, rocky, full of ravines and gorges at the back; wooded in parts and with a fair show of cultivation in the centre; rolling and fertile near the sea, with a long, wide beach.

Dyrrachium lies on a point of land at the northwest end

of the bow, confined by lagunes to a long triangular stretch of ground, bold and rocky at the seashore on the west. It can be besieged only by sea, for a force attempting to besiege it by land could itself be shut into the triangular foreland by fortifying the narrow land approaches at either end of the lagunes.

Now all the more confirmed in his plan of starving Cæsar in Epirus, and not of fighting him, Pompey ordered to Petra new provisions from Asia and other tributary countries. To get these was comparatively easy, as Pompey had plenty of ships. Cæsar, on the contrary, experienced difficulty in providing corn for a protracted campaign, for Illyricum was not a grain-bearing country, Epirus had little beyond its scant needs, and Pompey had already used up all there was on hand by foraging or devastation. Nor could Cæsar get any supplies from Italy, for Pompey ruled the sea.

In view of all these factors in his problem, it may be said that Pompey was not entirely short-sighted in his present method of gauging the probabilities of the war. It is only in contrasting his slowness and lack of initiative to the restless energy of Cæsar, that we feel like denying him his cognomen of Great. Still, the Fabian generals of the world are not without their justly earned laurels; nor must we underrate the ability of Pompey. But even if we esteem his present plan of starving out Cæsar to be a proper one, it is by no means to be admitted that Pompey was otherwise than lax in not forcing a decisive battle on Cæsar when the latter lay opposite him with but a third his force.

XXXII.

DYRRACHIUM. MARCH TO MAY, 48 B. C.

Cæsar lay between Pompey and Dyrrachium; but Pompey could reach the town from his camp by sea. Cæsar began to inclose Pompey in siege lines, — a hazardous task, as he was much the weaker. Pompey seized many hills around his camp to inclose as much ground as possible. Many skirmishes resulted. Pompey could victual plentifully from the sea; Cæsar had difficulty in gathering corn from the poor country in his rear. But he had good water and better forage for his animals, while able to cut off much of Pompey's water-supply by diverting streams which ran through his lines to the sea. In the fighting during the erection of the siege works, neither side won any marked advantage. Cæsar's veterans rather surprise us by not proving superior to Pompey's newer cohorts. During an absence of Cæsar's, Pompey attacked his lines, but after a long and heavy struggle the Cæsarians won a decided advantage. Cæsar's left reached the sea, but it was not strong.

IF Pompey lacked boldness in his conception and execution, Cæsar may be said to have been overbold. No sooner had he succeeded in thus cutting Pompey off from Dyrrachium than he undertook measures for blockading him in the position he had taken up. About Pompey's camp lay the threefold chain of hills already described; but his outlying parties had occupied no part of the watershed proper. As many of the hills of the outer curve as were available, Cæsar took, and on them built redoubts, — twenty-six in all were eventually constructed, — and these he began to join by a chain of earthworks more or less elaborate, according as the nature of the ground dictated. In inaccessible places this work was easy; in places less well defended by nature, art was called into play. Each end of the line was intended to lean on the seacoast; the north end at his camp east of

Dyrrachium; the south end at any place he could, in the course of the operations, most conveniently reach. Pompey at once perceived Cæsar's intention, but instead of resorting to active measures, he adopted the policy of one already besieged and endeavored to crowd Cæsar outward as much as practicable; and as Pompey still sought to avoid a general engagement, Cæsar was able to establish a fairly good line; not one, however, which prevented Pompey from holding, on the surrounding hills, an all but as good interior line.

Cæsar's object in this proceeding was to prevent Pompey, who was strong in cavalry, from cutting out his convoys of corn from Epirus or from devastating the country, for he needed the corn himself; and he desired to reduce Pompey's horse by want of forage. Again, he felt sure he should gain in reputation and Pompey correspondingly lose, if he hemmed him in, and thus showed that Pompey had not the vim to fight him.

Cæsar had for some time prescribed to his legions a set order of battle or encampment; and they now took up position accordingly. The Tenth, Thirteenth and Fourteenth legions formed the right wing; the Sixth and Seventh, the centre; the Eighth and Ninth, the left wing.

The line thus traced by Cæsar was nearly sixteen miles long, a vast stretch for twenty-two thousand men to defend. Pompey was anxious enough to regain Dyrrachium, for all his material was there; but he could not bring himself to hazard the battle which was necessary to arrest the completion of Cæsar's works. He likewise seized on as many hills as he could, and fortified them in such a way as to oblige Cæsar to divide his forces. He thus managed, by his own inner lines facing Cæsar's, to inclose a space of about fourteen miles in circuit, in which he was able to get quite an amount of forage for his cavalry. This inclosed line he for-

Dyrrachium Theatre of Operations.

tified by twenty-four redoubts and a line of ramparts. Pompey first completed his works, having a greater force and somewhat less extent to fortify. He made no organized sallies, but used his slingers and archers, of whom he had an efficient body, in a very harassing manner; and the Roman soldiers made themselves "coats or coverings of haircloth, tarpaulins and rawhide" to resist the darts. "In seizing the posts, each exerted his utmost power: Cæsar, to confine Pompey within as narrow a compass as possible; Pompey, to occupy as many hills as he could in as large a circuit as possible." Pompey had inclosed something like sixteen square miles; Cæsar twenty. It was on the terrain thus inclosed that there were constructed the most remarkable fortifications in antiquity.

It is not to be supposed that Pompey exhibited want of skill. On the contrary, whenever he put his hand to the work he showed it at every turn. With an ordinary opponent, with even an able one, he might have proved himself the general of old, who had conquered half the world. But Cæsar's matchless energy and skill overrode all his efforts; Pompey's *morale* was so much less than Cæsar's that he could not show to advantage. Pompey and Cæsar had long known each other, and though he had for many years held the stronger hand, Pompey no doubt recognized his superior, and was cautious accordingly. He simply remained inert.

Pompey's situation was markedly better than Cæsar's. He outnumbered him to a dangerous degree. He had much more cavalry. His ships brought him corn and material with ease and regularity from Dyrrachium and elsewhere. His position was central, each flank and all points being easily approached from the others by radial lines. And yet Pompey dared not make a determined attack upon his foe, even while the intrenchments were but half done.

During the erection of Cæsar's line of contravallation, skirmishing was constant. The Ninth legion occupied the then left of the works which Cæsar was gradually stretching out towards the sea. On one occasion when it had been ordered to take a certain hill that Cæsar desired to inclose, and had begun works (A on the chart), Pompey's men seized the adjoining heights to the west, set up a number of engines, and seriously annoyed Cæsar's men with their missiles and with archery. Their light troops could advance across the connecting hills to near the position of the Ninth. The reason for disputing Cæsar this height was that its possession would afford him a chance of cutting Pompey off from access to one of the streams most essential to his water supply (B), and confine the Pompeians within too narrow bounds. Cæsar's manifest purpose was to extend his left to the sea along this stream. He found it necessary to retire the Ninth legion from the place, and Pompey followed up Cæsar's legionaries vigorously and inflicted some losses on them. The retreat was down the rugged slope to the east, and gradually became difficult. It is reported that Pompey said that day in triumph to his friends about him, "that he would consent to be accounted a general of no experience, if Cæsar's legions effected a retreat without considerable loss from that ground into which they had rashly advanced," — an utterance which sounds as if Pompey still possessed something of the old spirit.

At this backset Cæsar became uneasy, for his veterans were exhibiting unusual lack of nerve. Hurdles were brought, and under their cover a trench was dug and the ends fortified with redoubts. This is one of the earliest recorded examples of field-fortifications made under fire for the purpose of temporarily holding a position, or of covering a retreat. The stand thus made was maintained for a period,

and later slingers and archers were thrown out so as to cover
a further retreat. The legionary cohorts were then ordered
to file off, but Pompey's men "boldly and tauntingly pursued
and chased" Cæsar's, leveling the hurdles and passing the
trench. Fearing that this might be the cause of serious

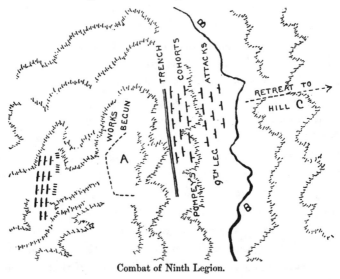

Combat of Ninth Legion.

demoralization in the army, and that retreat might degenerate into stampede, Cæsar ordered Antony, who was in
command, when in his withdrawal he reached a given place,
to turn and charge. This was gallantly done. At the
trumpet signal, the Ninth legion came to a right-about,
closed their files, — they were evidently still well in hand, —
paused but to cast their javelins, and then rushed upon the
enemy with the sword. Though as at Ilerda they were
charging up a steep incline, they drove everything before
them, and Pompey's men "turned their backs," retired in
confusion, and with no little loss, for the hurdles and trench
lay in the path of their retreat and tripped up many. Five
legionaries of Cæsar's were killed; of Pompey's, say the

Commentaries, many more. Another hill (C) was selected and fortified, Pompey retaining the one from which he had driven Cæsar. The loss of this hill was the first step in the disaster which was bound to result from Cæsar's over-confident undertaking in thus inclosing Pompey in siege lines. It enabled Pompey to occupy a larger extent of ground than Cæsar had hoped to confine him to, and obliged Cæsar to make his own the greater by nearly a half; and moreover it compelled him to close his left by a long line across an extended plain (D), where later Pompey found his weak spot. Had Cæsar been able to close his lines along the brook which has its sources at the hill just lost, there would have been more chance of success. But the operation was, from its inception, doomed to failure. Across the plain, when it was reached, Cæsar erected works, — a ditch fifteen feet wide and a parapet ten feet high and wide,— and garrisoned it with the Ninth legion.

The small loss in the late combat does not bespeak a very tenacious fight; but the retreat was as well managed on Cæsar's part as the attack had been smart on Pompey's. The number of the light troops killed or wounded is very rarely given. Only the legionaries killed are counted; so that a very small figure may sometimes express a material total loss. In this case the cohorts probably lost in killed and wounded fifty men; the light troops perhaps as many, making one hundred casualties in a force of not over four thousand men, say two and a half per cent., showing fairly smart fighting.

There was not what we should call picket-fighting between the two camps, but Pompey's men would often go out to a place where they saw camp-fires at night, and suddenly discharge at random a flight of arrows and stones towards it. Cæsar's soldiers were obliged to light fires in a place apart from where they mounted guard, to rid themselves of this dangerous annoyance. Petty war was constant.

This entire Dyrrachium proceeding, on Cæsar's part, was novel. Blockades are usually for the purpose of cutting off supplies, and are always conducted by larger forces than those inclosed or against an enemy demoralized by defeat. But here was Cæsar, with an army one half the size of Pompey's, and himself in need of supplies, blockading by exterior lines Pompey, who had supplies of everything brought to him by sea. The lines were long, and the Cæsarians had to work constantly to perform the guard-duty required of them. They stood their deprivations well. They lived on barley, pulse, and on rare occasions beef, and on a certain root named *chara*, of which they made mush and bread, and remembering the scarcity at Ilerda and Alesia and Avaricum, which had preceded great and important victories, lost not heart. The soldiers said to the Pompeians when they exchanged salutations on picket, that "they would rather live on the bark of the trees than let Pompey escape from their hands." The corn was beginning to ripen, and there was promise soon of plenty. And while the Pompeians had provisions in greater abundance, they were in serious want of water, for Cæsar had turned or dammed up all the springs and brooks which he could reach, and had obliged them to sink wells or rely on the brackish water of low, marshy pools. Pompey's men were not used to work, and it told on them. The health of Cæsar's men was perfect, owing to the large space they had for camping; that of Pompey's, cooped up in a small area and overworked, was questionable.

So short for forage was Pompey that he was constrained to send his cavalry to Dyrrachium by sea. Here it could be readily fed, and could, moreover, sally out in rear of Cæsar's lines and interfere with his foraging parties.

Cæsar was now called away from his army for a short time. At this point in the narrative of the Commentaries there is a gap, which we are compelled to supply by a hint or two in Appian and Dion Cassius, and by construing what is said in a fashion little short of guess-work. It is more than probable that Cæsar was on a diversion against Dyrrachium, to which he was led to believe that he would be given access if he essayed an attack out of hand. At the head of

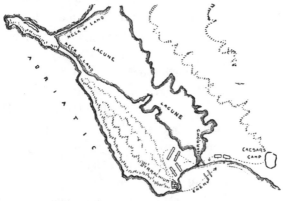

Cæsar before Dyrrachium.

a sufficient body of troops he advanced on the city, crossed the narrows at the south end of the lagunes, left his troops in hiding, and advanced with a small escort towards the walls. But his hopes were not realized. Instead of meeting a friendly reception from the party that had agreed to act with him, the Dyrrachium garrison issued from the gates suddenly and with hostile intent. A part took ship and sailed around to the narrows to cut him off. Another party moved around his right to prevent his making his way up to the north end of the lagunes. A third party attacked him in front. Cæsar quickly rallied his men, met these three attacks with three detachments from his forces, and a smart combat began with each body. The combat was without result. Fighting in his rear compelled Cæsar to retreat, which he did without meeting any particular difficulty.

Cæsar had left Publius Sylla in command of the big camp. Antony, though senior, was too far off on the left to exercise general control. Pompey, apparently soon made aware of the situation, seized the occasion as a good one to break through Cæsar's lines, reach Dyrrachium, and perhaps catch Cæsar near the city and shut him up with his small force in the Dyrrachium peninsula. Having a much larger army and interior lines, this attack on the legions left under Sylla was a comparatively easy matter. Pompey's plans were well conceived. Whenever he went at a tactical problem he did good work. He organized three attacks on Cæsar's siege lines. These were so nearly simultaneous to the ones opposite Dyrrachium that it looks as if Pompey purposely led Cæsar into an ambush, by himself dictating the false promise of opening the gates of that city.

The attacks were all against redoubts, and were so managed as to time, numbers and localities, as to make it probable that no reinforcements would be sent from one part of the line to the others. They were at points which lay east of Pompey's camp. There were two columns, of four legions in all. One column advanced up the ravine E, the other up by way of those marked F and G. Arrived on the high ground near H, the legions divided into three columns. By two of these columns attacks were only partially delivered. In one of the assaults, three of Cæsar's cohorts under Volca- tius Tullus easily beat back a legion which formed one col- umn; and in another, the German auxiliaries made a sally from the lines, defeated another legion with much loss, and retired safely. These were but demonstrations on Pompey's part.

The third or main assault was severe. Pompey's third

column of two legions had attacked in force at one of the
forts which was held by the second cohort of the Sixth legion —
— three hundred men under the centurion Minucius. The
legionaries resisted the assault with great stubbornness.
Pompey's cohorts had scaling ladders, mural hooks and a

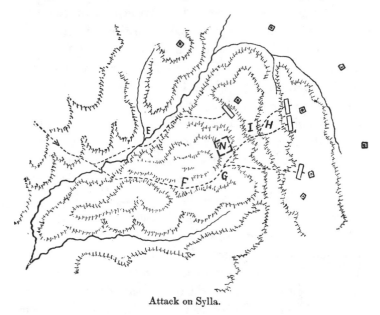

Attack on Sylla.

ram. They assaulted the towers of the castellum, tried to
set fire to the hurdles, filled up the trench, and exhibited the
utmost determination to break down the defenses. But the
Cæsarians held on so stubbornly and for so long a time that
Sylla was enabled to gather from adjoining works and to
lead up two legions to drive back the Pompeians. The latter, exhausted by their efforts, did not stand the charge, but
so soon as the front line was struck yielded ground. Sylla
had an excellent chance to bring on a general engagement
under auspicious conditions, and was loudly criticised in the
army for not having done so. But he deemed that he had

no right to deliver battle in Cæsar's absence, and was sustained by his chief.

The Pompeians, beaten back, had difficulty in making good their retreat. They were passing over a ridge (I); Pompey halted on the top, not daring to retire down it on the other side, lest he should be overwhelmed on the slope by Cæsar's men. He prolonged the combat till nightfall, and then seized an eminence out of engine-range from Minucius' redoubt (N) and fortified it. Cæsar's men remained in his front, hoping to have him at a disadvantage when he should retreat. During the night and following days Pompey built turrets and carried the works up fifteen feet, facing the exposed side with mantelets, so as to retire under their protection. On the fifth night, a cloudy one, at the third watch, he stole a march on Cæsar's cohorts which were in his front, and regained his old camp.

Defenses played a great rôle in those days. A general who wished to avoid battle had only to shut himself up in his camp, where, so long as provisions lasted, he was safe. But if his rival came forward and offered battle by marshaling his legions, it was considered as wanting in the nicest sense of honor to do less than accept it, by emerging from camp and drawing up in line, — unless, indeed, there were preponderating and sufficient reasons for not so doing. If, therefore, a general had camped in a plain, he might have battle forced on him on terms in which his only advantage lay in the proximity to his camp, to which he could retire at will. He was better placed if encamped on a height, with a slope down from the prætorian gate, so that when he drew up, the enemy, if he attacked, must do so uphill. The heavy-armed legionary did not like to fight uphill, as he got out of breath by the ascent, had to cast his missiles up at his enemy, who, meanwhile, hurled his own down to better effect, and being fresh, could at the proper moment rush in a counter-charge down upon him with perhaps fatal effect.

This action of Pompey's is another proof of the extreme difficulty experienced by the ancients in holding their men in hand when retiring from an enemy pursuing them down a slope. In attacking uphill the *élan* was helpful in over-coming the difficulty; in retiring downhill the equal loss of confidence bred a disastrous condition. To avoid being attacked on a descent was as important then as to avoid being enfiladed by the enemy's batteries is to-day. The position which afforded the soldier the chance to cast javelins downwards at the enemy was one not to be readily forfeited. The bulk of all fighting was at javelin range. In theory, after casting their javelins the two first ranks fell to with the sword; but practically the lines faced each other and sub-stantially remained in place for hours, with swayings to and fro as one or other side won a temporary advantage, or the rear ranks and lines moved to the front to relieve the weary. Although there were many duels among the more enterpris-ing in each line, it was as a last resort that the sword was drawn by all. A charge with the gladius was then much more frequent than charges are to-day with the bayonet; but it was the last act in the drama. If this failed, it was hard to restore the confidence of the men, and it was not lightly undertaken. If the second or third line was still fresh, they could be called on; but if these, sword in hand, were driven back, the battle was not easily redeemed, and as troops of olden days were quite as much subject to demoralization as our own modern soldiers, if not more so, a retreat down a slope was one of those critical movements which had to be conducted with scrupulous care.

The Cæsarians had gained a marked advantage. Pompey had lost nearly two thousand men, many *emeriti* and centu-

rions, and six standards, while only twenty Cæsarians were
missing, if the Commentaries are to be believed.   But in
Minucius' redoubt, not a soldier escaped a wound.   In one
cohort four centurions lost their eyes, — a curious coincidence.
The centurion Scæva, who had been largely instrumental
in saving the fort, produced to Cæsar his shield, which had
two hundred and thirty holes in it.   Cæsar presented Scæva
with two hundred thousand pieces of copper money, — about
thirty-six hundred dollars,— and promoted him from eighth
to first centurion (*primipilus*) as a reward for his exceptional
gallantry.   There were counted thirty thousand arrows
thrown into the fort.   The soldiers who had defended it
were rewarded with double pay, clothing and rations, and
with military honors.

Here is a curious discrepancy in the proportion of wounded
to killed.   Among the Greeks there was something approaching a general ratio — ten or twelve to one; among the Romans
there was scarcely any regularity.   In a late instance in the
Commentaries, — Curio's battle in Africa, — the losses were
given as six hundred killed and one thousand wounded.   In
this one we have a loss of only twenty legionaries killed
along the whole line, and yet every man wounded in the fort
which was most stoutly assailed.   Such statistics make it
difficult to compare ancient losses with modern.   In old
times wounds must often have been as slight as missiles
lacked in power.   In those days of hand weapons and good
armor, lines could fight at casting or shooting distance for
a long while with but small loss.   Had Scæva's shield been
struck by two hundred and thirty bullets he would scarcely
have lived to enjoy his munificent reward.

XXXIII.

CÆSAR'S DEFEAT. MAY, 48 B. C.

POMPEY was not abashed by his late defeat. He learned through certain
deserters that the left of Cæsar's line was not yet completed, and was in any
event weak. With excellent skill and by night he prepared an assault at this
quarter. He sent a large force of cohorts to attack the front of Cæsar's lines,
and auxiliaries and light troops to attack the rear. The assault was stoutly
given, and owing partly to accident, partly to poor preparation, partly to an
unexpected demoralization among the legions, Cæsar suffered a galling defeat,
with loss of one thousand killed. He had rashly ventured on the impossible,
and met the necessary consequence. Pompey considered the war at an end.
Not so Cæsar, whom disaster never abashed ; not so his men, who drank in his
unconquerable spirit.

DURING the weeks occupied by these operations at Dyrrachium, Ætolia, Acarnania and Amphilochis had been
reduced by Longinus and Sabinus. Cæsar, desiring to gain
a foothold in the Peloponnesus, sent these officers under the
orders of Calenus to take possession of Achaia. To meet
this threat Rutilius Rufus, Pompey's lieutenant, began to
fortify the Isthmus to prevent Calenus from entering Achaia,
for Cæsar had no fleet to cross the Corinthian Bay. Calenus
recovered Delphi, Thebes and Orchomenus by voluntary
submission. A large part of Hellas was under Cæsar's
control.

In order to leave no part of the responsibility for civil
bloodshed upon himself, Cæsar had still again made proposals to Pompey for an adjustment through their mutual
friend Scipio, when the latter reached Macedonia. He sent
Clodius, who was also an intimate of Pompey's, to Scipio.

But like the others, this effort at accommodation remained without effect. Whether these approaches were made because Cæsar knew they would not be accepted, as has been alleged by his detractors, or from a sincere desire for peace, will never be known. But the fact remains that Cæsar did make the proposals and that Pompey refused them. Nothing but the sword was left him.

Every day after the defeat of Pompey's late attack, Cæsar drew up his army on the level ground between the camps (K) and offered battle. He even led his lines up almost to the Pompeian ramparts, — at least to the edge of the zone of the engine-missiles. Though Pompey, to save his credit, would lead out his men, he would post them with the third line close against his camp, and under protection of the fire of the light troops from the ramparts. This precluded an attack by Cæsar.

As above related, the bulk of Pompey's horse had been sent to Dyrrachium. "Cæsar, that he might the more easily keep Pompey's horse inclosed within Dyrrachium and prevent them from foraging, fortified the two narrow passes already mentioned, *i. e.*, the narrows at the ends of the lagunes on the east and the northwest of Dyrrachium (L and M), with strong works and erected forts at them." This was about May 20. But when fodder thus became particularly hard to get and Pompey derived no advantage from his cavalry, he brought a large part of it back to his camp by sea. While shut off from Dyrrachium by land, his vessels allowed him a free access to it by sea, which Cæsar could not prevent. Within his lines, too, where even the young wheat had been eaten by the horses, it was difficult to keep them, and they were fed largely on leaves and plants. Barley and fodder were brought from Corcyra and Acarnania, but not in sufficient quantities. When even this supply gave out,

Pompey was left with no resource but a sally. To this he saw that he must sooner or later come.

About this time, though Pompey's men daily deserted to Cæsar, the first noteworthy desertions from Cæsar's camp to Pompey's occurred. But these were fatal ones. Two Allobrogians, commanders of cavalry, who had been of great service to Cæsar in Gaul and were men of birth, intelligence and courage, but, as it happened, had not been careful in their accounts of pay to their men, on being held to task by Cæsar, though mildly, for Cæsar preferred, he says, to make no scandal of the matter, deserted to Pompey, partly from shame and partly from fear, and conveyed to him detailed information about Cæsar's works. Such a desertion being rare (the very first, says Cæsar), Pompey made much of these men and took pains to exhibit them in every part of his lines.

Acting on the information obtained from these men, which was exact and thorough, Pompey gathered together a large amount of material for assaulting works, and at night transported his light troops and the material by sea to that part of Cæsar's works — on the extreme left — which was nearest the coast and farthest from Cæsar's greater camp. On the same night, after the third watch, sixty cohorts drafted from the north camp and the lines were marched to the same point, and the war-galleys were sent down the coast to anchor opposite. The foot soldiers were ordered to make ozier-shields to wear on their helmets. Stationed here was the Ninth legion under Lentulus Marcellinus, the quæstor, with Fulvius Posthumus second in command. Antony had general charge of the left wing. The contravallation works consisted of a rampart ten feet high and ten feet wide covered by a trench fifteen feet wide "fronting the enemy," *i. e.*, towards the north. Some six hundred feet back were similar

but less strong defenses backing on the others — the usual
circumvallation line. Cæsar had anticipated an attack from
the side of the sea and had recently erected these latter
defenses. The works which were to connect these two ramparts and defend the left of the line, *i. e.*, those facing the
sea, were not yet finished, and this fact Pompey had ascertained from the Allobrogians.

Pompey's attack was prepared at night and delivered at
daybreak on the weakest part of Cæsar's lines, was excellently planned, stoutly given, and was a complete surprise.
The archers and slingers who attacked from the south were
very active, and poured a galling fire upon the unprepared
defenders, whom they outnumbered six or eight to one. At

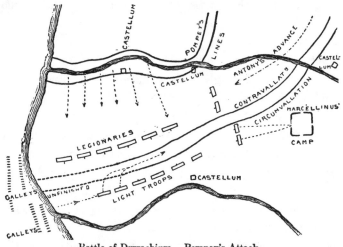

Battle of Dyrrachium.   Pompey's Attack.

the same moment the sixty legionary cohorts made a desperate onslaught from the north, using their weapons and
engines to great advantage; and began to set up their scaling
ladders after filling the ditch with fascines. The danger was
imminent enough, owing to the front and rear attack; but to

make the situation hopeless, a party of light troops discovered
the unfinished defenses on Cæsar's extreme left, and making
a gallant dash in between the two lines, took the legionaries
of the Ninth absolutely in flank. The Cæsarians appear to
have been slenderly supplied with missiles, for their chief
defense, thus taken unawares, was stones; and the ozier
headgear of the Pompeians saved them from the effect of
these. There appears clearly, from the Commentaries, to
have been a lack of readiness, against which, after the desertion of the Allobrogians, one would have supposed that
Cæsar would have provided. He knew his own weakest
spot, he knew that the deserters knew it, and he might have
guessed that an attack would be made here. Cæsar had
grown to believe that Pompey was loath to fight, and perhaps
was careless in consequence. In any event, Pompey's well-
conceived attack was fully successful. His men came on
with such a determined rush that the Cæsarians broke and
could not be rallied, and such cohorts as were sent to their
relief by Marcellinus, whose camp was near the left, also
caught the infection and retired in confusion. The Pompeians pressed on; the Cæsarians were suffering serious
losses, all the centurions but one of the leading cohort being
killed. He happily was the primipilus, and managed to
save the legionary eagle. The Pompeians did not stop until
they reached the camp of the Ninth legion. There Antony
was met debouching from the line of hills where had been
erected the circuit of castella, with a bold front of twelve
cohorts, and his brave stand on the enemy's flank checked
the latter's onslaught, drove back the enemy, rallied the runaways, and put an end to the present danger.

Cæsar, hearing of the disaster by the signals, which were
columns of smoke, usual in such emergencies, also came
speedily to the ground from the main camp with several

cohorts collected from the castella on the way. But it was
too late to save the day or the tactical loss. Pompey had
got a foothold from which he could not be ousted and from
which he could move in and out at will to forage, or to
attack Cæsar's rear. The work of months was rendered
nugatory. The blockade was practically broken.

At the end of Cæsar's late lines, Pompey at once intrenched a new and strong camp, utilizing for the purpose
part of the works Cæsar had erected. Its location was not
far from the seashore and somewhat over a mile south of the
river along which lay the right of his line. Opposite this
camp, Cæsar, nothing daunted and with the hope to neutralize the defeat by a success yet won before the day should
close, sat down and intrenched near Pompey. He had with
Antony's force and what he could safely and quickly draw
from the neighboring forts some thirty-five cohorts. He
placed his men between the two lines of circumvallation and
contravallation, the former on his right, the latter on his
left, and threw up a line between and perpendicular to them
within five hundred yards of the enemy.

Pompey's attack had been made at daylight and his initial
victory had been quickly won. It was yet early in the day.
There were many hours to retrieve the disaster. Pompey
had no doubt that the battle was over for that day; not so
thought Cæsar. Like Sheridan at Winchester, he determined to recover the field. Each of the armies was now
divided into two parts. One of each confronted the other at
the main camps on the north; one of each lay in fighting
contact with the other at the lines on the south plain.

There was near by this place an old encampment which
had an inner work. The latter had been a smaller intrenched camp of Cæsar's during the operation of the Ninth
legion a week or two back (A), and the outer wall had been

added by Pompey when Cæsar in changing his lines had
been compelled to abandon it and Pompey had occupied it
with a larger force. Later again Pompey had himself given

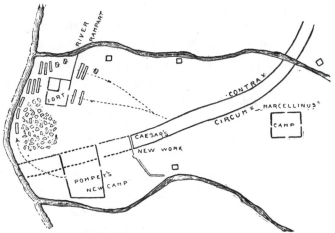

Battle of Dyrrachium. Cæsar's Attack.

up this double camp. "This camp joined a certain wood
and was not above four hundred paces distant from the sea."
When Pompey occupied the place, he "carried an intrenchment from the left angle of the camp to the river about four
hundred paces, that his soldiers might have more liberty
and less danger in fetching water," while Cæsar's men and
his were daily skirmishing over the ground each sought to
occupy in constructing their lines. It was now a sort of
redoubt, and was half a mile distant from Pompey's camp.
This general threw the legion commanded by L. Torquatus
into this camp as a convenient link between his north and
south camps, to make a wider front and to save his men the
labor of constructing a new one. Torquatus marched to the
place back of the wood in question.

Cæsar, who learned of this movement from his scouts,
thought he might attack this post with a good chance of suc-

cess, and by a brilliant stroke repair the effect of the disaster of the morning. His men had .finished their works, but Pompey's had not, and it would take them some time to drop their tools, make ready for battle, and reach the camp. Speed might serve him to crush Torquatus. He headed for this camp with thirty-three cohorts, some ten thousand men, among them the Ninth legion, much reduced by the recent fight. He left two cohorts in the trenches, which made enough of an appearance of working actively at the rampart to quiet Pompey's apprehensions, and, marching quickly but cautiously, reached the fort before Pompey could have notice of an advance.

Cæsar marshaled his men in two wings, each in two lines. The left wing was opposite the camp to be attacked; the right wing opposite the intrenchment which ran to the river. Attacking with the left wing, which he commanded in person, Cæsar carried the outer works with a rush, and pushing in, though the entrances were well barricaded by an *ericius*, or gate full of sharp spikes, forced the Pompeians from the front rampart of the inner one. So far the attack had succeeded. The right wing, however, in search of a gate by which to enter what they supposed to be part of the wall of the redoubt, and misled by following the new rampart which ran from the fort down to the river and was ten feet high, got separated from the left so far as to produce a serious gap in the line and make mutual support impossible. After following this river rampart a small distance, they climbed or broke through it, followed by the cavalry. This placed them no nearer the redoubt than they had been when in its front, and separated them from the left wing.

Pompey had soon learned of the attack on Torquatus, and recalling his five legions from their work of intrenching he marched to the rescue of his lieutenant. The garrison, now

sure of the support of Pompey, made a stout resistance to
Cæsar's left wing at the decuman gate and charged on the
Cæsarians with a will, while Pompey's cavalry advanced
against Cæsar's cavalry and his right wing. Cæsar's right-
wing soldiers by some strange fatality, or else seeing themselves cut off from their leader, were seized with a sudden
panic. They had not had time to recover from the morning's
disaster and their work was not crisply cut out. The cavalry
first caught the infection and fell back through a breach in
the river rampart which they had made and entered at. This
left the infantry of the right wing unsupported by the horse,
and it, too, drifted to the rear even before it had come within
sight of the enemy's line, and in retiring over the river rampart in disorder lost a vast number of men by being trodden
underfoot in the trenches. "Most of them, lest they should
be engaged in the narrow passes, threw themselves down a
rampart ten feet high into the trenches; and the first being
trodden to death, the rest procured their safety and escaped
over their bodies." Others, with no better result, tried to get
round the north end of the river rampart. It was clearly a
stampede. The men of the left wing, made aware that the
right wing and the cavalry were melting away, thus leaving
their own flank naked while they themselves had the garrison
to contend with, perceiving from the wall the advance of
Pompey in line of battle with bold and steady front, and
fearing to be inclosed between the outer and inner ramparts,
were seized with like terror and fell back in like confusion
before the enemy had hurled a single spear. Not even when
Cæsar laid hold of an eagle and personally called upon his
men to follow him could the panic-stricken troops be rallied.
One man, on whom Cæsar laid hands to restore him to a
sense of duty, is even said to have lifted his sword against
him in the violence of his fright. The men "continued to

run in the same manner; others, through fear, even threw away their colors, nor did a single man face about. At the prætorian gate of the outer redoubt the same scene of confusion and disaster was repeated. But as good luck would have it, Pompey suspected an ambuscade and did not rapidly advance. So sudden a success from so sudden a defeat constrained him to caution. His cavalry, eager to pursue, could not push through the breaches of the river rampart or the camp gates, which were all choked up with dead and wounded men. Cæsar was enabled to get the rest of his troops out of action without incurring the penalty of a pursuit, though he saved his cohorts from the enemy's cavalry, which finally came up, only just in time behind the contravallation wall.

In the two actions of this day Cæsar's losses were nine hundred and sixty men, several Roman knights, thirty-two military tribunes and centurions, and thirty-two maniple ensigns. Most of the men had been crushed to death in the ditch. All the prisoners who fell into Pompey's hands were put to death by Labienus with cruel taunts. Such was the hatred of the man whom Cæsar had delighted to honor. This heavy list of casualties, about eight per cent. in killed, cannot be counted as a battle loss in comparison with other general engagements. The men had scarcely fought. They had been cut down or perished in their flight.

The description of these two actions is somewhat lacking in clearness in the Commentaries. The terrain explains the story, however, and the few items given enable us to sketch out the scene of the combat very distinctly. This much is certain, — Cæsar was badly beaten, worse than he had ever been before. He himself came near losing his life. His troops had become utterly demoralized and could not be rallied, and as he is himself reported to have said, had Pompey known how to win a victory, he would have been

fatally defeated. There is not even an attempt in the
Commentaries to gloss over the matter. The two battles of
this day had been reverses which had been saved from
becoming irretrievable disasters solely by Pompey's lack of
enterprise. Excuse enough for the defeat existed in the
disparity of forces; there was no excuse for the demoralization of the troops.

All old soldiers know how irrational is the conduct of a
mass of fleeing soldiery; how each man seeks his own safety,
and all idea of discipline is for the moment lost. Cæsar's
descriptions give one a picture of an army very badly demoralized. There is a tendency in all old writers to make the
light and shade of their sketches very marked. The
gallantry displayed in unimportant affairs is brilliant; the
fear in slight reverses is excessive. Whether this habit of
statement overdraws the matter or not is doubtful. Disciplined and seasoned troops have been much the same in all
eras. Cæsar's men unquestionably lost heart at times in a
discreditable way. But Cæsar was always able to hold them
in hand and to shame their defeat into an encouragement for
the future. What the troops lose in honor, Cæsar gains in
courage and skill.

By his temerity in attempting a task, the impossibility of
which he should earlier have recognized, Cæsar had lost three
good months and all power of offense at this place. He was
back at his starting point, and with his communications with
Italy severed. He had failed in every sense, strategically
and tactically, and with Pompey's large force of cavalry
released he might be logistically compromised. His opponent's all but blameworthy deliberation had proven successful. Time did not work against him as against Cæsar. His
troops had behaved well; he had every reason to believe they
would do so again; and he could now credit Labienus' asser-

tion that Cæsar's Gallic veterans had disappeared. If Pompey should rouse himself for once and push home, Cæsar might be fatally struck. But Pompey did not do so. Fortune stood by Cæsar as she never has by any one; and the character of the two men now plainly appeared.

Aquilifer.

XXXIV.

RETREAT FROM DYRRACHIUM. MAY, 48 B. C.

CÆSAR retired from Dyrrachium with great skill. He so markedly impressed his own bearing on his soldiers as to shame them into the desire again to meet the enemy and retrieve their unsoldierly conduct. Pompey sought to pursue. but was not rapid enough. Cæsar picked up his detachments and headed towards Thessaly to concentrate all his legions and try conclusions afresh. Heretofore-friendly Greece now turned against him; and he was forced to capture Gomphi by assault. Other cities opened their gates. After some manœuvring between the rival lieutenants of either, Pompey and Cæsar both concentrated their forces and reached the neighborhood of Pharsalus. Cæsar had some thirty-five thousand men all told; Pompey, at least twice as many; while his cavalry was seven thousand to Cæsar's one thousand. Despite this superiority, Pompey waited for Cæsar to move upon him. Some manœuvring supervened for position near Pharsalus. Cæsar endeavored to bring Pompey to battle, but could not do so on even terms. He was about to shift his ground, when Pompey showed a disposition to fight. Cæsar at once accepted the challenge.

THIS double victory so elated Pompey and his party that he imagined the war already over. He was saluted as Imperator. He did not consider the difference in forces or the attendant circumstances. Cæsar, on the contrary, with the elasticity of the great soldier, rose to the occasion. By no means disheartened, he determined to change his plan, and at once. He was not slow to recognize that he had failed in his object. He was afraid to risk another battle here, lest from the recollection of the prior defeats his men should again grow demoralized. Even his hardened legionaries had shown that they were not above disgraceful panics. He concluded to give over what, after all, was practically an impossibility,

— the task with a much smaller force of shutting Pompey up
in his lines; to move away and to lure him out into the plain
country where he might out-manœuvre him as he could not
on the intrenched hills.   In the open field he felt a superiority he had been unable to show at Dyrrachium, where lines
and redoubts of such vast extent limited his movements and
his capacity to develop his resources.

Cæsar could not overlook all the acts of cowardice which
had been at the root of the Dyrrachium defeat.   He selected
those on whom reliance was wont to be placed, but who in
this instance had failed in their duty, and punished several of the standard-bearers by reducing them to the ranks.
This sufficed as an example.   He then addressed his men in
such wise as to rob them of the sting of defeat and inspire
them with fresh confidence.   Indeed, so soon as Cæsar's
legionaries had recovered from their first demoralization,
they became themselves and eager for a battle.   They begged
Cæsar to lead them against the enemy instead of leaving
Dyrrachium, promising to give a good account of themselves.   But Cæsar mistrusted not their good will but their
steadiness; he deemed his own plan wiser and adhered to it,
promising his men a victory the next time they struck the
enemy.   The question of victualing was, moreover, becoming difficult, and it was time to move away.

After taking only such few hours as were necessary to collect and care for the wounded, Cæsar quietly massed on his
left all his men and material, and sent forward at nightfall
on the day of the battle all his baggage and the wounded and
sick, in conduct of one legion, to Apollonia, ordering them
to make the distance in one march.   Then keeping two
legions under his own orders as rearguard in the camp, he
started the other seven on several roads, before daylight of
the next day, in the same direction, without signals or sound

of any kind. When they had got well on the way, he gave the usual signal for decamping, broke up with his two legions and rapidly followed the column. This sensitiveness as to the point of honor involved in giving the signal for the march is interesting. Cæsar was unwilling to slink away; but he came very close to doing so. It was the only wise thing to do.

Cæsar had a perilous task before him, — to retire from a victorious enemy over two bridgeless rivers, the Genusus and Apsus, both with rapid flow and steep banks. He reached the Genusus after about a five hours' march. Pompey sent his cavalry in pursuit, and followed with the entire army. The horse reached Cæsar's rear of column near the Genusus. But it accomplished nothing. Cæsar detached his own horse, intermixed with some four hundred legionaries, against Pompey's cavalry and threw it back with loss. He then put his legions across the Genusus, which was done without too much difficulty. This was the day's march he had planned, and he was now safe from Pompey's immediate pursuit, whose cavalry could not readily cross, as Cæsar had collected all the boats and the banks were very steep. He took up his post opposite Asparagium, in the old camp, whose wall and ditch still stood, with unusual precautions. He must steal another march on Pompey if he was to elude him. To induce Pompey to believe that he would stay where he was for a day or two, his horse was allowed to go out to forage; but it was soon quietly ordered in again. The infantry had been kept in camp ready to march. Pompey, who had followed Cæsar across the river, and had likewise camped in his old defenses at Asparagium, was deceived in effect. About midday, when Pompey's men were resting, and many of them had strayed back towards the old camp to collect their hastily left chattels, and were generally dispersed, owing to laxness of discipline, Cæsar stole his march on the enemy, and, making some eight miles before dark, got that much start. Then after a brief rest, at the opening of the night Cæsar sent forward his baggage, and followed by daylight with his legions. And this he did on the third day also, "by which means he was enabled to effect his march over the deepest rivers and through the most intricate roads without any loss." On the fourth day, Pompey gave over the pursuit, Cæsar having steadily out-marched him, and returned to Asparagium.

Immediately after the battle, Pompey had the choice of several plans by which to make use of his victory. He might cross to Italy, where he could count on a better reception now that Cæsar was defeated. He might sharply pursue Cæsar's army and perhaps destroy it before it could recruit, or, failing to reach it, might follow it inland and bring it to battle before it had recovered its tone. Having begun by pursuing Cæsar, though to no good effect, Pompey kept to the plan of a campaign in Greece. But he deemed it wise to reassemble his forces, which the pursuit had much scattered.

Cæsar had stopped at Apollonia only to leave his wounded under a suitable garrison and arrange for an indefinite absence. He left there June 1. He had determined to join Domitius, who, with the Eleventh and Twelfth legions, had succeeded in recovering all Macedonia, — a conquest Cæsar hoped not to forfeit, as its possession would enable him to concentrate his forces in a friendly country.

Domitius was on the Haliacmon, where he had towards the end of April been anticipating the arrival of Scipio from Syria with two legions and cavalry which the latter was bringing to Pompey. Scipio, about May 1, had reached the vicinity of Domitius, and had then turned south to surprise Longinus, who was in command of only a legion of recruits in Thessaly. He left his baggage under Favonius on the

Haliacmon, near Servia. Longinus, catching the alarm, retired across the Pindus Mountains to Ambracia. Scipio, sure of his prey, was about to follow, when Favonius called him back to present resistance to Domitius, who was threatening him. Returning thither, Scipio and Domitius indulged in several slight passages of arms, in which Domitius showed himself the more ready for combat; but nothing came of these exchanges. This was about the time when Cæsar had reached Apollonia.

So far as the general strategic scheme went, Cæsar's duty was plain. If Pompey pursued him, he would be cut off from his fleet and his dépôt at Dyrrachium, — from corn and war material, — and be thereby placed on equal terms with Cæsar. If Pompey crossed to Italy, Domitius and Cæsar would be forced to follow him through Illyricum to defend Italy, however difficult the task. If Pompey attempted to take Apollonia and Oricum, Cæsar would attack Scipio and compel Pompey to come to his relief. No other alternatives were apt to complicate the problem.

Cæsar left four cohorts at Apollonia, one at Lissus, and three at Oricum, not counting the wounded. This left him seven old legions, one of which had had three cohorts taken from it, — say eighteen thousand men. He expected two more legions from Italy; but these were intended to guard Illyricum under Cornuficius.

Pompey, on June 2, ascertained Cæsar's movements and elected to join Scipio. He feared that Cæsar had designs against his lieutenant and proposed himself to cut off Domitius if he could reach him before Cæsar. Many of his lieutenants strongly advised crossing the Adriatic and reconquering Italy, which they said would be the death-blow to Cæsar; but Pompey felt that he could not abandon Scipio and the many persons of note adhering to his cause who were still in Thessaly and Macedonia.   The majority approved his course.

Accordingly, leaving Cato with fifteen cohorts and three hundred vessels to guard the seashore and Dyrrachium, Pompey started from Asparagium June 3, towards Macedonia.   Cæsar's prompt action had forced Pompey to follow

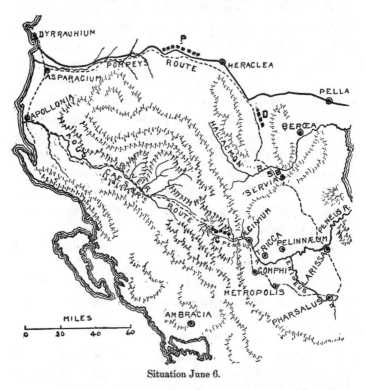

Situation June 6.

him.   It was he still, who, despite defeat, imposed the time and place of future manœuvres.   Pompey's was the weaker will.

The situation about June 6 was curious.   Pompey was marching along the Egnatian highway to join Scipio.   Cæsar was marching up the river Aous by a difficult road to join

Domitius. The latter, in search of victual and ignorant of
the recent events at Dyrrachium, was on the point of falling
into Pompey's clutches by a march on Heraclea.

The exaggerated rumors of Cæsar's defeat had weakened
the allegiance of many states in Greece. His messengers
had been seized, and it had been impossible for him to communicate with Domitius. Pompey, marching on the direct
road, reached Heraclea on June 8. As we have seen, Domitius
had been facing Scipio on the Haliacmon. When the latter
declined to come to battle, Domitius, pressed for rations, had
headed for Heraclea, where he thought he could revictual.
On the 9th of June he was close to the place. But just as
he was about to blunder into Pompey's column, some of the
Allobroges who had recently deserted to Pompey, and who
were with the latter's scouting parties, were captured by
Domitius' vanguard and revealed to him all the facts. Domitius quickly changed his course and filed south towards
Thessaly.

Cæsar had marched with clear purpose and corresponding
rapidity. His route was somewhat the same as that pursued
by Alexander when marching on Thebes. He reached the
watershed of the Aous and Peneus, and descended to Æginium in Thessaly, June 7. Here Domitius joined him June
13. Pompey had followed with for him unusual speed.
Fortune was kind to both. The threatened lieutenant of
neither was compromised. The situation had cleared itself.

Having joined his lieutenant, Cæsar had nine legions, of
which one was short three cohorts, — in all some twenty-four
thousand men. He had a few light troops and one thousand
horse. He decided to remain in Thessaly to recruit the
physique and *morale* of his army. He was where at need he
could rally his legates under Calenus, who had fifteen cohorts.

The alluvial plain of Thessaly was broad and well watered

by the Peneus and its affluents, was fertile and well-fitted for the operations of armies. The towns were active in partisanship of either Pompey or Cæsar, and as Scipio, on learning the movements of the rival generals, had marched to Larissa, Cæsar could scarcely count on much support after his late defeat. On debouching from the mountains he was confronted with four strong places lying on the foothills of Thessaly athwart his path, — Pelinæum, Trieca, Gomphi, Metropolis, — a quadrilateral of importance, but less then than it would assume to-day.

Cæsar left Æginium June 15 and marched to Gomphi, twenty miles distant. Here he found the gates shut on him, the news from Dyrrachium having in fact changed the minds of many of the Thessalians, who previously had been his allies. The inhabitants had sent for help to Scipio and Pompey; but Scipio had marched to Larissa, and Pompey had not yet reached the border of Thessaly.

Cæsar camped. His men had made a longer march than usual that day and had intrenched the camp; but he determined to assault Gomphi without delay. The men showed great alacrity. They were anxious to prove that the late defeat came not from lack of stomach. They prepared penthouses, scaling-ladders and hurdles, and were ready by four o'clock. After exhorting his cohorts to retrieve themselves, and win reputation and the provisions they needed at the same moment, Cæsar commanded an assault of the town, though it was protected by very high walls; and in the three remaining hours of the afternoon captured it. Then, as an example, and as encouragement to his men, he gave it up to plunder.

Next day he marched to Metropolis. Here, too, the inhabitants at first shut their gates, but on hearing of the fate of Gomphi, were wise enough to change their minds.

Cæsar scrupulously spared the place, and thereafter all towns
in Thessaly, except those near Larissa, where Scipio was
quartered, awed and persuaded by the examples of Gomphi
and Metropolis, opened their gates on his approach.

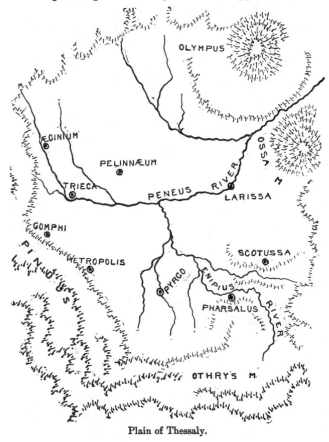

Plain of Thessaly.

Cæsar was cheered by the conduct of his men, and felt
that he might again trust to their steady bravery. He made
up his mind to await Pompey's arrival, while resting his
troops. He headed to the east, crossed the Apidanus at
Pyrgo, moved on farther into the level country and camped

north of Pharsalus in the plain on the left bank of the Enipeus. The camp appears to us to have been illy chosen, but Cæsar's reasons for placing it where he did are not given.

Pompey, when he found that Domitius had escaped him and that Scipio was safe, kept on his course with slow marches, southeast towards Larissa. It is hardly probable that he marched by way of Pella, as has been assumed. He at least knew that Scipio had been on the Haliacmon, and had probably heard that he had marched towards Larissa.

The event proved that Pompey would have been wiser to move into Italy. But he not unnaturally looked upon another victory as the certain consequence of his last, and we can but commend his purpose in following up an enemy whom every indication warranted him in believing he could overwhelm.

Again we see that the plan and sequence of the campaign were dictated by Cæsar's movements. Pompey might, by a diversion on Italy, have had things his own way, but he was too lax and indecisive. Even now he was giving his opponent too much time to recruit.

Pompey joined Scipio June 21, at Larissa, and assumed command of both the armies. Why Cæsar had not attacked Scipio before Pompey's arrival has been frequently asked. But such an act was not in accordance with ancient practice. Larissa was too strong a town to assault, and a siege was not possible at the moment when speed was of the essence. There may have been political grounds which we do not know. To attack a divided enemy, as we understand the phrase, is rather a device of the modern art of war than a habit of Cæsar's days. It had been done by Hannibal and by Alexander, but more often such an opportunity was neglected than improved. Moreover, Cæsar was reluctant to assault a well-defended city. Larissa, with Scipio's two legions, was a different task from Gomphi with its native population.

At all events, Cæsar remained *in situ* and awaited his enemy. Larissa was but twenty miles distant. The harvest was near at hand. His supplies were now certain and he was in open country where he could manœuvre at will. On the other hand, Pompey was in command of fifty thousand legionaries, seven thousand horse, and many light troops, — a force large enough to justify his belief that Cæsar was at his mercy. So certain was every one in Pompey's camp of victory, that already they saw their chief at the head of the Roman state, and quarreled about the disposal of honors, offices and spoils. The estates of the rich men in Cæsar's camp were cut up and divided, — on paper. Much wrangling was the result, and the cries to be led against Cæsar grew among soldiers, politicians and courtiers alike.

Labienus appears to have been the very worst of counselors for Pompey. Whatever his motives for his present hatred of Cæsar, the feeling was pronounced. He could scarcely himself believe, but he certainly led Pompey to believe, that Cæsar's troops were not of the best; that there were few Gallic veterans in the ranks; and that his young soldiers — *teste* Dyrrachium — would not stand fire. He dwelt on the fact that Pompey's cavalry was undoubtedly superior to Cæsar's; and alleged that with the preponderance of numbers there could be no doubt whatever of victory so soon as Cæsar was attacked. It is certain that Pompey was firmly convinced that he must now win. And there existed abundant reason for his conviction. There was but one weak premise in his argument. He forgot that he had Cæsar in his front, and that the personal factor is always the strongest in war. He took no steps to counterbalance the weight Cæsar's personality would have in the coming fray. The defect in Pompey's army was the lack of one head, one purpose to control and direct events.

Cæsar, on the other hand, *was* his army. The whole body was instinct with his purpose. From low to high all worked on his own method. He controlled its every mood and act. He was the mainspring and balance-wheel alike. And as he now felt that he could again rely upon his legions, — perhaps better than before their late defeat, — he proposed to bring Pompey to battle even though he had but half the force of his opponent.

Both armies had as by mutual consent approached each other and lay in the vicinity of Pharsalus. Cæsar, as we have seen, had first moved to this place and been followed at an interval of a few days by Pompey.

The forces of each can be fairly estimated. Some authorities claim that between three and four hundred thousand men faced each other on this field. This is absurd. Nearly all the ancient historians agree that Pompey had one hundred and ten cohorts, Cæsar, eighty-two cohorts, and that each had some auxiliaries. Pompey, whose cohorts were nearer the normal strength than Cæsar's, had not far from fifty thousand legionaries (the Commentaries state them at forty-five thousand men), some four thousand bowmen, seven thousand cavalry, and a host of auxiliaries, — a total certainly exceeding sixty thousand men. Cæsar's cohorts were small, scarcely more than three hundred men each. They had been much depleted and he had not been able to recruit them up to normal strength. He numbered in all not over twenty-five thousand legionaries (the Commentaries say twenty-two thousand), had but one thousand mounted men, and fewer auxiliaries than Pompey, — a total of some thirty thousand. All authorities are agreed that Pompey outnumbered Cæsar substantially two to one.

There is again, as so frequently occurs in ancient battles, some dispute as to which bank of the river the battle of Pharsalus was fought on. A study of the topography of the country and the field makes the matter perfectly clear. Pompey had come from Larissa, which lay north from Pharsalus; Cæsar had come from Metropolis, which lay to the west. These facts must be borne in mind; as also that the Enipeus, according to Strabo, springs from Mount Othrys and flows past Pharsalus; that the battle, according to Appian, was between Pharsalus and the Enipeus; and that according to the Commentaries Pompey's right and Cæsar's left flanks leaned on the river. We must find a site on which Pompey could suitably camp his large army and build certain castella we are told about, and a battle-ground between the rival camps which fits the relations which have come down to us. Unless we satisfy these points, as well as military probabilities, we are all at sea. The following theory of the battle is consistent with all these facts, and no other is. It has been the custom to throw aside one or other of these statements as inconsistent with the rest; but that theory which agrees with all of them is manifestly the best; especially when it accords with the terrain. As in the case of Cannæ, there is no need to discard any fact given by any reliable authority.

The Enipeus flows from its source through deep ravines until it emerges into the plain of Pharsalus. Here it turns to the west and incloses heights to-day known as Karadja Ahmet, some six hundred feet above the river-bed. On all sides, except on the west towards the plain, rises a heavy network of mountains. West of Karadja Ahmet there projects from this network the hill of Krindir, and between the two hills, bounded on the south by the mountains and on the north by the river, is a smaller plain, four miles long by two miles wide.

The Cynocephalæ Mountains — a range of gray, serrated peaks — lie to the north. On his way from Larissa Pompey had come across the plateau, leaving the Cynocephalæ hills on his left. He could not have camped here, with a view to battle, as alleged by Mommsen; it was far too rugged for operations. Pompey needed a battle-ground on which he could use his large body of cavalry. He sought a place whose slope was such that he could induce Cæsar to attack him, which on the rough and cut-up heights of Cynocephalæ Cæsar would certainly not have done. His enemy was already encamped in the narrows between the Enipeus and Krindir, with the citadel of Pharsalus — perhaps Homer's Phthia, dwelling of Achilles — frowning, with heroic memories, from its two-peaked hill five hundred feet above his camp. Pompey did what it was natural to do; he moved down and across the Enipeus, and pitched his camp on Karadja Ahmet, where he had in his front a suitable slope, with his flanks protected by the river on one side and the hills on the other, and with a good ford across the Enipeus at his back. On the flanking hills to the left of his camp he threw up a number of redoubts.

Cæsar faced east, Pompey west. The camps were five miles apart. Cæsar was intent on bringing Pompey to battle. He had kept his touch on the pulse of his army, and found that its beat was again strong and regular. This capacity to test the tone of an army's system is distinctly a proof of the great captain. Despite his late defeat, Cæsar was not misled in his estimate of his soldiers; despite his victory, Pompey's confidence in his cohorts was misplaced.

To bring Pompey to an issue, Cæsar each day led out his men and set them in array, at first on their own ground not far distant from Pompey's camp, but on succeeding days advancing up to the foot of the slope on which lay his power-

ful antagonist. His horse, of which he had but a handful
compared to Pompey, he mixed with the most active of the
light troops, and habituated them to this species of combat
by daily skirmishes. The cavalry, thus sustained, though
numerically weaker, felt confidence in its conduct, and in

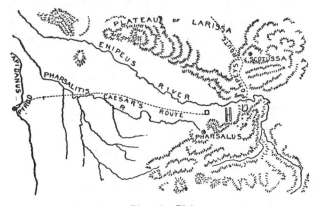

Pharsalus Plain.

one of its outpost combats defeated the enemy, killing one of
the Allobrogian deserter-chiefs. Cæsar's men thus gained
in self-poise from day to day.

Pompey did not leave the hill his camp lay on, but
uniformly drew up on the lower slope, hoping that Cæsar
would attack him at this disadvantage; but from his much
greater strength, Cæsar was far too wary to do so. Nothing
better shows Pompey's weaker *morale* than his indecision
here though every element was in his favor. Nor can it be
said that Pompey was still acting on his old theory of tiring
out Cæsar by non-action. For, whether of his own free will
or yielding to the importunities of his friends, he had come
hither especially to give Cæsar, sore hit in the late disaster,
the *coup de grâce*.

Unsuccessful in his attempt to bring Pompey to battle on

equal terms, Cæsar was about to change his tactics. He determined to shift his ground from day to day, and thus endeavor to catch Pompey under adverse conditions on the march. For Pompey's men were not used to hard marching, as were Cæsar's, and would be harassed by a series of forced manœuvres. And moreover, Cæsar, by keeping in motion, could more readily supply himself with corn without detailing a heavy force from camp each day. On the very morning when Cæsar proposed to put his new plan into execution he noticed that Pompey had advanced farther than usual from his camp and down the slope, as if willing finally to test the issue. This was actually the case, for Pompey's friends had unanimously demanded battle.

Pompey, though giving way to pressure, in his inner consciousness still clung to the value of his defensive views. This came partly from lack of initiative, partly from the fact that he was a good enough soldier to see that the victory at Dyrrachium had not been wholly without accident, that Cæsar's troops were really better than his own, and that to keep up a Fabian policy was safe, and more apt to win in the end, even if less commendable on the score of enterprise. This was a healthy view; but his lieutenants combated it, and Pompey's vanity yielded to their insistence.

Seeing Pompey's advance, Cæsar deferred his march to test the intention of the enemy and drew up over against them. It was the 29th of June, 48 B. C.

Coin with Civic Crown.

XXXV.

PHARSALUS. JUNE 29, 48 B. C.

THE Pompeians felt confident of victory. They were two to one, and had won the last fight. Pompey believed that by throwing his cavalry upon Cæsar's flank, he could rout his legions before they were able to close for battle. Pompey's right rested on the Enipeus, Cæsar's left; the cavalry was on the outer flanks. Each army had three lines, but Cæsar made a fourth line, perhaps a sort of a column of chosen troops, and posted it back of his right to hold head against Pompey's cavalry. Pompey allowed Cæsar to attack. The legions soon closed in fierce struggle. Meanwhile Pompey's cavalry rode round Cæsar's right, defeated his small body of horse, and, confident of victory, pushed in on the flank of the legions. But they were unexpectedly met by Cæsar's fourth line and checked; and, lacking cohesion, dispersed. The legions were alone left. Cæsar ordered in his third line. Its charge was stout, and the Pompeians gave way. Pompey fled. Following up his victory, Cæsar captured or dispersed the entire force. Pompey made his way first to Asia Minor, thence to Egypt, where he was assassinated. Cæsar followed him.

POMPEY had vauntingly declared to his men that he would make Cæsar's legions fly before their infantry came to action, and was unwise enough to explain to them how he proposed to do it. His plan was to place his heavy body of cavalry in one column on his own left wing and have it sally out and envelop Cæsar's right and rear, and charge in on the uncovered side, — of which all Romans had a dread, — before Cæsar's legions could reach his line of foot. It was his cavalry in which he particularly gloried. Nor did this seem an idle boast, for his horse was seven to one of Cæsar's and much of it was supposed to be and was indeed of high quality. Had he been an Alexander, and had he handled the cavalry himself as the Macedonian did at the Hydaspes, his theory would have been carried out in practice. Labienus, too, addressed the soldiers and told them that not only had the fight at Dyrrachium robbed Cæsar of all his best men, but that none of his old legionaries had come back with him from Gaul. Pompey and he and all the officers took an oath to return from the battle victorious or to perish. The Pompeians were in the highest elation and confidence.

Cæsar carefully reconnoitred Pompey's position. Pompey, instead of remaining on his inexpugnable heights, had descended to the plain and left his camp over a mile in his rear. Cæsar saw that Pompey's right wing leaned on the river where were steep banks which, with a force of six hundred cavalry from Pontus, abundantly protected it. This wing under Lentulus was composed of the Cilician and Spanish cohorts; these latter Afranius had brought from those discharged at the river Varus. Pompey considered these his steadiest troops. His left wing, under Domitius Ahenobarbus, contained the two legions sent him in the previous year by Cæsar, numbered the First and Third, and was accompanied by Pompey in person. The left flank was near the rising ground. Scipio held the centre with the two Syrian legions. Seven cohorts guarded the camp, which, as stated, was flanked by some redoubts. Many auxiliary and volunteer cohorts, including two thousand veterani, were interspersed in the line. Pompey's cavalry, under Labienus, and his archers and slingers, were on the left wing, which was in the air, for the hills were too easy to be any particular protection. The entire force comprised one hundred and ten complete cohorts of heavy troops numbering, according to Cæsar, forty-five thousand men in line, and stood in the usual three lines and ten-deep formation. The cavalry, light troops and auxiliaries swelled this number by one half. "Hercules Invictus" was the password.

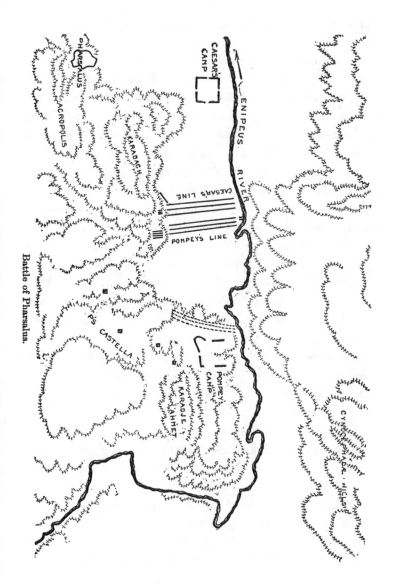

Battle of Pharsalus.

Cæsar, as was his wont, drew up his legions in three lines of cohorts, four in the first line, three in the second and third lines. The men may have stood eight deep. At all events, Cæsar must have deployed his cohorts so as to extend his front to equal that of Pompey. Had he not done so, the Commentaries would have stated the fact, as it would have had a marked effect on the tactics of the battle. It is to be regretted that we do not know how Cæsar covered so much front, Pompey so little, for the force each had in line. Cæsar placed the Tenth legion, despite its heavy losses, on the right, and the Ninth legion on the left. The depletion of the latter had been so severe that he placed the Eighth close by to support it and make up, as it were, one legion. Two cohorts — or as some think two thousand men, say six or seven cohorts — guarded the camp. Antony commanded the left; Sylla the right; Domitius the centre. Cæsar himself took post opposite Pompey, with the Tenth. He had eighty-two cohorts, including those in camp. Those in line numbered twenty - two thousand men, as he states in the Commentaries. With his cavalry, light troops and a few auxiliaries, he may have had thirty thousand men facing the enemy. The two lines stood within some three hundred paces of each other. Cæsar was outnumbered two to one. His situation and purpose recalls vividly to mind the iron will of Frederick who so constantly faced these and yet greater odds, and by unmatched determination wrested victory from the very jaws of disaster.

Cæsar foresaw that the main danger would come to his right flank from Pompey's cavalry force, for his left leaned on the steep river banks and was safe from such attack. Pompey at all events should not take him unawares. Recognizing the danger, he quickly made up a fourth line by drawing a choice cohort from the third line of each legion except

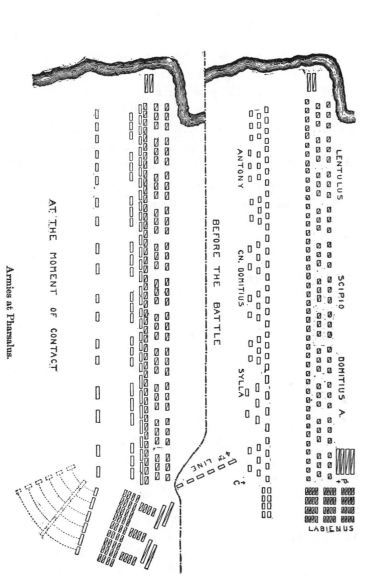

BEFORE THE BATTLE

LENTULUS
SCIPIO
DOMITIUS A.
ANTONY
CN. DOMITIUS
SYLLA
LABIENUS
P
C
4th LINE

AT THE MOMENT OF CONTACT

Armies at Pharsalus.

the Eighth and Ninth, and placed this fourth line of six
cohorts in support of his small body of horse on his right, —
"opposed them to Pompey's cavalry, and acquainted them
with his wishes." He gave this *corps d'élite* to understand
that on their steadiness, courage and rapid action would
depend the result of the day. He also distinctly required
of his main lines that they should not charge until ordered;
and especially so the third line, which he proposed to hold
strictly in reserve, lest he should have need of it to repair
an unexpected disaster. He then, as was usual, addressed
his army, exhorting them to display their ancient courage,
which had won on so many hotly contested fields, and called
on them to witness that it was not he who spilled Roman
blood, but Pompey, who persistently refused his overtures of
peace. We have no record of his words, but the enthusiasm
of the legionaries was marked. It was well typified by one
Crastinus, a volunteer who had been primipilus of the Tenth,
who, stepping from the ranks, voiced the ardent spirit of the
rest: "I will so act, Cæsar, that thou shalt be grateful to
me, living or dead," — which promise he redeemed with his
life. The trumpet signal for battle was then sounded. The
battle-cry was "Venus Victrix."

There was space enough between the armies for each to
advance part way upon the other, as was the usual manner
in ancient battles. But Pompey had ordered his legions to
await Cæsar's onset and to strike when the enemy should
reach them tired with the rapid charge and with ranks presumably disordered. Pompey thought "that the javelins
would fall with less force if the soldiers were kept on their
ground, than if they met them in their course; at the same
time he trusted that Cæsar's soldiers, after running over
double the usual ground, would become weary and exhausted
by the fatigue." But Cæsar knew well the value, moral and

physical, of impetus. "There is a certain impetuosity of spirit and an alacrity implanted by nature in the hearts of all men, which is inflamed by a desire to meet the foe. This a general should endeavor not to repress, but to increase; nor was it a vain institution of our ancestors, that the trumpets should sound on all sides, and a general shout be raised, by which they imagined that the enemy were struck with terror, and their own army inspired with courage." Every great general has understood this. Cæsar knew that his men could endure the fatigue and that they would be the more inspired by Pompey's line awaiting their attack, as if from fear.

The Cæsarians rushed forth with great bravery. It was Crastinus, with one hundred and twenty chosen volunteers on the right, who charged first. This was the place of honor, given to such men as, having discharged to the state all their military obligations, still preferred the career of arms. The Cæsarians, perceiving that Pompey's men did not advance of their own accord, and with the experience bred of many battles, paused as with one consent midway, lest they should reach the enemy out of breath. "After a short respite" they again advanced. When within distance they paused to let the front rank men cast their javelins, "instantly drew their swords, as Cæsar had ordered them," again sent their battle - cry resounding to the clouds and rushed upon their foemen with the cold steel. Pompey's legions received them manfully and with unbroken ranks, hurling their pila and quickly drawing swords. The battle was engaged with stanchness on either side. The two lines mixed in one, each intent on breaking down the other's guard, and swayed to and fro in the deadly struggle, neither able to wrest from the other an advantage which foretold success.

At the instant of the crash of meeting legions, the cavalry was launched from Pompey's left upon Cæsar's small body of horse, followed by his whole host of archers and slingers. The effect of the impact was never doubtful. Weight was superior to courage. Cæsar's cavalry was borne back, slowly but surely. It fought well, remembering the many fields on which it had held its own; but it soon began to lose formation, to melt into a disorganized mass, and finally broke up. The enemy, believing success within their grasp, commenced to file off in small troops to get into the rear of the army. The moment was critical. Was it a battle lost or won?

The foresight of Cæsar now proved his salvation. His fourth line of six cohorts, hitherto held behind the other three, came into play. We must presume them to have been either deployed, or so disposed that they could readily deploy, to face the probable direction of the charge of Pompey's horse. And cohorts such as they were had no dread of mounted men, in whatever number. Rushing forward at Cæsar's command when the Pompeian cavalry approached, this splendid body of men, who knew not fear nor ever doubted victory, charged with desperate purpose upon the front of the Pompeian cavalry, which, unsuspecting and in loose order, were wheeling in on the flank of the Tenth as if they believed the battle won. The Pompeian horse, startled at the unexpected sight of this firm array, at once drew rein. They were made up of many bodies from countries scarce knowing each other's names; and however effective as separate columns, they were bound together by no common purpose. Their speed once checked, their momentum was gone. There was no one again to launch them on the foe. Each squadron looked at the bold front of Cæsar's advancing men, paused, balanced. Who hesitates is lost. Cæsar's bold cohorts kept on until they reached the line of horse, and then, instead of hurling their pila, they closed with the enemy and, using them as spears, struck at the horses' breasts and the men's legs and faces. Not a man of all the seven thousand stood. Discountenanced, the squadrons, losing their heads, turned and fled towards the hills. Pompey's right arm was paralyzed. What a contrast to the cavalry at the Hydaspes, which, under Alexander's tremendous impulse, charged, and charged, and charged, and yet again charged home, until they pounded the flank of Porus' huge army to a jelly!

The cavalry disposed of, the six cohorts immediately advanced upon the slingers and archers, who, deprived of their mainstay, could offer no resistance, fell savagely on them and cut them to pieces where they stood. Then once more wheeling about upon the Pompeians' left wing, while the main lines were still locked in their bloody struggle, this gallant body furiously attacked the enemy's foot on the left and rear. The tables were turned.

Cæsar's plans had been welcomed by the smile of Fortune. The Pompeians, astonished beyond measure at the defeat of the horse, were visibly wavering under the blows of the flank attack. The second lines had already advanced into the fighting front. The moment had arrived for the home-thrust. Cæsar, who had until this moment directed his *corps d'élite*, now galloped over to his reserve third line and ordered it into action. Advancing with steady stride and perfect front upon the enemy, while the first and second lines fell back through the intervals and sustained them from the rear, these fresh and undaunted veterans deployed into battle order, and with one charge, delivered only as veterans can do it, broke through the Pompeian line as if it were but lacework, and tore it into shreds. It has been said that Cæsar's orders to his third line were to cut at the faces of the Pompeians, many of whom were young Roman fashionables, who dreaded a visible scar worse than a deadly wound. This lacks the semblance of truth; but true or false, no further resistance was attempted. Every man fled towards the camp. Nor was this all. When Pompey "saw his cavalry routed and that part of the army on which he reposed his greatest hopes thrown into confusion, despairing of the rest, he quitted the field and retreated straightway on horseback to his camp," ordered the gates closed and retired to his tent in apathy and despair.

The battle was won. Pompey was not only beaten but incapable of further action. But the camp must still be taken. Exhorting his men not to pause midway, Cæsar led them to attack its intrenchments. Though wearied by the heat, for they had fought from morn to midday, the legionaries obeyed with their wonted cheerfulness. The cohorts left in Pompey's camp fought well, but the best defense was made by the Thracians and auxiliaries, for the Pompeians who had taken refuge in it had mostly thrown away their weapons and standards, intent on further flight. The camp was captured, the foe fleeing to the hills beyond Karadja Ahmet.

The camp was full of the evidences of security and luxury. Tables loaded with plate and viands, tents covered with ivy and floored with fresh sods, testified to their false estimate of Cæsar's men, "distressed and suffering troops, who had always been in want of common necessaries." Pompey, so soon as the Cæsarians had forced the trenches, throwing aside his dress of general, mounted and fled to Larissa and thence to the coast, which he reached with but thirty horse, and embarked. He felt that his men had betrayed him.

Cæsar once again urged his legions not to pause for plunder, but to make an end of the whole war by capturing those who had fled to the mountain. In the persistency of his pur-

suit upon this field he resembles Alexander. Pursuit was
not as a rule his strong point. The men were most amenable
to discipline. They left Pompey's camp unplundered and
followed Cæsar, who set about drawing a line of works at the
foot of the hill where the runaways had taken refuge. Foreseeing their danger, as Cæsar's men threatened to surround

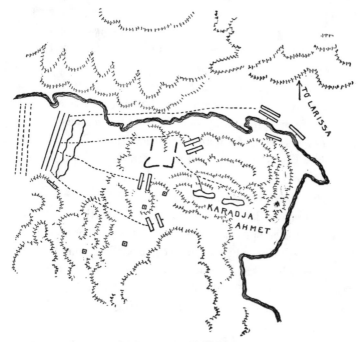

After the Battle of Pharsalus.

them and were advancing on three sides, there being no water
on the hills, the Pompeians sought to retreat by a circuit to
the river where it makes a bend. Here they hoped to cross
and get on the road to Larissa, in which place they might undertake renewed defense under another leader, or failing this,
might better plead for terms. But Cæsar, leaving a force in
Pompey's camp and another in his own, took four legions,

made a smart march up the river along the plain, and at a distance of six miles from his camp cut the fugitives off also from this retreat. The mass took refuge on still another part of the same hill. Though Cæsar's men were greatly exhausted, having fought and marched all day, he encouraged them to draw a work between the river and hill at the only available approach, to prevent the enemy from getting water during the night. This brought the Pompeians to immediate terms. They sent to treat for surrender. A few leading men of senatorial rank escaped.

Next morning all were ordered down from the hill and bid to pile their arms. Expecting retribution, they found clemency. Cæsar pardoned all, and forbade the soldiers to harm a man or take from them anything they had. Then, sending his weary troops to camp, and taking fresher ones, he pushed forward to Larissa.

In this noted battle Cæsar lost but thirty centurions and two hundred men killed, — a noteworthy proportion of officers, — while of Pompey's army there fell fifteen thousand men; twenty-four thousand prisoners were made; one hundred and eighty standards and nine eagles were taken. Domitius Ahenobarbus was killed while fleeing. The prisoners were sent to Asia and organized into new legions by Domitius Calvinus.

This splendid victory was won by Cæsar's admirable dispositions, the lack of vigor of Pompey's soldiers, and the want of steadfastness of Pompey's cavalry. Had this body done its duty the victory would have been more dearly purchased. Cæsar's quick detection of the weak point of his line; his disposal of the six chosen cohorts to resist the cavalry; and upon their overthrowing this body, his hurling them on Pompey's left flank, was a superb exhibition of grand tactics. It was entirely unexpected by Pompey, who believed his left flank to be his winning one, and upset all his calculations. It shows how a small body of determined men, well handled and thrown upon the foe at the critical instant, can change the tide of battle.

During this time at sea, Brundisium had been blockaded by Decimus Lælius, one of Pompey's admirals; and another of them, Cassius, had captured the harbor of Messana in Sicily, had destroyed by fire Pomponius' fleet and had later captured Vibo in Italy and in like manner damaged the fleet of Sulpicius. All these places would have fallen to the Pompeians but for the news of the victory of Cæsar at Pharsalus, upon receiving which Lælius and Cassius speedily decamped with their respective fleets.

Calenus, meanwhile, reduced much of Phocis and Bœotia; and after Pharsalus, Calenus and Cornuficius remained to complete the conquest of Greece and Illyria.

From Larissa Cæsar pursued Pompey with his cavalry to Amphipolis. Here he saw that Pompey had escaped him. The Sixth legion having come up, he kept on along the shore of Thrace; reached the Hellespont July 24; stopped to collect means of crossing; and finally put over in frail barks, — a most foolhardy operation. On the passage hazard threw in his way one of Pompey's minor fleets of ten galleys under L. Cassius. By good rights Cæsar should have succumbed; but the news of Pharsalus so utterly stupefied the Pompeian that Cæsar, with his matchless audacity, took the whole squadron prisoners. This windfall facilitated his progress to a degree.

Pompey had fled to points in the Ægean and Asia Minor, hoping in each place to run across friends and help. He dreaded to encounter Cato and his other lieutenants, after his disgraceful flight from Pharsalus. Cæsar felt that he must pursue him whithersoever he might fly, and finish the war without allowing him the opportunity to collect a fresh army. He marched on his track as fast as he was able, but was hampered by being tied down to an infantry column. He left Mark Antony behind to command the army, with orders to cross to Italy so soon as the enemy's fleet would permit it, and hold the peninsula. Cæsar took with him only the Sixth legion, and ordered Calenus to send him while *en route* another legion of young troops. He had a few hundred horse.

In his flight Pompey stayed one day, July 2, at Amphipolis, where he issued a proclamation calling all men to arms; and collecting moneys from the tax-farmers there, set sail for Mitylene, and thence to Pamphylia, Cilicia and Cyprus. Antioch having refused to receive him, he gave up a half-conceived design of going to Syria and thence to the Parthians; but collecting in Cyprus more money, and brass for military use, and raising two thousand troops, he sailed to Pelusium in Egypt, which he reached toward the end of September. Here he found the ten-year old Ptolemy, son of Ptolemy Auletes, engaged in war with his sister Cleopatra, who was seventeen, for the sole possession of the Egyptian throne. Cleopatra had taken refuge in Syria, and Ptolemy was at Pelusium holding the approaches to Egypt against her. Their respective armies now lay near the desert. To Ptolemy, Pompey applied for a refuge in Alexandria. Ptolemy received his application with openly expressed kindness, but fearing to associate with misfortune, he, or rather his tutor, the eunuch Photinus, caused Pompey to be put to death by Achillas, captain of the king's guard. L. Lentulus was likewise assassinated.

Thus miserably died in his fifty-ninth year, Pompey, surnamed the Great when but twenty-six years old. He had been the popular hero of the Romans. He had conducted

seventeen successful campaigns. He had thrice entered
Rome in triumph. He had thrice been consul. With Cæsar he could have divided the world. To what a pass had
he come, indeed!

"A good officer," says Mommsen, "but otherwise of
mediocre gifts of intellect and heart, fate had with superhuman constancy for thirty years allowed him to solve all
brilliant and toilless tasks; had permitted him to pluck all
laurels planted and fostered by others; had presented to him
all the conditions requisite for obtaining the supreme power,
— only in order to exhibit in his person an example of spu-
rious greatness to which history knows no parallel."

This contest for sovereignty between Cæsar and Pompey shows marked characteristics of the men themselves.
Whether right or wrong, Cæsar made great efforts to keep
the appearance of right on his side, and succeeded in so doing.
In this sense were made his reiterated appeals to Pompey for
a personal interview. He may, soon after the refusal of the
first one, have seen that his appeals would be fruitless, but
he nevertheless persevered, and no doubt his persistency,
coupled to success, gave him the shadow of right in the eyes
of many who had previously opposed him. For the same
purpose of persuading people to his cause Cæsar was generous
towards all Roman citizens who came under his control, as
prisoners or otherwise, even when they had been active foes.
Cæsar was not less inhuman than other Romans, but he was
wont to be politic in his actions, and he knew when and
how to be generous.

In warlike qualities the two generals are distinctly contrasted. Cæsar's broad and solid views, foresight and power
of reasoning out his course of action, were as marked as his
persistency, his wisdom and his strength. During much of
his Gallic campaign he had foreseen and been preparing for

this final struggle between Pompey and himself. And he had not reckoned in vain on the splendid legions he had created, nor on Gaul, which had afforded him his base for operations in Italy. Even Cæsar's foolhardy exploits never carried him out of the generally wise scope of his original plan. Pompey, on the contrary, while anticipating the coming struggle with equal certainty, had done absolutely nothing to enable him to cope with Cæsar. He had apparently not comprehended that he must undertake to hold Italy or forfeit the first and most important innings of the game. He had made preparations elsewhere for resistance, while he had failed to do so at the centre of the empire. He did not make use of his resources when collected. Instead of facing Cæsar and forcing him to pay dearly for success, he allowed him to snatch Spain from his lieutenants with apparently no effort to check him. One can scarcely imagine conduct more impotent than this. One can scarcely recognize the Pompey who conducted the war against the pirates.

Cæsar's directness of purpose in contrast to this is wonderful. In sixty days from crossing the Rubicon, he had conquered Italy. Then, shielding himself by a curtain of forces on the Adriatic, he turned to Spain in order to protect his rear and base from Pompey's legions in the peninsula. In six weeks more after reaching Iberia, this gigantic labor was also accomplished, and his course against Pompey was made clear. Then followed a period during which his hands were tied by Pompey's control of the sea. It was many months before he could cross both his detachments to Epirus, join them and stand face to face with his foe in command of such a force as would warrant him in fighting.

Cæsar knew his enemy. Though he was justified in relying on his inertia, he was unquestionably rash in moving with half his force, as he did, across the sea and running the chance of being beaten in detail. For if Pompey had but put forth his strength in a creditable manner, he could have crushed Cæsar and all his hopes. The position of Cæsar at Dyrrachium was a false one, brought on by conduct rash rather than judicious; and though its outcome was the victory of Pharsalus, it must be distinctly condemned as unsound military policy. This can scarcely be called the art of a great general, whose province is to play a bold but not rash part. Nor did Cæsar accomplish any substantial good by his haste in seeking Pompey in Epirus. The same time spent in Italy would have enabled him to prepare means of shipping his entire force at once to Greece, and thus have saved the grave risk he ran. Or better still, in much less time, he could have marched through Illyricum. The legions he needed all came from Spain and Gaul; they concentrated in the Padane country; it was not much farther from there to Epirus than to Brundisium. He would, indeed, have saved time if from this latter place he had made the overland march through Illyricum. This was his true road, for Illyricum was committed to his interests while Pompey held the Adriatic. There was no real danger of Pompey's crossing to Italy when he knew Cæsar was advancing to meet him in Greece. It was not his way. Good fortune alone saved Cæsar from the disaster which all but followed on his rashness in crossing to Greece by sea.

Cæsar's boldness in endeavoring, with his small force, to blockade Pompey near Dyrrachium, while it compels our admiration for its unwonted audacity, was none the less a reckless undertaking which of necessity sooner or later must and actually did come to grief. It entailed the loss of a large part of the flower of his army, not to mention the demoralization which it took no less than Cæsar's fluent tongue and able discipline to overcome. To undertake such an operation shows rather an excess of animal than a well-balanced moral courage, — or else an inexpertness in gauging his task which we know Cæsar was not subject to. In this operation, Cæsar was conducting war more on the physical than on the intellectual plan. It was not a case of necessity, which always excuses a desperate act, for he afterwards successfully tried another and better scheme, that of luring Pompey into the open country. His allowing his valor to override his discretion met with its proper check. Nothing but his luck saved him from fatal disaster. It was well that he was released from his false situation by a defeat which was not a final one.

An interesting circumstance in the campaigns of Cæsar, which cannot but impress itself on every American soldier, is the handiness exhibited by Cæsar's legionaries in the use of pick and shovel. Every Roman soldier knew how to use a spade. But Cæsar's men were even more expert. These intrenching tools, quite apart from the daily camping-work, seemed to be as important to the legions as their weapons or their shields. They dug their way to victory on more than one occasion.

The best illustration of Cæsar's character in the campaign against Pompey is his determination to fight at Pharsalus. Not every general is called upon or is ready to fight a decisive battle, which must make or mar his cause, against an army of twice his strength. In this determination one must recognize character sustained by intelligence of the first order. Cæsar had taken post at Metropolis, expecting to manœuvre with Pompey until he could place him at a disadvantage. Pompey, however, moved on him, and Cæsar without hesitation determined to take the initiative. This he boldly did; his men backed his courage by their gallantry, and leader and legions won. Pompey, on the contrary, while his plan of battle was good, showed in its execution that there was no stamina in his men, no such *esprit de corps* as emanates from contact with the great commander. His cavalry lacked the first elements of stanchness or discipline. It had no unity of action in the absence of a proper commander; and this was Pompey's fault. Orientals could not have behaved worse. And there appears to have been no mutual confidence which might be called on to resist disaster on the field. So soon as the first contrary incident occurred, there was neither head nor heart to stem the tide of defeat. Pompey beaten showed himself incapable of further exertion, mental or moral; his adherents decamped like a terror-stricken herd. Cæsar's loss in killed measures the fighting of the Pompeian army, and this measures the loss of *morale* of the great general.

In eighteen months from taking up arms Cæsar had made himself master of the world by defeating the only man who claimed to dispute this title with him. The battle of Pharsalus was fought just seven months from the landing in Epirus.

It must be said in Cæsar's honor that few conquerors of the ancient world made use of clemency after victory as did he. He knew its value, no doubt, but we must believe that with victory disappeared all feelings of animosity. This side of his character stands in curious contrast to that which urged him unnecessarily and by treachery to slay four hundred and thirty thousand defenseless Germans in one day.

The most marked result of the victory of Pharsalus was the transfer of allegiance by the provinces from the vanquished to the victor. These all recalled their military and naval contingents and refused to receive the refugees. Juba was the only man of consequence who stood to his guns. Most of the leading men escaped from Pharsalus and made

their way to Cato at Corcyra, — part of them by sea, part
over the mountains.   Here was held a conference at which
Scipio, Labienus, Afranius, Cnæus Pompey and others
were present.   Greece manifestly was lost.   Pompey's
whereabouts were unknown; large parts of the fleet had been
recalled by their respective provinces.   On the other hand,
Spain was largely favorable to Pompey.   In Africa Juba
was a strong centre-point; the Pompeian fleet was still larger
than Cæsar's.   There was no chance in surrender, — there
was one chance left in a partisan war.   But the Pompeians
no longer existed.   It was the aristocrats who continued the
war.

Ancient Helmet.

XXXVI.

ALEXANDRIA. AUGUST, 48, TO MARCH, 47 B. C.

CÆSAR now committed another of those foolhardy acts of which his career is full. He followed Pompey to Alexandria with but four thousand men, and attempted to dictate the succession to the throne of Ptolemy, about which Cleopatra and her brother were disputing. He was resisted by an Egyptian army of five times his force, and found himself beleaguered in Alexandria. He had great difficulty in holding himself. He sent for reinforcements, and managed to keep the eastern harbor and the Pharos tower. He burned the Egyptian fleet, and utilized his own fleet to great advantage. In a naval battle he defeated the Egyptians. These then essayed to cut off his water supply by pumping sea-water into the canals which supplied him; but Cæsar saved himself by digging wells. One legion soon reached him, and some vessels from Rhodes. In a second naval battle he was again successful; and he then captured the entire island of Pharos. But in a fight on the mole between the island and city Cæsar was defeated, as also in a third naval battle. Finally, Mithridates of Pergamos, with an army of relief, came to the Nile; Cæsar marched up the Delta, joined him, and, in a battle of considerable difficulty, decisively defeated the Egyptians, and recovered all the ground he had so nearly lost. But he had wasted the better part of a year by his carelessness in moving to Alexandria with so insufficient a force.

CÆSAR, in pursuit of Pompey, whom he thought to find in Ephesus, had crossed to Asia Minor. Here he heard that Pompey had been in Cyprus, and divined that he had gone to Egypt. He had with him the Sixth legion, and the one Calenus had been ordered to send him joined him August 8, at Rhodes. With these and eight hundred horse, he set out for Alexandria. He had ten ships of war from Rhodes and a few from Asia. The foot amounted to about thirty-two hundred men; the rest of the legionaries, "disabled by wounds received in various battles, by fatigue and the length of their march, could not follow him." With the eight hundred horse he boasted a bare four thousand men.

"Relying on the fame of his exploits, he did not hesitate to set out with a feeble force, and thought he would be secure in any place."

Reaching Alexandria about August 20, he was informed

of the death of Pompey. This was less than two months after the battle of Pharsalus. He anchored in the Great or eastern harbor, and took possession of the royal palace, which was half a fortress, situated near Cape Lochias, to the east of the artificial mole which divided the old and new harbors, and likewise of the arsenal, which was close by. Cæsar had supposed that to the conqueror of Pompey many troops would be unnecessary, but he was speedily and rudely undeceived. The tumult of the populace caused by the troubles raging in the land made even Cæsar unsafe. His entry into the place, preceded by the consular fasces, had in fact almost bred a riot, as the populace deemed such a display an infraction of their king's prerogative. Cæsar was called on to send immediately to Asia Minor for more legions, which he ordered collected by Domitius from some of the disbanded levies of Pompey.

Meanwhile Cæsar found himself in a most embarrassing situation. The troops he had sent for might be a long time reaching him. He himself had been detained by the periodical winds. But he was not the man to look back when his hand had been put to the plow. With the scanty means at his disposal, he determined to hold his ground. He could have at once retired before allowing a quarrel to breed. But Cæsar always settled all civil questions which came under his hand, *pari passu* with the military. He had undertaken to dictate a settlement of the troubles between young Ptolemy and Cleopatra. The late king had left his kingdom jointly to Ptolemy and Cleopatra, as king and queen, and had made the Roman people executors of his will. On this ground Cæsar, as consul representing the Roman people, deemed that he had the right to order these princely claimants to plead their cause before him and to disband their armies until he decided between them. Alexandria was a large, independent, turbulent city, full of able men. The population at once took alarm. It is possible that Cæsar might not have been able to get away had he been so inclined; he had run some personal danger from the populace in landing; and the Alex-

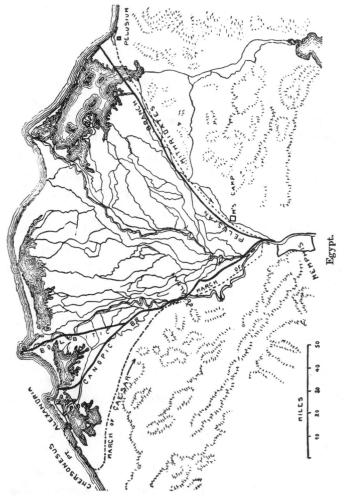

andrians had a large fleet, while he had next to none. Other motives than the Ptolemy-Cleopatra quarrel, or than the desire to gain his point, may have been the prevailing ones.

Cleopatra shortly arrived from Syria, and Cæsar's mandate was at first accepted; but Ptolemy and the eunuch Pothinus, his tutor and regent during his minority, soon adopted a less peaceful policy, secretly appointed Achillas, the captain of the guards and intimate friend of the king, commander of the army at Pelusium, and ordered it to advance on Alexandria. While the succession was being pleaded before Cæsar, news came that the king's army and all the cavalry were marching on the city.

Achillas had a motley force of eighteen to twenty thousand foot and two thousand horse, largely made up of freebooters, slaves and runaways, but among these were many of Pompey's disbanded legionaries. The Roman army of occupation had been largely Pompeian, and easily sided against Cæsar. "Cæsar's forces were by no means so strong that he could trust to them if he had occasion to hazard a battle outside the city. His only resource was to keep within the town in the most convenient places." So soon as Cæsar learned of the approach of Achillas he caused the king to send envoys to him. On these being assassinated by Achillas without even a hearing, Cæsar saw through the plot and seized on the persons of both Ptolemy and Pothinus, who had not left Alexandria, and held them as hostages, "both supposing that the king's name would have great influence with his subjects and to give the war the appearance of a scheme of a few desperate men, rather than of having been begun by the king's command." Pothinus was later executed by Cæsar.

Achillas had five times Cæsar's force, but the material of his army was poor. The old legionaries even, by long residence in Egypt, and many intermarriages with the native women, had lost all ideas of Roman discipline. Still Achillas was able to take possession of the larger part of the city of Alexandria, all except that small section which Cæsar had occupied on his arrival, and which was as much as his handful of men could defend. The part he occupied Cæsar at once put in a state of defense. He saw that his situation was questionable. However illy disciplined the Egyptian army, it was formidable in more than one way, and it was backed up by public sentiment.

Achillas' first effort was to force the palace, but he was unable to do so. Cæsar had occupied and barricaded all the streets leading to it. At the same time there was a desultory and obstinate combat at the port side of the town, fought in many streets at once and along the wharves, and difficult to manage. Achillas attempted to get possession of the Alexandrian war-galleys in the harbor, of which there were seventy-two, including many triremes and quinquiremes, but was foiled in his efforts. For fear they should fall into the enemy's hands, as he could not well guard the vessels, Cæsar put the torch to the entire fleet. It was in the conflagration thus begun that the Alexandrian library perished, together with many other public buildings and treasures. Had Achillas succeeded in getting hold of the ships, he could have closed the harbor and cut Cæsar off from receiving reinforcements or victualing the palace. Cæsar's act, however disastrous in its results, was a necessary method of protecting his position.

The action at this point was fraught with grave danger. "Accordingly that spirit was displayed which ought to be shown when the one party saw that a speedy victory depended on the issue, and the other their safety." Cæsar held his own, and took early occasion to occupy the Pharos tower. At that time, the Pharos was "a tower on an island, of prodigious height," claimed by a later historian to have been four hundred ells, or nearly six hundred feet, "built with amazing works and taking its name from the island. This island, lying over against Alexandria, forms a harbor; but on the upper side it is connected with the town by a narrow way eight hundred paces in length, made by piles sunk in the sea, and by a bridge. In this island some of the Egyptians have houses and a village as large as a town; and whatever ships from any quarter, either through mistaking the channel or by the storm, have been driven from their course upon the coast, they constantly plunder like pirates. And without the consent of those who are masters of the Pharos, no vessels can enter the harbor, on account of its narrowness. Cæsar being greatly alarmed on this account, whilst the enemy were engaged in battle, landed his soldiers, seized the Pharos, and placed a garrison in it. By this means he gained this point, that he could be supplied without danger with corn and auxiliaries; for he sent to all the neighboring countries to demand supplies." By holding the Pharos tower Cæsar commanded the entrance to the harbor, which secured his rear.

But though Cæsar had gained a footing in the harbor, he could gain nothing in the town. Here Achillas had a more than equal holding, Cæsar merely keeping what he had got, and fortifying the most necessary posts. Achillas, who, through the inhabitants, held all the Pharos island except the tower, as well as the Heptastadium, or mole, continued to push the attack on Cæsar by whatever means he could devise. Cæsar strongly fortified the theatre as a citadel, and the adjoining wing of the royal palace, so as to command the avenues to the port and docks.

Meanwhile Ptolemy's youngest daughter, Arsinoë, fled to Achillas in the camp, hoping herself to control the succession. But Achillas and she soon quarreled, which bred dissension in the native army, much to Cæsar's advantage.

Cæsar saw that he was in a perilous case, and that he must speedily gather more troops, or he could not rescue himself. By his utter lack of caution he had again blundered into a dilemma similar to the one he had barely escaped from at Dyrrachium. But Cæsar had one singular quality, — a certain test of the great captain. He was capable of the most reprehensible recklessness. But when, from the results of such conduct, he had forfeited almost every chance of success, he always rose to the occasion with a force, an intelligence which commanded the situation. When we have all but lost patience with his heedlessness, Cæsar compels our admiration by his energy, his courage, his resources. He was indomitable. When another man would have considered the question of surrender, Cæsar began to exert his splendid force, his absolute reliance on himself. Doubt as to eventual success never found rest in his unflinching soul.

So now. At the head of the Roman state, he had at his disposal the forces of the world; yet he was cooped up with four thousand men in one of the client-cities of Rome. But Cæsar was not for a moment doubtful of his ability to cope with the Egyptians. In how great soever danger he actually was, he gave no sign of it to his troops. His demeanor was at all times calm and self-poised, and no one could have read in his countenance or actions the least doubt as to the issue of the matter. He sent to Rhodes, Syria and Cilicia for all his fleet; to Crete for archers, and into Arabia Petræa, to Malchus, king of the Nabatheans for cavalry. Domitius, from whom he expected two legions from Asia Minor, was to send at the same time victual, material of war and military engines. Cæsar called on Mithridates, king of Pergamos, to march an army by way of Syria to his aid. He himself set to work to make ballistic machines and to collect from every source corn and soldiers. In Alexandria he took means to hold himself until relief should come. He razed many houses to the ground in order to gain elbow-room, and fortified the streets leading to the arsenal and palace, or wherever his line seemed weak, with sheds and mantelets, thus inclosing the entire smaller part of the town he had occupied. The walls were perforated for rams and missiles. The town, being built of houses whose floors were all vaulted, without wood of any kind, was peculiarly adapted to creating a good scheme of defense.

The smaller part occupied by Cæsar was "separated from the rest by a morass towards the south." This was a low and narrow piece of meadow land running north and south from the sea to Lake Mareotis, between the low hills on which the city is mainly situated. This lowland could be made to furnish the army both water and forage if it could be controlled. By dint of pushing forward works on either side of it from his own position southerly, Cæsar gradually gained a hold on a part of this lowland. Its possession in entirety would result in his being in a central position between the two wings of the enemy.

The Alexandrians, thoroughly roused by the seizure of their young prince, were equally active in collecting troops and material of war. From every part of Egypt which they could control, they levied troops. They accumulated and manufactured vast quantities of darts and engines in their part of the town, and increased their forces by a great multitude, including peasants and slaves. The raw levies they stationed in the least dangerous parts of the inclosing line; the veteran cohorts in the open squares. They shut up all the avenues and passes by a triple wall of hewn stones forty feet high, and built a number of ten-story towers in the lower part of the town. Some equally tall ones were made to move on wheels along the flat Alexandrian streets by horse-power.

The people were very ingenious, and not only imitated the
Romans in all they did, but devised many new things themselves.   The old art of the days when Archimedes studied
here was far from having died out.   They had resolved to be
rid, for once and all, of the Romans, who they felt were
trying to reduce Egypt to a mere province, as they had so
many other lands.   And their chiefs led them to believe that
Cæsar would soon be starved into surrender, because the
stormy season prevented him from getting supplies by sea.
Cæsar made an attempt to conciliate the Alexandrians
through the mediation of the young king; but the Alexandrians believed that what Ptolemy said was at Cæsar's
dictation, and would not listen to him.

Achillas was now murdered by the machinations of Arsinoë,
assisted by the eunuch Ganymed, her governor, whom she
raised to the command of the army.   Ganymed was a man
of fertile invention.   He determined to cut off Cæsar's water-
supply.   A good-sized canal or branch from the Nile Delta
ran into the quarter of the city held by the Alexandrians,
and yielded them abundance of water, though rather thick
and muddy.   The supply of Cæsar's part of the town was
stored up in cisterns which were filled through aqueducts,
likewise leading from the Nile.   The water was allowed to
settle and clarify in the cisterns.   Cæsar's narrow system of
defense had cut him off from the canal and reduced him to
use the cisterns alone.   Ganymed went to work on a large
scale.   He diverted the river water from these aqueducts and
reservoirs, by which he also cut off his own cistern supply,
and was forced to rely on the canal water.   But this was not
a grievous hardship.   Then, by water-wheels and other
engines, he raised sea water in large quantities and poured it
in a steady stream into the aqueducts leading to Cæsar's
cisterns.   By this clever means all the cisterns in the upper

town became gradually tainted and unfit for use. The water in that part of the lower town which was occupied by Cæsar was not reached by the salt water, but became brackish and unhealthful.

The impending danger of a water famine came close to occasioning a panic among the troops, which Cæsar had some difficulty in allaying. He could not safely retreat, for his small force, so soon as he left his defenses to embark, would be at the mercy of the Alexandrians, whose multitude could easily crush the retiring Cæsarians.

"Cæsar labored to remove his soldiers' fears by encouraging and reasoning with them. For, he affirmed, 'that they might easily find fresh water by digging wells, as all sea-coasts naturally abounded with fresh springs; that if Egypt was singular in this respect and differed from every other soil, yet still, as the sea was open and the enemy without a fleet, there was nothing to hinder their fetching it at pleasure in their ships, either from Parætonium on the left, or the island, Pharos, on the right, and as their two voyages were in different directions, they could not be prevented by adverse winds at the same time; that a retreat was on no account to be thought of, not only by those who had a concern for their honor, but even by such as regarded nothing but life; that it was with the utmost difficulty they could defend themselves behind their works; but if they once quitted that advantage, neither in number or situation would they be a match for the enemy; that to embark would require much time, and be attended with great danger, especially where it must be managed by little boats; that the Alexandrians, on the contrary, were nimble and active, and thoroughly acquainted with the streets and buildings; that, moreover, when flushed with victory, they would not fail to run before, seize all the advantageous posts, possess themselves of the tops of the

houses, and, by annoying them in their retreat, effectually
prevent their getting on board; that they must, therefore,
think no more of retreating, but place all their hopes of
safety in victory.'" The wonderful confidence of the troops
in their leader put an end to fear. Cæsar's promise was
redeemed by setting all hands which could be spared to digging wells. These he knew would be an effective means, and
in fact, during the very first night, the wells yielded plenty
of fresh, good water. "The mighty projects and painful
attempts of the Alexandrians were, with no great labor,
entirely frustrated."

The Thirty-seventh legion, part of Pompey's forces which
had surrendered to Cæsar, and were sent by Domitius Calvinus with full equipment of victuals, arms and enginery,
now arrived off the coast from Rhodes; but adverse east
winds kept it from making the harbor. It got blown westerly from the mouth. The ships could, however, safely ride
at anchor, and the commander sent a rowing galley to notify
Cæsar that they had arrived, but were in want of water. The
winds made no great odds to the rowing galleys. The transports, which relied upon sails, were at their mercy. Cæsar
determined to go to the fleet to take proper measures to bring
it into port. He left all the land forces at their posts,
unwilling to deplete the garrison. He embarked, and set out
with such galleys as he had ready, in search of his transports.

Sending some men on shore for water, as he was cruising
along the coast near Point Chersonesus, some seven leagues
west of Alexandria, these were captured, and the Alexandrians learned that Cæsar was on board the squadron, and
without legionaries. Here was too good a chance to miss.
Ganymed collected all the available ships and sallied out
from the Eunostos or western harbor, which the Alexandrians
had always held, to attack and haply capture him. Cæsar

would much have preferred not to fight, as he was intent on other things. When, on his return towards Alexandria with his fleet, he encountered the enemy, he at first declined the combat, as it was towards nightfall, and the enemy knew the coast better than he did. He, moreover, felt that he could get better work out of his men by daylight, and he had no soldiers on his war-galleys. The Thirty-seventh legion was in the transports. He drew in towards the shore.

But circumstances forced him to do battle. One Rhodian galley rashly separated from the fleet, and was attacked by several of the enemy's ships. Cæsar was forced to go to her relief, "that he might not suffer the disgrace of seeing one of his galleys sunk before his eyes." The Rhodians, always noted for naval pluck, here outvied each other in their gallantry. The Alexandrians could hold no head against them. The victory, largely by the good conduct of Euphranor, the Rhodian admiral, was complete. The enemy suffered grievous loss. Cæsar would have destroyed the enemy's entire fleet but for the approach of night. The adverse winds having happily abated, the transports, under convoy of Cæsar's galleys, reached their moorings in the Great harbor of Alexandria without mishap. Cæsar had now nearly doubled his force both on land and at sea.

At first this disaster to the Alexandrians appeared irremediable. They had lost one hundred and ten vessels since Cæsar came to Alexandria. They were peculiarly disheartened, because their defeat was not by soldiers but by seamen, and they prided themselves on their skill at sea. They "retired to the tops of their houses, and blocked up the entrances of their streets as if they feared the Cæsarian fleet might attack them on land." But this people was naturally a maritime race, and with great zeal, under the cheering words of Ganymed, they set to creating a new navy.

They saw that to blockade Cæsar by sea was their only sure means of reducing him. They brought together all the old vessels which could be refitted and made seaworthy, all those used as custom-house ships in the mouths of the Nile, and from whatever source they could gather craft, and equipped them as best they might, putting into use everything which could float in the harbor. To find material for oars they unroofed the porticoes, academies and public buildings, and made use of the plank thus obtained. They expected to fight in the port, where craft useless at sea would do well enough. In a few days they had fitted out twenty-two quadriremes, five quinquiremes and a vast number of small craft. These were manned by excellent seamen and the proper complement of soldiers. Cæsar had but ten quadriremes, five quinquiremes and, counting smaller ones without decks, thirty-four sail in all. Of these, nine were the Rhodian (one had been wrecked), eight from Pontus, five from Lycia, twelve from Asia.

Cæsar carefully made ready for a fresh naval engagement; for he saw that the Alexandrians, unless their fleet was dispersed, might succeed in blockading him in the harbor. He represented to all his troops the necessity of conquering. In case of defeat he showed them that each and every man was unquestionably lost. After due preparation, he sailed round Pharos and drew up in line facing the enemy opposite the Eunostos harbor. The Rhodians had the right, the Pontus galleys the left. Between these wings he left a distance of about four hundred paces for manœuvring, and marshaled the rest of his vessels in reserve, appointing to each ship in the fighting line another in the reserve for succor. The Alexandrians brought up their fleet, greatly more numerous, with abundant confidence. The twenty-two quadriremes were in front; the rest were in a second line.

A vast number of small craft accompanied the fleet. They had prepared a supply of flaming darts and combustibles on board the small craft to set Cæsar's vessels on fire.

Between the fleets lay certain shallows through which were

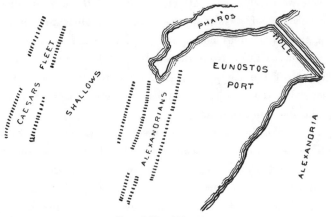

Second Naval Battle.

crooked channels. They are the same to-day. Each side waited for the other to pass these shallows, as each deemed it to be dangerous to fight with them in their rear. The fleet of Cæsar was commanded by Euphranor the Rhodian, who had been so useful in the late naval contest, and who was a man of no little ability and courage. After some hesitation, Cæsar, at Euphranor's suggestion, resolved to attack, and allowed the Rhodian galleys to lead the way through the shallows. The rest of the fleet followed hard upon. When the lines came into action, there was so little space to manœuvre that it became a question of bravery alone. This was an advantage for the Romans. The fight was witnessed from the housetops of Alexandria by Romans and Egyptians, people and soldiers alike. The Romans were really fighting for existence. If they lost this battle they would surely be shut off from the sea. This knowledge spurred them on to

exceed even their accustomed valor. After a long and rather
irregular battle, the Egyptians, despite their well-earned
reputation for gallantry at sea, and their far greater number
of ships, were signally defeated. A quinquireme and a
bireme were taken with all on board, and three were sunk,
without loss of a ship to the Romans. Measured by the
loss, the battle does not appear to have been as severe as
one is apt to infer from the wording of the Commentaries.
The rest of the Egyptian craft were driven into their port,
where they took shelter under the protection of the bowmen
on the mole and ramparts.

To deprive the enemy of this resource in the future, Cæsar
determined to make himself master of the entire island of
Pharos, and of the Heptastadium, which connected it with
the mainland. He already had the Pharos tower. He had
so far finished his works in the town as to think himself
able to hold his position there, and the mole and island as
well. He embarked in small vessels ten cohorts, a chosen
body of light troops, and some Gallic horse especially fit for
the work, and sent them against the south side of the island,
while with a few of the vessels of his fleet he attacked the
north side, promising rich rewards to those who should first
make themselves masters of it. The bulk of the ships had
to watch the Alexandrian fleet and keep it in the western
harbor. The defense at the Pharos village was stout, slingers and bowmen being stationed on the tops of the houses
along the shore, and it was difficult for the cohorts to land.
The coast was rocky, and every crag and inlet was defended
by boats and men, while five galleys patrolled the shore.
But at last a footing was secured, and the Pharians driven
to the town. On the harbor side of the island they had also
resisted the landing parties with some success; but Cæsar's
men pushed on vigorously, and though the town walls were

fairly strong and flanked by many towers, and the legionaries
had no ladders or fascines, a panic ensued among the inhabitants and they yielded up the town, with considerable loss in
killed and six hundred taken. Cæsar gave over the town
to plunder, and ordered it to be razed.

There was a fort on the island next the mole. This Cæsar
took and garrisoned. But the fort on the mainland at the

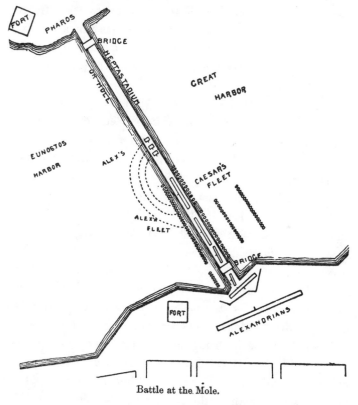

Battle at the Mole.

south end of the mole was held by the Alexandrians. It was
stronger than the other and situated in a large open place
outside the city proper. This he felt that he must have, for
by holding both ends of the mole he would substantially

control both the harbors.   Next day he attacked it.   At first
by a heavy fire of missiles he drove the garrison out of the
fort and towards the town and landed three cohorts to occupy
the mole and intrench, leaving the rest of his force in the
boats.   There was not room on the mole for a larger force
to operate to advantage.   The mole had near each end a
bridge built over an arch, through which the vessels could
pass to and from one harbor to the other, by which means
the Alexandrians could keep the Great port in a constant
state of uneasiness.   Cæsar threw up a work below the
south bridge and set the men at filling up the arch, so as to
cut off this communication.

While this was being done, the Alexandrians sallied out,
deployed in an open space opposite the end of the bridge,
and attacked the working party and force protecting it at
the bridgehead they had made.   At the same time they sent
the ships which they had in the west harbor alongside the
mole to attack the Romans on it, and seek to set fire to the
fleet on the other side.   The Cæsarians held the mole and
bridge; the Alexandrians attacked from the open space
facing the bridgehead and the ships.

While Cæsar's affairs were thus working to his advantage,
some additional men — rowers and mariners — landed from
the Roman galleys on the mole, unordered.   This diversion
at first materially aided the enterprise, for the men drove off
the enemy's ships, but being after a while taken in flank by
some enterprising Alexandrians who seized a footing on the
mole from small boats, this party, not under control, made a
hurried escape to their ships.   Seeing the success of this
flank attack, more Alexandrians landed on the mole and took
Cæsar's three cohorts at the bridge in the rear.   The soldiers
in the galleys, seeing the Alexandrians in force on the mole,
and fearful that they might board the galleys, withdrew the

ladders and put off from shore. The unusual commotion in
their rear of necessity produced among the three cohorts at
the bridge a flurry of which the Alexandrians were not slow
to take advantage; and pushing in heartily they forced
Cæsar's men back in marked disorder.

They now had Cæsar and his small force between two fires,
and though Cæsar himself was with them, the old spirit of
panic came up. Perceiving that the ships were shoving off
from the mole, and fearing that they would be left to their
fate, the cohorts began to fall back. Retreat soon became
flight, each man endeavoring to reach a vessel. Some made
for such galleys as were still alongside the mole and crowded
into them in such numbers as to sink them. Some swam out
to the galleys at anchor, buoying themselves upon their
shields. Some cast away their arms and swam out to the
fleet. Cæsar did his best to hold them in hand, but their
demoralization was as complete as at Dyrrachium. He could
not arrest the panic. It was another *sauve qui peut.*
Reaching his own galley, he found that so many had crowded
aboard her that she could not be got off the shore, and afterwards in effect she went down with all on board. Cæsar was
himself obliged to dive from the mole and swim for his life
out into the harbor to another ship. It was this occasion on
which he is said to have swum with one hand, holding aloft
a manuscript in the other lest he should lose it. Reaching a galley, he sent small boats to the rescue of those who
were floating in the water. Many were cut to pieces on the
mole; more were drowned. In all the loss was four hundred
legionaries, twice as many as had bit the dust at the great
victory of Pharsalus. More than that number of sailors
perished. This was the usual fate of the defeated in ancient
times, whether in a combat or a pitched battle. This victory
enabled the Alexandrians to retake and thenceforth to hold

the fort at the south end of the mole, the defenses of which they made too strong with enginery and works to again assault. They then reopened the bridge so as to have access through it to the east harbor.

The Roman soldiers appear to have been more ashamed than disheartened by this untoward defeat and anxious to wipe out their disgrace. They became so bent on fighting the Alexandrians, whom they assaulted on every possible occasion by sallies and cut off whenever they ventured beyond their works, that Cæsar was compelled to restrain rather than encourage them. For this quality of quick recovery from the demoralization of a defeat, Cæsar's legionaries were always distinguished. They had shown it markedly before Dyrrachium. They had caught the recuperative spirit of Cæsar.

In the peculiar elasticity which enables troops to recover their equipoise after a repulse, no soldier has ever equaled the American volunteer. All veterans of our civil war will remember occasions where, after being driven back from a position or an assault, in a disorder apparently fatal, the line, having reached shelter, would of its own accord recover, and in a few minutes be ready to renew the charge or retake the position, in better spirits than before the repulse. Nor was this so much due to the efforts of the officers as to the natural character of the men. So, in a lesser degree, with Cæsar's legionaries. They did get demoralized; but they speedily recovered their tone.

Seeing, then, that defeat neither weakened the enemy nor success threw him off his guard, some of the Alexandrians sent a secret deputation to Cæsar to ask that their young king be restored to them, for they were weary at the government of a woman and the tyrant Ganymed, promising that if they could have Ptolemy back they would shortly place themselves in a position to make terms with Cæsar. To this they solemnly bound themselves.

Cæsar had little faith in these promises, but thought that if the king were returned to the Alexandrians these would probably be less well led than they now were by Ganymed, in case they continued the war. He could not see in what manner he profited by Ptolemy's retention. Moreover, he had fully espoused the cause of Cleopatra, and with the young king well off his hands, he could the better place her in authority when he should have reduced the Egyptians to reason, — as he never for a moment doubted that he could do. Many thought that Cæsar had been overreached in these negotiations, but he probably saw through the matter with clean-cut purpose. He gave Ptolemy his freedom, and the young king left him with tears and vows to be grateful and friendly. But no sooner had he returned to his people than he in reality became more bitter than any one of the Alexandrian chiefs. As the courage of the Alexandrians was by no means raised by the recovery of their king, nor that of the Romans lowered, the surrender bore no part in the events which ensued.

The Alexandrians heard about this time a true rumor of an army marching overland to Cæsar's assistance, and a false rumor that a convoy of troops and victuals was on its way to him by sea. They took steps to intercept the latter. They ordered their fleet to cruise before the Canopic branch of the Nile, where they thought it could best watch its movements. Hearing of their expedition, Cæsar sent out his fleet to fall upon the Egyptian squadron, placing Tiberius Nero in command. Aboard the Rhodian galleys, which were with the fleet, was also Euphranor, who had rendered such exceptional services in the last naval battles. But fortune was unkind. In an action ensuing upon the fleets coming into each other's vicinity, Euphranor behaved with conspicuous gallantry and handled his own vessel to advantage; but for some reason not clearly set forth, he was not efficiently aided by the rest of the fleet. He was surrounded by the Alexandrian vessels and went down with his galley. The action had no particular result in affecting the war.

In January, 47, after Cæsar had for four months been carrying on this luckless war, which had been thrust upon him against his will, but as a result of his carelessness, Mithridates of Pergamos arrived across the desert from Syria with reinforcements for the Romans. This man, who had taken his name from Mithridates, king of Pontus, whose son he claimed to be, had warmly embraced Cæsar's cause in the Civil War, and enjoyed the consul's confidence. He had raised his army in Syria and Cilicia. Among the soldiers was a large body of Jews under Antipater. Mithridates began his campaign by assaulting and capturing Pelusium, where the Alexandrians had a small force, and leaving a garrison there, marched up the right bank of the Pelusian Branch towards Memphis, which was the nearest point where he could to advantage cross the Nile on his way to Alexandria, conciliating the regions he traversed, and gaining their allegiance to Cæsar "by that authority which always accompanies a conqueror." He soon approached the head of the Delta. King Ptolemy, on learning of his coming, dispatched a force from Alexandria, partly by boats up the Nile, partly up the left bank, to check Mithridates, whose advent threatened to transfer the balance of power into Cæsar's hands. This force crossed to the right bank, fell upon Mithridates in his camp, which he had fortified according to the Roman method, some thirty miles below Memphis. After repulsing them, Mithridates sallied out and inflicted on them a crushing defeat. But for their knowledge of the country and their vessels, none would have escaped. Mithridates was then enabled to get word to Cæsar of what had happened. This was near the end of January.

Cæsar and Ptolemy, on receipt of this news, both set out, Cæsar to aid, Ptolemy to destroy, the new arrival. Mithridates, meanwhile, marched to the head of the Delta and crossed the Nile. The king had sent his fleet up the Nile with the bulk of his army. Cæsar could not well march that way. Leaving a suitable garrison in his works at Alexandria, his fleet conveyed him along the shore to the west, where, disembarking at a convenient place on the coast, he marched around the south of Lake Mareotis, across the desert, and joined Mithridates on the fourth day, before the king could attack him, or was, indeed, aware of Cæsar's

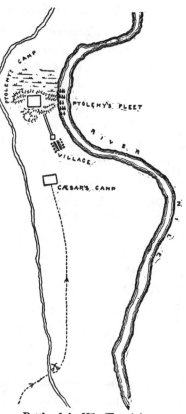

Battle of the Nile (Terrain).

whereabouts. How considerable an army he now commanded we cannot tell.

Ptolemy had encamped on a hill protected by the Nile on one side, by a morass on the other, and steep access on a third. Such a place is found near modern Alcam. Between this camp and the road upon which Cæsar was marching was "a narrow river with very steep banks," probably one of the numerous canals into which the Nile channel is constantly overflowing.   To this river, seven miles from his camp, Ptolemy sent his cavalry and some choice light infantry to oppose Cæsar's crossing and annoy him from the opposite bank. This force "maintained an unequal fight from the banks, where courage had no chance to exert itself and cowardice ran no risk." Cæsar found it an annoying undertaking to cross in the face of these troops, but he speedily sent some German cavalry upstream to make their way by swimming to the other shore and to take the enemy in reverse, and the legionaries, at the same time, felled some trees across the stream and forced the passage.   The enemy's cavalry fled in confusion, but were overtaken and mostly killed.   The light troops were cut to pieces.

Cæsar followed them up and at first blush thought he might assault their camp, as they seemed too much demoralized to defend it stanchly; but on arrival he found it so strongly intrenched, and the troops so alert, that he declined to risk the operation for the moment.   He camped.   There was a village and fort near by communicating with Ptolemy's camp by a line of works.   Cæsar next day made a demonstration here and forced an entrance to the village.   In the confusion resulting in the Alexandrian camp from this unexpected manœuvre, he ordered a general assault upon the latter. The camp had but two approaches, one in front from the plain and a narrower one facing the Nile.   The former approach was held in great force, as it was here the attack was anticipated; the latter was exposed to darts from the hill and from the ships in the river, on which the Alexandrians had stationed a large number of bowmen and slingers. When the troops made no headway, despite their utmost ardor, Cæsar, noticing that that side of the camp which had

rugged sides — the southerly one — was illy protected, "for
the enemy had all crowded to the other attacks, partly to
have a share in the action, partly to be spectators of the
issue," ordered a select force under Carfulenus, a soldier of

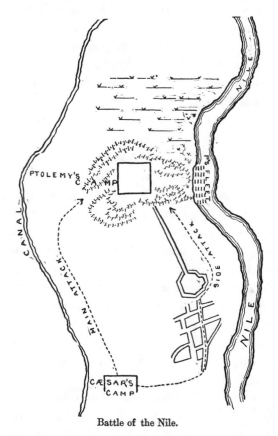

Battle of the Nile.

ability and experience, to scale the rocks in that place, where
an attack would be apt to fall on the defenders quite unprepared.   With the greatest effort the men were able to make
the ascent at all, but they succeeded in doing it in secrecy.
Taking the Alexandrian camp in reverse, they produced a

panic that enabled the legionaries who were delivering the front attack to succeed beyond expectation. The enemy fled in marked disorder, and in rushing over the ramparts towards the river, where they hoped to escape to their fleet, the trench was filled by men who fell and were trampled to death. There was fearful slaughter of the fugitives before they reached the river, and in the attempted escape to their ships a yet greater number perished by drowning. Among these was the king, whose ship was loaded down by terror-stricken men and sunk.

No sooner was the battle over than Cæsar advanced straight overland with his cavalry to Alexandria. Here the garrison and inhabitants, on hearing of the king's defeat, opened the gates of that part of the city which they had held and humbly sued for pardon. Cæsar placed the younger son and Cleopatra on the throne, as Ptolemy the late king had by will requested should be done, banishing Arsinoë. After remaining two months longer than necessary, — held, according to many ancient authors, by the blandishments of Cleopatra, — Cæsar departed by sea for Syria with the Sixth legion. He left the two legions which had been with him, and a third one from Syria, under Rufio, to sustain the new government of Egypt, for the young monarchs were unfavorably regarded by the people.

The Alexandrian war lasted six months. During the first five months Cæsar had been forced to hold himself on the defensive. This method he had largely transformed into offensive-defensive by his activity at sea. In the sixth month, on the arrival of reinforcements, he had assumed the offensive and ended the war by the battle of the Nile. He had not, on leaving for Egypt, anticipated being caught in the toils of a war; but from its inception he had foreseen that, with his mere handful of men, he would be cooped up until he could receive reinforcements. He made his plans accordingly, first to defend himself and then to carry on such an offensive as would forestall the offensive of the Alexandrians. As usual, he himself was the moving spring of action of both parties.

The six months thus spent, owing to Cæsar's lack of caution, and the two additional months given perhaps to Cleopatra, perhaps to political demands we do not know, afforded the Pompeian party a breathing spell, and the opportunity of taking firm root in Africa. This necessitated two additional campaigns, one in Africa and one in Spain. Had Cæsar, immediately after Pharsalus, turned sharply upon Pompey's adherents; or had he taken four or five legions with him — as he should have done in any event — to Alexandria; or had he for the moment put aside the question of the rule of Egypt by a temporizing policy and turned to the more important questions pressing upon him, he would have saved himself much future trouble.

The force he carried with him was so inadequate as to savor of foolhardiness. By crass good fortune alone was he able to seize the citadel and arsenal, and the tower on the Pharos, and save himself from utter ruin. It was a month after he arrived before the Egyptian army came from Pelusium and sat down before Alexandria. His own first reinforcements reached him shortly after. There seems to be nothing marvelous about the campaign, says Napoleon. And in view of the two months of unworthy dalliance, after the long and uncalled-for campaign had been ended, and other campaigns had become imperatively necessary, Egypt might well have become, but for Cæsar's wonderful good fortune, the very grave of his reputation.

XXXVII.

VENI, VIDI, VICI. 'MAY AND JUNE, 47 B. C.

PHARNACES, king of Bosphorus, taking advantage of the civil broils of Rome, had seized territory not his own. Cæsar's lieutenant had advanced against him and been defeated. Cæsar sailed from Egypt with a mere handful of men along the coast of Syria and through Cilicia to Pontus. With such troops as he collected on the way, he had but a few cohorts, of which all but one thousand men were raw levies. With this corporal's guard he set out to subdue the rebel, — another of his foolhardy operations, doubly so, because unnecessary. But Cæsar's luck did not desert him. In the battle of Zela, at great risk and with splendid courage, he snatched a victory and settled the Pontus question. Once on the ground, it had taken but four days. When he reached Rome, he found matters in Italy in much confusion. He suppressed a mutiny of the legions, who, deeming themselves the masters, had become unreasonable in their demands. He was then called to Africa, where the Pompeian chiefs had rendezvoused, and, owing to the defeat of Curio, had full sway. There was here a gigantic problem to solve.

PHARNACES, son of the great Mithridates, king of Pontus, had some years before risen against and made war upon his father, and on surrendering himself to Pompey had been made king of Bosphorus. On the outbreak of the Civil War, Pharnaces deemed the occasion suitable for acquiring further dominion, and had taken to threatening Armenia and Cappadocia. He had already made considerable headway with his conquests, when Pompey was defeated at Pharsalus, on which he became still more hardy, and laid his hands on everything within his reach. Deiotarus, king of Armenia and tetrarch of Galatia, and Ariobarzanes, king of Cappadocia, appealed for help to Domitius Calvinus, whom, from Epirus, Cæsar had sent to Asia, after the great victory.

Domitius, who had detached two of his three legions to Cæsar and was correspondingly weakened, sent a deputation to Pharnaces, commanding him to withdraw from Armenia and Cappadocia; and, knowing full well that the command alone

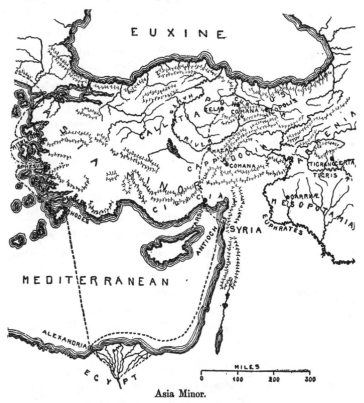

Asia Minor.

would be ineffectual, he at once backed up the embassy by arms. He rendezvoused, the end of October, 48 B. C., at Comana in Pontus, with the Thirty-sixth legion and two others which Deiotarus had drilled in the Roman fashion; he sent P. Sextus to C. Plætorius, the quæstor, for a legion which had been raised in Pontus, and Quinctius Particius in quest of auxiliaries in Cilicia. He had but two hundred

horse. To Domitius' message Pharnaces returned answer
that he had quitted Cappadocia, but that he claimed Armenia
as his inheritance; and that he would submit to Cæsar's
decision when he should personally arrive. Domitius gave no
credit to these protestations. He saw that Pharnaces had
merely vacated Cappadocia the better to concentrate his
forces on ground in Armenia, which was more easily defended.
He sent the monarch word that he would wait only when
matters were put on their old status, and at once marched on
Armenia. This was in the winter of B. C. 48–47.

The route lay along the very rugged mountain chain which
from Comana runs east and west, parallel to and south of the
river Lycus, and is a spur of Anti-Taurus. Domitius chose
this route because he would be less apt to be surprised on
the road and could the more readily victual from Cappadocia. Pharnaces sought to conciliate him by various flattering and costly presents, but Domitius kept on his way and
in due time reached a point west of Nicopolis, in Lesser
Armenia, and camped seven miles from the town. Nicopolis
lay in a plain flanked by mountains.

Between the Roman camp and Nicopolis lay a dangerous
defile. Here Pharnaces placed his cavalry and best foot in
ambush, but kept the flocks and herds in sight, so that if
Domitius "entered the defile as a friend, he might have no
suspicion of an ambuscade," "or if he should come as an
enemy, that the soldiers, quitting their ranks to pillage,
might be cut to pieces when dispersed" — a neat ruse quite in
the style of Hannibal. Meanwhile he sent repeated messengers to Domitius to allay his suspicions. Domitius kept to
his camp, fancying that negotiations might avail, and Pharnaces' clever design to entrap him failed. In a few days
Domitius advanced on Nicopolis and intrenched a camp near
by. Pharnaces drew up his army in line in front of the camp,

"forming his front into one line, according to the custom of the country, and securing his wings with a triple body of reserves," rather a curious order of battle for that day. No action supervened.

Rumors now arrived from Alexandria that Cæsar was in a

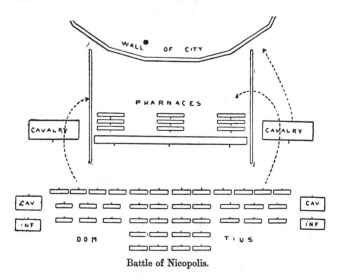

Battle of Nicopolis.

strait and had recalled Domitius to his aid, ordering him to move via Syria to Egypt. Pharnaces, who had learned the news from captured couriers, thought to embarrass Domitius by deferring battle, for delay would compromise him as well as Cæsar. He intrenched his position near the town with two ditches four feet deep, and between them daily drew up his foot in one long phalanx sustained by three bodies of reserves, with his cavalry on his flanks beyond the ditches, where they could charge to advantage. This was a clever defensive scheme and lacked not originality.

Domitius, more concerned for Cæsar than for himself, felt that he could not retreat without forcing and winning a battle against Pharnaces, equally as a measure of reputation and security. He accordingly drew up in front of his camp. The Thirty-sixth legion was posted on the right, that of Pontus on the left and Deiotarus in deep order in the centre. His front was narrow and his wings were protected with the cavalry and the cohorts not belonging to the legions named. Battle engaged. The Thirty-sixth seems to have been a fine body of men. Rushing upon the enemy, they entirely demolished Pharnaces' cavalry, — as Cæsar's fourth line had done Pompey's at Pharsalus, — and drove it back to the very walls of the town; then, turning, struck the foot in the rear. The Pontus legion, on the left, was of no such stuff. Its first line quickly gave way, and the second line, advancing to its support and making a circuit around the enemy's flank, was, though at first successful, finally overwhelmed by the multitude of darts. Deiotarus' legions offered scarcely a respectable resistance. Pharnaces' victorious right wing then swung round on the flank of the Thirty-sixth. Thus abandoned, this gallant body, undismayed, drew up in a circle, and, though with great loss, successfully retired from the field and retreated to the slope of a neighboring mountain, where Pharnaces, abashed by its firm aspect, did not see fit to pursue. It had lost two hundred and fifty killed and many Roman knights. The legion of Pontus was cut off and for the most part destroyed, as well as the bulk of the men of Deiotarus. Amid great hardships, Domitius retreated to Roman Asia.

In this battle, the difference between stanch and poor troops was made apparent. Pharnaces, expecting that Cæsar would be destroyed in Egypt, now marched into Pontus, inflicted cruelties and mutilations of the most galling atrocity on the Romans and leading Pontic citizens, and reëstablished in his own name the ancient limits of his father's kingdom.

The defeat of Pompey at Pharsalus by no means broke up

the combinations of the Pompeian party, — or rather of the aristocrats. While Cæsar was still working out the Egyptian problem in Alexandria, the Roman arms all but received a fatal check in Illyricum. Q. Cornuficius, with two legions, had established himself strongly and prudently in that region, where hordes of runaways from the beaten army at Pharsalus threatened trouble. Gabinius was sent from Italy by Cæsar to join him with two additional legions, newly raised. But Gabinius, undertaking an ill-advised winter campaign, was so harassed by the small-war of the Illyrian

Illyricum.

auxiliaries of Pompey, that he was brought to battle and defeated with a loss of two thousand men and many officers, and was happy to make good his retreat to Salona with the relics of an army. Here he was shut in while Octavius, Pompey's lieutenant, overran half Illyricum. The situation was, however, retrieved by the vigor of Vatinius, then at Brundisium. This officer collected boats, made his way, despite the fleet of Octavius, to Illyricum with a small force of convalescent veterans from the hospitals, and obliged Octavius to raise the siege of Epidaurus. Then, near the Isle of Tauris, though much weaker in numbers and vessels, he inflicted on his opponent a stinging naval defeat, — a very noteworthy act, as he had only a few hastily fitted merchantmen to oppose to Octavius' war-vessels. Thus having cleared the coast, Octavius retiring with a few vessels to Greece and thence to Africa, Vatinius turned over the province to Cornuficius and returned to Brundisium. Illyricum was saved to Cæsar.

From Alexandria, as already stated, Cæsar had taken ship to Syria. He arrived at Antioch May 23. Here was not much to do except to settle sundry political disputes and encourage the states in their dependence on the democratic party, — *i. e.*, on himself. He paused only when he must, for his presence was not only urgently needed in Pontus, but the affairs in Rome demanded his coming; and he must dispose of the Pontus question before he could return to the capital. Leaving Sextus Cæsar in command of the legions in Syria, he sailed to Cilicia on the fleet he had brought from Egypt. Summoning the states to meet him at Tarsus, he transacted the necessary business of the province and started at once for Pontus, via Mazaca in Cappadocia. Turning aside to Cappadocian Comana, he appointed a new priest for the temple of Bellona, pardoned and received again into favor Deiotarus, who had been seduced to join the cause of Pompey. Cæsar required him to join the army with all his cavalry and the two legions he had drilled in the Roman manner, but which had behaved with so little courage at Nicopolis. The relics of these had been collected and again recruited up to standard. With the Sixth and Thirty-sixth, this made a force of four legions, — two thirds of questionable stuff.

Of Cæsar's few men only the Sixth legion, which had been reduced to one thousand men by the drain of its campaigns, were veterans. Pharnaces, nevertheless, fearing a terrible retribution, at once sent in his submission and begged hard for forgiveness. This Cæsar granted upon certain promises of good behavior and restitution. But Pharnaces, foreseeing that Cæsar must soon leave for Rome, felt that he could afford to be slack in his performance, for he intended to keep none of his promises. Cæsar, well understanding his treachery, determined summarily to punish him, despite the fact that he had only the one thousand reliable men of the Sixth legion as a leaven to a small force of other troops to oppose to Pharnaces' considerable numbers. This was quite in Cæsar's style; it accords well with his bold disposition. When he had anything to do he felt that he could do it with the means at hand, — a marked characteristic of the great captain. When the able leader can readily concentrate larger numbers, he prudently does so. When he has but a limited force and work which must be done, he supplements his numerical weakness by his moral intelligence and strength instead of waiting for impossible reinforcements. But Cæsar was much at fault in entering into this campaign so illy equipped. It was not necessary, and to this extent he is blamable. No feature in his life is more peculiar than this habit of insufficient preparation.

Pharnaces lay encamped in a strong position, some miles north of the town of Zela. Here was the field on which his father, Mithridates, had vanquished Triarius, the lieutenant of Lucullus. Zela, fifty miles westerly of Comana, was a town of great natural and artificial strength, in a plain among the mountains, but with walls built upon a natural eminence. Cæsar approached, and camping, June 11, five miles from Pharnaces, and south of Zela, reconnoitred the ground. He ascertained that near the height forti- fied by Pharnaces was a hill separated from it by a steep ravine, and very suitable for defense. He was im- pressed by its natural tacti- cal advantages, as well as felt that its possession would yield him a certain moral advantage over Phar- naces; for the latter's fa- ther, Mithridates, in his victorious battle against Triarius, had held this lat- ter hill; but Pharnaces had neglected to occupy it.

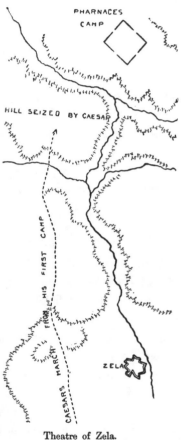

Theatre of Zela.

Cæsar quietly caused everything to be prepared for quickly intrenching a camp, and then by a night march passed over the Zela plain and, approaching the debouches on the other side, seized the height in question, unknown to Pharnaces. The material was speedily carried over to the new location by the camp-followers, while the legionaries to a man worked on the fortifications. Cæsar's idea was probably to prepare a thoroughly strong camp, from which as usual he could develop his plans and seek to wrest an advantage from the enemy. Pharnaces, seeing the non-combatants carrying material, thought it was the legionaries who were thus engaged, and deemed the occasion good to surprise the enemy.

Secure in his preponderating strength, and anxious to attack before Cæsar could complete his intrenchments, he drew up in four lines and advanced down his own slope and up the one on which Cæsar was at work, expecting to overwhelm him, though the position was strong (June 12). He felt that the fortune of his father would run in his favor; he remembered his own late victory, and he had had good omens in his sacrifices. Still the act was a foolhardy one.

At first Cæsar declined to believe that the attack was intended. He considered it a mere threat to interrupt his intrenching, and made the very natural mistake of only ordering out his first line. The Romans were almost unprepared when the shock came. They had really allowed themselves to be surprised.

The enemy's scythed chariots opened the action, but their advance was partially arrested by a heavy fire of darts. Cæsar's new troops were much alarmed at the suddenness of the attack, and threatened to become unmanageable. Pharnaces' infantry line soon closed in. The men came on with the utmost impetuosity, shouting their war-cry, as if victory was already secure. The impact was severe. The Sixth legion, on the right, stood like a stone wall, and the enemy recoiled from it; but in the centre the shock of the chariots had immediately broken through Cæsar's first line and, followed up by the infantry, the rush placed the Romans in the gravest danger; it required all Cæsar's presence of mind and skill to keep the troops on the left flank at work, and to fill the gap thus made in the centre. After a long and obstinate contest, the discipline of the Sixth legion — though but one thousand strong — prevailed over all odds; these brave men clung to their ground with a tenacity beyond words to praise, and by their example held the rest of the line to its work. Pharnaces, despite the splendid energy of

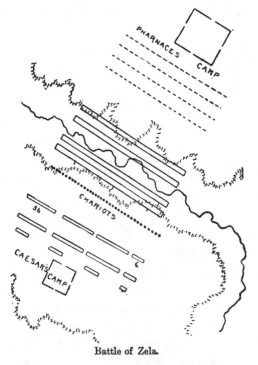

Battle of Zela.

his cohorts, could no longer maintain his ground, and was driven down the hill with great slaughter. The steadiness of this mere apology for a legion shows what a handful of good men may accomplish in the face of almost certain disaster. The Roman troops pursued the enemy to the camp, which, despite its strong location, they captured out of hand. Pharnaces escaped with a small troop of horse. His army was annihilated. Cæsar gave the enemy's camp up to plunder and the men found considerable spoil in it. The defeat was complete.

The king's army was quite broken up. Some months later, Pharnaces lost his life in battle against his brother-in-law, Asander, who had risen in opposition to his rule.

Having thus by the intervention of rare good fortune put an end to what promised to breed serious complications, Cæsar left two legions under Cælius to guard Pontus; sent the Sixth legion to Rome as a reward for its distinguished services; disbanded the cohorts of Deiotarus, and started the day after the battle with a cavalry escort for Rome. He paused only so long on the way as was essential to leave matters well settled in the several states through which he passed. Among other executive acts, he appointed Mithridates, who had served him so well in Egypt, king of Bosphorus and tetrarch of Gallogræcia, practically investing him with the dignities of Pharnaces.

It was with reference to the Pontus campaign that Cæsar, in a letter to his friend Amantius in Rome, made use of the words, " *Veni, vidi, vici !* " "Happy Pompey !" exclaimed he, "these are the enemies, for overcoming whom thou wast surnamed The Great!"

Cæsar always made great speed in his journeys. In going from Italy to Gaul and back, when in haste, he had the habit of traveling in a chariot or litter, and, alternating with riding or walking, moved day and night at the average speed of four miles an hour, or one hundred miles a day. Probably he did the same thing elsewhere. In the East he could get over still more ground. No doubt litter-bearers were then, as now, good travelers. His route was via Nicea (June 30), Athens (July 18), Tarentum (July 30), and Brundisium (August 2). He arrived in Rome August 11, much sooner than he was expected.

It was nearly two years since Cæsar had been in Rome when he again trod the sacred soil. It was time he should

return. The Senate was his tool. He had been made dictator, and Antony was his *magister equitum*, so that the latter
during his absence had exercised full sway. But Antony,
though officially a good servant, had subjected himself to
grave reproach for many breaches of decorum, legal, social
and political, and there was widespread discontent. The
legions which had fought in Gaul and Greece had not been
paid. To be sure they had all agreed to trust Cæsar for
their largesses until the end of the war, but there was no
doubt cause for complaint. The Second legion refused to
march to Sicily; others followed its example. Cæsar arrived
in the midst of all this tumult. He at once took measures
to settle the difficulties. For a time his presence sufficed to
restore quiet, but shortly a still graver trouble broke forth.
The legions which were stationed near Rome mutinied, murdered a number of their officers, who had tried to appease
them, seized their eagles and marched on Rome. They had
conceived the notion that Cæsar could not continue in power
without them; that they really were the fountain of authority; perhaps they flattered themselves that they could gain
greater rewards and more speedy payment by their threats.
The old legions which had placed Cæsar on the pinnacle of
fame and power felt that they were, in a fashion, masters of
the earth. Under Cæsar's sole charge they were tractable
and ready; under his lieutenants they had grown self-opinion-
ated and overbearing. Their officers grew to fear them, and
acts of violence even against these had become common.
The luxury of Campania had done them more injury than all
their campaigns, more than Livy alleges that sensuous Capua
did to Hannibal's veterans. Grave danger was imminent.
A spark might light the fire in this body of combustible soldiers and inaugurate a reign of terror.

Cæsar, on learning of their approach, caused the gates of

the city to be shut upon them and guarded by some cohorts
Antony had at hand; but when the legionaries asked leave to
assemble on Mars' field they were allowed to enter without
helmets, breastplates or shields, but wearing each his sword.
Disregarding the advice of his friends and scorning personal
danger, Cæsar at once went out to them, and, facing the turbulent, seething mass, asked their leaders sternly what it was
they desired. "We are covered with wounds," cried they,
"we have been long enough dragged about the world, and
have spilt sufficient of our blood. We ask our discharge."
"I give it you," replied Cæsar, with chilly deliberateness.
He then added that in a few weeks he was going on a new
campaign, that he would defeat the enemy with new legions,
and that when he returned and triumphed with a new army,
they, the old ones, should have the presents which had been
promised them "on his triumph," and unpromised land
beside. Expecting nothing less than that they would actually be discharged, and thus forfeit participation in the glo-
ries of Cæsar's triumph, — the one thing to which every Roman soldier looked cravingly forward, — and awed by the cold
demeanor of their great commander, the legionaries at once
showed signs of weakening. As Cæsar was about to go, the
legates begged him to say a few kind words to his veterans,
who had shared so many dangers with him. Cæsar turned
to them again, and quietly addressed them as "Citizens!"
(*quirites*) instead, as usual, as "Comrades!" (*commilitones*).
"We are not citizens," they exclaimed, interrupting Cæsar,
"we are soldiers!" Their ancient devotion to the splendid
chieftain who had so often led them to victory came welling
up; the cutting word of quirites, to them who were soldiers
first of all, and who had lost all pride in being burgesses of
the Roman republic, in an instant changed the current of
their purpose. A single word had conquered them whom arms

could not; Cæsar's indifference was their punishment. They could not bear that he should go forth to war with other troops. They crowded round him, and begged forgiveness and permission to continue in service and to accompany him whithersoever he might go. Cæsar, it is said, forgave all but the Tenth legion, his old favorite, whose mutiny he could not condone. All the ringleaders had a third docked from their largesses, and he threatened to muster out the Tenth. But later the Tenth followed him to Africa, and there did its service as of yore. Still one sees in after days that it was no more the Old Tenth of the times of the Gallic War.

The accounts of the suppression of this mutiny do not strike one as being so dramatic as Arrian's story of Alexander's suppression of the mutiny of his Macedonians, which threatened to be of even graver danger. But as both are but embellished statements of an actual fact, they can scarcely be compared as a measure of the men themselves. And each case was characteristic. It was certainly a great rôle for one man to appear before and control scores of thousands by the mere force of his disdain and his iron will.

Triumphal Car.

XXXVIII.

RUSPINA. OCTOBER AND NOVEMBER, 47 B. C.

CÆSAR commanded the resources of the world; yet he entered on the African campaign with his usual reckless disregard of suitable means. The Pompeians had assembled their forces in Africa, had accumulated a huge army and had been joined by King Juba as ally. Cæsar got together his legions in Sicily and set sail for Africa without giving his fleet any place as rendezvous. A storm dispersed his vessels, and he landed on the coast at Ruspina with but three thousand men, the rest having been blown he knew not whither. For weeks he lay on the seashore awaiting the rest of his forces, and, but for the hebetude of his enemies, in a state of greatest peril. Despite this blameworthy negligence, we are forced to admire the remarkable manner in which he imposed on his enemies and saved himself harmless from attack. From his camp near Ruspina he sent in all directions for victual and troops, and by and by — with Cæsar's own luck — the scattered fleet turned up, and ended the suspense. A battle shortly supervened, in which Cæsar ably rescued himself from a grave peril coming from too distant an advance inconsiderately undertaken. Scipio soon after came up with the bulk of the Pompeian forces. More serious work then supervened.

AT this time the northern part of the African continent, which alone was known to the Romans, was divided into Mauretania (Morocco), Numidia (Algiers), Gætulia (the Great Desert) and so-called "Africa" (Tunis). Libya was sometimes used as a name for all Africa, Egypt and Ethiopia. "Africa" was now a Roman province, ruled by a prætor in Utica. The country was in the hands of Pompey's adherents. The sovereign of Numidia, King Juba, was committed to the interests of the Pompeian party and held a large place in its councils.

Because Pompey was dead there was no reason why his followers should not assert the rights which he had represented. Whatever their dissensions among themselves, they were a unit in opposing Cæsar. The chiefs of the party, now a coalition of aristocrats rather than Pompeians, had severally fled to Africa. What they had lost in strength they gained in fanaticism. They could expect to make no terms with Cæsar. After Pharsalus, Metellus Scipio had collected

North Africa.

the relics of the Pompeian army and shipped them to Africa; and Cato, Labienus, Cnæus and Sextus Pompey, Afranius, Petreius, Octavius and others had joined him there. In Leptis, which they reached after great privations, these Pompeians spent the winter. Cato became prætor and took up his quarters in Utica. He unwisely declined the command in chief, luckily for Cæsar; for though Cato was not a soldier, he was a man of exceptional strength. Scipio was made commander of the armies. A new senate of "three hundred" was elected and convened. Juba was independent, but lent friendly assistance. This coalition of the aristocrats summarily called for Cæsar's presence in Africa.

The Pompeian army, as Cæsar was informed, consisted of a vast cavalry force; four legions, armed and drilled Roman fashion, under Juba, and a great number of light-armed troops; ten legions under Scipio, eight of which were from refugees and conscripts; one hundred and twenty elephants; and a numerous fleet, which under Octavius, Varus and Nasidius controlled the African and Sicilian shores and contained fifty-five war-galleys. This force, both on land and sea, was capable of immense mischief. Cæsar had thus far paid so little heed to the gathering danger that his enemies in Rome had feared that Scipio would invade Italy. This would have been practicable had Scipio worthily borne his name, — if his opponent had not been Cæsar. While Cæsar was in Alexandria and Asia Minor, what might not these legions, well led, have accomplished in Sicily and Italy? By a descent on Sicily and the occupation of its waters, Scipio could have practically nullified Cæsar's attempt to cross to Africa.

But boldness was no part of Scipio's programme. He contented himself with a mere holding of the African province. For this purpose his plan was to gather all obtainable victual in his cities, so as to rob Cæsar of the power to feed his troops, and to fortify all the coast towns. He was, however, unable to carry through his plan. Many of the towns were distinctly in Cæsar's favor, and Scipio's measures lacked both decision and efficacy.

With his main army, Scipio lay near Utica, protecting his magazines. Afranius, Petreius and other old Pompeian generals were stationed on the coast within concentrating distance. The cavalry scouted the seashore for many scores of miles. The fleet was cruising partly on the African and partly on the Sicilian coast. Apparently these precautions

were well taken.   But neither the fleet nor the cavalry were
sufficiently alert to fend off Cæsar's attack.   It was not
numbers they lacked; it was discipline and proper command.
There was not that push from headquarters which alone
keeps subordinates to their work.

Before leaving Rome, Cæsar divided up the provinces.
Allienus received charge of Sicily, Sulpicius of Achaia,
Sextus Cæsar and Dec. Brutus of Syria and Transalpine
Gaul, and M. Brutus of Cisalpine.   After collecting all the
transports he could lay his hands on, towards the end of October, B. C. 47, Cæsar gave a rendezvous to them and to his
army at Lilybæum.   He had at the time but one legion of
raw levies and six hundred horse at this port.   He expected
four legions to come to Africa from Spain, to work in connection with Bogud, king of west Mauretania.   The wind
was contrary, but such was his anxiety to reach Africa that
he kept his men in the ships ready to sail, and himself
watched them from his tent pitched on the seashore.   After
some days of impatient waiting, his levies and ships gradually
began to come in.   He soon had assembled six legions and
two thousand horse, among the legions the Fifth, a veteran
body.   Leaving Allienus, the prætor, strict orders to forward
more troops without delay, and having rendezvoused his
vessels at Aponiana, he set sail, October 30, for the promontory of Mercury (Cape Bon), hoping to land well south of
Scipio, whom he knew to be at Utica.   The troops were
embarked in light order, without servants or camp-kits, the
foot in galleys, the horse in transports.

The irregular winds of the season — they blow to-day as
they did then — separated his fleet.   He had failed to give
orders to his captains where to assemble in such a case, — a
very reprehensible oversight.   He was, says the author of
"The African War," in the Commentaries, unaware of the

location of the enemy's forces, and could not give a rendezvous. "Some blamed his conduct on this occasion, and
charged him with a considerable oversight, in not appointing
a place of meeting to the pilots and captains of the fleet, or
delivering them sealed instructions, according to his usual
custom, which being opened at a certain time, might have
directed them to assemble at a specified place. But in this
Cæsar acted not without design; for as he knew of no port in
Africa that was clear of the enemy's forces, and where the
fleet might rendezvous in security, he chose to rely entirely
upon fortune, and land where occasion offered." This is a
lame excuse, which Cæsar himself would never have made.
While he could not perhaps have assigned a very definite
rallying point, he knew where lay the bulk of the enemy's
forces, and, therefore, what ports to avoid; and in any case
he might have given better instructions than none at all.
He himself, after four days of tossing on the treacherous
waters of the Mediterranean, came in sight of land, attended
by a few galleys, sailed south along the coast past Clupea,
— where he saw the cavalry of the Pompeians and about
three thousand Moors scouting the shore, — past Neapolis,
and anchored near Hadrumetum (modern Sousa), November 3. Here was a Pompeian garrison of two legions and
seven hundred horse, under C. Considius. Having reconnoitred the coast and seen no enemy, though he had in his
company but three thousand men and one hundred and fifty
horse, the rest having been blown he knew not whither, he
concluded to land.

It was here that, in leaping on shore, Cæsar accidentally
fell, and lest the omen should dispirit the legions, he arose
with the cry, "Africa, I have embraced thee !" He
encamped where he had landed (a). He then made a reconnoissance, in person, of Hadrumetum, whose inhabitants at

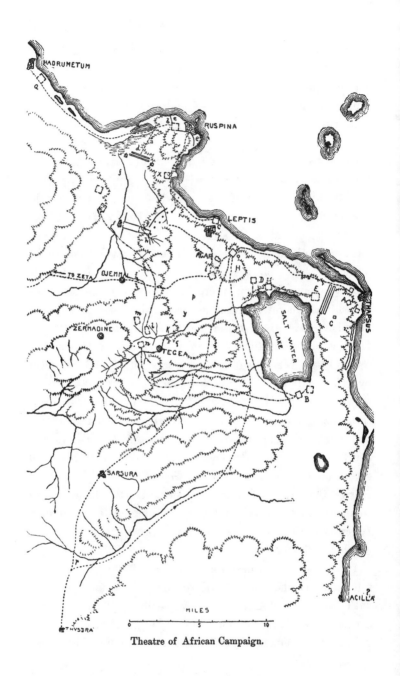

Theatre of African Campaign.

once manned the walls and prepared for defense. Desirous not to offend the population, he forbade any plunder to be taken by the men. L. Plancus, one of the legates, attempted to treat with Considius, by letter, but the advances were rejected by the sturdy Pompeian.

"The rest of the forces had not yet arrived; his cavalry was not considerable; he had not sufficient troops with him to invest the place, and these were new levies; neither did he think it advisable, upon his first landing, to expose the army to wounds and fatigue; more especially as the town was strongly fortified, and extremely difficult of access; and a great body of horse was said to be upon the point of arrival to succor the inhabitants; he therefore thought it advisable not to remain and besiege the town, lest, while he pursued that design, the enemy's cavalry should come behind and surround him." After remaining a day and night before the town, Cæsar retired down the coast to a more suitable place to collect his scattered fleet, perhaps thinking that he might find some city already committed to his interests, or which might be persuaded to join his cause.

He was in fact in a graver danger than at Alexandria. Considius' legions were ten thousand strong, and this force was soon increased by the arrival of Cnæus Piso with three thousand horse. The enemy had happily not attacked Cæsar, but had adopted means of defense themselves. It was part of his good fortune — even Alexander never boasted such — that he met so lax opponents on his first landing.

On Cæsar's retiring, Considius made a sally from the town, seized on the camp he had left and followed him up, sustained by Juba's cavalry, which had just come in to draw their pay; but Cæsar halted, and throwing his small body of horse sharply upon the Moors he drove them back to the town. "An incredible event occurred, that less than thirty

Gallic horse repulsed two thousand Moors." Incredible indeed! Mixing some cohorts of infantry with his horse as a rearguard, Cæsar retired to Ruspina (modern Monastir), a well-located and prosperous town on a headland, and camped (b). It was the 5th of November. Thence Cæsar, invited by its inhabitants, next day removed to Leptis, "a free city governed by its own laws," but far from a good place for defense, being situated on a flat part of the seashore. Leptis opened its gates to him. Cæsar posted guards to protect the town from the soldiery, and camped between it and the seashore (c). He kept his cavalry on board the transports, to prevent their roaming about and plundering the inhabitants, whom he wished to conciliate, — a matter which speaks poorly for the discipline under which he held them. Many towns came forward, furnished him victual, and assured him of their fidelity. Cæsar had by crass luck escaped the most serious danger. Shortly, a part of the fleet came up by the merest accident and reported the rest to be probably on the way to Utica, supposing Cæsar to be in that vicinity. Utica, since the destruction of Carthage, was the principal city on the coast, and, it will be remembered, was a usual place for a Roman army to disembark, when invading Africa from Sicily. Cæsar's failure to give a rendezvous to his ships was sending them into the very clutches of the enemy.

The Moorish horse appeared to keep afoot, and on one occasion fell from ambush upon a watering party from Cæsar's ships. Otherwise there were no armed exchanges.

Cæsar was compelled to remain near the coast to collect his scattered vessels, a fact which prevented his foraging largely in the interior, and threatened to cut his victual short. But he kept actively at work. He dispatched ten vessels in search of the missing fleet. He sent into Sardinia and elsewhere for men, corn and stores, with stringent orders to comply with his requisition. The vessels in which he had come he emptied and sent back to Sicily for a new load of troops. He gave strict orders to his men by no means to leave camp. He sent out a naval force to take possession of the well-filled magazines on the island of Cercina. He reconnoitred and informed himself from natives and deserters of the status of Scipio's army.

On the 7th of November, finding Leptis less available than he had thought it, Cæsar left six cohorts there under command of Saserna, and with some nine thousand men returned to Ruspina, "whence he had come the day before." He took steps to make this a dépôt for corn, of which he collected a large supply by using his soldiers and the inhabitants with all their wagons and sumpter-animals to forage. He was anxious to have an ample supply ready against his fleet should be collected. Ruspina was much more suitable for his purposes. It was nearer Sicily. It stood well out to sea so as to give a free view to a considerable distance. The anchorage, then as now, was on the south, and protected vessels from the north and west winds, which are those to be most dreaded.

Cæsar began to foresee trouble from the non-arrival of his vessels. He made up his mind to leave the bulk of his men in garrison in Ruspina and Leptis and to go himself in search of the missing fleet; failing to find which he would sail for Sicily to bring more legions. On the same day, therefore (November 7), the ten galleys sent after his fleet not having returned, Cæsar took seven of his choice cohorts, some of those which had behaved so well in the naval actions under Sulpicius and Vatinius, and embarked. He fully understood the danger in which he had placed himself. He said nothing of his destination to his army, which consequently felt much troubled at this proposed absence. For "they saw themselves exposed upon a foreign coast to the mighty forces of a crafty nation, supported by an innumerable cavalry. Nor had they any resource in their present circumstances, or expectation of safety in their own conduct; but derived all their hope from the alacrity, vigor and wonderful cheerfulness that appeared in their general's countenance; for he was of an intrepid spirit, and behaved with undaunted resolution and confidence. On his conduct, therefore, they entirely relied, and hoped, to a man, that by his skill and talents all difficulties would vanish before them."

Just as Cæsar was on the point of sailing next morning, the fleet appeared unexpectedly in view. This event was a fair sample of Cæsar's luck, to which he owed so much throughout his life. To whom else did such things ever happen? The troops were disembarked and encamped west of but close to Ruspina, and near the coast. His situation was now improved, having twenty thousand foot and two thousand horse; but it was still far from satisfactory. He was no longer in grave peril, but it seems inexcusable that he, practically the ruler of the world, should, by his own default, be so far beneath his opponents in strength. Scipio, Cæsar knew, was in Utica, nearly one hundred miles distant.

The whole coast here is flat. From the beach back there runs, as a rule, a line of slight hills, fifty or sixty feet high, and back of these, a flat country very slightly accentuated. The roll of the plain is no greater than the average of prairie land. Ruspina stands higher than most places on the coast.

So soon as the camp had been intrenched, on November 8, Cæsar, with thirty cohorts, one hundred and fifty archers, and four hundred horse in light marching order, set out at nine A. M. on another foraging expedition, and "advanced into the country." He could not send small parties, lest they should be cut off. Due south from Ruspina runs a line of coast hills. West of these hills is a flat plain, once the bed of an inlet of the sea. It is to-day just what Cæsar described it. Easy to march along and leading to a fertile section, he chose this plain for his advance. Some three miles out from camp a great dust announced the approach of an army. The Pompeians had moved up to his vicinity, camped, and were now coming out to meet him under command of Labienus, Petreius and other lieutenants of Scipio.

Cæsar's scouts and an advanced party of cavalry had but just discovered and reported this fact. The scouting service was apparently far from being good. It was well for Cæsar that Scipio had not been able to collect his force and reach the field a day or two before, when he was disembarking his troops. Scipio's legions had been occupying an extensive territory and had needed time to concentrate. He had heard of Cæsar's arrival from Considius, and of his lack of troops. He fancied he had an easy prey. He had probably expected Cæsar to land near Utica, and had only watched the gulf of Carthage.

It was too late to retire. Nor was it Cæsar's way. Ordering the horse forward, supported by archers, of whom but a few had accompanied the column, Cæsar himself rode out to reconnoitre, and ordered the legions to follow in line of battle (d). He soon saw that he had to do with a very large part of the enemy's force, and instructed the men to prepare for battle. His total number present was perhaps twelve thousand men. The Pompeians had marched with such precaution as not to be discovered, and had surprised Cæsar with an overwhelming body of men, stated in the Commentaries at ten thousand five hundred horse, forty-four thousand foot and a large array of light troops which were mixed in the line of battle with horse. Labienus was in command.

He had conducted his march with ability. Despite the defeat at Pharsalus, Labienus was full of courage and believed that he could crush Cæsar by numbers. He proposed to use his Numidian cavalry in their own hereditary fashion, by skirmishing round Cæsar's foot and tiring it out without even coming to combat ; and fight was the very thing the legionary must do, if he would succeed. Labienus had trapped Cæsar on the level, where his work was clear and easy.

Cæsar sent back for the rest of his horse, — sixteen hundred in number. The terrain was a perfectly flat, open plain somewhat over one and a half miles wide, and growing wider in Cæsar's front. On Cæsar's left were the slight hills of Ruspina; on his right was marshy ground, the relics of the old inlet. The enemy was drawn up in deep order, with heavy bodies of cavalry on the wings and Numidian horse interspersed with the light-armed Numidians and bowmen in the centre. Labienus intended to put horse rather than foot into action. His line was much longer than Cæsar's and overshot his flanks. Cæsar imagined that he would have only infantry to fight in the enemy's main line, but the latter had mixed horse with the foot so cleverly that at a distance it looked like an infantry line. To gain space, his numbers being small, Cæsar was obliged to draw up his army in one line. This he did by moving the fifteen cohorts of the second line up into the intervals of the first, or else by opening intervals between the cohorts, or by ordering the men to take open order. His line was covered by archers, out as skirmishers, and flanked by Cæsar's few horsemen on the wings. These were ordered to be particularly careful not to charge to a distance or to allow themselves to be surrounded. His line was probably about a mile long. His left wing and Labienus' right leaned on the Ruspina hills, but these were so very slight in elevation that they afforded scant protection. Why Cæsar did not send back to camp for the balance of his force is not explained. It may be of a part with his usual over self-reliance. Or he may have thought that in case of disaster he would be better off to have in camp a strong force of fresh and undemoralized men on which to retire. At all events, he concluded to fight it out against the odds before him.

Cæsar, owing to his limited numbers, was unable to take the offensive, but waited for the enemy to advance. He saw that he must depend more on tactics or stratagem than on strength. Presently the Pompeians began to extend their line to the right and left to lap Cæsar's flanks and surround his horse, which soon had difficulty in holding its ground. At the same time the centre of horse, interspersed with foot, adopted a new tactics, the horsemen rushing forward and casting their darts and, so soon as opposed, retiring under cover of the infantry through their intervals. When the legionaries

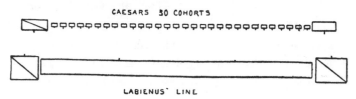

CAESARS 30 COHORTS

LABIENUS' LINE

Battle of Ruspina (first phase).

would advance beyond their line to drive off the horse, they would be taken in flank by the Numidian infantry and many wounded, while the horsemen easily escaped their darts by flight. And when the Cæsarians retired, the horse again advanced to the attack. This is similar to the tactics by which Hannibal's Numidians so frequently puzzled and defeated the legionaries of the Second Punic War. Labienus had boasted of this tactical attack by the novelty of which he believed he would certainly overwhelm Cæsar's legionaries.

Cæsar was obliged to forbid the men to advance more than four feet beyond the line of ensigns, — which from this we should imagine to be in the first rank.

Soon Labienus' force swept so far beyond Cæsar's flanks that the cavalry was crowded back upon the foot, many of the horses being wounded. The movement continued until the entire army of Cæsar was surrounded by the Pompeian hybrid squadrons. The cohorts "were obliged to form into

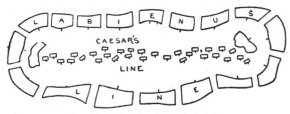

Battle of Ruspina (second phase).

a circle, as if inclosed by barriers." This they did rapidly and in good order. Despite all which, the battle had not yet advanced to hand-to-hand fighting; for these operations had been accompanied by only a skirmishing contact, and what Cæsar's men desired was to get at the enemy with the sword. They were placed at a grave disadvantage by this method of attack.

Cæsar's position was difficult and dangerous in the highest degree. The young soldiers appeared to be much demoralized, and looked only to him for countenance. Many, no doubt, thought of the massacre of Curio's army. But they found that in Cæsar's bearing which gave them confidence in him and in themselves. He was omnipresent, cheerful, active, full of encouragement. From him and the few old soldiers interspersed in the ranks the new levies took heart, and bore themselves like men.

Labienus made himself conspicuous by advancing beyond

the line and taunting Cæsar's men, over whom he imagined he was surely to obtain a complete and telling victory. In this vainglorious boasting he all but received a fatal check from a soldier of the old Tenth legion, who advanced, hurled a javelin at him, and wounded his horse. But Labienus was slow in attacking his old chief. He probably waited for a break in the lines so as to turn defeat into massacre. Cæsar saw that he must undertake some manœuvre to extricate his cohorts from their dilemma, or that he would soon succumb from some unexpected accident. As it was, it was becoming a question how long he could hold his new men in hand.

Cæsar's brain was fertile in expedients. What he did is explained at length in the Commentaries, but in such a manner as to be susceptible of several readings. In fact, many tactical manœuvres have been constructed to explain Cæsar's movement. Rüstow and Göler have each made an elaborate evolution, savoring, perhaps, a little too much of the drill-ground, of what was done. One thing may be assumed as certain. With new troops, Cæsar would be apt to undertake no very difficult tactical manœuvre; but to do that which was the simplest, and therefore most likely to work under the rather demoralizing circumstances.

The cohorts were huddled together so much that the men could not use their weapons to advantage. Cæsar saw that he must break the circle of the enemy, and was well aware that his interior position, so long as the cohorts kept their head, was much the stronger. He ordered alternate cohorts to face to the rear, and back up each against its neighbor, so as to form two fronts. The flank cohorts, presumably, as usual, of old troops, pushed their way to right and left, so as to give greater intervals to the centre cohorts; and by vigorous charges by horse and foot together, the circle of the enemy was ruptured at its two extremes. There were now two bodies of the enemy, which could not act together, and Cæsar could see that they, in their turn, were growing uneasy, while his own men, cheered by success, began to recover their elasticity.   Seizing the proper moment, Cæsar ordered both fronts to charge the enemy with a will.   The

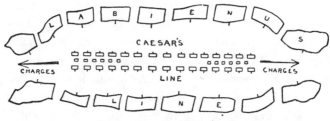

Battle of Ruspina (third phase).

result justified the order. The Pompeians turned and fled in all directions. Cæsar then faced the cohorts of the original front, which he had personally commanded, to the rear, and retired towards camp.

This manœuvre produced a temporary lull in the battle. It looked as if Cæsar could extricate himself. Just at this juncture a considerable body of foot and a select and fresh column of eleven hundred Numidian horse under M. Petreius and Cnæus Piso came up and rehabilitated matters for the enemy. Cæsar, during the lull, had begun to retire upon his camp in order of battle, and with unbroken ranks.   The enemy's newly arrived cavalry endeavored to harass his retreat and disorganize his line; but Cæsar's men had gained confidence in their chief, and in their own fighting capacity. Far from being nervous under the stress of their difficult situation, they promptly and cheerfully obeyed every order. There was no sign left of giving way. At command they sharply faced about and made bold to renew the battle in the middle of the plain. Labienus pursued the same policy of not coming to close quarters, but kept up a sharp skirmishing attack. Despite his boast, he seemed careful not to get within the reach of his old chief's arm. His presence was, however, harassing to a degree.

Cæsar saw that a supreme effort was essential if he would keep his forces so well in hand as to permit a retreat to camp. His cavalry was all tired out. On a given signal, and with a vim which only the true commander could impart, the whole force made about face, paused, and moved as one man forward at charging pace upon Labienus' line, which was now somewhat carelessly dispersed. Taken by surprise at this bold front by an enemy they supposed beaten and were waiting to see dissolve its ranks, the Pompeians were completely broken, and retired with loss beyond the hills on the west of the plain. The Cæsarians followed, and, taking possession of an eminence, held it until they could retire in order of battle. They then returned to camp in good condition. "The enemy, who in this last attack had been very roughly handled, then at length retreated to their fortifications," *i. e.*, their camp. The battle had lasted from eleven o'clock till sunset.

Cæsar's tactical manœuvre has been worked out by Rüstow to be something like this. From his one line of thirty cohorts he withdrew the even-numbered ones into a temporary second line, thus affording him a more open order which could better manœuvre. These latter cohorts then wheeled into two columns, those of the right wing to the right, those of the left wing to the left; and so soon as they were ready to charge, the horse retired around their flanks to the rear. The odd-numbered cohorts, now alone in the first line, also wheeled into column right and left, thus making two heavy columns facing outwardly to each flank. At the word of command these columns charged home right and left upon the wings of Labienus which had outflanked Cæsar's line, driving them well back but not advancing too far. Meanwhile, Cæsar collected the cavalry, which had retired behind the columns, into two bodies in the centre, and charged Labienus' centre to create a diversion there. The surprise of the whole manœuvre, particularly by troops which Labienus thought were all but defeated, was what gave it its success. So soon as the enemy had been thrown back, the cohorts again returned to their places in double line, and Cæsar began to withdraw. It cannot be said that this is accurate. It is one plausible explanation of the tactical manœuvre, and fits the description of the Commentaries, — as indeed more than one will do. But the manœuvre first given is more probable, as being simpler.

Many deserters came to Cæsar's camp. These reported that Labienus had expected to surprise and demoralize Cæsar's new troops by his unusual tactics, and then cut them to pieces as Curio had been. He had relied on his numbers rather than on discipline and his own ability, and had miscalculated Cæsar's resources of intelligence and courage when pressed. And yet he knew his old chief full well.

Cæsar had not won a victory, but he had, after being surprised, saved his army from possible annihilation by a very superior force. "Had Ruspina not been near, the Moorish javelin would perhaps have accomplished the same result here as the Parthian bow at Carrhæ," says Mommsen. But Cæsar was not a Crassus.

Cæsar now fortified his camp with great care, inclosing it with intrenchments flanked by towers which ran from the outer flank of Ruspina and that of the camp down to the sea, beside joining the town and camp (e). He could thus safely receive victuals and enginery of war and have safe access to his fleet. However strong Cæsar might make his works, the strength of his position lay in the man himself.

His own legions recognized his confidence and partook it; and in the enemy's camp, it may be presumed, the aristocrats equally felt the presence over against them of a great captain.

Cæsar did not deem it expedient just now to risk an attack on the enemy in the open field. Needing light troops, he armed many of the Gauls, Rhodians and other mariners in the fleet as slingers and archers, and drew from the fleet many Syrian and Iturean bowmen, who were serving as mariners. Though not very effective, they added a certain value to the army. He put up workshops to make engines, darts and leaden bullets, and sent to Sicily for corn, hurdles, wood for rams and other material of war. He insisted strictly on the performance of guard duty, saw to every detail himself, constantly visited the outposts, encouraged his men, and looked out for their wants with the utmost energy.

But Cæsar was unfortunate about his victual. Corn in Africa was scarce, for all the laboring population was under arms. He could not forage in the neighborhood; no corn had been left by the enemy. Many of his transports were taken by Scipio's fleet, for, not knowing where Cæsar was, the transports were uncertain where to land. Cæsar had to keep part of his fleet hovering along the coast to guide his incoming vessels. The question of subsistence taxed him to the utmost. The *motif* of the entire African campaign may be said to be the lack of victual in Cæsar's camp.

Scipio was heard to be on his way to reinforce Labienus with eight legions and three thousand horse. Cæsar, with his late arrivals, had less than thirty thousand men. Scipio and Labienus together had thrice the number. After the late battle, Labienus had sent his sick and wounded, many in number, to Hadrumetum, and made ready for a junction with Scipio. He posted cavalry outposts on all the hills around Ruspina to prevent victual from reaching Cæsar.

Scipio's intention had been to attack Cæsar before he got intrenched at Ruspina, but he was tardy. Cæsar's expedition was too great to allow of much delay by Scipio upon the march.

Scipio had left Utica with a strong garrison and marched

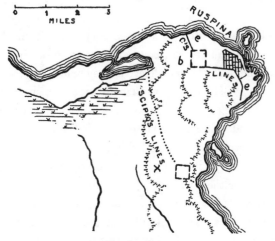

Ruspina Camp.

to Hadrumetum, where he arrived November 13. Thence, after a few days, he joined the forces under Labienus and Petreius, and all three fortified a camp about three miles south of Cæsar's works (x) before Ruspina. Scipio, no doubt, reconnoitred, but apparently did not care to attack Cæsar's intrenchments. They were too formidable. He thought he would try on Cæsar the same proceeding Cæsar had tried on Pompey at Dyrrachium, — blockade. In this he had a fair chance of success with his overwhelming odds. But he did not carry out his purpose with acumen nor with sufficient force. His guard-duties were laxly performed, and he had not the eye to seize on the salient topographical advantages of his position, though he established, apparently, a cordon about Cæsar's lines. Still, what he did soon began to interfere with Cæsar's foraging, — a serious matter, as no provisions had yet arrived from Sicily or Sardinia, and Cæsar "did not possess above six miles in each direction" from which to get corn. That he kept so much reflects small credit on Scipio's activity. Just what "six miles" may mean is subject to question. The circuit of Cæsar's inclosure was about six miles, but that he could forage much beyond is improbable in view of Scipio's great force of cavalry. The horses and cattle were largely fed on seaweed washed in fresh water, a fact which proves the considerable difficulties he was under. Cæsar was blockaded in earnest.

Young Pompey, meanwhile, in Utica, urged by Cato to do something worthy of his name, got together thirty sail, and, embarking two thousand men, invaded the land of King Bogud in Mauretania. Landing near Ascurum, the garrison allowed him to approach; then, sallying out, drove him back with confusion. Disheartened, he sailed to the Balearic Isles. Bogud was merely irritated into giving more earnest support to Cæsar, who made use of every means to which he could put his hand. P. Sitius, a soldier of fortune expatriated by the Catalinian *fiasco*, had collected a force of motley legionaries and served various African potentates for pay. Him Cæsar set to influence King Bogud to invade Numidia, whose king, Juba, was on the march to join Scipio. In this he succeeded. Sitius and Bogud advanced into Numidia, took Cirta (Constantine), put the citizens to the sword, and captured Juba's stronghold of provisions and war material. Juba was summarily called to defend his own territory. This defection was a serious blow to Scipio. Juba left but thirty elephants with the Pompeian army, out of the large number he had brought. Juba's approach had threatened to add the last straw to the load Cæsar had to bear; his change of mind distinctly modified the danger.

XXXIX.

INTRENCHED ADVANCE. DECEMBER, 47 B. C.

CÆSAR strongly intrenched himself in Ruspina to await the arrival of the rest of his legions. The country towns and people were mostly favorable to him, but under the control of the Pompeians. Scipio lay in a large camp three miles down the coast, with an outpost in Ucita, a small town in the middle of a plain surrounded by rolling hills. Cæsar was anxious to bring Scipio to battle, but on his own terms. All through this campaign he appeared to avoid a general engagement. He moved the bulk of his forces out to the heights east of Ucita, and intrenched. Between him and Ucita, in the plain and on the hills on its west, a number of skirmishes ensued, but no approach to a battle, though Cæsar frequently offered it. Cæsar determined to capture Ucita, which had been made the centre of Scipio's defensive line. He advanced a series of fieldworks from his intrenchments on the hills across the plain towards the town, so that he might not be attacked in flank. With a force all but equal, if not quite, to Scipio's, Cæsar, for some reason, did not force the fighting, though he restlessly manœuvred against the enemy.

So soon as the province of Africa was convinced of Cæsar's arrival in person, — this had not been believed, owing to the allegations of the enemy that only a legate was in command, until Cæsar communicated with the important towns himself, — many persons of rank sent in their offers of allegiance and complained bitterly of the cruelty of the Pompeian coalition, which had sucked the life-blood out of the land by their rapacity. Cæsar determined to undertake active operations as soon as the season would admit, and sent word to Alienus, the prætor in Sicily, that the troops must be forwarded, whatever the weather, if he was to preserve Africa from utter ruin. "And he himself was so anxious and impatient, that from the day the letters were sent he complained without ceasing of the delay of the fleet, and had his eyes night and day turned towards the sea." Meanwhile, the enemy continued to ravage the country, which Cæsar was forced to watch, and could not prevent owing to his small force. But he increased his works, and made his camp almost impregnable with redoubts and defenses, and carried the lines quite to the sea.

Cæsar's constrained position was due to his own overeager act in attacking the African problem with insufficient means. However justly we may admire Cæsar as perhaps the greatest man of ancient days, as indisputably one of the world's great captains, we cannot justly overlook his errors. Cæsar must be tried by his peers. His habit of undertaking operations with inadequate forces was a distinct failing from which only "Cæsar's fortune" on many occasions saved him. This characteristic of his military life cannot but be condemned. It is beyond question that all the danger and delay to which he had been subjected since sailing from Lilybæum were attributable to a carelessness which militates as much against his character as a captain as his subsequent splendid efforts to save himself from ruin and to defeat his enemies redound to his credit. His energy and skill in saving himself from self-imposed dangers are thoroughly admirable.

A great captain must face any odds of numbers or conditions when it is essential. But sound preparation is one of the corner-stones of his reputation. Foolhardiness may show courage; but it shows equal lack of discretion. Overhastiness is still worse. In the mixed caution and boldness of the captain, Hannibal far outranks Cæsar. But Hannibal had not the help of Fortune as Alexander and Cæsar always had.

It would seem clear that Scipio's best policy was the one which Cato urged upon him, — to move into the interior and, if possible, lure Cæsar away from the coast to a point where he would find it not only harder to victual, but to keep his army up to fighting level. But Scipio was not gifted with military sense. Instead of this course, he garrisoned Hadrumetum and Thapsus, and sought to shut Cæsar in. He spent much time in drilling his elephants in mock battles so as to train them to face the enemy. He knew that, as a rule, elephants in battle had proved as dangerous to one army as to another, — but Scipio could not give up his desire to put these beasts to use in his line.

As usual, the cavalry outposts of the two parties continually skirmished, and the German and Gallic cavalry occasionally exchanged greetings on a prearranged truce. Labienus tried on several occasions to surprise Leptis, but was beaten off by the three cohorts then in garrison under Saserna. The town was strongly fortified and well supplied with catapults and ballistas, which made up for its situation on the flat seashore where it had no natural defenses.

On one of these occasions when a strong squadron was before the gates, their chief was slain by a shaft from an engine which pinned him to his own shield. The whole body, terrified, took to flight, "by which means the town was delivered from any further attempts," — a fact which argues illy for the cool-headedness of Labienus' squadrons, and is a curious commentary on the value of the nomad cavalry of antiquity. When such a man as Hannibal headed it, it was alone effective; and then it was an arm of exceptional power.

When Scipio had finished his preparations and felt strong enough to fight Cæsar, he began about the 20th of November to draw up on successive days some three hundred paces from his own camp and to offer battle. This was invariably declined. Cæsar was awaiting his veterans and supplies, and could not be provoked into paying any attention to Scipio's taunts; and his works were impregnable. This "forbearance and tranquillity gave him (Scipio) such a contempt of Cæsar and his army" that on one occasion in a boastful spirit Scipio advanced with his whole army and towered elephants up to Cæsar's very ramparts. But Cæsar merely ordered in his outposts of horse when the enemy advanced to dart-throwing distance, called in his fatigue parties, posted his men, ordered his reserve cavalry under arms, and awaited the assault if they were foolish enough to make it.

"These orders were not given by himself in person, or after viewing the disposition of the enemy from the rampart; but such was his consummate knowledge of the art of war, that he gave all the necessary directions by his officers, he himself sitting in his tent and informing himself of the motives of the enemy by his scouts." This is the first instance in ancient military books where a commanding general is described as managing a battle just as he would do to-day. The Roman general was always at the front in person. Cæsar knew that the enemy would not dare to assault his works, for he had cross-bows, engines and other missile-throwing devices, besides abatis and *trous de loup* in plenty; but he was ready to receive them should they really attempt the storm. He did not desire a battle until he could make it a crushing defeat, and to insure this he waited for the veterans who were to arrive on the next embarkation. Scipio, out of this caution, made loud a claim of cowardice against Cæsar, exhorted his troops and promised them speedy victory. Cæsar resumed his work on the fortifications, and "under pretense of fortifying his camp, inured the levies to labor and fatigue."

But meanwhile many deserters, Numidians and Gætulians, came to Cæsar "because they understood he was related to C. Marius, from whom their ancestors had received considerable favors" during the Jugurthan wars. Many of these returned home and wrought up their friends to favor Cæsar's cause. Cæsar had spies in Scipio's camp in plenty and kept abreast with his purposes. Many tribes sent in offers of allegiance. Deputies came from Acilla, which perhaps has been identified with El Alia, some twenty miles south of Thapsus, and from other towns, requesting garrisons and promising supplies. Cæsar sent a small force to Acilla under C. Messius, who had been ædile. On the way, this body was all but intercepted by Considius, who was apparently on a general reconnoissance from his headquarters at Hadrumetum, with eight cohorts; but the garrison reached the town before him. Considius returned to Hadrumetum, whence, securing some horse, he again made his way to Acilla and laid siege to it.

About November 26 there arrived a large supply of corn from Cercina on board the fleet of transports which Cæsar had sent thither; and equally to be desired, the Thirteenth and Fourteenth legions, eight hundred Gallic horse, one thousand archers and slingers, and a great deal of war material from Alienus, the prætor at Lilybæum. The fleet laden with these troops had had a favorable wind and had made the passage in four days, — a distance of somewhat less than two hundred miles. This double arrival "animated the soldiers and delivered them from apprehensions of want." The cohorts, after a proper rest, Cæsar distributed on his works. He also ascertained that those of his ships which had not yet arrived were only detained by adverse winds, and that none had been taken by the enemy.

This failure to move greatly puzzled Scipio, all the more from Cæsar's usually all but abnormal activity. He sent two Gætulians as spies in the guise of deserters, and with promises of great rewards, into Cæsar's camp to discover what they could about the pitfalls and entanglements Cæsar had made; in what manner he proposed to meet the elephants, and what his dispositions were for battle. This only resulted in the men remaining in Cæsar's service and in increasing the number of real deserters. Of these there was daily a large number. But Cato at Utica supplied these gaps by the recruits he sent from there. These were mostly freedmen, Africans or slaves. The neighboring towns aided Cæsar as much as possible. Tysdra (modern El Djem), a town thirty miles to the south, pointed out to him a store of three hundred thousand bushels of corn belonging to Italian merchants, which he was, however, unable to seize. P. Sitius, still active, made an incursion into Numidia and captured an important castle of King Juba's, holding much victual and war material.

Cæsar now dispatched six of his transports to Sicily for the remainder of the troops. Though still far weaker in numbers he had enough men to face the enemy, and determined to manœuvre for a good chance to bring him to battle.

South of Cæsar's works at Ruspina lay "a fine plain, extending fifteen miles and bordering upon a chain of mountains of moderate height, that formed a kind of theatre." It is the same to-day as Cæsar describes it (f). The width of the valley is from two to five miles. The hills surrounding it vary from three hundred to six hundred feet. The northern outlet leads to a marsh near the sea. Six miles from the coast, in the centre of the plain, lay Ucita, a town held by a strong garrison of Scipio's. On the highest of the hills were watch-towers, and at various points of the valley Scipio had infantry guards and cavalry outposts. Cæsar did not propose to allow Scipio to inclose him in siege lines; he must break the growing circle, and this was a good place to do it. If Cæsar could gain possession of this plain it would also go far towards cutting Scipio off from Leptis, which he could

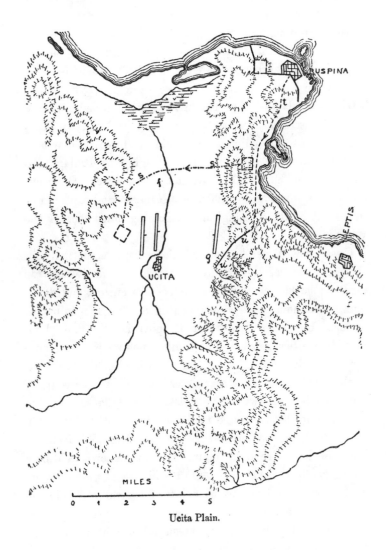

MILES

0   1   2   3   4   5

Ucita Plain.

then reach only by a long circuit and make it easier to hold
this place. This would secure him two good harbors, Ruspina and Leptis.

As Cæsar's good fortune would have it, Scipio was hard
up for water in his camp south of Ruspina, and determined to
move to a point where there was a better supply. He gave
up his camp November 27, and made for the hills on the west
of the Ucita plain (s s). This afforded Cæsar his opportunity, and he followed.

Cæsar's main purpose was probably to feel the enemy and
by a series of movements seek to put him at a disadvantage
so as to draw him into battle on terms helpful to himself.
Accordingly, on the last day of November, leaving a suitable
force in the Ruspina lines, he broke camp at midnight with
the rest of the infantry and all the cavalry and marched (t t)
away from Ruspina along the seashore, left in front, and,
striking the hills on the eastern side of the plain, he filed to
the south along them until his head of column neared Scipio's
cavalry outposts (g). He was careful to avoid the plain, for
fear of the Numidian cavalry, of which he had had so serious
a taste in the last encounter. Here Cæsar began to fortify
the most available line "along the middle of the ridge, from
the place at which he was arrived to that whence he set out;"
that is, he threw up works (u) crowning the slope of the hills
and facing substantially west. He was so placed as to prevent the enemy from cutting him off from Ruspina..

The "mountains" Cæsar refers to in all these operations
in the triangular theatre of Hadrumetum, Thysdra, Thapsus,
do not exist to-day, and from very evident geological conditions never did exist. There has been no change of topography since Cæsar's day. The highest point in this theatre
is six hundred feet; the highest point on which operations
were conducted is half that height. The ridge Cæsar occu-

pied is less than one hundred and fifty feet above the Ucita valley. Where Cæsar drew his lines is half way down the ridge, which here is cut up by ravines and is very stony. To read the Commentaries without knowledge of the topography is very misleading.

When dawn came on, Scipio and Labienus became aware of Cæsar's operations. Scipio's new camp was to the west of the valley, and Labienus appears to have had a supplementary camp near Ucita, between that town and the hills. The Pompeians at once determined to intercept the work. They advanced their troops in two lines, the cavalry in front

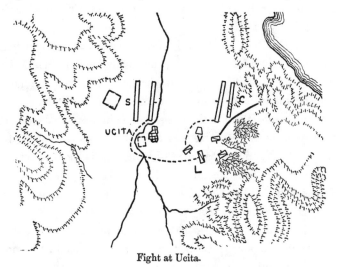

Fight at Ucita.

about a mile from their camp opposite Ruspina, the infantry one half mile in its rear. Scipio imagined that Cæsar's men would be exhausted by the night's work, and would fall an easy prey to an attack. When Cæsar saw that they had come within fifteen hundred paces, — a mile and a half, — a distance too small for him safely to continue his work on the intrenchments, he ordered some of his Spanish cavalry and

archers to attack the party of Numidian cavalry which held
a post on a hill near his own left, but on the enemy's right.
This was done in good form and the Numidians were quickly
driven off. Seeing this, Labienus led all his horse from the
right wing of his advance line to the assistance of this retiring force. So soon as this last detachment was separated
from the main army of Scipio, Cæsar threw forward his own
left wing to intercept them, and advanced a body of cavalry
to the right.

In the plain east of Ucita was a large villa and grounds
(v) which lay west of the hills where the cavalry skirmish
had just taken place. These grounds happened to hide from
Labienus the view of the movement of Cæsar's cavalry.
Under cover of this obstacle Cæsar's horse advanced, and
when Labienus had passed beyond the villa, presenting to
it his naked left, it wheeled round upon his flank and rear,
and charged home with a will. The astonished Numidians
at once broke and fled; but a body of Gallic and German
cavalry which Labienus had induced to accompany him from
Gaul, having stood their ground, Cæsar's men fell upon this
detachment, surrounded and cut it up. The sight of this
defeat so demoralized Scipio's legions that they could not be
held in hand, but retired in disorder from the plain and even
the hills. His loss had been very large. Cæsar did not
pursue, but retired to his lines and again set to work to complete his intrenchments.

This was an auspicious beginning. Cæsar had gained
possession of a foothold in the plain and a marked moral
advantage over Scipio. About December 4 he moved his
entire army, except the Ruspina garrison, into the new
intrenchments, which completely covered Ruspina and practically Leptis.

Next day Cæsar marched out from the new lines, drew up

and offered battle. He was anxious to see what Scipio would do. He had gained a strong point the day before and wanted to assert it for the influence on his young troops. But the Pompeian, discouraged by his defeat, declined the öffer. Cæsar marched along the foot of the hills to within a mile of Ucita, hoping he might take it by a *coup de main;* for not only had Scipio accumulated great stores in the town, but here, too, were the wells from which he drew the bulk of his

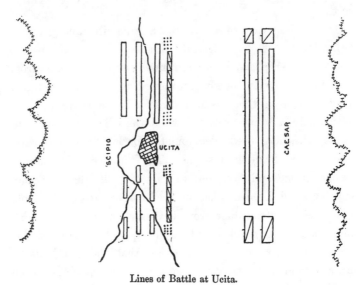

Lines of Battle at Ucita.

supply; and good water was so scarce along the coast that it was for this he had left his old camp.

Perceiving Cæsar's movement, Scipio, fearing to lose the place, at once marched out with his entire army to its defense, and drew up in four deep lines, "the first of cavalry, supported by elephants with castles on their backs." His depth made it impossible for him to outflank Cæsar. Cæsar stopped and waited for Scipio's advance. The latter, however, keeping Ucita as if it were a fieldwork in his centre, merely advanced his two wings on either side of the town, and remained in line. He had none too great confidence in his troops. Cæsar did not see a good chance of attacking both the town and the army on either side of it at the same time, and as it was now sunset and his men had fasted since morning, he withdrew to the intrenchments. But one good result of the last few days' manœuvring by Cæsar was to constrain Considius to abandon the siege of Acilla, ably defended by Messius, from which he retired with some loss to Hadrumetum by a long circuit "through the kingdom of Juba."

Nothing exhibits the fidelity of Cæsar's soldiers better than the capture about this time of one of his transports and a galley with some legionaries on board. These men were sent to Scipio, who offered them freedom and rewards if they would join his banner. Among them was a centurion of the Fourteenth legion. He answered Scipio's promises by a firm refusal to serve against Cæsar. He told the Pompeian that he quite underrated Cæsar's soldiers, and in proof challenged him to pick out the best cohort in his army and give him but ten of his comrades, and he would agree to destroy the cohort in open fight. The penalty of this faithful boldness was the death of all these veterans. Incensed at the capture of this transport, Cæsar broke the officers whose duty it was to patrol the coast to protect the landing of his vessels.

Cæsar's forces on this campaign, as already stated, were unprovided with baggage. So strict had he been in prescribing light order that even officers had been forbidden to take slaves or camp-kit. Moreover, he shifted his ground every few days, and thus prevented the men from thoroughly housing themselves from the weather, as they would have done if put into winter-quarters. They were reduced to making huts of brush, and to employing clothing or mats or

rushes as tent covering.   One severe hailstorm is mentioned
in the Commentaries, as occurring early in December,
which destroyed all the huts, put out the fires, soaked the
rations, laid the whole camp under water, and obliged the
soldiers to wander about with their bucklers over their heads
to protect themselves from the hailstones.   It reminds one
of the great storm which came so near demoralizing the phalanx of Alexander in the Hindoo Koosh.

Despite his numbers, Scipio felt that he was weak, and he
earnestly urged King Juba to join him.   The latter, well
aware that he ran greater danger from Cæsar's winning in
Africa than from any efforts of Sitius, left Sabura with part
of the army to protect his territory against this partisan chief
and King Bogud, and started with three legions, eight hundred regular and much Numidian horse, thirty elephants and
a vast number of light troops towards the Pompeian camp.
His arrival had been heralded with loud boasts which produced a certain uneasiness in Cæsar's camp, where daily
deserters spread all the rumors of Scipio's.   But when, about
December 20, Juba actually arrived, the legionaries, after a
glimpse at his undisciplined rabble, saw that they might
despise his numbers.   Scipio, however, celebrated this reinforcement by drawing up in line with the entire joint forces
and ostentatiously offering battle to Cæsar.   The only
response of the latter was a quiet advancement of his lines
along the ridge towards the south.   Juba camped north of
Scipio (j).

Scipio had now received all the reinforcements he could
expect and Cæsar believed that he could be brought to battle.
He had camped opposite Ucita, between two ravines, each
of which protected a flank.   He "began to advance along
the ridge with his forces, secure them with redoubts, and
possess himself of the hills between him and Scipio," who

still had outposts on the east slope of the valley, south of
Cæsar. The lattter could gain marked advantages by obtaining possession of this entire range of hills. He would be rid
of the cavalry outposts of the enemy which interfered with his

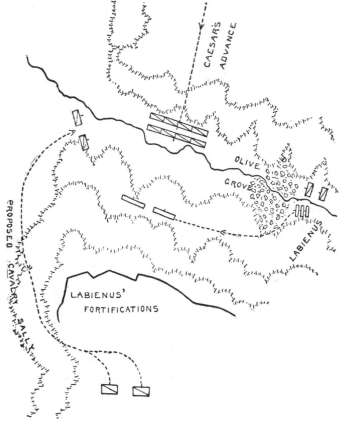

Ravine Fight.

watering parties. He would secure his left flank in case he
desired to advance against the enemy. He could seriously
impede the enemy's offensive movements, and perhaps, out of
some of the minor encounters, develop a general engagement
under favorable conditions. This advance of Cæsar's lines

Labienus sought to arrest by fortifying one of the hills beyond Cæsar's left (h). To reach this hill Cæsar had a rugged, rocky valley to pass, at the bottom of which was a thick grove of old olives. Here Labienus, anticipating Cæsar's manœuvre, about December 24 placed himself, with some horse and foot, in an ambuscade under cover of the grove, which lay well to the rear of the valley, and sent a body of cavalry to lie in hiding south of the fortified hill so as to be able to debouch on Cæsar's rear if he advanced so far as to attack it. Unaware of either ambush, Cæsar sent forward his cavalry, but Labienus' foot soldiers, fearing to encounter Cæsar's horsemen in the plain, began too soon to break out of cover in the olive wood in order to oppose them on the south bank of the ravine, where they had the advantage of height. This utterly upset Labienus' stratagem. Cæsar's horse easily dispersed this body of infantry in its scattered formation; the cavalry ambuscade also went wrong, and Labienus barely made good his own escape. This retreat having drawn from hiding the whole of Labienus' party, the Cæsarians captured the hill beyond as they had set out to do, and there Cæsar at once threw up a work and garrisoned it strongly. His camp was now inexpugnable.

Cæsar made up his mind to capture Ucita, a town which "stood between him and the enemy, and was garrisoned by a detachment of Scipio's army." But Scipio, with his numbers, was able to protect the town by such a long line of battle, that Cæsar's flanks would be exposed in advancing on Ucita across the plain. This led him to undertake another of those remarkable feats of field fortification for which the time was noted, and in which he especially excelled and carried out in all his campaigns. It is curious to see how Cæsar, who was capable of doing such hazardous things as to come to Africa with a mere handful of men, would resort to such hypercautious means of accomplishing an object, when his strength was greater, if properly gauged by quality, than the enemy's. We are not able to weigh all the existing conditions; we do not know them. But taking the Commentaries as the basis of our information, we are as much surprised at Cæsar's caution here as we were at his boldness in the operations at Dyrrachium. Still, we understand the situation fairly well; the topography and facts are before us, and we can only ascribe Cæsar's caution either to mood or to distrust of his newly raised legions. To give orders for a battle is as often a matter of inspiration as of calculation and preparation. Here Cæsar had an easier task than at Pharsalus, in luring Scipio into battle on the Ucita plain; and Scipio's troops were no better than his own. In Alexander there was but one mood: "de l'audace, encore de l'audace, toujours de l'audace!" In Hannibal's caution, when we know the facts, there is always a consistent reason and one which appeals to us. Cæsar's caution we are often put to it to explain. It was not perhaps so much the capture of Ucita at which Cæsar was aiming, as the chance in some manner of placing Scipio at a disadvantage so as to lead up to his defeat in a decisive engagement, — without too much risk.

To carry out his plan, about December 26 Cæsar began to throw out westward two parallel lines of works, facing north and south, from his camp at the foot of the slope across the plain in such a direction as to strike the outer corners of the town of Ucita. This, say the Commentaries, he did so that he might have his flanks amply protected from the enemy's vast force of cavalry in case he should besiege or assault the town; or, indeed, from any attempt by Labienus to outflank him. The proximity of these works facilitated desertion from the enemy to Cæsar. Within these lines he could sink wells, the plain being low, and he was in want of water at his camp upon the hills, and had to send to a distance for it.

The prosecution of the work was protected by a body of horse backed by some cohorts, which fended off the Numidian

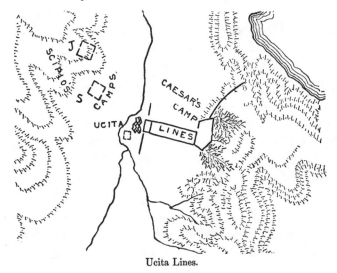

Ucita Lines.

cavalry and archers. The intrenchment was begun after dark, and was so far completed on two successive nights as to be occupied by the troops before the succeeding morning. During this work his men held frequent intercourse with the enemy's soldiers, — as, indeed, at all times when they could safely approach each other, — the result of which was almost invariably desertion to Cæsar. But of desertions from Cæsar there may be said to have been none. The Commentaries at least acknowledge no desertions, and their number was in any event small. A number of cavalry exchanges took place, in the majority of which the troops of Cæsar had the upper hand. Scipio's horse was much more numerous, but far from being as well drilled or steady. Nor had it that instinct which enables cavalry under a born leader to accomplish the wonders it sometimes does.

One day towards evening, — it may have been December 29, — as Cæsar was drawing off the fatigue parties, Juba, Labienus and Scipio, at the head of all their horse and light troops, fell upon the cavalry outposts and drove them in. But Cæsar quickly collected a few cohorts of legionaries, who always had their arms at hand, and leading them up to the assistance of the horse, reëstablished the combat. Seeing themselves well supported, the cavalry turned with a brilliant charge upon the Numidians, who were scattered over the plain by the pursuit they had just undertaken, slew a large number, and hustled the rest into rapid flight. Juba and Labienus barely escaped capture under cover of the dust. The result of this handsome interchange was that still more numerous deserters from the Fourth and Sixth legions came over to Cæsar, as well as a large number of Curio's horse.

Gætulia, roused by the leading citizens whom Cæsar had sent back to their homes for this purpose, now revolted from King Juba. This monarch, with three wars at once on his hands, was constrained to detach a considerable part of his force to protect his own borders. But he himself remained in the Pompeian camp with the remainder and made himself obnoxious by his insolence, meddling and vanity.

The Ninth and Tenth legions, on the last day of the year, arrived from Sicily, after a narrow escape from capture as the result of their own imprudence. The relics of their old spirit of mutiny were still evident in their undisciplined conduct. One of the military tribunes, C. Avienus, had gone so far as to fill one transport exclusively with his own slaves and camp-equipage. The legions had too long been on easy duty near Rome. In order to bring these men under curb, Cæsar resorted to sharp and decisive measures, and took the

case of Avienus as a pretext.   He broke this and one other
tribune and several centurions, and sent them out of Africa
under guard.   Among the Romans, to be cashiered was all
but the heaviest penalty which could be inflicted.   It was a
deprivation of all the culprit's civil rights, honor and character.   The cohorts of the Ninth and Tenth were put into the
trenches, with no more equipage or rations than the other
men.

Counting in the new arrivals, Cæsar's heavy infantry
force of five veteran and five new legions was nearly if not
quite equal to Scipio's.   The latter had more light troops,
but these were practically worthless in battle.   Cæsar still
looked for two more legions from Sicily, and Juba, having
been obliged to send away part of his army, depleted Scipio's
numbers.   The new year opened with Cæsar's chances fully
equal to those of the enemy.

Ancient Helmet.   (Louvre.)

XL.

UCITA.   JANUARY, 46 B. C.

THOUGH Cæsar's lines had reached Ucita, he still waited for more of his troops. These shortly arrived, though barely escaping capture. Each of the commanders daily drew up for battle, but neither attacked; and meanwhile further fortifying was their only activity. It had become difficult for Cæsar to victual his army. In foraging he was often reduced to fighting his way to and fro. Finally, between lack of corn and lack of a chance of battle on favorable terms, Cæsar gave up his designs on Ucita, and moved down the coast to near Leptis. His intrenchments had been made for naught. To all appearances Scipio had won the game. In a bold raid on Zeta, in which he ran an exceptional risk to procure victual, Cæsar had a brisk combat with the enemy; but nothing decisive came of it. He was still aiming to get a certain chance to thrust home. Scipio neither gave him an opening nor improved his advantages. Finally Cæsar determined upon a siege of Thapsus as a means of compelling Scipio to battle, and marched thither, reducing several towns on his way.

IN the early days of January, 46 B. C., having finished his works up to a point just beyond dart-throwing distance from Ucita, Cæsar built a line across the head of the works, mounted on the parapet and towers a number of military engines, and constantly plied these against the town. He brought five legions to the west end of the lines from the large camp at the east. The lines were almost two miles long. It speaks well for Cæsar's activity, skill and care that he was able to build and man such extensive works without affording an opportunity to Scipio to break through at any one point while incomplete. But Cæsar was the ablest engineer of his age, almost of any age.

When the lines were finished he was secure. It was generally deemed impossible to capture well-manned intrenchments, and Scipio was not the man to try. We have seen how reluctant Cæsar was to attempt such an assault, even when the defenders were savages. The successful completion of the lines produced other desertions of men of decided consequence to Cæsar's camp, and at the same time furnished him with one thousand more horse. Scipio, meanwhile, was not idle. He also undertook to fortify all available and useful points on his own front, and prepared for a vigorous and stout defense when Cæsar should attack Ucita.

The Seventh and Eighth legions now sailed from Sicily, and Varus at Utica thought there was a promising opportunity to intercept them. He weighed anchor with fifty-five vessels for this purpose and sailed to Hadrumetum. Cæsar had sent twenty-seven sail, under L. Cispius, to Thapsus, and thirteen sail under Q. Aquila to Hadrumetum with orders to anchor, watch for, and protect the convoys. Aquila's part of the fleet being unable to double the cape, they took shelter in an inlet near by. The mistral, or west wind on the Mediterranean, has always been a fruitful source of annoyance. To-day, large steamers often cannot land passengers at either Sousa (Hadrumetum) or Monastir (Thapsus). The balance of the fleet at Leptis was left riding at anchor; but the mariners were mostly ashore, some buying provisions, some wandering about, — a matter indicating poor discipline. A deserter notified Varus of these facts. He left Hadrumetum at night, — the mistral blew in his favor, — and next morning, January 9, reaching Leptis, came suddenly upon Cæsar's fleet in the same unprotected condition, burned all the transports, and carried off two five-benched galleys, "in which were none to defend them."

Cæsar heard of this misfortune while engaged inspecting his works at Ucita. Roused at the prospect of losing his men and victuals, he summarily took horse and rode to Leptis, happily only six miles distant, went aboard the most available galley, ordered his fleet to follow, joined Aquila, whom he found much demoralized in his retreat, pursued Varus, who, astonished, tacked about and made for Hadrumetum, recovered one of his galleys with one hundred and thirty of the enemy aboard, took one of the enemy's triremes,

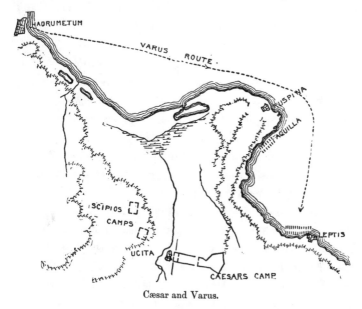

Cæsar and Varus.

which had fallen astern, and drove Varus into Hadrumetum. Cæsar could not double the cape with the same wind, which suddenly shifted; but, riding at anchor during the night, on the next day, when the east wind sprang up, he sailed near the harbor of Hadrumetum and burned a number of the enemy's transports lying outside. Aboard the captured galley was P. Vestrius, a Roman knight, who had been in Spain under Afranius, and after being paroled, had again joined Pompey in Greece, and later Varus, without exchange or ransom. Him Cæsar ordered to be executed for breach of his oath.

This fact shows that the paroling of prisoners was well understood, with at least some of its rights and liabilities.

This short expedition of Cæsar's exhibits the marvelous audacity, decision and skill of the man. Everything he undertook in person was carried through with an active intelligence which insured success. Whomever he attacked he was sure to defeat. Had he not done just this and done it in person, probably his transports, his fleets, his corn, his enginery, his legions would all have been liable to be cut off. Some of these minor expeditions of Cæsar show that if he had not been a great general, he would have made the very pattern of a partisan officer. All the more wonder that occasionally, as now before Ucita, Cæsar was almost a McClellan for his want of incisiveness.

Each commander now essayed to bring the other to battle on advantageous terms. Scipio, on a day shortly after the completion of Cæsar's lines, — January 7, — marshaled his army on a slight elevation running along the west bank of the brook which bisected the plain. Cæsar did the like on a parallel rise in the ground, but awaited the attack. On the floor of this valley can now be seen but slight indications of these eminences. It is nearly level. But a very little slope in the ground was of marked advantage to the Roman soldier, and the Commentaries often speak of hills which we should scarcely notice.

The enemy exceeded Cæsar in numbers; they had a strong garrison in Ucita opposite his right wing, so that if he defeated them and pursued beyond Ucita he might be compromised by a sally from the town; the ground in front of Scipio was rough and thoroughly bad for a charge. The valley in places is very stony. Where the brook had worn its way it was more so; and to attack required Cæsar to cross the brook. The two armies were marshaled within

three hundred paces of each other. Nothing divided them
but this slight depression in the ground. Scipio's left
leaned on the town, which was an advanced redoubt, as it
were, affording it ample protection. His own and Juba's
legions were in the front, the Numidians in a second line in

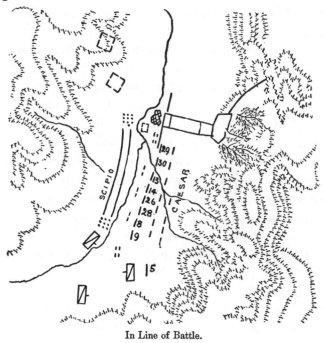

In Line of Battle.

reserve, but in an extended thin formation. "At a distance
you would have taken the main body for a simple line of
legionaries doubled only on the wings." On the right and
left at equal distances Scipio placed elephants supported by
light troops and auxiliary Numidians. The regular cavalry
was on the right in one body, not being needed or available
near Ucita. The Numidian and Gætulian horse, — irregulars, "without bridles," — sustained by a great body of light
troops, formed a flying right wing one thousand paces from

his right extending out towards the hills. Scipio's intention was to envelop Cæsar's left with all his cavalry and "throw it into confusion by their darts," when the action should begin.

In Cæsar's front line the Eighth and Ninth veteran legions were on the left, to-day the post of danger; the Thirteenth and Fourteenth, Twenty-sixth and Twenty-eighth, in the centre; the Twenty-ninth and Thirtieth on the right, leaning on the Ucita works. His second line was composed of the new levies, mixed with cohorts from the legions above named. His third line, composed of the third-line cohorts of the right legions, withdrawn for the purpose and replaced by some new cohorts, extended only from the centre of the line to the left, as the right was so strongly posted at the intrenchments opposite Ucita as to need no reserve. His right wing was thus in two, his left in three lines. All his cavalry stood on his left, opposite the enemy's, mixed with light foot; and because he put no great reliance on these, the Fifth legion was placed in reserve in their rear. The archers were principally on the wings, but bodies of them stood in the front.

The two armies thus drawn up remained in line all day, but three hundred paces apart, neither party willing to advance across the low ground, — a most unusual spectacle. It strikes one as curious, indeed, that Cæsar, who was so prompt in his attack at Pharsalus, where he had but half Pompey's force, and where excellent Roman legions under an able leader confronted him, should have been so slow at opening the battle here, when he was about on a par with his antagonists, a large part of whose troops were far from good either in quality or discipline. This is especially so as Pompey had recently beaten him at Dyrrachium, and in any event was far superior to Scipio in ability. Fighting a battle is, with any commanding general, often a matter of temporary vigor or lack of it, and Cæsar's indecision on this occasion may have depended on his state of health. An inspection of the terrain shows that there was nothing in any respect as disadvantageous to Cæsar as the hill at Pharsalus. And we seem to have all the details.

The simple fact is that Cæsar, in tactical attack, had far inferior initiative than Alexander, or than Hannibal, so long as the latter's conditions gave him anything approaching an equality to the Romans. In almost all Cæsar's battles, unless forced on him, he was slow in attack. In strategic initiative, on the contrary, Cæsar was admirable. It was one constant, never-ceasing push.

At night, when Cæsar was retiring to camp, the flying cavalry wing of the enemy moved out towards the works upon the hill. The heavy horse under Labienus remained opposite the legions. Seeing this, part of Cæsar's horse and light foot sallied out without orders to attack the Gætulians, and advancing through a morass, probably made by the brook, but which does not to-day exist, were driven in with a loss of a number of men and many horses wounded. Scipio, rejoiced at this success, retired to camp. This check was compensated for next day, when a party of Cæsar's horse, on their way to Leptis for corn, killed or captured an hundred of the enemy's troops who were straggling from camp.

Both armies now busied themselves with advancing their lines and intrenching new positions opposite each other. Scipio sought to strengthen his holding on the hills back of Ucita. Cæsar's especial endeavor was to cut Scipio's right off from the hills on his own left. He therefore "carried a ditch and rampart along the middle of the plain to prevent the incursions of the enemy." This phrase has been translated "quite across the plain," but that cannot be explained by anything which the probabilities or later events show us to have been done. There is no evidence that a ditch and rampart were carried across the Ucita plain from east to west; nor was there reason for it. The passage probably means that opposite Ucita Cæsar extended the head of his

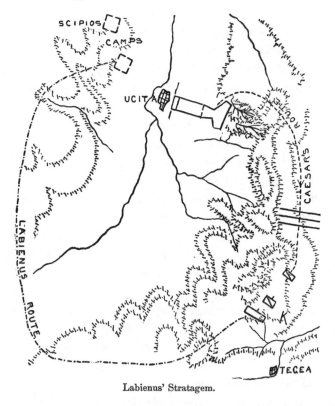

Labienus' Stratagem.

works in a long line north and south, — "along the middle of the plain." Scipio sought to anticipate any attack by Cæsar. The cavalry skirmished every day between the two parties.

The inhabitants of Africa, then as now, were wont to keep their corn in little caches or underground vaults for safety in time of war. Cæsar, who was in constant want of victual, sent out a party of two legions and some cavalry one night, which within a radius of ten miles in the fruitful region south of Agar collected a large supply of corn from these hiding-places and returned to camp. Labienus, expecting that Cæsar would again pursue the same road for the same purpose, laid an ambuscade for him on January 12 about seven miles from the plain where operations were being conducted. This was presumably in the vicinity of Tegea, where the plain narrows between two lines of hills (k).

Cæsar became aware of this stratagem through the medium of deserters. He waited a few days until Labienus' men should become a trifle careless. Sending forward part of his cavalry, he followed with eight legions and the rest of the squadrons. The cavalry came unexpectedly upon Labienus' outposts of light troops, which were taking their ease in their cover and paying small heed to the duty they were sent on, fell on them and broke them up with a loss of five hundred men. Labienus, near by, hurried up to their assistance with his own horse, and, by weight of numbers, had routed Cæsar's cavalry, when he suddenly ran against Cæsar's line of legions, which compelled him to beat a summary retreat to the west. His ambuscade had been a failure. Juba crucified all the Numidian runaways as an example.

Cæsar, despite all his efforts, was unable to collect the corn he needed to feed his men. He was reduced either to shift his ground or else to make an attack on Scipio in his defenses. On estimating the chances, Cæsar deemed the risk of the assault greater than the possible loss of *morale* incident to a change of base and the abandonment of the position gained by so much exertion and sacrifice. Besides, he knew how easy it was to him to persuade his army that they retired with honor, and the labor had really been useful in hardening the legions.

The whole matter is somewhat puzzling. Cæsar must have long ago foreseen that his supplies would be precarious. He had gone to incredible exertions to create works from which he could fight a battle with Scipio to advantage. The army opposing him was by no means as good and scarcely larger than his own. He had pushed his manœuvring at Ilerda; he had boldly attacked Pompey at Pharsalus, who had a superiority much more marked; here he declined the combat. It is unlike the Cæsar we are apt to believe in; and yet not unlike the real Cæsar. The best explanation lies in the probability that his intrenchments had been made in the hope that he could lure Scipio out into the open and there defeat him; that Scipio had erected excellent works and that Cæsar did not care for an assault. We must remember, too, that Cæsar did not have the same splendid body of men he had trained in the wars in Gaul and which he still commanded at Pharsalus, though relatively he was now better placed than then. The lack of initiative looks much like that of Napoleon in his later years. Was Cæsar tiring of war? Or was war sapping Cæsar's energies?

Leaving the garrisons at Leptis, Ruspina and Acilla, which were all strongly fortified, Cæsar ordered his fleet under Cispius and Aquila to blockade Hadrumetum and Thapsus and narrowly watch the coast to forestall attack on coming transports during his movements, set fire to his camp at Ucita, and started, January 14, before daylight, in column left in front and with baggage-train between his column and the sea, and marched westerly along the coast between the hills and the shore to Agar, a town near Leptis, on the southerly slope of the first line of small coast-hills. He was thus basing on Leptis rather than on Ruspina. He camped in the plain before Agar (i). In the neighborhood he found a large supply of barley, oil, wine and figs, with

some wheat. Scipio did not attempt to disturb the retreat,
or even send his horse in pursuit; but soon followed along
the hills, and, reaching the vicinity, camped a few miles
away and farther from the sea (1). His evident purpose was
to shut Cæsar out from getting corn in the interior. His

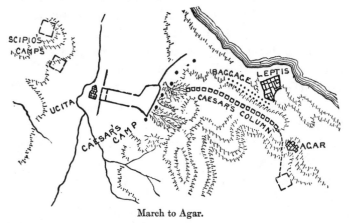

March to Agar.

force lay in three camps about six miles from Cæsar's on the
heights which stood back of the town of Tegea (1 m n). The
Numidian cavalry was posted on all advantageous heights,
to head off foragers from Cæsar's camp. But, for all their
care, Cæsar was able to collect a fair supply of victual, by
sending out large bodies on this duty.

It is evident, not only from the Commentaries, but from
the circumstances narrated, that Cæsar was very close-pressed
for rations; for, in order to fill his depleted magazines, he
now undertook one of the most hazardous operations of all
his campaigns. The town of Zeta (modern Bourdjine) in
rear of the enemy was ten miles from Scipio's camp, some
seventeen from Cæsar's. Deeming it secure beyond a peradventure, Scipio had made it a great magazine of corn and
had sent two legions to those parts to forage and protect the
corn collected. Of this fact Cæsar had notice by a deserter.

He made up his mind to try a raid on Zeta. To accomplish his purpose he was forced to make a flank march past Scipio's camps and to return by the same or an equally perilous road. Only famine staring him in the face, and the fact that supplies could not be got in sufficient quantity in the region to the south of Thapsus, explain the risk he took. He established his men in a new camp on a hill east of Agar (o) for greater security to the comparatively small number he was to leave behind in it, broke up January 17 at three o'clock A. M., with his entire cavalry force and a large body of foot, passed around Scipio's camp unobserved, reached and took the town of Zeta out of hand, with a number of prominent Pompeians, loaded an enormous train, including twenty-two camels, with breadstuffs, and put a garrison under Oppius in the place, with instructions to shift

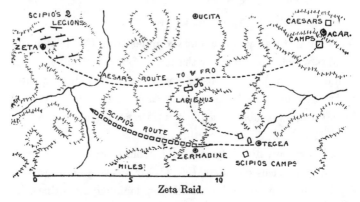

Zeta Raid.

for itself as best it might. Not content with this success, he moved on to attack the two foraging legions; but, on reaching their vicinity, Cæsar found that Scipio had learned of his diversion, and had marched to their support with his whole army. He wisely desisted from attack and began to retire with his booty.

Cæsar was obliged to pass near by Scipio's camp on the

way back to his own. Here a heavy force of Numidian horse
and light troops under Labienus and Afranius had been
placed by Scipio in ambush for him among the neighboring
hills about modern Djemmal. Just after he had got beyond
them they sallied out and attacked his rear. So far, Cæsar
had had extraordinarily good luck, but this diversion threatened trouble. He at once faced his cohorts towards the
enemy, and, moving the baggage to their rear, he threw his
cavalry out in their front, and prepared to defend his rearward march. No sooner did Cæsar's cavalry, sustained by
the legions, fall boldly upon the enemy than the troops of
Labienus and Afranius turned and fled; but when Cæsar
resumed his march they renewed the attack. These Numidians were wonderfully active and expert at their own method
of fighting. They so effectually harassed Cæsar in his
effort to retire that he "found he had not gained a hundred
paces in four hours." Moreover, he lost many horses, which
he could ill afford to spare. The enemy's purpose was to
force him to camp in that place, where there was no water;
and Cæsar's men had had nothing to eat from their start at
three A. M. till now, about three of the afternoon. Finally
his cavalry grew so exhausted with its efforts that he was
compelled to send it on ahead and make his rearguard of
infantry, which could better impose upon the Numidians.
The legionaries, though the ground was not much cut up,
were really more fitted for rearguard than the tired horsemen. The baggage was hurried on ahead. Cæsar was thus
able to advance, though with extreme slowness. For, if only
a handful of the legionaries faced about and flung their darts,
thousands of the Numidian light troops or cavalry would fly;
but so soon as the march was resumed, these warriors again
approached and showered darts, stones and arrows upon the
rear of column. Some of these worked their way around to

the flanks and van of Cæsar's column, and gave him the greatest trouble. Labienus and Afranius made an effort to inclose Cæsar's army by marching round his wings and through the hills to head him off, but unsuccessfully. Cæsar preserved his formation, which may have been the square usual in such cases, in unbroken order. "Thus Cæsar, at one time moving forward, at another halting, going on but slowly, reached the camp safe," about seven in the evening, a total march of over thirty-six miles, with a loss of only ten men wounded.

To judge from the description in the Commentaries one would have gauged the loss an hundred-fold this sum. It is not improbable that the number is erroneously given by the historian. Labienus, he says, had thoroughly tired out his troops and lost three hundred men, beside the wounded. The disparity in numbers is incompatible with the description of the raid. Cæsar was in a position to lose the larger number.

The distance marched in sixteen hours seems incredible. Assuming that the capture of Zeta, the loading of the train and the diversion against Scipio's two legions consumed but two hours, we have a large army, harassed by the enemy part of the way back, and delayed four hours by fighting, making a march of thirty-six miles in the remaining ten hours. There is probably exaggeration somewhere. Few bodies of foot can cover three and one half miles an hour except for a short stretch. Still, that the march was made from shortly before day to some evening hour is scarcely to be denied.

This raid exhibits in marked contrast the character and ability of Scipio and Cæsar. It is probable that Cæsar would not have dared undertake such a movement against an opponent more his equal. Scipio distinctly showed want of power to seize an advantage. Cæsar had passed over a range

of hills to the plain of Zeta, and must return through the
same path to regain camp. What more natural than for
Scipio to draw up his forces on suitable slopes and, by disputing his passage, bring him to battle on disadvantageous
terms? And during such an engagement, which Cæsar
would be forced to accept, Scipio had two legions at Zeta
which could fall upon his rear. But instead of this simple
plan, Scipio, apparently losing his head, marched off to the
assistance of the two legions on such an eccentric line that he
opened to Cæsar the very road of retreat which he should
have closed. Nor was Labienus any more skillful. He
should have disputed Cæsar's passage of the hills by attacking his head of column and not his rear. Instead of so
doing he allowed Cæsar's column to regain the road to camp,
and contented himself with simply attacking his rearguard.
It looks a trifle as if Cæsar had really sustained something
more of a defeat than the Commentaries are willing to
acknowledge. But the defeat was not a fatal one. Cæsar
had a way of extricating himself from desperate straits.

In justification of Cæsar's movement on Zeta it may be
said that the character of the country is such as to afford
more than one route for retreat. The whole surface of the
land is covered with carriage and mule roads now, and presumably was so then, when the population was larger and
even more intelligent. He could have returned by way of
modern Zermadina, Scipio being left at Zeta. He could
have moved north along the Ucita plain to his old camp and
thence to Agar, for on his left he would have Ruspina,
strongly garrisoned by his own troops, as a refuge in case of
danger.

Cæsar's own luck and the paltry conduct of his foes had
again saved him harmless. It is all the more strange that,
with such contemptible opponents, this great captain, who

was daring enough to undertake expeditions which might compel him to do battle with all the chances against him, should have so long delayed forcing on his enemy a decisive engagement which might terminate the war. For he now had twelve legions, and the difficulties of subsisting them were enough to make him above all desire a definite outlet to the matter. He indeed shortly undertook it in a way he had not before attempted.

While Labienus was fighting Cæsar on his retreat, Scipio, after returning from Zeta, had apparently drawn up before his camps, while Cæsar was filing by the flank in his front laden with baggage. But on Cæsar's approach he withdrew. This lack of force is of a part with Scipio's entire conduct.

Cæsar had run a grave danger, but at all events his legions had refilled their corn-bags.

Cæsar was obliged to instruct his men in new tactics to meet the new conditions thrust upon him. The enemy's light troops were so nimble as seriously to annoy the heavy-armed legionaries in a mere skirmish; and he deemed it wise to bring some elephants from Italy to accustom the troops and horses to their sight, and drilled the men in the best method of attacking them. In Gaul, Cæsar's troops had met a frank, courageous enemy who came out and fought hand to hand on the field; here they had to resist the devices of a crafty foe who relied upon artifice, not courage. The Commentaries acknowledge that Cæsar's horse was no match for the enemy's when sustained by light foot, and frankly confess that Cæsar was not certain that his legionaries were equal to the enemy's in the open. This again seems inexplicable. We are wont to think that Cæsar's raw levies soon became seasoned; Hannibal's did; and we have proof that Scipio's troops were none of them well disciplined.

Cæsar constantly marched his troops about the country, not only to drill and harden them, but in hope of compromising Scipio by some manœuvre and of bringing him to battle against his will. He drew up, three days after the Zeta raid, near Scipio's camp in the open plain south of Agar (p), but this general declined to come out and Cæsar did not care to assault his works. As a rule Cæsar was fortunate in securing the towns in the vicinity of which he was campaigning. Vacca sent to him for a garrison; but in this case Juba anticipated him, captured and razed the town.

Too great fault should not be found with Scipio's apparently inactive method. It was Fabian. Famine was doing the work of many a victory. But it was half indecision, half method, which governed Scipio's movements.

On the 22d day of January Cæsar held a grand review of his army, which now numbered some forty thousand legionaries, three thousand horse and some auxiliaries, and on the succeeding day, well satisfied with his legions, marched out to a distance of five miles from his camp and to within two miles of Scipio's camp north of Tegea (q) and offered battle. But again Scipio declined it. Cæsar saw that he was wasting his time in trying to lure Scipio into the open by merely offering battle, and as a last resort he planned a series of attacks on Scipio's strong places and dépôts, such as Sarsura, Tysdra and Thapsus, to provoke him to activity.

Thapsus was on the coast southeast of Leptis, a large magazine of military stores and a highly important point for Scipio, which he had strongly garrisoned and in whose harbor was a large number of vessels, at present blockaded by Cæsar's fleet. But to attack Thapsus was to play the great game for which Cæsar was apparently not yet ready. He preferred to raid the smaller towns, not only as being an easier prey, but above all because he needed the corn with which they were well supplied. It is altogether probable that at this moment Cæsar's legions were all but starving. He was on a tramp for victual. The strategy of the situation must yield to the logistics.

Cæsar broke up from Agar January 23 and marched on Sarsura over the eastern slope of the hill below Tegea. To Sarsura he was followed by Labienus who harassed his rear. Cæsar had on this occasion detailed three hundred men from each legion as rearguard. These do not, however, appear to have been able to hold Labienus in check, for this officer was able to cut out some of the train from the rear of column — probably animals which were ready to load in case Cæsar could capture Sarsura. In a rearguard engagement which ensued, the Numidians proved overanxious to secure booty and were severely punished by Cæsar's troops. They lost a number of men, and thereafter Labienus kept his distance, following along on Cæsar's right upon the hills. Arrived at Sarsura, Cæsar stormed and took it under the very eyes of Scipio and Labienus, put the garrison to the sword, and found a goodly supply of corn, which he distributed to the soldiers or loaded. Scipio observed him from above, not offering to interfere. Thence Cæsar marched next day to Tysdra, which he did not attempt to assault, the place having been very strongly fortified by Considius, a brave and stubborn officer who held it with his cohort of gladiators. There was no time, nor even engines, for a siege; and Cæsar had already got a fairly good supply of victual.

Cæsar started back and camped over night at the stream which ran midway between Tysdra and Sarsura (r). Thence he made his way to his camp at Agar, January 26, probably by a circuit round the foot of the hills he had marched across. Scipio did the like.

XLI.

THAPSUS. FEBRUARY, 47 B. C.

THE rest of Cæsar's reinforcements having arrived, he was ready, if ever, to try conclusions with Scipio. After some strategic manœuvring, Cæsar marched on Thapsus, and sat down before it. Scipio and Juba followed, lest they should lose this valuable city. Cæsar completed his lines. Scipio essayed to break through these on Cæsar's right, failing which, he tried the left, near the sea, and began to intrench a camp near his lines. Cæsar drew up for attack, while Scipio was at work, and compelled the latter to do the like. The Cæsarians were in high spirits; not so the Pompeians. The former were eager to attack, seeing the indecision of the enemy. Cæsar delayed. But the restless Tenth legion, on the right, gave a trumpet blast without orders, and this being repeated down the line, the whole army advanced on the Pompeians. These troops held their own some hours; but victory was finally won, and the ensuing slaughter was terrible. The entire army of Scipio was destroyed; the leaders fled. Cæsar had no difficulty in reducing Africa to his sway. The African campaign had been the direct result of Cæsar's going to Alexandria with an insufficient force and of the loss of time there encountered; and it was often characterized by a lack of decisiveness unlike Cæsar. The victory of Thapsus, "which Cæsar prepared, but his men won," rectified all his errors.

ABOUT these days Thabena, a town on the seacoast at the confines of King Juba's dominion, rose against its garrison, murdered it, and sent a deputation to Cæsar asking for protection, "as they had revolted from Juba's rule and therefore deserved well of the Roman people." Cæsar detailed thither the tribune M. Crispus with a cohort, some archers, and a number of engines of war.

The balance of the legionary soldiers who, by sickness, leaves of absence, or other causes had been detained in Sicily, arrived towards the end of January in one embarkation to the number of four thousand men, and with them four hundred horse and one thousand bowmen and slingers. Having all his forces in hand, Cæsar had no further excuse for not forcing Scipio to a decisive battle. Before resorting to the siege of Thapsus, which he had long contemplated, but had been prevented from undertaking on account of the necessity of procuring corn in towns more easily taken, he made one

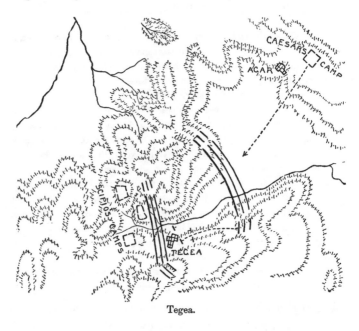

Tegea.

more effort to bring Scipio out on the open, and on the last day of January moved from his camp to a plain — which the Commentaries say was eight miles from his own and four from Scipio's, but the distances are actually less than six and two — not far from Tegea (y) and awaited the enemy.

Scipio was not willing to take any chances. The town of Tegea lay below his camp. Its garrison of four hundred horse he drew up on the right and left of the town, and formed his legions on a hill somewhat lower than his camp and about one thousand paces from it, as a reserve, the cavalry on both flanks, but so placed as to be able to sustain the Tegean horse in their front. From this place Scipio would not budge, nor Cæsar attack him in it. Finally, to tempt him out Cæsar sent some squadrons, about four hundred men, supported as usual by light troops, to charge the cavalry at Tegea. To meet this partial attack, Labienus sent some of the cavalry of his second line around the right and left of this body to take it in reverse. Cæsar ordered forward three hundred of the legionaries habituated to sustain the horse. Cæsar's men, not only greatly outnumbered but threatened in flank, began to give ground. Each side undertook to throw forward supports, and it looked for a short period as if the battle might become general. When Cæsar's line appeared to be all but overwhelmed, a further opportune reinforcement of foot carried the day. After a stout struggle Scipio's horse was broken and pursued, with loss of many officers, three miles to the mountains.

Cæsar kept his legionaries in line all day; but the enemy's foot, though the occasion appeared to be favorable to Scipio, he being on higher ground, could not be induced to come down to the plain to accept a general battle. Cæsar's efforts were all directed to trying to lure Scipio from his position. This, however, he could not accomplish, and as usual he was unwilling to attack equal numbers on ground above him. Though Fortune was wont to be on his side, he was manifestly disinclined to tempt her too far.

Cæsar finally withdrew his men to camp, "without the loss of a man," while "the enemy had many of his best officers either killed or wounded." A corresponding loss in men is to be presumed. This statement shows that the historian of the African War was subject to the weakness, observable in most chroniclers of modern contemporary military events, of understating the losses of his own side and overestimating those of the enemy. When a combat is presented in considerable detail and severe fighting is reported, we must assume some loss in killed. In most cases the wounded are not taken into consideration. Except in the case of a massacre, there are rarely large losses on one side without some equivalent on the other. It must, however, be remembered that with his good defensive armor and his skill in the use of his shield, the Roman legionary could fight, sometimes for many hours, without a wound. So long as ranks were kept unbroken, he was comparatively safe.

The siege of Thapsus now appeared to be the only means left of forcing Scipio into such activity as to give Cæsar a chance of fighting on at least even terms. If anything would bring Scipio to battle, the danger of losing this town and port would do so. And, water being scarce near Scipio's Tegean location, so that he could not sit down before him there, Cæsar broke camp in the night of February 3–4, "marched sixteen miles beyond Agar to Thapsus," — the distance is really ten, — and seizing the elevations back of it, immedi-

Thapsus and Vicinity.

ately began to draw lines of contravallation about the city to invest it, as well as lines of circumvallation with redoubts in proper places to prevent succor from reaching it (A).

Thapsus is situated at that point in the coast where, after having run to the southeast from Hadrumetum, it turns suddenly south. It was an old Carthaginian city and very strong. The ruins found to-day on the site of the city proper cover nearly one hundred and fifty acres. It had triple walls, and its harbor, natural and artificial, was excellent. The town lay on low land, but hills up to one hundred feet in height ran to the west and to the south along the coast. Thapsus could be approached only from the south or west, on account of a large salt lake three miles inland and seven miles long.

Cæsar's movement on Thapsus drove Scipio into action, "to avoid the disgrace of abandoning Virgilius and the Thapsitani who had all along remained firm to his party." After several councils of war in the Pompeian camp, it was determined to follow Cæsar along the line of the hills, and to avoid an attack unless on ground favorable to them. This was done, and the enemy intrenched eight miles south of Thapsus in two camps, one for Scipio and one for Juba (B).

There was, as stated, west of the town of Thapsus a salt-water lake, — the modern Sebka di Moknine, — separated from the sea by a strip of dry land from one to two miles wide. Cæsar had camped and thrown up his line around the entire town, but along this strip of land between the lake and the sea Scipio imagined that there was still access from his camps and that he could carry succor to the inhabitants. After renewed councils, it was determined to make a move in force up that way, — Juba remaining in his own camp to protect both. But Cæsar with his usual foresight had anticipated this very manœuvre, and had forestalled Scipio by the erection of a fort (C) in the centre of the strip of land and had placed a triple garrison in it which was ample to check the approach of an enemy as cautious as Scipio.

Scipio broke camp, and marching right in front up the narrow strip in question with his back to the sea, instead of being able to penetrate to Thapsus was astonished to run against Cæsar's redoubt.   It is altogether probable that vigorous measures might have captured or masked the fort, but its presence so entirely brought Scipio out of countenance that he scarcely knew what course to adopt.   He remained *in situ*, taking no action of importance during the entire day and night, but probably returned to his camp south of the lake. He now resolved to try the approach from the north, and early next morning he advanced round the lake to near Cæsar's camps.   Here, had he acted with vigor, he might have cut Cæsar off from Leptis and Ruspina, or by an attack on his works have added immensely to his task. But Scipio dallied, gave Cæsar time to finish his intrenchments, and undertook no diversion whatever.

Cæsar, in a day or two, got his army well intrenched and extended in a semicircle around the whole town from shore to shore.   The enemy was definitely excluded from Thapsus. Scipio set about constructing two camps north of the lake (D), one for Juba and one for himself, having done which, he marched his troops to a point about fifteen hundred paces from the sea and an equal distance from Cæsar's lines, and there, on the 6th of February, he began to intrench still another camp (E).   Just what his object may have been does not appear from the relation in the Commentaries, or from the topography.   Scipio's manœuvres were apt to be indefinite.   There were plenty of things to do, but Scipio was not given to vigor, and he was loath to approach Cæsar except under cover of heavy works.

Cæsar could not permit an intrenched camp to be placed in such dangerous proximity to his own lines, and determined to attack Scipio at once, though he would have preferred to defer a battle till he had taken Thapsus. The time for attack was manifestly before Scipio had completed his new works. Leaving Asprenas, the proconsul, with two legions, to look after the trenches of Thapsus, Cæsar drew out and marched upon Scipio with the rest of his forces. One half of the fleet he left before Thapsus, but ordered the other half to sail out beyond Scipio's camp, make in near the shore, and, upon a proper signal, to begin a noisy demonstration in Scipio's rear by shouting and getting ready to land men.

Scipio was drawn up before the half-made intrenchments in three lines, the third of which only was at work; the elephants, sustained by light troops, were displayed before his right and left wings. The Numidian cavalry was on the left, the rest of the cavalry and light troops on the right. His left all but reached the coast. Cæsar advanced likewise in three lines, with the Second and Tenth legions on the right, the Eighth and Ninth on the left, and five legions in the centre. His flanks opposite the elephants he covered each by five chosen cohorts of the Fifth legion aided by archers and slingers. His cavalry was mixed with light foot. He himself went on foot from legion to legion to encourage the veterans by reminding them of their past victories, and to stimulate the new levies by urging them to win equal glory. All perceived with glowing ardor that finally the battle was to come for which they had striven for so many weeks.

Not so the enemy. Scipio's men were seized with the trepidation of a surprise; they saw Cæsar about to attack when their camp was but half finished. They had been weakened by being kept behind intrenchments. There seemed to be no head or order. Cæsar's men could see the lines moving in and out of place as if entirely unprepared for the deadly work at hand. His legionaries and officers begged for an instant order to advance, for they saw in this

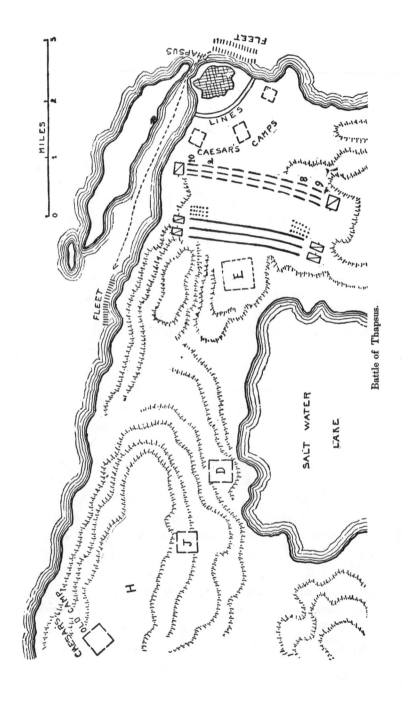

Battle of Thapsus.

uncertainty a sure sign of victory. Cæsar was anxious to
be deliberate, for the elephants were strange and awful to the
young troops, the Numidian cavalry was vast in number, and
had bred all but disaster at Ruspina, and the light troops
of the army were brave and nimble. While the captain was
thus hesitating, the men acted; the attack was actually precipitated by a trumpeter of the right wing, whom the soldiers
of the Tenth legion compelled to give the signal before Cæsar
commanded it. This is one of the most extraordinary
instances of slack discipline in all history. It reminds one
of the charge on Mission Ridge, — though, indeed, at the
latter place there was no actual breach of orders, but only
an excess of spirit in carrying them out.

The signal being repeated in the usual manner down the
line, the cohorts rushed forward, and could not be restrained.
Seeing this and taking advantage of his troops' enthusiasm,
Cæsar gave "Good fortune" (*Felicitas*) as the battle-cry,
"spurred on his horse" and joined the fray. The archers
and slingers and the cohorts on the right flank, set for this
particular duty and now well-trained to encounter elephants,
speedily overwhelmed these brutes with a shower of darts and
stones, and drove them trumpeting back upon their own lines,
where they trampled numberless men under foot, made their
way to camp, closed up the entrances, and utterly demoralized the Mauretanian horse in the left wing, which fled
incontinent. The lines of foot now clashed. That the Pompeian legions despite their surprise fought well is demonstrated by the fact that they held their own some hours. It
was sunset before Cæsar's legions could call the day their
own. But after a gallant struggle, Scipio's right wing partook the growing demoralization; then followed the centre.
In a short time thereafter the entire line was melting away
towards the half-completed camp (E). The legionaries of

Cæsar's right and left wings soon wheeled around the enemy's flank and captured the intrenchments which there was
scarcely an attempt to defend. The principal officers, fearful of their own fate if captured by Cæsar, and appalled at
this sign of disaster, without an effort to rally their men,
themselves fled from the field. Perceiving this desertion by
their chiefs, the whole army, seized with utmost panic, dissolved into formless squads and made its way from the field
as best it might. The struggle at the new camp was a short
one. The soldiers of Scipio were cut down *en masse;* all
who could still flee started towards the old camp north of the
lake (D).

The garrison of Thapsus had, meanwhile, made a sally
along the shore, wading through the surf to aid their friends;
but were beaten back by the camp-followers and non-combatants in the siege lines, which Cæsar had left to attack Scipio.

Cæsar's legionaries followed hard in pursuit. Scipio,
Labienus, Afranius, and other generals had already got
away; no sign of defense was made; their army was a mass
of fugitives. The men endeavored to rally at the old camp,
where they could still have shown a stout resistance, but
there was no one to head them. Seeing none of their officers
at this spot, they imagined that they had gone to Juba's
camp near by (J), and made their way thither to seek them.
Finding this camp already in the hands of Cæsar's men, who
had flanked them on their left, they at once fled to an adjoining hill (II), intending to defend themselves. On the approach of their pursuers they became panic-stricken, "cast
down their arms, and saluted them in a military manner,"
i. e., made the usual signal of surrender.

But surrender availed naught. Cæsar's soldiers were too
much wrought up to heed the signal. The Roman people
were by nature cruel; in common with all men of their trade

in ancient days, Cæsar's legionaries partook the national spirit and had long reproached him for clemency; they had been at war three long years; they now proposed to put an end to the matter, and broke quite beyond control. Cæsar, though anxious to spare Roman blood, was unable to stem the tide. The legionaries, glutted with passion and blood, not only slaughtered the armed men, pursuing them in every direction and cutting them down wholesale, but in their frenzy they killed a number of Roman citizens in their own camp, against whom the cry was raised that they were the authors of the war, or secret adherents of Pompey's cause. "This made several Roman knights and senators retire from the battle, lest the soldiers, who after so signal a victory assumed an unbounded license, should be induced by the hopes of impunity to wreck their fury on them likewise. In short, all Scipio's soldiers, though they implored the protection of Cæsar, were, in the very sight of that general, and in spite of his entreaties to his men to spare them, without exception put to the sword."

This escape from control by his legionaries is the most serious criticism on their discipline which can exist. One can scarcely associate such laxity with cohorts which had been even weeks under Cæsar. Plutarch says that several authors have claimed that Cæsar was not in this battle at all, but was down with an attack of epilepsy. This scarcely accords with the facts elsewhere set down, or with the probabilities; but if anything lends countenance to it, it is the remarkable lack of hold upon his men shown by Cæsar on this field, both at the inception and close of the engagement. Their conduct at Pharsalus stands out in marked contrast to it.

At least ten thousand men were slain and sixty-four elephants were taken. Scipio's whole force was annihilated. Cæsar's army, it is claimed in the Commentaries, lost not over fifty killed and some wounded. Fancy a decisive battle in the nineteenth century won by an army of forty odd thousand men at such a paltry cost!

The flight of the leaders, Scipio, Juba, Labienus, Afranius, Petreius and the others, availed them little. Most of them were unable to escape pursuing fate, whether by land or sea, and either fell that day or within a few weeks. Labienus made his way to Spain. Scipio reached his shipping, but was overtaken by bad weather, driven into Hippo, attacked by Sitius, and fell in the ensuing action. Some lesser chiefs reached Utica.

As Thapsus did not surrender after this signal victory, though formally summoned to do so, with a display of the captured elephants, Cæsar left the proconsul C. Rebellius with three legions to continue the siege, sent Cnæus Domitius to invest Considius in Tysdra with two, and having been lavish in praises and rewards to his troops, — the Fifth legion was allowed to adopt an elephant as ensign, — he set out for Ucita and Hadrumetum, which he took February 10 and 11, and where he found Scipio's stores and much military treasure. Thence he marched on Utica, with Messala commanding the cavalry in the van. He was anxious to capture Cato and a number of Scipio's lieutenants who had fled for refuge to its walls.

Scipio's cavalry escaped in a body from the battle as the foot could not, and started for Utica. On the way they were refused entrance to the town of Parada, but forced the place. In revenge for the refusal, they built a huge fire in the forum and into it cast the whole population bound hand and foot, with everything which they could not carry away as plunder. After this signal act of barbarity they marched to Utica, where they in like manner began to plunder and slaughter, and were only stopped by being bought off with money by

Cato and Sylla Faustus. Cato endeavored to arouse the inhabitants to resist Cæsar, but, unable to accomplish more than to gain permission from the city for all adherents of Pompey to leave for Spain, on February 12 he committed suicide.

Cato was Cæsar's most able opponent. Had he not yielded the military command to Scipio, Cæsar might not have put so easy an end to the campaign. After his death, L. Cæsar, his quæstor, determined to throw himself and the town on Cæsar's clemency. Sylla collected a body of men and retired into Juba's territory.

Messala, with Cæsar's cavalry-van, soon reached the city, and placed guards at the gates. Cæsar followed close upon his heels. Reaching Utica February 16, he was easily prevailed on to pardon the rebels their lives, but he amerced them in a heavy money - penalty of two hundred thousand sestertia to be paid the republic for having, while Roman citizens, furnished Varus and Scipio with funds.

King Juba and Petreius made their escape together, and hiding by day and traveling by night reached Zama, where were all Juba's treasures and his family. His subjects refused him admittance and appealed against him to Cæsar, — for Juba had threatened to consume himself, all his goods, and all the Zamians in one great conflagration should he return from this war other than victorious. On receiving this message Cæsar himself set out towards Zama. On the way many of Juba's officers and nearly all his cavalry came in and surrendered. Cæsar's pardon of all made them his firm adherents. Juba and Petreius killed each other. Reaching Zama March 6, Cæsar confiscated all the king's goods and those of Roman citizens who had borne arms against him and turned the kingdom into a province, leaving Crispus Sallustius as proconsul in command.

Considius, meanwhile, had abandoned Tysdra. On the retreat his forces assassinated him, seized his treasure and dispersed. Virgilius at Thapsus surrendered to Caninius. Sitius defeated Sabura, and on his return to Cæsar ran across Faustus and Afranius, who had escaped from Utica with the body of troops which tried to plunder the place, some fifteen hundred strong, surrounded and captured the entire force. The two chiefs were slain in a mutiny which occurred a day or two after. The services of Sitius were recognized by the gift of Cirta (Constantine) in which to settle his irregular cohorts.

Cæsar confiscated and sold the estates of the rebels in all the towns which had opposed him; and fined Thapsus and Hadrumetum and their merchants fifty thousand and eighty thousand sestertia respectively. Other towns were fined in proportion. He then embarked, April 14, for Sardinia, where he went through the same form of amercement of his enemies, and thence sailed for Rome, which city he reached on May 25. He had been absent six months, of which four and a half in Africa.

In Rome from June to November, Cæsar celebrated four triumphs, for his victories over the Gauls, Pharnaces, Egypt and King Juba. No triumph, under the Roman constitution, could be had for victories in civil wars. During the days of the triumphs Cæsar gave to the Roman people the most magnificent spectacles that had as yet been seen. Over four hundred lions and fifty elephants fought in the arena. The promised largesses were distributed to the soldiers, some nine hundred dollars to each old legionary, the centurions double, the tribunes and the chief of cavalry quadruple. Besides this, lands were distributed, though they had not been promised. For the next year, B. C. 45, Cæsar was elected consul and was made dictator for ten years. But his

stay in Rome was short. Seven months after his return
from Africa — November, 46 B. C. — he was called to Spain
to suppress the relics of the Pompeian insurrection in that
peninsula.

The African war is perplexing to gauge. From one point
of view it seems to have been a most difficult undertaking
and to have taxed Cæsar's ability to the utmost. From
another, when we note the low quality of the generals and
the legions opposed to him and the unusually cautious manner in which he handled his problem, it does not appear to
be a campaign as marked in excellence as others. That the
African war was ever waged was due to Cæsar's being caught
in unnecessary political and discreditable personal toils in
Alexandria. This delay gave the Pompeian conspirators the
better part of a year to hatch out their means of resistance,
and enabled them to organize and carry through a campaign
in Africa and still another in Spain. Both these campaigns
could have been avoided if at once on Pompey's death Cæsar
had turned against Cato and Scipio, his stoutest opponents;
or if he had at the outset gone to Alexandria with a number
of legions instead of less than one. We are not estimating
an ordinary man. We are gauging the work of perhaps the
greatest man the world has ever seen, of a soldier who has
few peers. What would escape notice in the average general, forces itself on our attention in the case of Cæsar.

At the root of all this lies Cæsar's reprehensible habit of
undertaking work with insufficient means. He moved to
Greece with half his force, and was compelled to wage a
defensive war for months. He sailed for Alexandria with
but four thousand men, a reckless act which gave rise to a
long and arduous struggle there. He moved into Pontus
with a ridiculously insufficient force and was saved from
disaster as by a miracle. He came to Africa under circum-

stances which, without Cæsar's own luck, must have resulted
in his defeat. This more than foolhardy conduct brought in
its train vastly greater complications than could have resulted
from a careful opening of each campaign. If the months
be counted, it will be seen that more than half of all Cæsar's
campaigns were consumed in extricating himself from the
results of his own mistakes.

It was either unnecessary delay or uncalculating haste
which made most of Cæsar's campaigns essential. At the
same time we cannot forget that it was these campaigns
which brought out his great qualities as a soldier, which have
taught us so many lessons in the art of war.

When Cæsar woke up to the danger of the African imbroglio, his impatience to seize upon and carry through the
matter led him to neglect the commonest precautions. He
must have known, or at all events he could have ascertained,
the numbers opposed to him in Africa. But apparently
without consideration, just as he had before started from
Brundisium against Pompey with half his force, he now set
sail from Lilybæum with but six legions and two thousand
horse, on a weaker fleet than Scipio's, at a season of the year
when storms were common, and, most extraordinary of all,
without a rendezvous if the transports should be separated,
as was not only probable but actually occurred. It needed
all Cæsar's luck to overcome such carelessness. It would
have been a much more expeditious plan to wait till he got
his forces together, till a season of better winds prevailed;
he could then have crushed out the opposition with a blow.
Most of the African campaign was taken up with manœuvring to avoid the natural results of Cæsar's numerical weakness, — Cæsar's, who controlled the vast resources of Rome,
— or else in search of corn which he should have collected
for shipment before he himself set sail. In this particular

characteristic — lack of preparation — Cæsar stands on a lower plane than any of his compeers. None of the other great captains was so unnecessarily reckless, ever tempted fortune so far; none ever had the fortune to be extricated from such dilemmas.

There is so curious a mixture of daring and caution in Cæsar that we are often tempted to believe that we do not understand the conditions under which he worked. The historian of the African War has an indefinite way of stating things which obliges us to complement much of his meaning by a study of the terrain. That the man who was bold enough to blockade Pompey at Dyrrachium with half his force, to attack Pompey uphill at Pharsalus with like odds against him, should be unwilling to attack Scipio under conditions far more favorable, is hard to explain. That the man who undertook and carried through the Zeta raid — the operation of a partisan corps by an entire army like that of Alexander at the Persian Gates — should have been unwilling to cross the valley at Ucita, or at least to attack Scipio when he had dug his way across, we can scarcely understand. Still the historian and the topography agree. We understand the conditions better than those under which Hannibal and Alexander worked. We are forced to ascribe Cæsar's hesitancy to mere mood.

Cæsar's manœuvring was always good. His reason for intrenching, instead of fighting, is harder to comprenend. Cæsar was a fighter, in his way; not like Alexander, not like Frederick, but still an able and antagonistic tactician. But often, without reason, he appeared to be disinclined to fight, even when his men were in the very tone to command success. He was so clever at manœuvring that he apparently desired for the mere art of the thing to manœuvre his enemy into a bad position before he attacked him. His pausing at Thapsus has led to the remark that, while he prepared for the battle, it was his men who won it. When Cæsar was weak in numbers, his caution was justifiable; but his caution was often less great with a handful than when his force was respectable. His opponent in Africa was far from being an able man; Scipio's legions were less stanch than Cæsar's; yet hypercaution gives Cæsar distinctly the appearance of having had more difficulty in mastering Scipio than in over-coming Pompey the Great. What difficulties he had were largely of his own creation. It is because he was Cæsar that we wonder at his hesitation.

This is one aspect of the case. On the other hand, Cæsar's activity, his intelligence, his skill and brilliant dash in the minor operations, his broad conceptions of the strategic necessities of the case, as well as the execution of all his plans, stamp him with the seal of genius. And if we con-sider the element of time, Cæsar is unapproachable. In the Civil War, from his arrival on the field, the Italian campaign lasted but sixty days; the Ilerda campaign six weeks; the Epirotic seven months; the Alexandrian six; the Pontus campaign a bare week; the African a little over three months; the Spanish an equal time. When we note that in the Epirotic and Alexandrian wars it was Cæsar's over-hastiness which consumed the bulk of each period, this rec-ord, added to the splendid work in Gaul, in this sense stands unequaled in the history of great captains.

XLII.

SPAIN. DECEMBER, 46, TO AUGUST, 45 B. C.

THE Pompeians had taken root in Spain, in doing which Cæsar's lieutenants had aided them by mismanaging his affairs. Pompey's sons, Cnæus and Sextus, were in command of large forces there. Cæsar, after triumphing in Rome, proceeded to Spain. The first manœuvring was near Corduba, with no marked advantage on either side, though Cæsar suffered a defeat in a combat near the bridge over the Bætis. Cæsar then moved away and attacked Attegua, and around this town there was a long interchange of hostilities, with frequent conflicts. Attegua finally surrendered. Ucubis was the next point of contest. Cæsar, as usual, skirmished for an opening, which Pompey was clever enough not to give. But unsuccessful at all points, and having been worsted in a battle of no great importance at Soricaria, Pompey finally determined to leave this part of Spain and retire to Carteia in the south.

SPAIN was divided by the Romans into Tarraconensis, or Hispania Citerior and Ulterior, in the north, Bætica in the south, Lusitania in the west. In this peninsula, while Cæsar had been preparing the defeat of Pompey in Greece, Q. Cassius Longinus, who, as tribune of the people, had so ably served him in the early months of the Civil War, and whom Cæsar had left in command, with the legions of Varro, after its conquest, had been acting with grave indiscretion. He had fallen into serious disfavor with the population, though he had kept the affections of the veterans in the army by exceptional largesses, — a course tending to the destruction of discipline. He had, for some time, by cruel extortions from the people, been raising moneys, which he squandered in needless equipments for his troops, and in supplying them with absurd extravagances. He had raised a fifth legion and three thousand horse, which he sumptuously paid and clad. Some time before the battle of Pharsalus, Cassius received orders from Cæsar to march through Mauretania on Numidia, where Juba was still in Pompey's favor, and was raising fresh troops to aid the cause. He was getting ready to march, for he lacked not vigor if there was work to do, when he was all but assassinated by some of the men he had injured. He was, however, rescued, and caused all the conspirators to be tortured and put to death, except some few whom he allowed to purchase their lives for sums varying

Spain.

from ten thousand to fifty thousand sestertii each. After this experience he became more tyrannical than ever. A mutiny and revolt ensued, which threatened to place Spain in the hands of the Pompeian faction; for these atrocities by one of Cæsar's lieutenants had brought the adherents of Pompey again to the front. At the request of his Spanish friends, Cæsar sent Trebonius, the conqueror of Massilia, to

displace Cassius. The latter, in sailing away from the
province where he had earned so much hatred, was drowned
in the Ebro.

Young Cnæus Pompey, after his *fiasco* in Mauretania, had
sailed for the Balearic Isles, and finally reached and taken
possession of Bætica in southern Spain, where he had been
well received by the larger part of the people whom Cæsar's
lieutenants had alienated, and had been saluted Imperator.
He had driven Trebonius out of that part of the country.
By seizing the wealth of many private citizens and by general
rapacity and high-handed measures, he managed to collect a
large army. After the defeat at Thapsus, many of the
fugitives — his brother Sextus, Labienus and Varus among
them — managed to make their way to young Pompey, with
such small relics of the army as they had saved. By all these
means a nucleus of parts of thirteen legions was collected and
put under supreme command of Cnæus, then a young man of
twenty-four, by no means lacking in boldness or ability.

In Bætica, which is a territory much cut up by hills and
rivers, with excellent resources, and strong towns and
positions, there was a promising chance for Pompey to drag
out a war of defense for an almost indefinite time. This
necessitated• Cæsar's at once leaving Rome. He had imagined the Civil War to be at an end, but he was rudely
undeceived by the news from Spain, received during October
and November, 46 B. C. He first dispatched Q. Fabius and
Q. Pedius to Spain with troops, and Didius with a fleet.
Didius beat Varus at sea and drove him into Carteia. Cæsar
left Rome early in December, 46. By what route he went
is not known. Appian, Strabo and Eutropius assert that
he reached his camp in Obulco (Porcuna) in twenty - seven
days from the city. It is thought that the trip was by sea
to Saguntum, which he reached in somewhat less than three

weeks, and thence to Obulco in a week more. One thing alone seems clear, that he reached Spain in less than a month after starting from Rome, certainly before he was expected,

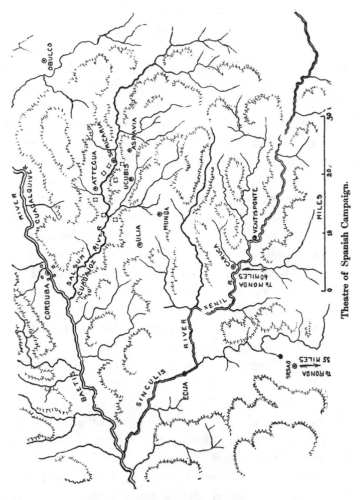

and in advance of his troops. He was on the ground prior to the rumor of his approach.

On arrival, Cæsar learned by ambassadors from Corduba

(Cordova) that the town was weakly defended by Sextus Pompey and might be captured out of hand. Pompey had sent out scouts to ascertain Cæsar's coming, but these had all been captured. Cnæus Pompey was besieging Ulia (Montemayor, twenty miles south of Corduba), the last town which had held out against him in Bætica. To the relief of Ulia Cæsar sent a force of eleven cohorts and a good body of horse under L. J. Paciecus, a man well known and acquainted with the province. Paciecus managed to enter the place during a storm which was accompanied by such darkness that the enemy was careless and readily deceived as to his presence and purpose. With this additional garrison, Ulia could probably have held out in any event; and moreover, to draw Pompey from the siege, Cæsar, about January 8, marched on Corduba, which he had some hope of capturing out of hand. He sent his cavalry on ahead, accompanied by a body of chosen heavy-armed foot, and adopted the stratagem of mounting a number of these behind the cavalrymen when they approached the city, so that their presence was not perceived by the enemy. The Cordubans thereupon sallied forth to attack what they supposed to be only horse intent on ravaging the country. The infantry, dismounting and forming, fell on the enemy with such effect that few returned to the town. But the victory obtained no result.

The presence of Cæsar near Corduba and the relief of Ulia, obliged Cnæus to raise the siege when Ulia was on the point of surrender and to march to Corduba, which was important as being the capital of the province, and which his brother Sextus had sent him word he feared he could not hold against Cæsar. It is very apparent that Cnæus had illy prepared for opposing, as well as little anticipated, Cæsar's arrival.

The description of the events which now took place is

given in the Commentaries in a manner very difficult to understand. These Commentaries, like the African War, were formerly ascribed to Hirtius Pansa, but it is certain that he did not write either; their author is unknown. One must decipher the matter as best one can. The bulk of the text is devoted to utterly trivial details, and the important movements are passed over with a word or altogether omitted. The topography is the only reliable guide so far as one can

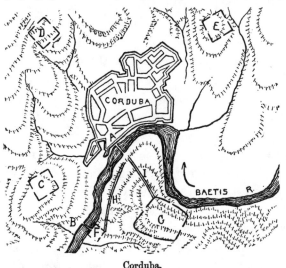

Corduba.

guess the localities or as they have been established by careful research and comparison of data. Few excavations have been made. It is necessary, sometimes, to do slight violence to the text in some one place in order to make the statements coincide with others equally positive. On the whole, however, we may feel reasonably sure of our general ground; but the details are wanting and any narrative of the campaign somewhat lacks sequence.

When, about January 10, Cæsar reached the Bætis (Guadalquiver), he found that the Pompeians held the only bridge

(A), and that the river was too deep to be forded. He accordingly built a number of piers for a bridge below the town (B) by sinking for foundations baskets of stones; and laying his roadway on these, crossed to the right bank in three successive divisions (C, D, E) and camped each in a suitable location strongly fortified. He then built a good bridgehead on the left bank (F). When Cnæus arrived from Ulia, he camped over against Cæsar's bridgehead, on the heights south of the town (G), hoping to get access to Corduba by the old bridge.

Cæsar began operations by an effort to cut Cnæus off from the town and prevent his entering it. "He ran a line from the camp to the bridge" (H) in such a manner as firmly to hold his bridgehead while threatening to cut Pompey off from easy access to the city and thus from his provisions. He might, perhaps, have thrown a force, by a night surprise, on the south end of the bridge and have quickly fortified it; but Cæsar was always fond of the security of earthworks. He ran his lines along the river towards the bridge at the foot of the hills on which sat Pompey.

Pompey's plan was of course to obtain control of his end of the bridge, whose farther end was near a tower of the town, a fact which would make his access all the safer. It would have been a simple matter for his brother Sextus to fortify the bridge at its southern extremity, but he kept comfortably within the town walls. Perceiving Cæsar's works, Pompey began a line of his own from his camp to the bridge (I). So long as neither cared to fight for the bridge, it became a question of speed in building works.

As a result of this intrenched race, a series of serious struggles occurred for the possession cf the bridge. Skirmishes near by were of daily occurrence, in which neither side could boast the upper hand. But it is evident that finally, about

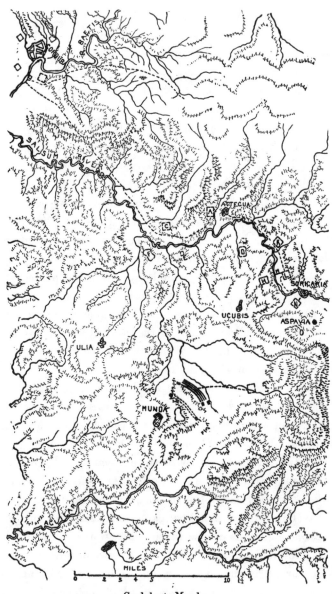

Corduba to Munda.

January 20, Cnæus broke down Cæsar's defenses by an attack in force and fought his way to the bridge. The battle here was desperate. The legionaries fought hand to hand. Hundreds perished not only by the sword but by falling from the bridge into the river. "On either side were heaps of slain." Despite stout fighting, it seems clear that Cæsar was defeated. Cnæus gained the bridge, and his entrance to Corduba. Cæsar stayed on awhile, hoping to force Pompey to an open-field engagement, which might terminate the war; but finding that he could not bring him to battle on advantageous terms, he gave up the hope of capturing Corduba, and, as a long siege was not advisable, he drew off his forces. When Cæsar left, Pompey strengthened Corduba by many engines.

Cæsar rightly believed that he could make better headway by attacking Pompey's minor strongholds to the south, and perhaps seize an opportunity for battle during the operations. Moreover, to get hold of some of these dépôts of provisions was the easiest way to ration his army. Southeast of Corduba lay Attegua (modern Teba), a town well fortified in a naturally strong and high position. This place he selected for a first attempt. On the 20th of January he quietly drew in his forces, after lighting the usual evening fires in the camp to deceive the enemy, crossed the river by night and marched on Attegua. There were plenty of provisions in the place, and as usual Cæsar lacked rations. The country was hilly and the town lay on a height a mile or so back from the river Salsum (modern Guadajoz), a narrow and not deep stream. Cæsar reached the place next morning and at once laid siege to it; he camped on the hills to its west (A), constructed strong lines about it with many redoubts to afford a shelter to the cavalry and infantry outposts, cast up a mound (B), brought up his vineæ and engines and made ready to

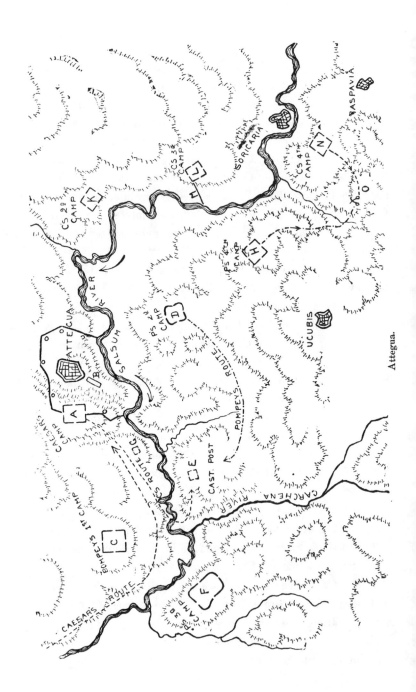

Attegua.

storm. The watch-towers built on nearly every height by the old inhabitants as a means of security against the barbarians came readily into play in Cæsar's work.

Pompey, on ascertaining next morning that Cæsar had decamped, at first entered Corduba amid much rejoicing. He felt that he had scored a point against the great soldier. Moreover, having possession of most of the towns, the winter season would work in his favor and not Cæsar's.

Attegua, against which he guessed Cæsar had marched, was strong and could hold out. But when he heard that the place was actually invested he followed Cæsar up and reached Attegua a week later, before the siege operations had advanced too far. By his sudden arrival on a foggy day he caught some stray parties of Cæsar's outpost horse and cut them to pieces. Not wishing to lose his communications with Corduba, he pitched his first camp on the hills to the west of Cæsar (C), but still north of the river Salsum. Changing his mind next day, perhaps January 28, he set fire to this camp, crossed the Salsum, and took up a new camp (D) south of Attegua, and in view both of it and of Ucubis (modern Espejo), another of his strong places to the south. But though his presence near Attegua with thirteen legions gave Cæsar and his troops much work, if not anxiety, Pompey could bring no assistance to the town, and in the outpost conflicts the Cæsarians generally had the best of it.

Pompey, to be sure, "had the emblems and standards of thirteen legions," but none of these were full, nor were they of good material. Two were native, had been under Varro, had deserted to Cæsar, had been given by him to Longinus and Trebonius, from whom they had revolted in favor of Cnæus Pompey; one was recruited among the Roman colonists in Spain; one had been in Africa with Afranius; the rest were mostly made up of fugitives from Pompey's old army, deserters and Spaniards. Thus four of his legions may be said to have been veteran, the rest raw. He had some thousands of horse, and about twelve thousand auxiliaries. Cæsar had eight legions, and with later reinforcements eight thousand cavalry. His light troops were probably of better quality and quite as many as those of Pompey. Each general had some fifty thousand men, not counting auxiliaries. The feelings of the old and weary legionaries were very bitter. The war promised not to lack atrocity.

The nature of the country, which is mountainous, with the towns built on easily defended heights, was such that Pompey was able to camp in positions to make an easy and protracted defense. Spain has always been noted for its defensive wars. The sharply accentuated country lends itself peculiarly to defense. Every small place remote from cities was built on an eminence, was fortified, and sentinels were kept constantly on the lookout. Whomever the native population befriended had strong and able allies.

Standing on any one of the numerous watch-towers of the country, one sees on every hand numberless round, woodless eminences, "like an immense city whose roofs are all cupolas." Nearly all these hills are fit for camping, and at every turn is a position easy to hold, difficult to capture.

In order to strengthen his own position, keep a good outlook, and hold more territory, Cæsar had taken possession of a suitable eminence — Castra Postumiana — some four miles from his main camp and fortified it (E). It was separated from his own camp by the river Salsum and was so placed as to be a threat to Pompey's camp. This general harbored the idea that Cæsar could not readily come to its relief in case he attacked it. It could be approached from his camp through the valleys without the troops being seen. He planned to fall upon this fort by night, as a means of creating a diversion in favor of Attegua, and, moving at midnight of February 4, reached the place without the cohorts being discovered. But before it was too late the garrison took alarm, flew to arms, and rained such numberless missiles on the Pompeians from the walls that Pompey was much delayed in his operations. Cæsar learned quickly of the attack, and with three legions hurried to the fort, already manfully defended by the garrison, where he inflicted a heavy loss on Pompey's troops and drove them off.

Cæsar at this time received reinforcements, especially of cavalry. Pompey, who again appears to have feared that Cæsar's position might enable him to move on Corduba and seize it out of hand, once more — on February 6 — set fire to his camp and made signs of retiring in the direction of that place, crossing the Carchena and actually camping south of his first location (F). He had been much harassed by Cæsar's cavalry in bringing victual from Corduba, and he appears to have retired the more readily to ration his men, for all his provisions were sent to him from the capital. Most of these convoys reached him, but Cæsar's cavalry on one occasion intercepted a train and pursued the guard back to the very walls of the city.

Cæsar pushed his works against Attegua. He daily added castella to his lines, and his terrace, surmounted by a tower, would shortly be able to fire upon the defenders of the city walls. To destroy these works the besieged made almost nightly sallies from Attegua, but these always resulted in their being driven back with loss. They employed every device to set fire to Cæsar's towers and engines. Pompey, who had not really left the vicinity, made sundry efforts to interfere with the siege, but to no serious effect. The besiegers proceeded with their operations, undermined and threw down a good part of the wall.

Pompey continued his activity. He seized a height on Cæsar's side of the river and erected a fort (G), hoping to place Cæsar at a disadvantage, and in many skirmishes near the town showed himself to be an efficient and capable soldier. A select body of his infantry one day lay in ambush for some of Cæsar's horse and suddenly attacked them. These troopers dismounted to fight on foot, and, not being as good infantry as cavalry, were as a consequence driven in nearly to Cæsar's lines; but being here reinforced they rallied and pushed back the enemy with a loss of some hundred men.

The garrison in the town was not only active but very obstinate and cruel. Cæsar's men were none the less so. The garrison consisted of Roman soldiers, and, mindful of the massacre of Thapsus, they dreaded any terms with Cæsar lest he should not be able to control his men. The soldiers murdered a great number of the citizens who were favorable to Cæsar, throwing some headlong from the walls. Flaccus, the commander of the garrison, organized the defense with skill, and a vast number of darts and missiles and much inflammable stuff was thrown at all times from the ramparts upon Cæsar's works.

One sally on February 15, at a time agreed upon with Pompey, — he being able occasionally by shooting darts or slinging bullets into the town to communicate with the garrison, — was made with particular vigor. The garrison had for object to cut its way out to join the main force. After having thrown a large number of fire-pots and flaming arrows upon the besiegers' lines at various places to create a diversion and uncertainty, they issued at midnight by the gate nearest Pompey's camp, carrying fascines to fill up the ditch, and mural hooks and fire to destroy Cæsar's works and the barracks of the men, which latter were mostly built of reeds.

They were sly enough to carry with them a large supply of silver and fine apparel with the intention of scattering these valuables in places where they would divert Cæsar's men from their work of resistance by thoughts of plunder. Pompey was in the fort he had erected on the Attegua side of the river Salsum, and bore his part in the fray. He remained all night in line to protect the retreat of the Atteguans, should they cut their way out. The military enginery of the town proved very efficient. One of Cæsar's wooden towers was battered so severely as to give way above the third story, and in fact the besiegers fired that and an adjoining tower. But the gallantry of the besieged was of no avail. The courage of the men and Cæsar's good leadership sufficed to drive them back into their lines and to hold Pompey in check at the same time.

The inhabitants now sent ambassadors to ascertain if Cæsar's clemency could be procured, and at the same time Pompey determined that he could do no more to afford the garrison relief. As a result, on February 19, the gates of the town were opened to his army. Cæsar behaved with conspicuous generosity.

When Cnæus learned of the surrender of Attegua, he felt convinced that Cæsar would advance on Ucubis. He moved his camp again up the river to a point northeast of the place, where he threw up works on all the hills around it which appeared to lend it strength. His weak conduct in not relieving Attegua had bred lack of confidence in him, and induced numberless desertions. These Pompey determined to punish. He selected a number of citizens of Ucubis supposed to be favorable to Cæsar's cause and put them to death. In all the towns and territories controlled by him similar cruelties were practiced. This was a short-sighted policy on his part, and materially helped Cæsar's cause.

After the capture of Attegua Cæsar moved his camp up the river nearer to and opposite Pompey's (K). He was puzzled how to proceed to draw Pompey into battle, which he sought as keenly as Pompey avoided it. Pompey, under the guidance of Labienus, was wisely avoiding open - field work and seeking to reduce Cæsar by famine. The experience of Africa and Greece was telling.

Cæsar within a few days (March 4) moved his camp somewhat nearer Pompey's, but still on the other bank (L), and his men drew an intrenched line to the river (M). This work, the object of which is not apparent, gave rise, after a while, to some heavy outpost combats.

On Cæsar's line was the town of Soricaria. Pompey had intrenched a dépôt at Aspavia, south of this place. The stores therein Cæsar wished to divert to his own uses. He moved to Soricaria, crossed the Salsum, and established a camp (N) whose position resulted in cutting Pompey off from his communications with Aspavia. Pompey broke camp and endeavored to reach the place, but found Cæsar athwart his path and intrenching his camp. Cnæus, thereupon, determined to offer battle, though on unequal terms to Cæsar's troops, as he sought the protection of the higher ground, in Cæsar's front (O). But Cæsar was on the alert. He sharply advanced on Pompey's cohorts, which were climbing the hill from the west, attacked them smartly, drove them from the heights and downward to the plain, occupied the upper ground himself, and, following down the slope, fell upon them as they were crossing the valley back to camp and defeated them with a loss of five hundred killed.

On the next day, March 6, Pompey, intending to retrieve himself, advanced on the same hill, anticipated Cæsar in its possession, and sent his cavalry to attack Cæsar's men, still working at their camp. Cæsar marched out and, drawing up on lower ground, invited Pompey to battle. This Pompey declined. After thus remaining some time, Cæsar retired to camp. Pompey attacked his rear with his cavalry, which bred a very severe combat, in which Cæsar's light troops had to mix to extricate the squadrons. The battle went no farther.

Soon after this action, Pompey retired to and held himself in Ucubis, and daily skirmishing was kept up between the armies, chiefly by the cavalry.

Desertions from Pompey grew in number alarmingly. To arrest these Pompey resorted to perversion of facts by writing to the towns which still held to him that Cæsar would not come down to the plain and fight, but stayed on the hills where he could not be attacked on anything like equal terms. Pompey was in his way energetic, and would have liked battle; but he was afraid of Cæsar. He determined to move from town to town, encourage some and punish others, hoping to gain some advantage by drawing out the war.

Roman Cuirass.

XLIII.

MUNDA. MARCH, 45 B. C.

THE Commentaries are very inexplicit on many of the facts of this campaign; they are made up of shreds and patches, which can be put together into one whole only by a knowledge of the topography. Cæsar followed up Pompey, and heading him off from crossing the Singulis, forced him to retrace his steps. Following him to Munda, — which place cannot well be at modern Monda, as it is usually assumed, — Cæsar attacked Pompey, and in a battle which came very close to being lost, by a happy accident cleverly utilized he eventually won a decisive victory. The entire Pompeian army was destroyed. It still took some five months for Cæsar to finish the settlement of Spain. He then returned to Rome.

ABOUT the 10th of March, Pompey, according to the Commentaries, which here become exceedingly sparse of details and unsatisfactory, broke camp and marched toward Hispalis, a place which, despite the name, cannot be modern Seville. Cæsar destroyed the camp at Ucubis, took Ventisponte, and following Pompey, marched to Carruca, still seeking opportunity to bring him to battle. Pompey moved to Munda. Cæsar followed and camped over against him. It is greatly to be regretted that the historian gives us no details of these manœuvres. Cæsar was evidently trying his best to drive Pompey into some position where he could have him at a disadvantage. And that he finally succeeded in so doing is evident from Pompey's concluding to fight at Munda. But the reasons for the marches and countermarches; as even these themselves, we have no means of positively knowing. All that we are sure of is that Cæsar finally succeeded in forcing Pompey into a position where the latter saw that subterfuge and retreat would no longer avail him; but that, in order to hold his allies to his cause, he must do battle for it. We are put to our inquiry from the topography and the probabilities.

Let us see whether we can supply the gap left by the historian of the Spanish War and reconstruct these manœuvres. The interest of the campaign justifies a digression from our narrative. First we must disprove some of the theories already advanced as to the location of Munda.

The entire Spanish campaign is involved in difficulties. As soon as we approach the battle of Munda, these difficulties multiply indefinitely. The question where Hannibal crossed the Alps is sufficiently puzzling, though it seems that the route of the Little St. Bernard may be considered as fairly established. In any event, there are but a few passes over which he could possibly have frayed a path. But within a radius of one hundred miles from Attegua and Ucubis there is scarcely a ruin-surmounted hill with a brook at its foot which has not laid claim to being the scene of Cæsar's great Spanish victory. And there are all but as many heights crowned by Roman ruins in Spain as in Italy.

The location of the battle of Munda has been the source of hundreds of essays and books, some indeed crowned by the Spanish Academy; it has been the subject of many topographical surveys and researches by the engineers of the Spanish army; it has been the cause of endless controversy. There is good reason to believe that the locality was not so far from that of the operations around Attegua and Ucubis as it is wont to be placed; certainly not so far as modern Monda, Osuna, or Ronda. There are dominant reasons for the belief that the battle was fought north of the Singulis (Xenil), rather than south of it. Let us glance at these.

Cæsar was constantly on the offensive, Pompey on the

defensive. This was Cæsar's strategic habit, or, at least, it was his habit to actively push his enemy by operations of some nature until he could force him to battle under suitable conditions. With none of his enemies did he long dally on the side of defense. We may fairly presume that this rule of conduct obtained in the present case. As we learn from the Commentaries, after the battle of Soricaria, "since which the enemy had been under continual alarms," and the succeeding operations, Pompey decamped. Cæsar followed, and "afterwards laid siege to Ventisponte, which surrendered; and, marching thence to Carruca, encamped over against Pompey, who had burned the city because the garrison refused to open the gates to him." Thence "Cæsar, still pursuing his march, arrived in the plains of Munda, and pitched his camp opposite to that of Pompey."

Now, none of these places have been identified by excavations or otherwise, and it is well not to give much heed to a similarity of names. It is safer to rely on military probabilities and to weigh each little item and word in the very short and unsatisfactory accounts which have been preserved to us.

There is an infinite number of arguments of more or less value, which can be framed to explain or sustain any given theory of the movements of the rival armies at this time. Let us keep in mind the leading statements concerning and characteristics of the campaign lest we go astray. These all point to the battlefield of Munda being not far from Corduba.

After his lack of success in the late operations, Pompey would not unnaturally determine to retire towards the sea, so as to have the proximity of his fleet to lean upon. Cæsar had a keen eye for the intentions of the enemy, and to have Pompey thus escape him would be the last thing he desired.

It is altogether probable that he narrowly watched his adversary and sought so to manœuvre as to head him off before he could cross the Singulis, which was a marked barrier between Pompey and the sea. Cæsar based on Obulco, and could hope to succeed better if he penned Pompey in the triangle made by it with the rivers Singulis and Bætis.

It is, therefore, a fair assumption that, so soon as Pompey showed the intention of definitively retiring from the theatre so marked out, Cæsar marched towards the river Singulis to head him off at the fords and compel him to do battle before he got away.

Had the rival armies passed the Singulis, the historian would have been likely to mention the fact as he does the passage of the Bætis. He does not mention the passage of the Salsum, because the latter is easily forded in many places. The Singulis has few fords, and at that time had doubtless few bridges, and is more or less difficult to cross.

Again: after the battle of Munda, the beaten Pompeians, we are told, took refuge in the cities of Munda *and Corduba*. Naturally enough in Munda, which they had at their back during the battle; but if we allow that Munda was far beyond the Singulis, and that Pompey was retiring from Corduba, while Cæsar followed him, how could large numbers of the Pompeians reach Corduba, through a country cut up by mountains and rivers and in possession of Cæsar's forces? Would they not rather have taken refuge in the towns nearer the battlefield, many, most of which, in fact, still held to Pompey's cause? That a very considerable number did reach Corduba appears plainly from what is told us about the siege of the town following the battle. A few stray fugitives from battle have often been known to reach very out-of-the-way places even through the enemy's lines, but not large bodies of men.

The text of the Spanish War is susceptible of meaning that some of these fugitives — among them Valerius — reached Corduba the night of the battle. This alone would prove Munda to be near Corduba. The text might also be held to imply that part of Cæsar's army marched from the battlefield to Corduba between the evening of the morrow of the battle and the next following noon, showing that but a short distance intervened. The text may be read to mean that Valerius escaped to Corduba, and that Cnæus took the road in the other direction, to Carteia (near modern Gibraltar), one hundred and seventy miles from Corduba, — as if Munda was near Corduba and Carteia very far away. But the text should not be forced. Let us consider some other items.

Cnæus Pompey, after the battle was lost, "attended by a few horse and foot, took the road to Carteia, where his fleet lay, and which was about one hundred and seventy miles distant from Corduba." He arrived there exhausted, showing that he had made a long journey, as his taking but a small party implied that he had a difficult march to make, — one much more tedious than the road from modern Monda to Carteia would be. Now, if the battlefield was not near Corduba, at least in the province of which Corduba was the capital, but far south of the Singulis, why should the historian give the distance of Carteia *from Corduba*, and not from some other well-known city nearer the battlefield?

Again: as Pompey's intention, unquestionably understood in the ranks of his army, was to make his way to Carteia, if he had passed the Singulis on his way thither, it seems certain that the fugitives would have sought to reach Carteia rather than distant Corduba. But except Cnæus, the historian speaks of no soldiers reaching any places other than Munda and Corduba.

The historian gives no details whatsoever of the march from Ucubis to Munda, except to say that Cæsar went to Ventisponte and Carruca. Had the distance been great, would not he have said something about it, especially as to pass the Singulis with an army is quite an operation, and the country beyond is very mountainous? He does describe the country near Attegua, and when he comes to speak of Munda he says: "*as we have observed before*, this country is full of hills which run in a continued chain without any plains intervening," as if Munda were still in the same section.

Again: Corduba surrendered easily after the news of the battle had reached it, as if from panic arising upon the presence of Cæsar's army near by. Orsao (Osuna), on the contrary, near which town many place Munda, stood a siege. May it not be assumed that it was too far off to be subject to immediate panic?

As to modern Monda, neither the topography of the section, nor the narration of the Spanish War, can be held to justify making it the locality of the battle. Mommsen is clearly wrong in this.

Ronda or Ronda la Vieja are still less available for both reasons. A few only have advocated these places.

The vicinity of the Rosa Alta mountains has been suggested. This will not do, because had this been the theatre of the battle, the town of Orsao would certainly have been a refuge for the beaten army. Nor does the topography of any particular place there correspond to what we are told of the battlefield.

Again: Many have claimed that Munda must be near Orsao, because the military engines used at Munda were brought to Orsao: "Fabius Maximus, whom he had left to continue the siege of Munda, conducted it with great zeal; so that the enemy, seeing themselves shut up on all sides, sallied out, but were repulsed with great loss. Our men seized this opportunity to get possession of the town, and took the rest prisoners, in number about fourteen thousand. Thence they retreated towards Orsao, a town exceedingly strong both by nature and art, and capable of resisting an enemy. Besides, there is not, within eight miles of the place, any spring but that which supplies the town, which was a decided advantage to the besieged. In addition to all this, the wood necessary for building towers and other machines had to be fetched from a distance of six miles. And Pompey, to render the siege more difficult, had cut down all the timber round the place, and collected it within the walls, which obliged our men to bring all the materials for carrying on the siege from Munda, the nearest town which they had subdued." But the Roman military engines were not difficult to transport. Alexander always carried his engines with him, like our field artillery. The legionary onagra were carried. Within six miles of Orsao there was wood left for the large framework, so that to carry all the parts of the big engines from Munda to Orsao was optional, and the operative parts could be carried almost any distance with ease. Orsao is, moreover, not on the road from Corduba to Carteia, the line of Pompey's retreat, but on that from Seville to Malaga, so that Munda can scarcely be assumed to have been near it. The Commentaries refer to Orsao as "the nearest town which they (*i. e.*, the besiegers of Munda) had subdued." But this does not necessarily imply that Munda was in the vicinity of Orsao. These two towns appear to have been the stoutest in their resistance to Cæsar. Had they been close to each other, it is probable that Cæsar would have done more than leave the sieges of Munda and Orsao to the management of Fabius, lest the one town should interfere with the siege of the other.

So much for the most important of the various places which lay claim to be the scene of this great battle. We can adduce only negative evidence at best to disprove their claims. The military probabilities furnish a stronger argument.

There is noticeable a certain similarity in some of Cæsar's campaigns, showing a method of work, — a type, — which it may be allowable to appeal to as a guide when we can find no certainty in the narration left to us. For instance, in the Ilerda campaign, Cæsar constantly kept Afranius and Petreius within certain bounds by manœuvring. He did not permit them to get beyond his easy reach. In Africa, too, all his manœuvres were within a comparatively small area. Without proof positive that the battle of Munda was fought south of the Singulis, may we not by analogy claim that it is more like Cæsar to have kept his opponent within the boundary prescribed by the Bætis and the Singulis?

If Pompey crossed the Singulis and made for Carteia, and Cæsar followed him and forced battle on him, how had he time to besiege Ventisponte on the way? For while he was doing so, Pompey would have certainly escaped him. Does it not seem more probable that Cæsar had headed Pompey off from crossing the Singulis on the way to Carteia, and had thus gained time for the siege? Is it not much more according to a Cæsarian model to imagine the great captain manœuvring Pompey into a place where he must fight, than to consider him as conducting a stern chase?

Such considerations as these make it altogether probable that the battle of Munda was fought north of the Singulis. The town of Montilla has been pointed out as a probable location. The topography is as satisfactory as we can ask, in view of the fact that the historian's description is not very close; and the strategic features tally well with what we may imagine Cæsar to have done. In order to construct a homogeneous whole out of the shreds of historical statement, we are compelled to assume something.

For the purpose, then, of planning a campaign which shall tally both with probability and with what we are told, let us assume that the three unidentified locations are: Ventisponte, modern Puente Vieja; Carruca, modern Puente Xenil; Munda, modern Montilla. The two former places are the only fords over the Xenil in this section, and have ruins of Roman bridges; the latter has a battlefield which chimes well with the narrative of the Spanish War. On his way towards Carteia after the battle of Soricaria, Pompey was heading for the bridges or fords of the Singulis. He chose Carruca for a crossing, but was stopped there by the garrison. Cæsar, meanwhile, moved on Ventisponte, took it, and moved against Pompey to Carruca. Thus cut off from his retreat towards Carteia, Pompey chose the only other alternative, turned in his tracks and headed by his left towards his old capital, Corduba. Cæsar met this manœuvre by moving by his right to cut him off from that city. Around modern Ecija are plains to which Cæsar may have been hoping to drive him. Pompey had told his allied cities so frequently that Cæsar would not fight when he offered him battle on equal terms, that he now felt compelled to make good his word. It is not impossible, too, that he saw no means of longer avoiding Cæsar's pursuit. In this way both armies reached Munda.

Cæsar had no special hope that Pompey would stand, but was surprised to see that his enemy had determined on battle. This was the thing he welcomed of all others.

The assumption thus made bears the stamp of accuracy, for it accords closely with the historian's relation, and still more closely with the military probabilities. No other does.

It was on the 15th of March that Pompey camped under

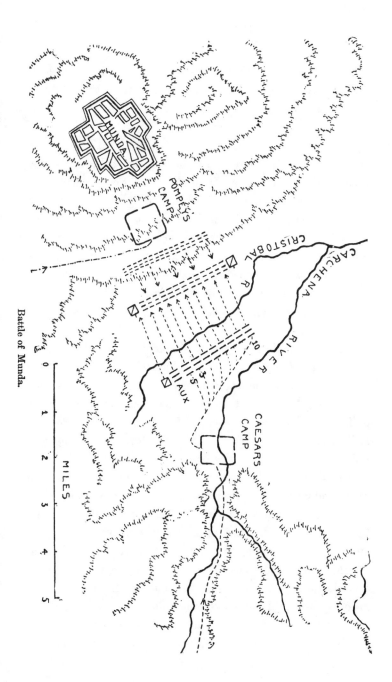

Battle of Munda.

the walls of Munda. Cæsar arrived next day and camped to the eastward, on a brook, to-day the Carchena. Back of Pompey lay his own intrenched camp and the town of Munda as a retreat in case of disaster. He did not feel that his position was disadvantageous.

The next day after Cæsar's arrival, March 17, as he was preparing for the route, — for he did not believe Pompey would fight, — he learned from spies that Pompey had been standing in battle array ever since midnight waiting for his approach. Cæsar "at once ordered the standard to be raised" for battle. Pompey had so long alleged that Cæsar preferred not to come to battle because his troops were raw levies that he had ended by half believing it; which idea, coupled to his present excellent tactical position, made him the more ready to chance matters on the result of a general engagement.

The town of Munda lay on a hill sloping towards the east. Between the two camps lay an undulating plain about five miles in width, through which ran a small rivulet, the modern Cristobal. Cæsar had had in mind some other plans for outmanœuvring his opponent, but on hearing that Pompey had prepared for battle, he himself drew up in line and waited for the enemy to descend to the plain, as he believed he would do; for Pompey had some cavalry which on the plain could act to better advantage than on the slope. But Pompey kept close to the hill and near the town on which his legions backed. His position was exceptionally strong, and he did not propose to forfeit it. He had all his thirteen legions in line. The cavalry was on his wings with six thousand light infantry and six thousand auxiliaries. He had probably been able to make good his losses, and may have still numbered fifty thousand men. The slope on which the Pompeians lay was rugged, excellent to defend, bad to attack. At its foot, on Cæsar's right, was low and marshy ground, fed by the brook. Cæsar had eighty heavy armed cohorts and eight thousand horse, — in any event under forty thousand effective. His light troops may have been eight thousand more.

As Pompey did not show any sign of advancing, Cæsar, on his part, marched across the plain to a point opposite Pompey, as a means of luring him forward. When the legions had reached the low ground and the brook, beyond which the hill where Pompey was posted began to ascend, and before crossing the brook, Cæsar halted the line and, calling together his officers, pointed out to them and to his troops the disadvantage under which they would attack if they did so now. As we have seen, Cæsar never favored attacking positions, and was reluctant to undertake an assault here. He had caution in certain contingencies equal to Hannibal's; but, unlike Hannibal, he alternated hypercaution with the extremity of recklessness.

"The army murmured greatly as if they had been kept back from a certain victory, when this was told them." The men were in excellent spirits and demanded but a chance to fight. The order to advance was accordingly issued, and the line promptly moved forward as with the will of one man, and crossed the brook. The pause which had thus occurred in the advance of the Cæsarians encouraged the enemy to believe that Cæsar's legions were hesitating from fear, and induced Pompey to order his line to move a short distance down the hill; but though they thereby yielded part of the strength of their position, the advantage still remained indisputably with them. Nor did they advance far from the protection of the walls of Munda, which was not exceeding a mile in their rear. Pompey proposed in any event to have this city as a harbor of refuge.

Cæsar's Tenth legion was on the right; the Third and Fifth legions were on the left with the cavalry and the auxiliaries drawn up beyond them. The other legions held the centre. The battle was engaged with extraordinary enthusiasm. The shout on each side came from men determined and expecting to conquer, — men who proposed to give no quarter. Cæsar's legions charged up the hill with consummate gallantry. Pompey's line met them at javelin-throwing distance by a storm of pila · and a counter - charge. Cæsar's men were superior in discipline and went at their work with cheerful courage; Pompey's troops fought with clenched teeth, in the belief that their only salvation depended on winning this battle. They remembered Thapsus.

At the instant before the impact the shower of darts was so heavy from above that the young troops wavered, and there was serious danger of Cæsar's line being broken before it had fairly engaged the enemy. Then came the charge down from the higher ground which struck like the blow of a ram. Its momentum fairly staggered Cæsar's line; the onset was checked. The two lines, like wrestlers, with a firm hold, swayed to and fro in fierce opposition. This lasted while the successive ranks and lines relieved each other and fought with lance and sword. But the position of Pompey's men was much in their favor. They pressed Cæsar's cohorts hard. After many hours of this close-locked fighting, Cæsar's line began to show serious signs of weariness; there were hints of that disintegration which appals the stoutest-hearted leader. Cæsar was taken aback. So grave, indeed, was the danger at this instant, that Cæsar afterwards stated that while he had often before fought for victory, this, his last battle, was the first occasion on which he ever fought for his life. He had forgotten the Sabis. But that wonderful magnetic energy of his was roused to its

highest pitch by the imminence of disaster. Never, since
the day when the Nervii all but annihilated his legions,—
save perhaps at Alesia, — had he been called upon to put out
his every power, physical and moral, as now. He rushed
through the ranks, shaming some, stimulating others,
reproaching the backward, praising the brave, and rousing
the courage of his men by every appeal. He fought, as at
the river Sabis, like a common soldier, with sword and shield
in the front rank before the ensigns. By his personal
endeavors the men were kept at their work.

There is no question that victory or defeat, for hours perhaps, hung by a hair. It was Cæsar, and Cæsar alone, who
kept the cohorts from stampede. It has been alleged by some
historians that at the most dangerous period of the battle Cæsar, in despair, was about to take his own life. But this is
so thoroughly unlike the man that we cannot accept it as true.
Cæsar was capable of falling at the head of his legions, but
not by his own hand in battle, unless he was taken prisoner.

Evening was approaching. The last man on both sides
had been put in. Not a cohort of reserves was left. The
battle was anybody's. No one could predict the result.
Cæsar's men had rallied, but they were fighting uphill, and
Pompey's men had been encouraged by holding their own so
long. The auxiliaries on both sides had fled. There was
no chance for manœuvring. It was a mere question of discipline and valor. An accident might break either line, and
such a breach would be surely fatal. Cæsar was still omnipresent. His efforts had never slackened. He clung to his
ground like one possessed. He would not face defeat. He
made a last appeal to his old favorite, the Tenth legion.
"Are you not ashamed to deliver your general into the
hands of boys?" he cried to his veterans. Stung to the
quick by the taunts of their general, for whom they had

wrested victory from desperate straits so many times before, these battle-scarred men now rose to their old standard of enthusiasm, and pressed the enemy hard. The rest of the line gained courage for redoubled effort. Pompey was compelled to draw a legion from his right to help sustain his left, which was battered by the heavy blows of the Tenth. Cæsar's cavalry of its own motion fell upon this depleted wing and created a distinct impression. The fighting "was hand to hand, foot to foot and shield to shield." On whose banners was victory to perch?

Finally chance decided the day. King Bogud with his Numidians, after the charge of the cavalry, made a circuit of the Pompeian right and marched upon their camp. Perceiving this, Labienus, who commanded on this wing, detailed five cohorts to head him off. Catching sight of these troops moving to the rear, Cæsar, who was in the thickest of the fray, though he comprehended the manœuvre, seized on it as an omen and shouted to his men: "Look you, comrades, the enemy flees!" The Pompeians at the same moment saw this rearward movement, and conceiving the idea that their line was somewhere broken, began to waver. This bred confusion in their ranks and enthusiasm in Cæsar's, — as small things will often do upon the battlefield. Here was Cæsar's opportunity. Under his powerful influence, the line was roused to one more almost superhuman effort. It was all that was required; the effort prevailed; the Cæsarians broke the Pompeian line and drove the enemy towards the town.

The victory was won, but the battle was not yet ended. Cæsar's eight thousand cavalry, which had so far done small work, now put in its heartiest blows, and soon broke up the cohorts of the aristocrats. Great slaughter ensued; thirty thousand Pompeians were cut down, among them Labienus and Varus, and three thousand Roman knights. Cæsar lost, according to the Commentaries, but one thousand killed, and five hundred wounded. This last item is another of those curious discrepancies between killed and wounded which make it so difficult to gauge the Roman losses in comparison to those of modern times. In some battles it can, from their peculiar tactics, be understood how there might be less wounded than killed; but at Munda the reason does not so plainly appear. It may have been due to the hand-to-hand fighting, which gave a wounded man small chance of getting to the rear.

Cæsar took the eagles of the thirteen Pompeian legions, an immense number of standards, and seventeen higher officers. The victory was overwhelming; the massacre decided the war. Most fugitives from Pompey's army made for Munda, which it became necessary to besiege. So heated were the passions of the Cæsarians, that the dead bodies of the slain were used as ramparts, and their javelins as palisades, and on these their bucklers were hung as breastworks. The heads of many were stuck on pikes and placed along the investment lines to strike terror into the besieged.

At Pharsalus Cæsar lost, according to the Commentaries, two hundred killed; at Thapsus, fifty; at Munda one thousand. The enemy, on the contrary, practically lost their entire army in each of these engagements. While these figures may not be accurate, it remains true that in ancient battles the vanquished lost to an extent impossible to-day. Defeat always meant massacre, — except to a Cæsar. There was no attempt to restrain the troops. To kill was one of the main purposes of an ancient battle; to-day, killing is an unfortunate incident of war, which is ended as soon as the army of the enemy is put as far as may be beyond usefulness for the campaign. Despite such fearful slaughter, the total losses of a campaign in ancient times were apt to be much less than they are to-day, when constant deadly fighting, with daily loss on both sides, is going on.

Cnæus Pompey fled from the field towards his fleet at Carteia, "which was about one hundred and seventy miles distant from Corduba," one hundred and forty-five from Munda; but, after some time, was overtaken and killed. Cæsar left Munda invested by Fabius Maximus, and marched to Corduba. Sextus Pompey had decamped. Here Cæsar was arrested some time by the gallant defense offered by the Thirteenth legion. We have no details whatever of the operations. But the adherents of Cæsar within the walls set fire to the place. Cæsar made his way in, and slew twenty-two thousand men, many of them runaways from the battle-field of Munda. This slaughter was uncalled for. It adds to the list of holocausts for which Cæsar was responsible.

The battle of Munda had by no means crushed out opposition. Pompey's adherents defended themselves to the last. Hispalis was the next city to be reduced. This occupied some time. Asta and Munda followed. Each was a task of some difficulty. Carteia had seized Cnæus Pompey. One party in the town wanted to give him up; one to assist him. His adherents got the upper hand, and, laying hands on all his adversaries, remorselessly slaughtered them. Cnæus escaped by sea, but Didius followed him up with Cæsar's fleet, and, after a series of romantic adventures and a brave fight for life, he was captured and killed. Didius' success was, however, short-lived; he was shortly after caught in an ambuscade and his fleet destroyed by the Lusitanians.

Fabius, after a long siege, took Munda, and later the city of Ursao fell to the Cæsarian arms. But the stanch defense of the towns adhering to Pompey is best shown by the fact that it took Cæsar or his lieutenants many months to accomplish their reduction.

The Spanish war was the last in which Cæsar was engaged. Having reduced the whole of Spain, there was now no organized opposition to his rule in any quarter of the world. He started for Rome the end of July. But his glory was short-lived. He was assassinated next Ides of March.

The sons of Pompey had many conditions in their favor at the beginning of the Spanish campaign, but they did not use them to advantage. One of their chief errors was of a kind not unusual at that day; they devastated the land and robbed the population of a country already half Cæsar's. This conduct incensed both their friends and foes, and enabled Cæsar to tamper with Pompey's adherents, who listened the more readily to him for having suffered at the hands of Pompey. Cnæus, who was the ruling spirit, conceived his military projects in a manner far from perfect and carried them out in still worse form. When the execution of a plan of campaign brought either Cnæus or Sextus into the presence of Cæsar, he seemed to be still less capable of intelligent action. Few generals shine when they are opposed to men like Alexander, Hannibal or Cæsar. Except Vercingetorix, scarcely one of Cæsar's opponents came out of the struggle with military reputation unscathed. Pompey had been a great man; but he was no longer such in Cæsar's front.

Cæsar never had to face such men as Marcellus, Nero and Scipio. Even in contrast with the greatest captain of antiquity, perhaps of all time, these Romans earned an abiding fame. Cæsar was never called on to oppose such generals; nor, indeed, such legions as were made up of the burgesses of the Second Punic War.

Cæsar encountered semi-barbaric tribes much as did Alexander, but not in as overwhelming numbers; he never encountered civilized armies under conditions by any means as unequal as Hannibal.

A marked distinction in ancient times between the great and the mediocre captain lay in the ability of the former to rescue himself from disaster if he happened to suffer defeat; to keep his men within the bounds of demoralization; to save them from a massacre. Alexander scarcely knew failure. Hannibal often looked defeat in the face, but never disaster, until Zama. Cæsar always rescued himself from defeat. Disaster never overtook him.

If, after the battle of Munda, Cnæus had not lost his head, he might have saved a portion of his army; have retired to one of half a dozen provinces or cities, and have raised troops to continue the struggle. He might not have been able to alter the outcome of the war, but he could have protracted it indefinitely, at this time a highly undesirable thing for Cæsar, who was needed at Rome to allay serious political troubles, and could not well afford military difficulties. Neither Cnæus nor Sextus were in any sense worthy antagonists of Cæsar. The former must not be underrated. He had some good points, and, under better conditions, might have shown for more. Sextus must be gauged lower. They could not expect to equal Cæsar; but they might have made his task a harder one.

The fact that Cæsar took from March to August after Munda to reduce Spain to complete subjection shows how strong a grasp the Pompeian element had got upon the peninsula, and proves that a good soldier, despite defeat, might well have held out an indefinite time. While it is true that Cæsar's luck generally pitted mediocre men against him during the Civil War, his genius was demonstrated as much in taking advantage of their shortcomings as it was in his so cutting out and doing his work as to reduce the length of his campaigns to such exceptionally short limits.

XLIV.

THE MAN AND SOLDIER.

CÆSAR was tall and slight, but strong and uniformly well. He was a good fencer and rider, and well up in athletic sports. His features were large but refined. In his last years he showed his age and grew bald. His dress was always elegant. Cicero was his only superior as an orator; in ordinary converse he was unequaled. His power of work and endurance were wonderful. He is charged with many *liaisons*, but they were the custom of the day. His domestic habits were simple, but he was extravagant in art. Some ancient authors charge him with many vices; he was, indeed, not perfect; but the sum of all is a well-balanced character. He was a good friend and bore no malice to enemies. He had no bigotry; his intellectual equipment was splendid. He did more cruel things than Alexander, but he was personally kind and generous. He had projected many great works in addition to those he had already performed when the end came. As a soldier, Cæsar's art was inborn. The ancients knew nothing beyond tactics and logistics. Strategy was not a recognized science. Cæsar was his own pedagogue; he learned from his own errors. The conception of the plan of the Civil War was on as high a plane as its execution; the rapidity of its campaigns has no equal; but it was marred by repeated instances of overhasty action barely pardonable in a tribune, inexcusable in a great captain. A large part of the time consumed by his work was due to these mistakes. Cæsar's objectives were always well chosen; he invariably struck at the key-point. His manœuvres and blockades were on a big scale. In adversity he was elastic; he never lost *morale*. His tactics was simple; such battle-tactics as that of Epaminondas, Alexander, Hannibal, we never see. His strategy was broad. Cæsar's opponents were not as a rule strong; but he made good use of their mistakes. Pompey was able; he was never great, and Cæsar's *morale* overrode him. Cæsar's influence over his men was marked. In peace he allowed laxity; in war he demanded strict discipline. With few exceptions his legions reflected his own splendid qualities.

"CÆSAR was born to do great things," says Plutarch. First of all a statesman, arms were to Cæsar a means of carrying out his political scheme, rather than statecraft an aid to his military policy. The portrait of this great man has been painted by able hands and in many colors. It is only sought to add to this portrait some touches which pertain to his military career.

Cæsar was tall and of slight but well-knit frame. Constant exercise and exposure had made him hardy; and his constitutional and nervous strength could not be overtaxed. Except that he had at times attacks of "the falling sickness," no illness save quartan ague is recorded of him during a life of infinite toil. He was skillful as a fencer, and in many of his battles exhibited an ability to wield arms, coupled to a personal gallantry and magnetic power rarely shown by the captain. To his boldness in swimming he owed his life in Egypt. He was a fine horseman. As Alexander had his Bucephalus, so Cæsar owned and rode in the Gallic War a much prized horse of his own raising who allowed no other man to mount him, and whose "divided hoof," which, it is said, resembled a human foot, made him singular, if adding no value to his other qualities. That Cæsar had great physical endurance is shown by the exceptional speed of his journeys. He often traveled day and night and worked on the road as if he had quietly sat in his tent.

Refinement and strength rather than beauty of feature characterized Cæsar's face. His portrait busts show a strong intellectual development with an abundance of will-power; and in some of them there is a singularly sweet expression of the mouth; but this detracts naught from its force. In the last few years he showed in the deep-cut lines of his face the severe strain to which he had so long been subjected; and his carriage was not as erect nor his gait as elastic as that of many men of his age. In middle life, much to his regret, his hair grew thin; and as he never quite lost the instincts of the dandy, he combed his locks forward with noticeable care, and to conceal his baldness was glad to wear upon his head the golden wreath of laurel voted him by the Senate. His eyes are variously spoken of as dark gray, or black and piercing. His face was pale when not bronzed by exposure; his dress had a touch of elegance all through life. He was a constant bather and never lost his liking for the niceties of the toilet.

Cæsar may not have possessed the grace of demeanor of Alexander; but he had the force of Hannibal, and a power of impressing himself on all who approached him in which neither the Macedonian nor the Carthaginian was his superior. His simple directness, his aptness at saying the right word in season, his persuasiveness, his broad culture and immense resources of thought and language charmed every one who was cast with him, whether the barbaric king of Gaul or the queen of Roman society. As an orator he was confessedly second to no one but Cicero; his voice was high-pitched and his manner animated. In personal converse he was, perhaps, the first man of his day. His high-bred courtesy and an easy manner never forsook him. He was gifted with a remarkable memory and power of concentration; he often dictated to two or more secretaries at the same time; and we can conceive how such a memory, stored with all that Greek culture and extensive travel could bestow, and drawn on by eloquent lips, must have lent an attractiveness none could approach. He was versatile; without an effort he attained the highest excellence in all he undertook.

Cæsar has been blamed for his relations to women. His habits were those of the day. Hannibal may be praised for his fidelity to Imilcea; Alexander for his scrupulous respect of Statira, the consort of fugitive Darius; but Cæsar is scarcely blameworthy for being a man of the world when what we call morality was not considered a virtue, and to be continent or scrupulous was to be out of fashion. It is no doubt true that Cæsar's *liaisons* extended far and wide. He is charged with intrigues with the wives of many of his friends; but, whatever the truth, it seems clear that his friends and he did not quarrel. He was assuredly not gross in his amours; and his bravery in refusing to divorce his wife at Sulla's nod, when other and then greater men did so, and in taking the consequences, scores a high mark in his favor. It is impossible to say how much of what has been charged against Cæsar is due to the idle gossip of the Roman *salons.*

Cæsar's domestic habits were not pretentious. When he was virtually king of Rome, when he had been called "the Divine" by an obsequious Senate, he is said to have lived simply, though Plutarch speaks of the general splendor of his manner of life, and he was extravagant in the purchase of statues, pictures, gems, and other objects of art. He kept a generous table, of the best to be had, but without ostentation. As *custos morum* he enforced the sumptuary laws with some severity. One of his tables was laid for his political friends, one for his military. He himself was moderate in food and drink, but enjoyed the mental friction of enlivening table-talk. That he had indulged in a youth of pleasure cannot be gainsaid; but that it left no trace on his body or mind is equally true. No vices had sapped his powers; his physical and mental structure rendered him proof against their effects.

Cæsar owed much to his mother, Aurelia; and he repaid her by the same devotion which Frederick showed to "the queen mother." Aurelia lived under her son's roof until her death. Cæsar exhibited equal affection for his sister.

The ancient authorities vary greatly in their estimates of this man. He is charged by some with all the vices; he is credited by others with all the virtues; still others ascribe all vices and virtues to him. It has been the habit until of late years to look upon Cæsar as "the monster," which the many-headed in Rome once dubbed him. The pendulum has now swung back, and we are threatened with forgetfulness of what many Roman authors tell us. Among others, Suetonius informs us that Cæsar exhibited great animosity as a judge; that he resorted to bribery; that he was hasty and violent; that he was suspected of ridding himself of an enemy by poison; that he lent money without interest in order to cater friendship; that he plundered Lusitania at the point of the sword and robbed temples in Gaul; that he was rapacious in character and extravagant in language; and that he incurred the suspicion of heading a conspiracy to murder his opponents in the Senate and resort to a *coup d'état*. Other authors give us many similar items. There is no certain means of weighing these allegations. We must note them all and give them a proper place in our estimate of what Cæsar was. But after so doing, the sum of all that is told us makes up a well-poised character, quite apart from Cæsar's gigantic intellect or moral force.

From youth up Cæsar avoided quarrels; he had other means of settling disputes, and could either assert his view with reasonable insistence or persuade his opponent by his superior skill. When angry he was easily appeased. When worsted he bore no malice.

Cæsar's friendships were sincere and durable, honest and above board. He was generous and kind. To sick Oppius he gave up his couch and slept on the ground. With few exceptions his friends remained his friends. He had no room for suspicion in his broad affection. He would not believe that Labienus meant to desert him. When he did so, Cæsar offered any friends of Pompey who might be in his service free conduct to join his opponent if they so chose.

He clung to his friends, not from calculation but affection; though he made use of them as he himself was useful to them. When he had pardoned an enemy, there was no further relic of ill-will. He took as much pride in restoring the statues of Sulla and Pompey as he had exhibited courage in replacing on the capitol-hill the trophies of Marius.

Had he been nothing but a soldier, Cæsar would still be the equal of the other great captains. Taking him as the statesman who built on the ruins of the Republic the foundations of the Empire, as the patron of learning who founded libraries in all the great towns, and filled Rome with men of science, culture and letters, as the legislator who drafted laws which still control the jurisdiction of the world, as the profound scholar who dictated the correction of the calendar, as the thinker, for the grasp of whose mind nothing was too intricate, nothing too broad, Cæsar was, indeed, "the foremost man in all this world."

Of the men of that generation, no one clung to fact as did Cæsar. As Carlyle says of Napoleon, "the man had a certain instinctive, ineradicable feeling for reality." He was no idealist, yet he had an abundant fund of imagination, as every creative mind must have. He coolly dissected things, and could look at them as they actually were. From a given array of facts Cæsar rarely failed to draw the correct conclusion. Traditions were of value to him for their influence on weaker minds. As *pontifex maximus*, he was neither bigoted nor over-liberal. The cult of the Roman gods had on his mind the proper influence, no more. It was of distinct value to the state; of no particular value to the indivdiual.

In gifts of intellect and character Cæsar was exceptional; his judgment was rarely at fault. He was of a reasonable turn of mind, and the harmony and consistency of his life were marked. In politics he was persuasive rather than dogmatic, but he had a way of carrying his point. His intuitions as well as his power of gauging men and of guessing their actions were keen.

While allowing all this, it must not be assumed that Cæsar was perfect in character. It is possible to make a glaring array of faults with which he may be charged. He was utterly unscrupulous as to the means he employed when he made up his mind to do a given thing, — a fact not palliated because it may be said to have been the fault of his age. He would allow nothing to stand in the way of the accomplishment of his purpose. When he deemed the thing he aimed at worthy to be done, every means was proper. He borrowed immense sums of money without other means of payment than what he anticipated might be ground out of the government of a province. Personally of a generous, kindly habit, he is chargeable with holocausts before which the devastations of Alexander shrink to naught. It is said of him that he never murdered a Clitus or savagely mutilated a Batis, or burned a Persepolis; but he executed Acco with extreme if legal cruelty; he put to death the whole Venetan Senate for their patriotic resistance; he again and again visited awful vengeance on the Eburones for the sins of Ambiorix; he cut the hands off all the prisoners taken at Uxellodunum, and in treacherous cold blood he massacred four hundred and thirty thousand defenseless men, women and children in the course of a short afternoon. The sum of his massacres in Gaul overruns a million souls, paying no heed to those who perished by a worse fate than the edge of the sword. Yet, though we view all these things in their proper light, we cannot withhold from Cæsar's personal character the meed of our respect and admiration.

Up to middle life, Cæsar was purely a statesman. He then had the fact brought home to him that he could no

longer win the success he sought unless he had at his command
the military resources which his enemies boasted. Those
who place Cæsar on the plane of pure patriotism, who claim
that the regeneration of Rome and Greece was his leading
object, must still allow that he sought it mainly by his own
elevation. What he sought he won. He was a born ruler,
and he became a republican king. The honors and titles
which were heaped upon him were lavish to absurdity. The
heretofore military title of Imperator became a prefix to his
name and was made hereditary in his family. He was styled
Pater Patriæ. He was saluted as Divus Julius. He was
made consul for ten years. His statue was erected in every
town and medals were struck in his honor. Chairs of gold
and gilded chariots were presented to him. Triumphal
arches arose in his honor, and a temple of Concord or Clemency. He was invested with tribunician honors which made
it sacrilege to injure his sacred person or character.

It is hard to say what part of all this proceeded from the
gratitude of the Senate, what part was fulsome and empty
adulation, what part the work of enemies who sought to sap
the autocrat's popularity with the people. It is hard to say
how much Cæsar enjoyed this worship, and how much he
despised it. He declined some of the honors; he accepted
others. He added his own to the seven statues of the kings
of Rome; he appeared in public in the garb of the old kings
of Alba. About all he did there was a certain ceremonial,
despite his natural personal simplicity. Cæsar was sole ruler
and the Senate became a mere council. He assumed their
political functions. A new patrician nobility was created.
Augustus was no more Emperor than Cæsar.

It is probable that Cæsar at heart cared little for much of
all this tinsel; it is certain that he felt out of place and far
from secure in the city. And yet he was covetous of honor;

he enjoyed the applause of the multitude. That he had a certain habit of simplicity is undeniable. He went about alone and unarmed, though well aware how numerous were his enemies. He refused the crown which was offered him, — perchance because he saw therein a snare. Had he lived he would no doubt have openly become what Augustus was, but he bided his time and the time never came.

He had good cause to be satisfied with what he had accomplished. Vast as his work had been, it had borne good fruit. Despite its fearful depopulation, Gaul was again flourishing and commerce and agriculture were on the increase. His changes in the laws were solid, — "the political life of nations has during two thousand years again and again reverted to the lines which Cæsar drew." As *custos morum* and in his other judicial characters, he punished severely but judiciously, and despite Suetonius we must believe impartially. It is certain that Rome was the better for his administration, at least for the foundations which he laid.

On Cæsar's final return to Rome, his physical strength, which had been upheld by nervous tension, sensibly declined; but his energy remained intact. He made vast projects for the future. He purposed to drain the Pontine marshes, to make a new channel for the Tiber, to improve the roads, to cut through the Isthmus of Corinth. He projected a campaign against the Parthians and was intending soon to start in order to secure this frontier of the state, as he had all the others — when the end came.

At the risk of repeating what has already been said in running comment, it is well to sum up the soldier. Cæsar had the inborn qualities of the great captain. When he received Gaul as his province he had had no training in the duties of a general officer except that gained in the Lusitanian campaign. There was no training for the larger operations of war known to the ancients. The management of a campaign depended solely on the ability of the leader. The grasp of a military problem came purely from his personal equipment. To-day, instruction is given to students of war in its broader phases, and precept is enforced by the example of great commanders. We hear of no such teaching among the ancients. Instruction there was, and perfect of its kind; but it went not beyond the tactical and logistic requirements of an army. Strategy was still unknown as a teachable science. It must not be assumed that to be an adept in the book-lore of strategy will make a great captain. Character counts for more than half. The personal equation is the one that tells. But character coupled to a well-trained intellect are essential to produce the greatest results. To-day only the highly-trained officer is efficient; it was less so in ancient days, but intellect then won as it does now and always will.

Cæsar was his own pedagogue in war. He taught himself his trade in Gaul. He accomplished this self-training by dint of many errors. In the Civil War, Cæsar committed fewer, and these were generally from overanxiety to get at his work. His operations, all things considered, were wellnigh faultless.

We have already considered the strategic plan of the Gallic War and incidentally that of the Civil War. Let us recapitulate the latter. In this war Cæsar wisely chose Italy, the centre point of the empire for which he was contending, as his first objective. This accords with his uniform habit of selecting for attack the most important point. He never adopted indirect means. His blows were always aimed at the key-point. In sixty days from crossing the Rubicon he had, by his directness and the moral ascendant which followed his vigorous initiative, acquired possession of the peninsula.

Once seated in Italy, Cæsar found the enemy on three sides of him, — in Spain, Greece, Africa. He had gained a central position from which to operate. If he could hold himself in Rome, he could attack each of his enemy's divisions in turn. To hold Rome and carry on an offensive, demanded two things, legions and speed. In the former, counting out essential detachments, he was weaker than his adversary; in the latter he proved himself far superior.

We have assumed that Cæsar's better plan was at once to move on Greece, where Pompey stood with his main force. This was of a part with Cæsar's common habit of aiming directly at his enemy's army. We are forced to guess at Cæsar's reasons for doing otherwise, — the Commentaries are not specific. They tell us that Pompey had command of the sea and that Cæsar feared that it would consume much time to gather a fleet; that meanwhile not only would he be forced to inactivity, but that Pompey's veteran legions might "confirm Spain in his interest," gather large levies, and, more dangerous still, invade Gaul from Spain, and arouse an enemy in his rear. Cæsar knew Pompey and gauged his temperament correctly. He could more safely rely on Pompey's keeping quiet in Epirus than on Pompey's lieutenants doing the same in Iberia. This reasoning does not convince us; but action under it was crowned with success; it may, therefore, be deemed to have been sufficient.

The Spanish campaign and the siege of Massilia, however rapid, took long enough to bring Cæsar back to Italy at an inopportune season. But Cæsar could never wait. Driven by exhaustless energy, he crossed the Adriatic to Epirus with half his army, because he had not transports for the whole. That he would have been wiser to march through Illyricum seems clear. It was his own province. From the Padus through Illyricum to Epirus was almost as short a march as to Brundisium, and the bulk of his army had rendezvoused on that river. Reaching Epirus with limited forces, Cæsar with energy and unequaled good fortune held his ground until, after the lapse of five months, he was joined by Mark Antony. How Cæsar would have fared with an abler opponent in his front is a matter of conjecture. He owed his safety to Pompey's laxness. Why Antony was not ordered to march by Illyricum when his presence was so essential in Epirus is explainable only in that Cæsar and he both hoped from day to day that chance would afford him the opportunity to cross the Adriatic.

The operation at Dyrrachium resulted in a marked defeat for Cæsar, directly due to his undertaking an operation which could succeed only by virtue of a miracle or an accident. He was able to rescue himself from disaster because he was Cæsar and had Pompey opposed to him. Having saved his army from this danger, he skillfully manœuvred to join Domitius, which done, with an audacity worthy of a Frederick, he attacked and beat Pompey at Pharsalus. All this is so splendid, the errors are so completely swallowed up in the well-deserved success, that criticism is put to the blush.

Upon this decisive victory followed Cæsar's overhasty and uncalculating pursuit of Pompey with a bare corporal's guard to Alexandria; his political mistake in mixing himself up in petty Egyptian affairs when the world was still at stake; his being blockaded in Alexandria by a horde of barbarians, whom three of his old Gallic legions might have overwhelmed; his holding himself by pure stubbornness until released by Mithridates; his two months' dalliance with Cleopatra while his enemies were daily gaining strength. Add to these delays the essential campaign in Pontus, and there was again a year consumed, during which the Pompeian party had acquired control of Africa. However much we may admire the skill exhibited in the details of the Alexandrian campaign, as well as the courage to see it through to a successful issue, it is clear that Cæsar for the moment lost sight of the broad plan of his mighty game which had the world for a theatre of operations. This error was the origin of the bitter struggle which it cost to reduce the Pompeians to terms in the succeeding years.

Again, when Cæsar was compelled to take up arms to bring Africa into subjection, his hyper-activity drove him to ship over to that continent at one of the worst seasons of the year, —and this without giving a rendezvous to his fleet; by which neglect the same untoward situation was brought about on the African coast which had happened a year before on the Epirotic. The man who held in his grasp the resources of the Roman state was reduced for months to a petty defensive scarcely befitting a legate, until he could gather forces sufficient to go over to the offensive; and during all this time he was in a danger which an able opponent might have rendered fatal. It was Cæsar's luck which placed Scipio in command instead of Cato. To this situation and the difficulty of procuring corn must be traced the narrowness of his movements. At the same time his danger showed up his fertility in resources in a wonderful measure. Having again recruited up his forces to a proper standard, we are led to look for an immediate and vigorous offensive. But we are disappointed. Though opposed by a less good army, and by trivial generals, Cæsar hazarded nothing. For the moment all his audacity disappeared. He played the game which Hannibal was forced to play when he was facing thrice his numbers of superior troops under consummate leaders; and he appears to small advantage when contrasted with the Carthaginian. But when the opportunity for which he had long manœuvred had come, and Scipio had been brought to battle on advantageous terms, Cæsar, or rather Cæsar's army, made short work of him in the brilliant victory at Thapsus.

Then came the Spanish campaign, to crush out the relics of the Pompeian party. The clever manœuvres on the Bætis, followed by the hard-won battle of Munda and the ensuing sieges, again took more than half a year. We know less about these movements than we could wish. What we do know shows Cæsar up in brilliant colors.

It is clear that the Civil War might have been carried through in half the time it actually consumed had Cæsar been more judicious. But he started with only a moiety of his army for Epirus at a bad season; he committed precisely the same error in opening the African war; the Alexandrian and Pontus campaigns came in between the other and more important ones and prevented the prosecution of the latter in due season. These events had depended upon Cæsar's own volition. Had he marched to Epirus overland before the fall of 49, had he in the spring of 48 gone with a respectable force to Africa, this year would probably have seen the end of the Pompeian coalition. That despite these mistakes he was victorious in each campaign in so comparatively short a time he owes to his extraordinary ability, his simply astonishing good fortune, and the weakness of his opponents. It is, perhaps, hypercritical to suggest errors in a record which history can scarcely equal. And yet the errors are glaring; they are such as Hannibal was never guilty of; such as cannot be traced to Alexander.

Speaking broadly, the Civil War was a war of conquest as much as the Gallic. Cæsar was content with no less than sole control of Rome. In accomplishing this end his political and military management were, as always, admirable. He was constantly on the offensive. Except as the result of an overeager movement, he was never put on the defense.

His constant endeavor, as in the Gallic War, was to surprise his opponents before they were ready. It may be claimed as a valid reason why he did not march overland against Pompey, that the latter, being master of the sea, would have ascertained his movements and prepared for them. It may be claimed that it was to take the enemy unawares that Cæsar moved on Pompey in Epirus in the winter season. It may be claimed that to surprise the aristocrats was the object of the winter movement on Africa. For as a rule Cæsar was careful to put his troops into winter-quarters. But to allow these claims does not palliate the lack of preparation.

Cæsar's scouting system was always good. In the Civil War he could more readily gather information of his enemy's plans than in Gaul. He was in countries where he had many adherents, sometimes the bulk of the population, in his favor. Deserters were more frequent from the enemy. Pompey had similar advantages in a lesser degree. The tide of desertion was apt to set in Cæsar's favor. Cæsar used his light cavalry for scouting purposes to better advantage and was generally more active in collecting information than his opponents.

Though Cæsar was always numerically the weaker, his troops were of a higher grade in discipline and *morale*. He had not many auxiliary troops. He felt that his legionaries were stronger without them. He kept enough for an efficient skirmishing line, but did not care for the hordes of them which were usual at his day.

In the Civil War Cæsar kept his troops well concentrated. He rarely made detachments from his army except those necessary for foraging. In the first Spanish campaign he left three legions in Massilia and took six to Spain; four remained in Sicily, one in Sardinia, and the rest in Italy. With less than these he could not hold the territory he had already conquered. While Cæsar concentrated his own, his constant endeavor was to make his opponents divide their forces or to keep them from concentrating, so as to beat them in detail.

His objectives were well chosen. They were generally the forces of his enemy. In 49 it was Brundisium, where Pompey was in force, seeking to leave Italy. Being the chief seaport, it had the advantage of protecting Rome if he drove Pompey across to Epirus. Later objectives were the passes of the Pyrenees, to open his route to Spain; Ilerda, where Afranius and Petreius lay in force; Dyrrachium, to rob Pompey of his base of supplies; Pharsalus, or in other words, the army of the enemy; Alexandria, to which place he thought Pompey had fled; the upper Delta, where Ptolemy was in force; Zela in Asia Minor, where he could strike Pharnaces without delay; Ruspina, as a secondary base near the enemy; Ucita and Thapsus, the enemy's dépôts; Ulia, Corduba and Attegua, important cities held by the enemy in force; and Munda, where he could force a decisive battle upon Cnæus; each and every objective he chose was a thrust at the heart of his adversary. Cæsar never looked askance at his work. His look, thought and act went to the very centre. *Veni, vidi, vici* might well have been his motto, instead of being applied to one campaign.

Cæsar was frequently in distress for rations. In victualing he was less apt than Alexander, less careful than Hannibal. Overanxiety to get into the field lay at the root of the evil; but, though often with difficulty and risk, Cæsar always managed to keep his men in food. In offensive campaigns the enemy is apt to control the supplies. Cæsar was fairly careful in victualing, but his movements were not wont to be controlled by the question of rations unless famine stood at the door. He was ready to take his chances of subsisting on the country or of capturing his enemy's supplies.

Not infrequently he made a mistake. On the whole he was a good provider.

As in Gaul so in the Civil War, Cæsar preferred combat in the open field; but he was at times compelled to sit down before fortified places and to waste time in besieging them. According to the custom of the time, he drew up near the enemy in the open in nearly all his battles. He had none of the sublime audacity of Frederick or Alexander; he was cautious not to be lured into an attack on intrenchments or difficult positions; but he was not slow to accept equal battle.

Cæsar's manœuvring and blockades were on a large scale. The object of his manœuvring was for battle, to compromise the enemy or to reach his magazines. In the Civil War this was more frequent than in Gaul; Cæsar had gained self-confidence. The earliest example of able manœuvring was at Ilerda. A good example was the operation at Zeta.

In adversity Cæsar was strong and elastic. He never weakened in *morale;* he was never disastrously defeated. After Dyrrachium he marched away rather like a victor than a badly beaten man. He showed no sign of loss of self-confidence; he cheered his legions by explaining away their defeat; he raised their courage by sundry small operations like the one at Gomphi, until they again felt that they could cope with the Pompeians even if outnumbered two to one. This ability to cope with adversity is more than any other a mark of Cæsar's genius. No one ever exhibited it as Hannibal did; but it was a distinct characteristic of Cæsar.

The tactics of Cæsar in the Civil War was substantially the same as in Gaul, somewhat altered to conform to the fact that he had Roman soldiers in his front. His attacks were less summary than on the Gallic barbarians. At Ilerda the cohorts fought five hours with the spear before they took to the sword.

In battle, flank movements were common. The general effort of each commander was to rupture the enemy's line or break down one of its flanks. The tactics of Cæsar was simple. There are few examples in his battles of splendid tactical formations like Epaminondas' oblique order at Leuctra or Mantinæa, Alexander's wedge at Arbela, or Hannibal's withdrawing salient at Cannæ. Cæsar's one instance of battlefield manœuvring was at Ruspina. This was good, but not on an extensive scale. Why he did not profit by the tactical lessons of other captains is not clear. He did not appear to think the grand-tactics of battle available for his purposes. Nearly all his engagements were in simple parallel order, coupled with prudent forethought against unusual danger, as in the creation of a fourth line at Pharsalus. What one admires in other captains as original grand-tactical combinations are absent in the case of Cæsar. The more usual combinations we do find. The orbis — or square — we saw used at Zeta with excellent effect. At Ilerda we saw Cæsar march in order of battle a much longer distance than usual, showing exceptional steadiness in his formation and discipline. In marching by the flank in two or three lines, peculiar heed was given to the flank which was toward the enemy; it was so formed that it could readily come to a front against a sudden attack.

Cæsar's ordinary formation was in three lines; but the accomplishment of the fourth line at Pharsalus is peculiarly noteworthy. Scarce another instance exists in which so great an effect has been produced by so small a body of men used at the right time in the right way. The Fifth legion at Ucita was a sort of fourth line; the same legion at Thapsus acted in a similar capacity against elephants; and we notice at Ucita that Cæsar had two lines in his left and three in his right wing, or with the Fifth legion really four. It was a species of a strengthened left wing, though not for the usual purpose of such a reinforced wing.

In formation for battle Cæsar's line of ten to twelve legions was generally divided into a centre and two wings, each of these under a legate. He had not enough legates to place one in command of each legion. One or other wing opened the battle. This duty was most frequently performed by the Tenth legion, whose post was wont to be on the right. Cæsar was always with the opening wing and gave the signal. From this there sometimes arose a sort of oblique order, because the wing which opened the battle pressed forward faster than the rest of the lines, much in the same way as in Alexander's battles; but this was not an oblique order in the same sense as the formations at Mantinæa or Leuthen.

The Romans were never able in the use of mounted men. Pompey's cavalry at Pharsalus was massed in one heavy body on one wing and should have gained the victory; but it was badly organized and commanded. Cæsar's small corps was employed to better advantage. Cæsar's Gallic and German horse — of which at times he had large bodies — was, in its way, efficient. Occasionally as many as four thousand men rode in one column. There had been an improvement in the Roman cavalry since the Punic Wars, principally due to the employment for that arm of the natives of countries which made a specialty of cavalry. But on the whole, Cæsar's cavalry was defective. It did not act the legitimate part of cavalry. It was often mixed with foot. Nothing in Cæsar's battles even faintly approaches the magnificent use of cavalry by Alexander or Hannibal.

A general must be gauged by his opponents. Pompey had long ranked as a great soldier; but he had ceased from war; he was resting on his laurels. He had never been noted for initiative, and the political intrigues of many years had unfitted him for the field. Cæsar had just emerged from an eight years' war in perfect training. His political scheming had gone hand in hand with war and had not weakened his soldier's habit. Add to each man's equipment his own peculiar qualities and Cæsar could scarcely help winning in the contest, if he had means at all equal to those of his adversary. There needs no proof of Cæsar's ability to cope with the difficulties which lay before him; and that Pompey looked quietly on at Cæsar's conquest of Spain is proof enough of the latter's hebetude. Cæsar had had the best training, actual war under, in this instance, the best master, — himself. His experience was bred of the errors he had made and intelligently profited by. Not that he now ceased to commit errors. Dyrrachium was a blunder of the first water. Cæsar needed a back-set to teach him caution. He got it at Dyrrachium; he at once adopted a more rational scheme, and won.

From the beginning Cæsar grew in every department of the art of war. His ability in strategy, tactics, fortification, sieges, logistics, was more marked at the end of his career than at any other period. It is a question as to whether his aggressiveness did not decrease towards the end of his campaigns. It would have been strange had it not done so. To Cæsar's personality his soldiers owed all they knew and all they were. They sometimes lacked the spirit of discipline, but they were remarkable for toughness, force, adaptiveness, patience in every matter of difficulty and self-denial, endurance and courage in battle, attachment to and confidence in their general. Cæsar's legionaries were an equal honor to Cæsar and to Rome. They were a standing reproach to Roman rottenness. Pompey's men could not compare with them in any sense, and this was because Pompey had created his soldiers and Cæsar had created his.

Pompey had never shown the highest order of ability, but it will not do to underrate him. He had at small outlay won his salute as Imperator; he had yet more easily come by his title of Magnus. Still some of Pompey's work was excellent, when he actually set to work and good luck ran in his favor. In what has been said it has not been intended to convey the idea that Pompey was not still a good, perhaps a great soldier, though he fell short of being a marvelous one. It is in comparison only to Cæsar that he pales. Had a lesser man opposed him, Pompey might have shown in higher degree the qualities he may fairly be credited with possessing. But Cæsar overshadowed him to a degree which made him not only seem but be less than himself. He dwindled because he met a moral force which bore him under. Cæsar, on the contrary, was and always will be simply Cæsar, — symbol of all that is greatest as a captain and a ruler.

Scipio lacked both energy and ability in any marked degree. He was merely a military hack. Solely as Pompey's father-in-law it was that he came by his command.

Cato, who was really the superior of all the Pompeians, refused the supreme command in favor of Scipio, made no use of his unquestioned powers, and avoided disaster by committing suicide.

Labienus showed much energy, but his skill was weakened by hatred of Cæsar. He was a fair sample of the excellent lieutenant, but poor captain. He had been a worthy and able soldier under Cæsar; against Cæsar he sank to a less than second-rate position. In every encounter with his ancient chief he lost his head.

Both of the young Pompeys showed at first some promise. But when taxed, Sextus dropped back to a low grade of skill. Cnæus exhibited more but not marked ability. Neither was a dangerous opponent.

The rest of the generals opposed to Cæsar were distinctly of a low order.

Cæsar's abilities stand out in singular contrast to all of these. Tried by the ability of his opponents, which is a tempting theme, but neither a fair test nor a fruitful subject, Cæsar ranks lower than Alexander, vastly lower than Hannibal. But as one of the marks of the great captain is to utilize the errors of opponents who lack high qualities, a thing which he always did, the soldier Cæsar cannot be placed on a level other than theirs. His wonderful power of mind and will produced a marked influence on everything he touched. Every one relied on him, all looked to him as the centre of motion. As has been before said, the test of greatness in a campaign may be applied by seeking the general who is the mainspring of the movement, the motive power which keeps the rest at work. This in all his campaigns was Cæsar. It was not what his enemies did, but what Cæsar did, which furnished the keynote of all that happened.

Cæsar was generous in rewards, praise and largesses to his soldiers. He was ever ready to distinguish the brave and thus incite others to imitate them. He had the rare capacity of winning his men's devotion to himself, both as a soldier and as a man; and this without losing his power or descending from the dignity of his position. He dressed and equipped his legions well, distinguished many by giving them weapons ornamented with gold and silver, took pride in seeing his men well-mounted and handsomely attired. Though his soldiers were dubbed "scented dandies," they yet knew how to fight. In this they were like their leader. Beware of underrating dandies. Some of the stoutest hearts and clearest heads have lurked under a foppish dress.

Cæsar never lacked a pleasant word for his men, remembered the face of any one who had done a gallant deed, and when not in the presence of the enemy encouraged amusements, in which he not infrequently personally joined. After the disaster to Sabinus and Cotta, Cæsar allowed his beard and hair to grow and vowed he would not cut them till his soldiers had revenged their comrades' death. This to us trivial act had its meaning to Cæsar's legionaries. Such things wrought up the feeling of his soldiers to a worship almost fanatical.

However lax when danger was not near, in the vicinity of the enemy Cæsar demanded discipline of the strictest. He required the most unheard-of exertions and sacrifices; he allowed no rest, day nor night; season or weather had no recognition. Every man must be ready at all times for duty. A willingness to do and suffer all this Cæsar comprehended in the name soldier. It was his use of "citizens" instead of "comrades" that broke up the mutiny of the Tenth legion. He was generous in overlooking smaller faults, but severe beyond measure in punishing larger ones. He was the more requiring of a man the higher he stood in office. His severest punishment was dismissal, as in the case of the tribunes and centurions of the Tenth legion when it came to Africa. In the Roman state this was political and social excommunication. Cæsar's officers were capable of more under his command than under any other conditions. Witness Labienus in Gaul and Labienus afterwards. This was owing not only to his gigantic personality but to the fact that he was ready and able at all times to do thrice the work that any one else could do. No one in the army labored so hard as Cæsar. All this makes it stranger that Cæsar's men more than once escaped from his control in a manner which showed a limit to their discipline. Of this Thapsus was the most noted example. The same may be said of their occasional demoralization, as at Dyrrachium.

Cæsar's career as a soldier shows to a marked degree how great in war is the factor of personal character. Cæsar's art was not a thing he had learned from or could impart to others. It was the product of his vast intellect and bore the seal of his splendid moral force.

Cæsar as Pontifex Maximus.
(Vatican Museum.)

XLV.

ALEXANDER, HANNIBAL, CÆSAR.

ALEXANDER had the most beauty; we think of him as the Homeric youth; of Hannibal and Cæsar as in sober maturity of years. In all his qualities, Cæsar is the most splendid man of antiquity; as a soldier he equals the others. Alexander's ambition and Cæsar's was coupled to self; Hannibal's pure. Cæsar the man was kindly; Cæsar the soldier ruthless. In capacity for work all were equal. Alexander's will was fiery; Hannibal's discreet; Cæsar's calculating. In battle Alexander was possessed of divine fury; Hannibal was cool but bold; Cæsar had not their initiative. In influence over men Hannibal was supreme. Cæsar was an orator; Alexander and Hannibal spoke simply and to the point. As statesmen, Alexander built on a mistaken foundation; Hannibal's work was doomed to fail; Cæsar's is everlasting. For performance with slender means and against great odds Hannibal stands the highest. Alexander had luck, but used it; Hannibal had no luck; Fortune smiled on Cæsar as on no other man. The strategy of each was the same. In extent of conquest Alexander was the most distinguished; in speed, Cæsar; in endurance, Hannibal. Alexander was the cavalry-leader; in tactics Cæsar was below the others; in sieges, Hannibal. As men Alexander and Hannibal stir us with the touch of nature, as Cæsar does not. Cæsar evokes our admiration; Alexander and Hannibal our sympathy.

IN beauty of person and stateliness of presence the king of Macedon was more distinguished than the Carthaginian general or the Roman imperator. Few of the heroes of history appeal to us in the physical sense so distinctly as Alexander; and, adding youth to splendid achievement and royal bearing, the conqueror of the Great King stands out the most lustrous of mortals. In bodily strength and endurance Hannibal was his equal; Cæsar, while gifted with unsurpassed nervous force, and physically able, does not wear the Homeric garb with the right of Alexander. Nor had he the youth of warlike glory of the son of Hamilcar. When our thoughts call up Cæsar or Hannibal, we are apt to see in our mind's eye the mature man, superb in his power of intellect and character; Alexander stands before us clad in a blaze of divine strength and youthful fervor. All Alexander's portrait-busts are those of the hero who subdued the world and died before he passed his youth; those of Cæsar and the sole authentic one of Hannibal show us the man of middle age, all the more powerful, perhaps, but less the demi-god than the son of Philip.

If we take him as statesman, jurist, author, thinker, soldier, Cæsar has no peer in antiquity. If we take him merely as the soldier, he stands beside the others. There are things which can be neither weighed nor measured. In intellectual activity and moral force these captains varied as their temperaments varied. In uprightness of purpose and purity of life neither Alexander nor Cæsar in any sense approached Hannibal, — the unselfish, model patriot, whose ambition was solely for his country, whose appetites were always curbed, whose life was one long and earnest effort, whom pleasures could not seduce, nor position warp, nor flattery turn.

Alexander was rash in temper and succumbed all too often to his love of wine. His ambition was a dream of personal greatness coupled to the hope of Hellenizing the world; and around this he cast the atmosphere of his all-pervading intellect, his boundless ability to conjure up mighty projects, his fabulous power of compassing the impossible. Cæsar was by nature cool and calculating. He neither resisted nor succumbed to temptation. To him there was no temptation; what he craved he took. It was his boundless egotism which made him Cæsar. His ambition was Rome; but Rome was not Rome without Cæsar as its guiding star. With many of the noblest personal qualities, which he manifested at every

turn, Cæsar had not a glint of patriotism in its finest sense.
All that he did or aspired to do was coupled to self. He
could not serve Rome, as Hannibal sought to serve Carthage,
though he himself was swallowed up. Generous and kindly
by nature, he yet has to his charge holocausts which stop
one's heartbeats. Cæsar, the conqueror, knew not Cæsar,
the man. If he felt a qualm at the treacherous butchery of
nearly half a million souls in a few hours, no one ever knew
it. Alexander was warm-hearted but hasty; generous at one
moment, violent at another. Hannibal had that gentle fibre
whose human kindness to fallen foemen overcame his hatred
of their race. Cæsar was gracious in his dealings with persons, ruthless to insensibility in his treatment of peoples.

Intellect and moral force alone do not suffice to make a
great man. Work is at the root of all that man has done or
will ever do. In his capacity for work Alexander drew on
a body and mind which never knew fatigue. If in any
respect Alexander came near to being the demigod he loved
to be thought, it was in his superhuman ability to labor. No
professional athlete was his superior in arms or games; no
philosopher had a clearer grasp of any new or knotty problem; no soldier was ever so truly instinct with the *gaudium
certaminis* as he; no one ever performed so much in so short
a life. Hannibal, in his youth, was much like Alexander;
but maturity early sat on Hannibal's brow; eternal youth
ever shone from Alexander's visage. Cæsar we only know
in youth as the dandy who was noted for bold political acts;
in manhood as the sublime orator, and as the statesman who
overrode all with whom he came in contact; in middle age as
the magnificent soldier, but the soldier whose boldness was
not Alexander's nor his caution Hannibal's; in old age as
the legislator, the governor, the creator of what to-day we
look upon as the foundation of our civilization.

The will-power of Alexander was that of a man who brooked not restraint; whose fiery purpose respected neither bosom friend nor ancient servitor; who would destroy even himself in seeking to compass his chosen end. Hannibal's will never outran an inborn discretion which subordinated even Hannibal. We do not know what Alexander might have become at the age of Hannibal's greatest power; we do know what Hannibal was at the age of Alexander's greatest performance. Alexander did his brilliant work in the twenties, Hannibal in the thirties and forties. Cæsar was well on in middle life before he wore the purple paludamentum. When he won his most splendid battle on the field of Pharsalus, he had by two years passed fifty; his best work followed this. His will-power was of a different kind. What he set out to do, he did, with the courage of Alexander, the persistency of Hannibal; but he could yield here a little, insist there a little, cajole, command, weave his way into opposition or tear its fabric into shreds, without for a moment losing sight of his once conceived, never forgotten purpose.

The courage of each was unsurpassed. So soon as battle was engaged, Alexander was possessed of a divine fury scarcely sobered by his divine intelligence. In the death struggle of legion and phalanx Hannibal never for a moment lost his quiet power of seeing and doing the proper thing; never failed to take advantage of the least error of his opponent, nor to force the fighting at the critical moment. In the execution of his projects he was obstinately bold; deliberate when doubtful, rapid at the instant when a blow would tell. Cæsar's courage as a soldier lay rather in the power to push a strategic advantage than in the longing to meet and annihilate the enemy. Alexander and Hannibal, like Frederick, never counted numbers; unless forced into action,

Cæsar sought to get the chances on his side before he fought.

Alexander's influence over others as a man, was marked; as a king, was supreme. He would have been the chief of any assembly had he not been king; but his royal character added to his manly force. Hannibal had no equal in his power over men. He who could hold together a motley array of diverse tribes, with clashing instincts and aspirations, weld them into an army and, though outnumbered many times by superior troops, could with it keep his clutch on the throat of Rome for half a generation, has no peer. By just what method he did it we do not know; but the bare fact suffices. Cæsar won his influence much as Napoleon did. His gigantic grasp, his fluent tongue, his plausible method, his suggestive mind, his appearance of reasonably yielding to those whom he desired to control, carried every point. He was truly Cæsar Imperator, embodiment of all which should be czar and emperor, — which, alas, so rarely is.

Cæsar was by nature and training an orator. His style was direct, convincing; his manner animated; he held his audience. Alexander and Hannibal were both intellectual and cultured; neither had studied rhetoric as an art; but each had the power of saying the right thing at the right moment and in such fashion as to sway his hearers and to compass his ends. None of these great men dealt in mere words. What they said proceeded from the glowing thoughts within. Who thinks clearly speaks clearly. None of these men spoke without due effect. Whoso listened was convinced, persuaded, or silenced. Alexander spoke as the master; Hannibal as the diplomat, with peace or war in either hand; Cæsar, however powerful, never lost his plausibility. No man ever conjured right to his side, ever made the worse appear the better reason, more surely than he.

That Alexander's statesmanlike projects left a permanent trace of Hellenism on every country he overran is praise enough. Hannibal was sagacious and far-sighted. Had he not been endowed with the craft of a Talleyrand as well as the purity of a Washington, he could never have come so close to upheaving the foundations of the Roman republic. But as a statesman Cæsar's work was the more enduring, as it had the better basis. He built on what was left of the solid Roman character; his corner-stones were well laid; his superstructure lasted for generations; the inner meaning of his work has modified all human endeavors towards civilization from his own age to ours. Alexander wrought like a giant, but on a mistaken plan. Traces of his work still stand, like the pyramids of Gizeh. Hannibal's work could not last; the Carthaginians were bound by the rule of progress to disappear from the world's economy. Baal could not endure; no Punic structure but must perish. Cæsar had a groundwork prepared for him by twenty generations of rational, honest thinkers, who builded even better than they knew. On this his perspicacity and wisdom erected what will ever be the pattern of growth in statecraft. That the Roman Empire did not last was due to other causes. The fabric wrought by Cæsar the statesman can never perish.

Apart from other work — as a soldier simply — no performance with slender means can equal Hannibal's. Alexander started worse handicapped than Hannibal, but circumstances favored him and, once he had attacked his problem, his material resources grew as he advanced into the bowels of the land. Hannibal's resources dwindled from the first; he was forced to create everything he had. He made bricks without straw; he himself forged every weapon with which he slew a Roman. We shall never see such soldier's art again. Cæsar's resources were ample. He could have drawn on

more than he put to use. Vast as was the result of his
achievements as a soldier, there is no part of his work which
can be fairly compared to the record of Hannibal. To win
is not the test of military skill.

Alexander had a way of courting Fortune so that she
always smiled on him. One's fancy readily ascribes her
fidelity to his fascinating influence; in truth, it was that he
never neglected a chance the fickle goddess offered. The
smallest favor he on the instant put to use. He never called
on Hercules until his own shoulder was at the wheel. How
could Fortune be fickle with such an ardent wooer? To
Hannibal the youth, Fortune was kind; on Hannibal, past
his youth, she turned her back, and never again smiled.
And yet this noble soldier wrought as persistently as if he
had basked in her favors from morn to sunset. No man ever
tempted Fortune as did Cæsar. He was successful beyond
any in his devotion to women; he obtained before he asked.
So with Fortune. She who forsook watchful Hannibal never
turned from reckless Cæsar. Always at hand and kinder
the more Cæsar neglected what she requires in all others, she
saved him a thousand times when his schemes deserved to
come to naught. History furnishes no instance of a great
man being so beholden to her whom he rarely sought to court.
Foolhardiness which in others Fortune would leave to the
punishment which ought to follow, in Cæsar she would favor.
He could not overtax her patience. And knowing that
Cæsar was happy in his conquests of women, we must allow
that his greatest was the easy conquest of this wont-to-be
hard-won goddess.

Though Alexander was outnumbered as no one else, he
fought only barbarians and semi - civilized armies; he
attacked an effete monarchy without cohesion, a structure
already toppling. Cæsar fought barbarians first and then

troops of his own kindred, though not so well equipped or commanded. The barbarians Cæsar showed less aptness in handling than Alexander or Hannibal; in the Civil War he had stancher forces to oppose him than Alexander. Hannibal fought barbarians in Spain, and in Italy troops far better than his own, the stoutest then on foot, under leaders who had been taught by himself and who had assimilated his method. Marcellus and Nero and Scipio learned Hannibal's lessons by heart as the Archduke Charles and Blucher and Wellington had mastered the art of Napoleon. Hannibal was overtaxed as no captain in the history of war has ever been and held his own a moment. The more we compare Hannibal with any other soldier, the brighter the effulgence of his genius.

The art of each of these captains was based on a rare combination of intellect and moral force; and in the case of each the third element, opportunity, was not wanting. Each had a method; he saw distinctly the point at which he aimed, and he drove his shaft straight and unerringly into the target, — and through it. Each was careful of his base; each saw and sought the enemy's weak spot; each kept his army well in hand. Alexander and Hannibal were better providers than Cæsar, whose army, from his overanxiety to grapple with his problem, was often on the point of starvation. Alexander won by bold strokes, the brilliancy of which can be found on no other historic page. Hannibal won by a careful study of the when and where to strike; his blow when delivered never failed to cripple the enemy. Cæsar was less bold than Alexander; in a way he was more cautious than Hannibal; but with his caution was mixed a precipitancy which should in many cases have wrecked his schemes. Alexander's first glance told him where to strike, and the blow fell with lightning speed and force. Hannibal was deliberate;

he lured his enemy into a false position and annihilated him. Cæsar, while never failing to grasp the whole, and to act on a method fully abreast of the problem, was so lax in many of the parts that to succeed required the intervention of a luck which often comes like a *deus ex machinâ.* Alexander would not steal a victory; Hannibal was the master of stratagem; Cæsar was by turns Quixotically bold and a very Fabius for lack of tactical enterprise. Yet *finis coronat opus;* Cæsar won, and he stands beside Alexander and Hannibal.

The element of speed in accomplishing a task is a test not to be overlooked. Cæsar took eight years to conquer Gaul; Alexander in eight years had conquered a vast territory of neighboring barbarians, had ground Hellas under his heel, had restored to the Ægean cities their independence, and had overrun Asia to the Jaxertes and India to the Hyphasis. In the Civil War, Cæsar was second in extent and rapidity of conquest only to Alexander. Hannibal must be tried by another standard. In five years he subdued half of Spain, crossed the Alps to Italy and, though reaching the Po with but twenty-six thousand men, throttled the gigantic power of Rome, — a city which could levy three quarters of a million men. This record for speed against odds excels that of Alexander and Cæsar. And when we take up the question of endurance, — the man who, forsaken by his own people and cast on his own sole resources, could hold Rome at bay and on the verge of dissolution for fifteen years has not, cannot have a peer.

Alexander had no confidant but Hephæstion. Hannibal never had a confidant. Cæsar had many friends to whom he confided his schemes in part; the whole he kept strictly to himself. Cæsar trusted men so far as he could use them. But though on the surface plausible, frank and open as few men ever are, no one knew Cæsar's ulterior purpose. What he aimed at as the result of all he did, no one divined. He was an adept at concealing his intentions under a veil of candor. It befits Alexander's sunny character to have a Hephæstion; it befits Hannibal's vast and trying task as well as his patient isolation that he should alone hold the key to his purpose. It befits Cæsar's versatility and self-reliance that he should use many friends to aid his kaleidoscopic plans. But under all a well-kept counsel added to his chances of success. Hannibal is said to have worn masks to conceal his person; Cæsar's face was always masked when it came to his inner motives.

Alexander's strategy was gigantic in conception; the theatre of his campaigns was the world. Hannibal's strategy differed from Alexander's as the problems of each differed; but it was equally skillful and bold; in a certain sense keener if not so vast. Cæsar's strategic push was always noteworthy. His apprehension of the strategy of the Gallic problem was as fine as his judgment of what was required by the conditions which faced him as he stood on the bank of the Rubicon. It could not be better.

As a cavalry leader Alexander cannot be equaled. No one ever repeated charges with the same body of horse on the same place in the enemy's line as he did at the Hydaspes. No one ever trained such squadrons; the "Companions" stand unrivaled in history. Next to him, but with a distinct interval, came Hannibal with his Numidians. Alexander's Companions won with naked blade in hand; the Numidians by clever tactics. Cæsar never knew the uses of cavalry in this sense. His Gallic and German horse were each excellent; but they cannot be mentioned beside the others.

Alexander's tactics was audacious and clean - cut. He thrust home on the instant, and blow succeeded blow until his enemy was a wreck. Hannibal studied his tactical problem with deliberation; he thrust not till by skillful feints he had found the weak side of his adversary's defense. But when he thrust, his blade never failed to find an opening. Cæsar's tactics was not strong. He had neither the audacity nor persistence of Alexander; he had none of the originality of Hannibal. His battles were not won because of his own perfect plan, but because of the weak behavior of the enemy. As a tactician Cæsar is far below Alexander; still farther below Hannibal. Alexander was boldness personified; Hannibal was careful in plan, strong in execution; Cæsar was neither. When Cæsar was forced to fight — as at the Sabis, or at Munda — he fought nobly; but he never fought as if he liked the task. Pharsalus is the only battle boldly planned and boldly carried through; and this was won by Pompey's laxness as much as by Cæsar's courage and good judgment.

In personal bearing, Alexander was, as he strove to be, an Achilles. Hannibal's gallantry in youth is testified to by Livy, but we forget it; we look on him as the thoughtful soldier, running no unnecessary risks, calculating his chances closely and then striking a blow marvelous for its effect. Cæsar never appeals to us as the *beau sabreur;* he is the intellectual captain. In the few instances in which his personal conduct was called upon he was acting in self-defense. He never led his men, as Alexander did at the city of the Malli, from sheer exuberance of courage. Cæsar won by brain tissue backed by strong moral force. He was not Homeric in his heroism.

In the history of sieges, Tyre and Alesia stand side by side. Hannibal never did such work. Saguntum, though fine, is on a lower level.

Alexander's opponents were far below him in capacity; Cæsar's rank higher. Vercingetorix was able; Pompey had been great, but his powers had waned. Neither Alexander nor Cæsar faced such men as Marcellus and Nero, Fabius and Scipio, or such troops as the burgess-legion. Tried by this standard Hannibal is the pattern of patterns.

In marches Alexander holds the record for great distances; his pursuit of Darius is hard to equal. Hannibal is unmatched for craft and skillful eluding of the enemy. Some of Cæsar's marches are remarkable. The march from Gergovia to the Æduan army and back — fifty miles in twenty-four hours, with a force of fifteen thousand foot — is only equaled by the Spartan march to Marathon. Alexander's passage of the Hindu-Koosh is like Hannibal's crossing of the Alps. Cæsar was never called on to do such work. Alexander was cautious on the march; Hannibal still more so. It was from Hannibal that the Romans learned to march an army. Cæsar began by being careless; but surprises taught him caution; he ended by conducting his marches in the ablest manner.

Alexander demanded of his men the severest exertions, without regard to season or circumstances, but took excellent care of them whether at work or rest. Hannibal was never out of bread, though living most of the time on the enemy's country. On occasion, as in crossing the Alps or the Arnus marshes, he called on his men for labor untold. Cæsar was not always a good provider; the African campaign was largely a tramp for victual. He was more apt to put his men in winter-quarters than Alexander or Hannibal.

In exerting influence over his men, each of these captains exhibited the highest power. That each was the hardest worked man in the army was apparent to all; each could do every part of a soldier's duty in a manner no man in his command could approach. Justice, generosity and high character made them the example all strove to imitate.

Each inculcated a spirit of emulation among his men; each rewarded gallantry and good service as they deserved.

As simple man, Hannibal far outranks the others in his purity of life and his elevated patriotism. Alexander had two sides — the one lovable, admirable; the other lamentable in its want of self-control. Cæsar the man lacks the one touch of nature. One can truthfully say a thousand admirable things of him. Quite apart from his greatness, — his reasonableness, his warm friendships, his generosity, the fine qualities of his mind, the many noble traits to which all testify, commend him to our admiration, to our regard. And yet there is to Cæsar, as there is to Napoleon, an artificiality which one never can forget. He wears an armor we cannot penetrate. We say much to praise him, but the epithets lack an inward meaning. Alexander, in his love for Hephæstion, in his violence to Clitus, was a man. Hannibal, in his hatred of Rome, in his self-immolation at the altar of Carthage, was a man. Gustavus, the Christian king, falling at the head of his squadrons at Lützen, and Frederick, the monarch of iron, writing poor French verses as a relief from his defeat, are both full of human nature. Cæsar and Napoleon impress us as characters in history. Each calls out a thrill of admiration; neither calls out a thrill of human sympathy.

Tried solely by the standards of the soldier, these equal captains, if one may pronounce between them, stand: Hannibal the peerless; Alexander the Homeric; Cæsar the unvanquished.

Taken in all his characters, Cæsar is the greatest man in antiquity.

XLVI.

THE ART OF WAR OF THE ROMAN EMPIRE.

AUGUSTUS formed from the relics of the legions of the civil wars a new standing army some three hundred thousand strong, which was distributed mostly on the frontiers. The Empire rested on the army; but Augustus' method was good. The prætorian guard gradually increased, acquired great power and used it illy. Later on, when there was a good ruler there was a good army; under weak emperors, the army was bad. On the whole the material degenerated; service was avoided, even by mayhem; barbarians filled the ranks. The use of the sword decreased in favor of jactile weapons; engines were employed in line of battle; elephants and trained wild beasts were used. Intervals decreased so that the legion again became a phalanx. Tactics reached a high point, but the soul of the army was not there. Baggage and non-combatants reached Oriental proportions. Pay and largesses were enormous. Camps were more strongly fortified. Fortification and sieges were expert. Theory was developed; practice retrograded. Standing armies called out regular fleets. Declining soldierly spirit was supplemented by petty defensive means. There were many and able generals during the first five centuries of our era; but there was no growth in the art of war.

FROM the history of the army of Julius Cæsar we have seen that it was the genius of the captain and not the personal qualities of the rank and file which won his splendid victories. When Cæsar Augustus became sole ruler of Rome, military matters were not long in being put on a new footing. The ancient army of the republic had been a burgess-militia, and it is only necessary to recall the events of the Second Punic War to show that, rather than the ability of any one leader, it was the steadfastness of the Senate and army — for the army was the people — that saved Rome from annihilation by Hannibal.

During the civil broils of Rome, professional soldiers and

mercenaries had gradually crept in until they formed the bulk of the rank and file; and these had prepared the way for the standing army which was now to form a part of the equipment of the empire, in peace and war alike.

Augustus went to work in a systematic way. From the forty-five legions and fifteen thousand cavalry remaining over from the civil wars, the slaves, freedmen and all of that ilk were discharged. Some one hundred and twenty thousand volunteers and veterans were settled in twenty-eight colonies on the lands in Italy donated to them. The remainder, mostly Roman citizens, were consolidated into twenty-five legions and a number of bodies of auxiliaries. These new legions and the cavalry attached to them were quartered in permanent camps, principally on the Rhine, Danube and Euphrates, to hold head against the inroads of foreign hordes. These troops were thus removed from the temptations of too great proximity of the capital or larger cities. Auxiliaries were raised in large numbers for service in their respective provinces.

For the protection of Italy there were raised ten prætorian cohorts, of one thousand men each. This was the famous body-guard of the emperor. Three of these cohorts formed the garrison of Rome; the seven others those of the principal near-by cities.

The sum total of all this standing force has been estimated at three hundred thousand men.

The soldier's oath had in early days been to the republic; from the time of Marius down it had been taken individually to the general who was raising legions to hold his province or to make war upon the neighboring nations; now that the emperor was the state, it ran: "In the name of the Emperor I swear unconditionally to obey him, never to leave the ensign, nor spare my life for Emperor and State."

The term of service varied from twelve to twenty years, and every third year a careful levy was held to fill the service gaps. The excessive privileges which the soldiers had enjoyed during the civil wars and gradually claimed as a condition of military life, were restricted, and a special fund, under the emperor's sole control, was created from which to pay, clothe and ration the troops.

Thus was the power of the Roman emperor as firmly grounded on the army as the power of the republic had been grounded on the burgess-soldier; and while the exceptional personal qualities of Augustus made this reorganization a benefit to Rome, the army, under later and less worthy rulers, became a curse. The ten prætorian cohorts were all drawn in to Rome by his successor, and from thence on remained there, and by their corruption and tyranny grew to be the terror of the land. Nearly the entire first century of our era was made unquiet by the antagonism between people and army.

During the second century, from Nerva to Marcus Aurelius, the army was held in better leash. But luxury and lax political morals had been doing their work in people and army alike. Both were degenerating. The citizens avoided military service to such a degree that the habit of self-mayhem became common. The succeeding period of threatened invasions by Germans and Parthians again obliged the emperors to resort to raising mercenaries, — and these among the barbarians, a necessary but dangerous practice.

The third century saw the power of Rome fallen practically into the hands of the prætorian guards, who made and unmade emperors at will. Though their abuses were somewhat reformed by Septimius Severus, the gulf between people and army had grown apace. The army was largely German, — the Roman Republic was fast drifting to its fall.

The ancient arms and equipment of the legionary were not changed until the second century, though the use of the sword was steadily decreasing in favor of the spear. As the material of the arms-bearing class decreased, the latter weapon grew lighter. As the discipline and character of the rank and file waned, so whatever intervals between cohorts were still left decreased, and in the third century, under Caracalla and Alexander Severus, an organization like the Grecian phalanx was adopted, though but temporarily. The general tendency was to make all weapons lighter, for the man himself had ceased to be the well-trained, strong and able citizen of old. The legions were no longer expected to close with the foe, and the men carried additional jactile weapons, rather than those of hand-to-hand conflict.

Cavalry was still as of old heavy, with man and horse in armor; or light, using only darts for weapons.

Artillery began to accompany the legions. This it will be remembered was no new thing. Alexander in the prime of his power had employed field artillery; in their decline the Greeks had employed it in line of battle to protect their foot. The same thing now occurred with the Romans. At first this purported to be only for use on the walls of the permanent camps. But later, in the third century, the onager or smaller ballista was transported on a two-ox cart, and the hand-ballista on a one-horse wagon. Each was served by eleven men. They could cast stones and darts three to four hundred paces. They were placed in line of battle, between the legions, to save these from too sudden or close contact with the enemy.

Elephants again appeared, and trained wild beasts and dogs were occasionally used against the enemy. These artificial aids exhibit the declining value of the legions.

The strength of the legions grew to be somewhat greater,

at the normal from six to seven thousand men. Armies rarely numbered more than eight or ten legions.

Flags replaced other ensigns, sometimes cut into dragon-shape; and the bust or likeness of the emperor took the place of the eagle. To the old military horns was added a peculiar flute.

A number of changes, owing largely to the new enemies encountered as well as the less good material of the legions, gradually took place. The third line of battle was given up so as to strengthen the first, and each line had five cohorts. The first cohort was doubled in number, was often as high as twelve hundred strong, and was composed of the best men. It was not infrequently divided into halves so as to be placed on the right and left of the first line, or the fifth cohort was made equally strong, so that a powerful body was on each extremity of the first line. The cohorts of the second line stood behind the intervals of the first so long as they existed, and these at a time not well settled appear to have been diminished by half. This was the Hadrian formation. The entire question of intervals and of the space occupied by the men is a puzzling one. Tribunes now commanded cohorts; legates legions; the prætorians were led by prætorian præ-fects, the army by imperial or consular legates. The staff-officers were quæstors and procurators.

Trajan introduced still another system. The ten cohorts of the legion were placed in one line. The first had nine hundred and sixty chosen men in ten centuries and two hundred and forty cavalry. The others had four hundred and eighty men in six centuries. Arrian says the men stood in eight, Vegetius in six ranks. The front ranks were of the heavier and older legionaries; the rear ranks of the younger and lighter. Each man occupied three feet in width, and the ranks were six feet apart from back to breast. Light troops stood behind the legionaries. The cohorts stood in order from one to ten with very small, next to no, intervals, and these were filled by horizontal-fire engines. Behind the line were engines of high trajectory which could fire above the line. Behind the flanks were special troops, such as the prætorians, and cavalry and bowmen were on the flanks.

This formation had its advantages against barbarian nations, such as the Dacians, Parthians and Germans. It suited either the offensive or defensive, any kind of ground, and could be used against cavalry or infantry. It had certain features of the old class ordering of the legion. Hadrian and Trajan were specially apt at utilizing the legion thus formed. It seems to have been an attempt to reconcile the useful side of the class organization of old burgess times with the necessarily growing phalangial idea.

Armies appear to have drilled, manœuvred and marched much as of old. The tactics of the parade-ground often reached a high point. But that old instinct for war which enabled a Roman consul to raise his army of citizens and leave Rome in one day was not present.

The hollow square for marches, on open plains and against sudden attacks, remained common. It was a safe defensive formation. The wedge or hollow wedge was successfully put to use. An instance of this was seen at Treviri, 70 A. D.

Josephus narrates how Vespasian and Titus disposed their armies. In the former's march from Syria to Galilee in 67 A. D., the column was as follows: the light troops (bowmen and slingers) sustained by a small body of heavy foot and some horsemen, in the van; following them the mechanics (*fabri*) like our pioneers, to repair bridges and roads; then the officers' baggage with cavalry, the emperor and staff, the military engines; then the bulk of the army, — the legions in a column of sixes; next the army-train. Last came the mercenaries, mixed with legionaries and cavalry to steady them.

Up to the third century the Roman armies marched rapidly; the speed and distances then decreased markedly, owing in part to the less good material, in part to the greater amount of baggage and enginery.

An army was marshaled for battle in much the same manner as a legion, and occasionally the position of the legions was determined by lot. When the army was in one line, the light troops and enginery opened the action. The heavy foot then advanced, and the light troops retired through them, — as there were no intervals, by the even-number men stepping for the moment behind the odd. The front ranks of legionaries closed and couched their spears, though these were not formidable, and the rear ranks fired above their heads. The light troops and engines which were in the rear aided the front lines by their fire. The mounted archers moved from point to point and the cavalry operated on the wings.

The farther the Roman army grew away from its old self-reliance the more it was sought to supplement this by enginery and defensive tactics of various useless sorts. The assault with naked weapon was now rarely seen. Distance weapons were preferred. Instead of the Roman soldier being more than a match for the barbarian so soon as he closed with his man, the reverse was now the case. The bulky German could laugh in earnest at the Roman legionary. Under able emperors this was not so apparent; but before the end of the third century the old-fashioned Roman organization, bravery and reliability had vanished, as had happened in Greece five hundred years before.

In the same measure as the evidences of the ancient

Roman gallantry in war, there disappeared from the legions the sense of discipline, order and good conduct. Cæsar Augustus had somewhat reëstablished the old Roman military virtues; but it was only for a time. The pay of the troops rose as their value decreased, and largesses became enormous. Under Domitian the foot soldier is said to have received four gold pieces (about twelve dollars) a month, the centurion eight, the mounted man or prætorian twelve; and the deductions for arms, equipment and rations were given up. This seems excessive, in view of the value of gold. Allowances were increased to a luxurious extent and the trains and non-combatants correspondingly increased, until they reached Oriental proportions, and of the nimbleness of the Roman army there remained but a tradition. Occasionally a vigorous emperor or an energetic general improved these conditions, but only during his period of control. The tendency was downward.

Augustus had brought back military gymnastics and drill; and under Vespasian, Titus and Antoninus these were encouraged; but in the third century they again disappeared. The drill-marches which Augustus compelled the legions to make three times a month, with baggage — sometimes doubled — and over all kinds of country, were forgotten; the army manœuvres which were then conducted on as large a scale as to-day in Germany or France became onerous and were dropped; and the splendid public works, especially military roads, were no longer built. The troops mutinied against such labors.

So far as military science and study were concerned, they were less practical and more pedantic. Though the empire produced numberless writers on military matters, there were none to approach Polybius or Cæsar. They admirably wrote up details, but they failed to give the soul of the matter.

So far as the moral tone of the army was concerned, it could not be worse. If the ancient burgess-legion of the Second Punic War was the type of all that is excellent from a military standpoint, so it may be said that the army of the later empire represented all that was vicious. It was a monster whose work was to destroy the structure of the empire, even as its predecessor had been the creator of the power and greatness of Rome. The army may be said to have been held together solely by a system of fearful punishments and unreasoning rewards.

Up to the era of Gratian, toward the end of the fourth century, the daily camp was still the rule and was made to conform to the ground with much skill, the ditch and wall being deeper and higher. The permanent camps were like regular fortresses, and enginery was much more abundant on the parapets. A system of such permanent camps was sometimes constructed as a military frontier, like Hadrian's wall from the Tyne to the Solway, or Trajan's wall from the Danube to the Euxine. On the whole, while no works exceeded in ability Cæsar's wonderful defenses, fortification grew in skill as troops grew in worthlessness. Terraces and rams increased in size. Titus built four huge terraces opposite Jerusalem, and Vespasian had a ram which weighed one hundred tons and required fifteen hundred men to set it in motion and one hundred and fifty pairs of oxen or three hundred pairs of mules to transport it. Mines were cleverly designed and executed. The subterranean war at Jerusalem in 70 A. D. was remarkable. Double tortoises for assaulting walls and the use of inflammables in ballistics are to be noted. The number of engines accompanying an army was huge. Titus had, says Josephus, before Jerusalem, three hundred catapults and forty ballistas. This would be called a very large artillery force for an army of equal size to-day.

In a certain sense, during this period, the art of war was not on the decline but rather on the increase. The theoretical was more highly developed, the practical simplicity was less. The ancient Roman habit of winning by hard knocks had given way to a system which protected the soldiers who were no longer ready to expose life and limb for the public weal. The gain in theoretical knowledge was but a cloak to cover the loss of the old military virtues.

Standing armies soon called for regular fleets. Augustus had two, — at Ravenna and Misenum, — in the Adriatic and Tyrrhenian seas respectively. A third was later placed on the coast of Gaul. Flotillas were on the Rhine, Danube and other rivers. The type of vessel was Illyrian, and it had from one to five rows of oars. Many light boats for reconnoitring and scouting and dispatch-bearing were in use. The material of the fleets was of the worst. Slaves and criminals made up the crews. The tactics remained as of old, so far as it could be utilized.

The changes in organization of the last two centuries of the Roman empire have no interest. They all tended to the same end, — to sustain a declining soldierly spirit by petty defensive inventions in tactics, ballistics and fortification. The old offensive tone of Rome had disappeared. The Roman soldier no longer felt that if he could but get at the enemy with sword and shield, he was more than a match for him. Everything tended to invite an attack by the enemy, and to an attempt to destroy him before he reached the line of battle.

To recapitulate, chronologically, the changes by which the old quincuncial legion of brave burgesses became the one line phalanx of unsoldierly mercenaries: Marius, a century before the Christian era, changed the class-rating of citizen-soldiers to one of mere physical capacity, and began to introduce a lessening of the intervals.   Cæsar fully matured Marius' plan, deployed his men for battle so that the front line, and perhaps the second, had no intervals, and changed the cohort from a body in three lines, with light troops and cavalry pertaining to it, into a body of heavy foot in one line eight or ten men deep.   His legion was habitually set up in three lines.   In the first century A. D. the ten legionary cohorts were set up in two lines, five in each, with whatever intervals there existed filled with ballistic machines.   In the second and third centuries the cohorts were gradually marshaled in one line without intervals, and the spears were lengthened.   In the fourth and fifth centuries the legion became absolutely a phalanx and a very poor one.   As we remember, the courageous and enterprising Roman citizens of the early republic had adapted the old Dorian phalanx to their own ideas of a quincuncial form; the gradual decline of the imperial army had, by converse causes, brought it back, not to the phalanx of Miltiades, Epaminondas and Alexander, but to the phalanx of the degenerate Greece of the second century B. C.   This was a noteworthy but a perfectly natural series of events.

It must not be forgotten that, during the five first centuries of the Christian era, there were many able generals, both among the Romans and their barbarian opponents; and that there was a skillful adaptation of means to end.   But there is nothing in the way of improvement to the art of war which claims our notice.   The fact that Augustus, Arminius, Civilis the Batavian, Tiberius, Drusus, Germanicus, Vespasian, Titus, Trajan, Marcus Aurelius, Diocletian, Constantine, Julian, Theodosius, Stilicho, Aëtius, Ricimer, Odoaker, Alaric, Attila, Belisarius commanded huge armies, conducted far-reaching campaigns, displayed military talents of a high order, does not concern us here.   Many of the lesser

lights of war at the inception of its story are of more consequence because in what they did we first discover some
principle which had its bearing on subsequent events. It is
not wars, but the art of war whose history we are tracing.
And if in a subsequent volume we devote but a passing notice
to the entire period from the fall of the Roman empire to
the invention of gunpowder, we shall not interrupt the sequence of events which have brought the art of war from its
crude beginnings in the age of Cyrus to its wonderful development in our own nineteenth century.

Triumphal Car.

APPENDIX A.

CASUALTIES IN SOME ANCIENT BATTLES.

Battle of	Date B. C.	Number Engaged.	Nationality.	Number Killed.	Per-centage.	Usual Per cent.[1]	Killed and Wounded.	Per-centage.	Usual Per cent.[1]	Loss of Enemy.	Remarks.
Marathon........	490	11,000	Greeks	192	1¾	5	2,100	19¼	13	6,400	
Platæa	479	*38,700	"	1,360	3½	4	15,000	13½	13	257,000	*Hoplites, who alone fought.
Chæronæa.......	338	50,000	"	2,000	4	4	18,000	36	13		
Thebes	335	33,000	Macedonians........	500	1¾	4	5,500	17	13	6,000	
Granicus	334	3,000	Macedonian Cavalry.	85	3	2	935	31	16	*19,000	*Mostly massacre of Greek Phalanx; 1,000 Persian horsemen fell.
Issus............	333	30,000	Macedonians........	450	1½	4½	5,000	16½	13	*100,000	*The usual massacre.
Arbela...........	331	47,000	"	500	1	4	5,500	12	13	*40,000	*The usual massacre. Diodorus says 90,000; Arrian says 300,000.
Megalopolis......	330	40,000	"	3,500	8¾	4½					
"	330	20,000	Spartans............	5,300	26½	5					
Jaxartes.........	329	6,000	Macedonians........	160	2¾	7	1,160	19⅓	20	1,000	
Hydaspes........	326	14,000	"	930	6¾	5	10,200	73	13	*12,000	*Arrian says 23,000.
Heraclea	280	25,000	Epirots.............	*4,000	16	5	–	–	–	–	*Dionysius says 13,000 loss.
"	280	20,000	Romans	*7,000	35	5	–	–	–	–	" " 15,000 "
Asculum	279	70,000	Greeks and Italians.	*3,550	5	4	–	–	–	–	" " " "
"	279	70,000	Romans and Italians.	*6,000	8½	4	–	–	–	–	" " " "
At Rhone........	218	500	Numidian Cavalry...	200	40	2					
"	218	300	Roman Cavalry	140	46½	2					
Geronium........	217	50,000	Carthaginians.......	6,000	12	4					
"	217	50,000	Romans	5,000	10	4					
Cannæ	216	42,000	Carth. and Gauls ...	6,000	14¼	4½	–	–	–	*40,000	*Some authors say 70,000.
" (Camp)...	216	11,000	Romans	2,000	18	5					
Nola, 2d.........	215	20,000	"	1,000	5	5	–	–	–	5,000	
Beneventum	214	20,000	"	2,000	10	5	–	–	–	15,000	Usual massacre.
Nola, 3d.........	214	20,000	"	400	2	5	–	–	–	2,000	
Asculum, 2d.....	209	20,000	"	2,700	13½	5					
" 2d day.	209	17,000	"	3,000	17½	5	–	–	–	8,000	
Grumentum	207	40,000	"	500	1¼	4½	–	–	–	8,000	
Metaurus........	207	40,000	"	8,000	20	4½	–	–	–	35,000	Usual massacre
Crotona	204	20,000	"	1,200	6	5					
Magos' Battle....	203	20,000	Carthaginians.......	5,000	25	5					
" "	203	40,000	Romans	2,300	5¾	4½					
Zama............	202	43,000	"	*2,000	4½	4½	–	–	–	20,000	*Clearly understated.
Aduatuca........	53	5,000	"	350	7	7½	4,450	89	13		
Gergovia.........	52	16,000	"	746	4⅔	5					
Ilerda	49	5,000	"	71	1½	7	671	1⅓	20	200	
Pharsalus........	48	22,000	"	230	1½	5	–	–	–	15,000	Usual massacre.
Thapsus.........	47	40,000	"	50	⅛	4½	–	–	–	10,000	" "
Munda	45	58,000	"	1,000	1¾	4	1,500	2½	13	30,000	" "

APPENDIX B.

SOME ANCIENT MARCHES.

By whom Made.	Where Made.	Date B.C.	Number and Kind of Troops.	Distance. Miles.	Time of March.	Distance Miles per Day.	Remarks.
Spartans	Sparta to Marathon	490	2,000 Infantry	150	3 days	50	
Ten Thousand Greeks	Myriandrus to Thapsacus	401	10,000	230	12 "	19	
"	Retreat	400	6,000	4,000	215 "	18½	
Macedonians	Drill Marches	c. 350	All arms	—	—	30	Mountain road.
"	Pelium to Thebes	335	33,000 all arms	300	14 days	21½	
"	Pella to Sestos	334	35,000	350	20 "	17½	
"	Phœnicia to Thapsacus	331	50,000	200+	11 "	19+	
"	Pursuit at Arbela	"	5,000	70	1 night and day	70	Bad mountain road.
"	Urians to Persian Gates	"	15,000	113	5 days	22½	
"	Persian Gates to Araxes	330	4,000 Cavalry	40	1 night	40	
"	Ecbatana to Rhagæ	"	30,000 all arms	220+	11 days	20	Hot, midsummer tropical weather.
"	Pursuit of Darius	"	3,000+Cavalry	400	11 "	36¼	Hot, sandy road, part desert.
"	"	"	3,000	175	4 "	44	
"	"	"	500	47	1 night	47	Desert. The end of thirty-six hours continuous marching; of eleven days at nearly forty miles a day.
"	Hecatompylos to Aria	"	23,000 all arms	500+	20 days	25	
"	To Artacoana	"	6,000+	75	2 "	37½	
"	Capture of Bessus	329	6,000	150	4 "	37¾	Ptolemy's march.
"	Jaxartes to Maracanda	"	15,000	170	3½ "	48¼	
"	Desert of Sandar	325	20,000+	57	1 day	57	Desert.
Romans	Lilybæum to Ariminum	218	20,000	650	40 days	16	13 marching days; 1 day of battle.
"	Canusium to the Sena and back	207	7,000	500	14 "	58½	
"	Vesontio to Axona	57	60,000	145	15 "	9¾	Winter roads.
"	Samarobriva to relief of Cicero	54	8,000	110	5	22	
"	Gergovia to Æduan army and back	52	16,000	50	24 hours	50	
"	Corfinium to Brundisium	49	25,000	290	17 days	17	
"	Asparagium to Dyrrachium	48	21,000	45	26 hours	41+	
"	Zeta raid	46	15,000	36	16 "	48	

INDEX.

LIST OF DATES.

LIST OF DATES.

LIST OF DATES.

* marks a certain date; others are approximate or estimated.